Praise for the Reformation Commentary on Scripture

"Protestant reformers were fundamentally exegetes as much as theologians, yet (except for figures like Luther and Calvin) their commentaries and sermons have been neglected because these writings are not available in modern editions or languages. That makes this new series of Reformation Commentary on Scripture most welcome as a way to provide access to some of the wealth of biblical exposition of the sixteenth and seventeenth centuries. The editor's introduction explains the nature of the sources and the selection process; the intended audience of modern pastors and students of the Bible has led to a focus on theological and practical comments. Although it will be of use to students of the Reformation, this series is far from being an esoteric study of largely forgotten voices; this collection of reforming comments, comprehending every verse and provided with topical headings, will serve contemporary pastors and preachers very well."

Elsie Anne McKee, *Archibald Alexander Professor of Reformation Studies and the History of Worship, Princeton Theological Seminary*

"This series provides an excellent introduction to the history of biblical exegesis in the Reformation period. The introductions are accurate, clear and informative, and the passages intelligently chosen to give the reader a good idea of methods deployed and issues at stake. It puts precritical exegesis in its context and so presents it in its correct light. Highly recommended as reference book, course book and general reading for students and all interested lay and clerical readers."

Irena Backus, *Professeure Ordinaire, Institut d'histoire de la Réformation, Université de Genève*[†]

"The Reformation Commentary on Scripture is a major publishing event—for those with historical interest in the founding convictions of Protestantism, but even more for those who care about understanding the Bible. As with IVP Academic's earlier Ancient Christian Commentary on Scripture, this effort brings flesh and blood to 'the communion of saints' by letting believers of our day look over the shoulders of giants from the past. By connecting the past with the present, and by doing so with the Bible at the center, the editors of this series perform a great service for the church. The series deserves the widest possible support."

Mark A. Noll, *Francis A. McAnaney Professor of History, University of Notre Dame*

"For those who preach and teach Scripture in the church, the Reformation Commentary on Scripture is a significant publishing event. Pastors and other church leaders will find delightful surprises, challenging enigmas and edifying insights in this series, as many Reformational voices are newly translated into English. The lively conversation in these pages can ignite today's pastoral imagination for fresh and faithful expositions of Scripture."

J. Todd Billings, *Gordon H. Girod Research Professor of Reformed Theology, Western Theological Seminary*

"The reformers discerned rightly what the church desperately needed in the sixteenth century—the bold proclamation of the Word based on careful study of the sacred Scriptures. We need not only to hear that same call again for our own day but also to learn from the Reformation how to do it. This commentary series is a godsend!"

Richard J. Mouw, *President Emeritus, Fuller Theological Seminary*

"Like the Ancient Christian Commentary on Scripture, the Reformation Commentary on Scripture does a masterful job of offering excellent selections from well-known and not-so-well-known exegetes. The editor's introductory survey is, by itself, worth the price of the book. It is easy to forget that there were more hands, hearts and minds involved in the Reformation than Luther and Calvin. Furthermore, encounters even with these figures are often limited to familiar quotes on familiar topics. However, the Reformation Commentary helps us to recognize the breadth and depth of exegetical interests and skill that fueled and continue to fuel faithful meditation on God's Word. I heartily recommend this series as a tremendous resource not only for ministry but for personal edification."

Michael S. Horton, *J. G. Machen Professor of Systematic Theology and Apologetics, Westminster Seminary, California*

"The Reformation was ignited by a fresh reading of Scripture. In this series of commentaries, we contemporary interpreters are allowed to feel some of the excitement, surprise and wonder of our spiritual forebears. Luther, Calvin and their fellow revolutionaries were masterful interpreters of the Word. Now, in this remarkable series, some of our very best Reformation scholars open up the riches of the Reformation's reading of the Scripture."

William H. Willimon, *Professor of the Practice of Christian Ministry, Duke Divinity School*

"The Reformation Scripture principle set the entirety of Christian life and thought under the governance of the divine Word, and pressed the church to renew its exegetical labors. This series promises to place before the contemporary church the fruit of those labors, and so to exemplify life under the Word."

John Webster, *Professor of Divinity, University of St. Andrews[†]*

"Since Gerhard Ebeling's pioneering work on Luther's exegesis seventy years ago, the history of biblical interpretation has occupied many Reformation scholars and become a vital part of study of the period. The Reformation Commentary on Scripture provides fresh materials for students of Reformation-era biblical interpretation and for twenty-first-century preachers to mine the rich stores of insights from leading reformers of the sixteenth century into both the text of Scripture itself and its application in sixteenth-century contexts. This series will strengthen our understanding of the period of the Reformation and enable us to apply its insights to our own days and its challenges to the church."

Robert Kolb, *Professor Emeritus, Concordia Theological Seminary*

"The multivolume Ancient Christian Commentary on Scripture is a valuable resource for those who wish to know how the Fathers interpreted a passage of Scripture but who lack the time or the opportunity to search through the many individual works. This new Reformation Commentary on Scripture will do the same for the reformers and is to be warmly welcomed. It will provide much easier access to the exegetical treasures of the Reformation and will hopefully encourage readers to go back to some of the original works themselves."

Anthony N. S. Lane, *Professor of Historical Theology and Director of Research, London School of Theology*

"This volume of the RCS project is an invaluable source for pastors and the historically/biblically interested that provides unparalleled access not only to commentaries of the leading Protestant reformers but also to a host of nowadays unknown commentaters on Galatians and Ephesians. The RCS is sure to enhance and enliven contemporary exegesis. With its wide scope, the collection will enrich our understanding of the variety of Reformation thought and biblical exegesis."

Sigrun Haude, *Associate Professor of Reformation and Early Modern European History,*
University of Cincinnati

"This grand project sets before scholars, pastors, teachers, students and growing Christians an experience that can only be likened to stumbling into a group Bible study only to discover that your fellow participants include some of the most significant Christians of the Reformation and post-Reformation (for that matter, of any) era. Here the Word of God is explained in a variety of accents: German, Swiss, French, Dutch, English, Scottish and more. Each one vibrates with a thrilling sense of the living nature of God's Word and its power to transform individuals, churches and even whole communities. Here is a series to anticipate, enjoy and treasure."

Sinclair Ferguson, *Senior Minister, First Presbyterian Church, Columbia, South Carolina*

"I strongly endorse the Reformation Commentary on Scripture. Introducing how the Bible was interpreted during the age of the Reformation, these volumes will not only renew contemporary preaching, but they will also help us understand more fully how reading and meditating on Scripture can, in fact, change our lives!"

Lois Malcolm, *Associate Professor of Systematic Theology, Luther Seminary*

"Discerning the true significance of movements in theology requires acquaintance with their biblical exegesis. This is supremely so with the Reformation, which was essentially a biblical revival. The Reformation Commentary on Scripture will fill a yawning gap, just as the Ancient Christian Commentary did before it, and the first volume gets the series off to a fine start, whetting the appetite for more. Most heartily do I welcome and commend this long overdue project."

J. I. Packer, *Retired Board of Governors Professor of Theology, Regent College*

"There is no telling the benefits to emerge from the publication of this magnificent Reformation Commentary on Scripture series! Now exegetical and theological treasures from Reformation era commentators will be at our fingertips, providing new insights from old sources to give light for the present and future. This series is a gift to scholars and to the church; a wonderful resource to enhance our study of the written Word of God for generations to come!"

Donald K. McKim, *Executive Editor of Theology and Reference, Westminster John Knox Press*

"Why was this not done before? The publication of the Reformation Commentary on Scripture should be greeted with enthusiasm by every believing Christian—but especially by those who will preach and teach the Word of God. This commentary series brings the very best of the Reformation heritage to the task of exegesis and exposition, and each volume in this series represents a veritable feast that takes us back to the sixteenth century to enrich the preaching and teaching of God's Word in our own time."

R. Albert Mohler Jr., *President, The Southern Baptist Theological Seminary*

"Today more than ever, the Christian past is the church's future. InterVarsity Press has already brought the voice of the ancients to our ears. Now, in the Reformation Commentary on Scripture, we hear a timely word from the first Protestants as well."

Bryan Litfin, *Professor of Theology, Moody Bible Institute*

"I am delighted to see the Reformation Commentary on Scripture. The editors of this series have done us all a service by gleaning from these rich fields of biblical reflection. May God use this new life for these old words to give him glory and to build his church."

Mark Dever, *Senior Pastor, Capitol Hill Baptist Church, and President of 9Marks.org Ministries*

"Monumental and magisterial, the Reformation Commentary on Scripture, edited by Timothy George, is a remarkably bold and visionary undertaking. Bringing together a wealth of resources, these volumes will provide historians, theologians, biblical scholars, pastors and students with a fresh look at the exegetical insights of those who shaped and influenced the sixteenth-century Reformation. With this marvelous publication, InterVarsity Press has reached yet another plateau of excellence. We pray that this superb series will be used of God to strengthen both church and academy."

David S. Dockery, *President, Trinity International University*

"Detached from her roots, the church cannot reach the world as God intends. While every generation must steward the scriptural insights God grants it, only arrogance or ignorance causes leaders to ignore the contributions of those faithful leaders before us. The Reformation Commentary on Scripture roots our thought in great insights of faithful leaders of the Reformation to further biblical preaching and teaching in this generation."

Bryan Chapell, *Chancellor and Professor of Practical Theology, Covenant Theological Seminary*

"After reading several volumes of the Reformation Commentary on Scripture, I exclaimed, 'Hey, this is just what the doctor ordered—I mean Doctor Martinus Lutherus!' The church of today bearing his name needs a strong dose of the medicine this doctor prescribed for the ailing church of the sixteenth century. The reforming fire of Christ-centered preaching that Luther ignited is the only hope to reclaim the impact of the gospel to keep the Reformation going, not for its own sake but to further the renewal of the worldwide church of Christ today. This series of commentaries will equip preachers to step into their pulpits with confidence in the same living Word that inspired the witness of Luther and Calvin and many other lesser-known Reformers."

Carl E. Braaten, *Cofounder of the Center for Catholic and Evangelical Theology*

"As a pastor, how does one cultivate a knowledge of the history of interpretation? That's where IVP's Reformation Commentary on Scripture and its forerunner, the Ancient Christian Commentary on Scripture, come in. They do an excellent job in helping pastors become more aware of the history of exegesis for the benefit of their congregations. Every pastor should have access to a set of each."

Carl R. Trueman, *Paul Woolley Chair of Church History, Westminster Theological Seminary*

REFORMATION
COMMENTARY
ON SCRIPTURE

NEW TESTAMENT
XII

1–2 THESSALONIANS,
1–2 TIMOTHY,
TITUS, PHILEMON

EDITED BY
LEE GATISS AND BRADLEY G. GREEN

GENERAL EDITOR
TIMOTHY GEORGE

ASSOCIATE GENERAL EDITOR
SCOTT M. MANETSCH

IVP Academic

An imprint of InterVarsity Press
Downers Grove, Illinois

InterVarsity Press
P.O. Box 1400, Downers Grove, IL 60515-1426
ivpress.com
email@ivpress.com

InterVarsity Press® is the book-publishing division of InterVarsity Christian Fellowship/USA®, a movement of students and faculty active on campus at hundreds of universities, colleges and schools of nursing in the United States of America, and a member movement of the International Fellowship of Evangelical Students. For information about local and regional activities, visit intervarsity.org.

This publication contains The Holy Bible, English Standard Version®, copyright © 2001 by Crossway, a publishing ministry of Good News Publishers. The ESV® text appearing in this publication is reproduced and published by cooperation between Good News Publishers and InterVarsity Press and by permission of Good News Publishers. Unauthorized reproduction of this publication is prohibited.

The Holy Bible, English Standard Version (ESV) is adapted from the Revised Standard Version of the Bible, copyright Division of Christian Education of the National Council of the Churches of Christ in the U.S.A. All rights reserved.

English Standard Version®, ESV® and ESV® logo are tradmarks of Good News Publishers located in Wheaton, Illinois. Used by permission.

Quotes from Luther's Works vols. 15, 19, 25, 28 and 29 © 1972, 1974, 1972, 1973, 1968 Concordia Publishing House, www.cph.org. Used by permission. All rights reserved.

Library of Christian Classics, Volume 25: Williams, George H., and Angel M. Mergal, eds. Spiritual and Anabaptist Writers. Philadelphia: Westminster, 1957.

CRR 6: Philips, Dirk. The Writings of Dirk Philips, 1504–1568. Translated and edited by Cornelius J. Dyck, William E. Keeney, and Alvin J. Beachy. CRR 6. © 2019 Plough Publishing House, Walden, NY.

CRR 5: Hubmaier, Balthasar. Balthasar Hubmaier: Theologian of Anabaptism. Translated and edited by H. Wayne Pipkin and John H. Yoder. CRR 5. © 2019 Plough Publishing House, Walden, NY.

CRR 12: Marpeck, Pilgram. The Writings of Pilgram Marpeck. Edited and translated by William Klassen and Walter Klassen. © 2019 Plough Publishing House, Walden, NY.

Design: Cindy Kiple
Images: wooden cross: iStockphoto
    The Protestant Church in Lyon: The Protestant Church in Lyon, called "The Paradise" at Bibliotheque Publique et Universitaire, Geneva, Switzerland. Erich Lessing/Art Resource, NY.

ISBN 978-0-8308-2975-0 (print)
ISBN 978-0-8308-7027-1 (digital)

Printed in the United States of America ∞

InterVarsity Press is committed to ecological stewardship and to the conservation of natural resources in all our operations. This book was printed using sustainably sourced paper.

Library of Congress Cataloging-in-Publication Data

Names: Gatiss, Lee, editor. | Green, Bradley G., 1965- editor.
Title: 1-2 Thessalonians, 1-2 Timothy, Titus, Philemon / edited by Lee Gatiss and Bradley G. Green ; general editor, Timothy George ; associate general editor, Scott M. Manetsch
Other titles: First and Second Thessalonians, First and Second Timothy, Titus, Philemon
Description: Westmont, Illinois : InterVarsity Press, 2019. | Series: Reformation commentary on scripture. New Testament ; XII | Includes bibliographical references and index.
Identifiers: LCCN 2019031162 (print) | LCCN 2019031163 (ebook) | ISBN 9780830829750 (hardcover) | ISBN 9780830870271 (ebook)
Subjects: LCSH: Bible. Thessalonians--Commentaries. | Bible. Pastoral epistles—Commentaries. | Bible. Philemon—Commentaries.
Classification: LCC BS2725.53 .A155 2019 (print) | LCC BS2725.53 (ebook) | DDC 227/.807—dc23
LC record available at https://lccn.loc.gov/2019031162
LC ebook record available at https://lccn.loc.gov/2019031163

P	27	26	25	24	23	22	21	20	19	18	17	16	15	14	13	12	11	10	9	8	7	6	5	4	3	2	1
Y	42	41	40	39	38	37	36	35	34	33	32	31	30	29	28	27	26	25	24	23	22	21	20	19			

Brad Green dedicates this work to

MILLARD J. ERICKSON
Theologian, Teacher, Mentor, Friend

Lee Gatiss dedicates this work to

the men and women of the
Junior Anglican Evangelical Conference (JAEC).
"And the things you have heard me say in the presence
of many witnesses entrust to reliable people who
will also be qualified to teach others."
2 Timothy 2:2 NIV

Reformation Commentary on Scripture
Project Staff

Project Editor
David W. McNutt

Managing Editor
Elissa Schauer

Copyeditor
Jeffrey A. Reimer

Assistant Project Editor
André A. Gazal

Editorial and Research Assistants
David J. Hooper
Ashley Davila
April Ponto

Assistants to the General Editors
Le-Ann Little
Jason Odom

Design
Cindy Kiple

Design Assistant
Beth McGill

Content Production
Maureen G. Tobey
Daniel van Loon
Jeanna L. Wiggins

Proofreader
Travis Ables

InterVarsity Press

Publisher
Jeff Crosby

Associate Publisher, Director of Editorial
Cindy Bunch

Editorial Director, IVP Academic
Jon Boyd

Director of Production
Benjamin M. McCoy

CONTENTS

ACKNOWLEDGMENTS

For the Pastoral Epistles, I (Lee Gatiss) particularly want to thank Robert Crellin and David Noe for their cheerful and careful assistance with some of the Latin translations of certain Lutheran and Catholic sources, and Nathalie Caplet for pardoning my French. Mark Smith and Tom Woolford saved me from egregious error with their knowledge of the early church and Richard Hooker respectively, for which I am very grateful. I owe a great debt of gratitude to John Percival for his eagle-eyed proofreading of an early draft and his rich knowledge of the Pastoral Epistles and their background. His works of supererogation usually created more work for me to do in clarifying things and adding footnotes, but they also most certainly helped to improve what you now read. I am also extremely grateful to all the men and women of the Junior Anglican Evangelical Conference (JAEC), which it has been my pleasure and privilege to lead over the last few years. As I was working on this commentary it was these Timothys, Tituses, Phoebes, and Priscillas that I kept in mind throughout, and their encouragement, example, and prayers helped sustain my efforts.

Several friends helped me (Brad Green) with the varied tasks of a project like this. There were a number of difficult pieces of Latin. Many thanks to Aaron Denlinger, Bradford Littlejohn, Michael Lynch, all with the Davenant Latin Institute, for their help with a few Latin words or phrases. I took a course with the Davenant folks, which helped me improve my translation skills. And thanks to Michael Sloan, who also helped me with some tricky Latin. I also want to thank Dirk Jongkind, of Tyndale House, Cambridge, for helping me make sense of the occasional Greek word or ligature that was difficult to read in an old sixteenth- or seventeenth-century manuscript. Much of the work was in fact completed at Tyndale House, Cambridge. Many thanks to the fine folks there—simply a wonderful place to study and write. Lee Gatiss helped me fine-tune and improve my portion of the assignment, and it was a joy to work with him. Many thanks to Union University, my employer, and its board of trustees, for supporting my scholarship. I dedicate this work to Millard J. Erickson. At two separate institutions I had the opportunity to either study with, or work for, Dr. Erickson. He was a great encouragement to me as a young theological student, and has continued to be a great encouragement to me. Thank you, Millard. Finally, my wife and children have always been supportive of my writing and scholarship. Thank you, Dianne, Caleb, Daniel, and Victoria, for everything.

ABBREVIATIONS

CCSL	Corpus Christianorum: Series Latina. Turnhout, Belgium: Brepols, 1953–.
CO	*Ioannis Calvini Opera quae supersunt omnia.* 59 vols. Corpus Reformatorum 29–88. Edited by G. Baum, E. Cunitz, and E. Reuss. Brunswick and Berlin: C. A. Schwetschke, 1863–1900. Digital copy online at archive-ouverte.unige.ch /unige:650.
CRR	*Classics of the Radical Reformation.* 12 vols. Waterloo, ON, and Scottsdale, PA: Herald Press, 1973–.
CTS	Calvin Translation Society edition of Calvin's commentaries. 46 vols. Edinburgh, 1843–1855. Several reprints, but variously bound; volume numbers (when cited) are relative to specific commentaries and not to the entire set.
EEBO	Early English Books Online. Subscription database, eebo.chadwyck.com.
EOO	Erasmus, Desiderius. *Desiderii Erasmi Roterodami Opera Omnia.* 10 vols. Edited by Jean LeClerc. Leiden: Van der Aa, 1706. Reprint, Hildersheim: Georg Olms, 1961–1962. Digital copy online at babel.hathitrust.org.
Geneva Bible 1560	Whittingham, William. *The Bible and Holy Scriptures conteyned in the Olde and Newe Testament.* Geneva: Rouland Hall, 1560. Digital copy online at EEBO.
Geneva Bible 1576	Whittingham, William. *The Bible and Holy Scriptures conteined in the Olde and Newe Testament.* London: Christopher Barkar, 1576. Digital copy online at EEBO.
Geneva Bible 1599	Beza, Theodore. *The New Testament of Our Lord Jesus Christ, Translated out of Greeke by Theodore Beza: With Brief Summaries and Expositions Upon the Hard Places by the Said Author.* Translated by L. Tomson. London, 1599.
LCC	John Baillie et al., eds. The Library of Christian Classics. 26 vols. Philadelphia: Westminster, 1953–1966.
LCL	Loeb Classical Library. Cambridge, MA: Harvard University Press; London: Heinemann, 1912–.
LW	*Luther's Works [American Edition].* 82 vols. planned. St. Louis: Concordia; Philadelphia: Fortress, 1955–1986; 2009–.

NPNF   A Select Library of the Nicene and Post-Nicene Fathers of the Christian Church. 28 vols. in two series, denoted as NPNF and NPNF². Edited by Philip Schaff et al. Buffalo, NY: Christian Literature, 1887–1894. Several reprints; also available online at www.ccel.org.

PL   Patrologia cursus completus. Series Latina. 221 vols. Edited by J.-P. Migne. Paris: Migne, 1844–1864. Digital copies online at books.google.com.

PML   The Peter Martyr [Vermigli] Library. 24 vols. projected in two series. Kirksville, MO: Truman State University Press, 1994–.

PRDL   Post-Reformation Digital Library. Online database at prdl.org.

Schaff   Philip Schaff, ed. *Bibliotheca Symbolica Ecclesiae Universalis: The Creeds of Christendom*. 3 vols. New York: Harper and Brothers, 1877. 6th ed., by David S. Schaff. Reprint ed. Grand Rapids: Baker, 1990. Available online at www.ccel.org.

WA   *D. Martin Luthers Werke, Kritische Gesamtausgabe*. 73 vols. Weimar: Hermann Böhlaus Nachfolger, 1883–2009. Digital copy online at archive.org.

WSA   John E. Rotelle, ed. Works of St. Augustine: A Translation for the Twenty-First Century. Hyde Park, NY: New City Press, 1995.

BIBLE TRANSLATIONS

ESV   English Standard Version
KJV   King James Version
NASB   New American Standard Bible
NIV   New International Version

A GUIDE TO USING THIS COMMENTARY

Several features have been incorporated into the design of this commentary. The following comments are intended to assist readers in making full use of this volume.

Pericopes of Scripture

The scriptural text has been divided into pericopes, or passages, usually several verses in length. Each of these pericopes is given a heading, which appears at the beginning of the pericope. For example, the first section in this commentary is 1 Thessalonians 1:1, "Introduction to Thessalonians and Greeting." This heading is followed by the Scripture passage quoted in the English Standard Version (esv). The Scripture passage is provided for the convenience of readers, but it is also in keeping with Reformation-era commentaries, which often followed the patristic and medieval commentary tradition, in which the citations of the reformers were arranged according to the text of Scripture.

Overviews

Following each pericope of text is an overview of the Reformation authors' comments on that pericope. The format of this overview varies among the volumes of this series, depending on the requirements of the specific book(s) of Scripture. The function of the overview is to identify succinctly the key exegetical, theological, and pastoral concerns of the Reformation writers arising from the pericope, providing the reader with an orientation to Reformation-era approaches and emphases. It tracks a reasonably cohesive thread of argument among reformers' comments, even though they are derived from diverse sources and generations. Thus, the summaries do not proceed chronologically or by verse sequence. Rather, they seek to rehearse the overall course of the reformers' comments on that pericope.

We do not assume that the commentators themselves anticipated or expressed a formally received cohesive argument but rather that the various arguments tend to flow in a plausible, recognizable pattern. Modern readers can thus glimpse aspects of continuity in the flow of diverse exegetical traditions representing various generations and geographical locations.

Topical Headings

An abundance of varied Reformation-era comment is available for each pericope. For this reason we have broken the pericopes into two levels. First is the verse with its topical heading. The reformers' comments are then focused on aspects of each verse, with topical headings summarizing the essence of the individual comment by evoking a key phrase, metaphor, or idea. This feature provides a bridge by which modern readers can enter into the heart of the Reformation-era comment.

Identifying the Reformation Authors, Texts, and Events

Following the topical heading of each section of comment, the name of the Reformation commentator is given. An English translation (where needed) of the reformer's comment is then provided. This is immediately followed by the title of the original work rendered in English.

Readers who wish to pursue a deeper investigation of the reformers' works cited in this commentary will find full bibliographic detail for each Reformation title provided in the bibliography at the back of the volume. Information on English translations (where available) and standard original-language editions and critical editions of the works cited is found in the bibliography. The Biographical Sketches section provides brief overviews of the life and work of each commentator, and each confession or collaborative work, appearing in the present volume (as well as in any previous volumes). Finally, a Timeline of the Reformation offers broader context for people, places, and events relevant to the commentators and their works.

Footnotes and Back Matter

To aid the reader in exploring the background and texts in further detail, this commentary utilizes footnotes. The use and content of footnotes may vary among the volumes in this series. Where footnotes appear, a footnote number directs the reader to a note at the bottom of the page, where one will find annotations (clarifications or biblical cross references), information on English translations (where available) or standard original-language editions of the work cited.

Where original-language texts have remained untranslated into English, we provide new translations. Where there is any serious ambiguity or textual problem in the selection, we have tried to reflect the best available textual tradition. Wherever current English translations are already well rendered, they are utilized, but where necessary they are stylistically updated. A single asterisk (*) indicates that a previous English translation has been updated to modern English or amended for easier reading. We have standardized spellings and made grammatical variables uniform so that our English references will not reflect the linguistic oddities of the older English translations. For ease of reading we have in some cases removed superfluous conjunctions.

GENERAL INTRODUCTION

The Reformation Commentary on Scripture (RCS) is a twenty-eight-volume series of exegetical comment covering the entire Bible and gathered from the writings of sixteenth-century preachers, scholars and reformers. The RCS is intended as a sequel to the highly acclaimed Ancient Christian Commentary on Scripture (ACCS), and as such its overall concept, method, format, and audience are similar to the earlier series. Both series are committed to the renewal of the church through careful study and meditative reflection on the Old and New Testaments, the charter documents of Christianity, read in the context of the worshiping, believing community of faith across the centuries. However, the patristic and Reformation eras are separated by nearly a millennium, and the challenges of reading Scripture with the reformers require special attention to their context, resources and assumptions. The purpose of this general introduction is to present an overview of the context and process of biblical interpretation in the age of the Reformation.

Goals

The Reformation Commentary on Scripture seeks to introduce its readers to the depth and richness of exegetical ferment that defined the Reformation era. The RCS has four goals: the enrichment of contemporary biblical interpretation through exposure to Reformation-era biblical exegesis; the renewal of contemporary preaching through exposure to the biblical insights of the Reformation writers; a deeper understanding of the Reformation itself and the breadth of perspectives represented within it; and a recovery of the profound integration of the life of faith and the life of the mind that should characterize Christian scholarship. Each of these goals requires a brief comment.

Renewing contemporary biblical interpretation. During the past half-century, biblical hermeneutics has become a major growth industry in the academic world. One of the consequences of the historical-critical hegemony of biblical studies has been the privileging of contemporary philosophies and ideologies at the expense of a commitment to the Christian church as the primary reading community within which and for which biblical exegesis is done. Reading Scripture with the church fathers and the reformers is a corrective to all such imperialism of the present. One of the greatest skills required for a fruitful interpretation of the Bible is the ability to listen. We rightly emphasize the importance of listening to the voices of contextual theologies today, but in doing so we often marginalize or ignore another crucial context—the community of believing Christians through the centuries. The serious study of Scripture requires more than the latest

Bible translation in one hand and the latest commentary (or niche study Bible) in the other. John L. Thompson has called on Christians today to practice the art of "reading the Bible with the dead."[1] The RCS presents carefully selected comments from the extant commentaries of the Reformation as an encouragement to more in-depth study of this important epoch in the history of biblical interpretation.

Strengthening contemporary preaching. The Protestant reformers identified the public preaching of the Word of God as an indispensible means of grace and a sure sign of the true church. Through the words of the preacher, the living voice of the gospel (*viva vox evangelii*) is heard. Luther famously said that the church is not a "pen house" but a "mouth house."[2] The Reformation in Switzerland began when Huldrych Zwingli entered the pulpit of the Grossmünster in Zurich on January 1, 1519, and began to preach a series of expositional sermons chapter by chapter from the Gospel of Matthew. In the following years he extended this homiletical approach to other books of the Old and New Testaments. Calvin followed a similar pattern in Geneva. Many of the commentaries represented in this series were either originally presented as sermons or were written to support the regular preaching ministry of local church pastors. Luther said that the preacher should be a *bonus textualis*—a good one with a text—well-versed in the Scriptures. Preachers in the Reformation traditions preached not only about the Bible but also from it, and this required more than a passing acquaintance with its contents. Those who have been charged with the office of preaching in the church today can find wisdom and insight—and fresh perspectives—in the sermons of the Reformation and the biblical commentaries read and studied by preachers of the sixteenth century.

Deepening understanding of the Reformation. Some scholars of the sixteenth century prefer to speak of the period they study in the plural, the European Reformations, to indicate that many diverse impulses for reform were at work in this turbulent age of transition from medieval to modern times.[3] While this point is well taken, the RCS follows the time-honored tradition of using *Reformation* in the singular form to indicate not only a major moment in the history of Christianity in the West but also, as Hans J. Hillerbrand has put it, "an essential cohesiveness in the heterogeneous pursuits of religious reform in the sixteenth century."[4] At the same time, in developing guidelines to assist the volume editors in making judicious selections from the vast amount of commentary material available in this period, we have stressed the multifaceted character of the Reformation across many confessions, theological orientations, and political settings.

Advancing Christian scholarship. By assembling and disseminating numerous voices from such a signal period as the Reformation, the RCS aims to make a significant contribution to the ever-growing stream of Christian scholarship. The post-Enlightenment split between the study of the Bible as an academic discipline and the reading of the Bible as spiritual nurture was foreign

---

[1] John L. Thompson, *Reading the Bible with the Dead* (Grand Rapids: Eerdmans, 2007).

[2] WA 10,2:48.

[3] See Carter Lindberg, *The European Reformations*, 2nd ed. (Malden, MA: Wiley-Blackwell, 2010).

[4] Hans J. Hillerbrand, *The Division of Christendom* (Louisville, KY: Westminster John Knox, 2007), x. Hillerbrand has also edited the standard reference work in Reformation studies, *OER*. See also Diarmaid MacCulloch, *The Reformation* (New York: Viking, 2003), and Patrick Collinson, *The Reformation: A History* (New York: Random House, 2004).

to the reformers. For them the study of the Bible was transformative at the most basic level of the human person: *coram deo.*

The reformers all repudiated the idea that the Bible could be studied and understood with dispassionate objectivity, as a cold artifact from antiquity. Luther's famous Reformation break-through triggered by his laborious study of the Psalms and Paul's letter to the Romans is well known, but the experience of Cambridge scholar Thomas Bilney was perhaps more typical. When Erasmus's critical edition of the Greek New Testament was published in 1516, it was accompanied by a new translation in elegant Latin. Attracted by the classical beauty of Erasmus's Latin, Bilney came across this statement in 1 Timothy 1:15: "Christ Jesus came into the world to save sinners." In the Greek this sentence is described as *pistos ho logos,* which the Vulgate had rendered *fidelis sermo,* "a faithful saying." Erasmus chose a different word for the Greek *pistos—certus,* "sure, certain." When Bilney grasped the meaning of this word applied to the announcement of salvation in Christ, he tells us that "immediately, I felt a marvellous comfort and quietness, insomuch as 'my bruised bones leaped for joy.'"[5]

Luther described the way the Bible was meant to function in the minds and hearts of believers when he reproached himself and others for studying the nativity narrative with such cool unconcern:

> I hate myself because when I see Christ laid in the manger or in the lap of his mother and hear the angels sing, my heart does not leap into flame. With what good reason should we all despise our-selves that we remain so cold when this word is spoken to us, over which everyone should dance and leap and burn for joy! We act as though it were a frigid historical fact that does not smite our hearts, as if someone were merely relating that the sultan has a crown of gold.[6]

It was a core conviction of the Reformation that the careful study and meditative listening to the Scriptures, what the monks called *lectio divina,* could yield transformative results for *all* of life. The value of such a rich commentary, therefore, lies not only in the impressive volume of Reformation-era voices that are presented throughout the course of the series but in the many particular fields for which their respective lives and ministries are relevant. The Reformation is consequential for historical studies, both church as well as secular history. Biblical and theological studies, to say nothing of pastoral and spiritual studies, also stand to benefit and progress immensely from re-newed engagement today, as mediated through the RCS, with the reformers of yesteryear.

Perspectives

In setting forth the perspectives and parameters of the RCS, the following considerations have proved helpful.

Chronology. When did the Reformation begin, and how long did it last? In some traditional accounts, the answer was clear: the Reformation began with the posting of Luther's Ninety-five

---

[5]John Foxe, *The Acts and Monuments of John Foxe: A New and Complete Edition,* 8 vols., ed. Stephen Reed Cattley (London: R. B. Seeley & W. Burnside, 1837), 4:635; quoting Ps 51:8; cited in A. G. Dickens, *The English Reformation,* 2nd ed. (University Park, PA: The Pennsylvannia State University Press, 1991), 102.

[6]WA 49:176-77, quoted in Roland Bainton, "The Bible in the Reformation," in *CHB,* 3:23.

Theses at Wittenberg in 1517 and ended with the death of Calvin in Geneva in 1564. Apart from reducing the Reformation to a largely German event with a side trip to Switzerland, this perspective fails to do justice to the important events that led up to Luther's break with Rome and its many reverberations throughout Europe and beyond. In choosing commentary selections for the RCS, we have adopted the concept of the long sixteenth century, say, from the late 1400s to the mid-seventeenth century. Thus we have included commentary selections from early or pre-Reformation writers such as John Colet and Jacques Lefèvre d'Étaples to seventeenth-century figures such as Henry Ainsworth and Johann Gerhard.

Confession. The RCS concentrates primarily, though not exclusively, on the exegetical writings of the Protestant reformers. While the ACCS provided a compendium of key consensual exegetes of the early Christian centuries, the Catholic/Protestant confessional divide in the sixteenth century tested the very idea of consensus, especially with reference to ecclesiology and soteriology. While many able and worthy exegetes faithful to the Roman Catholic Church were active during this period, this project has chosen to include primarily those figures that represent perspectives within the Protestant Reformation. For this reason we have not included comments on the apocryphal or deuterocanonical writings.

We recognize that "Protestant" and "Catholic" as contradistinctive labels are anachronistic terms for the early decades of the sixteenth century before the hardening of confessional identities surrounding the Council of Trent (1545–1563). Protestant figures such as Philipp Melanchthon, Johannes Oecolampadius and John Calvin were all products of the revival of sacred letters known as biblical humanism. They shared an approach to biblical interpretation that owed much to Desiderius Erasmus and other scholars who remained loyal to the Church of Rome. Careful comparative studies of Protestant and Catholic exegesis in the sixteenth century have shown surprising areas of agreement when the focus was the study of a particular biblical text rather than the standard confessional debates.

At the same time, exegetical differences among the various Protestant groups could become strident and church-dividing. The most famous example of this is the interpretive impasse between Luther and Zwingli over the meaning of "This is my body" (Mt 26:26) in the words of institution. Their disagreement at the Colloquy of Marburg in 1529 had important christological and pastoral implications, as well as social and political consequences. Luther refused fellowship with Zwingli and his party at the end of the colloquy; in no small measure this bitter division led to the separate trajectories pursued by Lutheran and Reformed Protestantism to this day. In Elizabethan England, Puritans and Anglicans agreed that "Holy Scripture containeth all things necessary to salvation: so that whatsoever is not read therein, nor may be proved thereby, is not to be required of any man" (article 6 of the Thirty-Nine Articles of Religion), yet on the basis of their differing interpretations of the Bible they fought bitterly over the structures of the church, the clothing of the clergy and the ways of worship. On the matter of infant baptism, Catholics and Protestants alike agreed on its propriety, though there were various theories as to how a practice not mentioned in the Bible could be justified biblically. The Anabaptists were outliers on this subject. They rejected infant baptism altogether. They appealed to the example of the baptism of Jesus and to his final words as recorded in the Gospel of Matthew (Mt 28:19-20): "Go therefore, and make disciples of all nations, baptizing them in the name of the Father, and of the Son, and of the Holy Spirit, teaching them to observe all that I have commanded you." New Testament Christians, they argued, are to follow not only the commands of Jesus in the Great Commission, but also the exact order in which they were given: evangelize, baptize, catechize.

These and many other differences of interpretation among the various Protestant groups are reflected in their many sermons, commentaries and public disputations. In the RCS, the volume editors' introduction to each volume is intended to help the reader understand the nature and significance of doctrinal conversations and disputes that resulted in particular, and frequently clashing, interpretations. Footnotes throughout the text will be provided to explain obscure references, unusual expressions and other matters that require special comment. Volume editors have chosen comments on the Bible across a wide range of sixteenth-century confessions and schools of interpretation: biblical humanists, Lutheran, Reformed, Anglican, Puritan, and Anabaptist. We have not pursued passages from post-Tridentine Catholic authors or from radical spiritualists and antitrinitarian writers, though sufficient material is available from these sources to justify another series.

Format. The design of the RCS is intended to offer reader-friendly access to these classic texts. The availability of digital resources has given access to a huge residual database of sixteenth-century exegetical comment hitherto available only in major research universities and rare book collections. The RCS has benefited greatly from online databases such as Alexander Street Press's Digital Library of Classical Protestant Texts (DLCPT) and Early English Books Online as well as freely accessible databases like the Post-Reformation Digital Library (prdl.org). Through the help of RCS editorial advisor Herman Selderhuis, we have also had access to the special Reformation collections of the Johannes a Lasco Bibliothek in Emden, Germany. In addition, modern critical editions and translations of Reformation sources have been published over the past generation. Original translations of Reformation sources are given unless an acceptable translation already exists.

Each volume in the RCS will include an introduction by the volume editor placing that portion of the canon within the historical context of the Protestant Reformation and presenting a summary of the theological themes, interpretive issues and reception of the particular book(s). The commentary itself consists of particular pericopes identified by a pericope heading; the biblical text in the English Standard Version (ESV), with significant textual variants registered in the footnotes; an overview of the pericope in which principal exegetical and theological concerns of the Reformation writers are succinctly noted; and excerpts from the Reformation writers identified by name according to the conventions of the *Oxford Encyclopedia of the Reformation.* Each volume will also include a bibliography of sources cited, as well as an appendix of authors and source works.

The Reformation era was a time of verbal as well as physical violence, and this fact has presented a challenge for this project. Without unduly sanitizing the texts, where they contain anti-Semitic, sexist or inordinately polemical rhetoric, we have not felt obliged to parade such comments either. We have noted the abridgement of texts with ellipses and an explanatory footnote.

While this procedure would not be valid in the critical edition of such a text, we have deemed it appropriate in a series whose primary purpose is pastoral and devotional. When translating *homo* or similar terms that refer to the human race as a whole or to individual persons without reference to gender, we have used alternative English expressions to the word *man* (or derivative constructions that formerly were used generically to signify humanity at large), whenever such substitutions can be made without producing an awkward or artificial construction.

As is true in the ACCS, we have made a special effort where possible to include the voices of women, though we acknowledge the difficulty of doing so for the early modern period when for a variety of social and cultural reasons few theological and biblical works were published by women. However, recent scholarship has focused on a number of female leaders whose literary remains show us how they understood and interpreted the Bible. Women who made significant contributions to the Reformation include Marguerite d'Angoulême, sister of King Francis I, who supported French reformist evangelicals including Calvin and who published a religious poem influenced by Luther's theology, *The Mirror of the Sinful Soul*; Argula von Grumbach, a Bavarian noblewoman who defended the teachings of Luther and Melanchthon before the theologians of the University of Ingolstadt; Katharina Schütz Zell, the wife of a former priest, Matthias Zell, and a remarkable reformer in her own right—she conducted funerals, compiled hymnbooks, defended the downtrodden, and published a defense of clerical marriage as well as composing works of consolation on divine comfort and pleas for the toleration of Anabaptists and Catholics alike; and Anne Askew, a Protestant martyr put to death in 1546 after demonstrating remarkable biblical prowess in her examinations by church officials. Other echoes of faithful women in the age of the Reformation are found in their letters, translations, poems, hymns, court depositions, and martyr records.

Lay culture, learned culture. In recent decades, much attention has been given to what is called "reforming from below," that is, the expressions of religious beliefs and churchly life that characterized the popular culture of the majority of the population in the era of the Reformation. Social historians have taught us to examine the diverse pieties of townspeople and city folk, of rural religion and village life, the emergence of lay theologies, and the experiences of women in the religious tumults of Reformation Europe.[7] Formal commentaries by their nature are artifacts of learned culture. Almost all of them were written in Latin, the lingua franca of learned discourse well past the age of the Reformation. Biblical commentaries were certainly not the primary means by which the Protestant Reformation spread so rapidly across wide sectors of sixteenth-century society. Small pamphlets and broadsheets, later called *Flugschriften* ("flying writings"), with their graphic woodcuts and cartoon-like depictions of Reformation personalities and events, became the means of choice for mass communication in the early age of printing. Sermons and works of devotion were also printed with appealing visual aids. Luther's early writings were often accompanied by drawings and sketches from Lucas Cranach and other artists. This was done "above all for the sake of children and simple folk," as Luther

---

[7]See Peter Matheson, ed., *Reformation Christianity* (Minneapolis: Fortress, 2007).

put it, "who are more easily moved by pictures and images to recall divine history than through mere words or doctrines."[8]

We should be cautious, however, in drawing too sharp a distinction between learned and lay culture in this period. The phenomenon of preaching was a kind of verbal bridge between scholars at their desks and the thousands of illiterate or semiliterate listeners whose views were shaped by the results of Reformation exegesis. According to contemporary witness, more than one thousand people were crowding into Geneva to hear Calvin expound the Scriptures every day.[9] An example of how learned theological works by Reformation scholars were received across divisions of class and social status comes from Lazare Drilhon, an apothecary of Toulon. He was accused of heresy in May 1545 when a cache of prohibited books was found hidden in his garden shed. In addition to devotional works, the French New Testament and a copy of Calvin's Genevan liturgy, there was found a series of biblical commentaries, translated from the Latin into French: Martin Bucer's on Matthew, François Lambert's on the Apocalypse and one by Oecolampadius on 1 John.[10] Biblical exegesis in the sixteenth century was not limited to the kind of full-length commentaries found in Drilhon's shed. Citations from the Bible and expositions of its meaning permeate the extant literature of sermons, letters, court depositions, doctrinal treatises, records of public disputations and even last wills and testaments. While most of the selections in the RCS will be drawn from formal commentary literature, other sources of biblical reflection will also be considered.

Historical Context

The medieval legacy. On October 18, 1512, the degree *Doctor in Biblia* was conferred on Martin Luther, and he began his career as a professor in the University of Wittenberg. As is well known, Luther was also a monk who had taken solemn vows in the Augustinian Order of Hermits at Erfurt. These two settings—the university and the monastery—both deeply rooted in the Middle Ages, form the background not only for Luther's personal vocation as a reformer but also for the history of the biblical commentary in the age of the Reformation. Since the time of the Venerable Bede (d. 735), sometimes called "the last of the Fathers," serious study of the Bible had taken place primarily in the context of cloistered monasteries. The Rule of St. Benedict brought together *lectio* and *meditatio*, the knowledge of letters and the life of prayer. The liturgy was the medium through which the daily reading of the Bible, especially the Psalms, and the sayings of the church fathers came together in the spiritual formation of the monks.[11] Essential to this understanding was a belief in the unity of the people of God throughout time as well as space, and an awareness that life in this world was a preparation for the beatific vision in the next.

---

[8]Martin Luther, "Personal Prayer Book," LW 43:42-43* (WA 10,2:458); quoted in R. W. Scribner, *For the Sake of Simple Folk: Popular Propaganda for the German Reformation* (Cambridge: Cambridge University Press, 1981), xi.

[9]Letter of De Beaulieu to Guillaume Farel (1561) in *Theodor Beza nach handschriftlichen und anderen gleichzeitigen Quellen*, ed. J. W. Baum (Leipzig: Weidmann, 1851), 2:92.

[10]Francis Higman, "A Heretic's Library: The Drilhon Inventory" (1545), in Francis Higman, *Lire et Découvire: la circulation des idées au temps de la Réforme* (Geneva: Droz, 1998), 65-85.

[11]See the classic study by Jean Leclercq, *The Love of Learning and the Desire for God* (New York: Fordham University Press, 1961).

The source of theology was the study of the sacred page (*sacra pagina*); its object was the accumulation of knowledge not for its own sake but for the obtaining of eternal life. For these monks, the Bible had God for its author, salvation for its end and unadulterated truth for its matter, though they would not have expressed it in such an Aristotelian way. The medieval method of interpreting the Bible owed much to Augustine's *On Christian Doctrine*. In addition to setting forth a series of rules (drawn from an earlier work by Tyconius), Augustine stressed the importance of distinguishing the literal and spiritual or allegorical senses of Scripture. While the literal sense was not disparaged, the allegorical was valued because it enabled the believer to obtain spiritual benefit from the obscure places in the Bible, especially in the Old Testament. For Augustine, as for the monks who followed him, the goal of scriptural exegesis was freighted with eschatological meaning; its purpose was to induce faith, hope, and love and so to advance in one's pilgrimage toward that city with foundations (see Heb 11:10).

Building on the work of Augustine and other church fathers going back to Origen, medieval exegetes came to understand Scripture as possessed of four possible meanings, the famous *quadriga*. The literal meaning was retained, of course, but the spiritual meaning was now subdivided into three senses: the allegorical, the moral, and the anagogical. Medieval exegetes often referred to the four meanings of Scripture in a popular rhyme:

> The letter shows us what God and our fathers did;
> The allegory shows us where our faith is hid;
> The moral meaning gives us rules of daily life;
> The anagogy shows us where we end our strife.[12]

In this schema, the three spiritual meanings of the text correspond to the three theological virtues: faith (allegory), hope (anagogy), and love (the moral meaning). It should be noted that this way of approaching the Bible assumed a high doctrine of scriptural inspiration: the multiple meanings inherent in the text had been placed there by the Holy Spirit for the benefit of the people of God. The biblical justification for this method went back to the apostle Paul, who had used the words *allegory* and *type* when applying Old Testament events to believers in Christ (Gal 4:21-31; 1 Cor 10:1-11). The problem with this approach was knowing how to relate each of the four senses to one another and how to prevent Scripture from becoming a nose of wax turned this way and that by various interpreters. As G. R. Evans explains, "Any interpretation which could be put upon the text and was in keeping with the faith and edifying, had the warrant of God himself, for no human reader had the ingenuity to find more than God had put there."[13]

With the rise of the universities in the eleventh century, theology and the study of Scripture moved from the cloister into the classroom. Scripture and the Fathers were still important, but they came to function more as footnotes to the theological questions debated in the schools and brought together in an impressive systematic way in works such as Peter Lombard's *Books of Sentences* (the standard theology textbook of the Middle Ages) and the great scholastic *summae* of the thirteenth

---

[12]Robert M. Grant, *A Short History of the Interpretation of the Bible* (New York: Macmillan, 1963), 119. A translation of the well-known Latin quatrain: *Littera gesta docet/Quid credas allegoria/Moralis quid agas/Quo tendas anagogia.*

[13]G. R. Evans, *The Language and Logic of the Bible: The Road to Reformation* (Cambridge: Cambridge University Press, 1985), 42.

century. Indispensable to the study of the Bible in the later Middle Ages was the *Glossa ordinaria*, a collection of exegetical opinions by the church fathers and other commentators. Heiko Oberman summarized the transition from devotion to dialectic this way: "When, due to the scientific revolution of the twelfth century, Scripture became the *object* of study rather than the *subject* through which God speaks to the student, the difference between the two modes of speaking was investigated in terms of the texts themselves rather than in their relation to the recipients."[14] It was possible, of course, to be both a scholastic theologian and a master of the spiritual life. Meister Eckhart, for example, wrote commentaries on the Old Testament in Latin and works of mystical theology in German, reflecting what had come to be seen as a division of labor between the two.

An increasing focus on the text of Scripture led to a revival of interest in its literal sense. The two key figures in this development were Thomas Aquinas (d. 1274) and Nicholas of Lyra (d. 1340). Thomas is best remembered for his *Summa Theologiae*, but he was also a prolific commentator on the Bible. Thomas did not abandon the multiple senses of Scripture but declared that all the senses were founded on one—the literal—and this sense eclipsed allegory as the basis of sacred doctrine. Nicholas of Lyra was a Franciscan scholar who made use of the Hebrew text of the Old Testament and quoted liberally from works of Jewish scholars, especially the learned French rabbi Salomon Rashi (d. 1105). After Aquinas, Lyra was the strongest defender of the literal, historical meaning of Scripture as the primary basis of theological disputation. His *Postilla*, as his notes were called—the abbreviated form of *post illa verba textus*, meaning "after these words from Scripture"—were widely circulated in the late Middle Ages and became the first biblical commentary to be printed in the fifteenth century. More than any other commentator from the period of high scholasticism, Lyra and his work were greatly valued by the early reformers. According to an old Latin pun, *Nisi Lyra lyrasset, Lutherus non saltasset*, "If Lyra had not played his lyre, Luther would not have danced."[15] While Luther was never an uncritical disciple of any teacher, he did praise Lyra as a good Hebraist and quoted him more than one hundred times in his lectures on Genesis, where he declared, "I prefer him to almost all other interpreters of Scripture."[16]

Sacred philology. The sixteenth century has been called a golden age of biblical interpretation, and it is a fact that the age of the Reformation witnessed an explosion of commentary writing unparalleled in the history of the Christian church. Kenneth Hagen has cataloged forty-five commentaries on Hebrews between 1516 (Erasmus) and 1598 (Beza).[17] During the sixteenth century, more than seventy new commentaries on Romans were published, five of them by Melanchthon alone, and nearly one hundred commentaries on the Bible's prayer book, the Psalms.[18] There were two developments in the fifteenth century that presaged this development and without which it

---

[14]Heiko Oberman, *Forerunners of the Reformation* (Philadelphia: Fortress, 1966), 284.

[15]Nicholas of Lyra, *The Postilla of Nicolas of Lyra on the Song of Songs*, trans. and ed. James George Kiecker (Milwaukee: Marquette University Press, 1998), 19.

[16]LW 2:164 (WA 42:377).

[17]Kenneth Hagen, *Hebrews Commenting from Erasmus to Bèze, 1516–1598* (Tübingen: Mohr, 1981).

[18]R. Gerald Hobbs, "Biblical Commentaries," *OER* 1:167-71. See in general David C. Steinmetz, ed., *The Bible in the Sixteenth Century* (Durham: Duke University Press, 1990).

could not have taken place: the invention of printing and the rediscovery of a vast store of ancient learning hitherto unknown or unavailable to scholars in the West.

It is now commonplace to say that what the computer has become in our generation, the printing press was to the world of Erasmus, Luther, and other leaders of the Reformation. Johannes Gutenberg, a goldsmith by trade, developed a metal alloy suitable for type and a machine that would allow printed characters to be cast with relative ease, placed in even lines of composition and then manipulated again and again, making possible the mass production of an unbelievable number of texts. In 1455, the Gutenberg Bible, the masterpiece of the typographical revolution, was published at Mainz in double columns in gothic type. Forty-seven copies of the beautiful Gutenberg Bible are still extant, each consisting of more than one thousand colorfully illuminated and impeccably printed pages. What began at Gutenberg's print shop in Mainz on the Rhine River soon spread, like McDonald's or Starbucks in our day, into every nook and cranny of the known world. Printing presses sprang up in Rome (1464), Venice (1469), Paris (1470), the Netherlands (1471), Switzerland (1472), Spain (1474), England (1476), Sweden (1483), and Constantinople (1490). By 1500, these and other presses across Europe had published some twenty-seven thousand titles, most of them in Latin. Erasmus once compared himself with an obscure preacher whose sermons were heard by only a few people in one or two churches while his books were read in every country in the world. Erasmus was not known for his humility, but in this case he was simply telling the truth.[19]

The Italian humanist Lorenzo Valla (d. 1457) died in the early dawn of the age of printing, but his critical and philological studies would be taken up by others who believed that genuine reform in church and society could come about only by returning to the wellsprings of ancient learning and wisdom—*ad fontes*, "back to the sources!" Valla is best remembered for undermining a major claim made by defenders of the papacy when he proved by philological research that the so-called Donation of Constantine, which had bolstered papal assertions of temporal sovereignty, was a forgery. But it was Valla's *Collatio Novi Testamenti* of 1444 that would have such a great effect on the renewal of biblical studies in the next century. Erasmus discovered the manuscript of this work while rummaging through an old library in Belgium and published it at Paris in 1505. In the preface to his edition of Valla, Erasmus gave the rationale that would guide his own labors in textual criticism. Just as Jerome had translated the Latin Vulgate from older versions and copies of the Scriptures in his day, so now Jerome's own text must be subjected to careful scrutiny and correction. Erasmus would be *Hieronymus redivivus*, a new Jerome come back to life to advance the cause of sacred philology. The restoration of the Scriptures and the writings of the church fathers would usher in what Erasmus believed would be a golden age of peace and learning. In 1516, the Basel publisher Froben brought out Erasmus's *Novum Instrumentum*, the first published edition of the Greek New Testament. Erasmus's Greek New Testament would go through five editions in his lifetime, each one with new emendations to the text and a growing section of annotations that expanded to include not only technical notes about the text but also theological comment. The influence of Erasmus's Greek New

---

[19]E. Harris Harbison, *The Christian Scholar in the Age of the Reformation* (New York: Charles Scribner's Sons, 1956), 80.

Testament was enormous. It formed the basis for Robert Estienne's *Novum Testamentum Graece* of 1550, which in turn was used to establish the Greek *Textus Receptus* for a number of late Reformation translations including the King James Version of 1611.

For all his expertise in Greek, Erasmus was a poor student of Hebrew and only published commentaries on several of the psalms. However, the renaissance of Hebrew letters was part of the wider program of biblical humanism as reflected in the establishment of trilingual colleges devoted to the study of Hebrew, Greek and Latin (the three languages written on the *titulus* of Jesus' cross [Jn 19:20]) at Alcalá in Spain, Wittenberg in Germany, Louvain in Belgium, and Paris in France. While it is true that some medieval commentators, especially Nicholas of Lyra, had been informed by the study of Hebrew and rabbinics in their biblical work, it was the publication of Johannes Reuchlin's *De rudimentis hebraicis* (1506), a combined grammar and dictionary, that led to the recovery of *veritas Hebraica*, as Jerome had referred to the true voice of the Hebrew Scriptures. The pursuit of Hebrew studies was carried forward in the Reformation by two great scholars, Konrad Pellikan and Sebastian Münster. Pellikan was a former Franciscan friar who embraced the Protestant cause and played a major role in the Zurich reformation. He had published a Hebrew grammar even prior to Reuchlin and produced a commentary on nearly the entire Bible that appeared in seven volumes between 1532 and 1539. Münster was Pellikan's student and taught Hebrew at the University of Heidelberg before taking up a similar position in Basel. Like his mentor, Münster was a great collector of Hebraica and published a series of excellent grammars, dictionaries and rabbinic texts. Münster did for the Hebrew Old Testament what Erasmus had done for the Greek New Testament. His *Hebraica Biblia* offered a fresh Latin translation of the Old Testament with annotations from medieval rabbinic exegesis.

Luther first learned Hebrew with Reuchlin's grammar in hand but took advantage of other published resources, such as the four-volume Hebrew Bible published at Venice by Daniel Bomberg in 1516 to 1517. He also gathered his own circle of Hebrew experts, his *sanhedrin* he called it, who helped him with his German translation of the Old Testament. We do not know where William Tyndale learned Hebrew, though perhaps it was in Worms, where there was a thriving rabbinical school during his stay there. In any event, he had sufficiently mastered the language to bring out a freshly translated Pentateuch that was published at Antwerp in 1530. By the time the English separatist scholar Henry Ainsworth published his prolix commentaries on the Pentateuch in 1616, the knowledge of Hebrew, as well as Greek, was taken for granted by every serious scholar of the Bible. In the preface to his commentary on Genesis, Ainsworth explained that "the literal sense of Moses's Hebrew (which is the tongue wherein he wrote the law), is the ground of all interpretation, and that language hath figures and properties of speech, different from ours: These therefore in the first place are to be opened that the natural meaning of the Scripture, being known, the mysteries of godliness therein implied, may be better discerned."[20]

The restoration of the biblical text in the original languages made possible the revival of scriptural exposition reflected in the floodtide of sermon literature and commentary work. Of even

---

[20]Henry Ainsworth, *Annotations upon the First Book of Moses Called Genesis* (Amsterdam, 1616), preface (unpaginated).

more far-reaching import was the steady stream of vernacular Bibles in the sixteenth century. In the introduction to his 1516 edition of the New Testament, Erasmus had expressed his desire that the Scriptures be translated into all languages so that "the lowliest women" could read the Gospels and the Pauline epistles and "the farmer sing some portion of them at the plow, the weaver hum some parts of them to the movement of his shuttle, the traveler lighten the weariness of the journey with stories of this kind."[21] Like Erasmus, Tyndale wanted the Bible to be available in the language of the common people. He once said to a learned divine that if God spared his life he would cause the boy who drives the plow to know more of the Scriptures than he did![22] The project of allowing the Bible to speak in the language of the mother in the house, the children in the street and the cheesemonger in the marketplace was met with stiff opposition by certain Catholic polemists such as Johann Eck, Luther's antagonist at the Leipzig Debate of 1519. In his *Enchiridion* (1525), Eck derided the "inky theologians" whose translations paraded the Bible before "the untutored crowd" and subjected it to the judgment of "laymen and crazy old women."[23] In fact, some fourteen German Bibles had already been published prior to Luther's September Testament of 1522, which he translated from Erasmus's Greek New Testament in less than three months' time while sequestered in the Wartburg. Luther's German New Testament became the first bestseller in the world, appearing in forty-three distinct editions between 1522 and 1525 with upward of one hundred thousand copies issued in these three years. It is estimated that 5 percent of the German population may have been literate at this time, but this rate increased as the century wore on due in no small part to the unmitigated success of vernacular Bibles.[24]

Luther's German Bible (inclusive of the Old Testament from 1534) was the most successful venture of its kind, but it was not alone in the field. Hans Denck and Ludwig Hätzer, leaders in the early Anabaptist movement, translated the prophetic books of the Old Testament from Hebrew into German in 1527. This work influenced the Swiss-German Bible of 1531 published by Leo Jud and other pastors in Zurich. Tyndale's influence on the English language rivaled that of Luther on German. At a time when English was regarded as "that obscure and remote dialect of German spoken in an off-shore island," Tyndale, with his remarkable linguistic ability (he was fluent in eight languages), "made a language for England," as his modern editor David Daniell has put it.[25] Tyndale was imprisoned and executed near Brussels in 1536, but the influence of his biblical work among the common people of England was already being felt. There is no reason to doubt the authenticity of John Foxe's recollection of how Tyndale's New Testament was received in England during the 1520s and 1530s:

---

[21]John C. Olin, *Christian Humanism and the Reformation* (New York: Fordham University Press, 1987), 101.

[22]This famous statement of Tyndale was quoted by John Foxe in his *Acts and Monuments of Matters Happening in the Church* (London, 1563). See Henry Wansbrough, "Tyndale," in *The Bible in the Renaissance*, ed. Richard Griffith (Aldershot, UK: Ashgate, 2001), 124.

[23]John Eck, *Enchiridion of Commonplaces*, trans. Ford Lewis Battles (Grand Rapids: Baker, 1979), 47-49.

[24]The effect of printing on the spread of the Reformation has been much debated. See the classic study by Elizabeth L. Eisenstein, *The Printing Press as an Agent of Change* (Cambridge: Cambridge University Press, 1979). More recent studies include Mark U. Edwards Jr., *Printing, Propaganda and Martin Luther* (Minneapolis: Fortress, 1994), and Andrew Pettegree and Matthew Hall, "The Reformation and the Book: A Reconsideration," *Historical Journal* 47 (2004): 1-24.

[25]David Daniell, *William Tyndale: A Biography* (New Haven: Yale University Press, 1994), 3.

The fervent zeal of those Christian days seemed much superior to these our days and times; as manifestly may appear by their sitting up all night in reading and hearing; also by their expenses and charges in buying of books in English, of whom some gave five marks, some more, some less, for a book: some gave a load of hay for a few chapters of St. James, or of St. Paul in English.[26]

Calvin helped to revise and contributed three prefaces to the French Bible translated by his cousin Pierre Robert Olivétan and originally published at Neuchâtel in 1535. Clément Marot and Beza provided a fresh translation of the Psalms with each psalm rendered in poetic form and accompanied by monophonic musical settings for congregational singing. The Bay Psalter, the first book printed in America, was an English adaptation of this work. Geneva also provided the provenance of the most influential Italian Bible published by Giovanni Diodati in 1607. The flowering of biblical humanism in vernacular Bibles resulted in new translations in all of the major language groups of Europe: Spanish (1569), Portuguese (1681), Dutch (New Testament, 1523; Old Testament, 1527), Danish (1550), Czech (1579–1593/94), Hungarian (New Testament, 1541; complete Bible, 1590), Polish (1563), Swedish (1541), and even Arabic (1591).[27]

Patterns of Reformation

Once the text of the Bible had been placed in the hands of the people, in cheap and easily available editions, what further need was there of published expositions such as commentaries? Given the Protestant doctrine of the priesthood of all believers, was there any longer a need for learned clergy and their bookish religion? Some radical reformers thought not. Sebastian Franck searched for the true church of the Spirit "scattered among the heathen and the weeds" but could not find it in any of the institutional structures of his time. *Veritas non potest scribi, aut exprimi*, he said, "truth can neither be spoken nor written."[28] Kaspar von Schwenckfeld so emphasized religious inwardness that he suspended external observance of the Lord's Supper and downplayed the readable, audible Scriptures in favor of the Word within. This trajectory would lead to the rise of the Quakers in the next century, but it was pursued neither by the mainline reformers nor by most of the Anabaptists. Article 7 of the Augsburg Confession (1530) declared the one holy Christian church to be "the assembly of all believers among whom the Gospel is purely preached and the holy sacraments are administered according to the Gospel."[29]

Historians of the nineteenth century referred to the material and formal principles of the Reformation. In this construal, the matter at stake was the meaning of the Christian gospel: the liberating insight that helpless sinners are graciously justified by the gift of faith alone, apart from any works or merits of their own, entirely on the basis of Christ's atoning work on the cross. For Luther especially, justification by faith alone became the criterion by which all other doctrines and

---

[26]Foxe, *Acts and Monuments*, 4:218.
[27]On vernacular translations of the Bible, see *CHB* 3:94-140 and Jaroslav Pelikan, *The Reformation of the Bible/The Bible of the Reformation* (New Haven: Yale University Press, 1996), 41-62.
[28]Sebastian Franck, *280 Paradoxes or Wondrous Sayings*, trans. E. J. Furcha (Lewiston, NY: Edwin Mellen Press, 1986), 10, 212.
[29]BoC 42 (BSLK 61).

practices of the church were to be judged. The cross proves everything, he said at the Heidelberg disputation in 1518. The distinction between law and gospel thus became the primary hermeneutical key that unlocked the true meaning of Scripture.

The formal principle of the Reformation, *sola Scriptura*, was closely bound up with proper distinctions between Scripture and tradition. "Scripture alone," said Luther, "is the true lord and master of all writings and doctrine on earth. If that is not granted, what is Scripture good for? The more we reject it, the more we become satisfied with human books and human teachers."[30] On the basis of this principle, the reformers challenged the structures and institutions of the medieval Catholic Church. Even a simple layperson, they asserted, armed with Scripture should be believed above a pope or a council without it. But, however boldly asserted, the doctrine of the primacy of Scripture did not absolve the reformers from dealing with a host of hermeneutical issues that became matters of contention both between Rome and the Reformation and within each of these two communities: the extent of the biblical canon, the validity of critical study of the Bible, the perspicuity of Scripture and its relation to preaching, and the retention of devotional and liturgical practices such as holy days, incense, the burning of candles, the sprinkling of holy water, church art, and musical instruments. Zwingli, the Puritans, and the radicals dismissed such things as a rubbish heap of ceremonials that amounted to nothing but tomfoolery, while Lutherans and Anglicans retained most of them as consonant with Scripture and valuable aids to worship.

It is important to note that while the mainline reformers differed among themselves on many matters, overwhelmingly they saw themselves as part of the ongoing Catholic tradition, indeed as the legitimate bearers of it. This was seen in numerous ways including their sense of continuity with the church of the preceding centuries; their embrace of the ecumenical orthodoxy of the early church; and their desire to read the Bible in dialogue with the exegetical tradition of the church.

In their biblical commentaries, the reformers of the sixteenth century revealed a close familiarity with the preceding exegetical tradition, and they used it respectfully as well as critically in their own expositions of the sacred text. For them, *sola Scriptura* was not *nuda Scriptura*. Rather, the Scriptures were seen as the book given to the church, gathered and guided by the Holy Spirit. In his restatement of the Vincentian canon, Calvin defined the church as "a society of all the saints, a society which, spread over the whole world, and existing in all ages, and bound together by the one doctrine and the one spirit of Christ, cultivates and observes unity of faith and brotherly concord. With this church we deny that we have any disagreement. Nay, rather, as we revere her as our mother, so we desire to remain in her bosom." Defined thus, the church has a real, albeit relative and circumscribed, authority since, as Calvin admits, "We cannot fly without wings."[31] While the reformers could not agree with the Council of Trent (though some recent Catholic theologians have challenged this interpretation) that Scripture and tradition were two separate and equal sources of divine revelation,

---

[30]LW 32:11-12* (WA 7:317).
[31]John C. Olin, ed., *John Calvin and Jacopo Sadoleto: A Reformation Debate* (New York: Harper Torchbooks, 1966), 61-62, 77.

they did believe in the coinherence of Scripture and tradition. This conviction shaped the way they read and interpreted the Bible.[32]

Schools of Exegesis

The reformers were passionate about biblical exegesis, but they showed little concern for hermeneutics as a separate field of inquiry. Niels Hemmingsen, a Lutheran theologian in Denmark, did write a treatise, *De methodis* (1555), in which he offered a philosophical and theological framework for the interpretation of Scripture. This was followed by the *Clavis Scripturae Sacrae* (1567) of Matthias Flacius Illyricus, which contains some fifty rules for studying the Bible drawn from Scripture itself.[33] However, hermeneutics as we know it came of age only in the Enlightenment and should not be backloaded into the Reformation. It is also true that the word *commentary* did not mean in the sixteenth century what it means for us today. Erasmus provided both annotations and paraphrases on the New Testament, the former a series of critical notes on the text but also containing points of doctrinal substance, the latter a theological overview and brief exposition. Most of Calvin's commentaries began as sermons or lectures presented in the course of his pastoral ministry. In the dedication to his 1519 study of Galatians, Luther declared that his work was "not so much a commentary as a testimony of my faith in Christ."[34] The exegetical work of the reformers was embodied in a wide variety of forms and genres, and the RCS has worked with this broader concept in setting the guidelines for this compendium.

The Protestant reformers shared in common a number of key interpretive principles such as the priority of the grammatical-historical sense of Scripture and the christological centeredness of the entire Bible, but they also developed a number of distinct approaches and schools of exegesis.[35] For the purposes of the RCS, we note the following key figures and families of interpretation in this period.

Biblical humanism. The key figure is Erasmus, whose importance is hard to exaggerate for Catholic and Protestant exegetes alike. His annotated Greek New Testament and fresh Latin translation challenged the hegemony of the Vulgate tradition and was doubtless a factor in the decision of the Council of Trent to establish the Vulgate edition as authentic and normative. Erasmus believed that the wide distribution of the Scriptures would contribute to personal spiritual renewal and the reform of society. In 1547, the English translation of Erasmus's *Paraphrases* was ordered to be placed in every parish church in England. John Colet first encouraged Erasmus

---

[32]See Timothy George, "An Evangelical Reflection on Scripture and Tradition," *Pro Ecclesia* 9 (2000): 184-207.

[33]See Kenneth G. Hagen, "'De Exegetica Methodo': Niels Hemmingsen's *De Methodis* (1555)," in *The Bible in the Sixteenth Century*, ed. David C. Steinmetz (Durham: Duke University Press, 1990), 181-96.

[34]LW 27:159 (WA 2:449). See Kenneth Hagen, "What Did the Term *Commentarius* Mean to Sixteenth-Century Theologians?" in *Théorie et pratique de l'exégèse*, eds. Irena Backus and Francis M. Higman (Geneva: Droz, 1990), 13-38.

[35]I follow here the sketch of Irena Backus, "Biblical Hermeneutics and Exegesis," *OER* 1:152-58. In this work, Backus confines herself to Continental developments, whereas we have noted the exegetical contribution of the English Reformation as well. For more comprehensive listings of sixteenth-century commentators, see Gerald Bray, *Biblical Interpretation* (Downers Grove, IL: InterVarsity Press, 1996), 165-212; and Richard A. Muller, "Biblical Interpretation in the Sixteenth and Seventeenth Centuries," *DMBI* 22-44.

to learn Greek, though he never took up the language himself. Colet's lectures on Paul's epistles at Oxford are reflected in his commentaries on Romans and 1 Corinthians.

Jacques Lefèvre d'Étaples has been called the "French Erasmus" because of his great learning and support for early reform movements in his native land. He published a major edition of the Psalter, as well as commentaries on the Pauline Epistles (1512), the Gospels (1522), and the General Epistles (1527). Guillaume Farel, the early reformer of Geneva, was a disciple of Lefèvre, and the young Calvin also came within his sphere of influence.

Among pre-Tridentine Catholic reformers, special attention should be given to Thomas de Vio, better known as Cajetan. He is best remembered for confronting Martin Luther on behalf of the pope in 1518, but his biblical commentaries (on nearly every book of the Bible) are virtually free of polemic. Like Erasmus, he dared to criticize the Vulgate on linguistic grounds. His commentary on Romans supported the doctrine of justification by grace applied by faith based on the "alien righteousness" of God in Christ. Jared Wicks sums up Cajetan's significance in this way: "Cajetan's combination of passion for pristine biblical meaning with his fully developed theological horizon of understanding indicates, in an intriguing manner, something of the breadth of possibilities open to Roman Catholics before a more restrictive settlement came to exercise its hold on many Catholic interpreters in the wake of the Council of Trent."[36] Girolamo Seripando, like Cajetan, was a cardinal in the Catholic Church, though he belonged to the Augustinian rather than the Dominican order. He was an outstanding classical scholar and published commentaries on Romans and Galatians. Also important is Jacopo Sadoleto, another cardinal, best known for his 1539 letter to the people of Geneva beseeching them to return to the Church of Rome, to which Calvin replied with a manifesto of his own. Sadoleto published a commentary on Romans in 1535. Bucer once commended Sadoleto's teaching on justification as approximating that of the reformers, while others saw him tilting away from the Augustinian tradition toward Pelagianism.[37]

Luther and the Wittenberg School. It was in the name of the Word of God, and specifically as a doctor of Scripture, that Luther challenged the church of his day and inaugurated the Reformation. Though Luther renounced his monastic vows, he never lost that sense of intimacy with *sacra pagina* he first acquired as a young monk. Luther provided three rules for reading the Bible: prayer, meditation, and struggle (*tentatio*). His exegetical output was enormous. In the American edition of Luther's works, thirty out of the fifty-five volumes are devoted to his biblical studies, and additional translations are planned. Many of his commentaries originated as sermons or lecture notes presented to his students at the university and to his parishioners at Wittenberg's parish church of St. Mary. Luther referred to Galatians as his bride: "The Epistle to the Galatians is my dear epistle. I have betrothed myself to it. It is my Käthe von Bora."[38] He considered his 1535 commentary on Galatians his greatest exegetical work, although his massive commentary on Genesis

---

[36]Jared Wicks, "Tommaso de Vio Cajetan (1469-1534)," *DMBI* 283-87, here 286.

[37]See the discussion by Bernard Roussel, "Martin Bucer et Jacques Sadolet: la concorde possible," *Bulletin de la Société de l'histoire de protestantisme français* (1976): 525-50, and T. H. L. Parker, *Commentaries on the Epistle to the Romans, 1532–1542* (Edinburgh: T&T Clark, 1986), 25-34.

[38]WATR 1:69 no. 146; cf. LW 54:20 no. 146. I have followed Rörer's variant on Dietrich's notes.

(eight volumes in LW), which he worked on for ten years (1535–1545), must be considered his crowning work. Luther's principles of biblical interpretation are found in his *Open Letter on Translating* and in the prefaces he wrote to all the books of the Bible.

Philipp Melanchthon was brought to Wittenberg to teach Greek in 1518 and proved to be an able associate to Luther in the reform of the church. A set of his lecture notes on Romans was published without his knowledge in 1522. This was revised and expanded many times until his large commentary of 1556. Melanchthon also commented on other New Testament books including Matthew, John, Galatians, and the Petrine epistles, as well as Proverbs, Daniel, and Ecclesiastes. Though he was well trained in the humanist disciplines, Melanchthon devoted little attention to critical and textual matters in his commentaries. Rather, he followed the primary argument of the biblical writer and gathered from this exposition a series of doctrinal topics for special consideration. This method lay behind Melanchthon's *Loci communes* (1521), the first Protestant theology textbook to be published. Another Wittenberger was Johannes Bugenhagen of Pomerania, a prolific commentator on both the Old and New Testaments. His commentary on the Psalms (1524), translated into German by Bucer, applied Luther's teaching on justification to the Psalter. He also wrote a commentary on Job and annotations on many of the books in the Bible. The Lutheran exegetical tradition was shaped by many other scholar-reformers including Andreas Osiander, Johannes Brenz, Caspar Cruciger, Erasmus Sarcerius, Georg Maior, Jacob Andreae, Nikolaus Selnecker, and Johann Gerhard.

The Strasbourg-Basel tradition. Bucer, the son of a shoemaker in Alsace, became the leader of the Reformation in Strasbourg. A former Dominican, he was early on influenced by Erasmus and continued to share his passion for Christian unity. Bucer was the most ecumenical of the Protestant reformers seeking rapprochement with Catholics on justification and an armistice between Luther and Zwingli in their strife over the Lord's Supper. Bucer also had a decisive influence on Calvin, though the latter characterized his biblical commentaries as longwinded and repetitious.[39] In his exegetical work, Bucer made ample use of patristic and medieval sources, though he criticized the abuse and overuse of allegory as "the most blatant insult to the Holy Spirit."[40] He declared that the purpose of his commentaries was "to help inexperienced brethren [perhaps like the apothecary Drilhon, who owned a French translation of Bucer's *Commentary on Matthew*] to understand each of the words and actions of Christ, and in their proper order as far as possible, and to retain an explanation of them in their natural meaning, so that they will not distort God's Word through age-old aberrations or by inept interpretation, but rather with a faithful comprehension of everything as written by the Spirit of God, they may expound to all the churches in their firm upbuilding in faith and love."[41] In addition to writing commentaries on all four Gospels, Bucer published commentaries on Judges, the Psalms, Zephaniah, Romans, and Ephesians. In the early years of the Reformation, there was a great deal of back and forth between Strasbourg and Basel, and both

---

[39]CNTC 8:3 (CO 10:404).

[40]DMBI 249; P. Scherding and F. Wendel, eds., "Un Traité d'exégèse pratique de Bucer," *Revue d'histoire et de philosophie religieuses* 26 (1946): 32-75, here 56.

[41]Martin Bucer, *Enarrationes perpetuae in sacra quatuor evangelia*, 2nd ed. (Strasbourg: Georg Ulrich Andlanus, 1530), 10r; quoted in D. F. Wright, "Martin Bucer," *DMBI* 290.

were centers of a lively publishing trade. Wolfgang Capito, Bucer's associate at Strasbourg, was a notable Hebraist and composed commentaries on Hosea (1529) and Habakkuk (1527).

At Basel, the great Sebastian Münster defended the use of Jewish sources in the Christian study of the Old Testament and published, in addition to his famous Hebrew grammar, an annotated version of the Gospel of Matthew translated from Greek into Hebrew. Oecolampadius, Basel's chief reformer, had been a proofreader in Froben's publishing house and worked with Erasmus on his Greek New Testament and his critical edition of Jerome. From 1523 he was both a preacher and professor of Holy Scripture at Basel. He defended Zwingli's eucharistic theology at the Colloquy of Marburg and published commentaries on 1 John (1524), Romans (1525), and Haggai–Malachi (1525). Oecolampadius was succeeded by Simon Grynaeus, a classical scholar who taught Greek and supported Bucer's efforts to bring Lutherans and Zwinglians together. More in line with Erasmus was Sebastian Castellio, who came to Basel after his expulsion from Geneva in 1545. He is best remembered for questioning the canonicity of the Song of Songs and for his annotations and French translation of the Bible.

The Zurich group. Biblical exegesis in Zurich was centered on the distinctive institution of the *Prophezei*, which began on June 19, 1525. On five days a week, at seven o'clock in the morning, all of the ministers and theological students in Zurich gathered into the choir of the Grossmünster to engage in a period of intense exegesis and interpretation of Scripture. After Zwingli had opened the meeting with prayer, the text of the day was read in Latin, Greek, and Hebrew, followed by appropriate textual or exegetical comments. One of the ministers then delivered a sermon on the passage in German that was heard by many of Zurich's citizens who stopped by the cathedral on their way to work. This institute for advanced biblical studies had an enormous influence as a model for Reformed academies and seminaries throughout Europe. It was also the seedbed for sermon series in Zurich's churches and the extensive exegetical publications of Zwingli, Leo Jud, Konrad Pellikan, Heinrich Bullinger, Oswald Myconius, and Rudolf Gwalther. Zwingli had memorized in Greek all of the Pauline epistles, and this bore fruit in his powerful expository preaching and biblical exegesis. He took seriously the role of grammar, rhetoric, and historical research in explaining the biblical text. For example, he disagreed with Bucer on the value of the Septuagint, regarding it as a trustworthy witness to a proto-Hebrew version earlier than the Masoretic text.

Zwingli's work was carried forward by his successor Bullinger, one of the most formidable scholars and networkers among the reformers. He composed commentaries on Daniel (1565), the Gospels (1542–1546), the Epistles (1537), Acts (1533), and Revelation (1557). He collaborated with Calvin to produce the *Consensus Tigurinus* (1549), a Reformed accord on the nature of the Lord's Supper, and produced a series of fifty sermons on Christian doctrine, known as *Decades*, which became required reading in Elizabethan England. As the *Antistes* ("overseer") of the Zurich church for forty-four years, Bullinger faced opposition from nascent Anabaptism on the one hand and resurgent Catholicism on the other. The need for a well-trained clergy and scholarly resources, including Scripture commentaries, arose from the fact that the Bible was "difficult or obscure to the unlearned, unskillful, unexercised, and malicious or corrupted wills." While forswearing papal claims to infallibility, Bullinger and other leaders of the magisterial Reformation saw the need for a kind of Protestant magisterium as a check against the tendency to read the Bible in "such sense as everyone shall be persuaded in himself to be most convenient."[42]

Two other commentators can be treated in connection with the Zurich group, though each of them had a wide-ranging ministry across the Reformation fronts. A former Benedictine monk, Wolfgang Musculus, embraced the Reformation in the 1520s and served briefly as the secretary to Bucer in Strasbourg. He shared Bucer's desire for Protestant unity and served for seventeen years (1531–1548) as a pastor and reformer in Augsburg. After a brief time in Zurich, where he came under the influence of Bullinger, Musculus was called to Bern, where he taught the Scriptures and published commentaries on the Psalms, the Decalogue, Genesis, Romans, Isaiah, 1 and 2 Corinthians, Galatians and Ephesians, Philippians, Colossians, 1 and 2 Thessalonians, and 1 Timothy. Drawing on his exegetical writings, Musculus also produced a compendium of Protestant theology that was translated into English in 1563 as *Commonplaces of Christian Religion*.

Peter Martyr Vermigli was a Florentine-born scholar and Augustinian friar who embraced the Reformation and fled to Switzerland in 1542. Over the next twenty years, he would gain an international reputation as a prolific scholar and leading theologian within the Reformed community. He lectured on the Old Testament at Strasbourg, was made regius professor at Oxford, corresponded with the Italian refugee church in Geneva and spent the last years of his life as professor of Hebrew at Zurich. Vermigli published commentaries on 1 Corinthians, Romans, and Judges during his lifetime. His biblical lectures on Genesis, Lamentations, 1 and 2 Samuel, and 1 and 2 Kings were published posthumously. The most influential of his writings was the *Loci communes* (*Commonplaces*), a theological compendium drawn from his exegetical writings.

The Genevan reformers. What Zwingli and Bullinger were to Zurich, Calvin and Beza were to Geneva. Calvin has been called "the father of modern biblical scholarship," and his exegetical work is without parallel in the Reformation. Because of the success of his *Institutes of the Christian Religion* Calvin has sometimes been thought of as a man of one book, but he always intended the *Institutes*, which went through eight editions in Latin and five in French during his lifetime, to serve as a guide to the study of the Bible, to show the reader "what he ought especially to seek in Scripture and to what end he ought to relate its contents." Jacob Arminius, who modified several principles of Calvin's theology, recommended his commentaries next to the Bible, for, as he said, Calvin "is incomparable in the interpretation of Scripture."[43] Drawing on his superb knowledge of Greek and Hebrew and his thorough training in humanist rhetoric, Calvin produced commentaries on all of the New Testament books except 2 and 3 John and Revelation. Calvin's Old Testament commentaries originated as sermon and lecture series and include Genesis, Psalms, Hosea, Isaiah, minor prophets, Daniel, Jeremiah and Lamentations, a harmony of the last four books of Moses,

---

[42]Euan Cameron, *The European Reformation* (Oxford: Oxford University Press, 1991), 120.

[43]Letter to Sebastian Egbert (May 3, 1607), in *Praestantium ac eruditorum virorum epistolae ecclesiasticae et theologicae varii argumenti*, ed. Christiaan Hartsoeker (Amsterdam: Henricus Dendrinus, 1660), 236-37. Quoted in A. M. Hunter, *The Teaching of Calvin* (London: James Clarke, 1950), 20.

Ezekiel 1–20, and Joshua. Calvin sought for brevity and clarity in all of his exegetical work. He emphasized the illumination of the Holy Spirit as essential to a proper understanding of the text. Calvin underscored the continuity between the two Testaments (one covenant in two dispensations) and sought to apply the plain or natural sense of the text to the church of his day. In the preface to his own influential commentary on Romans, Karl Barth described how Calvin worked to recover the mind of Paul and make the apostle's message relevant to his day:

> How energetically Calvin goes to work, first scientifically establishing the text ("what stands there?"), then following along the footsteps of its thought; that is to say, he conducts a discussion with it until the wall between the first and the sixteenth centuries becomes transparent, and until there in the first century Paul speaks and here the man of the sixteenth century hears, until indeed the conversation between document and reader becomes concentrated upon the substance (which must be the same now as then).[44]

Beza was elected moderator of Geneva's Company of Pastors after Calvin's death in 1564 and guided the Genevan Reformation over the next four decades. His annotated Latin translation of the Greek New Testament (1556) and his further revisions of the Greek text established his reputation as the leading textual critic of the sixteenth century after Erasmus. Beza completed the translation of Marot's metrical Psalter, which became a centerpiece of Huguenot piety and Reformed church life. Though known for his polemical writings on grace, free will, and predestination, Beza's work is marked by a strong pastoral orientation and concern for a Scripture-based spirituality.

Robert Estienne (Stephanus) was a printer-scholar who had served the royal household in Paris. After his conversion to Protestantism, in 1550 he moved to Geneva, where he published a series of notable editions and translations of the Bible. He also produced sermons and commentaries on Job, Ecclesiastes, the Song of Songs, Romans and Hebrews, as well as dictionaries, concordances, and a thesaurus of biblical terms. He also published the first editions of the Bible with chapters divided into verses, an innovation that quickly became universally accepted.

The British Reformation. Commentary writing in England and Scotland lagged behind the continental Reformation for several reasons. In 1500, there were only three publishing houses in England compared with more than two hundred on the Continent. A 1408 statute against publishing or reading the Bible in English, stemming from the days of Lollardy, stifled the free flow of ideas, as was seen in the fate of Tyndale. Moreover, the nature of the English Reformation from Henry through Elizabeth provided little stability for the flourishing of biblical scholarship. In the sixteenth century, many "hot-gospel" Protestants in England were edified by the English translations of commentaries and theological writings by the Continental reformers. The influence of Calvin and Beza was felt especially in the Geneva Bible with its "Protestant glosses" of theological notes and references.

During the later Elizabethan and Stuart church, however, the indigenous English commentary came into its own. Both Anglicans and Puritans contributed to this outpouring of biblical studies.

---

[44]Karl Barth, *Die Römerbrief* (Zurich: TVZ, 1940), 11, translated by T. H. L. Parker as the epigraph to *Calvin's New Testament Commentaries*, 2nd ed. (Louisville, KY: Westminster John Knox, 1993).

The sermons of Lancelot Andrewes and John Donne are replete with exegetical insights based on a close study of the Greek and Hebrew texts. Among the Reformed authors in England, none was more influential than William Perkins, the greatest of the early Puritan theologians, who published commentaries on Galatians, Jude, Revelation, and the Sermon on the Mount (Mt 5–7). John Cotton, one of his students, wrote commentaries on the Song of Songs, Ecclesiastes, and Revelation before departing for New England in 1633. The separatist pastor Henry Ainsworth was an outstanding scholar of Hebrew and wrote major commentaries on the Pentateuch, the Psalms, and the Song of Songs. In Scotland, Robert Rollock, the first principal of Edinburgh University (1585), wrote numerous commentaries including those on the Psalms, Ephesians, Daniel, Romans, 1 and 2 Thessalonians, John, Colossians, and Hebrews. Joseph Mede and Thomas Brightman were leading authorities on Revelation and contributed to the apocalyptic thought of the seventeenth century. Mention should also be made of Archbishop James Ussher, whose *Annals of the Old Testament* was published in 1650. Ussher developed a keen interest in biblical chronology and calculated that the creation of the world had taken place on October 26, 4004 B.C. As late as 1945, the Scofield Reference Bible still retained this date next to Genesis 1:1, but later editions omitted it because of the lack of evidence on which to fix such dates.[45]

Anabaptism. Irena Backus has noted that there was no school of "dissident" exegesis during the Reformation, and the reasons are not hard to find. The radical Reformation was an ill-defined movement that existed on the margins of official church life in the sixteenth century. The denial of infant baptism and the refusal to swear an oath marked radicals as a seditious element in society, and they were persecuted by Protestants and Catholics alike. However, in the RCS we have made an attempt to include some voices of the radical Reformation, especially among the Anabaptists. While the Anabaptists published few commentaries in the sixteenth century, they were avid readers and quoters of the Bible. Numerous exegetical gems can be found in their letters, treatises, martyr acts (especially *The Martyrs' Mirror*), hymns, and histories. They placed a strong emphasis on the memorizing of Scripture and quoted liberally from vernacular translations of the Bible. George H. Williams has noted that "many an Anabaptist theological tract was really a beautiful mosaic of Scripture texts."[46] In general, most Anabaptists accepted the apocryphal books as canonical, contrasted outer word and inner spirit with relative degrees of strictness and saw the New Testament as normative for church life and social ethics (witness their pacifism, nonswearing, emphasis on believers' baptism and congregational discipline).

We have noted the Old Testament translation of Ludwig Hätzer, who became an antitrinitarian, and Hans Denck that they published at Worms in 1527. Denck also wrote a notable commentary on Micah. Conrad Grebel belonged to a Greek reading circle in Zurich and came to his Anabaptist convictions while poring over the text of Erasmus's New Testament. The only Anabaptist leader with university credentials was Balthasar Hubmaier, who was made a doctor of theology (Ingolstadt, 1512) in the same year as Luther. His reflections on the Bible are found in his numerous

---

[45] *The New Scofield Reference Bible* (New York: Oxford University Press, 1967), vi.
[46] George H. Williams, *The Radical Reformation*, 3rd ed. (Kirksville, MO: Sixteenth Century Journal Publishers, 1992), 1247.

writings, which include the first catechism of the Reformation (1526), a two-part treatise on the freedom of the will and a major work (*On the Sword*) setting forth positive attitudes toward the role of government and the Christian's place in society. Melchior Hoffman was an apocalyptic seer who wrote commentaries on Romans, Revelation, and Daniel 12. He predicted that Christ would return in 1533. More temperate was Pilgram Marpeck, a mining engineer who embraced Anabaptism and traveled widely throughout Switzerland and south Germany, from Strasbourg to Augsburg. His "Admonition of 1542" is the longest published defense of Anabaptist views on baptism and the Lord's Supper. He also wrote many letters that functioned as theological tracts for the congregations he had founded dealing with topics such as the fruits of repentance, the lowliness of Christ, and the unity of the church. Menno Simons, a former Catholic priest, became the most outstanding leader of the Dutch Anabaptist movement. His masterpiece was the *Foundation of Christian Doctrine* published in 1540. His other writings include *Meditation on the Twenty-fifth Psalm* (1537); *A Personal Exegesis of Psalm Twenty-five* modeled on the style of Augustine's *Confessions*; *Confession of the Triune God* (1550), directed against Adam Pastor, a former disciple of Menno who came to doubt the divinity of Christ; *Meditations and Prayers for Mealtime* (1557); and the *Cross of the Saints* (1554), an exhortation to faithfulness in the face of persecution. Like many other Anabaptists, Menno emphasized the centrality of discipleship (*Nachfolge*) as a deliberate repudiation of the old life and a radical commitment to follow Jesus as Lord.

Reading Scripture with the Reformers

In 1947, Gerhard Ebeling set forth his thesis that the history of the Christian church is the history of the interpretation of Scripture. Since that time, the place of the Bible in the story of the church has been investigated from many angles. A better understanding of the history of exegesis has been aided by new critical editions and scholarly discussions of the primary sources. The *Cambridge History of the Bible*, published in three volumes (1963–1970), remains a standard reference work in the field. The ACCS built on, and itself contributed to, the recovery of patristic biblical wisdom of both East and West. Beryl Smalley's *The Study of the Bible in the Middle Ages* (1940) and Henri de Lubac's *Medieval Exegesis: The Four Senses of Scripture* (1959) are essential reading for understanding the monastic and scholastic settings of commentary work between Augustine and Luther. The Reformation took place during what has been called "le grand siècle de la Bible."[47] Aided by the tools of Renaissance humanism and the dynamic impetus of Reformation theology (including permutations and reactions against it), the sixteenth century produced an unprecedented number of commentaries on every book in the Bible. Drawing from this vast storehouse of exegetical treasures, the RCS allows us to read Scripture along with the reformers. In doing so, it serves as a practical homiletic and devotional guide to some of the greatest masters of biblical interpretation in the history of the church.

The RCS gladly acknowledges its affinity with and dependence on recent scholarly investigations of Reformation-era exegesis. Between 1976 and 1990, three international colloquia on the

---

[47]J-R. Aarmogathe, ed., *Bible de tous les temps*, 8 vols.; vol. 6, *Le grand siècle de la Bible* (Paris: Beauchesne, 1989).

history of biblical exegesis in the sixteenth century took place in Geneva and in Durham, North Carolina.[48] Among those participating in these three gatherings were a number of scholars who have produced groundbreaking works in the study of biblical interpretation in the Reformation. These include Elsie McKee, Irena Backus, Kenneth Hagen, Scott H. Hendrix, Richard A. Muller, Guy Bedouelle, Gerald Hobbs, John B. Payne, Bernard Roussel, Pierre Fraenkel, and David C. Steinmetz (1936–2015). Among other scholars whose works are indispensible for the study of this field are Heinrich Bornkamm, Jaroslav Pelikan, Heiko A. Oberman, James S. Preus, T. H. L. Parker, David F. Wright, Tony Lane, John L. Thompson, Frank A. James, and Timothy J. Wengert.[49] Among these scholars no one has had a greater influence on the study of Reformation exegesis than David C. Steinmetz. A student of Oberman, he emphasized the importance of understanding the Reformation in medieval perspective. In addition to important studies on Luther and Staupitz, he pioneered the method of comparative exegesis showing both continuity and discontinuity between major Reformation figures and the preceding exegetical traditions (see his *Luther in Context* and *Calvin in Context*). From his base at Duke University, he spawned what might be called a Steinmetz school, a cadre of students and scholars whose work on the Bible in the Reformation era continues to shape the field. Steinmetz served on the RCS Board of Editorial Advisors, and a number of our volume editors pursued doctoral studies under his supervision.

In 1980, Steinmetz published "The Superiority of Pre-critical Exegesis," a seminal essay that not only placed Reformation exegesis in the context of the preceding fifteen centuries of the church's study of the Bible but also challenged certain assumptions underlying the hegemony of historical-critical exegesis of the post-Enlightenment academy.[50] Steinmetz helps us to approach the reformers and other precritical interpreters of the Bible on their own terms as faithful witnesses to the church's apostolic tradition. For them, a specific book or pericope had to be understood within the scope of the consensus of the canon. Thus the reformers, no less than the Fathers and the schoolmen, interpreted the hymn of the Johannine prologue about the preexistent Christ in consonance with the creation narrative of Genesis 1. In the same way, Psalm 22, Isaiah 53, and Daniel 7 are seen as part of an overarching storyline that finds ultimate fulfillment in Jesus Christ. Reading the Bible with the resources of the new learning, the reformers challenged the exegetical conclusions of their medieval predecessors at many points. However, unlike Alexander Campbell in the nineteenth century, their aim was not to "open the New Testament as if mortal man had never seen it before."[51]

---

[48]Olivier Fatio and Pierre Fraenkel, eds., *Histoire de l'exégèse au XVIe siècle: texts du colloque international tenu à Genève en 1976* (Geneva: Droz, 1978); David C. Steinmetz, ed., *The Bible in the Sixteenth Century* [Second International Colloquy on the History of Biblical Exegesis in the Sixteenth Century] (Durham: Duke University Press, 1990); Irena Backus and Francis M. Higman, eds., *Théorie et pratique de l'exégèse. Actes du troisième colloque international sur l'histoire de l'exégèse biblique au XVIe siècle, Genève, 31 aôut–2 septembre 1988* (Geneva: Droz, 1990); see also Guy Bedouelle and Bernard Roussel, eds., *Bible de tous les temps*, 8 vols.; vol. 5, *Le temps des Réformes et la Bible* (Paris: Beauchesne, 1989).

[49]For bibliographical references and evaluation of these and other contributors to the scholarly study of Reformation-era exegesis, see Richard A. Muller, "Biblical Interpretation in the Era of the Reformation: The View From the Middle Ages," in *Biblical Interpretation in the Era of the Reformation: Essays Presented to David C. Steinmetz in Honor of His Sixtieth Birthday*, ed. Richard A. Muller and John L. Thompson (Grand Rapids: Eerdmans, 1996), 3-22.

[50]David C. Steinmetz, "The Superiority of Pre-Critical Exegesis," *Theology Today* 37 (1980): 27-38.

[51]Alexander Campbell, *Memoirs of Alexander Campbell*, ed. Robert Richardson (Cincinnati: Standard Publishing Company, 1872), 97.

Rather, they wanted to do their biblical work as part of an interpretive conversation within the family of the people of God. In the reformers' emphatic turn to the literal sense, which prompted their many blasts against the unrestrained use of allegory, their work was an extension of a similar impulse made by Thomas Aquinas and Nicholas of Lyra.

This is not to discount the radically new insights gained by the reformers in their dynamic engagement with the text of Scripture; nor should we dismiss in a reactionary way the light shed on the meaning of the Bible by the scholarly accomplishments of the past two centuries. However, it is to acknowledge that the church's exegetical tradition is an indispensable aid for the proper interpretation of Scripture. And this means, as Richard Muller has said, that "while it is often appropriate to recognize that traditionary readings of the text are erroneous on the grounds offered by the historical-critical method, we ought also to recognize that the conclusions offered by historical-critical exegesis may themselves be quite erroneous on the grounds provided by the exegesis of the patristic, medieval, and reformation periods."[52] The RCS wishes to commend the exegetical work of the Reformation era as a program of retrieval for the sake of renewal—spiritual ressourcement for believers committed to the life of faith today.

George Herbert was an English pastor and poet who reaped the benefits of the renewal of biblical studies in the age of the Reformation. He referred to the Scriptures as a book of infinite sweetness, "a mass of strange delights," a book with secrets to make the life of anyone good. In describing the various means pastors require to be fully furnished in the work of their calling, Herbert provided a rationale for the history of exegesis and for the Reformation Commentary on Scripture:

> The fourth means are commenters and Fathers, who have handled the places controverted, which the parson by no means refuseth. As he doth not so study others as to neglect the grace of God in himself and what the Holy Spirit teacheth him, so doth he assure himself that God in all ages hath had his servants to whom he hath revealed his Truth, as well as to him; and that as one country doth not bear all things that there may be a commerce, so neither hath God opened or will open all to one, that there may be a traffic in knowledge between the servants of God for the planting both of love and humility. Wherefore he hath one comment[ary] at least upon every book of Scripture, and ploughing with this, and his own meditations, he enters into the secrets of God treasured in the holy Scripture.[53]

Timothy George
General Editor

---

[52]Richard A. Muller and John L. Thompson, "The Significance of Precritical Exegesis: Retrospect and Prospect," in *Biblical Interpretation in the Era of the Reformation: Essays Presented to David C. Steinmetz in Honor of His Sixtieth Birthday*, ed. Richard A. Muller and John L. Thompson (Grand Rapids: Eerdmans, 1996), 342.
[53]George Herbert, *The Complete English Poems* (London: Penguin, 1991), 205.

INTRODUCTION TO 1–2 THESSALONIANS, 1–2 TIMOTHY, TITUS, AND PHILEMON

The volume in your hands includes Reformation-era commentary on 1 and 2 Thessalonians, 1 and 2 Timothy, Titus, and Philemon. As these letters do not necessarily *organically* belong together in a volume like this—other than all being Holy Scripture, and all coming from the pen of the apostle and his various coworkers to the Gentiles—this introduction will at times speak of them together, but will largely treat them in their natural groupings: (1) 1 and 2 Thessalonians; (2) 1 and 2 Timothy and Titus; and (3) Philemon.

The reformers all believed that the apostle Paul penned these six letters, and in the sixteenth and seventeenth centuries there appears to have been little to no questioning of Pauline authorship of any of the letters in this volume. Of course, the interpretation of Paul was key to the Reformation and its insights and impulses, so it is no surprise that there is a significant tradition of early modern commentary on both Paul and his letters.

Paul and the Reformation

It is almost cliché to state the obvious: the apostle Paul and his writings were central to the Reformation. Huldrych Zwingli once said, "We shall try everything by the touchstone of the Gospel and by the fire of Paul."[1] And of course it was Luther's wrestling with Romans 1:17, the *dikaiosynē theou*—the righteousness of God—that was central to his own theological development. In the light of Luther's wrestling with this text, F. F. Bruce has remarked, "The consequences of Luther's grasp of the liberating gospel according to Paul are writ large in history."[2] Bruce recognized that there might be some truth in the position taken by Krister Stendahl and other proponents of the so-called new perspective,[3] that one misses Paul by reading the apostle to the Gentiles through the lens of an Augustine and/or Luther. Nonetheless, Bruce writes,

> Paul's gospel of salvation by divine grace has a living relevance not only to people who, like him, supposed they had attained a satisfactory standard of righteousness by law-keeping but also to

---

[1]See Samuel M. Jackson, ed., *The Latin Works and the Correspondence of Huldreich Zwingli: Together with Selections from His German Works* (London: G. P. Putnam's Sons, 1912), 1:280. See also Bruce Corley, "Interpreting Paul's Conversion—Then and Now," in *The Road from Damascus: The Impact of Paul's Conversion on His Life, Thought, and Ministry*, ed. Richard N. Longenecker (Grand Rapids: Eerdmans, 1997), 9.

[2]F. F. Bruce, *Paul: Apostle of the Heart Set Free* (Grand Rapids: Eerdmans, 1977), 471.

[3]Krister Stendahl, "The Apostle Paul and the Introspective Conscience of the West," *Harvard Theological Review* 56 (1963): 199-215.

those who, in one way or another, have known themselves to fall far short of such a standard and have suffered agonies of conscience as a result.[4]

We suspect that B. B. Warfield's comment is fundamentally correct: "The Reformation, inwardly considered, was just the ultimate triumph of Augustine's doctrine of grace over Augustine's doctrine of the Church."[5] What Warfield was arguing is that what one sees in the Reformation is the full flowering of a certain understanding of grace—not that the Reformation was *only* such a full flowering. But if Warfield is right, that in the Reformation we see the working out of central insights from Augustine, the next obvious question is: Whence did Augustine get his doctrine of grace? If Augustine is fundamentally a "Paulinist," then it is a short step to arguing that in the Reformation there is a certain trajectory at work: from Paul to Augustine, then onward to the Reformation. This is no doubt an oversimplification, as one could—and should—argue that there were a number of "Augustinian" streams at work in the late medieval world.[6] Is it not likely that almost any traditional Christian could—rightly—be called "Augustinian" in some sense? Nonetheless, we also suspect that those who have read Paul and Augustine closely will likely see numerous commonalities in these two seminal Christian thinkers. And it is also the case that Augustine, that lover and propagator of Paul, is the most central patristic thinker influencing the reformers.

Although our focus is on 1 and 2 Thessalonians, the Pastoral Epistles, and Philemon, we rightly draw notice to the centrality of Paul in the Reformation, as seen in various comments on *other* Pauline books. For example, Luther can write of Romans, "This epistle is in truth the most important document in the New Testament, the gospel in its purest expression."[7] In his Preface to Romans Luther explores several key terms at great length: "sin," "grace," "faith," "righteousness," "flesh" and "spirit." These Pauline (but not only Pauline) terms are central to the central tenets of the Reformation.

But all is not quiet, or unanimous, on the front of contemporary Pauline studies. A significant swath of Pauline scholars is quite adamant that the reformers—and those who self-consciously align themselves with the reformers—have seriously misread Paul by seeing the apostle to the Gentiles as a kind of proto-reformer. Jonathan Linebaugh has recently recounted something of the main contours of this attempt to rescue Paul from such a Reformation reading.[8] Albert Schweitzer's perspective is particularly pointed: "The Reformation fought and conquered in the name of Paul. . . . Reformation exegesis reads its own ideas into Paul, in order to receive them back again clothed with Apostolic authority."[9] E. P. Sanders similarly could write, "Luther sought and found

---

[4]Bruce, *Paul*, 471.

[5]B. B. Warfield, *Calvin and Augustine*, ed. Samuel G. Craig (Philadelphia: P&R, 1956), 322.

[6]See Heiko A. Oberman, *The Dawn of the Reformation: Essays on Late Medieval and Early Modern Thought* (Grand Rapids: Eerdmans, 1986), 8-12.

[7]Martin Luther, "Preface to the Epistle of St. Paul to the Romans," in *Martin Luther: Selections from His Writings*, ed. John Dillenberger (New York: Doubleday, 1962), 19.

[8]Jonathan A. Linebaugh, introduction to *Reformation Readings of Paul: Explorations in History and Exegesis*, ed. Michael Allen and Jonathan A. Linebaugh (Downers Grove, IL: IVP Academic, 2015), 11-19.

[9]Albert Schweitzer, *Paul and His Interpreters: A Critical History*, trans. William Montgomery (New York: Schocken, 1964), 2; quoted in Linebaugh, introduction, 11.

relief from guilt. But Luther's problems were not Paul's, and we misunderstand him if we see him through Luther's eyes."[10]

But the reformers *were* certainly reading Paul. And many would still affirm that the Reformation was something of a working out of a close (and generally faithful) reading of Paul. As Gerald Bray has noted, "That the Reformation was in large measure a movement of Pauline theology can scarcely be doubted, and this was affirmed by the reformers themselves." Indeed, "the reformers concentrated on the Pauline epistles, which to their minds expressed the heart of the gospel message."[11] We should also note the obvious: even if the reformers did not get Paul right, they certainly *thought* their movement was in large part anchored in the thought of the apostle. Bray also writes, "Advocates of the 'new perspective' on Paul who criticize Luther for failing to understand the spiritual nature of Second Temple Judaism do not show that they realize this [i.e., the similarities between the Judaism of the first century and the late medieval Catholic church], and so they fail to grasp just how much Luther's background resembled that of Saul the Pharisee."[12]

There are a couple of issues to consider here: (1) A question: How faithfully did the reformers understand Paul? (2) A simple historical observation: the reformers were reading Paul closely, and trying to understand him. The second point is simply that we must recognize that the reformers saw themselves as attempting to come to terms with the writings of the apostle Paul, and the Reformation was in many ways *an outworking of the reformers' exegetical engagement with the apostle.* The first point above—the question of how well the reformers actually interpreted or understood Paul—is a separate question.

In the end, a volume like this, indeed the whole Reformation Commentary on Scripture, will hopefully be helpful in providing some answer to the first question above. The second point above will certainly be demonstrated—there is really little question of whether the reformers were seriously engaged with the writings of the apostle Paul. The first question above—did the reformers get Paul right?—will not necessarily be settled in a volume like this. The most we editors can do is hopefully provide a fair representation of the exegetical labors of the reformers. That is, we can provide a (hopefully helpful and judicious) selection of commentary from both more well-known and lesser-known reformers as *they* wrestled with the apostle. Let the reader decide. However, we are convinced, with Stephen Chester, that one of the most significant weaknesses of historical-critical interpretation has been "the tendency to ignore all but recent interpreters," and that

> the Protestant Reformers of the sixteenth century have insights into the interpretation of the Pauline letters that can assist us as we attempt to interpret the same texts in and for contemporary

---

[10]E. P. Sanders, *Paul: A Very Short Introduction* (Oxford: Oxford University Press, 1991), 53; quoted in Linebaugh, introduction, 13.

[11]Gerald Bray, "In Conclusion: The Story of Reformation Readings," in Allen and Linebaugh, *Reformation Readings of Paul*, 259.

[12]Bray, "Story of Reformation Readings," 272. See Lee Gatiss, "Justified Hesitation? J. D. G. Dunn and the Protestant Doctrine of Justification," in *Cornerstones of Salvation: Foundations and Debates in the Reformed Tradition* (Welwyn, UK: Evangelical Press, 2017), 69-92, on the weakness of some new perspective dismissals of Reformation readings of Paul. Moreover, Timothy Wengert has argued that the "new perspective on Paul" is a revival of an ancient approach to the apostle's writings known to Luther and Melanchthon, and rejected by both, but defended by the humanist scholar Erasmus of Rotterdam. See Timothy J. Wengert, *Reading the Bible with Martin Luther* (Grand Rapids: Baker Academic, 2013), 92-122.

contexts. This does not mean that they are right on every issue. It also does not mean that we may merely repeat what they said. . . . To make effective use of the resources offered by the Reformers requires us instead to sift their exegetical conclusions critically and to bring them into conversation with our own questions and concerns, sharpening our own focus as we stage a dialog with them about interpretative issues.[13]

Ultimately then, as Timothy George has said, "We read the reformers for the same reason that we pay attention to the church fathers: we share with them a common patrimony in the sacred Scriptures. We listen to their struggles, musings, and debates about the written Word of God as a way of better attending to the thing itself."[14]

Reformation Reception of 1–2 Thessalonians

Historical context. The reformers were reading Paul closely, and trying to understand the apostle to the Gentiles, while certainly coming to Paul with unique concerns as well as universal and transcendent questions. Paul and Silas had visited Thessalonica (Acts 17:1-10) during Paul's second missionary journey. Paul and Silas were likely in Thessalonica around AD 49 or 50, and Paul then wrote the Thessalonians soon after his departure from Thessalonica and arrival at Corinth (putting the date of authorship likely around AD 49–51). Thessalonica was the capital city of Macedonia, a Roman province. There was a genuine saving response to the gospel message (Acts 17:4). However, the Jews became jealous (Acts 17:5), and incited opposition to Paul and Silas. The missionaries eventually left the city—perhaps with a pledge not to return (Acts 17:9). This somewhat sudden departure means that the Thessalonians had not been instructed and taught perhaps as much as Paul might have wished (1 Thess 2:17–3:5). Thus, while the Thessalonians were not, it seems, facing a controversy like we find in Corinth, Galatia, or Philippi, Paul nonetheless was eager to give instruction to help with some issues the Thessalonians were facing. He desired to return to see the Thessalonians, in order to check on them, and to encourage and exhort them. When Paul had left Thessalonica, and arrived in Athens, he sent Timothy to the Thessalonians to check on them (1 Thess 3:5). Paul was encouraged by Timothy's good report (2 Thess 3:6), but this report nonetheless gave him some insight on issues that apparently needed addressing:

1. Eschatology
2. Encouragements and warnings
3. The question of death and the state of the dead
4. The nature of the "lawless one/man of lawlessness," or "son of destruction," or "Satan"
5. The danger of idleness

Perhaps in terms of historical context—at least for parts of 1 and 2 Thessalonians—the key *unique* historical issue for Reformation commentators, which relates to issue four above, was

---

[13]Stephen J. Chester, *Reading Paul with the Reformers: Reconciling Old and New Perspectives* (Grand Rapids: Eerdmans, 2017), 1-2. Chester is mostly concerned with some issues in soteriology, above all the meaning of "righteousness," but his argument here applies to many other loci in Pauline theology too.

[14]Timothy George, *Reading Scripture with the Reformers* (Downers Grove, IL: IVP Academic, 2011), 42.

coming to terms with the reality of the Roman Catholic Church, especially the role, place, and authority of the pope. Clearly, for the reformers, understanding their movement and understanding the nature of pastoral ministry and preaching and church life required them to ask central questions. Who are we as Protestants in relationship to the Roman Catholic Church? What is the authoritative grounds for our ministry, if it is not organically and institutionally related to the Roman Catholic system? What do *we* think are the ways people receive grace if it is *not* through the late medieval Roman Catholic sacramental system? Reformation commentators were writing during a time of much turmoil and unrest.

Calvin, for example, had begun the process of reform at Geneva, but he and Guillaume Farel were told in no uncertain terms to leave in April 1538. In March 1539, Jacopo Sadoleto had written the Genevans attempting to woo the city back to Rome. Why follow "innovators" (the Protestants) who seek to rip the church from the womb of its mother, when mother is calling her children gently home? The Genevans decided to write to Calvin, who was then in Strasbourg, to ask him to write a response to Sadoleto—which he did in the span of six days. All this is to say: *generally*, the Reformation commentators were writing in a time where Reformation "ground" was still being staked out, and it took strenuous effort to keep such well-earned ground.[15] The Protestants—according to Sadoleto—were endangering the souls of the poor Genevans. Calvin's response is that Sadeloto's gospel is really no gospel at all, for it does not root forgiveness in the death, burial, and resurrection of Jesus. And to the charge of "innovation," Calvin argues that it is the *reformers* who stand closest to the theological tenets of the earliest Christians and earliest church fathers. Thus, in a rather strong counterattack, Calvin argues that it is the Protestants who are the ones most committed to ancient, classical Christianity.[16]

More specifically in terms of the Reformation exegetical approach to 1 and 2 Thessalonians, the key *unique* historical context must be the role of the Roman Catholic Church—especially the pope, and how to make sense of the Roman Catholic Church and the pope in light of Paul's teaching in 2 Thessalonians 2:1-12. Having worked through numerous Reformation commentators who wrestled with Paul's teaching in the second chapter of 2 Thessalonians, we were struck again and again at the amount of attention given to these key verses. If contemporary Protestants at times have become perhaps "settled" into a kind of easy coexistence with Rome, this was most certainly *not* the case with the reformers. Making sense of the pope in light of their reforming efforts was an intellectual, exegetical, and perhaps existential issue of the greatest import, and that is reflected in the amount of effort spent wrestling with Paul's teaching in 2 Thessalonians.

Five hundred years is a long time ago, but is it *that* long ago? Reformation commentators were fully capable of understanding and relating to the eschatological framework of 1 and 2 Thessalonians (number one above)—even if scholars like Geerhardus Vos[17] and George Eldon Ladd[18]

---

[15]See John Calvin and Jacopo Sadoleto, *A Reformation Debate*, ed. John C. Olin (Grand Rapids: Baker, 1976). The introduction helpfully outlines some of the history surrounding this debate between Calvin and Sadoleto.

[16]Calvin and Sadoleto, *A Reformation Debate*, 49-94.

[17]Geerhardus Vos, *The Pauline Eschatology* (Phillipsburg, NJ: P&R, 1979).

[18]George Eldon Ladd, *A Theology of the New Testament*, ed. Donald A. Hagner, 2nd ed. (Cambridge: Lutterworth, 2001); Ladd, *Gospel of the Kingdom: Scriptural Studies in the Kingdom of God* (Grand Rapids: Eerdmans, 1990).

were not yet around to help readers unpack and understand the "already, not yet" eschatological structure of the New Testament. Christians of the sixteenth and seventeenth centuries were looking forward to the future coming of Christ as much as we do. And such sixteenth- and seventeenth-century Christians needed to hear about the coming judgment of the returning Lord as much as we do.

Likewise, Reformation commentators were writing at a time when the encouragements and warnings given from Paul to the Thessalonians (number two above) would have been particularly meaningful. The reform movement was by no means a fait accompli, especially in the sixteenth century itself, and thus Paul's various encouragements to the Thessalonians would have been naturally (and appropriately in our view—*mutatis mutandis*) applied to their context in order to encourage the reform movement to carry on in its precarious efforts.

With number three above—the question of death and the state of the dead—there is also significant continuity between first-century concerns and sixteenth- and seventeenth-century concerns. Certainly it is a perennial question of virtually all persons: What happens when we die? Additionally, given that the Reformation commentators were writing against the backdrop of a culture that had experienced massive death and disease in the Middle Ages, they understandably would have found assurance in Paul's teaching that our future being with the Lord is dependent on his command, the voice of an archangel, and God's trumpet (1 Thess 4:16)—rather than the medieval sacramental system.

With number five above—the danger of idleness—we again see an issue of discontinuity and continuity between the first century and the sixteenth and seventeenth centuries. Whereas Christians in the first century were political and religious minorities,[19] the political realities had of course changed dramatically by the sixteenth and seventeenth centuries—the church having experienced significant phases of cultural dominance and influence, although this dominance and influence had always been historically marked by ongoing wars, threats, and extreme challenge. But perhaps in the sixteenth and seventeenth centuries the Reformation commentators would have felt themselves to be something of a bedraggled minority once again? It is the case that in the first century some Thessalonians might have thought the Day of the Lord had already come (2 Thess 3:6-15). We have no reason to think Christians in the Reformation era were making this mistake. Nonetheless, the encouragement to avoid idleness would have still applied to the Christians of the sixteenth and seventeenth centuries.

Theological themes and interpretive issues. 1. *The eschatological framework of 1–2 Thessalonians.* When one reads Paul's first letter to the Thessalonians, especially when read in relationship to Paul's other letters, it is easy to be struck by one key note: 1 Thessalonians does not ring with

---

[19]Rodney Stark suggests that by AD 40 Christians were 0.0017 percent of the entire population of the Roman Empire, and by AD 100 that number had risen to 0.0126 percent of that same population. See Rodney Stark, *The Rise of Christianity: How the Obscure, Marginal Jesus Movement Became the Dominant Religious Force in the Western World in a Few Centuries* (San Francisco: HarperSanFrancisco, 1997), 7.

the conflict that so often courses through Paul's other letters. Things may not be perfect in Thessalonica, but one is struck by how much Paul is encouraging his readers to stay the course. He is encouraging them—in many ways—to continue doing what they are doing. Nonetheless, there are key issues Paul wants and needs to address with the Thessalonians. It is often noted that Paul, in both 1 and 2 Thessalonians, has a concern with, or interest in, eschatology. At or near the end of each chapter of 1 Thessalonians Paul speaks of the return of the Lord. And in 2 Thessalonians, there is significant treatment of the "lawless one," "the mystery of lawlessness," "the son of destruction," and Satan, all in relation to the "Day of the Lord" and the "coming of our Lord Jesus Christ" (2 Thess 2:1-12). But rather than see eschatological concerns as one of many, it may be more helpful to start with grasping the eschatological nature of the New Testament and its theology. That is, it would seem to be the case that to understand 1 and 2 Thessalonians correctly, one must grasp the eschatological structure and nature of the New Testament as a whole.[20] Thus, rather than an eschatological concern simply being one of several concerns that Paul wants to address in 1 and 2 Thessalonians, it may be the case that the eschatological structure and backdrop of the whole New Testament is central to understanding all of Paul's concerns in this correspondence.

As noted above, Reformation commentators spent a tremendous amount of energy and space on 2 Thessalonians 2:1-12. This should not be surprising. But the obvious should not be missed. The Reformation commentators—when they treated this passage in depth (which was often!)—are virtually unanimous in the broad contours of their thought. "Antichrists" have been present since the first century, yet they often identify the pope or the office of the papacy as the antichrist. Why? Because, they argue, his message differs so starkly from the message of Jesus. The pope is simply one more person in history whose message differs starkly from that of Christ. The Reformation commentators do not seem to see the pope as *particularly* special. He is one in a myriad of "antichrists" throughout history. If our Roman Catholic friends think Protestants make too much of the pope, the Reformation commentary tradition might legitimately respond: "He really is simply one of a long line of persons who is opposed to the person and message of Jesus."[21]

---

[20]Scholars like Herman Ridderbos, E. Earle Ellis, and Gregory K. Beale for some time have argued this point. Still helpful is Herman Ridderbos, "Fundamental Structures," in *Paul: An Outline of His Theology* (Grand Rapids: Eerdmans, 1997), 44-90; E. Earle Ellis, *Christ and the Future in New Testament History* (Leiden: Brill, 2001); Gregory K. Beale, "The Eschatological Conception of New Testament Theology," in *"The Reader Must Understand": Eschatology in the Bible and Theology*, ed. Kent E. Brower and Mark W. Elliott (Leicester: Apollos, 1997), 11-52; Beale, *New Testament Biblical Theology: The Unfolding of the Old Testament in the New* (Grand Rapids: Baker Academic, 2011). In terms of 1 and 2 Thessalonians itself, Beale's comments in the following are very helpful: *1 and 2 Thessalonians*, IVP New Testament Commentary (Downers Grove, IL: InterVarsity Press, 2003), 18-23.

[21]The nature of the polemical battles between Protestantism and Roman Catholicism is of course an absorbing pastime, but any sustained attention to this polemic is beyond the scope of this volume. Somewhat older critics of Protestantism, like Hilaire Belloc, could call Protestantism a "heresy," and spend many pages trying to illustrate the many negative consequences of Protestantism in the history of Western culture. See Hilaire Belloc, *The Great Heresies* (London: Sheed and Ward, 1938; repr., Milwaukee, WI: Cavalier, 2015). Perhaps somewhat less polemical is the recent work of Brad S. Gregory, *The Unintended Reformation: How a Religious Revolution Secularized Society* (Cambridge, MA: Belknap Press of Harvard University Press, 2012). The thesis is succinctly stated in the title itself, and Gregory writes, "This book's principal argument is that the Western world today is an extraordinarily complex, tangled product of rejections, retentions, and transformations of medieval Western Christianity, in which the Reformation era constitutes the critical watershed" (2). The best responses to Gregory include the review by Carl Trueman, "Pay No Attention to That Man Behind the Curtain! Roman Catholic History and the Emerald City Protocol," *Reformation 21*, April 2012,

This attention to eschatology was often seen in relation to other central theological themes. For example, in his commentary on 1 Thessalonians 1:10, Calvin can write, "Let everyone, therefore, who would persevere in a course of holy life, apply their whole mind to an expectation of Christ's coming."[22] Similarly, Martin Bucer, commenting on the same verse, can write, "The people are to be exhorted to repent of their sins and to hope firmly in the life of heaven, and also to foster an earnest zeal and longing for this life to come, with the constant mortification of the old Adam and advancement of the new."[23]

2. *Encouragement and warnings.* Paul seems particularly concerned in 1 and 2 Thessalonians to encourage (and occasionally warn) the Thessalonians, at times encouraging them to remain on the path they are walking.

The Reformation commentators did not look on Paul's encouraging words as somehow extraneous or peripheral to, the gospel message. Instead, Paul's encouraging words in the Thessalonian letters could be linked inextricably to the gospel itself. For example, Jerome Zanchi, in his comments on 1 Thessalonians 2:3, writes, "As a synecdoche [i.e., a part referring to the whole, or the whole referring to a part], [Paul] signifies [with the word "encouragement," *paraklēsis*] the whole teaching of the gospel. First dogmatic things, then moral things, *didache*.[24] Since Paul not only passed on a simple teaching, but also exhorted, and implored people, that they might apprehend it [i.e., the dogmatic teaching]." Thus for Zanchi, "The action of ministry ought not simply to put forth [dogmatic/doctrinal] teaching, but also exhorts and entreats."[25]

Among Paul's exhortations (e.g., 1 Thess 2:13) is his encouragement to the Thessalonians to see his teaching for what it is: the word of God. Although there is a difference between (1) an apostle and (2) the sixteenth- or twenty-first-century preacher of Scripture, the Reformation commentators saw this passage as a touchstone for the centrality for Christian preaching. At least some of the Reformers could move somewhat seamlessly from Paul's preaching to Reformational preaching. Thus Bullinger can write, "Although the word of God be preached unto us by human beings, yet we receive it not as the word of human beings, but as the word of God, according to the saying of the apostle, 'When they had received the word of God which they heard from us, they received it not as a human word (but as it is indeed) the word of GOD.'"[26]

---

www.reformation21.org/articles/pay-no-attention-to-that-man-behind-the-curtain-roman-catholic-history-and-the-e.php, and the review by D. G. Hart, "Hyper About Pluralism: A Review Essay," *Humanitas* 27, nos. 1 and 2 (2014): 153-61. A mid-century volume by Louis Bouyer is more irenic in general, putting forward a more intriguing thesis, captured nicely in the title of the foreword by Mark Brumley: "Why the Catholic Church Is Necessary for the Full Flowering of the Protestant Reformation." In other words, for the legitimate insights and gains of the Reformation to fully flower, it is ultimately the Roman Catholic Church that is necessary. See Louis Bouyer, *The Spirit and Forms of Protestantism*, trans. A. V. Littledale (San Francisco: Ignatius, 2017), originally published as *De Protestantism à l'Eglise* (Paris: Cerf, 1954).

[22]CTS 42:245-47* (CO 52:142-43).

[23]Bucer, *A Brief Summary of Christian Doctrine*, 27.

[24]*Didache* simply means "teaching," though here it is used in the sense of "moral teaching."

[25]Zanchi, *Thessalonicenses*, 504-5.

[26]Bullinger, *Fifty Godly and Learned Sermons*, 963*.

3. The question of death and the state of the dead. As noted above, Paul appears to be addressing a concern about the state and future of believers who have died (e.g., 1 Thess 4:13). What happens to Christians who have died? Paul's key insight is that the future of all Christians hinges on the death and resurrection of Christ. Just as Christ died and rose again, so those who are in him die (and some will "literally" die before the Lord's return) and are raised up. Paul continues this general theme in 1 Thessalonians 5:1-11, where he encourages them in relationship to the Day of the Lord.

For Reformation commentators, lament is appropriate—only inordinate sorrow is to be put aside. Thomas Poole writes, "To mourn for the dead, especially the dead in the Lord, is a duty that both nature and grace teach, and God requires; and the contrary is reproved by God himself . . . and to die unlamented is reckoned as a curse."[27] Luther similarly writes, "Grieve in such a way, therefore, as to console yourselves even more. For you have not lost him, but have sent him on ahead of you to be kept in everlasting blessedness."[28] Perhaps most importantly, Reformation commentators were convinced that those who where Christ's would be raised up with him. As Robert Rollock notes, "In the resurrection all senses will be satisfied with God, that is, from that very source of rejoicing and happiness: For God will be all in all."[29]

4. The nature of the "lawless one," "man of lawlessness," or "son of destruction," or "Satan." In 2 Thessalonians 2:1-12 we find a particularly fascinating eschatological passage having to do with the "coming of the Lord" (2 Thess 2:1). Apparently some person or persons have suggested that the Day of the Lord has already come. In light of this confusion, Paul replies that there must be a "rebellion" before the Day of the Lord comes. Attendant to that rebellion, Paul speaks of the revelation of the "man of lawlessness," who is the same person as "the son of destruction" (2 Thess 2:3). This person is not necessarily the same as "Satan," but this "man of lawlessness" is "by the activity of Satan"[30] (2 Thess 2:9). Whatever the exact identity, this person is clearly opposed to the things of God. Interestingly, there is also a "mystery of lawlessness," which is already at work, although this "mystery of lawlessness" is currently being restrained (2 Thess 2:7). Eventually the "lawless one" will be revealed, and will be defeated by Jesus when he comes.

The commentators were keen to comment on these verses, and to do so at great length. A few patterns should be noted.

First, the Reformation commentators fairly consistently identified the "man of lawlessness," "son of perdition" (and sometimes "antichrist" was included in these discussions) as the pope or the institution of the papacy. Some commentators would go on at great length to make the argument. Robert Rollock,[31] Heinrich Bullinger,[32] Erasmus Sarcerius,[33] and others wrote at length identifying this figure as the pope.

---

[27]Poole, *Annotations*, 744*.

[28]LW 50:52.

[29]Rollock, *Ad Thessalonicenses*, 148.

[30]The Greek behind "by the activity of Satan" is *kat energeian tou satana*. The NASB of 2 Thess 2:9 reads, "the one whose coming is *in accord with the activity of Satan*."

[31]Rollock, *Ad Thessalonicenses*, 292-301.

[32]Bullinger, *Second Thessalonians*, 2:1-12.

[33]Sarcerius, *Ad Thessalonicenses*, 544-57.

Second, a rather sophisticated hermeneutic was often at work in the Reformation commentators. In 2 Thessalonians 2, as we have noted, there are several overlapping terms being used: "man of lawlessness," "son of destruction," "mystery of lawlessness." Again, the term "antichrist" also made it into these discussions, not surprising, especially given 2 Thessalonians 2:4. Also, the Reformation commentators did their work with a couple of key texts in mind:

- 1 John 2:18: "Children, it is the last hour, and as you have heard that antichrist is coming, so now many antichrists have come."

- 1 John 4:2-3: "By this you know the Spirit of God: every spirit that confesses that Jesus Christ has come in the flesh is from God, and every spirit that does not confess Jesus is not from God."

When one combines all of this, an interesting pattern emerges. Reformation commentators, in general, argued that there has been a pattern of opposition to the things of God since the first century.[34] Likewise, there have been many "antichrists" throughout history. Thus there has been opposition to the things of God going on throughout the history of the church, and there have been figures who could rightly be called "antichrists" throughout the church. In the sixteenth and seventeenth centuries, many Reformation commentators saw the pope as one more of this long line of figures. Interestingly, a number of Reformation commentators based their case for identifying the pope as "antichrist" on a rather simple method: they would often summarize the teachings of Christ, and summarize the teachings of the pope(s), and simply conclude that the pope seems clearly to be opposed to the teachings of Christ himself.

Third, while Reformation commentators did not deny a final, future "antichrist," there seems to be little theorizing about this future figure.

Fourth, it is also worth noting that beside the pope, the other major figure who is identified as antichrist is Muhammad. Often the line of argument is similar to that used when discussing the pope. Muhammad can be seen as antichrist because when one compares the teachings of Muhammad and Jesus, they are clearly contradictory teachings.

And fifth, the Roman Empire functioned as "that which restrained" until its eventual dissolution, which enabled the papacy to usurp its authority over Christendom.

5. *The danger of idleness.* Finally, one last item to mention is the issue of idleness. This, like the other themes, is perhaps only fully understood when seen in relationship to the eschatological realities manifested in the New Testament. Paul addresses this issue in 2 Thessalonians 3:6-15 and, perhaps more subtly, in 1 Thessalonians 4:9-12.

At times Reformation commentators treat these passages in relation people who refuse to work, and at other points they read them in light of the monastic life. Thus Bullinger can write, "Also this place Paul does condemn all sturdy beggars. I need not to speak anything of monks and such sacrificers, as are unprofitable to the godly ministration of the church, seeing that nothing can be feigned that condemns them more than this." Bullinger encourages the civil rulers to take

---

[34]This is *not* to say such opposition to the things of God does not push back further in history as well. One sees this in, among others, the commentary by Robert Rollock, Erasmus Sarcerius, and Heinrich Bullinger just mentioned in the previous notes.

this text seriously: "You princes and rulers of cities take good heed that this law of God be put in use and have place among you, if you love the health of the commonwealth."[35] Bullinger takes the importance of work very seriously, as he goes on to write: "As many of you as are chargeable to the people, as many of you as do not work at all, but go about things that are to no purpose, think that this is spoken to you also. Christ shall punish you unless you leave your dishonest and most uncomely idleness, and get you to labor. And here is a goodly place to speak of the kinds of labors and business, and of the helping and duties to the poor also."[36]

Historical reception. These letters have always been thought to have been written by Paul, and there was never serious doubt as to their inclusion in the canon. The Reformation commentators, as all traditional Christians have done, viewed these books as the divine Word of God, and they were worthy of close attention and study. We draw attention to 1 Thessalonians 2:13, which reads, "And we also thank God constantly for this, that when you received the word of God, which you heard from us, you accepted it not as the word of men but as what it really is, the word of God, which is at work in you believers." At times, Roman Catholic apologists use this passage to point to an early oral or unwritten apostolic message that was considered to be the "word of God." The argument is then made: if there was an early, oral, apostolic "word of God" that *preceded* the actual written New Testament documents, why could there not be such an oral word of God that *follows* the possession of the New Testament documents, namely, the Roman Catholic magisterium?

Contemporary Protestants have addressed this issue, and the Reformation commentators were not blind to the implications of a passage like this. In our own day, Robert Sloan (among others) has argued that there certainly was a precanonical, oral, apostolic theology that led to the formation of the New Testament documents. If Paul, Peter, Luke, and the other authors of the New Testament were actually theologians (and surely they were), then it is of course the case that it was their theologizing that led to writing of the New Testament documents, which was followed by the formation of the Christian canon.[37] The Protestant need not get nervous when Roman Catholics or others appeal to 1 Thessalonians 2:13 as somehow challenging a traditional Protestant affirmation of *sola Scriptura.* Heinrich Bullinger says about this passage, "Although, therefore, the apostles were men, nevertheless their doctrine, first of all, taught by a lively expressed voice and after that set down in writing with pen and ink, is the doctrine of God and the very true word of

---

[35]Bullinger, *Second Thessalonians*, 3:10*.

[36]Bullinger, *Second Thessalonians*, 3:11-12*.

[37]See Robert B. Sloan, "Unity in Diversity: A Clue to the Emergence of the New Testament as Sacred Literature," in *New Testament Criticism and Interpretation*, ed. David S. Dockery and David Alan Black (Grand Rapids: Zondervan, 1991), 437-68. E. Earle Ellis has also written on these issues in his *The Old Testament in Early Christianity: Canon and Interpretation in the Light of Modern Research* (Grand Rapids: Baker, 1991); Ellis, *The Making of the New Testament Documents* (Leiden: Brill, 2002). Also helpful is a classic essay by Richard Gaffin, "New Testament as Canon," in *Inerrancy and Hermeneutic: A Tradition, a Challenge, a Debate,* ed. Harvie Conn (Grand Rapids: Baker, 1998), 165-83. The works on canon by F. F. Bruce and Bruce Metzger are still helpful, although Michael Kruger's recent volumes might be just as, if not more, crucial reading for readers today. See F. F. Bruce, *The Canon of Scripture* (Downers Grove, IL: InterVarsity Press, 1988); Bruce M. Metzger, *The Canon of the New Testament: Its Origin, Development, and Significance* (Oxford: Clarendon, 1992); Michael J. Kruger, *Canon Revisited: Establishing the Origins and Authority of the New Testament Books* (Wheaton, IL: Crossway, 2012); Kruger, *The Question of Canon: Challenging the Status Quo in the New Testament Debate* (Downers Grove, IL: IVP Academic, 2013).

God."[38] In short, Bullinger is quite happy, as a Protestant, to affirm that the apostles taught "by a lively expressed voice" (orally, in their teaching) their doctrine. This doctrine was "after that set down in writing with pen and ink." This teaching, first given orally, then written down, is "the very true word of God." In short, in the case of 1 Thessalonians 2:13, Paul could consider his apostolic teaching "the word of God," and this apostolic message was eventually committed to writing, and this writing comes to us as the document we now call 1 Thessalonians.

For the reformers, the Thessalonian epistles, along with Paul's other letters, communicated the truth of the gospel message and provided guidance for both the church's faith and practice—guidance that was as applicable to sixteenth-century Christians as it was to the first-century church.

Reformation Reception of 1–2 Timothy and Titus

It is now common for commentators to doubt that the apostle Paul was the author of the Pastoral Epistles of 1–2 Timothy and Titus, employing categories such as "literary deceit" or "pseudonymity" or "allonymity" to explain Paul's name at the beginning and their circulation as part of the Pauline corpus.[39] Reformation-era exegetes, however, did not do so in the way that they did question the authorship of Hebrews (traditionally assigned to Paul, but without his name specifically attached).[40] Even those with an impressive knowledge of Greek literature did not raise questions about the Pauline character of the Greek in these letters.[41] Their larger concern was to locate the letters in the ministry of Paul and to learn from them as part of Christian Scripture.

Timothy and Titus were certainly associates of the apostle Paul, being mentioned extensively in the New Testament.[42] Timothy is acknowledged at the beginning of some of Paul's epistles as a coauthor (2 Corinthians, Philippians, Colossians, 1 Thessalonians, 2 Thessalonians, and Philemon), and both Timothy and Titus were clearly trained and trusted coworkers with the apostle in his missionary endeavors, as sixteenth-century interpreters all recognized.

Some modern commentators have drawn attention to the plural "Grace be with *you*" at the end of 1 Timothy 6:21, as if it indicates a plural audience reading over Timothy's shoulder, so to speak.[43] On the basis of content and context, Calvin argues that each epistle was "so addressed to one man that it is also addressed to all, and that it ought to profit the children of God generally."[44]

---

[38]Bullinger, *Fifty Godly and Learned Sermons*, 12*.

[39]See, e.g., Bart G. Ehrman, *Forgery and Counterforgery: The Use of Literary Deceit in Early Christian Polemics* (Oxford: Oxford University Press, 2013). "Allonymity" is the term preferred by I. Howard Marshall, *The Pastoral Epistles*, International Critical Commentary (London: T&T Clark, 2004), 84, because it avoids the nuance of intentional deceit.

[40]See Ronald K. Rittgers, ed., *Hebrews, James*, Reformation Commentary on Scripture, New Testament XIII (Downers Grove, IL: IVP Academic, 2017), 1-6. Erasmus, Luther, and Calvin were all against Pauline authorship of Hebrews.

[41]Luke Timothy Johnson, *The First and Second Letters to Timothy: A New Translation with Introduction and Commentary*, Anchor Yale Bible 35A (New Haven, CT: Yale University Press, 2008), 37n72.

[42]See Acts 16:1; 17:14-15; 18:5; 19:22; 20:4; Rom 16:21; 1 Cor 16:10; 2 Cor 1:19; Phil 2:19; 2:22; 1 Thess 3:2, 6 (Timothy); and 2 Cor 2:13; 7:6, 13-14; 8:6, 16-17, 23; 12:18; Gal 2:1, 3; and 2 Tim 4:10 (Titus).

[43]See George W. Knight III, *The Pastoral Epistles: A Commentary on the Greek Text*, New International Greek Testament Commentary (Carlisle, UK: Paternoster, 1992), 277. The word "you" was not, however, in the plural form in the Textus Receptus used by our Reformation-era commentators, but in the singular. See Bruce M. Metzger, *A Textual Commentary on the Greek New Testament*, 2nd ed. (Stuttgart: Deutsche Bibelgesellschaft, 1994), 577.

[44]CO 53:5.

Of Titus, he said it "was not so much a private epistle of Paul to Titus, as it was a public epistle to the Cretans."[45]

The phrase "Pastoral Epistles" to describe 1 Timothy, 2 Timothy, and Titus together was not a Reformation invention, but probably originates from the eighteenth century.[46] Nevertheless, these three related but distinct epistles to the apostle Paul's colleagues in pastoral ministry clearly have a number of common themes, which *were* noted by Reformation-era exegetes. Of particular importance are church order, ministry, false teaching, and soteriology.

Church order. The exact status of Timothy and Titus (as presbyters, evangelists, or bishops) is a question on which Reformation-era commentators disagreed. Some very firmly said that they were archbishops (Erasmus) or bishops (Tyndale, Luther, Scultetus, Hooker). Others of a more Presbyterian frame of mind were adamant that they were better labeled evangelists (Calvin, Cartwright, Diodati, Dickson), though they invested that title with more dignity and duties than many commonly do today because they considered it a temporary and extraordinary office, unique to the early days of the church. Clearly, issues of church polity were key for Protestant churches as they broke from Rome in the sixteenth century or argued over the best way to organize themselves going forward; the Pastoral Epistles were an important battleground as different conceptions of ideal polity were debated.

In 1 Timothy, Paul lays out a charge to Timothy to help him govern the church at Ephesus in the midst of various false teachings. Luther went so far as to say that the letter "is not didactic, and it does not strive to establish basic teaching. Rather, it establishes the church and sets it in order." True, he said, "in the midst of this process Paul does not neglect to add very important doctrinal subjects," but the key thing was to set the church in good order.[47] To use a metaphor from Matthew Poole's commentary, Paul the conquering general left Titus in Crete and Timothy in Ephesus as garrison governors, with instructions on how to behave in post.[48] The unfinished business in Crete was putting things in good order with regard to the governance of the church.

Ministry. A key part of church governance is, of course, establishing properly constituted leadership and ministry. The Pastoral Epistles, being written to Paul's fellow ministers who also had a certain oversight over others and a responsibility in appointments (e.g., 1 Tim 1:3; 3:1-15; 5:17-22; 2 Tim 2:2; Titus 1:5-9) are a vital place to find biblical teaching on this subject. The reformers were pleased to discover that the ministry described here does not appear to be focused on the Mass, but on the word of God being read and preached, and prayer being offered for all (1 Tim 2:1-2).

Jay Twomey has drawn attention to a great number of poetic and fictional appropriations of the Pastoral Epistles through the centuries.[49] That is not so much our interest here, but the idea of looking beyond commentaries and sermons to understand how and where the biblical text was

---

[45]CTS 42:277-78 (CO 52:401-2).

[46]According to Donald Guthrie, *The Pastoral Epistles*, Tyndale New Testament Commentaries (Downers Grove, IL: InterVarsity Press, 1990), 19, the term originates with D. N. Berdot (1703) and Paul Anton (1726).

[47]LW 28:217 (WA 26:4).

[48]Poole, *Annotations*, Introduction to Titus.

[49]Jay Twomey, *The Pastoral Epistles Through the Centuries* (Oxford: Wiley-Blackwell, 2009).

interpreted in this period is a very important one. As Ashley Null says, Thomas Cranmer "looked to the Pauline epistles for his reforming approach to the office of a bishop as much as he would later do for his reconsideration of the nature of salvation."[50] Or as Jonathan Linebaugh puts it, "Cranmer's second prayer book is, in part, a liturgical expression of his reading of Paul. . . . Paul, in other words, is among those who taught Cranmer to pray."[51] Hence, in the commentary, we have sometimes used liturgical and confessional material that alludes to or applies 1 Timothy, 2 Timothy, or Titus. The Books of Common Prayer (especially the Ordinal), the Anglican Homilies, the Belgic Confession, and the Westminster Directory of Public Worship are all key places where the teaching of the Pastoral Epistles was expounded and applied in our period. These often provide suitable examples of the reception and use of these epistles, and ones that became extremely influential through repeated use and widespread familiarity, even more so than interpretations locked away in commentaries. Also widely influential were the notes found in the margins of the popular Geneva Bible, which tried to steer readers very much in a Reformed direction on certain key topics.

One aspect of ministry in the Pastoral Epistles that has become particularly important in the last century is the role of women in the church.[52] Reformation-era commentators were also interested in this aspect of the epistles' teaching in 1 Timothy 2–3 and Titus 1–2, though it was less controversial in their days. What Paul says about women learning but not teaching in the public meetings of the church, and, what precisely Paul meant by them being "saved through childbearing" raised many interpretive questions, not least by comparison with Paul's teaching in 1 Corinthians. So as Peter Martyr Vermigli comments, "If at that time it was lawful for a woman to pray and prophesy openly, why does Paul, writing to the Corinthians and to Timothy, admonish that a woman should not speak in the church? These two sayings, although they may seem somewhat repugnant [to each other], may be reconciled in several ways."[53] He is also aware of arguments citing Deborah's role as a judge in the Old Testament, but concludes that unusual privileges do not set regular examples.[54] It was the common position of most of the interpreters in the sixteenth century, who also looked back to the early church for example and precedent,[55] to rule out women as presbyters or public preachers however godly and learned they might be. As evidenced by the commentary below, however, there were others—including female commentators—who did not interpret Paul's guidance in 1 Timothy 2 as universally prescriptive and who argued, on the basis of Scripture, that women could—indeed, should—be full participants in the ministry of the gospel.

---

[50]Ashley Null, "Thomas Cranmer's Reading of Paul's Letters," in Allen and Linebaugh, *Reformation Readings of Paul*, 213.

[51]Jonathan Linebaugh, "The Texts of Paul and the Theology of Cranmer" in Allen and Linebaugh, *Reformation Readings of Paul*, 253.

[52]Andreas J. Köstenberger and Thomas R. Schreiner, eds., *Women in the Church: An Analysis and Application of 1 Timothy 2:9-15*, 3rd ed. (Wheaton, IL: Crossway, 2016) has an extensive bibliography and a number of chapters on aspects of 1 Tim 2:9-15. Philip B. Payne, *Man and Woman, One in Christ: An Exegetical and Theological Study of Paul's Letters* (Grand Rapids: Zondervan, 2009) develops an egalitarian reading of the relevant sections in 1 Timothy and Titus.

[53]Vermigli, *Commonplaces*, 1:20*.

[54]Vermigli, *Commonplaces*, 4:7.

[55]See Grotius, *Annotationes*, 7:226-27, for example, who cites Tertullian.

False teaching. The nature of the opposition Timothy and Titus faced has been of perennial interest.[56] William Tyndale saw 1 Timothy as a call for Bishop Timothy to "resist false preachers who make the law and works equal with Christ and his gospel."[57] These insatiably covetous false prophets, as he describes them, sound remarkably like the often-parodied Roman priests who opposed Tyndale himself and the gospel of salvation by grace alone. The tempting parallels between the enemies of the gospel in the Pastoral Epistles and the enemies of contemporary Protestantism was hard to resist for many commentators. Calvin saw the sophistical theologians of the Sorbonne in 1 Timothy 1:6-7 and 1 Timothy 6:4.[58]

Erasmus saw the apostates as those who "slide back into a certain Jewishness,"[59] while Giovanni Diodati described the avaricious heretics as "false Christianized Jews, perpetual corrupters of the pureness of the gospel in those days."[60] Their interest in genealogies (1 Tim 1:4) and abstinence from certain foods (1 Tim 4:1-3) as well as their fascination with circumcision and "Jewish myths" (Titus 1:10-14) provided ready evidence for this identification. Some also pointed out links to Gnosticism and other ancient groups such as Encratites, Essenes, and Manichees. Noting the prevalence of conscience language (e.g., 1 Tim 1:19), some such as Calvin noted how greed and ambition function within false teachers and conclude that "a bad conscience is, therefore, the mother of all heresies."[61]

Given what they saw as the prevalence of false teaching all around them, our commentators were keen to identify based on the Pastoral Epistles when the time is right to fight for the faith and how to do so. "The world is full of unprofitable questions," wrote Tilemann Hesshus, and so we must major on "the chief Christian teachings" and not on idle, unnecessary speculations.[62] False teachers are to be avoided and disciplined, but also at times reasoned with, taught, and prayed for. "Christian love itself prevents us from rashly losing hope in someone," asserted Bullinger, who speaks against "the excessive ferocity of certain bishops who are quicker to condemn than to teach, to reprove and bite than to take hold and restore to health."[63]

Soteriology. Twomey writes that in general, patristic interpreters used the Pastorals in christological and trinitarian debates while Enlightenment readers focused on political aspects of these letters. Reformation writers, however, "key in on soteriological concepts."[64] It is certainly noteworthy how much attention our interpreters gave to certain sections of these letters with implications for the doctrine of salvation, such as 1 Timothy 1:15 and 1 Timothy 2:4—texts that had been

---

[56]Recently, Dillon Thornton, *Hostility in the House of God: An Investigation of the Opponents in 1 and 2 Timothy*, Bulletin for Biblical Research, Supplements 15 (Winona Lake, IN: Eisenbrauns, 2016) has persuasively presented the opponents as being paid Christian teachers active within the congregation at Ephesus who had distorted Paul's eschatological teaching.

[57]Tyndale, *The Newe Testament*, cccii*.

[58]CTS 43:29 (CO 52:254); CTS 43:154-55* (CO 52:324-25).

[59]Erasmus, *Paraphrases*, 47-49.

[60]Diodati, *Pious Annotations*, NT 37-38*.

[61]CTS 43:45-46 (CO 52:263-64).

[62]Hesshus, *Commentarius*, 303-4.

[63]Bullinger, *Apostolicas Epistolas*, 611-12.

[64]Twomey, *Pastoral Epistles Through the Centuries*, 4.

keenly fought over in earlier debates in church history, such as the semi-Pelagian controversy.[65] What did it mean for God to desire "*all* people to be saved and to come to the knowledge of the truth" (1 Tim 2:4), or for Jesus to give himself as "a ransom for *all*" (1 Tim 2:6), or for God to be "the Savior of *all* people, especially of those who believe" (1 Tim 4:10)?

Reflection on these texts inevitably led to a great deal of time and energy being expended in an attempt to harmonize them with the rest of Scripture and an individual commentator's wider theological commitments. Precisely how we are meant to understand God's will here in the context of the rest of the Bible's teaching on God's sovereignty was something of a contentious issue among our interpreters, requiring some careful distinctions and discussion of the precise meaning of the deceptively simple word "all." Jacobus Arminius, for example, saw Calvin's doctrine of predestination as openly hostile to the ministry of the gospel and to the command to pray for all, while Conradus Vorstius focused on the universal offer of the gospel and its sufficient provision for salvation.[66] Others restrict salvation proper to the elect alone, noting that this happy company consists of *all kinds* of people.[67] Still others, also represented here, attempted a "middle way" of one sort or another.

At the same time, the uniqueness and sufficiency of Christ's mediation and intercession raised by 1 Timothy 2:5 was an issue of major disagreement between Protestants and Romans Catholics and so merited extensive discussion. In the fourteenth century, John Wycliffe had objected to the supposed mediation of saints. "So he would be a fool who sought some other intercessor," wrote Wycliffe, because it is not fitting for Christ "to mediate in company with other saints, since he is kinder and more likely to help than any other." Such practices are confusing to the pious mind and "can lead to a twisted devotion in which one stupidly worships canonized demons, esteeming them as blessed."[68] The Counter-Reformation Council of Trent (session 25, 1563) exhorted Roman Catholic priests to instruct the faithful diligently regarding the intercession of the saints, "teaching them that the saints who reign together with Christ offer up their prayers to God for human beings, that it is good and beneficial suppliantly to invoke them and to have recourse to their prayers, assistance, and support."[69] So all Protestant commentators felt it was incumbent on them to show how 1 Timothy 2:5 excludes all other mediators and heavenly intercessors.

Reformation Reception of Philemon

Historical context. The book of Philemon is also attributed to Paul, and there is no good reason to doubt Paul's authorship. Paul is writing as a prisoner (Philem 1, 9, 10, 23), and perhaps the best

---

[65]See Francis Gumerlock, *Fulgentius of Ruspe: On the Saving Will of God; The Development of a Sixth-Century African Bishop's Interpretation of 1 Timothy 2:4 During the Semi-Pelagian Controversy* (Lewiston, NY: Mellen, 2009). Roland Teske, "1 Timothy 2:4 and the Beginnings of the Massalian Controversy," in *Grace for Grace: The Debates After Augustine and Pelagius*, ed. Alexander Y. Hwang, Brian J. Matz, and Augustine Casiday (Washington, DC: Catholic University of America Press, 2014), 14-34.

[66]Arminius, *Writings*, 1:232-33. Vorstius, *Commentarius*, 462.

[67]See Martin Foord, "God Wills All People to Be Saved—Or Does He? Calvin's Reading of 1 Timothy 2:4," in *Engaging with Calvin: Aspects of the Reformer's Legacy for Today*, ed. Mark D. Thompson (Nottingham, UK: Apollos, 2009), 179-203.

[68]Wyclif, *Trialogus*, 188-89 (3.30).

[69]See *The Canons and Decrees of the Council of Trent*, trans. H. J. Schroeder (Rockford, IL: Tan Books, 1978), 215.

option for locating the place of his imprisonment is Rome. The letter is from Paul and Timothy, though Paul is clearly playing lead, given the prominence of the first-person-singular "I" throughout the letter. It is a short letter with a very particular focus: Onesimus, Philemon's runaway slave who is being returned to Philemon (Philem 8-22).

Colossians 4:7-17 can be illuminating in understanding some of the background. In Colossians 4:7 Paul writes that one Tychicus has been sent to Colossae with Paul's letter to that community. Also traveling with Tychicus is Onesimus. Thus, if Onesimus is traveling with Tychicus, it would make sense that Tychicus is carrying the letter from Paul to Philemon. Also, it would make sense to posit that Philemon himself was a part of the Christian community in Colossae and lived there. The letter is likely dated around AD 60–61.

The historical context of the Reformation-era commentators is such that they have slightly different emphases in their approach to Philemon than we do. Whereas contemporary exegetes are often interested in the question of slavery, the Reformation commentators seem to be drawn to the striking love that Paul has for Onesimus. This is not to imply an endorsement of slavery, but it does not seem to be an especially pressing issue for the Reformation commentators. Tyndale speaks of Paul's "godly example of Christian love," and Calvin speaks of the "singular loftiness of the mind of Paul, though it may be seen to greater advantage in his other writings that treat of weightier matters, it is also attested by this epistle, in which, while he handles a subject otherwise low and humble, he rises to God with his customary elevation."[70] As is so often the case, we may approach this text with different questions than the Reformers, but we can still learn from the questions they were asking.

Theological themes and interpretive issues. Paul's letter to Philemon in one sense has a single focus: Onesimus and his relationship to Paul and Philemon. After Paul's greeting (Philem 1-3) and encouraging words to Philemon (Philem 4-7), Paul moves to the heart of the letter: Onesimus (Philem 8-22). Paul is sending Onesimus, a runaway servant or slave, back to Philemon. Onesimus had been apparently converted under Paul's ministry while Paul was in prison (Philem 10). Paul desires to make an appeal rather than a command (Philem 8-9). It is interesting to ask: What exactly is the appeal? Before one actually reads the letter, if one simply knows some of the background one might suspect that the letter is going to "deal" with slavery. But even when one has read this letter dozens upon dozens of times, one must conclude that Paul does not seem here particularly driven to "deal" with a particular social or moral issue. The actual appeal does not appear to come until Philemon 17: "So if you consider me your partner, receive him as you would receive me."

One might think that there would be in-depth or sustained analysis to the question of slavery per se, but this does not seem to have been the case with the Reformation commentary tradition. As F. F. Bruce notes, "The letter throws little light on Paul's attitude to the institution of slavery."[71] But that does not mean that the letter is without benefit or theological significance. As Luther

---

[70]CTS 43:347-48* (CO 52:441).
[71]Bruce, *Paul*, 400.

states, "Paul cannot refrain from inculcating the general doctrine concerning Christ even here in treating a private matter."[72]

Historical reception. As with 1 and 2 Thessalonians, the Reformation commentators affirmed the Pauline authorship of Philemon, as do most scholars today. It is interesting that N. T. Wright chose to begin his magnum opus, *Paul and the Faithfulness of God*, with a treatment of the book of Philemon. Wright is not alone in noting that there is some similarity between Paul's letter to Philemon and similar ancient literature, where one person is writing to a particular bondservant's owner, on behalf of the bondservant. Wright notes a certain letter from Pliny the Younger (AD 61–113). In this letter, Pliny the Younger addresses the owner of a servant on behalf of the bondservant.[73] But Wright's goal is to point out the differences between Pliny and Paul. If the one (Pliny) essentially says, "Now, my good fellow, let me tell you what to do with your stupid freedman and then we'll all be safely back in our proper positions," the other (Paul to Philemon) says, "Now, my brother and partner, let me tell you about my newborn child, and let me ask you to think of him, and yourself, and me, as partners and brothers."[74] In short, as Wright notes, "the shortest of all Paul's writings that we possess, gives us a clear, sharp little window into a phenomenon that demands a historical explanation, which in turn, as we shall see, demands a *theological* explanation." Indeed, "if we had no other first-century evidence for the movement that came to be called Christianity, this letter ought to make us think: Something is going on here. Something is different. People don't say this sort of thing."[75]

A Note on Methodology

Readers might be interested in something of the methodology utilized in the writing of this volume. For the commentary on 1 and 2 Thessalonians and Philemon, I (Brad Green) attempted to follow the directives of the publisher by seeking a broad spectrum of Reformation-era writers. Generally I focused on sixteenth-century commentary, with a few forays into the early seventeenth century for a few writers (e.g., Matthew Poole and David Dickson). I did use some material from reform-minded Roman Catholics like Jacques Lefèvre d'Étaples, a fascinating figure.[76] I also tried not to allow Luther and Calvin to predominate. There is more (percentage-wise) of Calvin in Philemon than in 1 and 2 Thessalonians. I generally wrote the volume without at first utilizing much from Luther and Calvin. I then turned to Luther and Calvin to supply commentary where perhaps I needed to. There were some works I used in translation (e.g., Luther, Calvin, and Bullinger) and some needed no translation (the various English texts). There was a good bit of material translated from Latin, and all Latin translations are my own, much of which has not been published in English.

---

[72]LW 29:93.
[73]N. T. Wright, *Paul and the Faithfulness of God*, Christian Origins and the Question of God 4 (Minneapolis: Fortress, 2013), 3-7.
[74]Wright, *Paul and the Faithfulness of God*, 6.
[75]Wright, *Paul and the Faithfulness of God*, 6.
[76]Lefèvre was fascinating indeed. Guy Bedoulle concludes that Lefèvre "made no statement of a break with the Church of Rome, but neither did he make any declaration—as he was apparently asked to do—of conformity to the doctrines of the Church of Rome." See Guy Bedouelle, "Lefèvre d'Étaples, Jacques," in *The Oxford Encyclopedia of the Reformation*, ed. Hans J. Hillerbrand (New York: Oxford University Press, 1996), 2:415.

On the Pastorals, I (Lee Gatiss) worked in a very similar way to Brad, though with a slight balancing tendency toward more seventeenth-century sources. As mentioned above, I utilized a number of confessional sources as well as commentaries and sermons, especially since the Pastorals are such a rich source of reflection on pastoral ministry, which underwent a significant reconfiguration in Protestant contexts. I occasionally glance back at Jan Hus (1372–1415) or John Wycliffe (1330–1384), who was considered by the reformers themselves as "the Morning Star of the Reformation," though of course they had their own contexts in the fourteenth and fifteenth centuries too. I have also tried to note some other significant medieval texts in the footnotes where appropriate (e.g., Peter Lombard and Thomas Aquinas) since it is increasingly noticed by scholars that the reformers painted on a medieval canvas whose contours and textures can still be observed in their fresh appreciation of Paul. The reformers were also deeply learned in classical texts, and I have tried to locate their significant quotations and allusions (e.g., to Seneca, Cicero, and Plutarch) in the footnotes, using the widely available Loeb editions where possible (and correcting their misattributions where necessary).

Commentary from Roman Catholic writers such as Cardinal Cajetan, Cardinal Bellarmine, Gregory Martin, Petrus Stevartius, François Carrière, Libert Froidmont, and Alfonso Salmerón is included, often for its own insights into the text, but also because this gives valuable polemical and theological context to the interpretations advanced by Protestant commentators. Also included is Erasmus, who is difficult to characterize but whose *Paraphrases* were to be found in churches all over England and all over Europe. There are several Latin sources translated here into English for the first time and a deliberate variety of Protestants from different denominations and doctrinal perspectives (e.g., Arminius and Amyraut as well as Davenant and Vermigli, Hooker as well as Cartwright, Zwingli as well as Luther and various Lutherans). After assembling the sixteenth- and seventeenth-century cast of men and women, I also made a pass over ancient commentaries (such as Chrysostom's) and more modern text-critical and theological scholarship on these epistles (e.g., Metzger, Knight, Towner, and Marshall) in order to identify things that may particularly stand out in Reformation comments.

All of the overviews, headings, and summaries are intended to clarify the texts here assembled and make the commentary as useful and user-friendly as possible. We hope and pray that you will enjoy it, and put it to good and edifying uses in the service of God's church and the truth of his word. May this prayer from the Anglican Ordinal guide your reading:

> Most merciful Father, we beseech you, so to send upon these your servants your heavenly blessing, that they may be clad about with all justice, and that your word spoken by their mouths may have such success, that it may never be spoken in vain. Grant also that we may have grace to hear and receive the same as your most holy word and the means of our salvation, that in all our words and deeds we may seek your glory and increase of your kingdom, through Jesus Christ our Lord. Amen.[77]

---

[77]*Forme and Maner, Ordering of Priests**.

COMMENTARY ON 1 THESSALONIANS

1:1 INTRODUCTION TO
1 THESSALONIANS AND GREETING

Paul, Silvanus, and Timothy,
  To the church of the Thessalonians in God the
Father and the Lord Jesus Christ:
  Grace to you and peace.

OVERVIEW: As they introduce Paul's first epistle to the Thessalonians, the commentators below highlight the apostle's pastoral concern for the church of Thessalonica. In so doing, they observe that such concern shows itself in strengthening the faith of others and exhorting them to pursue lives of holiness. In this regard, these commentators attribute the holy lives of believers to the preaching of the Word, which simultaneously refutes false doctrine, the antithesis of holiness. While commenting on this opening verse, these expositors point out the prayerful nature of Paul's greeting and emphasize the church as a spiritual entity that is united in fellowship with the Father, Son, and Holy Spirit.

Introductory Comments

PAUL'S LOVE AND CARE FOR THE THESSALONIANS. WILLIAM TYNDALE: This epistle Paul wrote out of exceeding love and care: and he praises them in the two first chapters because they received the gospel earnestly, and had in tribulation and persecution continued therein steadfastly, and became an example to all congregations, and they had also suffered [at the hands] of their own kinsmen as Christ and his apostles did of the Jews, putting them also in mind how purely and godly

he had lived among them to their example, and thanked God that his gospel had brought forth such fruit among them.

In the third chapter, he shows his diligence and care, lest his great labor and their blessed beginning should have been in vain, Satan and his apostles persecuting and destroying their faith with human doctrine. And therefore he sent Timothy to them to comfort them and strengthen them in the faith, and thanked God that they had so constantly endured, and desired God to increase them.

In the fourth he exhorts them to keep themselves from sin and to do good one to another. And he also informs them concerning the resurrection.

In the fifth he writes of the last day, that it should come suddenly, exhorting them to prepare themselves thereafter and to keep a good order concerning obedience and rule. A PROLOGUE TO THE FIRST EPISTLE OF ST. PAUL TO THE THESSALONIANS.[1]

THE NEED FOR CONSTANCY AND A HOLY LIFE. DAVID DICKSON: Thessalonica in times past was the metropolis of all Macedonia, in which Paul and Silas . . . converted many in a little time among the Jews, and also the Gentiles, to the Christian faith. But afterward a sedition being stirred up by those

---

[1]*Tyndale's New Testament*, prologue*.

who did not believe, they were by force cast out from that place. The apostle first of all went to Berea, afterward to Athens. And in the first place he sends away Timothy to them, that he might comfort the afflicted. Afterward, Timothy being returned, and he, understanding the constancy of the Thessalonians, sends this epistle, in which he confirms them in the faith, and exhorts them to a life worthy of their holy profession. There are two principal parts of the epistle. In the first, after his endeavor to confirm them in the faith of Christ, and persuasion of his affection toward them, he encourages them to constancy (chapters 1–3). In the second part, he instructs and exhorts them to a holy life, inserting consolation touching the resurrection of the dead (chapters 4–5). The First Epistle of Paul to the Thessalonians[2]

The Preaching of Paul and the Example of the Thessalonians. Johannes Bugenhagen: The Thessalonians, since they had heard the preaching of Paul, stood firm in the faith. Paul was not afraid on account of certain false apostles. Stirring up confidence for works, since he himself had, as he says elsewhere, concern for the churches, truly exhorting (as he was accustomed) with rejoicing over two things: The one: both the Thessalonians and their own example, displayed in notable places. The other: [being] more effective, more certain, more persuasive and which might be fitting the gospel of Christ among those who hear: those who truly receive it [the gospel] through the Holy Spirit, who with no shame, no loss, or injury, not even death, depart with the Spirit, whom they receive through the hearing of the word of God. Annotationes in Epistolas Pauli.[3]

1:1 Greetings from the Apostle and His Coworkers

Why Multiple Authors? Jerome Zanchi: These [i.e., Silvanus and Timothy] he [i.e., Paul]

added as common authors. Why? Because they were also with Paul in Thessalonica, and he converted them. Therefore, in order that the epistle might have more authority, he added them, these known servants, to himself. Commentary on First Thessalonians.[4]

The Church Is in the Father and the Son. Robert Rollock: There are three in this greeting, the apostle Paul and the evangelists Silvanus and Timothy. The one greeted is the church of the Thessalonians. The blessings that are wished from the greeters to those they are greeting are grace and peace, and the author of this grace and peace is first God the Father, the source of all good things. Next, it is the Lord Jesus Christ, to whom all things have been given first by the Father, so that out of his fullness we all might receive. The cause and foundation for choosing these particular blessings for the Thessalonian church by the Father and his son Jesus Christ is because the church is in the Father and the Son, that is, it is in fellowship and communion with the Father and the Son. Commentary on First Thessalonians.[5]

What Makes a Church a Church. John Calvin: The brevity of the inscription clearly shows that Paul's doctrine had been received with reverence among the Thessalonians, and that without controversy they all rendered to him the honor that he deserved. For when in other epistles he designates himself an apostle, he does this for the purpose of claiming authority for himself. Hence the circumstance that he simply makes use of his own name without any title of honor is an evidence that those to whom he writes voluntarily acknowledged him to be such as he was. The ministers of Satan, it is true, had endeavored to trouble this church also, but it is evident that their machinations were fruitless. He associates, however, two others along with himself, as being, in common with himself, the authors of the epistle. Nothing

---

[2]Dickson, *Exposition*, 146*; citing Acts 17.
[3]Bugenhagen, *Annotationes in Epistolas Pauli*, 67.

[4]Zanchi, *Thessalonicenses*, 485.
[5]Rollock, *Thessalonicenses Commentarius*, 7*.

further is stated here that has not been explained elsewhere, except that he says, "the Church *in God the Father, and in Christ*"; by which terms (if I am not mistaken) he intimates that there is truly among the Thessalonians a church of God. This mark, therefore, is as it were an approval of a true and lawful church. We may, however, at the same time infer from it that a church is to be sought for only where God presides, and where Christ reigns, and that, in short, there is no church but what is founded on God, is gathered under the auspices of Christ, and is united in his name. THE FIRST EPISTLE OF PAUL TO THE THESSALONIANS 1:1.[6]

GREETING AS A TYPE OF PRAYER. ROBERT ROLLOCK: Greeting is a proof of benevolence from those who give a greeting to those who are being greeted, and not only that, but it is also an instrument ordained by God to point to the grace of the Father and the Son in those to whom we wish well. Thus it is a certain type of prayer. Grace and peace are chosen by God the Father and by the Lord Jesus Christ. There is no grace and peace if it is not from these authorities, as they are the source, and so no wish of the same things ought to be except from these authorities. However, those particular things of the church of the Thessalonians, which is in the Father and the Son, which in themselves are infinite, this grace and peace pertains only to those who are in fellowship. Therefore, these things are not to be wished unless they are in relationship with them. I understand with the names of grace and peace those benefits of Christ which follow the faith and fellowship that is with the Father and Son, that is, remission of sins, justification, regeneration, peace, joyfulness, and finally, eternal life. For this reason, that kind of greeting does not pertain to the Jews and Turks, who are not in fellowship with the Father and the Son. What, if anything, should be wished for them? First of all, it is to be wished to be introduced to the Father and the Son, and to be united with them, then grace might flow and be derived to them by the Father

and the Son. And also that greeting might pertain to those who seem to be Christian and seem to be united to the Father and the Son, but in their heart have no conjunction with them. These are hypocrites, and in vain grace from Christ is earnestly desired by them. COMMENTARY ON FIRST THESSALONIANS.[7]

THE CHURCH AS THE COMPANY OF THE FAITHFUL IN CHRIST. JOHN JEWEL: The church of God is in God the Father, and in the Lord Jesus Christ by his word and by the Holy Spirit, to honor him as he himself has appointed; this church hears the voice of the Shepherd. It will not follow a stranger, but flies from him; for it knows not the voice of strangers. Of this church St. Jerome says: . . . "The church of Christ, which contains the churches through all the world, is joined together in the unity of the Spirit, and has the refuge of the law, of the prophets, of the gospel, and of the apostles. The church does not goes forth, or beyond her bounds, that is, the holy Scriptures."[†] It is the pillar of the truth; the body, the fullness, and the spouse of Christ: it is the vine, the house, the city, and the kingdom of God. They who dwell in it "are no more strangers and foreigners, but citizens with the saints, and of the household of God; and are built upon the foundation of the apostles and prophets, Jesus Christ himself being the head cornerstone; in whom all the building coupled together grows into a holy temple in the Lord." This church "Christ loved, and gave himself for it; that he might sanctify it and cleanse it by the washing of water through the word, that he might make it for himself a glorious church, not having spot, or wrinkle, or any such thing; but that it should be holy and without blame." Such a church was the church of God at Thessalonica: such a church are they, whosoever in any place of the world fears the Lord, and call upon his name. Their names are written in the book of life: they have received the Spirit of adoption by which they cry, "Abba

---

[6]CTS 42:236-37* (CO 52:139).

[7]Rollock, *Thessalonicenses Commentarius*, 8-9*.

Father:" they grow from grace to grace, and abound more and more in knowledge and in judgment: they cast away the works of darkness, and put on the armor of light: they are made absolute and perfect for all good works: they are evermore comforted in the mercies of God, both by the holy Scriptures, wherein God declares his gracious goodness toward them, and by the sacraments, which are left to the church to be witnesses and assured pledges for performance of the promise of God's goodwill and favor toward them. Upon the First Epistle to the Thessalonians.[8]

An Effective Greeting. Robert Rollock: Finally, observe here the form of an effective greeting. First, when the godly ones Paul, Silvanus, and Timothy salute, what do they wish? They wish grace, and the benefits that are advanced by the gratuitous favor of God, not out of some human merit. They chose grace, not to anyone, but to those who are in fellowship with the Father and his Son Jesus Christ. To them alone it pertains. Therefore it follows that the greeting is ineffective for the heathen and profane of humankind, for they do not understand grace and they do not know the church and the fellowship of Christ. Commentary on First Thessalonians.[9]

---

[8]Jewel, *Works*, 2:819-20*; citing 1 Tim 3:15; Eph 2:19-21; 5:25-27; Phil 4:3; Rom 8:15. †Jerome, *Commentariorum in Michaeum* 1.1.

[9]Rollock, *Thessalonicenses Commentarius*, 9*.

1:2-10 THE THESSALONIANS HAVE SET AN EXAMPLE IN THEIR FAITH

²*We give thanks to God always for all of you, constantlyᵃ mentioning you in our prayers, ³remembering before our God and Father your work of faith and labor of love and steadfastness of hope in our Lord Jesus Christ. ⁴For we know, brothersᵇ loved by God, that he has chosen you, ⁵because our gospel came to you not only in word, but also in power and in the Holy Spirit and with full conviction. You know what kind of men we proved to be among you for your sake. ⁶And you became imitators of us and of the Lord, for you received the word in much affliction, with the joy of the Holy Spirit, ⁷so that you became an example to all the believers in Macedonia and in Achaia. ⁸For not only has the word of the Lord sounded forth from you in Macedonia and Achaia, but your faith in God has gone forth everywhere, so that we need not say anything. ⁹For they themselves report concerning us the kind of reception we had among you, and how you turned to God from idols to serve the living and true God, ¹⁰and to wait for his Son from heaven, whom he raised from the dead, Jesus who delivers us from the wrath to come.*

a Or *without ceasing*   b Or *brothers and sisters*. In New Testament usage, depending on the context, the plural Greek word *adelphoi* (translated "brothers") may refer either to *brothers* or to *brothers and sisters*

OVERVIEW: Throughout their expositions of this passage, these Reformation-era commentators stress the exemplary faith of the Thessalonians as the result of Paul's prayers, thanksgiving, and preaching. Moreover, they emphasize the efficacy of the preached Word in producing a lively faith that vividly demonstrates itself in love, accompanied by hope. As they discuss extensively the nature and interrelationship of faith, hope, and love, these exegetes confirm the position of these three as the chief Christian virtues, thus appropriating to an extent the teaching of medieval moral theology, which regarded them as the "theological virtues," while classifying wisdom, temperance, prudence, justice, and fortitude as the "cardinal virtues." Furthermore, these expositors highlight the role of the Holy Spirit both in giving the Word its efficacy and producing the above Christian virtues in believers. Finally, the commentators call attention to the importance of living a life of faith in light of the inevitability of death and the certainty of Christ's return.

1:2 *Praying for the Thessalonians*

THANKS TO ENCOURAGE PERSEVERANCE.
JOHN CALVIN: He praises, as he is in the habit of doing, their faith and other virtues. Not so much, however, for the purpose of praising them, but to exhort them to perseverance. For it is no small excitement to eagerness of pursuit when we reflect that God has adorned us with signal endowments, that he may finish what he has begun, and that we have, under his guidance and direction, advanced in the right course, in order that we may reach the goal. For as a vain confidence in those virtues, which humans foolishly arrogate to themselves, puffs them up with pride, and makes them careless and indolent for the time to come, so a recognition of the gifts of God humbles pious minds, and stirs them up to anxious concern. Hence, instead of congratulations, he makes use of thanksgivings, that he may put them in mind, that everything in them that he declares to be worthy of praise is a kindness from God. He also turns immediately to the future, in making mention of his *prayers*. We thus see for what purpose he

commends their previous life. COMMENTARY ON
1 THESSALONIANS 1:2.[1]

THE THESSALONIANS ARE A FEAT OF PAUL'S
APOSTLESHIP. MATTHEW POOLE: After his
salutation, he adds his thanksgiving and prayer for
them. He saw them as an eminent feat of his
apostleship and effect of his ministry, and as an
advantage to the gospel in their example, and so
gives thanks. His thanks is to God, because the
success of the gospel was more from his blessing
than his own ministry. *Pantote* [always], that is, in
constant course, or *affectu* [with affection], though
not *actu* [by action/deed], by a grateful sense he
had of it continually on his heart. He had a good
report of them all from Timothy, and we find not
one reproof to anyone in this first epistle, as in the
second. He adds also his prayer for them, wherein
he made mention of them by name, as some
understand the words *mneian hymōn poioumenoi*
[making mention of you (all)], prayer and thanksgiving ought to go together, especially in the
ministers of the gospel and in the work of the
ministry, and thus the apostle practiced this toward
other churches also. ANNOTATIONS UPON THE
HOLY BIBLE.[2]

1:3 Faith, Hope, and Love

TRUE CHRISTIANITY. JOHN CALVIN: From this
we may gather a brief definition of true Christianity—that it is a faith that is lively and full of vigor,
so that it spares no labor, when assistance is to be
given to one's neighbors, but, on the contrary, all the
pious employ themselves diligently in offices of love,
and lay out their efforts in them, so that, intent on
the hope of the manifestation of Christ, they
despise everything else, and, armed with patience,
they rise superior to the wearisomeness of length of
time, as well as to all the temptations of the world.
COMMENTARY ON FIRST THESSALONIANS.[3]

THE CHARACTER OF TRUE FAITH, LOVE, AND
HOPE. MATTHIAS FLACIUS: Truly faith is not
inactive, but active; it prays, confesses, and is
steadfast by fighting the world and Satan. Faith
produces various good fruits. Love works in many
ways, by preserving one's brothers and sister from
troubles, and by lifting their burdens. Hope
patiently tolerates and bears those inconveniences
by expecting most constantly good to come from
dangerous storms and persecutions. But we want to
understand that the one fully in Christ, or the one
who flows from him to whom is entirely given all
glory, will not be mowed down because of his hope,
though the unworthy will be made nothing by
wrath. [Paul] adds further: In the presence of God,
who for sure considers the struggles of his own,
helps and rewards them. Paul then says next, "The
Lord knows the way of the righteous." You have
here the whole reason for the life of Christians that
is made firm by the constancy of faith, and that
through love and hope are preserved by God. The
life of this person bears fruit that is proved throughout its entirety for the edification of brothers and
sisters. And truly the words to the Hebrews refer to
these: a powerful faith, a working love, and an
enduring hope. GLOSS ON 1 THESSALONIANS.[4]

FAITH, HOPE, LOVE. MATTHEW POOLE: "Your
work of faith, or the work of faith of you." That is,
their faith and the work of it, whereby he intimates
their faith was true and real; a faith unfeigned, the
faith of God's elect, and so distinguished from
dead faith. They received the work in much
affection, with joy of the holy Ghost. They turned
from idols to the service of the true God, they
waited for the coming of Christ, and so on. Here
was the work of faith.

And a labor of love, a labor of weariness. As
the word imports, laborious love. True faith has
its work, but love has its labor, and when faith
works by love it will work laboriously. The apostle
declares the reality of their love as well as their
faith. It was unfeigned love, yea, fervent love, the

---

[1]CTS 42:237-38* (CO 52:139-40).
[2]Poole, *Annotations*, 732*; citing 1 Thess 3:6; Rom 1:8; Phil 1:3.
[3]CTS 42:239 (CO 52:141).

[4]Flacius, *Glossa Compendaria*, 1006; citing Heb 10:22-24.

labor of it went forth toward that true God whom they now worshiped, that Jesus Christ on whom they now believed, to the saints that were now their fellow brethren, and particularly to the apostle himself, as in other ways, so particularly in the pains and labor that some of them took to conduct and travel alone with him from Thessalonica to Athens. Annotations upon the Holy Bible.[5]

Virtues of Christ. David Dickson: Your sincere faith, which has showed itself lively, and efficacious by works, your indefatigable charity visible in your daily labors, and diligence, especially in your liberality toward the saints. And last, your lively hope shown in patience and suffering afflictions for Christ have left in me an indelible impression that I cannot but make mention of them before God and humankind. Therefore it is right that you be strengthened in faith. But he calls them the virtues of Christ, because they sprang from Christ, and tend to him. But he says in the sight of God, because they were of that sort that were in the sight of God, genuine and no ways counterfeit. The First Epistle of Paul to the Thessalonians.[6]

The Word of the Gospel Received Through the Power of the Holy Ghost. Jacobus Arminius: In this passage he openly attributes to the power of the Holy Ghost the certainty by which the faithful receive the word of the gospel. The papists reply, "Many persons boast of the revelation of the Spirit, who nevertheless are destitute of such a revelation. It is impossible, therefore, for the faithful safely to rest in it." Are these fair words? Away with such blasphemy! If the Jews glory in their Talmud and their Kabbala, and the Muslims in their Alcoran,[†] and if both of these boast themselves that they are churches, cannot credence therefore be given with sufficient safety to the scriptures of the Old and New Testaments, when they affirm their divine origin? Will the true church be any less a church because the sons of the stranger arrogate that title to themselves? This is the distinction between opinion and knowledge. It is their opinion that they know that of which they are really ignorant. But they who do know it have an assured perception of their knowledge. "It is the Spirit that bears witness that the Spirit is truth," that is, the doctrine and the meanings comprehended in that doctrine are truth. The Internal Witness of the Holy Spirit.[7]

1:4-7 Imitators of Paul and of the Lord

The Fruit and Effects of Election. Matthew Poole: By the manner of their receiving the gospel and the evident operation of the graces of God's Spirit, the apostle knew their election was from God. We cannot know election as in God's secret decree, but as it is made manifest in fruit and effects. As there is a knowledge of things a priori, when we argue from the cause to the effect, things can also be known a posteriori, when we argue from the effects to the cause. And thus the apostle came to know their election. Not that we hope it or conjecture it, but we know it, and not by extraordinary revelation, but by evident outward tokens. And if the apostle knew this, why should we think they themselves might not know also? The words may be read, "You, knowing your election of God." And election imports the choosing of some out of others; for election cannot comprehend all. Some deny eternal election of particular persons; and make it a temporal separation of persons to God in their conversion; but is not this separation from a preexisting decree? "God doing all things according to the counsel of his own will." Or they will allow for an eternal election of persons, but only conditional.

---

[5]Poole, *Annotations*, 732*; citing 2 Tim 1:5; Titus 1:1; Jas 2:26; 1 Thess 4:10; Acts 17:15, 1-21.
[6]Dickson, *Exposition*, 146.

[7]Arminius, *Works*, vol. 1, 398-99; citing 1 Jn 5:8. [†]According to the *Oxford English Dictionary*, *alcoran* is an older term for the Qur'an. The etymology of *alcoran* goes back to Middle French, and before that to the Arabic word *al-qur'ān* (*al* = "the" and *qur'ān* = "Qur'an").

One condition whereof is perseverance to the end. But the apostle asserts their election at present before he saw their perseverance. ANNOTATIONS UPON THE HOLY BIBLE.[8]

SIGNS OF THE EFFICACY OF THE GOSPEL.
DAVID DICKSON: I plainly perceive that my gospel has been efficacious among you, for there did accompany my preaching (1) strength and spiritual virtue to the begetting of faith in you; (2) the Holy Ghost by his inward testimony together with his gifts bestowed on you sealed the truth received by you; (3) much assurance and persuasion in your hearts ensued, which has freed you from all doubting; (4) such was the work of and presence of God in you that heard, as was to be seen in us apostles that taught, as you yourselves have known. Therefore you ought to be strengthened in faith. THE FIRST EPISTLE OF PAUL TO THE THESSALONIANS.[9]

PREACHING AND FAITH. JOHN CALVIN: With the view of increasing their alacrity, he declares that there is a mutual agreement, and harmony, as it were, between his preaching and their faith. For unless people, on their part, answer to God, no proficiency will follow from the grace that is offered to them—not as though they could do this of themselves, but inasmuch as God, as he begins our salvation by calling us, perfects it also by fashioning our hearts to obedience. The sum, therefore, is this—that an evidence of divine election showed itself not only in Paul's ministry, insofar as it was furnished with the power of the Holy Spirit, but also in the faith of the Thessalonians, so that this conformity is a powerful attestation of it. COMMENTARY ON FIRST THESSALONIANS.[10]

1:8-10 The Report of the Faith of the Thessalonians

WHAT TRUE SERVICE TO GOD IS. HEINRICH BULLINGER: The true service of God is divided again, for perspicuity or plainness's sake, into the inward service of God, and the outward. The inward service is known to God alone, who is the searcher of hearts. For it is occupied in the fear of God, and perfect of obedience, in faith, hope, and charity, from whence springs the worshiping of God, the calling on him, thanksgiving, patience, perseverance, chastity, innocence, well doing, and the rest of the fruits of the Spirit. For with these gifts of God and spiritual things, God, who is a Spirit, is truly served. Without these there is no service allowed of God, however much in the sight of human beings it seems joyful, glorious, and pure.

This service of God has testimonies both divine and human, but first of all the Law, the Prophets, and the apostles. OF ADORING OR WORSHIPING.[11]

THE FAITH OF THE THESSALONIANS GOES FORTH BY REPORT. MATTHEW POOLE: How could the Thessalonians be examples to persons so remote, with whom they did not speak? The apostle resolves it here: it was by way of report. Things that are eminent, and done in eminent places, such as Thessalonica was, easily spread abroad, either by merchants, travelers, or correspondence by letters. And this report is compared to a sound that is heard far off, that made an echo, as the Word implies. And that which sounded out from you was the "word of the Lord." The Word is said to sound by the voice of the preacher, and by the practice of the hearers. The might, power, and efficacy of it was made known abroad, not only in Macedonia and Achaia, but in every place, not strictly everywhere, but here and there, up and down in the world. As it is said of the apostle's ministry, "Their sound went into all the earth, and their words to the end of the world." The report of the gospel went further than the preachers of it, and their receiving the gospel sounded abroad far and near. That you believed so soon at our first entrance, and though we had been shamefully

---

[8]Poole, *Annotations*, 733*; citing Eph 1:11.
[9]Dickson, *Exposition*, 146*.
[10]CTS 42:242-43 (CO 52:142-43).

[11]Bullinger, *Fifty Godly and Learned Sermons*, 668. In this passage Bullinger speaks in general terms of service to God. He then quotes several passages that speak to such true service, including 1 Thess 1:8-9.

entreated at Philippi a little before our coming to you, yet you believed, and your faith was eminent in the fruits and operations of it also, as was mentioned before, and was afterward in the epistle. And it was faith Godward. It rested not on human beings, no, nor only the man Christ Jesus whom we preached to you, but on God himself, though through Christ you became worshipers of the true God, and believed on him with an exemplary faith. Annotations upon the Holy Bible.[12]

Waiting for the Son and Perseverance. John Calvin: As, however, it is a thing that is more than simply difficult, in so great a corruption of our nature, he shows at the same time what it is that retains and confirms us in the fear of God and obedience to him—"waiting for Christ." For unless we are stirred up to the hope of eternal life, the world will quickly draw us to itself. For as it is only confidence in the divine goodness that induces us to serve God, so it is only the expectation of final redemption that keeps us from giving way. Let everyone, therefore, that would persevere in a course of holy life, apply their whole mind to an expectation of Christ's coming. It is also worthy of notice that he uses the expression "waiting for Christ" instead of the hope of everlasting salvation. For, unquestionably, without Christ we are ruined and thrown into despair, but when Christ shows himself, life and prosperity at the same time shine forth upon us. Let us bear in mind, however, that this is said to believers exclusively, for as for the wicked, he will come to be their Judge, so they can do nothing but tremble in looking for him.

This is what he afterward adds—that Christ "delivers us from the wrath to come." For this is felt by none but those who, being reconciled to God by faith, have their conscience already pacified; otherwise, his name is dreadful. Christ, it is true, delivered us by his death from the anger of God, but the import of that deliverance will become apparent on the last day. This statement, however, consists of two departments. The first is that the

wrath of God and everlasting destruction are impending over the human race, inasmuch as "all have sinned, and come short of the glory of God." The second is that there is no way of escape but through the grace of Christ; for it is not without good grounds that Paul assigns to him this office. It is, however, an inestimable gift that the pious, whenever mention is made of judgment, know that Christ will come as a Redeemer to them.

In addition to this, he says emphatically, "the wrath to come," that he may rouse up pious minds, lest they should fail from looking at the present life. For as faith is a "looking at things that do not appear," nothing is less befitting than that we should estimate the wrath of God according as anyone is afflicted in the world; as nothing is more absurd than to take hold of the transient blessings that we enjoy, that we may from them form an estimate of God's favor. While, therefore, on the one hand, the wicked sport themselves at their ease, and we, on the other hand, languish in misery, let us learn to fear the vengeance of God, which is hidden from the eyes of flesh, and take our satisfaction in the secret delights of the spiritual life. Commentary on First Thessalonians.[13]

Both Divine and Human Agency. Matthew Poole: The believers of Macedonia and Achaia do speak of these things *apangellousin*, openly. It is evident the word of the Lord sounded forth to them from you, and they without any information from us declare the great provision you gave us and our gospel at our first entrance among you. Particularly your forsaking your former idolatry, when you worshiped idols, which were either the images or shapes of the true God formed by human beings, or human beings whom they deified, and set up as gods, and worshiped them and their images, or inanimate creatures, as sun, moon, and stars, or whatever creature they found beneficial to them, the heathens made idols of them. "These you turned from." Though it was by the power of God and the gospel on your hearts, it was

---

[12]Poole, *Annotations*, 733*; citing 1 Cor 14:8-9; Gal 6:6; Rom 10:18.

[13]CTS 42:245-47 (CO 52:142-43); citing Rom 3:23; Heb 11:1.

an act of your own. And though it was the worship of these idols you had been trained up in and generally practiced, you turned from it. ANNOTATIONS UPON THE HOLY BIBLE.[14]

WATCH, BE CAREFUL. DAVID JORIS: See in this way all things have their fulfillment and full perfection in three, according to which we should work with many tears. We who will, desire, and seek to uphold the Holy One in Israel and to bring honor, glory, and strength, thanksgiving and praise to the Lord of hosts. Who (I say), seek the kingdom of God and his righteousness. Take heed. Therefore, seek humility, seek righteousness, all of you who are kept by the Lord's right hand, so that you may be protected in the day of the wrath of the Lord. Watch out, pay attention. OF THE WONDERFUL WORKING OF GOD.[15]

ON HOW DEATH CAN REMIND US OF THE COMING OF THE LORD. MARTIN BUCER: Concerning those whom the Lord takes from this world in the confession of his name, we teach that they should be buried in the ground with all reverence and decency, and the people present reminded from the Word of God of his severe judgment against sin, and also of the redemption of Christ who has redeemed us from death, and to the resurrection to eternal life, which he has won for all who believe in him. . . . In addition, the people are to be exhorted to repent of their sins and to hope firmly in the blessed resurrection and the life of heaven and also to foster an earnest zeal and longing for the life of heaven, and also to foster an earnest zeal and longing for this life to come, with the constant mortification of the old Adam and advancement of the new. Next should follow prayer for true repentance and strength of faith, and also for the blessed resurrection of the departed and of those present, and alms are to be given to the poor. A BRIEF SUMMARY OF CHRISTIAN DOCTRINE.[16]

WAITING IN FAITH AND EXPECTANCY FOR THE LORD'S RETURN. MATTHEW POOLE: This is added to show the further power of the gospel on them, they had not only faith toward God, as was said before, but also toward Christ. They did not only turn to the true God, in opposition to the heathen, but to the Son of God as the true Christ, in opposition to the heathen, and also to the Son of God as the true Christ, in opposition to the unbelieving Jews. For though he was the Son of David after the flesh, yet he was the Son of God also, and not by creation, as the angels are called the sons of God, nor by adoption, as the saints are, but by eternal generation, though the man Christ Jesus by his personal union is the Son of God. And their faith respecting the Son of God was their waiting for him from heaven; not that their faith consisted only in this, but it suited their present state of affliction to wait for Christ's coming as a deliverer and rewarder, therefore here mentioned by the apostle, and their faith, hope, love, patience, may all be included in it. They believed that he was gone to heaven, and would come again, which are two great articles of the Christian faith. And though there was nothing in sense or reason or any tradition to persuade them of it, yet they believed it upon the apostle's preaching. And though the time of his coming was unknown to them, yet their faith presently put them upon waiting for it. And the certain time of his coming is kept secret, that the saints in every age may wait for it. Though he will not come until the end of the world, yet the saints ought to be influenced with the expectation of it in all generations that precede it. It is to their advantage to wait for it, though they do not live to see him come. ANNOTATIONS UPON THE HOLY BIBLE.[17]

THE ASSURANCE OF GOD'S WORK IN US. DAVID DICKSON: Your conversion to God was not without his Son Christ, as the unbelieving Jews falsely boast on their conversion. But to God in Christ, or to the Father, and to Christ, as the

---

[14]Poole, *Annotations*, 734*.
[15]CRR 7:123-24; citing Mt 6:33; Rom 5:9.
[16]Bucer, *A Brief Summary of Christian Doctrine*, 27.

[17]Poole, *Annotations*, 734*.

incarnate Son of God, the Redeemer, dead and risen for us, who shall come from heaven, a judge to destroy all unbelievers, and to deliver his own from the wrath that is to come upon the rest; this faith alone is saving. Therefore, you ought to be

confirmed in faith, reminding those works of God in you. The First Epistle of Paul to the Thessalonians.[18]

---

[18]Dickson, *Exposition*, 147.

2:1-16 THE MINISTRY OF PAUL
TO THE THESSALONIANS

For you yourselves know, brothers,[a] that our coming to you was not in vain. [2]But though we had already suffered and been shamefully treated at Philippi, as you know, we had boldness in our God to declare to you the gospel of God in the midst of much conflict. [3]For our appeal does not spring from error or impurity or any attempt to deceive, [4]but just as we have been approved by God to be entrusted with the gospel, so we speak, not to please man, but to please God who tests our hearts. [5]For we never came with words of flattery,[b] as you know, nor with a pretext for greed—God is witness. [6]Nor did we seek glory from people, whether from you or from others, though we could have made demands as apostles of Christ. [7]But we were gentle[c] among you, like a nursing mother taking care of her own children. [8]So, being affectionately desirous of you, we were ready to share with you not only the gospel of God but also our own selves, because you had become very dear to us.

[9]For you remember, brothers, our labor and toil: we worked night and day, that we might not be a burden to any of you, while we proclaimed to you the gospel of God. [10]You are witnesses, and God also, how holy and righteous and blameless was our conduct toward you believers. [11]For you know how, like a father with his children, [12]we exhorted each one of you and encouraged you and charged you to walk in a manner worthy of God, who calls you into his own kingdom and glory.

[13]And we also thank God constantly[d] for this, that when you received the word of God, which you heard from us, you accepted it not as the word of men[e] but as what it really is, the word of God, which is at work in you believers. [14]For you, brothers, became imitators of the churches of God in Christ Jesus that are in Judea. For you suffered the same things from your own countrymen as they did from the Jews,[f] [15]who killed both the Lord Jesus and the prophets, and drove us out, and displease God and oppose all mankind [16]by hindering us from speaking to the Gentiles that they might be saved—so as always to fill up the measure of their sins. But wrath has come upon them at last![g]

a Or brothers and sisters; also verses 9, 14, 17   b Or with a flattering speech   c Some manuscripts infants   d Or without ceasing   e The Greek word anthropoi can refer to both men and women   f The Greek word Ioudaioi can refer to Jewish religious leaders, and others under their influence, who opposed the Christian faith in that time   g Or completely, or forever

---

OVERVIEW: Our commentators note that Paul can claim that his teaching (1 Thess 2:13) was actually the Word of God. Even though Roman Catholic apologists have used this passage to argue against a traditional Protestant affirmation of *sola Scriptura*, Protestant writers were happy to affirm that the apostolic message of Paul was indeed the Word of God and that this message was eventually written down and inscripturated. The commentators go on to call attention to the spiritual motives of pastors as ones entrusted with the sacred task of proclaiming the Word with the view that their primary concern is to be the church's well-being. Furthermore, these expositors identify as one of the distinguishing characteristics of the church a willing reception of the Word of God. Finally, they candidly acknowledge that faithful preaching of the Word incurs persecution.

2:1-6 Entrusted with the Gospel

PAUL'S PREACHING WAS NOT IN VAIN. JEROME ZANCHI: This is the explication of the schoolmen, and particularly that he maintained walking in the name. The doctrine is, as the Thessalonians walked, they preached. And in particular, that he desired to signify with the name *kenos* [vain], it is that this doctrine is not made by humans and thus "vain," but divine, in that it is truly effective for salvation. And other things also he desires to signify by these words.

First therefore with the name *tēs eisodou*,[†] the apostle understood not simply in the sense of having come bodily to the city, but having come with so great a teaching, as they preached, since their teaching was joined with so many divine signs. For they preached, and hostile ones among the Thessalonians were turned from every greed and scorn. They became calm, humble, no one hesitating to work, but rather with their own hands laboring. Thus they were nurses, permanently nourishing their own children. With holiness, with justice, blamelessly living. And thus, holiness of life, with the teaching of the gospel, to the great glory of God, and then edification, joining together. And everything, both universally and individually, are paternally to witness, so that they might walk worthily before that God, into whose reign they were called. These things, however, all things in themselves, are explicated in context. Therefore, this thing grasps the name *eisodou*, that is, coming in order to preach the gospel, in all their qualities and circumstances. But the name *kenos* refers not only to the arrival itself per se, that it was not in vain. But also to their leaving to preach, that certainly it was not foolish, and being devoid of their own reward, but effective. On the First Epistle of Paul to the Thessalonians.[1]

Sacraments, Like Paul's Teaching, Are Not in Vain. The English Annotations: The meaning is either that he did not preach vain things to them, like poetic fictions or curious speculations, but true and necessary doctrines, or that his preaching among them was not without fruit, but, through the operation of the Spirit, fruitful and effectual. In this sense, the sacred symbols or elements are truly affirmed not to be *kina*, the word used here, that is, "bare," "vain," or "empty" signs, because the Spirit works by them, and they really exhibit to the soul that which is signified by them. Annotations on 1 Thessalonians 2:1.[2]

The Apostolic Use of Words. Heinrich Bullinger: They are greatly deceived and mad who think the church can either be gathered together or, being gathered, can be maintained and preserved with practices, that is to say, with crafty counsels and subtle deceits of human beings. It is truly said of the common people that the same is overthrown again by human wisdom, which was first built by human wisdom. Besides this, the Lord himself both removes force and arms from the building of the church, since he forbids his disciples the use of sword and to Peter, who is ready to fight, says, "Put up your sword into the scabbard." Neither do we ever read that any were sent by the Lord as soldier, by which armed force should bring the world into subjugation. But rather that Scripture witnesses that the great enemy of God, antichrist, shall be destroyed with the breath of God's mouth. For this reason there is no doubt that all those things which are read in different places of the prophets, and chiefly in Zechariah 12, concerning wars to be made against all nations, by the apostles and apostolic men, ought to be figuratively expounded. For the apostles according to their manner fight as apostles, not with spear, sword, and bow of carnal warfare, but of spiritual. The apostolic sword is the Word of God. Of the Holy Catholic Church.[3]

Paul's Boldness a Result of His Teaching the Gospel. Jerome Zanchi: The commentators [= *scholia*] prefer that the argument with constancy of the apostle in persisting amid all kinds of evil is for the sake of the free preaching of the gospel. That certainly the apostle would not

---

[1]Zanchi, *Thessalonicenses*, 503-4. [†]A "coming in" or "entrance." Zanchi consistently renders *tēs eisodou* in the genitive, even though in the Greek text it is in the accusative.

[2]Downame, ed., *Annotations*, 3K2r*.
[3]Bullinger, *Fifty Godly and Learned Sermons*, 831*; citing Jn 18:11.

have done unless he had been persuaded that his teaching is the very gospel of God. From here therefore the Thessalonians, who were not ignorant of these things, had been able plainly to understand that the apostle had not come to them in vain, and that his teaching was not human, but divine. On the First Epistle of Paul to the Thessalonians.[4]

God Empowered Paul amid Persecution. John Calvin: Paul now, leaving out the testimony of other churches, reminds the Thessalonians of what they themselves had experienced, and explains at large the way he, and in like manner his two associates, had conducted themselves among them, inasmuch as this was of the greatest importance for confirming their faith. For it is with this view that he declares his integrity—that the Thessalonians may perceive that they had been called to the faith, not so much by a mortal, as by God himself. . . .

He proves this by two arguments. The first is that he had suffered persecution and ignominy at Philippi, the second that there was a great conflict prepared at Thessalonica. We know that human minds are weakened, nay, are altogether broken down by means of ignominy and persecutions. It was therefore an evidence of a divine work that Paul, after being subjected to evils of various kinds and ignominy, did, as if in a perfectly sound state, show no hesitation in making an attempt upon a large and opulent city with the view of subjecting the inhabitants to Christ. Commentary on 1 Thessalonians 2:1-2.[5]

Bold Though Persecuted. Jerome Zanchi: The apostle on his own allowed that he had suffered many evil things on account of his own preaching, and in Philippi was afflicted with many injuries. Nevertheless, he did not doubt, but immediately contended at Thessalonica and there indeed preached the same gospel, and that indeed

with many contests. The Thessalonians were able to gather, and he was not afraid of them. He came to them not in fear, and not with human counsel, but rather with divine. Nor was his teaching a human teaching, and therefore vain, but divine, and therefore effective for the salvation of souls. However, the apostle alludes to the commandment of the Lord that he received in a vision, that without doubt he might go to Macedonia, and there preach. (See Acts 16 for these things.) Not therefore in vain did he come to the Philippians and to Thessalonica, particular cities of Macedonia. But he was sent by God. Here it occurred that he did no harm to any of his adversaries, among whom he freely preached. From this therefore we see the constancy of the apostle in enduring so many calamities and struggles on account of the preaching of the gospel. The Thessalonians understood that his coming to them was not undertaken with vain counsel. Nor was his teaching in vain. . . .

He says two words, *prospathontes kai hybristhentes* [already suffered and shamefully treated], since in Philippi they suffered many blows on the body, as well as jail time. And besides these great injuries afflicted against one's honor, they were stripped naked and struck with rods in public.

Therefore what then? Should they cease preaching, having been made fearful? Truly not at all. On the First Epistle of Paul to the Thessalonians.[6]

Removing Corrupt Motives for Ministry. Matthias Flacius: First note here once more that he [Paul] again describes himself negatively or rather as one lacking, as in the second verse. He removes from himself the causes of corrupt doctrine of whatever kind they are: flattery, avarice, and ambition. For whoever works by these vices, the same one in their own function unavoidably obeys those who preach insincerely or allow corruption, or certainly others who badly occupy themselves with their own service, speaking pleasing

---

[4]Zanchi, *Thessalonicenses*, 504.
[5]CTS 42:248* (CO 52:146).
[6]Zanchi, *Thessalonicenses*, 504-5.

things, and those who give life to souls worthy of death, and set themselves against those mortifying themselves to whom life is owed, as Ezekiel says. Indeed, Paul proves that the particular testimony of some is from flattery. In truth he proves that the testimony, or rather, the oath of others is from avarice. Gloss on 1 Thessalonians.[7]

What Paul Means by "Exhortation" or "Appeal." Jerome Zanchi: "For our exhortation," *paraklēsis* (thus 1 Thess 2:12, *parakalountes hymas*, "we exhort you").

As a synecdoche,[†] he signifies [with the term *paraklēsis*] the whole teaching of the gospel. First dogmatic things, then moral things, *Didache*.[‡] This is indeed why he describes what the distinction between *didache* and *paraklēsis* actually is. Paul not only passed on a simple teaching but also exhorted and implored the people that they might apprehend it [i.e., the teaching]. For example, 2 Corinthians 5. God was in Christ. This is a simple teaching. He applies it, and in the name of Christ, he discharges it as an ambassador, just as with God's exhortation through you. We entreat before Christ, be reconciled to God. This is *paraklēsis*.

The action of ministry ought not simply to put forth teaching, but also exhorts and entreats.

Thus Acts 2. Peter first encourages by saying, "Repent [Lat.: *agite poenitentiam*], and be baptized each one of you." Next, he applies, saying, "Indeed, for you the promise was made, and for your children." Luke puts forth: "And in many other words, *parakalei* [he encourages], saying: 'Be on guard from that kind of wickedness.'" Therefore, the whole doctrine of Paul, as the scholia[††] explain, is understood: since the total reason [for Paul's coming and teaching] was without error, without *akatharsia* [uncleanness]. On the First Epistle of Paul to the Thessalonians.[8]

Heretics and False Apostles Seek Three Things. The English Annotations: The heretics and false apostles proposed to themselves chiefly three ends: applause, gain, and voluptuousness. The first they sought to attain by soothing their hearers and conspiring with them. The second, by crafty fetches and cloaks of covetousness, and the third by sewing pillows under men's elbows and preaching doctrines tending to carnal liberty. From all of these things, the Apostle calls God to be his compurgator.[†] Annotations on 1 Thessalonians 2:3.[9]

Fitted and Approved. Jerome Zanchi: Now a certain thing must be diligently examined and observed. Above he demonstrated negatively that his own teaching is pure and sincere. That is, having removed those things that are able to taint the teaching—error, *akatharsia*—by cunning, here he confirms the same thing with another reason. Now he affirms these five things:

1. He himself was approved by God, that is, besides being chosen, so that he might be a worthy preacher of his own gospel. Then again he himself was made suitable, and an approved minister of God, *dedokimasmetha* [having been approved], it is said, *hypo tou theou* [by God].

2. To him has been entrusted the gospel of God, and with that he has grasped the most pure teaching, *tou pisteutēnai to euangelion* [to be entrusted with the gospel].

3. Likewise, not that he preaches another teaching, nor with another intention, than that which he received. And as from that intention, so that he might preach, was approved by God, *hypo*, it is said, *laloumen* [we speak] truly as *dedokimasmetha* [having been approved].

4. Explicating the quality of his own mind, he affirms that he does not speak and preach so as to please human beings (which would certainly be against God), but God.

---

[7]Flacius, *Glossa Compendaria*, 1010.

[8]Zanchi, *Thessalonicenses*, 507; citing 2 Cor 5:19; Acts 2:38-40.
[†]Synecdoche is a figure of speech in which a part is made to represent the whole or vice versa. [‡]*Didache* means "teaching."
[††]Scholia were collections of comments on Scripture.

[9]Downame, ed., *Annotations*, 3K2r*. [†]A compurgator is a sworn witness who testifies to the innocence and good character of a defendant.

5. He affirms his own heart and his own mind, by which he preaches the gospel, still by God. With this Paul therefore said and affirmed: he knows that he has a good conscience in this work of his own apostleship. Another thing follows from these things, as his own teaching is sincere, divine, and effective for the salvation of souls, and in that gospel is going to persevere.

God does not entrust his own gospel except to those who are approved, and to those sufficient, as we see here. Since we are by our nature unsuitable, he, for that reason, makes us, who are unsuitable, suitable, and approved, so that he may commit his own gospel to none except to those approved and suitable. Therefore the church ought to consent with the example of God, so that persons are not received into ministry, unless they have been approved and found worthy, as also the apostle commands in 1 Timothy 3. ON THE FIRST EPISTLE OF PAUL TO THE THESSALONIANS.[10]

EXPERIENCE EMPHASIZES TRUTH. JOHN CALVIN: It is not without good reason that he repeats so frequently that the Thessalonians know what he states is true. There is no surer attestation than the experience of those with whom we speak. This was of the greatest importance to them, because Paul relates with what integrity he had conducted himself, and with no other intention than that his doctrine may have the greater respect for the building up of their faith. It is, however, a confirmation of the foregoing statement, for he who is desirous to please others must of necessity stoop shamefully to flattery, while those who are intent upon duty, with an earnest and upright disposition, will keep at a distance from all appearance of flattery. COMMENTARY ON 1 THESSALONIANS 2:5.[11]

PAUL'S CLAIM TO BE GENTLE. JEROME ZANCHI: "To be gentle": This has a twofold signification, as we show above from the scholia[†] and the Fathers.

One, to be a burden. Certainly Paul was able with the Thessalonians, as an apostle of Christ, to request the necessary things. But he did not want to. And this signification fits that which he said before, and not *en prophesai plenexias* [with a pretext of greed].

And with that, he says in verse 9 that he worked day and night, so that he wouldn't burden anyone. And Theodore Beza and others follow this sense. The other signification is, to be "gentle," that is, in authority. Certainly Paul was able, as an apostle of Christ, to conduct himself with great weightiness and authority, but did not want to. And this fits with that which precedes: "I did not seek glory from human beings." Besides with that, what immediately follows, "*alla egenēthēmen nēpioi* [but we were children] in your midst." And this follows Photius, Chrysostom, Syrus, Calvin, and others. ON THE FIRST EPISTLE OF PAUL TO THE THESSALONIANS.[12]

THE ORAL WORD MUST BE HEARD. MARTIN LUTHER: I shall not speak of the Anabaptist scoffers at the oral word. . . . The Sacramentarians impudently dare to reject the oral Word. They argue thus: No external thing is salvatory. The oral word and the sacraments are external things, therefore [they are not salvatory]. . . .

I reply: There is a great difference between the external things of God and of human things. God's external things are salvatory and efficacious. The poor people used to think that the external ministry of God was the same as the unfruitful traditions of the papists. The devil worked through such childish inferences: "the flesh is of no avail." If one drew conclusions from this way of reasoning, unspeakable consequences would follow, so one would reject all external means and ultimately even the humanity of Christ. Satan has considered this, for it is his way to begin with lowly things and eventually climb up to the heights. TABLE TALK.[13]

---

[10]Zanchi, *Thessalonicenses*, 510.
[11]CTS 42:250-51* (CO 52:147).

[12]Zanchi, *Thessalonicenses*, 511. [†]Scholia were collections of comments on Scripture.
[13]LW 54:318; citing Rom 10:14; 2 Thess 2:4; Rom 1:16; Mt 10:20; Jn 6:63.

2:7-12 *Like a Nursing Mother or a Caring Father*

REGARDING THE WELFARE OF THE CHURCH MORE THAN ONE'S OWN WELFARE. JOHN CALVIN: "As if a nurse." In this comparison he takes in two points that he had touched on—that he had sought neither glory nor gain among the Thessalonians. For a mother in nursing her infant shows nothing of power or dignity. Paul says that he was such, inasmuch as he voluntarily refrained from claiming the honor that was due to him, and with calmness and modesty stooped to every kind of office. Second, a mother in nursing her children manifests a certain rare and wonderful affection, inasmuch as she spares no labor and trouble, shuns no anxiety, is wearied out by no assiduity, and even with cheerfulness of spirit gives her own blood to be sucked. In the same way, Paul declares that he was so disposed toward the Thessalonians that he was prepared to lay down his life for their benefit. This, assuredly, was not the conduct of a man who was sordid or avaricious, but of one who exercised a disinterested affection, and he expresses this in the close—"because ye were dear to us." In the meantime, we must bear in mind that all who would be ranked among true pastors must exercise this disposition of Paul—to have more regard to the welfare of the church than to their own life, and not be impelled to duty by a regard to their own advantage, but by a sincere love to those to whom they know that they are conjoined, and laid under obligation. COMMENTARY ON FIRST THESSALONIANS.[14]

NOT ACTS OF SUPEREROGATION. MATTHEW POOLE: To make good what had asserted before about their integrity in preaching the gospel, that it was without covetousness, vainglory, and so on, and about their great affection for them, he appeals to their own memory. "Labor," in what we suffered, attended with care and solicitude of mind; as the word means. "Travail" in what we did, attended

with weariness, as some distinguish of the words. This refers to some bodily labor they used, which I find not mentioned in the story while they were at Thessalonica, though Paul did practice at Corinth. He did so to prevent scandal and misconstruals that may arise from receiving support, and in case of the churches poverty, the apostle would refuse it, but in the absence of this he accepted it as his due. And his refusing was no work of supererogation,[†] as the papists plead here; for in such cases it was a duty with respect to the honor of his ministry, so that it ought not to pass into a rule, either that ministers in no case may labor with their hands to get their bread, or that they ought always to do, as some would conclude here, and preach freely. However, he commends them that they did not forget the labor and travail they underwent for their sake, and that both night and day, which implies assiduity and diligence. ANNOTATIONS UPON THE HOLY BIBLE.[15]

THE WORLD SPEAKS EVIL AGAINST US, CHRISTIANS DO NOT. JOHN CALVIN: "You are witnesses." He again calls God and them to witness, with the view of affirming his integrity, and cites, on the one hand, God as a witness of his conscience, and them, on the other hand, as witnesses of what they had known by experience. "How holily," he says, "and justly," that is, with how sincere a fear of God, and with what fidelity and blamelessness toward others; and third, "unreproachably," by which he means that he had given no occasion of complaint or obloquy. For the servants of Christ cannot avoid calumnies and unfavorable reports; for being hated by the world, they must of necessity be evil-spoken of among the wicked. Hence he restricts this to

---

[14]CTS 42:252 (CO 52:148).

[15]Poole, *Annotations*, 737*; citing Acts 18:3; 1 Cor 9:1; Ps 1:2; Lk 2:37; 1 Thess 3:10. †Richard C. Muller defines "works of supererogation" as follows: "works beyond those required for salvation." In short, the Roman Catholic Church has access to "extra" works, and hence a store of extra merit, which can in various ways (e.g., indulgences) be distributed to certain persons. See "*Opera supererogationis*," in Richard C. Muller, *Dictionary of Latin and Greek Theological Terms Drawn Principally from Protestant Scholastic Theology*, 2nd ed. (Carlisle, UK: Paternoster, 2000), 212.

"believers," who judge uprightly and sincerely, and do not revile malignantly and groundlessly. COMMENTARY ON FIRST THESSALONIANS.[16]

GOD CALLS PERSONS INTO HIS OWN KINGDOM AND GLORY. JACOBUS ARMINIUS: The efficient cause of this vocation is God the Father in the Son. The Son himself, as appointed by the Father to be the Mediator and the King of his church, calls people by the Holy Spirit; as he is the Spirit of God given to the Mediator; and as he is the Spirit of Christ the King and the head of his church, by whom both "the Father and the Son hitherto work." But this vocation is so administered by the Spirit, that the Holy Spirit is himself its effector: for he appoints bishops, sends forth teachers, endues them with gifts, grants them his assistance, and obtains authority for the word and bestows efficacy on it. DISPUTATION 16. ON THE VOCATION OF MEN TO SALVATION.[17]

A MORE INTIMATE ANALOGY. THE ENGLISH ANNOTATIONS: Before he compared himself to a nurse, who tenderly affects and carefully attends and cherished the infant committed to her. But because the nurse cannot be of the same natural affection as the parent, nor has the same power to do the infant good, nor has authority over it, he improves the former metaphor and amplifies his love for them, by comparing his care over them and affection toward them to that of a father. Truly pastors are like spiritual fathers, bit in respect to their fatherly affection and fatherly power, and especially because in Christ Jesus they beget us through the gospel. ANNOTATIONS ON 1 THESSALONIANS 2:11.[18]

2:13 Receiving the Word of God

THE TRUE CHURCH AND PAUL'S TEACHING. MARTIN BUCER: The church is the pillar of the truth and has no fellowship with error. This church is to be heeded, because God uses its ministry in calling us. As Scripture has it, "They believed the Lord and Moses his servant," and hence that dictum of Augustine's so misunderstood by his opponents, "I would not believe the gospel unless the church moved me." Paul praises those who receive his preaching as the word of God, for we cannot believe in God if we do not give credence to the person who proclaims him. LECTURES ON EPHESIANS.[19]

THE APOSTLES BELIEVED THEIR MESSAGE WAS FROM GOD. HEINRICH BULLINGER: Neither is it to be marveled at that the Forerunner and the apostles of Christ had always very great dignity and authority in the church. For, even as they were ambassadors of the eternal King of all ages, and of the whole world, so, being imbued with the Spirit of God, they did nothing according to the judgment of their own minds. And the Lord by their ministry wrought great miracles, thereby to garnish the ministry of them, and to commend their doctrine to us. And what may be thought of that, moreover, that by the word of God they converted the whole world gathering together, and laying the foundations of notable churches throughout the compass of the world, which truly by human counsel and words they had never would have been able to bring to pass. So this is further added, that they who once leaned to this doctrine as a doctrine giving life did not refuse to die. Besides that, however many believed in the doctrine of the gospel were not afraid though water, fire, and swords to cut off their life, and to lay hand on the life to come. The faithful saints could in no way have done these things, unless the doctrine they had believed had been of God.

Although, therefore, the apostles were men, their doctrine, first of all taught by a lively expressed voice and after that set down in writing with pen and ink, is the doctrine of God, and the very true word of God. For therefore the apostle left this saying in writing: "When they received the

---

[16]CTS 42:254 (CO 52:149).
[17]Arminius, *Works*, 2:232; citing Eph 2:17; 4:11-12; Rev 3:20; Jn 5:17; Heb 3:7; Acts 13:2; 20:28; 1 Cor 12:4, 7, 9, 11; Heb 2:4.
[18]Downame, ed., *Annotations*, 3K2r*.

[19]Bucer, *Lectures on Ephesians*, 212; citing Ex 14:31.

word of God they heard from us, they received it not as a human word but as it is indeed, the word of God, which effectually works in you who believe." OF THE WORD OF GOD.[20]

RECEIVING THE WORD OF GOD AND THE REALITY OF DIVINE GRACE. MATTHEW POOLE: The apostle, having given the reasons on the part of himself and his fellow ministers, as to why the gospel had such effect on them, he next proceeds to show the reason for which he gives God thanks, that is, from their manner of receiving it, though this as well as the former are only subordinate reasons. First, they heard it. Some will not do that: and therefore the apostle here calls it a word of hearing, a Hebraism as in Romans 10, "Faith comes by hearing." Second, they received it. The word implies a receiving with affection, as Joseph the Virgin Mary to his wife. Third, they "received it not as a human word," which we receive sometimes doubting, sometimes disputing it; or believing it only with a human faith, on grounds of reason, as the dictates of philosophy, or on the reports of human beings; and without the impression of the authority of God on our minds, or when we receive the word of God because of the eloquence or learning of the preacher, and the affection we bear to him, or admiration of his person, or as the papists, we believe it because the church believes it.

"But as it is in truth, the word of God," they received it with a divine faith, ready subjection of our souls to it, and with reverend attention, as a word that is from heaven, which the apostle positively asserts in a way of parenthesis.

"As it is in truth," or truly, they believed, so he dispersed the Word to them, and so they received it. And for this cause he "gave thanks to God." Having mentioned before the subordinate reasons of the efficacy of the word, he now mentions the principal, which is God himself. That any receive the word as the word of God, it is not from the preachers so much as from God. And it is a great cause of thanksgiving to God, when ministers find

a people receive the word with a divine faith, which is not done without divine grace. ANNOTATIONS UPON THE HOLY BIBLE.[21]

RECEIVING THE WORD OF GOD AND THE SACRAMENTS. HEINRICH BULLINGER: As we do receive the word of salvation and grace, so it is needful also that we receive the signs of grace. Although the word of God be preached to us by a human being, we receive it not as a human word, but as the word of God, according to the saying of the apostle: "When they had received the word of God which they heard of us, they received it not as a human word (but as it is indeed) the word of GOD." It behooves us to have respect to the first author thereof, who when he sent abroad his disciples, said, "Go into the whole world, and preach the gospel to all creatures, teaching them to observe whatsoever I have commanded you, and I baptizing them in the name of the Father, and of the Son, and of the Holy Ghost. Those who hear you, hear me, and those who despise you, despise me." And therefore although the sacraments are administered by human hands, they are not received by the godly and religious as proceeding from human beings, but as it were from the hand of God himself, the first and principal author of the same. OF SACRAMENTS.[22]

THE AUTHORITY OF GOD BINDS THE CONSCIENCE. JACOBUS ARMINIUS: When this authority is once known, it binds the consciences of all those to whom the discourse or the writing is addressed or directed to accept it in a becoming manner. But whoever receives it as if it were delivered by God, who approve of it, publish, preach, interpret, and expound it, who also distinguish and discriminate it from words or writings that are supposititious and adulterated; these persons add not a tittle of authority to the sayings or writings, because their entire authority, whether contemplated separately or conjointly, is

---

[20]Bullinger, *Fifty Godly and Learned Sermons*, 12*.

[21]Poole, *Annotations*, 739-40*; citing Rom 10:17; Mt 1:20.
[22]Bullinger, *Fifty Godly and Learned Sermons*, 963*.

only that of mortals. Things divine neither need confirmation, nor indeed can receive it, from those that are human. But this whole employment of approving, preaching, explaining, and discriminating, even when it is discharged by the church universal, is only an attestation by which she declares that she holds and acknowledges these words or writings, and these alone, as divine. ON THE AUTHORITY AND CERTAINTY OF THE SACRED SCRIPTURES.[23]

PAUL'S PREACHING WAS THE WORD OF GOD.
JOHN CALVIN: "For this reason we give thanks." Having spoken of his ministry, he returns again to address the Thessalonians, that he may always commend that mutual harmony of which he has previously made mention. He says, therefore, that he gives thanks to God, because they had "embraced the word of God which they heard from his mouth, as the word of God, as it truly was." Now, by these expressions he means that it has been received by them reverently, and with the obedience with which it ought. For as soon as this persuasion has gained a footing, it is inevitable that a feeling of obligation to obey takes possession of our minds. For who would not shudder at the thought of resisting God? Who would not regard contempt of God with detestation? The circumstance, therefore, that the Word of God is regarded by many with such contempt, that it is scarcely held in any estimation—that many are not at all actuated by fear—arises from this, that they do not consider that they have to do with God.

Hence we learn from this passage what credit ought to be given to the gospel—that it does not depend on human authority, but, resting on the sure and ascertained truth of God, raises itself above the world; and, in conclusion, is as far above mere opinion as heaven is above earth; and, second, that it produces of itself reverence, fear, and obedience, inasmuch as humans, touched with a feeling of divine majesty, will never allow themselves to sport with it. Teachers are, in their turn,

admonished to beware of bringing forward anything but the pure word of God, for if this was not allowable for Paul, it will not be so for anyone in the present day. He proves, however, from the effect produced that it was the Word of God that he had delivered, inasmuch as it had produced that fruit of heavenly doctrine that the prophets celebrate, in renewing their life, for human doctrine could accomplish no such thing. The relative pronoun may be taken as referring either to God or to his word, but whichever way you choose, the meaning will come all to one, for as the Thessalonians felt in themselves a divine energy, which proceeded from faith, they might rest assured that what they had heard was not a mere sound of the human voice vanishing into air but the living and efficacious doctrine of God.

As to the expression "the word of the preaching of God," it means simply, as I have rendered it, "the word of God preached by human beings." For Paul meant to state expressly that they had not looked on the doctrine as contemptible, although it had proceeded from the mouth of a mortal, inasmuch as they recognized God as the author of it. He accordingly praises the Thessalonians, because they did not rest in mere regard for the minister but lifted up their eyes to God that they might receive his word. Accordingly, I have not hesitated to insert the particle *ut* (that), which served to make the meaning more clear. There is a mistake on the part of Erasmus in rendering it "the word of the hearing of God," as if Paul meant that God had been manifested. He afterward changed it thus: "the word by which you learned God," for he did not advert to the Hebrew idiom. COMMENTARY ON FIRST THESSALONIANS.[24]

A MESSENGER OF GOD MUST SPEAK AS GOD SPEAKS. JOHN JEWEL: The servant and messenger of God must so speak as God speaks. God speaks deeply, and to the heart. He lances the spirit, and wounds the inward parts. He bids Isaiah to show the people their transgressions, and the house of

---

[23]Arminius, *Works*, 2:81*.

[24]CTS 42:256-58 (CO 52:151-52); citing Is 55:11, 13; Jer 23:29.

Jacob their sins. God himself says, "I visit the sin of the fathers upon the children to the third and fourth generation of those who hate me." Again he says, "If you will despise my ordinances, either if your soul abhors my laws so that you will not do all my commandments . . . I will set my face against you, and you will fall before your enemies, and they who hate you will reign over you." But to those who repent of their sins and turn to him, God says, "Turn to me, you will be saved." Again: "You disobedient Israel, return, says the Lord, and I will not let my wrath fall upon you." So must the minister of God: he must show forth the mercy of God, not hide his judgments. He has the Lord's business in hand; he may not do it negligently. A flatterer makes it their greatest care to please people; they seek their favor; they fear to displease, and dare not speak as to whether something undertaken is evil. When they see a thief, they run with him, and partake with the adulterers: they sew pillows under the arms of sinners. Whoever says, "No," their "no" is ready; and if any say, "Yes," they are ready to say, "yes." They change as often as the weathercock. They dare not strive against the stream. Their heart is at the will of others. They seek some gain; they seek their own glory, and not the glory of God. They who are such are called in the Scriptures "hirelings," "dumb dogs that cannot bark." They deny God, betray his truth, and deceive the people. They lock up the truth in lies. Of such the Spirit of God says, "Woe to them who have a double heart, and wicked lips!" And, "A double-minded person is unstable in all their ways." And, "He who is not with me is against me, and he who gathers not with me scatters." And, "How long will you hesitate between two opinions? If the Lord is God, follow him, but if Baal be god, then go after him." And again, "What fellowship does light have with darkness? And what concord has Christ with Belial?" Cursed is that one who flatters the people, and is unfaithful in the Lord's work. Upon the First Epistle to the Thessalonians.[25]

2:14-16 *Suffering for the Gospel*

The Necessity of Perseverance. Heinrich Bullinger: Let the faithful think on these sayings and others like them and have them in their minds, and let them persevere still with constancy and patience to spread abroad the doctrine of the gospel, no matter what the world creates and what offenses it casts in the way. Fifty Godly and Learned Sermons.[26]

The Errors of the Jews. David Dickson: That he may remove the scandal of persecution whereby the Christian churches were vexed by the unbelieving Jews, who called themselves the people of God, he takes off the vizard[†] from those perverse enemies of the gospel, by setting out their sins with a most severe accusation, of which there are seven branches: (1) The unbelieving Jews killed Christ himself. (2) They have not spared their own prophets, being their countrymen. (3) They persecute us apostles who they say that the Thessalonians should receive consolation from the fellowship of the sufferings of Christ, and the sufferings of his servants. (4) They are adversaries of God, and they think that they please God most when they persecute his servants. (5) That as public enemies of humankind, they hinder as much as they can, the common salvation of humankind. (6) They are enemies to the Gentiles to their utmost, forbidding the apostles to preach the gospel of salvation to the Gentiles, lest they should be saved, so far is it lies in them. (7) By doing these and many other things, they daily more and more fill up the measure of their sins. Having recited their faults he annexes the judgment and wrath of God, which now had come on them even to the utmost. The First Epistle of Paul to the Thessalonians.[27]

---

[25]Jewel, *Works*, 2:832**; citing Ex 20:5; Lev 26:14-17; Jer 3:12; Sir 2:14 (see Douay-Rheims); Jas 1:8; Lk 11:23; 1 Kings 18:21; 2 Cor 6:15.

[26]Bullinger, *Fifty Godly and Learned Sermons*, 453*.
[27]Dickson, *Exposition*, 148. †According to the *Oxford English Dictionary*, *vizard* is a common sixteenth-century word for "mask" (i.e., an older sense of "visor" denoted something that covered one's face).

The Jews Filled Their Measure of Sin.
The English Annotations: The Jews did not intend to fill up the measure of their sins by persecuting the church, and so to draw vengeance from heaven onto themselves. The apostle's meaning is that God in his just judgment permitted them to make up the full measure of their own sins and those of their forefathers, because he intended to sweep them away with the broom of destruction in the hand of the Romans. Annotations on 1 Thessalonians 2:16.[28]

God's Judgment on Unbelieving Jews.
Theodore Beza: He [Paul] prevents an offense that might be taken, for that the Jews especially above all others persecuted the gospel. That is no new thing, he says, seeing that they slew Christ himself and his prophets, and have banished me also.... He foretells the utter destruction of the Jews, lest anyone should be moved by their rebellion. Until the wickedness of theirs that they have by inheritance as it were of their fathers, becomes so great that the measure of their iniquity being filled, God may come forth in wrath.... The judgments of God being angry, which indeed appeared shortly after in the destruction of the city of Jerusalem, whether many resorted then out of diverse provinces, when it was besieged. The New Testament of Our Lord Jesus Christ.[29]

Rome Seems to Be Beyond Reform. Martin Luther: The pope in Rome leads the life of ease; by right and wrong he strives to make his [sons] richer and more important, bravely killing or poisoning those whose property his sons eagerly covet. Rome is so incomparably bad that God is in no position to consider it worthy of any opportunity for reform: "God's wrath has come upon it at last." Letter to James Propst.[30]

---

[28]Downame, ed., *Annotations*, 3K2r*; citing Gen 15:16; Mt 23:32.

[29]Beza, *New Testament*, 91.
[30]LW 50:181.

2:17–3:13 PAUL'S DESIRE TO SEE THE THESSALONIANS AGAIN

[17]But since we were torn away from you, brothers, for a short time, in person not in heart, we endeavored the more eagerly and with great desire to see you face to face, [18]because we wanted to come to you—I, Paul, again and again—but Satan hindered us. [19]For what is our hope or joy or crown of boasting before our Lord Jesus at his coming? Is it not you? [20]For you are our glory and joy.

3 Therefore when we could bear it no longer, we were willing to be left behind at Athens alone, [2]and we sent Timothy, our brother and God's coworker[a] in the gospel of Christ, to establish and exhort you in your faith, [3]that no one be moved by these afflictions. For you yourselves know that we are destined for this. [4]For when we were with you, we kept telling you beforehand that we were to suffer affliction, just as it has come to pass, and just as you know. [5]For this reason, when I could bear it no longer, I sent to learn about your faith, for fear that somehow the tempter had tempted you and our labor would be in vain.

[6]But now that Timothy has come to us from you, and has brought us the good news of your faith and love and reported that you always remember us kindly and long to see us, as we long to see you— [7]for this reason, brothers,[b] in all our distress and affliction we have been comforted about you through your faith. [8]For now we live, if you are standing fast in the Lord. [9]For what thanksgiving can we return to God for you, for all the joy that we feel for your sake before our God, [10]as we pray most earnestly night and day that we may see you face to face and supply what is lacking in your faith?

[11]Now may our God and Father himself, and our Lord Jesus, direct our way to you, [12]and may the Lord make you increase and abound in love for one another and for all, as we do for you, [13]so that he may establish your hearts blameless in holiness before our God and Father, at the coming of our Lord Jesus with all his saints.

a Some manuscripts *servant* b Or *brothers and sisters*

OVERVIEW: As Paul emphasizes his desire to see the Thessalonians again, these early modern commentators remind readers that as their desire to serve God increases so does the ferocity of Satan's attacks. Yet amid these attacks, the Spirit of God strengthens faith, which produces mutual love, and the authority of God is supreme over all wickedness, providing motivation for believers to persevere in their faith. The exegetes go on to explore different types of faith as well as the role of the sacraments and prayer in fortifying faith. Timothy's report of the faith of the Thessalonians also gives occasion for the reformers to call attention to the happiness that comes from observing the spiritual growth of others.

2:17-20 *Paul's Glory and Joy*

GOD'S SUPREME AUTHORITY OVER SATAN'S WORK. JOHN CALVIN: Whenever the wicked harass us, they fight under Satan's banner, and are his instruments for harassing us. More especially, when our endeavors are directed to the work of the Lord, it is certain that everything that hinders proceeds from Satan; and would to God that this sentiment were deeply impressed on the minds of all pious persons—that Satan is continually contriving, by every means, in what way he may hinder or obstruct the edification of the church! We would assuredly be more careful to resist him; we would take more care to maintain sound doctrine, of which that enemy strives so keenly to deprive us. We would also, whenever the course of the gospel is retarded, know whence the hindrance proceeds. He says elsewhere that God had not permitted him, but both are true: for although Satan does his part, God retains supreme authority, so as to open up a way for us, as often as he sees good, against Satan's will, and in spite of his opposition. Paul accordingly says truly that God does not permit, although the hindrance comes from Satan. Commentary on First Thessalonians.[1]

Glorying in God's Favors. John Calvin: He confirms that ardor of desire of which he had made mention, inasmuch as he has his happiness in a manner treasured up in them. Unless I forget myself, I must necessarily desire your presence, "for you are our glory and joy." Further, when he calls them his "hope and the crown of his glory," we must not understand this as meaning that he gloried in anyone but God alone, but because we are allowed to glory in all God's favors, in their own place, in such a manner that he is always our object of aim, as I have explained more at large in the first epistle to the Corinthians. We must, however, infer from this that Christ's ministers will, on the last day, according as they have individually promoted his kingdom, be partakers of glory and triumph. Let them therefore now learn to rejoice and glory in nothing but the prosperous issue of their labors, when they see that the glory of Christ is promoted by their instrumentality. The consequence will be that they will be actuated by that spirit of affection to the church with which they ought. The particle "also" denotes that the Thessalonians were not the only persons in whom Paul triumphed, but that they held a place among many. The causal particle *gar* (for), which occurs almost immediately afterward, is employed here not in its strict sense, but by way of affirmation— "*assuredly* you are." Commentary on First Thessalonians.[2]

3:1-5 Establish the Faith

The Sacraments and the Establishing of Faith. Heinrich Bullinger: Unless the inward force of the Spirit draws and quickens the hearts of the hearers, the outward persuasion of the teacher, though ever so forcible and vehement, shall avail nothing. But if the Holy Spirit shows forth his might and works with the word of the preacher, the souls of the hearers are most mightily strengthened. And so it stands with the mystery of the sacrament. For if the inward anointing and sealing of the Holy Ghost is wanting, the outward action will be counted but a toy to the unbelievers; neither does the sealing of the sacraments work anything at all. But when faith, the gift of the Holy Spirit, goes before, the sealing of the sacraments is very strong and sure.

Some also have said very well that if our minds are destitute of the Holy Ghost, the sacraments do no more profit us than it does a blind man to look upon the bright beams of the sun. But if our eyes are opened through the illumination of the Spirit, they are wonderfully delighted with the heavenly light of the sacraments.[†] And although sacraments do not seal the promises to the unbelievers because they mistrust them, the sacraments were nevertheless instituted by God, that they might be seals. Of Sacraments.[3]

Paul Sacrifices Companionship for the Thessalonians. John Calvin: By the detail that follows he assures them of the desire of which he had spoken. If, on being detained elsewhere, had he sent no other to Thessalonica in his place, it might have seemed as though he were not so much concerned with them. When he substitutes Timothy in his place, he removes that suspicion, more especially when he prefers them before himself. Now that he esteemed them above himself,

---

[1]CTS 42:263* (CO 52:154-55); citing Rom 1:13.
[2]CTS 42:263-64 (CO 52:155).

[3]Bullinger, *Fifty Godly and Learned Sermons*, 1016-17*. [†]At this point Bullinger quotes Zwingli, *Libello ad princips Germania*: "It does not offend us, though all those things that the Holy Ghost works be referred to the external sacrament, as long as we understand them to be spoken figuratively, as the Fathers spoke."

he shows from this that he chose rather to be left alone than that they should be deserted, for these words, "we judged it good to be left alone," are emphatic. Timothy was a most faithful companion to him. He had at that time no other companion with him, hence it was inconvenient and distressing for Paul to be without him. It is therefore a token of rare affection and anxious desire that he does not refuse to deprive himself of all comport with a view to relieving the Thessalonians. COMMENTARY ON I THESSALONIANS 3:1.[4]

PAUL DOESN'T WANT HIS CHALLENGES TO DISCOURAGE OTHERS. THE ENGLISH ANNOTATIONS: The troubles and afflictions that befell the apostle, their teacher, were likely to unsettle the faith of the weak and discourage them in their holy course that he had set them in. Therefore out of wisdom and love he sent Timothy seasonably to them, both to strengthen them in their faith, comfort them in their fears, and arm them against the temptations of Satan. ANNOTATIONS ON I THESSALONIANS 3:2.[5]

PERSECUTION A CONDITION OF THE FAITH. JOHN CALVIN: As all would gladly exempt themselves from the necessity of bearing the cross, Paul teaches that there is no reason why believers should feel dismayed on the occasion of persecutions, as though it were a thing that was new and unusual, inasmuch as this is our condition that the Lord has assigned to us. For this manner of expression, "we are appointed to it," is as though he had said we are Christians on this condition. He says, however, that they know it, because it became them to fight more bravely, inasmuch as they had been forewarned in time. In addition to this, incessant afflictions made Paul contemptible among rude and ignorant persons. On this account, he states that nothing had befallen him but what he had long before, in the manner of a prophet, foretold. COMMENTARY ON I THESSALONIANS 3:3.[6]

3:6-8 *Timothy Brings Good News*

PAUL ENCOURAGED BY TIMOTHY'S REPORT. BENEDICT ARETIUS: He speaks of the return of Timothy, and how he was moved to much praise. This pertains to the occasion of the letter of Scripture. Hereafter he commended three things in Timothy's return, each of which pertains to their praise. And therefore they have the strength of argument to constancy. Indeed the praised virtue increases in good qualities.

1. First, he speaks of their faith, that is, its constancy in profession.

2. Then, their mutual love, which is the fruit of faith.

3. Third, of himself, the desire of Paul, by whom the honest judgment of the good teacher is commended. They do not find fault with him on account of his absence, but think piously of him, even though he is far removed from their own trials. However, this desire of mutual affection compensated [for Paul's absence], and there ought to be with love *antiphilēsis*,[†] that is, mutual love.

THE FIRST EPISTLE TO THE THESSALONIANS.[7]

SATAN IS MOST ACTIVE DURING PERSECUTION. JOHN JEWEL: The tempter waits all occasions to draw us from our faith and steadfastness in the Lord. Yet he is never so busy as when any persecution is raised against the truth. Then he is in his best attire. Then he plays his part, and leaves nothing undone whereby he may move us to forsake the truth. Will you (he says) be so foolish so as to lose your life, and not know why? Are you wiser than your forefathers? Why should you not be content to do as your father, mother, friends, and kinsfolk? Do you think that they do not care for their souls as much as you do yours? Will you make them pagans and infidels? Do you think they are damned? Be wise and do not cast yourself away. Flesh is frail, life is sweet, death is dreadful; but to

---

[4]CTS 42:264-65* (CO 52:155-56).
[5]Downame, ed., *Annotations*, 3K2v*.
[6]CTS 42:266* (CO 52:156).

[7]Aretius, *Thessalonicenses*, 215-16. [†]*Antiphilēsis* = "a return of affection" (so Liddell and Scott). To paraphrase: "there ought to be a return of affection with love, that is, mutual love."

die in the fire, to be burned alive, to see your arms and your legs quite burnt from your body, and yet you cannot die; this is most terrible. You can never abide it. Behold so many kings, princes, nobles, cardinals, bishops, doctors, and learned people as well as whole kingdoms and countries of the contrary opinion. Be not willful. Do not think that you are wiser than all of the world. What is it for you to come to the church and show yourself obedient, and to do as others do? It is a small matter to look up and hold up your hands at the elevation of the host. If it is an offense, you will be excused because you are forced to do it by author- ity. God is merciful. He will forgive you.

Thus and thus does Satan tempt us, and sifts us, to lead us from our steadfastness. He practices these devices in these late days before our eyes, with many constant professors of Christian religion; but through the mighty power of God, they [faithful Christians] quenched all his fiery darts, and through many tribulations enter into glory. UPON THE FIRST EPISTLE TO THE THESSALONIANS.[8]

TIMOTHY ENCOURAGES PAUL. BENEDICT ARETIUS: The effect that follows of the narration of Timothy was wonderfully rebuilt and re-created by the commemoration of those words to you. *Thlipsis* [affliction, trouble, persecution] here is the spiritual concern for the constancy of the churches. *Ananke* [necessity or distress], however, means external care, as that he might work in the mean- time with his very own hands, he wrote separate messages, so he might send messages himself, with which he himself was not able to visit. THE FIRST EPISTLE TO THE THESSALONIANS.[9]

SUPREME HAPPINESS OVER OTHERS' SPIRI- TUAL GROWTH. MATTHIAS FLACIUS: Paul says . . . that he lives, or does well and happily if that one presently stands bravely in Christ; that is, he counts as his highest felicity their constancy and progress in true piety. To stand in the Lord is to

persevere and to flourish in true faith in Christ, wherefore the best fruit of all virtue is brought forth. Note the metaphor that must be observed even in Latin, as Cicero[†] himself says that the cause of day stands beautifully, but conversely, much is known from things lying down. GLOSS ON 1 THESSALONIANS.[10]

PAUL'S WELL-BEING CONNECTED TO THE THESSALONIANS. BENEDICT ARETIUS: Another argument to constancy, as if he says: I seem to live as long as you are enduring. Otherwise life is hard and bitter. And it is as if it is your lot in relation- ship to me to give and take away life. THE FIRST EPISTLE TO THE THESSALONIANS.[11]

3:9-13 *Abounding in Love*

THE NECESSITY OF INCREASING ONE'S FAITH. HEINRICH BULLINGER: So long as we live, we learn that our faith may not be perfect, and if at any time it shall be weakened by temptations, then it may be repaired, and again confirmed. And in this diversity, I mean in this increase and weakness of faith, there is no partition or division, for the selfsame root and substance of faith both always remain, although it is sometimes more, and sometimes less. In like manner, faith is not therefore changed or cut in sunder because one is called general faith and another particular faith. For general faith is other than that which believes that all the words of God are true, and that God has a good will to humankind. Particular faith believes nothing contrary to this, only that which is common to all, the faithful applies particularly to himself, believing that God is not well-minded toward others alone, but even to him also.

So then, it brings the whole into parts, and that which is general to particularities. For whereas by general faith he believes that all the words of God are true, in the same sort by particular faith he believes that the soul is immortal, that our bodies

---

[8]Jewel, *Works*, 2:846.*
[9]Aretius, *Thessalonicenses*, 216.

[10]Flacius, *Glossa Compendaria*, 1016. [†]Cicero, *Divinatione* 1.10.
[11]Aretius, *Thessalonicenses*, 216.

rise again, that the faithful shall be saved, the unbelievers destroyed, and whatsoever else is of this sort taught to be believed in the Word of God. Moreover, the disputation touching faith that is poured into us, and faith that we ourselves get, touching formal faith, and faith without fashion, I believe to be beaten out of them who of themselves bring these new disputations into the church.

True faith is obtained by no strength or merit of human beings, but is poured into him of God, as I declared in my last sermon, and though humans obtain it by listening to the Word of God, it is nevertheless wholly imputed to the grace of God. For unless this grace works inwardly in the heart of the hearer, the preacher that labors outwardly both brings no profit at all. THAT THERE IS ONLY ONE TRUE FAITH.[12]

FILLING UP WHAT IS LACKING. CORNELIUS À LAPIDE: In Greek it is *kai katartisai ta hysterēmata tēs pisteōs hymōn* [and to supply the things lacking in your faith], as if it says, "that I might perfect the body parts, the members, and the joints, which thus far your faith is lacking, so that the body of your faith might be integrated,[†] and with all its parts as though the members might be completed." For the Greek *katartisai* is speaking about the body that is integrated, completed, and perfected

with its own body parts and members. In the same sense Paul says that he fills up what is lacking, that is, those things that are lacking in the sufferings of Christ, as in Colossians 1:24. As if he says, "I want you to see that this is why I was compelled to throw off the persecution of the Jews, that I might perfect and complete my imperfect preaching and instruction of you." COMMENTARY ON 1 THESSALONIANS.[13]

SUPPLYING THE LACK THROUGH PRAYER. CARDINAL CAJETAN: "Night and day praying abundantly." Consequently, he treats that particular proposition from the beginning, "making memory of you in our prayers, without ceasing." Since he said, "without ceasing," he explains the manner—night and day abundantly (that is, frequently, diligently, daily) praying, indeed, in extraordinary ways. For the saying that is interpreted "abundantly" signifies "to exceed," and it makes evident excessive prayer. "So that we might see your face." Not that they lack anything necessary for faith, but that they were lacking something to be known, concerning the mysteries of faith, or of the work and of this sort. ON 1 THESSALONIANS.[14]

---

[12]Bullinger, *Fifty Godly and Learned Sermons*, 41*.

[13]Lapide, *Commentaria In Omnes D. Pauli Epistolas*, 731 (pdf 755).
  [†]The Latin word here, *integretur* (a verb in the passive voice), can also mean "to renew" or "to refresh."
[14]Cajetan, *In Omnes*, 279 (pdf 286); citing 1 Thess 1:2.

4:1-12 A LIFE PLEASING TO GOD

Finally, then, brothers,[a] we ask and urge you in the Lord Jesus, that as you received from us how you ought to walk and to please God, just as you are doing, that you do so more and more. [2]For you know what instructions we gave you through the Lord Jesus. [3]For this is the will of God, your sanctification:[b] that you abstain from sexual immorality; [4]that each one of you know how to control his own body[c] in holiness and honor, [5]not in the passion of lust like the Gentiles who do not know God; [6]that no one transgress and wrong his brother in this matter, because the Lord is an avenger in all these things, as we told you beforehand and solemnly warned you. [7]For God has not called us for impurity, but in holiness. [8]Therefore whoever disregards this, disregards not man but God, who gives his Holy Spirit to you.

[9]Now concerning brotherly love you have no need for anyone to write to you, for you yourselves have been taught by God to love one another, [10]for that indeed is what you are doing to all the brothers throughout Macedonia. But we urge you, brothers, to do this more and more, [11]and to aspire to live quietly, and to mind your own affairs, and to work with your hands, as we instructed you, [12]so that you may walk properly before outsiders and be dependent on no one.

a Or brothers and sisters; also verses 10, 13   b Or your holiness   c Or how to take a wife for himself; Greek how to possess his own vessel

---

OVERVIEW: Throughout their expositions of this passage, these early modern commentators devote their attention to the subject of sanctification, portraying it as the long, convoluted, but certain path to final spiritual victory. In their discussion, they explore various impediments to sanctification, among which is wrong ambition. It is within the broader context of sanctification that the commentators extensively discuss the subject of marriage and the function of sexuality within it. As a significant feature of the Reformation debates, the authors contrast the genuine spirituality of marital vows with the allegedly carnal monastic ones. Also, these expositors examine the social dimensions of sanctification, having in view the salvation of the Christian commonwealth. In this regard, they condemn sins that prove socially destructive, especially usury. Finally, the authors strive to preserve the pastoral office by affirming its spiritual authority within what they understand as biblical parameters.

4:1-2 Walking to Please God

THE LONG VICTORY OF CHRISTIANS. BENEDICT ARETIUS: This place begins with metabasei,[†]

because the figure is suitable for diverse connected members. However, he says to loipon [i.e., "finally" in the ESV],[‡] by which part of the innocence of life is to be upheld; the other is the members of the whole of Christians. First is to know Christ. The second is following after what we know to do, as if you said: theory and practice have been renewed completely with humankind. Therefore rightly it is said to loipon, since now knowledge precedes. And truly with the Christian world it lacks nothing than solely to loipon. Truth is portrayed, is written, is recited publicly and privately in meetings, in parties, in streets with the poor. Indeed, as is known by children. But that "finally" [to loipon] to be preserved concerning the innocence of life is still desired among that particular part of the world. Therefore the work has completely succeeded.

Then the supplication is added that pertains to the argument. And as the strength of the arguments is able to be understood the proposition can be established. The apostle maintains this to the end of the period. Therefore translate it in this way here. It is placed with these words, hina perisseuēte mallon [in order that you may abound all the more], for instance, and it is the end of superior arguments.

The sense will therefore be: to you is to be given works, so that having been born again, you might increase in good morals among humankind.

In these days increase more and more, says the apostle, *perisseuein mallon,*[††] to abound, that is, in other things to excel those who have not been born again, as they see the notorious good works of these ones. Then they themselves attempt in these days to be abundant. Thus it ought to be a perpetual struggle in faithful acts, since they are to overcome themselves, besides other ones, who have not yet been born again. This victory at length is spectacular. The First Epistle to the Thessalonians.[1]

Right Ambition Is Not Sinful. Viktorin Strigel: Since foolish ambition is bad and customarily made evident by many things from a swelled heart, Paul opposes it with a contrary ambition. This is the contrary way of seeking glory, and so he retains the name of ambition, because it is common to vice and virtue, indeed in the old manner of speaking. Nevertheless, so that the admonition would be more clear, he retains the same name because he was ambitious for applause and thanks, as if he were to say, that he should be without some ambition for splendid things, or desire for glory, neither do I censure glory, but rather that the desire for glory should be rightly ordered. Exposition on 1 Thessalonians.[2]

4:3-5 Sanctification Is the Will of God

A Zeal for Sanctification. Thomas Müntzer: O most beloved, see to it that you prophesy, otherwise your theology will not be worth a cent. Think of your God as at hand and not distant; believe that God is more willing to speak than you are prepared to listen. We are brimful of desires. This hinders the finger of the living God from piercing his tablets. By your arguments you drag men to matrimony although the bond is not yet an immaculate one, but a satanic brothel, which is as harmful to the church as the most accursed perfumes of the priests. Do not these passionate desires impede your sanctification? How can the spirit be poured out over your flesh, and how can you have living colloquy with God when you deny such things? There is no precept (if I may put it like this) that so firmly binds the Christian as that of our sanctification. Müntzer to Melanchthon.[3]

Avoid Mixed Marriages. Dirk Philips: Everyone who fears God, who seeks and has love for God's honor and the welfare and improvement of the congregation, consider how openly and stubbornly outside marriages work against other marriage admonitions and warnings of the apostles. And if one will confess the truth rightly, what is being sought with the outside marriages and what is otherwise contained in them than that one gives room for the evil stubborn flesh (that will not be obedient to the Spirit because it has not been sufficiently disciplined but much more bound to sensuality) to complete its evil and unbecoming lusts. And what can result from it but aggravation and evil examples? Now the Lord said in the Gospel: "If anyone offends the least of those who believe, it were better that a millstone be bound to his neck and he be sunk and drowned in the deepest of the sea." From this is to be noted: if it is such an abominable and blameworthy sin to offend one of the littles of the Christian believers, how much more is it an abomination that one offends, saddens, and burdens to death not one but so

---

[1] Aretius, *Thessalonicenses,* 219. [†] According to the *Oxford English Dictionary, metabasis* is "a transition from one subject or point to another." [‡] *To loipon* would translate something like "the remaining," "the rest." In various English translations the phrase *loipon oun* is translated "finally" (esv), "as for other matters" (niv), "finally then" (nasb). [††] Aretius has here taken the Greek text, which reads *hina perisseuēte mallon* (that you may abound all the more), and simply changed the second-person-plural verb *perisseuēte* (you might abound, [or] be rich in) and made it an infinitive, *perisseuein* ("to abound" or "to be rich in").
[2] Strigel, *Hypomnenta in omnes Epistolas,* 283.

[3] Müntzer, *Collected Works,* 44. Müntzer begins this letter to Melanchthon as follows: "To the Christian man Phillip Melanchthon, professor of the sacred Scriptures. Greetings, instrument of Christ. Your theology I embrace with all my heart for it has snatched many souls from the snares of the hunters."

many God-fearing hearts with [the practice of] outside marriage? About the Marriage of Christians.[4]

Different Aspects of the Will of God. Jacobus Arminius: The will of God is also distinguished into that by which he wills to do or to prevent something, which is called "the will of his good pleasure," or rather "of his pleasure"; and into that by which he wills something to be done, or to be omitted, by creatures endued with understanding, and which is called "the will that is signified." The latter is revealed; the former is partly revealed, and partly hidden. The former is efficacious, for it uses power, either so much as cannot be resisted, or such a kind as he certainly knows nothing will withstand: The latter is called "inefficacious," and resistance is frequently made to it, yet so that when the creature transgresses the order of this revealed will, the creature by it may be reduced to order, and that the will of God may be done on those by whom his will has not been performed. To this twofold will is opposed the remission of the will, which is called "permission," and which is also twofold. The one, which permits something to the power of a rational creature by not circumscribing its act with a law, is opposed to "the revealed will." The other is that by which God permits something to the capability and will of the creature, by not interposing an efficacious hindrance; this is opposed to "the will of God's pleasure," which is efficacious. On the Nature of God.[5]

Proper and Improper Abstention in Marriage. Martin Luther: We shall now consider how to live a Christian and godly life in that [married] estate. I will pass over in silence the matter of conjugal duty, the granting and withholding of it, since some filth-preachers have been shameless enough in this matter to rouse our disgust. Some of them designate special times for this, and exclude holy nights and women who are pregnant. I will leave this as St. Paul left it when he said in 1 Corinthians 7:9, "It would be better to marry than to burn"; and again, "To avoid immorality, each man should have his own wife, and each woman her own husband." Although Christian married folk should not permit themselves to be governed by their bodies in the passion of lust, as Paul writes to the Thessalonians, nevertheless all must examine themselves so that by their abstention they do not expose themselves to the danger of fornication and other sins. Neither should they pay any attention to holy days or work days, or other physical considerations. The Estate of Marriage.[6]

The Importance of Controlling One's Own Vessel. Benedict Aretius: *Skeuos.*[†] Some here take for "wife" as it is understood in 1 Peter 3, where the woman is called the weaker vessel, whose honor is to be had in marriage. If thus you accept, this will be the sense: fornication is to be avoided. Do not offend your own legitimate wife. For to this they often credit the sicknesses of lustful marriage: ulcers, a French itch, to other ailments, only to be spoken of reluctantly.[‡] And reasonably this argument is important, if from yourselves you do not want to refrain, at least you refrain from the marriage of your most distinguished. But another sense is better, that you accept the vessel as your very own body, as it is understood in 2 Corinthians 4. We have a treasure in a hard container. Thus 2 Timothy 2. In the house of God it says that there are vessels are of honor, and others are vessels of dishonor. Vessels of wrath, that is, which God uses as if they were instruments. Therefore a vessel might be a human instrument, that is, a spiritual instrument, as really it is a body, as a body uses an organ. Therefore, the sense is, bodies themselves are influenced for dishonor through being a user of a prostitute. Therefore it is to be eagerly avoided. Because here dishonor is meant is able to be proved. First, since

---

[4]CRR 6:563*; citing Mt 18:6-7; Lk 17:2; Mk 9:42.
[5]Arminius, *Works*, 2:128-29; citing Ps 115:3; Mk 3:35; Deut 29:29; 1 Cor 2:11-12; Ps 33:9; Rom 9:19; 2 Sam 17:14; Is 5:4-5; Mt 21:39-41; Acts 5:4; 1 Cor 7:28; Acts 14:16; Ps 81:13.

[6]LW 45:35-36*; citing 1 Cor 7:2.

abuse of the body is against the law of the creator God. Abuse however yields to dishonor, as if you have a gold bowl in a place of dishonor. Certainly here the abuse of gold leads to its dishonor. Thus vases have their own ordinary use, that in which they are honestly preserved. Here it is said that the bodily vessel is spoken of: Therefore as a vessel for certain use is preserved. Then, for dishonor, since good health is stricken, stricken of that good and healthy constitution, stricken with a thousand ailments, itches, poverty, ulcers, paralysis, leprosy, which turns the body nasty and abominable. Therefore it is to be avoided. Likewise, observe in this phrase the special diligence that is required to seize the vessel. For certain vessels are fragile that are preserved with a special care, and how great are the fragile ones, and with great subtlety we treat such things. Thus a blue bowl rather than a gold one. Thus as long as a vessel is fragile, and is easily polluted, it is zealously to be preserved. For indeed the vessel is polluted with an appetite of illegitimate thought, as the Lord Christ says. THE FIRST EPISTLE TO THE THESSALONIANS.[7]

MARITAL FAITHFULNESS BETTER THAN MONASTIC VOWS. MARTIN LUTHER: God forbids a man to transgress and wrong his brother in any matter. This must be observed over and above all the ordinances of all men. Therefore I believe that such a man cannot with a good conscience live in marriage with a second woman, and this impediment should be completely reversed. For if a monastic vow makes a man no longer his own, why does not a pledge of mutual faithfulness do the same? After all, faithfulness is one of the precepts and fruits of the Spirit, in Galatians 5:22,

while a monastic vow is of human invention. And if a wife may claim her husband back, despite the fact that he has taken a monastic vow, why may not an engaged woman claim back her betrothed, even though he has intercourse with another? But we have said above that he who has plighted his troth to a girl may not take a monastic vow, but is in duty bound to marry her because he is in duty bound to keep faith with her; and this faith he many not break for any ordinance of men, because it is commanded by God. Much more should the man here keep faith with his first betrothed, since he could not plight his troth to a second except with a lying heart; and therefore did not really plight it, but deceived her, his neighbor against God's command. Therefore, the "impediment of error" enters in here, by which his marriage to the second woman is rendered null and void. THE BABYLONIAN CAPTIVITY OF THE CHURCH.[8]

4:6-8 Do Not Sin Against a Brother or Sister

NUMEROUS REASONS NOT TO CHEAT A BROTHER. BENEDICT ARETIUS: The third part of the heading is against deceits. The particular proposition is: All the faithful ought to avoid deceit in all matters. Paul says this: *mē hyperbainein* [do not transgress], and *me pleonektein* [do not take advantage]. The former word signifies a way of crossing over, the latter word to want more than equity permits to have. Therefore, whether it signifies with a just proportion, and to dismiss rules of equity. For Scripture does not deny buying and selling, or other business enterprises, but it desires that we stay within boundaries of equity, as it removes deceits. Collect therefore arguments *pros thesin*.[†]

1. First, deceit destroys the rule of equity and justice, for it is positioned in *hyperbasei*,[‡] and it accepts more than it ought, destroys that principal, which you ought not to desire to be among you, nor ought you to do to others. Therefore, it is to be avoided.

---

[7]Aretius, *Thessalonicenses*, 225-26; citing 1 Pet 3:7; 2 Cor 4:7; 2 Tim 2:20-21; Rom 9:21. [†]A *skeuos* is a "container" of some sort. In this context it denotes "body" or "vessel," or perhaps simply "person." [†]"French itch," "French boils," and *mal Francese* were terms used during the early modern era to denote a wide variety of symptoms, though often coalescing around sexually transmitted diseases, particularly what is now known as venereal syphilis. See Jon Arrizabalaga, John Henderson, and Roger French, *The Great Pox: The French Disease in Renaissance Europe* (New Haven, CT: Yale University Press, 1997).

[8]LW 36:101.

2. Then, the brother is the one with him you engage in matters. Therefore, you ought not to violate them. For it is not the case that the civil laws allow one to cheat a brother or sister. Moses allowed usury for the Jews against the Greeks,[††] but toward a Jew he did not permit a Jew to do this. Christ removed all deceit, since he commanded everyone to recognize brothers indiscriminately. Therefore, it ought to be avoided.

3. Third, God is defender of the oppressed, as of widows, of orphans, and all who suffer from deceit. Therefore, deceit is to be avoided lest you meet the punishment of God. Or the sense can be that God punishes great imposters through the ordinary magistrate. God is judge.

The First Epistle to the Thessalonians.[9]

Usury Is Fraud. John Jewel: Let no one defraud their brother, neither by false weight, nor by false measure, nor by lying words. Let your measures and weights and words be true: let your gains be just and true, that God may bless them. His blessing will make you rich; and whatever he does not bless will waste and consume and do you no good. Do to others as you would they do to you. This is true dealing and upright.

If you speak more than is true, if you take more than your merchandise is worth, your conscience knows it is not yours. God will destroy all the workers of iniquity. He who delights in sin hates his own soul. The mouth that is accustomed to lying slays the soul.

Defraud not your brother: he is your brother, whether he is rich or poor: he is your brother, and a child of God. Will you do wrong to your brother? Will you oppress the child of God, and that even in the sight of God? God is that person's Father: he will not leave you unpunished. If someone is simple and unskillful, do not abuse

that person's simplicity. God is the God of righteousness. Deal justly so that your own conscience does not accuse you. Do not teach your children or your servants to deceive others, and to gain by wickedness. After they have learned from you to deceive others, they will deceive you also. Job prayed daily for his children. Be careful that your children and servants deceive no one nor hurt anyone. Their sins will be laid to your charge. Why do you ask God to feed you, and give you daily bread, and do not wait on his will, but feed on the bread of iniquity? This food will not nourish you; this wealth will not stand by you; God will not prosper it. The wise one says, "The bread of deceit is sweet to a person; but afterward his mouth will be filled with gravel. Ill-gotten goods have an ill end." God has said by his prophet Haggai, "You have sown much, but you have brought in little: you brought it home, and I did blow on it." We have examples hereof daily. We have seen great heaps of wealth suddenly blown away, and consumed to nothing; great houses decayed, and the hope of the wicked quite overthrown.

Here I will speak somewhat of the unhappy trade of usury, because therein stands the most miserable and shameful deceiving of the brethren.... Usury is a kind of lending of money, or corn, or oil, or wine, or of any other thing, wherein, upon covenant and bargain, we receive again the whole principal that we delivered and somewhat more for the use and occupying of the same: as, if I lend 100 pounds, and for it covenant to receive 105 pounds, or any other sum greater than was the sum that I loaned. This is that which we call usury: such a kind of bargaining as all people that ever feared God's judgment have always abhorred and condemned. It is filthy gains, and a work of darkness. It is a monster in nature, the overthrow of mighty kingdoms, the destruction of flourishing states, the decay of wealthy cities, the plagues of the world, and the misery of the people. It is theft; it is the murdering of our brethren; it is the curse of God and the curse of the people. This is usury....

From where does usury spring? It is soon shown. From the same place where theft, murder,

---

[9] Aretius, *Thessalonicenses*, 226-27*; citing Rom 13:1-7. [†]*Pros thesin* would translate woodenly something like "to the arrangement," or paraphrastically, "Here is the structure of the argument." [†]That is, in "an overstepping" or "transgression of law," a "trespass" (so Liddell and Scott). [††]Here, *ethnikos*.

adultery, the plagues, and destruction of the people spring. All these are the works of the devil and the works of the flesh. Christ tells the Pharisees, "You are of your father the devil, and the lusts of your father you will do." Even so may it be truly said to the usurer, You are of your father the devil, and the lust of your father you will do, and therefore you have pleasure in his works. The devil entered into the heart of Judas, and put in him this greediness and covetousness of gain, for which he was content to sell his master. Judas's heart was the shop: the devil was the foreman to work in it. St. Paul says, "They who desire to be rich fall into temptation and snares, and into many foolish and noisome lusts, which drown people into perdition and destruction. For the desire of money is the root of evil." And St. John says, "Whoever commits sin is of the devil." Thus we see that the devil is the planter and the father of usury.

Covetousness, desire of money, insatiable greediness, deceitfulness, unmercifulness, injury, oppression, extortion, contempt of God, hatred of the brethren, and hatred of all people are the nurses and breeders of usury. It springs from Satan, and grows, is watered, and fed and nourished by these cruel and damnable monsters.

Let us see further as to what the fruits of usury are. For perhaps it does some good, and you may think that many are better for it. These therefore are the fruits. It dissolves the knot and fellowship of humanity: it hardens the human heart. It makes people unnatural, and bereaves them of charity and love to their dearest friends. It breeds misery, and provokes the wrath of God from heaven. It consumes rich people, it eats up the poor, it makes people bankrupt, and undoes many households. The poor occupiers are driven to flee, their wives are left alone, their children are helpless, and driven to beg their bread through the unmerciful dealing of the covetous usurer. Upon the First Epistle to the Thessalonians.[10]

---

[10]Jewel, *Works*, 2:850-52*; citing Prov 20:17; Hag 1:9; Jn 8:44; 1 Tim 6:9-10; 1 Jn 3:8. Throughout the Middle Ages theologians like Thomas Aquinas (1225–1274) and the church in general regarded usury as a sin. The Council of Vienne (1311–1312) went

THE PROPER AUTHORITY AND ROLE OF THE MINISTER UNDER GOD. HEINRICH BULLINGER: Some wresting these places of the holy Scripture against the natural sense give the ministers an equal power in a manner with Christ, and that which only pertains to him they communicate also to them. But they say that by such means the ministry must be set out, lest it were vile and of no estimation among profane people. Or again to speak of the inward drawing of the Spirit, that they seem as it were to make superfluous, or to take clean away the outward ministry, and to attribute nothing at all to it.

Therefore the minister must be limited with his bounds, lest he be drawn hither and thither, with the affections and lusts of humankind, and either too much or too little be attributed to it. Let the ministry indeed be beautified, and kept in authority, but let it be done without the dishonoring of God. Neither indeed does it become us, under the pretense of the ministry, to attribute to human labor that which is only God's office, on whom all people ought to depend, and to whom, as the only wellspring and giver of all godliness, they ought to have respect. Therefore, the faithful ministers of the Lord Jesus ought only to have regard to this, that they may keep the glory and authority of

---

as far as to condemn usury as heretical. In the sixteenth century, the reformers were divided on the issue of loaning money at interest. Whereas some, like Calvin, gave some qualified support for it, others, like Luther and Jewel, strongly and uncompromisingly opposed it. Usury was subject to shifting legislation in Tudor and early Stuart England. See Charles R. Geist, *Beggar Thy Neighbor: A History of Usury and Debt* (Philadelphia: University of Pennsylvania Press, 2013), 41-57; for general studies on the reformers and usury, see David W. Jones, *Reforming the Morality of Usury: A Study of the Differences That Separated the Protestant Reformers* (Lanham, MD: University Press of America, 2004); Eric Kerridge, *Usury, Interest, and the Reformation* (Aldershot: Ashgate, 2002); for the usury issue in Tudor and early Stuart England, see Norman Jones, *God and the Moneylenders: Usury and Law in Early Modern England* (Oxford: Blackwell, 1989). For Jewel on usury, see John Jewel, "Commentary on 1 Thessalonians 4:4" and "A Paper on Usury," trans. and ed. Andre A. Gazal, *Journal of Markets and Morality* 15, no. 1 (2012): 273-313; Andre A. Gazal, "'Profit That Is Condemned by the Word of God': John Jewel's Theological Method in His Opposition to Usury," *Perichoresis* 13, no. 1 (2015): 37-54.

Christ unblemished, and his priesthood sound to himself in every point. For the Lord Jesus himself sitting at the right hand of the Father, in the true tabernacle, which God fixed and not man remains a priest, yes, the only high priest of his church forever, executing as yet all the duties of a priest in the church. For he as the only teacher and master in the church teaches his disciples, that is, the church, or congregation of the faithful, inducing them with the Holy Ghost, regenerating and drawing them, sanctifying and making them free from their sins. Which thing the Scripture in every place plainly teaches. OF THE MINISTRY AND THE MINISTERS OF GOD[11]

4:9-12 Loving One Another and Working with Your Hands

THANKS TO THE SPIRIT, PAUL DID NOT NEED TO TEACH LOVE. JOHN CALVIN: Having previously, in lofty terms, commended their love, he now speaks by way of anticipation, saying, you do not need me to write to you. He assigns a reason—because they had been divinely taught—by which he means that love was engraved upon their hearts, so that there was no need of letters written on paper. For he does not mean simply what John says in his first canonical epistle, that the anointing will teach you, but that their hearts were framed for love, so that it appears that the Holy Spirit inwardly dictates efficaciously what is to be done, so that there is no need to give injunctions in writing. He subjoins an argument from the greater to the less; for as their love diffuses itself through the whole of Macedonia, he infers that it is not to be doubted that they love one another. Hence the particle for

means likewise, or nay more, for, as I have already stated, he adds it for the sake of greater intensity. COMMENTARY ON 1 THESSALONIANS 4:9.[12]

A PROPER KIND OF CHRISTIAN LIVING. DAVID DICKSON: There follows three exhortations briefly conjoined in these two verses. (1) That you should not be curious, looking into other people's business, but carry yourselves quietly, and pleasingly. (2) That you should not be idle, but take care about your private matters, and do your business, work with your own hands, as I have commanded you before. (3) Carry yourselves decently toward those, and before those, that are not in the church, and in all these duties strive among yourselves as it were for matter of honor; for this end especially besides others, that you may have no need to beg anything from the household of faith, or of those that are without. THE FIRST EPISTLE OF PAUL TO THE THESSALONIANS.[13]

TWO REASONS TO WORK. JOHN CALVIN: He recommends manual labor on two accounts—that they may have a sufficiency for maintaining life, and that they may conduct themselves honorably even before unbelievers. For nothing is more unseemly than someone who is idle and good for nothing; they profit neither themselves nor others, and seem born only to eat and drink. Further, this labor or system of working extends far, for what he says as to hands is by way of synecdoche; but there can be no doubt that he includes every useful employment of human life. COMMENTARY ON 1 THESSALONIANS 4:12.[14]

---

[11]Bullinger, *Fifty Godly and Learned Sermons*, 871-72*.

[12]CTS 42:276-77* (CO 52:163); citing 1 Jn 2:27.
[13]Dickson, *Exposition*, 150*.
[14]CTS 42:278* (CO 52:164).

4:13-18 THE COMING OF THE LORD

¹³*But we do not want you to be uninformed, brothers, about those who are asleep, that you may not grieve as others do who have no hope. ¹⁴For since we believe that Jesus died and rose again, even so, through Jesus, God will bring with him those who have fallen asleep. ¹⁵For this we declare to you by a word from the Lord,ᵃ that we who are alive, who are left until the coming of the Lord, will not precede those who have fallen* asleep. ¹⁶*For the Lord himself will descend from heaven with a cry of command, with the voice of an archangel, and with the sound of the trumpet of God. And the dead in Christ will rise first. ¹⁷Then we who are alive, who are left, will be caught up together with them in the clouds to meet the Lord in the air, and so we will always be with the Lord. ¹⁸Therefore encourage one another with these words.*

a Or *by the word of the Lord*

OVERVIEW: As they interact with this passage, these early modern interpreters discuss at length the relationship between nature and grace in the resurrection. Throughout their expositions, the commentators examine extensively the meaning of Paul's reference to "sleep." Moreover, they provide pastoral instructions on mourning, highlighting the differences between the sorrow of believers, which is accompanied by the hope of the resurrection, and that of unbelievers, which is attended by dread of the final judgment. In this regard, the commentators utilize the hope of the resurrection as incentive for believers to persevere in their faith. Very significantly, these authors expound at length on the nature of the resurrection and the manner in which deceased and living believers will be transformed by Christ's own words at his second coming. Notably, they emphasize the Christian's union with Christ by faith even in death while awaiting the resurrection. Finally, the commentators discuss the function and mission of angels.

4:13 Those Who Are Asleep

THE FAITHFUL WHO HAVE DIED. ROBERT ROLLOCK: At this point there is instituted a digression from the doctrine of sanctification to the doctrine concerning the state of the faithful who have died. Either the Thessalonians were ignorant, or certainly they had not examined it deeply enough, nor had they thought enough about these things. With their immoderate suffering and grief they have over death,† he alleges that they are ignorant of the state of the dead, as though there should be no more of them, and they perished like beasts. First is a proposition, in which the apostle says that he himself is unwilling that they be ignorant of the state and condition of those who are finished with this life. Finally it is added that they do not grieve as the Gentiles who do not have the hope of life and of the future resurrection; that is, they do not grieve immoderately and desperately, and cry desperately [at the] death of their own. Indeed, it is not the case that they are entirely forbidden to grieve, nor is it required that they set aside completely the condition of suffering, which is by nature engrafted into us, and, just as all other affections of our heart, is capable of sanctification. Having observed this proposition, by ignorance of the truth you might often create trouble and suffering, and without cause. Wherefore, that we might be immune from unnecessary pain, and from the empty annoyance of the heart, we ought to seek to be freed from ignorance, so we might know from the light of the Word of God all those things that pertain either to life or to death. The apostle commands that we always rejoice. Not however by another route do we rightly follow it, as if we might pay attention so that the truth of whatever things God revealed in his own Word he might make known to us. For in the Word and revelation of God, this matter is of continual rejoicing. Next, learn to what end and in what order knowledge dispels ignorance, and at the same time begets joy. Knowledge of the state of the dead brings about hope of life and of the future resurrection. Hope is the cause of joy, indeed of boasting. Let us glory in the hope of the glory of God. Indeed let us glory in afflictions. Commentary on First Thessalonians.[1]

Nature and Grace and Resurrection.

Matthew Poole: Grace does not destroy nature, but regulates it; nor does it destroy reason, but rectifies it; nor does it take away the affections, but moderates them. It does not make us Stoics. Affections are good when set upon right objects, and kept within due bounds; and this Christianity does teach, and grace does effect. And to mourn for the dead, especially the dead in the Lord, is a duty that both nature and grace teach, and God requires; and the contrary is reproved by God himself, and to die unlamented is reckoned as a curse. It is only then immoderate sorrow the apostle here means. And to prevent it, or remove it, gives many instructions and arguments. And he supposes their ignorance might be a great occasion of it, and so instructs them about the doctrine of the resurrection, and Christ's personal coming again, which by the light of nature Gentiles knew nothing of, or were very uncertain in. And the apostle, because of his short stay among them, had not had opportunity to instruct them about these things, and therefore does it here distinctly and fully, as he does for the Corinthians, hearing there were some among them, even of the church itself, who said there was no resurrection. It is such a mystery to reason that it is hard to believe it; and the most learned of the heathen doubted it, and some exploded and scoffed at it, as we find, even

such as that held the immortality of the soul. Annotations upon the Holy Bible.[2]

Death Referred to as Sleeping. Robert

Rollock: In this idea of falling asleep the established doctrine concerning the state of the dead comes to a head. It is because with this life finished, it is not so much that they died, as they are sleeping. Indeed, death signifies particularly the destruction of the created thing. And truly the bodies of the dead as long as they lie in the tomb do not undergo destruction. Certainly they are dissolved into dust, but this dissolution is not perdition of the substance of the body, but rather its certain purgation of the corruption and mortality which is in the substance, perdition. However, in the tomb the body itself is not absorbed, but certainly the mortality of the body is absorbed, so that mortality might be absorbed by life. For this reason bodies are said correctly to sleep in the tomb rather than to die. As indeed after sleep is waking, so after this death and burial is making alive and resurrection of bodies. As with sleep the bodies of the sleeping are recreated and made, so also in a certain way in the grave the bodies of the faithful dead are recreated and renovated. But as concerning this word of the sleeping, since with this life ended it is presented in Scripture, I will say a few things. Sometimes you will discover this yourself without any addition. Lazarus our friend sleeps. Concerning Stephen it says that he fell asleep. In the Old Testament generally you read this word with an addition: He slept with his fathers. Commentary on First Thessalonians.[3]

A Proper Kind of Mourning. Martin

Luther: You should also consider how grateful you ought to be, and how much comfort you ought to derive from this, that he (unlike many others) did not perish in a dangerous and pitiful way. Even

---

[1]Rollock, *Ad Thessalonicenses*, 144*; citing Thess 5:16; Rom 5:2.
†I.e., with the deaths of certain of the Thessalonians.

[2]Poole, *Annotations*, 744*; citing Is 57:1; Jer 22:18-19; 1 Cor 15:12; Acts 17:18.
[3]Rollock, *Ad Thessalonicenses*, 146*; citing 2 Cor 5:4; John 11:1; Acts 7:60.

if he had lived a long time, you could not with your efforts have helped him to anything higher than some sort of office or service. Now, however, he is in a place that he would not wish to exchange for all the world, not even for a moment. Grieve in such a way, therefore, as to console yourselves even more. For you have not lost him, but have sent him on ahead of you to be kept in everlasting blessedness. St. Paul says, "You should not mourn over the departed, or those who have fallen asleep, as the heathen do." LETTER 248 TO THOMAS ZINK, APRIL 22, 1532.[4]

BURYING, SUFFERING, AND DEATH. ROBERT ROLLOCK: This word of sleeping in Scripture does not refer to souls of people, which themselves after death live either in a sense of suffering, as with the soul of the wicked (see the parable of rich man and of Lazarus) or in the sense of rejoicing, as the souls of the faithful. "I desire to be unloosed and to be with Christ." "We esteem it better to depart and go to live with the Lord." God is not the God of the dead, but of the living, where concerning the souls of the saints who have died Christ says in Matthew 22:32 that they live with God in heaven. This word of sleeping however is referred to the bodies of people, whether of the faithful or of the wicked. Many, he says, sleeping in the dust of the earth will rise; some certainly to life, others truly to disgrace. It is allowed that this word is said more frequently about the bodies of the faithful, and also to a greater extent more properly. For as people for that reason seize sleep and they sleep, so the more eager and confident ones return to the actions of this life. As the bodies of the faithful are resting in the grave, the eager ones return and are confirmed in a certain way to the actions of this future life. Of the wicked truly the bodies are not the same, where sorrowful ones rise rather than lie down in the grave. But concerning the word thus far from this first head of doctrine, he desires them to understand before God, in order that actually they might have a certain consolation in their own death and

observe this. He actually grants consolation and moderated mourning, so that we know their bodies, which are dear to us, without a certain sense of suffering, will take repose in the ground until the day of the resurrection. Dissolution and resolution of the body in the dust, apart from any sense of suffering, will happen. In fact, I doubt that at a distance, if we have believed that burying is conjoined with suffering, and that thing[†] has carried suffering with us into death and burial. COMMENTARY ON FIRST THESSALONIANS.[5]

COMFORT ROOTED IN HOPE. MARTIN LUTHER: St. Paul exhorts the Thessalonians not to sorrow over the dead as others who have no hope, but to comfort each other with God's Word as having a certain hope of life and of the resurrection of the dead.

It is little wonder if those are sad who have no hope. Nor can they be blamed for it. Since they are beyond the pale of faith in Christ, they must either cherish this temporal life as the only thing worthwhile and hate to lose it, or they must expect that after this life they will receive eternal death and the wrath of God in hell and must fear to go there.

But we Christians, who have been redeemed from all this by the dear blood of the Son of God, should by faith train and accustom ourselves to despise death and to regard it as a deep, strong, and sweet sleep, to regard the coffin as nothing but paradise and the bosom of our Lord Jesus Christ, and the grave as nothing but a soft couch or sofa, which it really is in the sight of God; for he says, "Our friend Lazarus has fallen asleep," and, "The girl is not dead but sleeping." PREFACE TO THE BURIAL HYMNS TO THE CHRISTIAN READER.[6]

4:14 Jesus Brings the Dead with Him

THE HOPE OF THE RESURRECTION. ROBERT ROLLOCK: This is the second head of the doctrine

---

[4]LW 50:52.

[5]Rollock, *Ad Thessalonicenses*, 147-48*; citing Lk 16:19-31; Phil 1:23; 2 Cor 5:8; Dan 12:2. [†]"That thing" appears to be here simply "dying."
[6]LW 53:325; citing Jn 11:1; Mt 9:24.

of the apostle concerning the state of faithful dead. However, it pertains to the condition following burial, which is that they rise in their own time. And this head of doctrine also allows suffering to be mitigated even more, for in that there is a certain consolation, because we know that bodies rest and sleep without any sense of suffering. Even more it conveys consolation, because we know that those very bodies will finally rise up and once more to conquer with an ineffable sense of rejoicing. Indeed in the resurrection all senses will be satisfied with God, that is, from that very source of all rejoicing and happiness. For God will be all in all. To the resurrection of bodies he spreads out two fundamental things. First, faith in Christ. Having died first, and having died for us, then having been made alive, and having been made alive for us, his death indeed being on account of our sin, he arose on account of our justification. The other fundamental thing is perseverance in that faith all the way to the last breath, namely, to fall asleep in Christ. Commentary on First Thessalonians.[7]

Paul's Purpose Is to Comfort Believers.
The English Annotations: He will raise their bodies and join their souls to them and so bring them to heaven, or, to see the face of God. And it is to be observed that the apostle here speaking of the resurrection makes no mention at all of the resurrection to condemnation, but only the resurrection of the elect to life and glory. The reason for this is twofold. First, because his purpose in this part of the epistle is to comfort the Thessalonians, whereas the doctrine of the raising of the wicked to their condemnation and everlasting punishment is a doctrine of terror. Second, because he directs his speech here to those who lived and died in the faith of Christ, who as members of Christ shall be raised with him to everlasting glory and will never experientially know any condemnation. Annotations on 1 Thessalonians 4:14.[8]

The Necessity of Perseverance. Robert Rollock: Note how necessary perseverance is in faith, so that we might rise to eternal life, and that it is required so that in that very moment of death we might adhere to Christ, and we might apprehend him alone by faith. For how very many temptations offer themselves in death that would tear us apart from Christ, if that could happen. Wherefore in death we are greatly to be armed with faith. I concede truly, we do not stand through our faith—that is, through our apprehension, by which we comprehend Christ, so that we serve either in life or in death—but our salvation is to be ascribed properly to the apprehension of Christ himself, by which he himself apprehends us. It follows, it is said, proving whether by what way I might apprehend, for the sake of which thing we have been apprehended by Christ Jesus. However, being apprehended by Christ, it is impossible that from him we might be separated. "Who will separate us from the love of Christ?" "No one takes my sheep from the hand of the Father." Commentary on First Thessalonians.[9]

Christ's Death and Resurrection an Axiom of Faith. John Calvin: He assumes this axiom of our faith, that Christ was raised up from the dead so that we might be partakers of the same resurrection. From this, he infers that we shall live with him eternally. This doctrine, however, as has been stated in 1 Corinthians 15:13, depends on another principle, that is was not for himself, but for us, that Christ died and rose again. Hence those who have doubts about the resurrection do great injury to Christ. Nay, more, they do in a manner draw him down from heaven. Commentary on 1 Thessalonians 4:14.[10]

The Resurrection of Believers and of the Wicked. Robert Rollock: With more fundamental things he builds up from the resurrection of the dead, which he understands to be truly

---

[7]Rollock, *Ad Thessalonicenses*, 148*; citing 1 Cor 15:28; Rom 4:25.
[8]Downame, ed., *Annotations*, 3K2v*.
[9]Rollock, *Ad Thessalonicenses*, 149*; citing Phil 3:12; Rom 8:35; Jn 10:9.
[10]CTS 42:280* (CO 52:165); citing Rom 10:6.

adduced from this place. For the resurrection of the bodies of the faithful, which is different from the leading of them to God himself, is that the blessed union with God? For how long will bodies sleep in the dust, for so long in a certain way they have been separated from God. For they lie down with some ignominy, and they are called up with the full glory of God, although in other respects the grave itself for them might be sanctified through Christ. This word "to be lead" [i.e., speaking of those God "leads"/brings with Jesus] is not read as concerning the bodies of the wicked, although also those too will rise at the coming of Christ. Certainly not in the resurrection are those [i.e., the wicked] to be lead to God or conjoined with him, rather from him to be separated, and pushed away from his face for eternity. COMMENTARY ON FIRST THESSALONIANS.[11]

BELIEVERS REMAIN UNITED TO CHRIST BETWEEN DEATH AND RESURRECTION. JOHN CALVIN: To sleep in Christ is to retain in death the connection we have with Christ. Those that are by faith ingrafted into Christ have death in common with him, that they may ever be partakers of life with him. It is asked, however, whether unbelievers will also rise again, for Paul does not affirm that there will be a resurrection, except in the case of Christ's members. I answer that Paul does not here touch on anything but what suited his present design. He did not design to terrify the wicked, but to correct the immoderate grief of the pious and cure it, as he does, by the medicine of consolation. COMMENTARY ON 1 THESSALONIANS 4:14.[12]

RESURRECTION TO BLESSING OR TO JUDGMENT. ROBERT ROLLOCK: Naturally with Christ, in whom, if they were inserted through faith, they fell asleep and therefore with him who is of the first to rise, they will rise. For that cord by which they were tied with him in death will remain in the resurrection. Thus in him they fell asleep; thus with

him they will rise to life. Note, therefore, the body being free from the soul and all its functions is not however separated from Christ, if merely it will sleep with him. By the strength of that faith which was in that death, it also adheres in that very tomb, and finally with the same it will rise, just as a part and member of the same body. It is so much to believe, and in that same death to believe, that still remains a union of the body and the soul! Note the following, resurrection to life is to be by the virtue of Christ, with whom we ourselves are united through faith, that is, it shall be by that reason, by which we are members of his body. The wicked also will rise, but not with Christ, and not in the strength of the head, truly by the power of God the judge, who summons them to that judgment. COMMENTARY ON FIRST THESSALONIANS.[13]

4:15-16 *The Coming of the Lord and the Resurrection of the Dead*

THE PRIORITY OF THOSE WHO HAVE DIED IN CHRIST. ROBERT ROLLOCK: This third head of established doctrine concerns the state of the dead. However, it comprises the order in which the dead, those who are going to meet the Lord, are found after the resurrection.† The knowledge of this thing also pertains to consolation and the reduction of suffering. These words seem to have been exposed through their application. Indeed, it could conceivably be thought that those who are first in death will be the latter in glory, and that the grave will be an impediment, by which those having died will less quickly go in the way of the Lord, and participate in his glory than those who are found alive at the coming of the Lord. The apostle opposes this, and he teaches that we who have fallen asleep shall go before those who in that day will be left alive. Indeed (it is well known from the following things) those who will have died in Christ [are the] first [of] those who are going to rise and be seized in the clouds at the meeting of the Lord. With them, however, in the second place,

---

[11]Rollock, *Ad Thessalonicenses*, 149-50*.
[12]CTS 42:281* (CO 52:165).

[13]Rollock, *Ad Thessalonicenses*, 150*.

shall be others, who at that time will be found alive. Note: appearance is of a certain prerogative, prior ones [i.e., the dead in Christ] themselves shall meet first at the coming of the Lord. Note on the other hand that desire to meet with Christ is required in us, so that likewise we might contend that the prior ones are with others in coming to him, and by his delighting to see them. COMMENTARY ON FIRST THESSALONIANS.[14]

HOPE FOR BOTH THE DEAD AND THE LIVING. MATTHIAS FLACIUS: Having asserted most gloriously the resurrection of the godly, Paul now in his way depicts, as it were, the form: What he does in this verse negatively, or deficiently, he soon does in the following two verses affirmatively, or positively. In truth he adds by the grace of authority that he speaks the Word of God to them, just as the prophets immediately repeated: "Thus says the Lord." Moreover, that preaching observes that they should thus not mourn the dead as though they will be neglected on the last day. On the contrary, he says that they will be glorified first, and made alive like us. Moreover, Paul speaks in this manner about those living in his times as though by chance the [second] advent of Christ is about to come because we ought thus piously to expect the Lord every hour. Yet even this way of saying something should be possible because just as he counts all the dead among those who are to be resurrected, so he places all the living in another category that is truly theirs, which at the time will be adjacent to the time that the dead will be glorified. GLOSS ON 1 THESSALONIANS.[15]

JESUS RAISES THE DEAD THROUGH HIS OWN WORD. ROBERT ROLLOCK: The testimony of the Lord confirms this future prerogative of the dead in the resurrection. How the apostle received this from the Lord, whether by an ordinary or extraor-dinary revelation, is not to be inquired. . . . However, it is probable that the words of the Lord were in this sense, which follows in the succeeding verses, in which we have a description of the very coming of the Lord, and the order by which the dead will rise,[†] and also how they are gathered at his meeting. Only observe this: since it is an admirable thing he narrates, and he overcomes the man, therefore for him he mentions the testimony of the Lord in the middle, by which the incredible thing is naturally believed. These things indeed pertain to another life [i.e., the afterlife], and these things indeed fight at every point with nature and human character so that insofar as he is a man no human words are able to persuade a person, except God himself, who alone is able to go against nature, and to accomplish all things that he himself speaks, in which God is heard, either through himself, or through a human being, to set forth his own voice. COMMENTARY ON FIRST THESSALONIANS.[16]

AN EXTRAORDINARY TEACHING ABOUT THE RETURN OF THE LORD. MATTHEW POOLE: The apostle here sets down particularly the manner of the Lord's coming, the method and order how all the saints shall then meet with him, and with one another, which we find not so distinctly in any other Scripture; and whereby he further develops the argument he is making. That they might not think that what he speaks was either by some tradition from others, or an invention of his own; and this is ground enough for faith, to which our judgment and reason ought to be captivated. That which he says here about the resurrection, Christ's coming, the ministry of angels, the sound of a trumpet, and the voice of Christ at that day we have in the evangelists; but the method and order of all the saints meeting together, and meeting the Lord in the air, we find not in any express words written before. The apostle speaks if here by extraordinary revelation, which is the "word of the

---

[14]Rollock, *Ad Thessalonicenses*, 151-52*; citing Mt 11:12; Rom 16:7.
   [†]That is, Paul is not simply giving us *general* information about the state of the dead, but is giving his readers some information related to *order* or *sequence*. What is happening to whom and when.
[15]Flacius, *Glossa Compendaria*, 1019.

[16]Rollock, *Ad Thessalonicenses*, 152-53*. [†]There is a note in the margin of Rollock's Latin text at this point, where he (or an editor perhaps) writes, "He does not make that saying to the proposition: since he speaks concerning the gracious reign in his life."

Lord," though not then written. And this order is expressed, first, negatively. The saints then living upon the earth shall not be with Christ sooner than those that were fallen asleep, and be caught up into the air, while the others are in the grave; and the apostle speaks as if he should be one of that number; sure he could not think the coming of Christ should be in the age wherein he lived; he speaks otherwise. Or that his life should be prolonged to that day. For the time of his "departure," he says, "was at hand." But he looks upon the whole body of saints together, and himself as one of that number, and so speaks, "We who live and remain." . . . "We shall not all die, but we shall all be changed." Second, affirmatively, "the dead in Christ" shall rise first, that is, before they that are alive shall be caught up into the air. They shall stay until the rest be risen. "We shall not all die, but be changed, and in a moment," which the apostle calls "clothing upon," and which he rather desired than to be unclothed, and then they who are dead in Christ shall rise, and be united, to these in one visible body.† ANNOTATIONS UPON THE HOLY BIBLE.[17]

IN TRUE PREACHING ONE HEARS THE WORD OF THE LORD. MARTIN LUTHER: Here it is unnecessary, even bad, to pray for the forgiveness of sins, as if one had not taught truly, for it is God's word and not my word, and God ought not and cannot forgive it, but only confirm, praise, and crown it, saying, "You have taught truly, for I have spoken through you and the word is mine." Whoever cannot boast like that about this preaching, let him give up preaching , for he truly lies and slanders God. AGAINST HANSWURST.[18]

THE LORD COMES WITH AUTHORITY. DAVID DICKSON: "Christ shall descend from heaven with all his angels . . ." The manner of his coming shall be with much expression of authority and majesty,

for as the chief Judge he shall command by his authority, that every element give up their dead, from whereupon all the dead shall be gathered together to his tribunal, but his command shall be promulgated by some chief angel, the trumpet shall sound, or a voice instead of a trumpet, and the sound shall be heard in all places where the dead are to be raised. . . . The dead in Christ shall arise, before the living shall be changed. THE FIRST EPISTLE OF PAUL TO THE THESSALONIANS.[19]

THE ARCHANGEL WARNS THOSE WHO SEEK HOLINESS. DAVID JORIS: Behold the voice of the archangel, namely, the earthly angel, who will make a command or warning to all who desire to become holy and to remain standing in the face of the Lord. If they will follow and fulfill his voice, then they will be the humble and the sincere of heart. HEAR, HEAR, HEAR, GREAT WONDER, GREAT WONDER, GREAT WONDER.[20]

THE BRIDE WILL BE DRAWN UP INTO THE CLOUDS. BALTHASAR HUBMAIER: This is the very power of the church about which I wrote similarly in my booklets on the sword and ban, namely, that before the incarnation of Christ, God the Father dealt with all matters related to sin, as we find it in Moses and the Prophets. Afterward he transferred the authority to Christ. In the third place, Christ hung these keys at the side of the church, his bride, to teach, rebuke, bind, loose, admit, and exclude according to this word. This power the church on earth now possesses until Christ returns in the clouds. Then the bride will be drawn up into the clouds to meet her bridegroom Christ and will hand over these keys again to him, while he will then judge the living and the dead and after this give all power back to his heavenly Father. For in this way God will become all in all. THE SIXTEENTH ARTICLE, ON CONFESSION.[21]

---

[17]Poole, *Annotations*, 745*; citing 2 Thess 2:2; 2 Tim 4:6; 1 Cor 15:51; 2 Cor 5:2. †Even though it is 1 Thess 4:17 that speaks of believers being "caught up together . . . in the clouds . . . in the air," Poole speaks to this language here in his comments on 4:15. [18]LW 41:216.

[19]Dickson, *Thessalonians*, 150.*
[20]CRR 7:140.
[21]CRR 5:546*; Jn 20:23; 1 Cor 15:22-58.

4:17-18 *Being Caught Up with the Lord*

Believers to Ascend. Matthew Poole:
Christ will have a church to the end of the world,
and some will be found alive at his coming, and will
be "caught up," or snatched up, to denote its
suddenness. It may be in the arms of angels, or by
some immediate attractive power of Christ; and it
will be together with those who are now raised
from the dead. They shall all ascend in one great
body, and it will be together with those who are
now raised from the dead; they shall all ascend in
one great body, and it will be "in the clouds." As
Christ himself ascended in a cloud, and so will he
return again, making the clouds his chariots. "To
meet the Lord in the air." First, to congratulate his
coming, when others shall flee and tremble. Second,
to honor him; as the angels will also attend him for
that end. Third, to receive their final discharge.
Fourth, to be visibly joined to their head. Fifth, to
be assistants with him in judging of the world, and
to reign with him upon earth. And whether the last
judgment will be upon the earth, or in the air, I
shall not determine. But after this Christ and his
saints shall never part. Their first meeting shall be
in the air, and their continuance will be with him
while he is in this lower world, and after that they
shall ascend with him into heaven, and so "be
forever with him." Augustine imagined that the
saints that are found alive shall in their rapture die,
and then immediately revive, "because it is appointed to all men once to die"; but the apostle says
expressly, "We shall not all die, but we shall all be
changed." Annotations upon the Holy Bible.[22]

To Be Caught Up with the Lord. Heinrich
Bullinger: We confess therefore in this article
that Jesus Christ being taken up into heaven is
Lord of all things, the King and Bishop, the
Deliverer and Savior of all the faithful in the whole
world. We confess that in Christ and for Christ we
believe in the life everlasting, which we shall have
in this body at the end of the world, and in soul so
soon as we are once departed out of this world.

But now by the way we must weigh the very
words of this article. "He ascended," we say. Who
ascended, I pray you? He who was born of the
Virgin Mary, who was crucified, dead, and buried,
who rose again from the dead. He (I say) ascended
truly both in body and soul. But to where did he
ascend? Into heaven. Heaven in the Scriptures is
not taken always in one signification.

First it is put for the firmament, and that large
compass that is over our heads, wherein the birds
fly to and fro, and in which the stars are placed,
that are called the furniture and host of heaven. For
David says, "God is clothed with light as with a
garment, he spreads forth the heaven as it were a
curtain." He says also, "I shall see your heavens, the
work of your fingers, and the moon and stars,
which you have laid." And again, "Who covers
heaven with clouds, and prepares rain for the earth."
And again, "The heavens declare the glory of God,
and the firmament shows forth the work of his
hands." Then also, heaven is taken for the throne
and habitation of God. And last, for the place, seat,
and receptacle of those who are saved, where God
gives himself to be seen and enjoyed by those who
are his. For David witnessing again, says, "The Lord
has prepared his seat in heaven." Whereupon the
Lord in the Gospel says, "Swear not by heaven, for
it is God's seat." And the apostle Paul says, "We
know if our earthly mansion of this tabernacle be
destroyed, that we have a dwelling place forever in
heaven, built by God, not made by hands."

And therefore in this signification heaven is
called the kingdom of God, the kingdom of the
Father, joy, happiness, and felicity, eternal life, peace,
and quietude.

God indeed is not shut up in any place. For he
says, "Heaven is my seat, and the earth, the
footstool of my feet." Yet because the glory of God
does most of all shine in the heavens, and because
that in heaven he gives himself to be seen and
enjoyed by those who are his, according to the
saying, "We shall see him even as he is." And again,
"No one shall see me," says the Lord, "and live."
Therefore God is said to dwell in heaven.

---

[22]Poole, *Annotations*, 745-46*; Mt 24:30; Ps 104:3; Hebrews 9:27;
    1 Cor 15:52.

Moreover, Christ our Lord touching his divinity is not shut up in any place, but according to his humanity once taken, which he drew up into heaven, he is in the very local place of heaven, neither is he in the meantime here in the earth and everywhere bodily, but being severed from us in body remains in heaven. For he ascended, leaving that which is below both go to that above.

Christ therefore leaving the earth has placed a seat for his body above all heavens. Not that he is carried up beyond all heavens, but because ascending up above all the circles into the utmost and highest heaven, he is taken (I say) into the place appointed for those who are saved. For Paul the apostle speaking plainly enough to be understood, says, "Our conversation is in heaven, from whence we look for the Savior to come." OF THE LATTER ARTICLES OF THE CHRISTIAN FAITH.[23]

THOSE GRANTED ETERNAL LIFE ARE ETERNAL. JOHN CALVIN: To those who have been once gathered to Christ he promises eternal life with him, by which statements the reveries of Origen and of the chiliasts are abundantly refuted. For the life of believers, when they have once been gathered into one kingdom, will have no end any

more than Christ's. Now, to assign to Christ a thousand years, so that he would afterward cease to reign, were too horrible to be made mention of. Those, however, fall into this absurdity who limit the life of believers to a thousand years, for they must live with Christ as long as Christ himself will exist. We must observe also what he says—"we shall be," for he means that we profitably entertain a hope of eternal life, only when we hope that it has been expressly appointed for us. COMMENTARY ON I THESSALONIANS 4:17.[24]

ON THE REALITY AND PURPOSE OF ARCH-ANGELS. HEINRICH BULLINGER: He shows that we must not busily and curiously search after these things. Whose counsel we willingly obey, perceiving that the Scriptures, which minister to us all things necessary and healthful, has set down nothing concerning them. Yet this we cannot deny, that those names (or if you will so call them, orders of angels) are expressed in the holy Scriptures; whereupon for our weakness, it is acceptable after a sort to expound them as we may. These blessed spirits of heaven seem generally and simply to be called angels, because they are the messengers and ambassadors of the Most High God, who it appears are called archangels, when they are sent in message in God's greatest matters, to show or do things altogether hard and heavenly. OF GOOD AND EVIL SPIRITS.[25]

---

[23]Bullinger, *Fifty Godly and Learned Sermons*, 70-71*; Ps 104:2; 8:3; 147:8; Ps 19:1; 103:19; Mt 5:34; 2 Cor 5:1; Is 66:1; I Jn 3:2; Ex 33:20; Phil 3:20. In this sermon, Bullinger is commenting on a portion of the Apostles' Creed: "The third day he rose again from the dead, he ascended into heaven." In this context, when he references I Thess 4:17, he focuses on the nature of heaven.

[24]CTS 42:284* (CO 52:167).
[25]Bullinger, *Fifty Godly and Learned Sermons*, 737-38.

5:1-11 THE DAY OF THE LORD

Now concerning the times and the seasons, brothers,ᵃ
you have no need to have anything written to you.
²For you yourselves are fully aware that the day of the
Lord will come like a thief in the night. ³While people
are saying, "There is peace and security," then sudden
destruction will come upon them as labor pains come
upon a pregnant woman, and they will not escape.
⁴But you are not in darkness, brothers, for that day to
surprise you like a thief. ⁵For you are all childrenᵇ of
light, children of the day. We are not of the night or of
the darkness. ⁶So then let us not sleep, as others do,
but let us keep awake and be sober. ⁷For those who
sleep, sleep at night, and those who get drunk, are
drunk at night. ⁸But since we belong to the day, let us
be sober, having put on the breastplate of faith and
love, and for a helmet the hope of salvation. ⁹For God
has not destined us for wrath, but to obtain salvation
through our Lord Jesus Christ, ¹⁰who died for us so
that whether we are awake or asleep we might live
with him. ¹¹Therefore encourage one another and
build one another up, just as you are doing.

a Or *brothers and sisters*; also verses 4, 12, 14, 25, 26, 27   b Or *sons*; twice in this verse

OVERVIEW: Throughout their discussions of this passage, these early modern commentators stress the urgency for Christians to live in light of the coming Day of the Lord. In highlighting the coming judgment, they examine extensively Paul's simile of a "thief in the night" to describe the unexpected nature of its arrival. Though Christians are freely justified by grace through faith, and thus spared God's wrath that awaits the ungodly, they nevertheless must vigilantly walk according to the knowledge of God that they have through the preached Word. Such vigilance manifests itself in a life of sobriety. In short, the death of Christ provides incentive for the living of a holy life in response to a God who has not "destined us for wrath."

5:1-3 Like a Thief in the Night

WHAT A THIEF ACTUALLY DOES. BENEDICT ARETIUS: The logic is of the proposition, "you yourselves learned the truth of the thing." Therefore, a long oration or teaching is not necessary. He attributes a full knowledge of the truth, therefore that by praising it might excite. *Akribōs* ["carefully" or "exactly"] is said correctly. Thus in Ephesians 5, see

that *akribōs* you walk, that is, circumspectly and faithfully. What, however, do they know? Thus: that the Day of the Lord will come as a thief in the night. See Matthew 24:43; Luke 12:13-48; 2 Peter 3:10, in which passages is a similar thing. However, that similitude signifies [Christ's] sudden coming, accompanied by the damnation of the world. For a thief comes not at all expected, and comes with damage to the house, and ambushes the most precious things. Thus Christ will come to the world not at all expectantly, and he will come with great damage for the wicked. He threatens in this way in Revelation 3 and Revelation 16. THE FIRST EPISTLE TO THE THESSALONIANS.[1]

BE PREPARED FOR THE COMING OF THE LORD. WILLIAM TYNDALE: Let your care be to prepare yourself with all your strength to walk the way he will have you and to believe that he will go with you and assist you and strengthen you against all tyrants and deliver you out of all tribulation. But what way or by what means he will do it, that leave to him and to his godly pleasure and wisdom and cast that care upon him. And though it seem ever so unlikely or ever so impossible to natural reason, yet believe steadfastly

---

[1]Aretius, *Thessalonicenses*, 239.

that he will do it. And then shall he according to his old use change the course of the world, even in the twinkling of an eye, and come suddenly upon our mighty ones as a thief in the night, and compass them in their wiles and worldly wisdom: when they cry peace and all is safe, then shall their sorrows begin, as the pangs of a woman that travails with child. And then he shall destroy them, and deliver you to the glorious praise of his mercy and truth. Amen. The Obedience of a Christian Man.[2]

The Sudden Coming of the Lord. Benedict Aretius: There is confirmation of the logic with which he abundantly explicates the sudden coming. "They proclaim peace, peace." . . . They eat and drink, and so on. That is, the sum of things will be secure. Therefore, he will come suddenly . . . as a trap. A new likeness is used: as pain crushes a pregnant woman. Pain is here expressed, as in Luke 23: "They will say to the mountains, fall upon us." Ōdin is the pain of pregnancy, which Christ uses as a similitude in Matthew 24 and Mark 13. *Panta tauta archēōdinōn,*[†] are the beginnings of pains. Likewise, *archaiōdinōn tauta.*[‡] Thence the word is *ōdinō,* as it is placed in Galatians 4. My sons again *ōdinō,*[††] "I brought forth in pain." And thence, composed as *synōdinō.* The whole creation is *synōdinei*[†††] with us, "groans as one." The First Epistle to the Thessalonians.[3]

5:4-5 Children of Light

Those Who Walk in the Knowledge of God Are Not Surprised. Niels Hemmingsen: He consoles the faithful who in the day, that is, in the clear sight of God live piously by faith. By

"darkness" is signified the ignorance of God, carelessness. Thus by "light of God" he understands the knowledge and enjoyment of God. Paul does not here say that the coming Day of the Lord is known to the faithful, but he admonishes them to be truly watching, so that those in the clear day watching might in true fear be expecting it. For those watching and living in the light, if a certain thief comes to attack, stumbles accidentally and is met, nothing will be able to devastate that which is theirs. But if he catches those sleeping in the darkness, having taken the goods, he will withdraw right away. Commentary on First Thessalonians.[4]

The Day Is Close. Balthasar Hubmaier: Although Christ gave us many signs whereby we can tell how near at hand the day of his coming is, nevertheless no one but God knows the exact day. . . . For you yourselves know well that the Day of the Lord will come like a thief in the night. When people say, "There is peace and security," then sudden destruction will come as travail comes upon a woman with child, and there will be no escape. But you are not in darkness, brethren, that that day should surprise you like a thief. Out of these words I have always and everywhere formulated the article as is stated above, but said that the Day of the Lord is closer than we know; therefore we should persist in daily contemplation, righteousness, and the fear of God. Apologia.[5]

The Need to Be Vigilant. Niels Hemmingsen: He explains the general duties of the faithful. And first in a kind of beautiful likeness. The sense of this is as follows. To the extent that the days for working and watching, not for sleep nor laziness were fixed, so having been called to the light of the gospel through the preaching of the word during the reign of darkness, now indeed they ought in the bright day to watch and to offer their own great worthy works to which they were called. And he calls all things to vigilance and sobriety. It is a

[2]Tyndale, *The Obedience of a Christian Man,* 13.
[3]Aretius, *Thessalonicenses,* 239-40; citing Lk 17:27; 2:35; 23:30; Gal 4:9 Rom 8:22. [†]From Mt 24:8. *Panta tauta archēōdinōn* translates "all these [are] the beginning birth pains." [‡]From Mk 13:8. Aretius here appears to follow the Byzantine text (*archaiōdinōn* rather than *archēōdinōn*). *Archaiōdinōn tauta* translates "these [are] the beginning birth pains." [††]This is the Greek verb *ōdinō,* from Gal 4:9. The term means "suffer birth pains, be in travail" (so Friberg's lexicon). [†††]From Rom 8:22. The Greek verb *synōdinō* translates as "suffering birth pangs in common with others" (so Friberg's lexicon).
[4]Hemmingsen, *Ad Thessalonicenses,* 545*.
[5]CRR 5:541-42*; citing Mt 24; Lk 21; Mk 13.

certain vigilance, provided that having thrown off a carnal carelessness, we consider the Lord with certain hope. To this is opposed sleeping, which is a passive neglect of one's own salvation. Sobriety truly is that by which this is avoided, for we do not walk with the drunken allurements of this world, nor do we sleepwalk in carelessness, but preferably we are eager to do our duty. So then this distinction between the faithful and the unfaithful is observed. There are those who walk near the light of the gospel; and there are those enveloped in the toils of the world, the care of their own salvation thrown away. COMMENTARY ON FIRST THESSALONIANS.[6]

5:6-8 Stay Awake!

ALWAYS BE READY. THE ENGLISH ANNOTATIONS: Returning to exhortation, he warns us who are enlightened with the knowledge of God that it is our duty not to live securely and deliciously, lest we be suddenly taken in a dead sleep in pleasures. On the contrary, we are wisely to have an eye on the Lord, and to take care in our consumption and drunkenness and occupation with the cares of this life, and that day come upon us unawares. ANNOTATIONS ON 1 THESSALONIANS 5:6.[7]

THE WAKEFULNESS OF THE DAY SYMBOLIZES THE GOSPEL. JOHN CALVIN: He adds other metaphors closely allied to the preceding one. For as he lately showed that it was by no means seemly that they should be blind in the midst of light, so he now admonishes that it is dishonorable and disgraceful to sleep or be drunk in the middle of the day. Now, as he gives the name of "day" to the doctrine of the gospel, by which the Christ, the "Sun of righteousness" is manifested to us, so when he speaks of sleep and drunkenness, he does not mean natural sleep, or drunkenness from wine, but stupor of mind, when, forgetting God and ourselves, we regardlessly indulge our vices. "Let us not sleep," says he; that is, let us not, sunk in

indolence, become senseless in the world. "As others," that is, unbelievers, from whom ignorance of God, like a dark night, takes away understanding and reason. "But let us watch," that is, let us look to the Lord with an attentive mind. "And be sober," that is, casting away the cares of the world, which weigh us down by their pressure, and throwing off base lusts, mount to heaven with freedom and alacrity. For this is spiritual sobriety, when we use this world so sparingly and temperately that we are not entangled with its allurements. COMMENTARY ON 1 THESSALONIANS 5:6.[8]

CHRISTIANS SHOULD BE AWAKE AND SOBER. NIELS HEMMINGSEN: The argument is similar. So people sleep at night and watch during the day. They are at night drunk, and sober during the day. Thus it befits us who now have overcome the night of ignorance to strive for vigilance and sobriety. It requires that light of the gospel, not with a mind weighed down with the sleep of ignorance, and with an intemperate heart and with tired drunkenness obscenely we bring ourselves thus into the clear light of the gospel. The exhortation in Ephesians 5 is similar. You ought not to be consorts of them, for you were once of the darkness, but now light in the Lord, so walk as sons of the light. COMMENTARY ON FIRST THESSALONIANS.[9]

BE PREPARED AS IF FOR BATTLE. JOHN CALVIN: He adds this so that he may the more effectually shake us out of our stupidity, for he calls us as it were to arms, that he may show that it is not a time to sleep. It is true that he does not make use of the term "war"; but when he arms us with a "breastplate" and a "helmet," he admonishes us that we must be ready for warfare. Whoever, therefore, is afraid of being surprised by the enemy must keep awake, that they may be constantly on watch. As, therefore, he has exhorted us to vigilance, on the ground that the doctrine of the gospel is like the light of day, so he now stirs us up by another

---

[6]Hemmingsen, *Ad Thessalonicenses*, 545*.
[7]Downame, ed., *Annotations*, 3K3r*.
[8]CTS 42:288* (CO 52:169); citing Mal 4:2.
[9]Hemmingsen, *Ad Thessalonicenses*, 545*.

argument—that we must wage war with our enemy. From this it follows that idleness is too hazardous a thing. For we see that soldiers, though in other situations they may be intemperate, do nevertheless, when the enemy is near, from fear of destruction, refrain from gluttony and all bodily delights, and are diligently on watch so as to be on their guard. As, therefore, Satan is on the alert against us, and tries a thousand schemes, we ought at least to be not less diligent and watchful.

It is, however, in vain that some seek a more refined exposition of the names of the kinds of armor, for Paul speaks here in a different way from what he does in Ephesians 6:14, for there he makes "righteousness" the "breastplate." This, therefore, will suffice for understanding his meaning, that he designs to teach, that the life of Christians is like a perpetual warfare, inasmuch as Satan does not cease to trouble and molest them. He would have us, therefore, be diligently prepared and on the alert for resistance: further, he admonishes us that we have need of arms, because unless we be well armed we cannot withstand so powerful an enemy. He does not, however, enumerate "all the parts of armor," but simply makes mention of two, the "breastplate" and the "helmet." In the meantime, he omits nothing of what belongs to spiritual armor, for the person who is provided with "faith," "love," and "hope" will be found in no department unarmed. COMMENTARY ON 1 THESSALONIANS 5:8.[10]

5:9-11 Destined for Salvation, Not Wrath

FOOLISH TO OPPOSE GOD'S OFFER OF SALVATION. WOLFGANG MUSCULUS: He returns to this other reason, on account of that vigilance and sobriety in faith, with desire, and with the hope of salvation we ought to watch over. He takes this up with the counsel and proposition of the will of God toward us, by which he called us to himself through his own gospel, and he constituted us sons of the kingdom. We ought however (he says) to apply ourselves, having been positioned by the

grace of God, by which he called us out of darkness, and constituted us sons of the light. That is not, however, so that we might stir up his own wrath and die, but so that remaining in grace, we might grasp salvation. To this manner of God we will oppose, if instead of salvation we deserve wrath and perdition. We will fight against this statement of God if we acquire wrath and damnation instead of salvation because we cause it if, since we are are children of darkness, we are zealous for the works of darkness. What however he has expressed is enough, how great this perversity is, if God appointing us to salvation, we then spurn his plan and prefer to perish for eternity, through wrath in the reign of Satan, than to be saved through his own reign through grace. COMMENTARY ON FIRST THESSALONIANS.[11]

GOD APPOINTS US FOR SALVATION. WOLFGANG MUSCULUS: In Greek it is, *etheto*,[†] that is, *posuit*. The place here ought diligently to be noted. It is admonished that we Christians have been placed by God, and not to perdition, but to salvation. In what way has God placed us, and in what has he placed us, and to what? He placed us by choosing, by predestining, by calling, by drawing, by regenerating, and by justifying. Not ourselves, to the extent that neither were we born, nor are we placed by ourselves, but we receive both from God. However, he appointed us not to fear anything, but as if members in the body of Christ. Twigs and branches on a tree, and members in a body, which he desires with time, number and way to appoint and arrange. It is the same in the body of Christ, clearly the church—he constitutes and arranges Christians. Third, he appoints us not to perdition but to salvation. Otherwise he would appoint us to the reign of Satan, rather than into the body and reign of Christ, in which the end is not to perdition, but to salvation and eternal life. We should reflect upon these things who are Christians. We should certainly relinquish contentions, and curiosity of them, we who contend with many

---

[10]CTS 42:288-89* (CO 52:169-70).

[11]Musculus, *Thessalonicenses*, 270-71.

things (that is, somethings and not all things). He appointed such great things, and not divisive things. With such debates the faith of ignorant people is not edified, but is destroyed. Commentary on First Thessalonians.[12]

Christ's Death Drives Pious Living. Matthias Flacius: Paul shows the reason for the purchase of salvation for us through Christ. Truly he says that he, by his death and obedience, satisfied for us debts for obedience and death, or eternal punishment so that with him we may be eternally blessed. Christ's death here comprehends simultaneously the acquisition of all benefits themselves for us. This is not received in order to be awake and sleep, at once to live either piously or impiously, but in order to live for this common life rather than death. Gloss on 1 Thessalonians.[13]

The Medicine of the Lord Brings Healing. Wolfgang Musculus: It is in Greek, not however that God appointed us *eis orgēn* [i.e., "positioned, set, placed"], that is, for wrath, anyone to be acquired with a word, since the interpreter appointed his own, he supposes to philosophize. However, he appointed wrath for vengeance and perdition. By this small thing it is admonished, although God did not appoint us for wrath, nevertheless it is to be feared by us, lest with the impious sons of darkness we are intoxicated and we sleep in sins, in the same way if also in the nights of darkness we are sons and we incur the wrath of God instead of grace, and perdition instead of salvation. Just as, however, where delight is changed into a deserved hatred, the more seriously hate is rendered, the greater the delight was. Thus also the change of grace was compared, by which into deserved wrath for our vice it [i.e., grace] is changed. He returns a mighty wrath upon that one for contempt of the grace of God. Wherefore it is not that you say to a brother: There is no danger, no

matter how I live. God appoints me not to wrath, but to attainment of salvation. It is necessary to be firm on this: that one is appointed by God. Wherefore, I am not able to incur the wrath of God. It is necessary so that I might be saved. If you are not appointed by God for wrath, but to salvation, you recognize rather the grace and will of God, and you say from the spirit: God forbid that I sin in the grace and will of God, and that I stir up the wrath of that one to me, and I die. Why not rather I will fit myself for the grace and will of that one, who does not wish that I might die, but that I might be saved. In this he appointed my end, and he desires that I be a Christian. Therefore, I conduct myself, as is fitting to a person, not a pagan person, but a Christian person. If a sick man says, "He [i.e., God] does not deal with me in terms of how I conduct myself. I eat, I drink, I do what pleases me. Indeed he appointed me for health, not for death, but in wellness and life, and therefore I will be cured and I will live." Whether or not words of this sort are either of a demented person or of a worthless person, such a person is worthy of destruction, wouldn't you say? He [i.e., God] obtains certainly medicine for the sick person, not for death, but for wellness and life, and he gives to that one medicine, not for death, but for life. Truly next he prescribes still to that one nevertheless to be made as living and he requires as is fitting to one's own prescription. Such we think to be our condition. God appointed us not for wrath, but for salvation. We ought to admire greatly all his benevolence with a grateful spirit. Then he gave to us not only a word of grace but also precepts of life. We cherish [these precepts] by believing, and truly obeying. If we were to do this, we would avoid being known to be guilty. But if we do any less, having departed from grace, we incur the wrath of that one. Commentary on First Thessalonians.[14]

This Sleep Is Not Ordinary Sleep. John Calvin: From the design of Christ's death he confirms what he has said, for if he died with this

---

[12]Musculus, *Thessalonicenses*, 271. †This is a form of the Greek word *tithēmi*, meaning "to put, to place, to lay."
[13]Flacius, *Glossa Compendaria*, 1022.

[14]Musculus, *Thessalonicenses*, 271*.

view—that he might make us partakers of his life, there is no reason why we should be in doubt as to our salvation. It is doubtful, however, what he means now by sleeping and waking, for it might seem as if he meant life and death, and this meaning would be more complete. At the same time, we might not unsuitably interpret it as meaning ordinary sleep. The sum is this—that Christ died with this view, that he might bestow upon us his life, which is perpetual and has no end. It is not to be wondered, however, that he affirms that we now live with Christ, inasmuch as we have, by entering through faith into the kingdom of Christ, passed from death into life. Christ himself, into whose body we are ingrafted, quickens us by his power, and the Spirit that dwells in us is life, because of justification. COMMENTARY ON 1 THESSALONIANS 5:10.[15]

CHRIST DID NOT SIMPLY DIE, HE DIED FOR US. WOLFGANG MUSCULUS: He did not simply say "who died," but, "who died for us." The attainment of salvation is not simply in the fact that Christ died, the just and innocent Son of God, by whose name he endured a great condemnation in his death, and acquired salvation for this world. But in that he died *for us*. Hitherto, because the death of that one, redemption is for the world. We ourselves were on account of sin guilty of death, and sons of wrath. Therefore he endured death for us, by which death we were preserved, liberated from death. Likewise, if anyone is liberated from debt, he frees the debt credited to that person. COMMENTARY ON FIRST THESSALONIANS.[16]

---

[15]CTS 42:290* (CO 52:170-71); citing Jn 5:24.

[16]Musculus, *Thessalonicenses*, 272*.

5:12-28 FINAL INSTRUCTIONS AND BENEDICTION

[12]*We ask you, brothers, to respect those who labor among you and are over you in the Lord and admonish you,* [13]*and to esteem them very highly in love because of their work. Be at peace among yourselves.* [14]*And we urge you, brothers, admonish the idle,[a] encourage the fainthearted, help the weak, be patient with them all.* [15]*See that no one repays anyone evil for evil, but always seek to do good to one another and to everyone.* [16]*Rejoice always,* [17]*pray without ceasing,* [18]*give thanks in all circumstances; for this is the will of God in Christ Jesus for you.* [19]*Do not quench the Spirit.* [20]*Do not despise prophecies,* [21]*but test everything; hold fast what is good.* [22]*Abstain from every form of evil.*

[23]*Now may the God of peace himself sanctify you completely, and may your whole spirit and soul and body be kept blameless at the coming of our Lord Jesus Christ.* [24]*He who calls you is faithful; he will surely do it.*

[25]*Brothers, pray for us.*

[26]*Greet all the brothers with a holy kiss.*

[27]*I put you under oath before the Lord to have this letter read to all the brothers.*

[28]*The grace of our Lord Jesus Christ be with you.*

a Or *disorderly*, or *undisciplined*

OVERVIEW: As they examine the concluding words of this epistle, these early modern commentators stress the importance of supporting a learned ministry. Moreover they urge their readers to compensate ministers adequately so as to sustain their labors in the Word. The authors also explore the manner in which churches maintain doctrinal and moral purity. Most noteworthy in this regard are the comments by some of the radical expositors related to separation from the world. On this same subject, other commentators assign authority to the church to maintain theological integrity by means of the illumination of the Spirit through the Word. Among the people of God, preserving truth and life entails willingly hearing and receiving the preaching of the Word. Finally, the authors consider various aspects of sanctification and the efficacy of prayer.

5:12-13 *Respecting Those in Pastoral Ministry*

PROVIDING FOR BOTH MINISTERS AND THEO-LOGICAL STUDENTS. HEINRICH BULLINGER: Let enough of the church goods as is sufficient be given to the ministers and teachers, so far as honest necessity requires. Thus have we spoken much about the proportion that is due to pastors.

In times past, the second part of ecclesiastical goods was allotted to the clerics. And clerics are the harvest of pastors, studious of divinity, and wholly disposed to the holy ministry. And seeing that these have dedicated themselves and all that they have wholly to the church and the ministry thereof, it is most fit that they should be nourished and maintained by the costs of the church. But it is convenient they be nourished meanly, as they ought to be an example of mean and thrifty living to others.

To be brought up delicately does not agree with the ministries of the church. Therefore Amos found fault that the Nazirites drank wine, for that he meant that drunkards did not maintain the church, but utterly destroy it. Of this we spoke in another place. Moreover, it is fit that due portions be paid to priests, schoolmasters, scholars, and to all other ecclesiastical persons whatsoever. OF THE INSTITUTIONS OF THE CHURCH.[1]

---

[1]Bullinger, *Fifty Godly and Learned Sermons*, 1123.

MINISTERS MUST BE SUPPORTED. LEUPOLD SCHARNSCHLAGER: There is a shortage of faithful workers who correctly, wisely, and in good conscience faithfully seek the lost and labor for the Lord in his vineyard. Every day this shortage causes much confusion, error, and offense. Thus, when such a faithful worker is found and discovered, there is an urgent need that he be given due respect and obeyed, for he is worthy of a double honor, according to the words of Paul. Share every good thing and all the support possible with him, as he may need in addition to work he is able to do on the side. Our concern is not that we depreciate the messengers and workers of the Lord for whom we pray daily, lest the Lord allows us to be scattered abroad without shepherds. This applies not only for the sake of the ones who have seen the truth, but also for the sake of the weak, milk-drinking vegetarians and for the sake of those who will be gathered to the Lord in the future. CONGREGATIONAL ORDER.[2]

5:14-15 Admonish, Encourage, Help, Be Patient

THE NECESSITY OF EVANGELICAL SEPARATION. DIRK PHILIPS: The fourth ordinance is evangelical separation, without which the congregation of God cannot stand or be maintained.[†] For if the unfruitful branches of the vine are not pruned away they will injure the good and fruitful branches. If offending members are not cut off, the whole body must perish; that is, if open sinners, transgressors, and the disorderly are not excluded, the whole congregation must be defiled, and if false brethren are retained, we become partakers of their sins. Of this we have many examples and evidences in the Scripture. THE CHURCH OF GOD.[3]

KNOWING PEOPLE BY THEIR FRUITS. PILGRAM MARPECK: We have examples of those who have had evil semblances, leaves, or blossoms, and in whom all the good was hidden by the secret counsel of God, whose hand, even today, is not so shortened that it cannot help. Therefore, as already said so often, Christ has commanded us to know them by their fruits, not by the leaves or blossoms that precede the fruit. Those who judge by leaves or blossoms, that is, by the appearances of evil, presume to know God's hidden judgment, just as the Jews did with respect to Christ when He ate with sinners, did not observe food laws, healed the sick on the Sabbath, and much more. From these acts, they judge him to be a Gentile and demon-possessed. JUDGMENT AND DECISION.[4]

THE POWER OF SEPARATION GIVEN BY THE LORD. DIRK PHILIPS: The Lord Jesus Christ gave his congregation the power and established the ordinance that she should separate, avoid, and shun the false brethren, the disorderly and disobedient, contentious and heretical people, yea, all in the congregation who are found wicked, as has already been said; what is done over and above this is not Christian, evangelical, or apostolic. THE CHURCH OF GOD.[5]

5:16-18 Rejoice, Pray, Give Thanks

THERE IS ALWAYS A REASON TO PRAY. JOHN CALVIN: In the first place, he would have us hold God's benefits in such esteem that the recognition of them and meditation upon them shall overcome all sorrow. And, unquestionably, if we consider what Christ has conferred upon us, there will be no bitterness of grief so intense as may not be alleviated and give way to spiritual joy. For if this

---

[2]CRR 12:408*; citing 1 Tim 5:17; Heb 13:7; Lk 10:2.
[3]LCC 25:246; citing Jn 15:6; Mt 5:30; 18:7-9; 1 Cor 5:13; 2 Jn 10-11.
[†]Philips lists seven ordinances of the true church. In addition to the fourth ordinance listed here are the following: first, "that the congregation above all other things must have the pure and unfalsified doctrine of the divine Word"; second, "the proper, scriptural use of the sacraments of Jesus Christ, that is, of

baptism and the Supper"; third, "the foot washing of the saints"; . . . fifth, "the command of love that Christ gave his disciples"; sixth, "the keeping of all his commandments"; seventh, "all Christians must suffer and be persecuted, as Christ has promised them and said thus (Jn 16:33)." See LCC 25:240-53.
[4]CRR 2:347-48.
[5]LCC 25:252; citing Rom 16:17; 1 Cor 5:10; Titus 3:10.

joy does not reign in us, the kingdom of God is at the same time banished from us, or we from it. And very ungrateful is that person to God who does not set so high a value on the righteousness of Christ and the hope of eternal life, as to rejoice in the midst of sorrow. As, however, our minds are easily dispirited, until they give way to impatience, we must observe the remedy that he subjoins immediately afterward. For on being cast down and laid low we are raised up again by prayers, because we lay upon God what burdened us. As, however, there are every day, nay, every moment, many things that may disturb our peace and mar our joy, he for this reason bids us pray without ceasing. Now, as to this constancy in prayer, we have spoken of elsewhere. Thanksgiving, as I have said, is added as a limitation. For many pray in such a manner as at the same time to murmur against God, and fret themselves if he does not immediately gratify their wishes. But, on the contrary, it is befitting that our desires should be restrained in such a manner that, contented with what is given us, we always mingle thanksgiving with our desires. We may lawfully, it is true, ask, nay, sigh and lament, but it must be in such a way that the will of God is more acceptable to us than our own. COMMENTARY ON 1 THESSA-LONIANS 5:16.[6]

The Effectual Prayers of God's People.
HEINRICH BULLINGER: The prayers of the faithful are effectual, staying the wrathful judgments of God, yea, and taking them clean away. For whereas they object again that prayer is a declaration of things that we require of the Lord, and that God foreknows all things, therefore that those things are unprofitably and superfluously declared to him, which he already knows, and so for that cause that prayer is unprofitable; it is confuted of Christ our Lord himself, who when he had plainly said, "Your heavenly father knows what things you have need of before you ask him," but nevertheless adding a form of prayer he teaches us to pray. In another place he commands us and stirs us up to pray often,

"Watch, and pray," says he, "lest you enter into temptation." And Paul says, "Rejoice always, pray continually." In every place there are many precepts of this kind. OF PRAYER.[7]

Rejoice in Lasting Things. THE ENGLISH
ANNOTATIONS: Carnal joys are but like a blaze of a fire nourished with stubble, which soon goes out. They who rejoice in their foods, in their children, in their peace and worldly safety, in their honor and preferments, or the descent of their pedigree, their joy is transitory. Those who rejoice in the Holy Ghost and the comforts of the Spirit, their joy is everlasting. Wherefore though you find many troubles in the world and causes of grief, yet still rejoice in the Lord and comfort yourself with the hope of a better life. Even when you grieve and mourn for your sins, rejoice in this, that you grieve in a godly way, and that the more abundantly you sow in tears, the more plentifully you will reap in joy. ANNOTATIONS ON 1 THESSALONIANS 5:16.[8]

Sanctified by the Blood of Christ.
HEINRICH BULLINGER: Now this purging or purification, which is made by our care and our industry, is called by the name of sanctification, not because it is made by us as of ourselves, but because it is made of those who are sanctified by the blood of Christ, in respect of Christ his blood.

For unless that sanctification, which is the very true and only sanctification indeed, goes before our sanctification (I mean that which we work), it is nothing at all. But if that [i.e., the sanctification from Christ's blood] goes before, then is this ours imputed for sanctification, although in the meanwhile the spots of sin remaining in us defile it, and that we do put no confidence in it. Therefore so often as you shall read in the holy Scriptures that righteousness is attributed to our good works, you shall think straightaway that it is done for no other cause than those which I have hitherto

---

[6]CTS 42:296-97* (CO 52:174-75).

[7]Bullinger, *Fifty Godly and Learned Sermons*, 917; citing Mt 6:8; Mk 14:38.
[8]Downame, ed., *Annotations*, 3K3r*; citing Eccles 7:6; Phil 4:4.

already declared to you. For the apostolical spirit cannot be repugnant or contrary to itself.

This will then be made a great deal more manifest if we call to remembrance and consider that the apostles had to deal with two kinds of people, the one sort affirming that they were sufficiently able of their own strength to satisfy or fulfill the law, and that they could by their deserts and good works merit eternal life, and affirming that the merit of Christ was not sufficient enough to acquire salvation, unless human righteousness were added to it.

Against these Paul disputed very constantly and pithily in all his epistles. For they made Christ and the grace of God of no effect. The other sort were such as abusing the doctrine of grace and faith, wallowing like swine in all filthy sins, because they thought that it was sufficient to salvation if they said that they believed. OF CHRISTIAN LIBERTY, WORKS, AND MERITS.[9]

A CALM MIND IS THE SOURCE OF JOY. JOHN CALVIN: "Rejoice Always." I refer this to moderation of spirit, when the mind keeps itself in calmness under adversity, and does not give indulgence to grief. I accordingly connect together these three things: "rejoice always," to "pray without ceasing," and to "give thanks to God in" all things. For when he recommends constant praying, he points out the way of rejoicing perpetually for by this means we ask from God alleviation in connection with all our distresses. In like manner, in Phil 4:4, having said, "Rejoice in the Lord always; again I say, Rejoice. Let your moderation be known to all. Be not anxious as to anything. The Lord is at hand," he afterwards points out the means of this: "But in every prayer let your requests be made known to God, with giving of thanks." In that passage, as we see, he presents as a source of joy a calm and composed mind, that is not unduly disturbed by injuries or adversities. But lest we should be borne down by grief, sorrow, anxiety, and fear, he bids us repose in the

providence of God. And as doubts frequently obtrude themselves as to whether God cares for us, he also prescribes the remedy—that by prayer we disburden our anxieties, as it were, into his bosom, as David commands us to do in Psalm 37:5, and 55:22; and Peter also, after his example (1 Peter 5:7). As, however, we are unduly precipitate in our desires, he imposes a check upon them—that, while we desire what we are need of, we at the same time do not cease to give thanks.

He observes here, almost the same order, though in fewer words. For, in the first place, he would have us hold God's benefits in such esteem, that the recognition of them and meditation upon them shall overcome all sorrow. And, unquestionably, if we consider what Christ has conferred upon us, there will be no bitterness of grief so intense as may not be alleviated and give way to spiritual joy. COMMENTARY ON 1 THESSALONIANS 5:16.[10]

AT ALL TIMES, WE SHOULD DIRECT OUR EYES TOWARD CHRIST. JOHN CALVIN: God has such a disposition toward us in Christ that even in our afflictions we have large occasion of thanksgiving. For what is fitter or more suitable for pacifying us, than when we learn that God embraces us in Christ so tenderly, that he turns to our advantage and welfare everything that befalls us? Let us, therefore, bear in mind that this is a special remedy for correcting our impatience—to turn away our eyes from beholding present evils that torment us, and to direct our views to a consideration of a different nature—how God stands affected toward us in Christ. COMMENTARY ON 1 THESSALONIANS 5:18.[11]

5:19-22 Test Everything

THE SPIRIT IS LIKE FIRE. THE ENGLISH ANNOTATIONS: Do not stop the motions of the Spirit in yourselves, nor restrain its gifts in others. This speech is metaphorical, taken from the fire of the altar, which was to never go out. The Spirit is

---

[9]Bullinger, *Fifty Godly and Learned Sermons*, 464.

[10]CTS 42:296 (CO 52:174).
[11]CTS 42:297 (CO 52:175).

compared to fire both in the light that it gives to understanding, and the heat and fervor of our affections. When we feel this fire within us, either in out private meditations or at the hearing of the word, we must endeavor to keep it burning, and if it slacks, we must . . . stir it up in us, but such means as God has ordained for this end. ANNOTATIONS ON I THESSALONIANS 5:19.[12]

REJECTING THE PAPISTS AND THE LUTHERANS. MICHAEL SATTLER: Unless both, the papist and Lutheran, yea, also all others, who are of their nature, creatures who proclaim letter for spirit and the command of human beings for the command of God, when Christ speaks clearly to such people, "You brood of vipers, how can you speak good when you are evil." Wherefore he also says, "Beware of the scribes, who walk around in long garments, and receive greetings in the marketplace, and gladly take the highest seats in the synagogues, and eat up the houses of widows. . . ." Therefore Paul also says, "Beware of the dogs. Look out for the evil workers, watch out for the circumcision." . . . But now it is said everywhere (in order not to be persecuted by the false prophets and to avoid the cross) that such a prohibition of love does not forbid the bodily attendance but only the assent and agreement of the heart, as it stands written, "Test everything, and accept that which is good."† ON FALSE PROPHETS AND EVIL OVERSEERS.[13]

SETTING FORTH A WITNESS. PILGRAM MARPECK: According to our duty and covenant in Christ we have felt the need to send forth this witness along with other witnesses included herein, published by others and (according to the words of Paul) tested by us and purged of all the errors that we have in part found among them, for these errors do not agree with our faith, love, and patience in Christ. These other witnesses we have cleansed and corrected, omitting the mistakes and

errors in them, in order that we may give a free testimony only to that which is good and pure without any mixture of error. In this way, truth will not be mixed with its opposite, nor will it be despised through the blasphemers and impure judges of the truth, who habitually spoil the good by mixing it with the evil and cast it aside without distinguishing or protecting the good and the truth. THE ADMONITION OF 1542.[14]

BE CAUTIOUS WITH NEW TEACHINGS. CARITAS PIRCKHEIMER: God's Word shall and must be our judge. . . . This alone must rule our conscience. To it alone we must open our hearts and not plug up our ears. . . . It means nothing when the people say they will interpret the Scriptures however they want to. For this reason they even form parties among themselves. This is what we find now in the case of Karlstadt, Zwingli, and so on. Now it is impossible for simple people to form an opinion about that. Therefore we must wait until the question is decided in a council or by knowledgeable people. For what should the simple people do if such explanations are delayed? How could they protect themselves from false prophets and listen to no other voice but the voice of Christ. Yet St. Paul teaches we should test everything and accept what is right. In this matter Christ says that the Father will reveal the gospel to the simple people. . . . Together we will faithfully seek to give honor solely to the Word of God and not persist in our wicked delusion. In this way we will find the truth. May God help us all. Amen. JOURNAL.[15]

DO NOT IGNORE THE SPIRIT, BUT CAREFULLY EXAMINE HIS WORK. PILGRAM MARPECK: Truly, my dear brothers and sisters, in a variety of ways, the Lord sends a concise, direct word to those people to save their souls. Regardless of the form, whether it be in writing or in speech, it behooves us to accept (as Christ himself) whatever

---

[12]Downame, ed., *Annotations*, 3K3r*; citing 2 Tim 1:6.
[13]CRR 1:128; citing Mt 12:34; Mk 12:38-39; Phil 3:2. †The CRR text identifies this text as coming from 1 Thess 2, but the reference is clearly 1 Thess 5:21.

[14]CRR 2:166. The editors of this CRR volume note that *The Admonition of 1542* "is the longest and most detailed statement of the Anabaptists on baptism and the Lord's Supper" (CRR 2:159).
[15]Pirckheimer, *Journal of the Reformation Years*, 128-29*; citing Mt 11:25.

in them is the testimony and the truth. Even though because of our carnal mind many things are difficult to understand and incomprehensible, and even though because of guilt and human weakness we may not immediately be able to understand or grasp, the time does come when we grasp and receive it with thanksgiving, and when, in tribulation under the rod in the school of Christ, we truly learn to understand and become wise with the wise. Thus St. Paul says, "Test everything, keep the good and discard the evil." He has written many things in great wisdom and divine earnestness, some of which are hard to understand. Peter also testifies to this when he says, "About which our dear brother Paul writes much (notice, much), of which some things are hard to understand, and which the ignorant twist—as they do other Scriptures—to their own destruction."

Thus it behooves us that we carefully examine and test all things, and that we do not judge, reject, misinterpret, or falsify what we do not understand, in order that in doing so we do not condemn ourselves and be plunged into error. For the gifts of the Holy Spirit are weighty. He moves as, when, and where he wills, giving them to whomever he desires, through Scriptures, speech, discipline, fear, tribulation, and judgment as he desired and pleases. He gives through profound and mediocre understanding, in length and breadth, in height and depth. Everything is His. He is Lord and Sovereign over all, over written and spoken Scriptures that human beings test, learn, experience, witness to, and judge to the praise of God and their own salvation, and from them judge themselves and others. To THE CHURCH IN ST. GALL AND APPENZELL.[16]

THE AUTHORITY OF THE CHURCH TO GIVE JUDGMENT. HEINRICH BULLINGER: Finally, that the church has power to give judgment on doctrines appears from the one sentence of the apostle Paul: "Let the prophets," says he, "speak two or three, and the other judge." And in another place he says, "Prove all things, and keep that which is good."

And St. John says, "Dearly beloved, do not believe every spirit, but try the spirits, whether they are of God." But of this kind of power to judge, there is also a certain order. For the church does not judge according to her own pleasure, but according to the sentence of the Holy Ghost, and according to the order and rule of the holy Scriptures. And here also order, moderation, and charity is observed. Therefore if at any time the church of God, according to the authority that she has received from the Lord, calls a counsel together for some weighty matter, as we read that the apostles of the Lord did in the Acts of the Apostles, it leans not here to her own fleshly judgment, but gives over herself to be guided by the Spirit, and examines all her doings by the rule of the Word of God, and of the twofold charity [i.e., love of God and love of neighbor]. Therefore the church does not make any new laws, for the church of Jerusalem, or rather the apostolic church, says "that it seems good both to the Holy Ghost and to the church, that no other burden should be laid upon" faithful Christians, but only a few and those very necessary things, and neither beside nor contrary to the holy Scriptures. Now ecclesiastical matters are of diverse sorts, the good ordering and well disposing whereof, for the commodity of human beings is in the power of the church, of which sort those things are that concern outward worship, in place and in time, as is prophesying, or interpretation of tongues, and schools. Also the church has to judge in causes of matrimony, and chiefly it has correction of manners, admonitions, punishments, and also excommunicating or cutting off from the body of the church. For the apostle also says that his power is given him, and yet to the intent he should therewith edify and not destroy. For all these things that we have remembered, and so on, are limited with the rule of the word, and of love, also with holy examples and reasons deduced out of the holy Scriptures, of all which we will perchance more largely speak, in their place. OF THE HOLY CATHOLIC CHURCH.[17]

[16]CRR 2:504-5; citing 2 Pet 3:15-16.

[17]Bullinger, *Fifty Godly and Learned Sermons*, 839; citing 1 Cor 14:29; 1 Jn 4:1; Acts 15:28.

Do Not Despise the Preaching of the Word. John Jewel: Prophecy is the preaching and expounding of the Word of God, and the one who prophesies is called a "prophet," who opens to us the will of God. This is not meant of fond and vain and lying prophecies, as were those of Merlin and others like him, who tell you tales of lions and bears and goats, of the sun, of the moon, and many strange devices. Such prophecies must be despised; they are works of darkness, and forged by the devil to make uproars, and to beguile the people.

But despise not prophesying: that is, despise not to hear the word of God: turn not away your ear from understanding. God gives power to his word, that it may work according to his good pleasure. It will let you see the weakness of your error, and settle you in the way wherein you should walk. If it had been dangerous for the people to hear the preaching of the gospel, he would not have sent his apostles into all the world. If Lydia should not have liked to hear Paul prophesy, how might she have known God? If those great numbers who heard Peter and were converted had despised prophesying, and would not have heard him open the gospel to them, they would have never considered the great mercy of God, nor would they have sought to be instructed in their salvation. "Faith comes by hearing." This has been the means by which Christ has given knowledge to kings and princes and all nations. "It has pleased God," says St. Paul, "by the foolishness of preaching to save those who believe." Despise not then to come to the church of God, to pray in the congregation of the faithful, to hear the Scriptures of God read and expounded: it is the blessing of God offered to you. Where there is no prophecy, the people perish. The one who despises it shall be despised of the Lord: they shall be cast into darkness, because they would not delight in the light. Upon the First Epistle to the Thessalonians.[18]

On Abstaining from the Appearance of Evil. Pilgram Marpeck: In anyone who, following an evil appearance or blossom, remains arrogant and puffed up in spite of brotherly admonition and warning, good fruit will rarely be found. Pride should be dealt with by discipline and repentance; otherwise, we must wait for the time of the fruit, which will certainly come and not delay. Thus, one is sure in one's judgment. Certainly, the true shepherds will not drive a patient, humble, meek, and loving heart any further than the chief Shepherd, Christ has driven and bound it, but will let it go out and in, find full and sufficient pasture, and be and remain victorious over all temptation in Christ Jesus. Judgment and Decision.[19]

Hold Fast to the Good, Reject the Bad. Thomas Müntzer: The damnable monastic ecstatics have not known how they ought to await the power of God. Over it they have become hardened into a contrary mind and have become for the whole world nothing but a mass of sin and shame like sluggish wastrels. Also they are blind in their folly. Nothing else has misled them and nothing else misleads them further in the present day than this wrong belief. For without any experience of the arrival of the Holy Spirit, they overcome of the fear of the God, they fail to separate (in their disdain for divine wisdom) the good from the bad, which is camouflaged under the appearance of good. Over such as these God cries out through Isaiah: "Woe to you who call good bad and bad good." Therefore it is not the habit of pious people to reject the good with the bad, since St. Paul says to the Thessalonians: Despise not prophesyings. Prove all things; hold fast that which is good. Sermon Before the Prince.[20]

Test Everything, Keep the Good, and Discard the Evil. Pilgram Marpeck: Truly,

---

[18]Jewel, *Works*, 2:880-81*; citing Acts 16:13-15; Acts 2:14-41; Rom 10:17; 1 Cor 1:21.

[19]CRR 2:345-46. This is the first of four letters written by Marpeck to the Swiss Brethren. The section quoted above comes during Marpeck's comments on the Ten Commandments.
[20]LCC 25:56-57; citing Is 5:20.

my dear brothers and sisters, in a variety of ways the Lord sends a concise, direct word to those people to save their souls. Regardless of the form, whether it be in writing or in speech, it behooves us to accept (as Christ himself) whatever in them is the testimony and the truth. Even though because of our carnal mind many things are difficult to understand and incomprehensible, and even though because of guilt and human weakness we may not immediately be able to understand or grasp, the time does come when we grasp and receive it with thanksgiving and when, in tribulation under the rod in the school of Christ we truly learn to understand, and become wise with the wise. Thus St. Paul says: "Test everything, keep the good, and discard the evil." He has written many things in great wisdom and divine earnestness, some of which are hard to understand. To the Church in St. Gallen and Appenzell.[21]

Await Fruit Before Judging. Pilgram Marpeck: Many evil blossoms could still turn out to be good or evil, but we do not have fruit by which one could make a judgment. Similarly, there are many—all liars, dissemblers, and hypocrites— who pretend to desire to bring forth good fruit but never can bring forth good fruit.

Yet we are forbidden to judge all such individuals before the time of the fruit. We are faithfully warned not to judge prematurely what is hidden but commit it to the Lord. This is especially the case with those who appeal to the Lord regarding their evil appearance. Paul commands us to avoid such people but not to ban them. These are to be left to the Lord until the revealing of the fruit and are not to be separated from the congregation. However, good fruit will rarely be found in anyone who remains arrogant and puffed up in spite of brotherly admonition and warning, following an evil appearance or blossom. Concerning Hasty Judgments and Verdicts.[22]

5:23-28 Paul's Benediction

Body, Soul, Spirit. Balthasar Hubmaier: Humans are corporal and rational creatures, made up by God of body, spirit, and soul. These three things are found to be essential and distinct in every person, as the Scriptures plainly demonstrate. When the Lord God made man of the dust of the earth, he breathed into him the breath of life, and thus man became a living soul. Here Moses points out three things with distinct names. First, the flesh or body, made of earth. This clod or lump of earth is called in Hebrew ʿāphār [dry earth, dust] and ʾereṣ [earth, land]; in our language, dust, ashes, or dirt from the earth. Second, there was then the breath of life, in Hebrew, nəšāmâ [breath]; in our language, blowing, breathing, or spirit. Third, the soul, which animates the body, is expressed separately, and called nepeš [soul, living being, person]. St. Paul plainly named these three essential substances by special distinct Greek names when he wrote to the Thessalonians about pneuma, psychē, and sōma; in Latin, spiritus, anima, corpus; in our language: spirit, soul, body. He said: May he, the God of peace, sanctify you wholly; and your spirit, soul, and body must be preserved blameless unto the coming of our Lord Jesus Christ. On Free Will.[23]

God's Own Righteousness Is Manifested in His Words and His Deeds. Jacobus Arminius: Righteousness or justice in God is an eternal and constant will to render to every one their own: to God himself that which is his, and to the creature what belongs to it. We consider this righteousness in its words and in its acts. In all its words are found veracity and constancy; and in its promises, fidelity. With regard to its acts, it is twofold, disposing and remunerative. The former is that according to which God disposes all the things in his actions through his own wisdom, according to the rule of equity, which has either been prescribed or pointed out

---

[21]CRR 2:504-5.
[22]CRR 12:175-76*; citing 1 Cor 4:5; 2 Thess 3:6; Tit 3:3, 10.

[23]LCC 25:116; citing Gen 2:7.

by his wisdom. The latter is that by which God renders to his creatures that which belongs to it, according to his work through an agreement into which he has entered with it. DISPUTATION 4. ON THE NATURE OF GOD.[24]

THE SPIRIT OF HUMANITY HAS REMAINED UPRIGHT. BALTHASAR HUBMAIER: The spirit of humankind has remained utterly upright and intact before, during and after the fall, for it took part, neither by counsel nor by action, yea, it did not in any way consent to or approve of the eating of the forbidden fruit by the flesh. But it was forced, against its will, as a prisoner in the body, to participate in the eating. But the sin was not its own, but rather that of the flesh and of the soul, for the latter had also become flesh. St. Paul demonstrates this integrity and uprightness of the spirit especially in writing to the Thessalonians: "May your whole spirit and soul and body be preserved blameless unto the coming of our Lord Jesus Christ." He says, your "whole spirit," not your whole soul or your whole body; for anything that has once fallen and been broken is no longer whole.[†] ON FREE WILL.[25]

EFFECTUAL CALLING AND THE MORAL CHARACTER OF GOD. THEODORE BEZA: The goodwill and power of God is a sure confirmation against all difficulties, whereof we have a sure witness in our vocation. . . . Always one and ever like himself, who performs indeed whatsoever he promises, and an effectual calling is nothing else but a right declaring and true setting forth of God's will. And therefore the salvation of the elect is safe and sure. THE NEW TESTAMENT OF OUR LORD JESUS CHRIST.[26]

---

[24]Arminius, *Works*, 2:132-33; citing Ps 11:7; 2 Tim 2:13; Num 23:19; Rom 3:4; Heb 6:10, 17-18; Ps 145:17; 2 Thess 1:6; Rev 2:23.
[25] LCC 25:120. [†]George H. Williams notes, "As Vedder has pointed out, Hubmaier improperly construes the *integer* of the Vulgate text of 1 Thess 5:23 to apply only to *spiritus*." See LCC 25:120 n. 5. The Latin word *integer* can be translated variously as "untouched, entire, whole, complete." The question would be (in the Latin text): Is (1) the text speaking of the "whole" spirit, or (2) to the whole person—who is spirit, soul, and body. Williams is suggesting that Hubmaier goes astray in opting for the first option, in the notion that Paul is speaking of the "whole" spirit, rather than the "whole" body/soul/spirit.
[26]Beza, *New Testament*, 92.

COMMENTARY ON 2 THESSALONIANS

1:1-4 INTRODUCTION TO
2 THESSALONIANS AND GREETING

Paul, Silvanus, and Timothy,

    To the church of the Thessalonians in God our Father and the Lord Jesus Christ:

    ²Grace to you and peace from God our Father and the Lord Jesus Christ.

    ³We ought always to give thanks to God for you,

brothers,ᵃ as is right, because your faith is growing abundantly, and the love of every one of you for one another is increasing. ⁴Therefore we ourselves boast about you in the churches of God for your steadfastness and faith in all your persecutions and in the afflictions that you are enduring.

a Or *brothers and sisters.* In New Testament usage, depending on the context, the plural Greek word *adelphoi* (translated "brothers") may refer either to *brothers* or to *brothers and sisters*

OVERVIEW: In introducing this epistle, these commentators preview its largely eschatological themes, among which are concerns about the nature of Christ's second coming and the kingdom of the antichrist. Regarding the latter, the question of the identity of the antichrist occupies considerable attention from these commentators, with most of them tending to identify it with the papacy, Muhammad, or both. Moreover, the authors explore the provenance of the epistle. Turning their attention to Paul's greeting, the commentators examine what they consider to be the chief Christian virtues: faith, love, and patience. In so doing, they emphasize patience amid suffering as evidence of a lively, justifying faith.

Introductory Comments

ESCHATOLOGICAL REALITIES AND WISDOM.
WILLIAM TYNDALE: Because in the previous epistle he had said that the last day should come suddenly, the Thessalonians thought that it should

have come shortly. Wherefore in this epistle he declares himself.

And in the first chapter he comforts them with the everlasting reward of their faith and patience in suffering for the gospel, and with the punishment of their persecutors in everlasting pain.

In the second he shows that the last day should not come till there is first a departing (as some people think) from under the obedience of the emperor of Rome, and that antichrist should set up himself in the same place as God and deceive the unthankful world with false doctrine, and with false and lying miracles wrought by the working of Satan, until Christ should come and slay him with his glorious coming and spiritual preaching of the word of God.

In the third he gives them exhortation and warns them to rebuke the idle who would not labor with their hands, and avoid their company, if they would not mend. A PROLOGUE TO THE SECOND EPISTLE OF ST. PAUL TO THE THESSALONIANS.[1]

---

[1] *Tyndale's New Testament,* prologue*.

The Agreement of the Two Letters.

Heinrich Bullinger: A commentary upon the second epistle of St. Paul to the Thessalonians. In the which, besides the sum of our faith, there is sincerely handled and set forth at large not only the first coming up and rising with the full prosperity and dominion but also the fall and utter confusion of the kingdom of antichrist, that is to say, of Muhammad and the bishop of Rome....

It seems that this latter epistle of St. Paul to the Thessalonians was written directly after the first, in the place of a defense or bulwark to the same. For in that he handed certain things at large, and in this he touches them more scarcely. And in the beginning he does yet still publish and praise the faith of the Thessalonians because they had endured constantly in much temptation and affliction. For this he promises them refreshing and eternal life, and to their adversaries fierce and utter confusion, to the end that he might strengthen their minds. Furthermore, because in his first epistle he had made mention of the coming of the Lord, and the resurrection of the dead, some understood that they were even then at hand. Therefore he shows in this that the Lord shall not come before the child of perdition be revealed, that is to say, antichrist, whose coming and kingdom, yea also the destruction, he does cunningly paint forth truly, even that the world then to come, being warned, might beware of that pestilence. Last of all he very often inculcates that such people ought to be brought into an order that with their idleness and curiosity troubled the public or commonwealth. For he had made mention of such in the fourth chapter of his first epistle. This epistle truly is short, but yet very profitable and learned. In the style it differs nothing from the first, neither is it of any less erudition than that. They say that this also was written by Paul at Athens, and sent by men of the same town: Theophilactus thinks that it was sent by Titus and Onesimus. Commentary on Second Thessalonians.[2]

Confusion Concerning the Return of Christ.

David Dickson: The occasion of writing this epistle seems to have been this: some of the Thessalonians abused the doctrine touching the sudden coming of Christ, even to negligence in their vocations, and to the wasting of their goods, as if there was no need that they should care for their estates any more, seeing Christ was about to come, perhaps the day after, as they did suppose, but others did abuse the simplicity and mistake of some, and intending to live upon the goods of others, left off working. In the meanwhile the persecution of enemies raged, and concurred to cherish this error. Wherefore the apostle writes this second epistle to them, solves the difficulty, and first of all comforts them against persecutions or afflictions (chapter 1). Second, he explains the doctrine concerning Christ's coming, which will approach before the antichristian apostasy from the true faith of Christ should appear, and be discovered to the world (chapter 2). Last, he exhorts them to Christian duties, and namely, to diligence in every one's vocation (chapter 3). The First Epistle of Paul to the Thessalonians.[3]

Paul's Love for the Thessalonians.

Martin Luther: In the first epistle, Paul had resolved for the Thessalonians the question of the last day, telling them that it would come quickly, as a thief in the night. Now as is likely to happen—that one question always gives rise to another, because of misunderstanding—the Thessalonians understood that the last day was already at hand. Thereupon Paul writes this epistle and explains himself.

In chapter 1 he comforts them with the eternal reward of their faith and of their patience amid sufferings of every kind and with the punishment of their persecutors in eternal pain.

In chapter 2 he teaches that before the last day, the Roman Empire must first pass away, and antichrist set himself up as God in Christendom and seduce the unbelieving world with false

---

[2]Bullinger, *Second Thessalonians*, introduction*.

[3]Dickson, *Exposition*, 152.

doctrines and signs—until Christ shall come and destroy him by his glorious coming, first slaying him with spiritual preaching.

In chapter 3 he gives some admonitions, especially that they rebuke the idlers who are not supporting themselves by their own labor. If the idlers will not reform, then the faithful shall avoid them. And this is a stiff rebuke to the clergy of our day. PREFACE TO THE SECOND EPISTLE OF ST. PAUL TO THE THESSALONIANS.[4]

SUM OF THE ARGUMENT. JOHN CALVIN: It does not appear to me probable that this epistle was sent from Rome, as the Greek manuscripts commonly bear; for he would have made some mention of his bonds, as he is accustomed to do in other epistles. Besides, about the end of the third chapter, he intimates that he is in danger from unreasonable men. From this it may be gathered that when he was going to Jerusalem, he wrote this epistle in the course of the journey. It was also from an ancient date a very generally received opinion among the Latins, that it was written at Athens. The occasion, however, of his writing was this—that the Thessalonians might not reckon themselves overlooked, because Paul had not visited them, when hastening to another quarter. In the first chapter, he exhorts them to patience. In the second, a vain and groundless fancy, which had got into circulation as to the coming of Christ being at hand, is set aside by him by means of this argument—that there must previously to that be a revolt in the church, and a great part of the world must treacherously draw back from God, nay more, that antichrist must reign in the temple of God. In the third chapter, after having commended himself to their prayers, and having in a few words encouraged them to perseverance, he commands that those be severely chastised who live in idleness at the expense of others. If they do not obey admonitions, he teaches that they should be excommunicated. COMMENTARY ON SECOND THESSALONIANS.[5]

1:1-4 To the Church in Thessalonica

THE CHURCH OF BOTH THE FATHER AND THE SON. JOHN CALVIN: "To the church of the Thessalonians that is in God." As to the form of salutation, it were superfluous to speak. This only it is necessary to notice—that by a "church in God and Christ" is meant one that has not merely been gathered together under the banner of faith, for the purpose of worshiping one God the Father, and confiding in Christ, but is the work and building as well of the Father as of Christ, because while God adopts us to himself, and regenerates us, we from him begin to be in Christ. COMMENTARY ON SECOND THESSALONIANS.[6]

THANKFUL FOR THE VIRTUE OF OTHERS. HEINRICH BULLINGER: He praises and rejoices at the Thessalonians, and gives thanks unto God for their constancy and increase of virtue. From this we may first learn that if we do anything well we should give the thanks to God, and not ascribe it to our virtue, but attribute unto him the principal effects of all things. We should in no way wax proud for anything that we do well, nor yet think ourselves any way perfect, if we seem ourselves somewhat to have profited in virtue and goodness. Rather let us think to go forward every day, and study to pass our own selves in all kind of virtues. Second, we may learn hereof that we should not envy at other people's virtues, but rather rejoice with them, yes and to give thanks for the going forward and good example of our brethren. COMMENTARY ON THE SECOND EPISTLE OF PAUL TO THE THESSALONIANS.[7]

THE CHIEF POINTS OF OUR RELIGION. HEINRICH BULLINGER: Here are also recited the chief points of our religion, faith, charity, and suffering for other manner of things, than those that the bishop of Rome, and many monks have rehearsed to us. And in that he calls the churches, not his but

---

[4]LW 35:389-90; citing 1 Thess 5:2.
[5]CTS 42:309 (CO 52:185-86). This is Calvin's introduction to his commentary on 2 Thessalonians, what he calls his "Argument."

[6]CTS 42:310-311 (CO 52:187).
[7]Bullinger, *Second Thessalonians*, 1:3.

God's, it comes of humility and faith. Commentary on the Second Epistle of Paul to the Thessalonians.[8]

Patience Is the Fruit and Evidence of Faith. John Calvin: He could not have bestowed higher commendation upon them than by saying that he sets them forward before other churches as a pattern, for such is the meaning of those words: "We glory in you in the presence of other churches." For Paul did not boast of the faith of the Thessalonians from a spirit of ambition, but inasmuch as his commendation of them might be an incitement to make it their endeavor to imitate them. He does not say, however, that he glories in their faith and love, but in their "patience" and "faith." Hence it follows that "patience" is the fruit and evidence of "faith." These words ought, therefore, to be explained in this manner: "We glory in the patience that springs from faith, and we bear witness that it eminently shines forth in you"; otherwise the context would not correspond. And undoubtedly, there is nothing that sustains us in tribulations as faith does; which is sufficiently manifest from this, that we altogether sink down so soon as the promises of God leave us. Hence, the more proficiency anyone makes in faith, they will be so much the more endued with patience for enduring all things with fortitude, as on the other hand, softness and impatience under adversity betoken unbelief on our part; but more especially when persecutions are to be endured for the gospel, the influence of faith in that case discovers itself. Commentary on Second Thessalonians.[9]

True Faith Grows Continually. John Jewel: "Your faith grows exceedingly." That is the will of God, that we grow and increase in all holiness. Hereby we know whether we be of God or no. We may not stand at a stay but must be renewed. Someone has said: *In via virtutis qui non proficit, deficit,* "Whoever does not mend himself in the practice of virtue grows worse."[†] God has placed us in a race to run: we must so run that we may attain the prize. We are grafts of the Lord's planting: we must grow to the height and breadth of a tree, and bring forth fruit. We are pilgrims and strangers, and pass by the wilderness of this world into our heavenly resting place: we may not stay by the way, but must remove our tents, and continually march forward until that day come when we shall enter into the land of promise. Upon the Second Epistle to the Thessalonians.[10]

Perseverance in Suffering. Cardinal Cajetan: "Therefore also, we ourselves boast about you in the churches of God." Continuously your faith toward God and your mutual love is honored, and we ourselves boast about you in the various churches of God.

"For your patience, and faith in all your persecutions and tribulations." Behold the material evidence of your glory, the exterior patience proceeding from your constancy of faith—not in certain things, but in all of your persecutions and afflictions from your fellow tribespeople. For this then was unusual at the time among the Gentiles, for until now persecution against the Christians had not been stirred up by the rulers. And the first Gentiles who were gathered and afflicted for the faith, were the Thessalonians. Therefore Paul rightly boasts about them among the various churches. On Paul's Epistle to the Thessalonians.[11]

---

[8] Bullinger, *Second Thessalonians*, 1:3.
[9] CTS 42:312 (CO 52:189).

[10] Jewel, *Works*, 2:889*. [†] Leo the Great, *De Passione Domini*, serm. 8.
[11] Cajetan, *In Omnes*, 284 (pdf 291).

1:5-12 THE COMING JUDGMENT
WHEN CHRIST RETURNS

⁵This is evidence of the righteous judgment of God, that you may be considered worthy of the kingdom of God, for which you are also suffering— ⁶since indeed God considers it just to repay with affliction those who afflict you, ⁷and to grant relief to you who are afflicted as well as to us, when the Lord Jesus is revealed from heaven with his mighty angels ⁸in flaming fire, inflicting vengeance on those who do not know God and on those who do not obey the gospel of our Lord Jesus. ⁹They will suffer the punishment of eternal destruction, away from^a the presence of the Lord and from the glory of his might, ¹⁰when he comes on that day to be glorified in his saints, and to be marveled at among all who have believed, because our testimony to you was believed. ¹¹To this end we always pray for you, that our God may make you worthy of his calling and may fulfill every resolve for good and every work of faith by his power, ¹²so that the name of our Lord Jesus may be glorified in you, and you in him, according to the grace of our God and the Lord Jesus Christ.

a Or *destruction that comes from*

OVERVIEW: Throughout their expositions of this passage, these commentators starkly contrast the effect of the coming judgment on the godly and ungodly. Whereas Christ's return will serve as the occasion for the final deliverance of believers, it will bring everlasting damnation to unbelievers. In their discussions, the authors argue that God appoints his people to suffering because suffering is a means of strengthening and maturing faith in anticipation of Christ's return. However, in stressing the role of suffering in maturing faith, the commentators insist that all of this is solely the work of God's grace. In short, by God's grace, justifying faith demonstrates itself through perseverance.

1:5-8 Worthy of the Kingdom of God

JESUS AND HIS MIGHTY ANGELS. HEINRICH BULLINGER: The firstborn of the Egyptians are smitten by the angel. In the Acts of the Apostles the angel of the Lord smites Herod Agrippa. It is said that in the camp of the Assyrians many were smitten and slain by one angel. And David saw an angel with a sword drawn, hovering between heaven and earth, afflicting the people with most grievous plague. So we believe that the holy angels shall come with the Son of Man to judgment, as Paul witnesses and says, "Our Lord Jesus Christ shall be revealed from heaven, with the angels of his power, in flaming fire, rendering vengeance to them who do not know God, and who do not obey the gospel of our Lord Jesus Christ." For in the revelation of Jesus Christ also the angels pour out vials full of the wrath of God upon the heads of false Christians.

Moreover, they take upon them the charge and defense of us, God so commanding; they are our keepers, ready at hand watching over us that no adversity happens to us, and guide our ways. For hitherto belong the testimonies of the Psalms, and very many examples of the Scripture. FIFTY GODLY AND LEARNED SERMONS.[1]

COUNTED WORTHY TO SUFFER. HEINRICH BULLINGER: This place also teaches that saints or holy people are appointed to persecution, and to be exercised with continual afflictions, and that those tribulations are a token or demonstration of the

---

[1]Bullinger, *Fifty Godly and Learned Sermons*, 741*.

righteous judgment of God, that is, that wicked people perish justly, but the godly are counted worthy of the kingdom of God, for which they have suffered much adversity. For after this manner does he comfort and lift up the saints, setting the pains and rewards before their eyes. But if anyone through the help of this place will contend, that salvation is due to our afflictions, and not to the passion and blood of Christ only, let them mark this also, that the very same person said to the Romans that we are justified by the benefit of faith, and not by the merit of our works. It is therefore of the fatherly liberality and goodwill of God that it is here said that eternal life is given us by right, and we made worthy of the kingdom of God through afflictions: where as it is plain that all our aptness is of God, and that we are made happy by the grace of God. But the goodness of God would not discomfort our minds, and as it were through our inability, provoke us to slackness or weariness. And therefore the Scripture speaks as though we deserved somewhat, and were worthy of the kingdom of God, that we should do all things with a glad and merry mind. COMMENTARY ON THE SECOND EPISTLE OF PAUL TO THE THESSALONIANS.[2]

Two Marks of an Unbeliever. JOHN CALVIN: He distinguishes unbelievers by these two marks—that they "do not know God," and "do not obey the gospel of Christ." For if obedience is not rendered to the gospel through faith, as he teaches in the first and in the last chapters of the Epistle to the Romans, unbelief is the occasion of resistance to it. He charges them at the same time with ignorance of God, for a lively acquaintance with God produces of itself reverence toward him. Hence unbelief is always blind, not as though unbelievers were altogether devoid of light and intelligence, but because they have the understanding darkened in such a manner, that "seeing they do not see." It is not without good grounds that Christ declares that "this is life eternal, to know the true God. . . ." Accordingly, from the want of this

salutary knowledge, there follows contempt of God, and in fine, death. COMMENTARY ON FIRST THESSALONIANS.[3]

Judgment for the Godly and the Ungodly. HEINRICH BULLINGER: Here he paints and with express and very notable words sets forth before our eyes the coming of the Lord Jesus and the manner of the judgment. The same coming shall be to all saints very acceptable and most welcome, and to the ungodly very sour and sorrowful. And every word has his strength and weight. Now (says he) the matter goes all by words. But when the end of all things shall come, those things about which all saints have disputed so long and many years shall appear manifestly. For the Lord Jesus himself, to whom all power is given in heaven and on earth, and to whom all judgment belongs, shall appear in a corporal form and likeness to judge all flesh. And now he describes the behavior of this mighty Judge, that to all his enemies shall be so terrible, and so desirous and longed for by his friends. He shall come (I say) from heaven, not now (as once) creeping upon the earth, nor then low and despised as he appeared in his first coming, but compassed about with the host of angels. COMMENTARY ON THE SECOND EPISTLE OF PAUL TO THE THESSALONIANS.[4]

1:9-10 Glorified with the Saints

The Return of the Lord Is a Blessing to His People. HEINRICH BULLINGER: His coming shall not only be fearful to the wicked, but glad also and glorious to the godly. He shall come (says he) to be glorified in his saints. As though he would say: when he shall come forth to render vengeance to the wicked, he shall show himself glorious to the saints also, and make their vile bodies like his glorious body, for which cause he shall be marvelous in all those who believe, who then shall praise and magnify his very great goodness and power?

---

[2]Bullinger, *Second Thessalonians*, 1:5.

[3]CTS 42:317-18 (CO 52:191); citing Mt 13:13; Jn 17:13.
[4]Bullinger, *Second Thessalonians*, 1:7.

And this shall be so (says he) because you believed our witness, that is, our preaching, which I preached to you, telling you that that should come to pass, which God shall do in that day. There are those which think that these words—"because you believed our testimony"—are put in by a parenthesis, and that to declare who be the true believers, that is to say, such as give credence to the apostle's witness. St. Ambrose says that it may be expounded two ways. For he shall come (says he) to punish the evil and glorify the good. For he shall seem and show himself glorious and marvelous toward those who believe, after the example and faith of the apostles, at what time they shall be crowned with glory, the gospel bearing witness to them in the Day of the Lord. And he shall appear to the unfaithful a sore and heavy Judge, when they shall begin to feel the bitterness of everlasting pain. For the glory of the master is a thing of rejoicing and in manner of a crown to the disciples, and his truth the extreme pain and misery of the unbelievers: because they believed not the true preachers. COMMENTARY ON THE SECOND EPISTLE OF PAUL TO THE THESSALONIANS.[5]

THE RETURN OF THE LORD SHOULD ENCOURAGE COMFORT AND FAITH. DAVID DICKSON: God in his justice will punish your persecutors in the day of judgment, and will set you at liberty from all evil. Therefore you ought to be comforted, and strengthened in faith.... You shall at last obtain, together with us, and with other martyrs of Christ, as your fellow soldiers, rest from all evil and misery. Therefore you ought to be comforted together with us, and strengthened in faith.... From those circumstances of last judgment, which makes the revenge terrible, that shall be taken upon them. The Lord Jesus (1) shall be made manifest and visibly come from heaven, a Judge and avenger of injuries. (2) The mighty angels shall accompany him, who shall execute the sentence of Judge. (3) He shall kindle a flaming fire, wherein this whole world shall burn. (4) He shall be revenged of

all those who are found destitute of saving knowledge (which is joined with faith and obedience) and who have not obeyed the gospel. (5) Then the wicked shall be punished with everlasting destruction. (6) This punishment shall be inflicted by an angry Judge, who shall eternally cast them out from his presence.... (7) The Lord shall manifest how glorious his power is by punishing them mightily. Therefore you ought to be comforted and confirmed in faith. THE SECOND EPISTLE OF PAUL TO THE THESSALONIANS.[6]

PUNISHMENT DUE TO UNBELIEF AND SINS COMMITTED AGAINST THE LAW. JACOBUS ARMINIUS: By faith in Jesus Christ the remission of all sins is obtained, and sins are not imputed to those who believe; yet the reprobate will be compelled to endure the punishment, not only of their unbelief (by the contrary of which they might avoid the chastisement due to the rest of their sins), but likewise of the sins they have committed against the law, being "everlasting destruction from the presence of the Lord, and from the glory of his power." ON DIVINE PREDESTINATION.[7]

1:11-12 *Paul's Prayer for the Thessalonians*

GOD'S GRACE IS WHAT MAKES US WORTHY. HEINRICH BULLINGER: To hard things he always adds prayer. For faith itself and the reverence we owe unto God teaches us that through prayer we ought to go about to obtain the chief gifts of God. And we should pray without ceasing. For St. Paul says, "We pray always for you. And what we should pray or desire, it follows: That our God will count you worthy of this calling." What calling, I ask you? The same no doubt wherewith he shall call the blessed into his kingdom, saying, "Come the blessed children of my father, possess the kingdom that is prepared for you, from the beginning of the world." Compare now this place with that: You suffer that you might be counted worthy of the kingdom of

---

[5]Bullinger, *Second Thessalonians*, 1:9-10.

[6]Dickson, *Exposition*, 153.
[7]Arminius, *Works*, 2:228-29; citing Rom 4:2-11; Jn 8:24; 9:41.

God, and you shall perceive that the free grace of God makes us worthy of the kingdom of God. For if our merits make us worthy, what need is there to pray the LORD that he would count us worthy of his calling? That worthiness therefore hangs upon the free liberality of God. After this we must pray that God will fulfill all our good purposes to goodness: That is, that according to his goodness, wherewith he loves us, he will fortunately perform that which he has begun in us. For the one who continues to the end shall be saved. It is not unlike to this that follows: That he will fulfill your work of faith in power. That is, he will make our faith perfect through constancy and strength of mind: the thing once put into our minds by God overcomes all adversities. Last of all we must pray that the name of our LORD, not our name may be glorified through our hope, and that he may glorify us in his coming, that is, make us safe in soul and body. He adds through that grace of our God and Lord Jesus Christ, admonishing us that all these things do depend upon the grace of God, and not of our own merit. This is also to be marked, that in this place also he in all things makes the Son equal to the Father: whereupon it follows that the unity of God in the Trinity is rightly defended by us. COMMENTARY ON THE SECOND EPISTLE OF PAUL TO THE THESSALONIANS.[8]

COUNTED WORTHY OF HIS CALLING. DAVID DICKSON: Of comforting and confirming them in faith. You have our continual prayers, that you may happily attain your end. Therefore you ought to be comforted in your afflictions, and strengthened in faith. There are [three] articles of this prayer.

Article 1. I pray that God (who is ours by a free covenant) would vouchsafe to make you meet for the vocation or glory to which you are called. This article ascribes as well the glory to which we are called, to the grace or favor of God, as well as the preparation that leads us to it.

Article 2. I pray that God would fulfill all the good pleasure of this goodness according to his

free bounty toward you. In which article he shows that not only salvation, but all means to salvation, are founded in the good pleasure of God, acknowledging nothing except the grace of God in the whole course of salvation, and in all the parts of it.

Article 3. I pray that God would complete the word of faith with power in you. In which article he affirms faith to be the work of God, which he works in his people, and he determines the beginning, increase, and perfecting of faith, as part of his good pleasure. Last, he shows that faith is not only not a work of power, but exceeds whatsoever can be in us, and requires the power of God, without which it can neither be begun, or continue, or be increased, or completed. . . . I pray that both in this life and in that which is to come Christ may be glorified in you, as in his members, and you may be glorified in him, as in your head, which is the end of the former articles. Neither in this article will he have the grace of God concealed, but teaches that the whole glory that Christ receives from his people, or which he communicates to them, is to be ascribed to the grace of God only. In all which the Thessalonians had no mean support for their consolation and confirmation in the faith. THE SECOND EPISTLE OF PAUL TO THE THESSALONIANS.[9]

HOW GOD'S GRACE WORKS IN PERSEVERANCE. THEODORE BEZA: Seeing that we have the mark set before us, it remains that we go to it. And we go to it by certain degrees of causes. First, by the free love and good pleasure of God, by virtue of which all other inferior causes work. From thence proceeds the free calling of Christ in us, and us in Christ. By calling he means not the very act of calling, but that selfsame thing to which we are called, which is the glory of that heavenly kingdom, which he determined long since, only upon his precious and merciful goodness toward you. So then, faith is an excellent work of God in us, and we see here plainly that the apostle leaves nothing to free will, to make it checkmate with God's

---

[8]Bullinger, *Second Thessalonians*, 1:11-12; citing Mt 25:34; 24:13.

[9]Dickson, *Exposition*, 153-54*.

working therein, as the papists dreamed. The New Testament of Our Lord Jesus Christ.[10]

To Truly Love Someone Requires Seeking Their Salvation. Dirk Philips: The fifth ordinance is the command of love that Christ gave his disciples, saying: "A new commandment I give unto you, that you love one another, as I have loved you, that you also love one another. By this shall all people know that you are my disciples, if you have love to another." From this it is easy to understand that pure brotherly love is a sure sign of genuine faith and true Christianity. But this is true brotherly love, that our chief desire is one another's salvation, by our fervent prayers to God, by scriptural instruction, admonition, and rebuke, that thereby we may instruct the one who is overtaken in a fault, in order to win their soul. And all this [we do] with Christian patience, having forbearance toward the weak and not simply pleasing ourselves. The Church of God.[11]

---

[10]Beza, *New Testament*, 92.

[11]LCC 25:248-49; citing Jn 13:34-35; 15:12, 17; Gal 6:3; Jas 5:16. For the complete list of seven ordinances, see n. 3 on 1 Thess 5:14.

2:1-6 THE MAN OF LAWLESSNESS

Now concerning the coming of our Lord Jesus Christ and our being gathered together to him, we ask you, brothers,ᵃ ²not to be quickly shaken in mind or alarmed, either by a spirit or a spoken word, or a letter seeming to be from us, to the effect that the day of the Lord has come. ³Let no one deceive you in any way. For that day will not come, unless the rebellion comes first, and the man of lawlessnessᵇ is revealed,

the son of destruction,ᶜ ⁴who opposes and exalts himself against every so-called god or object of worship, so that he takes his seat in the temple of God, proclaiming himself to be God. ⁵Do you not remember that when I was still with you I told you these things? ⁶And you know what is restraining him now so that he may be revealed in his time.

a Or *brothers and sisters; also verses 13, 15*   b Some manuscripts *sin*   c Greek *the son of perdition* (a Hebrew idiom)

Overview: Early modern commentators devoted significant attention to explaining this passage. Most of their expositions concern the identity of the antichrist, the events leading to his temporary dominance, and the nature of "apostasy," or "falling away." Concerning the antichrist's identity, some authors maintain that he is the pope or the institution of the papacy. Others contend that Muhammad, or the religion of Islam, is the antichrist, while some apply the term to both. Many of the authors contend that the antichrist is not one, but many individuals working through institutions to undermine the true church and Christendom. In this regard, the expositors trace the development of the antichrist, beginning with the false prophets. The authors furthermore discuss the various characteristics of the antichrist. In discussing "apostasy," some commentators generally view it as a departure from the faith precipitating the rise of the antichrist, while other expositors conceive of it as the gradual dissolution of the Roman Empire, which enabled the eventual supplanting of temporal authority by the pope, who would assert his universal rule over Christendom.

2:1-2 Do Not Be Quickly Shaken

The Thessalonians Shaken Unnecessarily. Matthew Poole: *Saleuthēnai* [shaken] is an

allusion to the waves of the sea that are tossed with the winds, as false doctrines tend to unsettle the mind, rather than to be established in the truth, as is often commanded. By "mind" here is either meant the faculty itself, and then the apostle beseeches them to keep company with their understanding, not to be removed from their mind. As false doctrine is said to bewitch people, and to make people foolish, as madness is called "amentia" or "dementia,"† as what it does is, as it were, unmind people, corrupt the mind, and pervert the judgment, as Jannes and Jambres‡ deceived the people by their enchantments, as the apostle there mentions. Or else, "mind" here means the sentence and judgment of the mind; and then they are beseeched to hold fast to the right judgment they had entertained about Christ's coming, and not to hesitate and waver about it, so the word is taken.§ Annotations upon the Holy Bible.[1]

---

[1]Poole, *Annotations,* 758*; citing Eph 4:14; Heb 13:9; 1 Cor 16:13; Phil 4:1; Col 1:24; Gal 3:1; 2 Tim 3:8-9; 1 Cor 2:16. †While *dementia* is a common word, *amentia* is not used as often today. *Amentia* denotes a lack of intellectual development, or simply a particularly strong mental malformity. ‡Jannes and Jambres are mentioned in 2 Tim 3:8-9: "Just as Jannes and Jambres opposed Moses, so these men also oppose the truth," referring to Ex 7:8-13, where Moses confronts Pharaoh and Pharaoh's servants—the "magicians of Egypt." The names Jannes and Jambres themselves come from extrabiblical Jewish material. §In emphasizing the importance of holding fast to right judgment, and of not becoming "unminded" (hence the reference to "amentia" and

A Problem in Thessalonica. David Dickson: An error had crept in among the Thessalonians concerning Christ's coming immediately, while they were alive, an error the devil cherished, that as for other causes, so also for this, that at leastwise after that age he might expose the whole Christian doctrine, together with this article, to a mockery. Therefore the apostle admonishes them not to be moved from the sound sense and faith of this article. In the meanwhile he affirms two things as most certain, wherefore he would not have them doubt. The first was that Christ will come, as he had taught before, in his appointed time. The other was that it will come to pass that all the faithful should be gathered together from the four quarters of the world to meet the Lord. But he beseeches them, if they would be wise for themselves in that day, that they would have a care of that error whereof we speak. The Second Epistle of Paul to the Thessalonians.[2]

False Teachers with a False Word at Thessalonica. Matthew Poole: The opinion of Christ's coming to be at hand might occasion this trouble in them, either lest they might be surprised by it and unprepared for it, or by judging themselves mistaken in their former apprehensions about it; and those false teachers that broach this opinion did also perhaps so represent this coming in such terror as to cause this trouble, as false teachers in general are said to cause trouble. The coming of Christ is in itself the saint's hope and joy rather than the ground of trouble. It may be some did pretend this opinion was from the Spirit, or some letter from the apostle, either the former epistle to them, or some letter that was forged, or some word he had spoken, or preached. And those words "as from us" may refer to all these: The Spirit "as from us"; or word, "as from us"; or letter "as from us."

Some extraordinary revelation may have been said to have come from the Spirit, which the false teachers pretended to, especially in the primitive times, when they were more ordinary, as in the church of Corinth and the churches of Galatia. Some would pretend that the Spirit called Jesus accursed, and therefore the apostle bids, "Try the Spirit." Simon Magus pretended to it, and had his Helene, Montanus his Paraclete,[†] Muhammad his Dove.[‡] The sinful person pretends to be this Spirit, though it is in truth the spirit of antichrist, and the spirit of Satan in the next chapter of this epistle, as was foretold that in the last times there would arise seducing spirits, as there were in the times of the Old Testament false prophets who pretended to the Spirit. And the very heathen would pretend to divine oracles, inspirations, and revelations, especially their kings and lawgivers, as Numa Pompilius, Lycurgus,[††] and so on, and still there are enthusiasts who make these pretenses. *Dia logou* [i.e., "through [the] word"], whereby some understand calculation by astrological rules, that the day of Christ was at hand; others render the word "reasoning"; and so from the declining of the vigor of the earth, and the nearer approach of the sun to it, as Ptolemy observed in his time, or some other natural causes, they reasoned the coming of Christ, and the dissolution of the world to be nigh at hand. Instead we understand it as some word from the apostle's own mouth, which it was pretended he had spoken, or preached somewhere, though not written. In thus way, the church of Rome pretends to traditions besides the written Word, upon which they ground many of their superstitions and idolatries not warranted by Scriptures. Similarly the Jews had a second Mishnah, and their kabbala, collected in part from the sayings of Moses, or some other of their prophets, which they did not write. "Nor by letter";

"dementia"), Poole appears to be referring to Paul's use of *symbibazō* in 1 Cor 2:16, where Paul says, "For who has understood the mind of the Lord, so as to *instruct* [*symbibasei*] him?" It is an interesting reference for Poole to make. Most English translations take the word to mean "instruct." Other senses of the word found in lexicons like Friberg and Liddle-Scott include options like: "cause to stand together, unite, bring together," or "be united together, joined" (of the body of Christ), as well as "prove conclusively," "demonstrate," "infer." Poole does reference 1 Cor 2:16, in which most English translates prefer "instruct," but Poole prefers the sense of holding the mind together—hence the mention of not being "unminded," and that the Thessalonians must "hold fast to the right judgment."
[2]Dickson, *Second Thessalonians*, 154.

some letter that was sent to them from some other hand, or else by some forged letters as from the apostle himself, or his former epistle misunderstood. Annotations upon the Holy Bible.[3]

Discerning What Is from The Lord.
Heinrich Bullinger: It cannot be spoken how shamefully you certain unthrifty knaves through this craft have mocked the church of God. You have thrust in among us many books, many epistles and works as though they had come from the apostles or apostolic men, sayings from writers that were noble and excellent in authority, learning, and holiness, which they never knew or could approve, even if they were yet alive. For there are abroad certain canons of the apostles, certain epistles of apostolic men, yet and many little books also under the name of Augustine and Ambrose that these men never saw. What shall I say of certain sermons garnished with the title of Cyprian and Augustine. The negligence of the age that is passed, and the covetousness of writers and printers, with their ignorance and shamelessness was so great that no one can detest it enough. Those who have read the writings of the old doctors, and have seen any of Erasmus's judgments upon the works of Jerome and Austen,[†] understand what I say. And yet you shall find them, who with the help of this passage, they will thrust into the church of God everything that they lust, objecting that all things necessary to true godliness are not written in the Scriptures, because the mention is made here of the spirit of the word, and of the epistle, by which a more perfect doctrine might be delivered to the world then to come. But these men do not see that this same place admonishes us, that people should not be drawn away from their mind, that is, the wholesome faith once received, through their traditions, which being covered with the cloak of the spirit, of the word, or of a decretal epistle, these men cast to us as apostolic and most holy doctrine. For after this manner they advance and only set forth to us both their popish Masses and all other things they cannot prove by the testimony of Scriptures. Instead they affirm that they were instituted by the tradition of the apostles, and afterward confirmed by the epistles of apostolic men, and by the revelation of the Holy Ghost. Let us beware therefore of these ravishing wolves, who being clothed with sheep's clothing, do come to spoil, to cause trouble, and to devour. Let us keep faithfully the meaning of Christ, with the wholesome and apostolic points of true and undefiled religion, and then shall no one deceive us by any means. That learned man Tertullian has spoken more of this matter in his book that he made about the banishment of heretics. Commentary on the Second Epistle of Paul to the Thessalonians.[4]

Two Signs Precede the Coming of the Day of the Lord. Erasmus Sarcerius: Why the Thessalonians are not suddenly to be moved, and not to be disturbed, and ought not to be seduced from their understanding concerning the Day of the Lord, selected from certain signs of the last day.

He points to two signs: (1) defection from sincere doctrine and true understanding of doctrine, and also (2) the revelation of that defection.

The abomination of desolation about which Daniel writes, and the revelation of the same, was a type of this defection, and a revelation of the same, and in what way immediately perdition and the end of Jerusalem follows the revelation of abomination, and thus the Day of the Lord immediately follows the revelation of this defection.

---

[3]Poole, *Annotations*, 758*; citing Gal 1:7; 5:12; 1 Thess 1:10; 4:18; 1 Cor 14:6; Gal 3:2, 5; 1 Cor 12:3; 1 Jn 4:1, 3; 1 Tim 4:1; 1 Kings 22:24; Mic 2:11. [†]Montanus was a second-century figure who purportedly claimed to have access to direct divine revelation. *Paraclete* comes from the Greek word for "comforter," and is one of the New Testament words used for the Holy Spirit. [‡]A dove purportedly gave Mohammed divine revelation. [††]These are perhaps references from Plutarch's *Lives*. Numa Pompilius was the second king of Rome (reigned 715–673 BC), following Romulus. Lycurgus of Sparta was the (legendary?) ruler of Sparta in the eighth century BC. Poole is here using them as examples of lawgivers.

[4]Bullinger, *Second Thessalonians*, 2:1-2*. [†]"Austen" here refers to Augustine.

By "defection" they understand defection of the Roman Empire, which under Phocas and Heraclius,[†] emperors who were yawning and neglecting what was happening in the East, when Muhammad, the chief member of antichrist, to be exact the image of the king, of antichrist, arose.

I understand "defection" to be a defection from sincere doctrine, and truly it touches the understanding of sincere doctrine around that time, in which Phocas and Heraclius brought together the empire [and] when Boniface took the name "Universal Roman Bishop," so that he might be the head of the universal church, by which he was able with power to oppress sincere doctrine at the same time with sincere understanding of the same, and he did nothing to turn from the duties of antichrist. Afterward other pontiffs followed this one, who afterward unless they are truly worshiped as God immediately seek to overturn, and to substitute their own traditions, to profane the sacraments, destroy the true use of them, and so on.

Nor are the pontiffs able to free themselves from the name of antichrist. The truth is that Daniel writes the same thing in chapter 2:9-11, and the apostle in this place, and in others, for example, 1 Timothy 4, and 2 Timothy 3; also see Matthew 24. The Second Epistle to the Thessalonians.[5]

2:3-6 Do Not Be Deceived

Do Not Let Anyone Seduce You in Any Way. Robert Rollock: He repeats the same thing with a few words that he said in the preceding verse. For we are not able to ever ask or admonish ourselves enough that we might guard ourselves from false teachers. Certainly by no means does it pain me to write you about the same; though certainly it is to protect you. Beware the dogs, the workers of evil, beware the mutilation. While he asks that they not allow themselves to be deceived, he mentions neither who deceives a person, nor in what way they are deceived, but he says: do not allow anyone in any way to deceive you. The apostle no doubt knew that any person is more than capable of deceiving than another, and one way of deceiving may be more effective than another (there are a thousand ways of deceiving). Therefore, he asked, whether through any person or through any way—do not allow yourselves to be deceived. For there is more evil and loss in deception than is able to be compensated either with the personal dignity of anyone who is deceiving, or in any matter whatsoever through which we are deceived. No king, or kingdom, will be able to compensate that loss, which overflows in ourselves after we were deceived, and lead into errors. Certainly insane are those who barter faith in Christ for all the kingdoms of the earth. Commentary on 2 Thessalonians.[6]

God Provides Theologians to Preserve the Truth. Heinrich Bullinger: The last thing to be noted is this: that not only of old and up to the present time, but in these days too the Lord God gives doctors and pastors to the church: doctors, I say, and not leaders and captains of hosts, not princes, not soldiers, not crafty people using deceitful means that nowadays they call practices. For by no other means and manner, by no other instrument than by the doctrine of truth and sound and simply godliness, is that holy and catholic church of God built up, fenced and preserved, of which at the beginning simple men and Christ's apostles laid the foundation. Paul therefore sets aside all worldly wisdom and says, "I was among you, Corinthians, in weakness and in fear, and in much trembling; neither stood my word and my teaching in the enticing speech of human wisdom, but in plain evidence of the Spirit and of power; that your faith should not be in human wisdom, but in the power of God." The same apostle also banishes all crafty counsel with all kinds of deceit when writing to the Thessalonians he says, "Our

---

[5]Sarcerius, *Ad Thessalonicences*, 544-45; Mt 24:15; Dan 9:27; 11:31; 12:11. [†]Phocas was emperor of the Byzantine Empire (the eastern half of the Roman Empire) from AD 602 to 610. He was overthrown by Heraclius, who then ruled as emperor from 610 to 641.

[6]Rollock, *Ad Thessalonicenses*, 292-93*; citing Phil 3:1.

exhortation was not by deceit, nor by uncleanness, nor by guile. But as we were allowed of God that the gospel should be committed to us, even so we speak; not as they that please people, but God, who tries our hearts. Neither yet did we use flattering words, as they know; nor colored covetousness, God is witness; neither did we seek praise of men." Of the Holy Catholic Church.[7]

The Day of the Lord Is Still to Come. Robert Rollock: A refutation follows about that false opinion of the coming of the Lord, which he pursues, and with the same prophetic work concerning the coming of the antichrist, which will precede the coming of the Christ. It is as if it says, "This is false what they say, that the Day of the Lord approaches." That is what thus I demonstrate: If the Day of the Lord will not come unless the first defection comes, . . . certainly, the Day of the Lord does not approach, as they teach. But there is the first truth. . . . The proposition of this syllogism is not considered in the text. Therefore, however, it is true, because the coming apostasy and unveiling of the antichrist demands ample time. Therefore it follows that if the apostasy is to come before the Day of the Lord, that Day of the Lord does not come first. The assumption of the syllogism expressed in the text is considered. I observe this before I come to the words: the church will not be glorified in heaven unless the faith and the patience of the church are exercised on the earth. There is no victory before a contest, and there is no triumph before victory. Commentary on 2 Thessalonians.[8]

Apostates Begin Within the Church. The English Annotations: Some understand by the word *apostasia* a falling away of many kingdoms from the Roman Empire, but the word *apostasy* in the New Testament is taken for falling away from the truth of doctrine and the purity of the gospel. Such a kind of general and universal revolt and defection from true faith, love, and obedience to

the gospel of Christ is foretold to come to pass in the latter days by the apostle. Annotations on 2 Thessalonians 2:3.[9]

A Coming Apostasy. Robert Rollock: By the name of apostasy I understand the defection not of any certain person, or even of a small number of people, but of a multitude. For the term "defection" is in the text only, and is taken as a type, without regard to addition or certain restriction. Therefore, a universal defection of many is signified by that word [i.e., apostasy]. The whole question is, what then might that apostasy be, which the apostle predicts to be coming? It does not escape my notice that the Latin fathers understand by that apostasy the defection of many nations from the Roman Empire. How well and true thus they might be, I now do not know. I am amazed, however, how many learned and acute men have been led into common error. Truly it is possible that when out of these a certain one erred, others by squadrons without judgment followed. But enough concerning this. By the name of apostasy in this place it is to be understood as many persons turning from faith in Christ, as the following verses, and the custom of the apostle in this place, and other places of the Scripture finally demonstrate. In 1 Timothy 4:1 and following the apostle says the same thing as here, as he teaches about apostasy, and he calls this the apostasy from faith. The Spirit, however, elegantly says that certain ones in the latter times will fall away from the faith, attending closely to deceptive spirits and to the doctrines of demons, through the hypocrisy of liars, whose conscience with a branding iron has been trimmed, leading to the prohibition of marriage, and commands to abstain from foods, which God created to share with the action of thanks. About this also see 2 Timothy 3:1 and following: "I know that, however, in the last days troubled times approach. . . ." Likewise 2 Timothy 4:3: "For there will be a time when they will not tolerate sound doctrine. . . ." Concerning the same thing see 2 Peter

---

[7]LCC 24:313; citing 1 Cor 2:3.
[8]Rollock, *Ad Thessalonicenses*, 294*.

[9]Downame, ed., *Annotations*, 3K3v*; citing 1 Tim 4:1.

2:1: "Among you there will be false teachers who will secretly introduce destructive heresies. . . ." And before these things, Christ himself teaches the same thing to come. Notwithstanding the Son of Man, when he comes, will faith be found on the earth? Apostasy, therefore, in this place is to be taken of those who at first are to give their name with Christ, then renounce faith in him. Commentary on 2 Thessalonians.[10]

Expect the Church to Apostatize. John Calvin: That they may not groundlessly promise themselves the arrival in so short a time of the joyful day of redemption, he presents to them a melancholy prediction as to the future scattering of the church. This discourse corresponds with that which Christ held in the presence of his disciples when they asked him about the end of the world. He exhorts them to prepare for enduring hard conflicts, and after he has spoken of the most grievous and previously unheard calamities, by which the earth was to be reduced almost to a desert, he adds "the end is not yet," but that "these things are the beginnings of sorrows." In the same way, Paul declares that believers must exercise warfare for a long time before gaining a triumph.

We have here, however, a remarkable passage, and one that is in the highest degree worthy of observation. This was a grievous and dangerous temptation, which might shake even the most confirmed and make them lose their footing, to see the church, which had by means of such labors been raised up gradually and with difficulty to some standing fall down suddenly, as if torn down by a tempest. Paul, accordingly, fortifies beforehand the minds, not only of the Thessalonians, but of all the pious, so that when the church should come to be scattered, they might not be alarmed, as if it were a thing new and unlooked for.

As, however, interpreters have twisted this passage in various ways, we must first of all endeavor to ascertain Paul's true meaning. He says that the day of Christ will not come until the world has fallen into apostasy and the reign of the antichrist has obtained a footing in the church. The exposition that some have given this passage as referring to the downfall of the Roman Empire, it is too silly to require a lengthened refutation. I am also surprised that so many writers, in other respects learned and acute, have fallen into a blunder in a matter that is so easy, were it not that when one has committed a mistake, others follow in troops without consideration. Paul, therefore, employs the term *apostasy* to mean a treacherous departure from God, not on the part of one or a few individuals, but spread far and wide among a large multitude of persons. For when apostasy is mentioned without anything being added, it cannot be restricted to a few. Now, none can be termed "apostates" except those that have previously made a profession of Christ and the gospel. Paul, therefore, predicts a certain general revolt of the visible church. The church must be reduced to an unsightly and dreadful state of ruin before its full restoration may be effected.

From this we may readily gather how useful this prediction from Paul is. It might have seemed as though it could not be a building of God that was suddenly overthrown and laid so long in ruins had Paul not long before intimated that it would be so. Nay, more, many in the present day, when they consider themselves the long-continued diaspora of the church, begin to waver, as if this had not been regulated by the purpose of God. The Romanists also, with the view of justifying the tyranny of their idol, make use of this pretext, that it was not possible that Christ forsake his spouse. The weak, however, have something here on which to rest when they learn that the unseemly state of matters that they behold in the church was long foretold. On the other hand, the impudence of the Romanists is openly exposed, inasmuch as Paul declares a revolt will come when the world has been brought under Christ's authority. Commentary on 2 Thessalonians 2:3.[11]

---

[10]Rollock, *Ad Thessalonicenses*, 293-95*; citing Lk 18:8.

[11]CTS 42:325-26* (CO 52:196-97); citing Mt 24:6.

Defection from Universal Faith in Christ. Robert Rollock: Now it ought to be asked whether this prophecy of the apostle concerning apostasy and defection from universal faith in Christ has yet been fulfilled, and if it has, where on earth and at what time has it been fulfilled? I respond, the beginning of this universal apostasy was accomplished from Muhammad, who seduced the oriental churches from the fundamental things of the apostle, not only from faith in Christ, but also from his name and profession. The Roman popes followed this, who seduced the oriental churches, if not from the name and external profession of Christ, from true faith in Christ himself.[†] And now, enough of these things about that apostasy. Out of which, observe by that preaching, what the condition is of this visible church of Christ, which is on the earth. Without doubt it is guilty with errors, heresies, and also with universal defection, to such a degree that as long as they regard this and consider themselves also faithful, sometimes they are offended and they doubt among themselves, whether this is of the church of Christ, or this structure is of God, that so suddenly is pulled down, that for so long lies buried in its own ruins. God therefore, in order that he might in a timely manner oppose this stumbling block through his own apostle taught this coming universal apostasy, in order that people might know, nothing here is done short of the special providence of himself, and in those things they repose. Adversaries fight for this thought, truly because that visible church is not able to err. Which I ask, how well it corresponds with that prediction of the apostasy of the universal and visible church? But they use this, as it were, as a pretext, by which they hold their own miserable church in its own apostasy, while they persuade their own miserable and apostate church not to be able to degenerate into apostasy, or entirely to err. For well is it brought about with that misery, if perhaps this manages to persuade first of all that the church is able to err and to defect from the faith. Then, for instance, it is able to be made to descend into itself, and it might see finally whether that apostasy pertains to itself. Commentary on Second Thessalonians.[12]

Popery, Islam, and Heresy Draw People from the Church. John Calvin: It was no better than an old wives' fable that was contrived about Nero, that he was carried up from the world, destined to return again and harass the church by his tyranny, and yet the minds of the ancients were so bewitched that they believed Nero would be the antichrist. Paul, however, does not speak of one individual but a kingdom that was to be taken possession by Satan that he might set up a seat of abomination in the midst of God's temple. This we see accomplished in popery. The revolt, it is true, has spread more widely, for Muhammad, as he was an apostate, turned away the Turks, his followers, from Christ. All heretics have broken the unity of the church by their sects, and thus there have been a corresponding number of revolts from Christ.

Paul, however, when he has given warning that there would be such a scattering, that the greater part would revolt from Christ, adds something more serious—that there would be such a confusion that the vicar of Satan would hold supreme power in the church and would preside there in the place of God. He describes that reign of abomination under the name of a single person because it is only one reign, though one succeeds another. My readers now understand that all the sects by which the church has been lessened from the beginning have been so many streams of revolt which began to draw water away from the right course, but that the sect of Muhammad was like a violent bursting forth of water that took away about half of the church by its violence. It remained also that the antichrist should infect the remaining part with its poison. Thus we see with our own eyes that this memorable prediction of Paul has been confirmed by the event.

In the exposition I bring forward, there is nothing forced. Believers in that age dreamed that

---

[12]Rollock, *Ad Thessalonicenses*, 295-96*. [†]This is a type of a fortiori ("with greater force") argument, or argument by implication.

they would be transported to heaven after having endured troubles during a short period. Paul, however, foretells that after they have had foreign enemies molesting them for some time, they will have enemies to endure at home, inasmuch as many of those that have made a profession of attachment to Christ would be hurried away into base treachery and as the temple of God would be polluted by sacrilegious tyranny so that Christ's greatest enemy would exercise dominion there. The term "revelation" is taken here to denote manifest possession of tyranny, as if Paul had said that the day of Christ would not come until this tyrant had openly manifested himself and had designedly overturned the whole order of the church. Commentary on 2 Thessalonians 2:3.[13]

The Revealing of the Man of Lawlessness. Robert Rollock: This is the same as that thing that was said recently. For apostasy and the coming of the antichrist are clearly the same revelation. For what indeed is the antichrist than the head of this universal apostasy? By the name of antichrist, who here is called the man of sin, is it not to be understood one particular person, as they wish; but truly a certain succession of persons in one rule or tyranny: Therefore in the Scriptures it is expressed and signified of one certain person by the name, because one to this extent is the power of those persons following him, one proposition certainly, this without doubt, that they exercise tyranny in the church of Christ. And who says those things as disclosing or revealing the antichrist? To be disclosed or revealed is called antichrist, since at the peak or summit of his own power or tyranny he arrives, and it is that at that time that he begins to be. For the antichrist began to be in the times of the apostles, in his own forerunners indeed, with false prophets and heretics, who paved the road itself. He was not, however plainly disclosed, except in the year of our Lord, 666, which is called his number.[†] That is, explicable and easy, but concerning this afterward it

will be said to have spread out. First it is said, the antichrist is to come. Then through correction is subjected, and already now many antichrists have emerged. There are many antichrists; there were those who from the times of the apostles paved the way for that great future coming antichrist, about which that prophecy of the apostle is to be understood. However, that coming antichrist, it is the great antichrist, who is the head of apostasy, and who is the middle and mediator between the dragon and the anti-Christian church. Commentary on 2 Thessalonians.[14]

The Antichrist Revealed. Matthias Flacius: That adversary of Christ is called "the son of perdition" not only because he will be wretched, and because as did Judas by his kiss, that is, by the highest pretense of love toward Christ, he will betray him, for which reason that one, Judas is called "the son of perdition," but also because he will infinitely destroy people with eternal death forever. Yes, indeed he will devastate and make desolate all religion and the church. For this reason this is also called "the abomination of desolation," or "the desolation." What is next said about his revealing could be understood that either he will appear, or rather prepare, or that it [his revealing] will be produced mostly by some sort of hidden treacheries. Other deceivers will rage when that one, sitting in the church, or temple of God, rages publicly against true godliness; or finally, this revealing is disclosed by the Word of God so that the true enemy of God may be exposed. And also by this exposure, understand that first it is necessary that [the antichrist] emerge and reign because also it says, concerning his revealing, that it pertains especially to our times. Yea indeed formerly many would understand and argue that it is copiously demonstrated in my evidentiary catalog of truth. Nevertheless, now at last he has taken possession of all the earth as exposited and

---

[13]CTS 42:325-26* (CO 52:197-98).

[14]Rollock, *Ad Thessalonicenses*, 296-97*; citing Rev 13:18; 1 Jn 2:18; Rev 13:16. [†]In the margin of Rollock's Latin text here (either by Rollock or an editor), it reads, "But thereby a number is not signified any year, but the antichrist himself."

interpreted in the writings and sermons of our churches because he himself would be the true, primary antichrist. And all his abominations are brought forth and refuted in the light because he has made known things formerly hidden and scarce. Gloss on 2 Thessalonians.[15]

How to Recognize the Man of Lawlessness. Robert Rollock: Here is considered a description of the antichrist according to his own name. The name is certainly not expressed by the apostle, but rightly from the description rather than from the name it can be understood who the apostle placed before us. First, he is described from his nature and essence. Then from two qualities. Third from four actions. Concerning nature, the apostle teaches that he was going to exist as a man, and not a devil by his nature and essence, as some stupidly think. He is not indeed a beast by nature, though it is allowed in Revelation by that name that he is distinguished on account of the most degenerate habits, by which he refers to the beast as more learned than a man. By his own nature therefore a man at that time to come was, and not is, the antichrist. From this learn that while that antichrist has been destroyed, there is the capacity for such great evil from one with human nature, who in the beginning was created in the image of God.

"Wicked." This is the first quality by which the antichrist to come is described. The man of sin is to come, that is, the servant of sin, and the most addicted to sin, thus not from the thing it calls itself on this day a servant of servants. If the enslavement is rightly understood, it is in fact not in respect of God, but in respect of sin.

"Son of perdition." This is the second quality, which by itself is attributed to the traitor Judas. He is called however the son of perdition, who was formerly destined for perdition and destruction. Thus Jude spoke in his own epistle concerning heretics in his own time, in verse 4, whom earlier he calls already formerly designed to this damnation. And Peter's second epistle says concerning the

same things that their previous damnation was not idle, and their destruction does not sleep. Having been subjected, however, this quality is as a fundamental cause of the prior one. For whoever in the plan of God has been destined to eternal destruction, in all the time of their whole life thus have been addicted to sin, such that they are able to do nothing except sin.

"Opposing himself." In this place the antichrist is described from his own actions, with which this first is that he places against himself whatever is called God or divinity, an object of awe [i.e., *sebasma*, an object of worship], that which is honored. That is, he positions himself against whatever powers and majesties, earthly things and heavenly things. For as the devil is an adversary with God, therefore he is called Satan. Thus the antichrist is the adversary with God and with Christ, and also for this reason he has obtained the name of antichrist. This opposition, as the apostle teaches, is characteristic of the antichrist, as whatever at last he might be, whoever opposes himself against whatever is called God or divine, he truly is to be judged to be the antichrist. Commentary on 2 Thessalonians.[16]

Antichrist Is a Destroyer. Erasmus Sarcerius: "And is lifted up": Another duty of antichrist. To be lifted up over all which is called God, or what is worshiped [as God]. He is not content with the true God, he is not content with true worship of God, he cultivates idolatry, and so on.

Daniel 11. And the king will do as he pleases, and will be elevated and will be magnified against every god, and against the God of gods will speak magnificently and will be guided, until wrath is completed....

In that very instant, he will not reflect upon the God of his own fathers, and he will be filled with desires for women. Nor will he care for anything of the gods, since he will rise up against all things. Commentary on the Second Epistle to the Thessalonians.[17]

---

[15]Flacius, *Glossa Compendaria*, 1029.

[16]Rollock, *Ad Thessalonicenses*, 297-99*; citing Jn 17:12; 2 Pet 2:3.
[17]Sarcerius, *Ad Thessalonicenses*, 549.

THE MAN OF SIN WILL BE REVEALED. DAVID DICKSON: He gives a reason of his dehortation,[†] because Christ would not come before the antichristian defection should be, and antichrist should be revealed, the chief captain and patron of this apostasy. Therefore it behooves two things to precede Christ's coming, [1] a falling from the received faith and [2] the revelation of the chief or great antichrist. That which concerns the falling away, he does not understand the falling away of one or a few, or of many in many churches, for day by day in those times there were not a few renegades from the tent of Christ, almost through all the churches, and many followers of many errors, but he understands the universal falling away of many errors, but he understands the universal falling away of the external or visible church, so that false opinions contrary to the gospel should be received, and openly defended, and that commonly in the visible Christian church, by those that should boast in the name of the Christians.

As concerning him, who should be the head of this apostasy, he foretells that he shall be revealed by God, partly by permitting him to erect his kingdom in his church, and openly, and in very deed shows himself to be antichrist, partly by making of him manifest by the doctrine of the gospel (which should make his impostures manifest, and open to all those that are unwilling to be deceived) of which antichrist, or head of apostates, that he may be better discerned in his time by those that he may be better discerned in his time by those that were circumcised, the apostle propounds seven articles.

Article 1 contains the description, and nine notes of antichrist, all which, every one, agree to none better, yes, to none others than to the pope of Rome, as it will appear by those who observe them. "Man." Note 1. He shall be a "man," in spite of those that in favor of the pope, feign, that the evil spirit antichrist is to come. Therefore he is called *anthrōpos*, a "man," both in nature and kind, and *ho anthrōpos*, "the man," in the singular number, that he may show that the famous, chief, and great antichrist in kind so called is described. He

does not only intimate some individual man, or a single person, but the series of shavelings[†] that were to succeed in one feat. *Ho archiereus* [Gk., "the high priest"].

"The High Priest" denotes the whole series or succession of priests, and *ho anthrōpos tou theou*, "The man of God," signifies not one pastor, but the series of faithful ministers, and that according to the title of the prophets when they speak concerning the order of kings.

"Of sin." Note 2. He shall be the "man of sin," as well because he is a notable sinner, yes highly addicted to sin, as because both by fraud and impostures and by force and tyrannical compulsion, he was to be the famous author of sinning to others.

"The son." Note 3. He shall be the son of perdition, or the successor of Judas the traitor. For by his title Christ heretofore noted Judas in the New Testament, which Judas antichrist resembles, partly in the assumed title of the apostolic calling, partly by dissimulation, covetousness, cruelty, obstinacy, and final perdition, bringing destruction upon many, and principally upon himself, destroying others, and destroyed himself. THE SECOND EPISTLE OF PAUL TO THE THESSALONIANS.[18]

IS THE POPE THE ANTICHRIST? ROBERT ROLLOCK: Let us investigate that man who bears this known thing of the antichrist, so that from this known thing we might discover that he is the antichrist. Who is therefore, of all people anywhere, who is an adversary of both the doctrine and the entire life of Christ? What thus might we do? First a certain application of parts of the teaching of Christ, in order that we might recognize the antichrist from the opposite teaching.

First, it is the teaching of Christ, that we only adore our Lord alone, and that we might serve him only. Who it is who shares in the proper worship of Christ with angels, with people finished in this life, with imaginary artifacts, with the remains of

---

[18]Dickson, *Exposition*, 154*; citing 1 Tim 4:1; Heb 9:7-25; Dan 7:2; Jn 17:12. [†]A "dehortation" is a "dissuasion" (i.e., the opposition of persuasion). [†]Probably here being used in an older, derogatory sense: a priest with a shaved, or tonsured, head.

the dead, and most of all with the bread of God in the sacrifice of the Mass? Can it be that he is the Roman pontiff?

Second, Christ prohibits superstitious observances [*ethelothrēskeias*] and invented teachings and human traditions in the worship of God. Who is it who thrusts infinite superstitious observances [*ethelothrēskeias*], traditions and human inventions into the church of Christ? Can it be that same pope?

Christ teaches that the Scriptures are perfect, sufficient, and abundantly contains all things that are necessary for faith and salvation. Who is it who defends those things which are obscure, mutilated, and crippled, finally having befouled the matter, and the mother of all heresies? Can it be the pope?

Christ says that he only is the mediator between God and humankind. Who is it who beyond Christ teaches that innumerable others are intercessors? Can it be the pope?

Christ teaches that on account of only the merit of his own blood are human beings to be justified and saved. Who is it who divides up justification and salvation between the merit of Christ and the merit of people? Can it be the pope?

Christ commends trust† to each one, that one's own sins might be forgiven, and that he might achieve eternal life. And who is it who calls this trust presumption, and commends the contrary doubt of miserable people to trust? Can it be the pope?

Christ teaches that it is impossible for human beings to fulfill the universal law of God. And who is it who passes on that it is possible? Can it be that same pope?

Christ teaches that our sins are remitted only by the price of his own blood. And who is it who teaches that large monetary indulgences redeem? Can it be the pope?

Christ instructed the disciples to serve the meal of the Lord under either kind. And who is it who commands that another kind, of course a cup, be withheld from the laity, whom they call? Can it be the pope?

Finally, Christ permits the use of marriage and of whichever foods you wish. And who is it who prohibits entering into marriage (as the apostle says),

and who commands to abstain from foods which God created for partaking. . . . Can it be the pope?

Who leaves no part of healthy and Christian doctrine unharmed at all, who fights the true and natural sense of all articles of faith? As no one does not know these known things from oppositions, he himself is the antichrist. What might I say about his life and habits with which he publicly denies Christ? What law is there, whether of the first, or of the second table, in which he does not sin, and which he does not violate conspicuously? Who is the head of all the apostate? Who the heresiarch? Who the idolater? Who the magician? Who the blasphemer against God? Who the rebel against the magistrate? Who the murderer? Who the adulterer? Who the thief? Who the perjurer? Who is filled with every evil of concupiscence, if not the same pope? It would take a long time to adduce the history of the life of the Roman pope for the common good, which witness is richly provided of all of them, which now we ourselves assert. Commentary on 2 Thessalonians.[19]

The Man of Sin Comes from the Catholic Bishops. Heinrich Bullinger: From bishops, and from those who advance bishops, came forth this man of sin, who places himself in the throne of the Lamb, and challenges those things to himself, which are proper only to the Lamb; of which sort are the supreme government, priesthood, lordship, and full power in the church. Whereof I have spoken enough in the former sermons. Whom does it now not move to think that saying of Paul is fulfilled: "The adversary or enemy of Christ shall be revealed, and shall be exalted above all that is called God, or that is worshiped; so that he as God sits in the temple of God, showing himself, that he is God." But the pope's champions dispute that it is for the profit and salvation, yea necessary for the church to have some one bishop, to have preeminence over

---

[19]Rollock, *Ad Thessalonicenses*, 299-301*. †Here and following *fiducia* is rendered as "trust" rather than "faith." See helpful entry by Richard C. Muller, "Fiducia," in *Dictionary of Latin and Greek Theological Terms Drawn Principally from Protestant Scholastic Theology*, 2nd ed. (Carlisle, UK: Paternoster, 2000).

the other [bishops] both in dignity and power. But let them dispute and set forth this their idol as they please; those who will simply confess the truth must freely acknowledge that the pope is antichrist. For that which these men babble of the supremacy of the pope is flatly repugnant to the doctrine of the gospel, and of the apostles. For what more evident thing can be alleged against their disputations than that which the Lord said to his disciples when they strived for sovereignty: "The kings of the Gentiles rage over them, and they that bear rule over them, are called gracious Lords. But you shall not be so, but let the greatest among you, be as the least; and the greatest, as he that serves. For who is greater, he that sits at table or he that serves? Is it not he that sits at table? And I am among you as he that serves." This place is alleged and discussed briefly also in my former sermon. This simple and plain truth shall continue invincible against all the disputations of these Harpies.[†] The most holy apostle of our Lord Christ, will not be Lord over anyone under pretense of religion, yea, St. Peter in plain words forbids lordship over God's heritage, and commands bishops to be examples to the flock. Whereas they object that Christ says to Peter, "You are Peter, and upon this rock I will build my church; and I will give to you the keys of the kingdom of heaven. . . ." And, "Feed my sheep." And thereupon that St. Peter was appointed over all the apostles, and in them over all priests, ministers, and bishops, the chief and prince, yea, and the monarch of the whole world, it makes nothing at all to establish their dominion or lordship. We willingly grant that St. Peter is the chief of the apostles, and we also ourselves do willingly call St. Peter, the prince of the apostles, but in that sense that we call Moses, David, Elijah, or Isaiah, the chiefs or princes of the prophets, that is to say, such as have obtained far more excellent gifts than the rest. Fifty Godly and Learned Sermons.[20]

---

[20]Bullinger, *Fifty Godly and Learned Sermons*, 887-88*; citing Lk 22:25-27; Mt 16:18; Jn 21:17. [†]Clearly a derogatory term here. A harpy is a mythological creature—half woman, half bird. Sometimes they are portrayed as particularly ugly, sometimes as particularly beautiful.

The Man of Lawlessness and His Obstinacy.

David Dickson: Note 4: He will be *antikeimenos*, an "adversary," who really and indeed will be opposite to God and his ordinances, whatsoever he pretends he will really prove and show himself an adversary, who will also oppose the gospel of Christ in fundamentals, such the apostle shows some of his forerunners. For he will be an adversary to Christ himself, as to the carriage, offices, and benefits of Christ. We see that the Roman bishop is such a one, who has opposed himself against Christ more, and in more things, and more cruelly and subtly[†] and longer than anyone ever did.

"Exalts." Note 5. He exalts himself by his pride above all that is called God, or everything that is worshiped, namely, above all magistrates, princes, kings, and emperors, who in Scripture are called gods, or are worshiped as it were *sebastos* [Gk., "reverenced, awful, august"], august or illustrious.

"In the temple." Note 6: He will be in the temple of God, or in the visible external Christian church, which will profess indeed the faith of Christ, and vaunt himself to be the temple of God.

"Sits." Note 7. He will sit in that society which profess themselves the temple of God; that is, he will possess the public ecclesiastical office, the episcopal seat or chair.

Note 8. He will sit in the temple, he will set himself over the temple, he will sit superincumbent over the church, arrogating to himself the chief seats, the preeminence, the bishopric, the prelacy in the Christian church.

"Showing himself." Note 9. He will boast himself, as if he was God, that is, not thinking that he is sufficiently exalted above the commonwealth, and the church of God, as the prince and chief governor thereof, he will also endeavor to carry himself as God, partly by falsely boasting himself to have all the power of Christ communicated to him, and that is by delegation, the vicar of Christ, that is, vice Christ, or antichrist according to the signification of the preposition, *anti*, in the words, *antitheou*, "like to God, equal with God" [or "in place of God"] and *antibasileus*, a "viceroy," partly by assuming the titles that are proper to God, as the chief pastor, or prelate, the head of the church, and so on, which titles are due only to Christ. Last, by arrogating to himself the privileges in heaven, earth, and hell, which belong to God alone, such as now the pontificians acknowledge without shame in the Roman pope. The Second Epistle of Paul to the Thessalonians.[21]

Christ Rules Over the Evil One. Heinrich Bullinger: Christ truly and the apostle Paul foretold that even the last times should be wonderfully bewitched with deceitful signs and powers. Most evident places touching that thing are extant in Matthew 24 and 2 Thessalonians 2. More might be spoken (dearly beloved) and that at large concerning the operations or workings of the devil. But I trust these things being gathered together in brevity are sufficient, and give occasion to muse on higher things. But let no one so understand these things, as if the devil were able to do all things, in that what he will he can also do by and by. For his power is definite, or limited and restrained, so that he cannot do so much as he would. Otherwise all things would have been overthrown and perished long ago. Therefore not without consideration I added in the describing of the devil, that he is subject to God, for he can do nothing without God's permission. Holy God permitted him either to exercise and try the patience of these that are his, and to halt their salvation, as it is manifest in the history of Job, and in the words of Paul to the Corinthians, saying, "Lest I should be exalted out of measure through the abundance of the revelations, there was given unto me a prick to the flesh, the messenger of Satan to buffet me." Neither is it doubtful that in most grievous torments of persecutions be exalted many notable martyrs, yes and at this day both and in times past has exalted such unto glory and everlasting rest. Or else he gives the devil leave to execute violence and cruelty upon human beings, by that means to chastise their wickedness, or to punish their unbelief. For truly devils are the instruments of God's wrath, to execute his vengeance. For Paul says, "The coming of antichrist is after the working of Satan, in all power and signs, and wonders of lying, and in all deceivableness of unrighteousness in those who perish; because they received not the love of truth, that they might be saved. And therefore God shall send them strong delusion, that they should believe lies, that all they might be damned which believes not the truth, but had pleasure in unrighteousness." And this in a manner is the strength and power of sorcery or enchanting, which his feeble in the faithful. Fifty Godly and Learned Sermons.[22]

The Roman Empire Restrained the Antichrist. The English Annotations: That which now hinders and keeps him back at present, until the time prefixed by God. This, by the judgment of Tertullian, Jerome, and Chrysostom, and other ancient doctors of the church, was the Roman Empire, which subsisting and flourishing then, withheld the manifestation of the antichrist, who shall rise upon the ruins of that empire. Annotations on 2 Thessalonians 2:6.[23]

Not Simply One Person. Heinrich Bullinger: Now shall we speak of the coming up of the antichrist, that is to say, of the revelation of that sinful man. There grew up a certain foolish opinion that the antichrist should be one only man, who should be born in Babylon and of the tribe of Dan, and that he should reign a certain number of years to the great hurt of the faithful. But the foolish people do not see that Daniel understood all the kings, emperors, or head rulers of the Babylonians, Persians, Macedonians, and Romans were under the names of one lion, bear, leopard, and other beasts. Therefore it must be understood that he meant by that little horn, by antichrist, not one man only, but whole kingdoms and a whole body which should fight against Christ with their laws, constitutions, manners, and strength. Let us

---

[21]Dickson, *Exposition*, 154-55*; citing 1 Cor 16:9; Acts 25:21-25; Ps 82:1. †The meaning of this term is uncertain.

[22]Bullinger, *Fifty Godly and Learned Sermons*, 753*; citing 2 Cor 12:7.
[23]Downame, ed., *Annotations*, 3K3v*; citing Rev 13:1-11; 17:9-11.

therefore mark the words of the prophet: "I marked the horns (says he) and behold another little horn came up among them, before whom three of the horns were plucked away." And again: "Another (says he) shall arise after them and shall be greater than the first, and shall subdue three kings." You have now the mystery, and the exposition of the same. For the horns do signify the dividing and confusion of the kingdoms. And in this confusion of things, little by little springs up another kingdom in the world which subdues three other kings. COMMENTARY ON THE SECOND EPISTLE OF PAUL TO THE THESSALONIANS.[24]

THE BISHOP OF ROME AND THE ANTICHRIST.
HEINRICH BULLINGER: For there is another certain thing also, which pertains to the perfection of this body of the antichrist. Therefore while these things were in hand in the Eastern region, the bishop of Rome goes about dominion of the West in the Western region. You did not like that I should say such things of the bishop, but yet they are true. And who would ever have thought that the ministers of God's Word and of the churches should once have come to such madness as to think about how they might get the governance of the city and of the world? Especially inasmuch as Christ had said so in plain words: "The kings of the Gentiles do rule, but so you shall not: but I have chosen you, that you should go and bring forth much fruit. And he that is greatest among you shall be a servant to you all." But with these commandments of the Lord being neglected, certain men began to dispute about the primacy of the bishop of Rome, at such time as that little horn was coming forth, because it was written: "You are Peter, and upon this rock will I build my church. And I will give the keys of the kingdom of heaven and what so ever you bind upon earth, shall be bound in heaven." And again because that Achasias the bishop of Constantinople and Timothy the man of Greece did desire of Simplicius the bishop of Rome that he also would condemn Peter the bishop of

Alexandria the follower of Eutyches† of heresy, as one who had rule over the chief church and whose authority was of great value among all people, certain men concluded upon this that the seat of Rome was the chief of all churches, and that the bishop of Rome was the head ruler over all bishops. You see here also how that little horn began to lift up itself. COMMENTARY ON THE SECOND EPISTLE OF PAUL TO THE THESSALONIANS.[25]

THE ROMAN EMPIRE IS THE RESTRAINING FORCE. JOHN JEWEL: "Only he who now withholds will restrain until he is taken out of the way." Now the emperor holds the whole power and authority over the world, but it will be taken away from him, and then will the antichrist come, when all stops and constraints will be removed. Who is he who stops him and restrains his coming? The emperor of Rome. So says Tertullian,† so Augustine,‡ Ambrose,†† and Chrysostom.††† Antichrist will possess a great part of the Roman Empire; yet, so long as the emperor shall stand and prosper, he will not allow part of his empire to be abated. So long as the emperor will be able to bear himself, antichrist will never be able to grow. But a time will come when the empire of Rome will be torn asunder: then the authority of the emperor will decay, then antichrist will gather strength, and will place himself where the emperor was. A traitor cannot usurp the crown so long as the right king is able to stand and maintain his state. Antichrist is a traitor; a traitor both to God and humanity. When the emperor shall fall into decay, then he shall rise up: when the emperor becomes weak, then he shall grow strong. Therefore Paul says, antichrist will not come yet; for the emperor restrains him: the emperor will be removed, and then shall the antichrist come. UPON THE SECOND EPISTLE TO THE THESSALONIANS.[26]

---

[24]Bullinger, *Second Thessalonians*, 2:3a-5*; citing Dan 7:8, 24.

[25]Bullinger, *Second Thessalonians*, 2:3a-5*; citing Jn 15:16; Mt 16:18. †Eutyches was condemned at the Council of Chalcedon in 451 for affirming monophysitism, which blends the divine and human natures of Christ into one nature.
[26]Jewel, *Works*, 2:913-14*. †Tertullian, *De resurrectione carnis* 24. ‡Augustine, *De civitate Dei* 20.19.3. ††Ambrose, *In ad Thessalonicenses* 2.2.7. †††Chrysostom, *In II Epistolae ad Thessalonicenses* 2, homily 4.

THE BISHOP OF ROME IS THE LITTLE HORN.
HEINRICH BULLINGER: Hitherto[†] have we shown at length the beginnings and order in which that little horn crept and achieved such great power. Neither was there then truly any power so great in all the Western region as the bishop of Rome. At their command, mighty kingdoms were changed. First Chilperic, born king of France, was cast off, then the bishop of Rome craftily made Pipin his governor in the king's stead. And after that he had taken away the power of the election and ordering of the emperor from the heads of Constantinople and the Romans, and he gave Charles the king of France the name of Augustus. For this he himself got the rule of that city [Rome], which is the lady of the world, for a reward for this happily accomplished deed. Furthermore he wasted that strong nation and mighty kingdom of the Lombards through his request and counsel. Therefore he that once obtained Rome, he threw down and exalted emperors at his own pleasure, and gave Frenchmen a king, and used their service as if they had been his servants. For with their armies he tamed the Lombards, that he might afterward reign safely over all Italy. He, I say, that rules over so many and so great kingdoms, it is not by good right that we are a glistering diadem with a triple crown. No doubt the providence of God would, that this bishop of Rome (with this manner of apparel fit for a king) should show forth to all the world what he was, that is to say, that little horn that Daniel speaks of, which came forth and put aside three other horns, and with wondrous subtlety subdued them under him. COMMENTARY ON THE SECOND EPISTLE OF PAUL TO THE THESSALONIANS.[27]

THE GOSPEL MUST FIRST GO OUT. JOHN CALVIN: *To katechon* means here properly an impediment or occasion to delay. Chrysostom, who thinks that this can only be understood as referring to the Spirit or to the Roman Empire, prefers to lean on the latter opinion.[†] He assigns a plausible reason—because Paul would not have spoken of the Spirit in enigmatic terms, but in speaking of the Roman Empire wished to avoid exciting unpleasant feeling. He also states the reason why the state of the Roman Empire retards the revelation of the antichrist—that, as the monarchy of Babylon was overthrown by the Persians and the Medes, and the Macedonians, having conquered the Persians, again took possession of the monarchy, and the Macedonians were at last subdued by the Romans, so the antichrist seized hold for himself the vacant supremacy of the Roman Empire. There is not one of these things that was not afterwards confirmed by actual occurrence. Chrysostom, therefore, speaks truly insofar as concerns history. I am of the opinion, however, that Paul's intention was different from this—that the doctrine of the gospel would require to be spread hither and thither until nearly the whole world were convicted of obstinacy and deliberate malice. For there can be no doubt that the Thessalonians had heard of this impediment from Paul's mouth, of whatever sort it was, for he recalls to their remembrance what he had previously taught in their presence.

Let my readers now consider which of the two is more probable. Either that Paul declared that the light of the gospel must be diffused through all parts of the earth before God would give loose reins to Satan, or that the power of the Roman empire stood in the way of the rise of the antichrist, inasmuch as he could only break through to a vacant possession. I seem at least to hear Paul speaking of the universal call of the gentiles, that the grace of God must be offered to all, that Christ must enlighten the whole world by his gospel, in order that the impiety of men might be more fully attested and demonstrated. This, therefore, was the delay, until the career of the gospel should be completed, because a gracious invitation to salvation was first in order. Hence he adds "in his time" because

---

[27]Bullinger, *Second Thessalonians*, 2:3a-5*. [†]In a lengthy section, Bullinger offers a reading of certain strands of Western history, trying to show a pattern whereby the various Roman governments utilized political power in various ways, resulting in the kind of centralized Roman power that developed, with the primacy of Rome as well as the pope at times possessing significant political power.

vengeance was ripe after grace had been rejected. COMMENTARY ON 2 THESSALONIANS 2:6.[28]

THE KINGDOM OF MUHAMMAD IS THE ANTI-CHRIST.

HEINRICH BULLINGER: The disposition and kingdom of antichrist.[†] For holy St. Paul sets forth antichrist in diverse ways as it were in his colors: that he might paint forth, and as it were set out before our eyes to behold, his disposition and kingdom. And to begin with, he gives him to name "the sinful man." And after that, as it were expounding himself, the "child of perdition." These names after the property of the Hebrew tongue, are as much to say, as if one in our tongue should call any man, most ungracious patron, or unhappy person: yes and as it were mischief itself and perdition itself: as you would say, such a man as were the cause of wickedness, and perdition both to himself, and also to another. If any man would read the history of Muhammad or of the Turks, . . . and would ponder it with a diligent judgment, he would swear that this antichrist were the sink of all mischief, and the greatest destruction of all humankind, for he had trodden down the law of God and had published his own, that is to say, a most superstitious law, in which hypocrisy is mightily set forth, but yet in the mean season a way opened unto all wickedness. He has also subverted most mighty cities and laid them flat upon the ground: he has destroyed the most holy congregations of God, Antioch, Alexandria, Jerusalem, and Constantinople with all the congregations of Greece and Egypt: for I will rehearse no more. Truly within these years he has invaded, beaten down, and spoiled more kingdoms than ever any mighty princes or cruel tyrant had done before him. We have heard such examples of his cruelty that we may very well understand by this child of perdition and sinful man, the kingdom of Muhammad. COMMENTARY ON THE SECOND EPISTLE OF PAUL TO THE THESSALONIANS.[29]

THE POPE AND MUHAMMAD ARE ALIKE ANTICHRIST.

HEINRICH BULLINGER: Paul calls the antichrist "Adversary," that is to say, an adversary. And he calls him an adversary or antichrist, as though one should say he is set plain contrary against Christ, as one whose wit, manners, life, doctrine, deeds, lawlessness, and institutions fight against Christ. Thus let us make a comparison between Christ and the antichrist. Christ came to show peace to all the world, as of whose coming the prophets had shown before that the most cruel nations should turn their swords into plowshares, and their spears into pruning hooks, but Muhammad boasts himself to be sent of God in the power of armor. Christ taught that people are not defiled with those things that go into the mouth, but Muhammad has forbidden to his people wine and other meats, which God ordained to be received with giving of thanks. Likewise, Muhammad has given to his people circumcision and admits polygamy: that is more wives at once than one, which Christ has abrogated, and taught out of the old law, that one flesh only and not two or more, ought to be in matrimony. In short, all the life and doctrine, all the laws, institutions, and deeds of Muhammad are against Christ. Neither do the sayings, deeds, doctrines, and rites of the bishop of Rome with all his body agree any better with Christ. Christ has given us in the prophets and by the preaching of the apostles an absolute and perfect doctrine, which alone is sufficient enough to get everlasting life. But the bishop of Rome says that to that perfection we must have the traditions of fathers, I write not what, as things without which no one can be saved, and as though those holy people who lacked them were damned. Christ taught that one only God ought to be worshiped and called upon, by the means and intercession of his name. But the bishop of Rome has thrust into the churches the praying and worshiping of saints more diligently than the true religion of God. The apostles out of the tradition and spirit of Christ

---

[28]CTS 42:332-33* (CO 52:200); [†]See John Chrysostom, *Homilies on 2 Thessalonians*, NPNF 13:388-92.
[29]Bullinger, *Second Thessalonians*, 2:3a-5*. [†]When Bullinger speaks of a "horn" or "little horn," he has Dan 7:1-8 in mind. There are

ten horns on the fourth beast (Dan 7:8). This "little one [horn]" is being interpreted as the antichrist.

taught that there was but one only high priest, and one everlasting sacrifice only, that is Jesus Christ. But the bishop of Rome subverting that order of Melchizedek has consecrated innumerable sacrifices for to sacrifice daily for the sins of the quick and the dead. The apostles taught that God only does remit sins, and that to him only people ought to confess them. But the bishop of Rome has set forth unto the churches wondrous lies of the power of the keys, of auricular confession, of cases reserved, and of the market of pardons. The apostles commended to the churches the grace of God; they taught that the believers were justified by faith. But the bishop of Rome has boasted the merits of saints, yes and has sold them too. Commentary on the Second Epistle of Paul to the Thessalonians.[30]

Muhammad the Antichrist. Jacques Lefèvre d'Étaples: Moses and Christ, man, and man above man through the fullness of God. First and second beast, beast, and beast below every beast through the fullness of the wickedness of Satan. In short, repeatedly and thoroughly in the empire of the Greeks, Christ came. Continually lifted up deep within the Roman Empire, a second beast came, who is antichrist. Not therefore so that the Thessalonians have a just cause of fear as we, who ought to fear the vicinity of the man of sin, and the coming of the son of perdition, since with the sign of Paul, we move the eye to the Roman monarch. Where now I ask, the monarch? Where is he who is in that role, who rules the reins of the world? And since we see the head of the monarch, even now in that role acts as God. How much obedience, I pray, does Rome present to its king, to its monarch? And I do not know in which times, the great defection is able to appear. But since Muhammad is the beast of beasts, and antichrist of antichrists, nothing is absurd if what the apostle adduces seems just about to fit him. Who denies that he is the man of sin, and the son of perdition, who from the reign of Christ and of God, drags

Africa, Asia, and a great part of Europe down to eternal perdition? And who, with the Roman Empire, causes apostasy through such a great fullness of the earth. Nevertheless, who arose an adversary of Christ? Who nevertheless rose above all who are called God? The Father is called God, and truly is. The Son is called God, and truly is. The Holy Spirit is called God, and truly is. And these three in fact are God, and are one God. And the Father he denies to be God, the Son he denies to be God, the Holy Spirit he denies to be God. He denies the three, and he denies that Christ is God, and lifts up himself against Christ. He lifts himself up against the angels. Before Christ, before angelic supplications and also demons, as superior, he deceptively claims that he is worshiped. Is he not therefore lifted up above all who are truly called God, and since above angels and demons, also above those who are ostensibly called "god"? Concerning idols it is no work for mention to be made. For he condemns every likeness. His only idol, that is a hanging grave, full of unhappy bones, and with many pernicious idols, foolish and bestial people venerate.[†] The place of veneration in happy Arabia, indeed, in that very unhappy place, they call Mecca. Commentary on the Second Epistle to the Thessalonians.[31]

There Is One Holy Catholic Church. Heinrich Bullinger: Here we may not pass over the fact that the papists expound this place of Paul upon us. For now they ask, is this departing fulfilled, when the Lutherans and the Zwinglians depart from the holy seat of Rome, and is their liberty open a gate to all sin and mischief, and are they against the prelates of the church? Besides this, they are lifted up against the vicar of God himself, defiling the authority of the church, which never erred, and sitting in the temple of God, boast that they themselves preach the Word of God, and therefore they think themselves worthy to be worshiped as God. But they do us wrong, because

---

[30]Bullinger, *Second Thessalonians*, 2:3a-5*.

[31]Lefèvre, *Epistola secunda ad Thessalonicenses*, 508. [†]D'Étaples here seems to be referring to Muhammed's burial site.

we never departed a straw's breadth from the truth of the canonical Scripture. For although we do not know the church of Rome as it is now ordered, yet we do acknowledge the holy catholic church and the only head thereof, Jesus Christ. COMMENTARY ON THE SECOND EPISTLE OF PAUL TO THE THESSALONIANS.[32]

THE ANTICHRIST IS NOT JUST ONE MAN.
ERASMUS SARCERIUS: It is a fable that the antichrist is going to be one certain person. In fact, since John's time antichrists were in the church. . . .

Antichrist is said of everyone who is opposed to the person and doctrine of Christ, indeed for everything said, instituted, and done by Christ.

At the time of the apostles, with many things certainly he alluded to this defection, which afterward in the sayings of the emperors themselves, and as it followed universally.

Truly this defection was in only a few things before these times recognized, as also in only a few things formerly was the abomination of desolation known standing in the holy place, whereby Christ speaking about those things, said: "He who has hears to hear, let him hear."

I understand "revelation" to be the open and public preaching of the gospel, to which makes known the defection spoken of, and restores true doctrine, true understanding of him, true worship of God, true use of the sacraments, and so on.

Christ predicted this revelation of defection being spoken of in Matthew 24, with these words: "And the gospel will be preached in the whole world," in testimony. . . . John reminds of this in his Apocalypse, chapter 12, with the fight holy Michael and his associates had with that dragon and his associates, in order to uphold sincere doctrine, and whatever adheres to this [i.e., to sincere doctrine]. Truly holy Michael conquered with his associates, and more of this revelation in Daniel 11 and 12. THE SECOND EPISTLE TO THE THESSALONIANS.[33]

NO NEED FOR A VICAR WHEN CHRIST IS PRESENT.
HEINRICH BULLINGER: Inasmuch as he promised that he would abide with us unto the end of the world, we need not believe that he has put a vicar or deputy in his stead. For a vicar stands in the stead of him that is absent. But Christ is evermore present with his church: him only do we preach, commend, and inculcate to our churches. We move people continually to believe in him, and we teach most diligently charity, innocence, and pure living. Neither do we teach any other liberty than that of which the apostle spoke: "You are called into liberty, but see that you give not your liberty an occasion to the flesh, but through charity serve you one another." And we are against none of the chief teachings of the church. For the prelates of the church are the ministers of the Word and teachers of the truth of the gospel: And who despises such? Who is against such? But if any under the pretense of the church and of ministration seek their own, rule, oppress the truth, and setting godly things aside, teach human traditions, therefore they are of good right despised through their own default. For Peter says, "We must obey God more than human beings." And our Lord in the Gospel, "See that no one deceives you. For many shall come in my name, saying 'I am Christ,' and shall deceive many." Furthermore we did never defile the authority of the catholic church. For we do highly esteem Christ himself and the canonical truth. Now the strength and foundation of the church is Christ and the truth. How should we not then judge honorably of the church? We have never sat in the temple of God, but have ministered always: and for this cause have we chiefly cried against you, because you will bear rule or sit, and not minister as we do. Moreover we do freely confess having left human traditions, we do purely and simply (that is to say as much as the grace of God and our frailness will suffer) preach the canonical Scripture, and for the establishing not of our authority but of it, do often say with St. Paul: "The one who refuses these things refuses not human beings, but God, who has given his Holy Spirit" to the prophets and

---

[32]Bullinger, *Second Thessalonians*, 2:3a-5*.

[33]Sarcerius, *Ad Thessalonicenses*, 545-46; citing 1 Jn 2:18-27; Mt 24:15, 14.

apostles, that they should teach these things to us. Yet we do give all honor to God only in all things, and to ourselves nothing but confusion. Our churches, which are Christ's, will testify this. Commentary on the Second Epistle of Paul to the Thessalonians.[34]

The Revealing of the Man of Lawlessness. Erasmus Sarcerius: Christ alluded to such types, to this revelation in Matthew 24. And since you will see the abomination of desolation standing in the holy place (of which Daniel spoke) he who reads, let him understand. Then those who are in Judea, let them flee to the mountains, and so on.

The revelation of the abomination of desolation was a sign nearest to the end and destruction of Jerusalem, and a revelation of the defection spoken of is a sign of the end and also of the destruction of the world, and after this sign another one is certainly not to be expected, excepting those which simultaneously are contained in the coming of Christ itself.

Correctly our preachers warn and say today: Those who have ears, let them hear, and whoever is able to flee, let them flee from the impiety of antichrist.

"And he will be revealed": Through the open and sincere preaching of the gospel.

Thereafter this revelation showed that the defection spoken of was known only to a few, as furthermore it was really true, you might say with all of our predecessors and to our very selves ultimately, blind and ignorant as a pair of dice.

At length now is it certainly not seen that which now we see, indeed with those approving the impiety of antichrist, as if offering piety to God himself. The author of this revelation is God himself, and our Lord Jesus Christ, who today destroys, and still destroys antichrist and his reign by the spirit of his own mouth. The Second Epistle to the Thessalonians.[35]

Drawn to False Worship by the Antichrist. Dirk Philips: The spiritual falling away from the kingdom of Christ has also taken place in the demolishing of the teaching and faith through the antichrist who has forsaken true worship in the temple at Jerusalem and set up for himself a false worship. For all that Christ has taught and commanded, that he [the antichrist] has imitated in appearance in a hypocritical manner, with his priests, altars, sacrifices, and church services, and with great pomposity he has abominably distorted the sacraments of Jesus Christ. This he always adorns with twisted Scriptures, just as though it were true worship and as though the almighty God in heaven will be served therewith. But when it is carefully examined, it is nothing other than an abominable idolatry and blasphemy of God, for it is always openly opposed to the gospel of Christ, as also what Jeroboam did in his own discretion was against the law of Moses. Concerning Spiritual Restitution.[36]

Signs of Antichrist. Erasmus Sarcerius: "Man of sin": antichrist with his defection.

Allow me here to summarize the description of antichrist and his reign. Antichrist is the man of sin, the son of perdition, who opposes and destroys.

The reign of antichrist is the reign of sin and perdition, since he opposes and destroys truly all things. . . .

The apostle proposes through a certain impersonation a certain person of antichrist, while nevertheless it is not a certain particular person, indeed it is a certain filth of many adversaries and Christ and his doctrine.

He calls the man of sin "antichrist" or his member, since he is himself sin and a sinner, and he gives to others the occasion to sin and makes others to sin.

Much better concerning this saying, "man of sin," if you were to say, "man the sinner." Paul however wants to exaggerate the malice of antichrist and his members.

---

[34]Bullinger, *Second Thessalonians*, 2:3a-5*; citing Mt 28:20; Gal 5:13; Acts 5:29; Mt 24:5; 1 Thess 4:8.
[35]Sarcerius, *Ad Thessalonicenses*, 547-48; citing Mt 24:15-16.

[36]CRR 6:341-42*; citing 1 Tim 4:1; Tob 1:5-6.

"Son of perdition": By nature perdition, which itself wastes, and makes others to waste.

"Sin" and "perdition" furthermore have provide to be helpful words.

"Who opposes": And this is one of the duties of antichrist, to oppose God and his worship.

Paul attributes three chief vices to antichrist: (1) to oppose God and the doctrine of God, (2) not to be content with the true worship of God, (3) and to be arrogant and to rule over faith, as if a kind of god.

He attributes three other things to the antichrist in Daniel 11.

The duties of antichrist point to certain signs that are to be known. Thus, he who opposes God and his doctrine is certainly antichrist. THE SECOND EPISTLE TO THE THESSALONIANS.[37]

WHEN CAN A CHURCH SECEDE? JACOBUS ARMINIUS: These things having been thus affirmatively premised, let us now come to the hypothesis of our question, according to the conditions which we said must necessarily be ascribed to the church that may justly be said to have made a secession from another. With regard to the First, which we have said was required as necessarily precedent, we own, that the churches which are now distinguished by the title of "the reformed," were, prior to that reformation, one with the church of Rome, and had with her communion of faith and of worship, and of the offices of charity; nay, that they constituted a part of that church, as she has been defined in the second thesis of this disputation. But we distinctly and expressly add two particulars. (1) That this union and communion is as that between equals, collaterals, sisters and members; and not as the union which subsists between inferiors and a superior, between sons and their mother, between members and their head: that is, as they speak in the schools of philosophy, the relation between them was that of equiparancy,† in which one of the things related is not more the foundation than the other, and therefore the obligation on both sides is

equal; yet the Roman pontiff, seated in the chair which he calls apostolical, and which he says is at Rome, affirms the church of Rome to be the mother and head of the rest of the churches. (2) That this union and communion is partly according to those things which belong to God and Christ, and partly according to those things which appertain to the defection or "falling away" predicted by the apostle as about to come: for "the son of perdition" is said to be "sitting in the temple of God." As far therefore as the doctrine of the true faith sounded in these churches, and as far as God and Christ were worshiped, and the offices of charity were legitimately exercised, so far were they One Church of Christ, who patiently bore with them and invited them to repentance. But as far as the faith has been interpolated with various additions and distorted interpretations, and as far as the divine worship has been depraved by different idolatries and superstitions, and the tokens of benevolence have been exhibited in partaking of the parts offered to idols, so far has the union been according to the spirit of defection and the communion of iniquity. DISPUTATION 22. THE CASE OF ALL THE PROTESTANT OR REFORMED CHURCHES, WITH RESPECT TO THEIR ALLEGED SECESSION.[38]

THE ANTICHRIST IS ARROGANT AND HAUGHTY. ERASMUS SARCERIUS: "Over all which is called 'God'": That is, opposes every god, as David has said. "Or what is worshiped [as God]." With a polishing rhetoric he says the same thing, lest anyone looks back to these things as a means of worshiping God.

"So he might sit in the temple of God," showing himself to be as God. Exaggeration of the raising up of antichrist. This duty of antichrist Paul stakes up greatly, his arrogance and rule in faith and conscience.

---

[37]Sarcerius, *Ad Thessalonicenses*, 548-49.

[38]Arminius, *Works*, 2:279*; citing Song 8:8; 1 Cor. 12:12-13, 17; Rev 2:20-21, 14. †This appears to be an archaic word that, in context, means something like "equal standing." Arminius is denying the supremacy of the Roman Catholic Church and affirming the "equiparancy" of various churches.

But I heard these same things in description, by which antichrist himself, or certainly the head of the reign of antichrist, he describes. The pope is lord both of spiritual things, and of civil things, who has power over all clerics and lay persons, since with authority preserving or establishing laws, by which people are guided then to salvation, then to tranquility, and so on. . . .

Antichrist there sits in the temple of God, and reveals himself to be as God, he, instead of the state, is arrogant and haughtily dominates over the Christians and the conscience of Christians.

Of which vice the apostle says it is unworthy.

"To sit" is to rule and to dominate.

"To display" is to be arrogant and haughty. COMMENTARY ON THE SECOND EPISTLE TO THE THESSALONIANS.[39]

THE ROMAN PONTIFF SHOWS HIMSELF TO BE ANTICHRIST. JACOBUS ARMINIUS: He is also deservedly called the destroyer and subverter of the church. For since the superstructure of the church "is built by the faith of the doctrine of the apostles and prophets, which rests on Jesus Christ himself, the chief cornerstone," since it likewise increases more and more through the obedience of faith in the right worship of the deity and in the pursuit after holiness; and since it is built up in the Lord, being fitly framed together into one body through the bond of peace and concord; the Roman pontiff demonstrates himself to be, in a fourfold manner, the subverter of this edifice. First, by perverting the faith. This he effects (1) by adding the books of the Apocrypha and unwritten traditions to the prophetical and apostolical scriptures; (2) by joining himself, as another foundation, with Christ who is the only foundation; (3) by mixing numerous false dogmas with those which are true; and (4) by taking away some things that are true, or corrupting them by false interpretations. Second, by adulterating the integrity of divine worship. This he does (1) by an addition to the persons who alone, according to God and his command, are to

be objects of worship; (2) by the introduction of a method that is expressly forbidden by God; (3) by introducing vain, ridiculous, and old wives' superstitions; and (4) by the institution of various peculiar societies of devotees, separate fraternities, and newly fabricated religious orders of Francis, Dominic, and so on. Third, by vitiating the purity or soundness of holiness and morals. This he accomplishes chiefly by the following acts: (1) by inventing easy methods of obtaining remission of sins and plenary indulgences; (2) by declaring certain precepts in the name of councils; (3) by absolving many persons from the obligation of their duties; (4) by binding people to [the performance of] those things that no one whatever is capable of understanding or accomplishing; and (5) by bringing into the Christian world the worst examples of all wickedness. Fourth, by breaking the bond of concord and unity. This he effects chiefly by these acts and artifices: (1) When he arrogates to himself a power over others, which by no right belongs to him; (2) when he obtrudes many false dogmas to be believed as true, and unnecessary things as absolutely necessary; (3) by excommunications and senseless fulminations, by which he madly rages against those who have not deserved such treatment, and who are not subject to his diocese; (4) when he excites dissensions between princes, republics, and magistrates and their subjects; or when he foments, increases, and perpetuates such dissensions, dissensions, after they have been raised in other quarters. DISPUTATION 21. ON THE ROMAN PONTIFF, AND THE PRINCIPAL TITLES WHICH ARE ATTRIBUTED TO HIM.[40]

WHEN DID SECESSION FROM THE APOSTOLIC FAITH TAKE PLACE? JACOBUS ARMINIUS: With regard to the third condition, . . . the reformed churches deny that they were the first to make the secession. That this may be properly understood, since a separation consists in a variation of faith and worship, they say that the commencement of

---

[39]Sarcerius, *Ad Thessalonicenses*, 550.

[40]Arminius, *Works*, 2:271-72*; citing Eph 2:20-21; 4:3; 2 Pet 2:5-6.

such variation may be dated from two periods: (1) Either from the time nearest to the apostles, nay at a period which came within the age of the apostles, when the mystery of anomian [i.e., lawlessness], that is, of iniquity, or rather (if leave may be granted to invent a word still more significant) when "the mystery of lawlessness began to work," which mystery was subsequently revealed, and which lawlessness was afterward openly produced by "that man of sin, the son of perdition," who is on this very account called "that wicked" or "that lawless one," and is said to be "revealed." The reformed say that the personage thus described is the Roman pontiff. (2) Or the commencement of this variation may be dated from the days of Wycliffe, Huss, Luther, Melanchthon, Zwingli, Oecolampadius, Bucer, and Calvin, when many congregations in various parts of Europe began, at first secretly, but afterward openly, to recede from the Roman pontiff. The reformed say that the commencement of the defection and secession must be dated from the former of these two periods; and they confess and lament that they were themselves, in conjunction with the modern church of Rome, guilty of a defection from the purity of the apostolic and the Roman faith, which the apostle Paul commended in the ancient church of Rome that existed in his days. The papists say that the commencement of the defection and secession must be dated from the latter period, and affirm that they are not to be accounted guilty of any defection. DISPUTATION 22. THE CASE OF ALL THE PROTESTANT OR REFORMED CHURCHES, WITH RESPECT TO THEIR ALLEGED SECESSION.[41]

THE HINGE OF THE ENTIRE CONTROVERSY. JACOBUS ARMINIUS: This is the hinge of the entire controversy. Here, therefore, we must make our stand. If the reformed churches place the beginning of the defection at the true point, then their separation from the modern church of Rome is not a secession from the church of Christ, but it is the termination and completion of a separation

formerly made, and merely a return and conversion to the true and pure faith, and to the sincere worship of God—that is, a return to God and Christ, and to the primitive and truly apostolical church, nay to the ancient church of Rome itself: But, on the other hand, if the beginning of the defection is correctly placed by the papists, then the reformed churches have really made a secession from the Romish church, and indeed from that church which still continues in the purity of the Christian religion. But the difference consists principally in this, that the Romish church is said to have added falsehoods to the truth, and the reformed churches are said, by the opposite party, to have detracted from the truth: this controversy, therefore, is of such a nature that the burden of proof lies with the church of Rome as affirming that those things of her own which she has added are true. Yet the reformed churches will not decline the province of proof, if the Romish church will permit the matter to be discussed and decided from the pure Scriptures alone. Because the church of Rome does not consent to this, but produces another unwritten word of God; she thus again imposes on herself the necessity of proving, not only that there is some unwritten word of God, but also that what she produces is the real word of God. DISPUTATION 22. THE CASE OF ALL THE PROTESTANT OR REFORMED CHURCHES, WITH RESPECT TO THEIR ALLEGED SECESSION.[42]

WHY IT IS HELPFUL TO KNOW SOMETHING OF THE ANTICHRIST. ERASMUS SARCERIUS: "As if he is God": Who has the power of preserving statutes, and the traditions of salvation, the worship of God, and so on.

With the official sayings of the antichrist, since the pontiffs do not shrink back from them, wherefore we do not incorrectly judge that they [the various pontiffs] are antichrists, until they lay aside the official sayings [of the antichrist].[†]

There is need of a full description of antichrist and his reign, so that from that and from his reign

---

[41]Arminius, *Works*, 2:280-81*.

[42]Arminius, *Works*, 2:281-82*.

over us we learn how to take precautions, and we might understand him and his reign, from which we know how to beware. COMMENTARY ON THE SECOND EPISTLE TO THE THESSALONIANS.[43]

THE PONTIFF EMPLOYS THE NAME OF CHRIST AS A PRETEXT. JACOBUS ARMINIUS: It is demonstrable by the most evident arguments that the name of antichrist and of the Adversary of God belongs to him. For the apostle ascribes the second of these epithets to him when he calls him "the man of sin, the son of perdition, who opposes and exalts himself above all that is called God, or that is worshiped; so that he, as God, sits in the temple of God, showing himself that he is God." It was he who should arise out of the ruins of the Roman Empire, and should occupy its vacant dignity. These expressions, we assert, must be understood, and can be understood, solely respecting the Roman pontiff. But the name of "the antichrist" belongs to him preeminently, whether the particle *anti* signifies opposition or the substitution of one thing for another; not indeed such a substitution as is lawfully and legitimately made by him who has the power of placing things in subordination, but it signifies one by which anyone is substituted, either by themselves or by another person through force and fraud. For he is both a rival to Christ, and his adversary, when he boasts of himself as the spouse, the head, and the foundation of the church, endowed with plenitude of power; and yet he professes himself to be the vicegerent of Christ, and to perform his functions on earth, for the sake of his own private advantage, but to the manifest injury of the church of Christ. He has, however, considered it necessary to employ the name of Christ as a pretext, that under this sacred name he may obtain that reverence for himself among Christians, which he would be unable to procure if he were openly to profess himself to be either the Christ, or the adversary of Christ. DISPUTATION 21. ON THE ROMAN PONTIFF, AND THE PRINCIPAL TITLES WHICH ARE ATTRIBUTED TO HIM.[44]

---

[43]Sarcerius, *Ad Thessalonicenses*, 551*. †Both instances of "sayings" in this paragraph could also be translated as "teachings."

[44]Arminius, *Works*, 2:272*.

2:7-12 FALSE SIGNS AND WONDERS

⁷For the mystery of lawlessness is already at work. Only he who now restrains it will do so until he is out of the way. ⁸And then the lawless one will be revealed, whom the Lord Jesus will kill with the breath of his mouth and bring to nothing by the appearance of his coming. ⁹The coming of the lawless one is by the activity of Satan with all power and false signs and *wonders, ¹⁰and with all wicked deception for those who are perishing, because they refused to love the truth and so be saved. ¹¹Therefore God sends them a strong delusion, so that they may believe what is false, ¹²in order that all may be condemned who did not believe the truth but had pleasure in unrighteousness.*

OVERVIEW: Throughout their expositions of this passage, these Reformation commentators examine the antichrist's brief reign and its end. In this regard, they discuss extensively the nature of false miracles and their role in deceiving those who reject the truth of God's Word. Such delusion, the authors allege, serves as a means of God's judgment on unbelievers. Moreover, they highlight the manner in which Christ will destroy the kingdom of the antichrist through the Word. Some of our commentators interpret this as the overthrow of the papacy's control of Christendom through the preaching of the Word. For several Protestant interpreters, the work of Christian magistrates in fostering the church's renewed teaching of the Word will be instrumental in Christ's triumph over the papal antichrist's kingdom. Furthermore, these authors largely regard this overthrow of the antichrist as a gradual process. Since their expositions deal with the role of sin and unbelief in receiving the antichrist, these writers provide detailed discussions concerning God's control over sin and reprobation.

2:7 Restrained for a Time

THE REALITY OF THE MYSTERY OF LAWLESSNESS. HEINRICH BULLINGER: A person cannot deny that even now the power of iniquity does work by them, but they now set forth their strength more covertly than they shall do when

their time comes. For to the body of the antichrist belongs blasphemies, cruel persecutions, heresies, and other similar iniquities. But these things began to bud and spring up by and by, even in the time of the apostles. In this regard, John the apostle says, "My little children, it is now the last time, and as you have heard, that the antichrist shall come, even now there begins to be many antichrists already." Therefore Paul more clearly signifies to us the same as the antichrist, that is to say, the perfection of all iniquity should be uttered, saying, when that shall be taken away, which now withholds or lets him reign, then shall the wicked be opened. That is to say, when the empire of Rome shall be taken out of the way, or at the least significantly troubled, then shall the antichrist reign, and after that shall Christ come to destroy this enemy of all saints, and also to judge all flesh. For he does now expound that more plainly that about which he spoke of before. The words corresponding to the Greek text make those things more plain for thus they signify: holding that now, until it is out of the way. Which is as much to say as that that thing which now only is allowed shall be taken out of the way. And then shall the wicked appear. Or else (to say it more plainly) that thing which now only is allowed shall be allowed so long, until it is taken away. And when it is taken away, then shall the antichrist come forth. COMMENTARY ON THE SECOND EPISTLE OF PAUL TO THE THESSALONIANS.[1]

---

[1]Bullinger, *Second Thessalonians*, 2:7*; citing 1 Jn 2:18.

The Reign of Antichrist and the Reign of Christ. Erasmus Sarcerius: "For the mystery of iniquity even now proceeds, so far he who restrains will hold prisoner until he is taken out of your midst." So,[†] why not now? But in his own time antichrist will be revealed, taken up from the circumstances of time, to which from according to the promise of God antichrist will reign.

This argument[‡] shows a certain defection to last a long time; the antichrist will reign for a considerable time, and will greatly flourish for a time.

Therefore the defection proceeded publicly with Phocas, Heraclius, and Boniface,[††] and all the way down. And Daniel predicted a certain intervening time, during which the antichrist would reign.

Paul declares with a mysterious voice that the reign of Christ cannot be understood except by revelation, and that reason does not perceive it.

Likewise, it is communicated with a mysterious voice, nothing extraordinary, and if our things come before, indeed we ourselves did not understand the impiety of antichrist, since it was a mystery. Commentary on the Second Epistle to the Thessalonians.[2]

2:8 Destroyed by the Breath of the Lord

The Lord's Victory over the Lawless One. Heinrich Bullinger: They are greatly deceived and mad who think the church can either be gathered together or, being gathered, can be maintained and preserved with practices, that is to say, with crafty counsels and subtle, human deceits. It is truly said of the common people that "the same is overthrown again by human wisdom that which was first built by human wisdom." Besides this, the Lord himself removes force and arms from the building of the church, since he forbids his disciples the use of sword and to Peter ready to fight, says, "put your sword into your scabbard." Neither do we ever read that any were sent by the Lord as soldiers, which with armed force should bring the world in subjection. But rather that Scripture witnesses the great enemy of God, antichrist, shall be destroyed with the breath of God's mouth. Wherefore there is no doubt that all those things which are read in diverse places of the prophets, and chiefly in Zechariah 12, concerning wars to be made against all nations, by the apostles and apostolic men, ought to be figuratively expounded. For the apostles according to their manner fight as apostles, not with spear, sword, and bow of carnal warfare, but of spiritual. The apostolic sword is the Word of God. Yet in the meantime no one denies that the weapons of carnal or corporal warfare have been profitable sometimes to apostolic men, and to the church, that do good even at this day. No one denies that God often uses the help of soldiers and magistrates in defending the church against wicked tyrants. Yes, rather all people will confess that a good and godly magistrate owes a duty toward the church of God. For not without great cause that worthy prophet of God, Isaiah, calls "kings nourishing fathers, and queens nourishing mothers." Paul, being opposed by the Jews in the temple of Jerusalem for preaching of the gospel among the Gentiles, is taken away and rescued by the army of Claudius Lysias the Roman tribune. Of the Holy Catholic Church.[3]

A Faithful Man. Jacques Lefèvre d'Étaples: In truth, as Christ with the spirit of his mouth will come to annul and destroy, thus he already cast down that idol (if the things I have heard told are true, and indeed having heard, the written things I

---

[2]Sarcerius, *Ad Thessalonicenses*, 552-53; citing Dan 11. [†]Sarcerius uses the Latin term *aetiologia*, which denotes a figure of reasoning that gives the cause (i.e., ground) of an argument. [‡]Sarcerius again uses *aetologia*. See previous note. [††]Sarcerius is here likely referring to the following persons: Flavius Phocas Augustus had usurped power in the Byzantine Empire from Maurice, and reigned from 602 to 610. Flavius Heraclius August conquered Phocas, and was emperor of the Byzantine Empire from 610 to 641. There have been a number of Bonifaces in church history, including St. Boniface (c. 675–754) and eight popes of that name. Despite the lack of clarity, Sarcerius's point is fairly straightforward: There has been a long history of defection from biblical faithfulness throughout history. The "mystery of lawlessness" might indeed climax in a certain way, and in a certain person at some point, but there have been since the first century numerous manifestations of this mystery of lawlessness. Phocas, Heraclius, and Boniface are particular manifestations of this unfaithfulness.

[3]Bullinger, *Fifty Godly and Learned Sermons*, 831-32*; citing Jn 18:11; Is 49:23.

collected) by the Spirit with lightning for which he prepared the schemes of the world to whatever things he is always prepared to serve. I saw a man of Felcina[†] now almost (if I am not mistaken) in his twentieth year. He was clothed in a sack, with a bare head, with no shoes, and always marching, enclosed in a twisted twig, a wooden cross carried in his hands, not shuddering at the cold or snow (which at that time was great), wandering from shrine to shrine, where if a doorway was not open he was praying in the snow on his knees. His food was cabbage and bread, after fasting for many days. A lake for his drink, the land for his bed. It is said this man suffered for seven years in servitude in Constantinople in confession of the name of Christ. After which time, although the merchants of Turkey did not know him, for the sake of simplicity of morals and fidelity brought him to Mecca. They indeed advanced to the temple, then he alone advanced, with his knees bent in front of the wild beast, and he himself bowed, adored the beast, and he, truly in silent speech to Christ, prayed with tears, so that in his strength he might reveal a sign, and he cast down that body who had seduced so great a number into perdition, and with the light of his grace he illuminated that same land, and people knew him, and they truly gave glory to God who alone is worthy of glory. Observers found that they would cut him in half with a saw [used] for wood. For this is the penalty for those daring to enter the temple—those opposed to Muhammad are cut in two. [This man] truly exulted as he waited patiently to be cut in two for the name of Christ. COMMENTARY ON THE SECOND EPISTLE TO THE THESSALONIANS.[4]

THE BREATH OF THE MOUTH OF THE LORD IS HIS OWN WORD.

HEINRICH BULLINGER: He shall not fall by and by after he is stricken with a stroke or weapon, but by little and little, and after he has been made weak by many battles he shall at the last perish. But he shall not be cast down with human hands, neither yet by the multitude of hosts, nor strength of soldiers, or gun strokes, but by the hand and power of God. For Christ shall first consume him with the spirit of his mouth, and after that shall he put him clean out of the way, with his most glorious coming into judgment. The first of these two Paul took out of the eleventh chapter of Isaiah, whose words are these: "With righteousness shall he judge the poor, and with equity shall he contend for the meek of the earth, he shall strike the world with the rod of his mouth, and with the spirit of his lips shall he slay the wicked." Now "the spirit of the mouth" or of "the lips of God" is the true exposition of the Word of God. For the Word of God is the same sword with which the head of this proud Goliath shall be stricken off. For antichrist speaks on the side of the highest, and he says that all that he does is deduced or taken out of the decrees of the holy Scripture. For under the pretense of this has he hitherto reigned safely. But when through the goodness of God, the light of the gospel, that is, God's Word, begins to shine, the clouds of this deceiver vanish straightway. For it is plain to all people that this fellow in his manners and laws is clean contrary to Christ. Therefore, it comes to pass that all godly witted people (the truth once known) abhor and forsake him. Therefore, the sword with which this man is slain is the Word of God, for then is he most surely slain, when his nature and disposition are manifestly known by the doctrine of truth. The knowledge of him kills him and casts him down, and the cloaking and ignorance of him sets him up. For those who do not know him do believe that he is an apostolic prophet, yes and a god too; but those who know him truly are sure that he is antichrist. COMMENTARY ON THE SECOND EPISTLE OF PAUL TO THE THESSALONIANS.[5]

IN TIME CHRIST DESTROYS THE REIGN OF ANTICHRIST.

ERASMUS SARCERIUS: "Whom the Lord will kill with the spirit of his mouth": antichrist in his own reign is not overcome through human strength, but by the power of Christ.

The Lord will kill antichrist by the spirit of his mouth; he will reveal, confound, and expose him by

---

[4]Lefèvre, *Epistola Secunda ad Thessaloninces*, 506-7. [†]A city in Italy.

[5]Bullinger, *Second Thessalonians*, 2:6-8; citing Is 11:4.

his own word. What today has been openly done we discern, truly likewise by our children now might be known: who is antichrist? What is his reign? What are its impieties, and finally, what are its members?

It is the Lord Jesus, whom here Paul calls "spirit of his mouth," as Isaiah 11 says, "the spirit of lips."

"And he will destroy at the appearance of his coming": His utter destruction does not follow suddenly at the same time the revelation and confusion of antichrist, but antichrist will reign all the way down to the last day.

There is a false opinion that the reign of impiety until revelation, about which Paul until this point spoke, will absolutely be ruined. Rather, it will endure utterly to the end of the world, because finally at his coming, Christ will extinguish this impious reign completely. In the meanwhile, it certainly remains, and at the revelation of antichrist, a great part of humankind from it will defect, and we see this with the world. COMMENTARY ON THE SECOND EPISTLE TO THE THESSALONIANS.[6]

THE DESTRUCTION OF THE EVIL ONE. DAVID DICKSON: Article 5. It contains the visible kingdom of antichrist, or the beginning, middle, and end of his kingdom. What pertains to the beginning of his kingdom, so soon as the Roman Empire, or the Roman emperor shall be removed from that which was to be the seat of antichrist, that is, Rome, then in that city of the patron of antichristianism will advance and discover himself, by exalting himself above all laws, and he is bound to none, neither civil nor ecclesiastical, and also has power in dispensing in divine matters, openly professing himself to the *anomos*, that lawless one (whereof the Spirit of God had foretold) this shall be the manner of revealing him, and the beginning of the clear possession of his kingdom. The Roman pope hitherto boasts himself to be such a one from that time wherein Rome ceased to be the seat of empire, who impudently does break in pieces the bars of laws, extols himself above the right and the laws, he disannuls the laws made by God, and dispenses concerning them, as they say, and establishes others

in their stead; he determines his will for reason, as the Orthodox have made manifest in their controversies. The pontificians are not ashamed to confess these, and many others of the like concerning their bishops, and publicly in their writings, so that there is no further need to inquire who he is, that sits antichrist in the temple, or in the visible church, as to his title, when we know that the name *antichrist* may signify two things, according to the various acceptation of the preposition *anti*, that is, the "vicar of Christ," and the "adversary of Christ," and we hear the pope of Rome boasting himself antichrist in one of these significations, that is, professing himself the vicar of Christ, but in the meanwhile we apprehend the same as it were in the very act, openly affirming himself to be among Christians, that he is neither subject to civil nor ecclesiastical laws, but without blushing to profess himself above them. And whereas now it is manifest to the world that the authority of the pope of Rome is by himself, and by his attendants, extolled above Scripture, or divine laws, as to the constitution of the canon, determination of the sense, judgment and deciding of controversies, dispensation (as it is called) about divine commands, and so on, shall we doubt who he is that sits lawless in the temple of God, or among the professors of Christian religion? As to what concerns the second, or the possession of his kingdom, antichrist shall not possess his kingdom without war, Christ shall fight against him, with the sword of his mouth, that is, by preaching of the truth revealed in the gospel, and by the power of his Spirit concurring with the Word.

As to the third, touching the end of antichrist's kingdom, or the issue of his war and kingdom. Christ will detect and confute the lies of antichrist, the deceits, wickedness, tyranny, false interpretations, and allegations of Scriptures, and will by degrees demolish, consume, and waste his kingdom, and at length will destroy and abolish it by the illustrious manifestation of his coming to the last general judgment. THE SECOND EPISTLE OF PAUL TO THE THESSALONIANS.[7]

---

[6]Sarcerius, *Ad Thessalonicenses*, 555; citing Is 11:4-5; citing Is 11:4.

[7]Dickson, *Exposition*, 155.

2:9-12 *Refusing the Truth*

The Judgment of God for Refusing to Love the Truth. Heinrich Bullinger: You have now a reason how it comes to pass that the world nowadays is so ready to believe the miracles, doctrines, and rites of antichrist. It is the judgment of God, who has shown miracles enough by his Son, by his prophets and apostles, and has also prescribed us doctrines and rites clearly and sufficient enough. But all these things set aside, we would rather be deceived. Therefore these priests and monks, antichrist's knights, deceived us by taking away our money, and never ceased to thrust in their lies to us, until that they had emptied all people's coffers. Such things as might be brought out of the Bible seemed old, worn things. All people daily desired to hear new matters, and therefore it was free for every person that would to invent everything that they liked. That one was favored who brought in any new thing into the church: and so through their shamelessness, and our curiosity and foolishness, it came to pass, by the righteous judgment of God, that all truth was banished many years since, and error has reigned mightily throughout the congregations. Now though it be thus, and that experience itself proves these things to be true, yet are there certain evil occupied persons, which go about to bolster up the corrupt captains of the most corrupt religion, which are bent to destroy the spirit of the mouth of God. But the truth which is invincible shall overcome both those vain prelates of the church, and also their foolish defenders and shall also overthrow them and bruise them all to pieces, except they convert to the Lord. Hitherto have we disputed more at large than we thought to have done at the beginning, of the coming of antichrist, of his kingdom and confusion, for the reader's pleasure, and for the erudition and warning of the simple people. Now will we return unto Paul and the Thessalonians. For Paul himself after he has finished his disputation of antichrist turns to the Thessalonians. Commentary on the Second Epistle of Paul to the Thessalonians.[8]

God's Rule over Sin. Jacobus Arminius: This is the efficiency of divine providence concerning sin, which cannot be accused of the least injustice. (1) For with respect to the hindering of sin, that which is employed by God is sufficient in its own nature to hinder, and by which it is the duty of the creature to be hindered from sin, by which also he might actually be hindered unless he offered resistance and failed of the proffered grace. But God is not bound to employ all the methods that are possible to him for the hindrance of sin. (2) But the cause of sin cannot be ascribed to the divine permission. Not the efficient cause; for it is a suspension of the divine efficiency. Not the deficient cause; for it presupposed that human beings had a capability not to commit sin, by the aid of divine grace, which is either near and ready, or if it is wanting, it is removed to a distance by the fault of the persons themselves. (3) The presenting of arguments and occasions does not cause sin, unless, *per accidens*, accidentally. For it is administered in such a manner as to allow the creature not only the spontaneous but also the free use of their own motions and actions. But God is perfectly at liberty in this manner to try the obedience of his creature. (4) Neither can injustice be ascribed with any propriety to the divine concurrence. For there is no reason in existence why God ought to deny his concurrence to that act which, on account of the precept imposed, cannot be committed by the creature without sin; which concurrence God would grant to the same act of the creature if a law had not been made. (5) Direction and determination have no difficulty. (6) Punishment and pardon have in them manifest equity, even that punishment which contains blinding and hardening; since God is not wont to inflict it except for the deep demerit and the almost desperate contumacy of his intelligent creature. Disputation 10. On the Righteousness and Efficacy of the Providence of God Concerning Evil.[9]

---

[8]Bullinger, *Second Thessalonians*, 2:9-12*.

[9]Arminius, *Works*, 2:188-89*; citing Rom 1:1–2:29; Is 5:4; Mt 11:21-23; Gen 2:16-17; Is 6:7; Rom 1:1-32; 2 Thess 2:9-12.

Christ the Lord of His Word. Pilgram Marpeck: O, you deceptive serpent, how dare you so forcefully employ your old craft in order to throw us from the word of medicine by which we may have life and become healthy; from the beginning, through your deceptive speech, you have thrown us from the word of life and death! The Lord must speak to you the word which says "I am," and so expose you and cast you down with all your cunning; you do not seek to learn of Christ; you seek only to capture the consciences. If you do not give yourself as a captive to Christ, the antichrist will nevertheless give himself captive to your thought and reason in order that you will also partake of innocent blood, for all those who struggle against innocent blood are guilty of innocent blood. A Clear and Useful Instruction.[10]

On Reprobation. Jacobus Arminius: From the law of contraries, we define reprobation to be a decree of the wrath, or of the severe will, of God; by which he resolved from all eternity to condemn to eternal death unbelievers, who, by their own fault and the just judgment of God, would not believe, for the declaration of his wrath and power.

Though by faith in Jesus Christ the remission of all sins is obtained, and sins are not imputed to them who believe; yet the reprobate will be compelled to endure the punishment, not only of their unbelief (by the contrary of which they might avoid the chastisement due to the rest of their sins), but likewise of the sins they have committed against the law, being "everlasting destruction from the presence of the Lord, and from the glory of his power." Disputation 15. On Divine Predestination.[11]

The Antichrist Can Perform Miracles, Signs, and Wonders. Erasmus Sarcerius: "Whose coming according to the working of Satan, in every strength and with signs, and with lying wonders, and in every seduction of sin for those who are perishing." A description follows of the power of antichrist, and of his reign, so that the Thessalonians will not think the antichrist impotent, or that his reign is impotent.

Paul attributes in this description to antichrist being a satanic ruler, through which antichrist will be effective in deceiving others.

Nothing is impossible for Satan on account of the permission of God, thus neither is anything for antichrist with God permitting. This is the place for the power of antichrist, and his reign, which reasonably ought to be feared, not lightly neglected. He pertains to this place at Ephesians 2. The devil is effective in his unbelief.

Formerly since also antichrist is effective to produce miracles, signs, and wonders, therefore it is not the case that certain miracles, signs, and wonders are enough for a sincere preacher, and also a witness to Christ; as in Matthew 7, where in these words he responds to impious hypocrites with his own sincerity, with displays of miracles in contrast to false [displays]. "I never knew you. Depart from you who work iniquity."

Also, Christ commands the false prophets to flee, even if they do miracles and signs.

This issue is not settled with the question, *whether* it is possible, that false prophets do miracles, but *if* therefore they are sincere and better, and *to whom* are miracles of false prophets to be ascribed? To Satan of course, not to God.

You have the same description on antichrist also in Matthew 24, in the description of the false prophets. Commentary on the Second Epistle to the Thessalonians.[12]

---

[10]CRR 2:87*; citing Gen 3:1-7; Mt 23:34-36. Editor William Klassen suggests that Marpeck (and perhaps others in the Marpeck circle) wrote this letter with Kaspar von Schwenckfeld in view. In the passage above, Marpeck's polemic is directed to those who—like the serpent in Gen 3—draw attention from God's clear communication to humankind, here holy Scripture.

[11]Arminius, *Works*, 2:228-29*; citing Jn 3:18; Lk 7:30; Jn 12:37, 40; Rom 9:22; 4:2-11; Jn 13:24; 9:41.

[12]Sarcerius, *Ad Thessalonicenses*, 555-57; citing Mt 7:23; 25:41-46; 24:1-51.

2:13-17 STANDING FIRM IN THE FAITH

¹³But we ought always to give thanks to God for you, brothers beloved by the Lord, because God chose you as the firstfruits[a] to be saved, through sanctification by the Spirit and belief in the truth. ¹⁴To this he called you through our gospel, so that you may obtain the glory of our Lord Jesus Christ. ¹⁵So then, brothers, stand firm and hold to the traditions that you were taught by us, either by our spoken word or by our letter.

¹⁶Now may our Lord Jesus Christ himself, and God our Father, who loved us and gave us eternal comfort and good hope through grace, ¹⁷comfort your hearts and establish them in every good work and word.

a Some manuscripts *chose you from the beginning*

OVERVIEW: Election and perseverance are the two primary themes drawn from this passage by our sixteenth-century commentators. A link is made between God's choosing of his people for salvation and the operation of his external word, particularly in preaching, as the means by which he establishes this end. Similarly, in Paul's call for believers to stand firm to the traditions they had been taught, Scripture in its divine perfection is emphasized as an appointed means by which believers are enabled to persevere in faith. Also particularly noteworthy is the manner in which these Reformed commentators interact with the Catholic view on the role of tradition, as they argue traditions can be acceptable, even if not explicitly established in Scripture, as long as they are judged by Scripture and not in conflict with its teachings.

2:13-14 *Elected unto Salvation*

ELECTION AND PREACHING. HEINRICH BULLINGER: This is a notable place teaching the election of God. God has chosen us unto salvation, not that we should say, "If God has chosen me, I need not fear damnation, and though I sin, never so much." But God has chosen us unto salvation, says Paul, which is finished in us through the sanctifying of the Spirit and believing the truth, that is to say, by the Spirit himself, who purifies our hearts and gives us true faith. For faith that is the gift of God is mighty in operation. Paul therefore sets true faith against the false persuasion, of that which James speaks, saying "faith without works is dead." To this matter of election belongs the preaching of the gospel also. For through the preaching of the gospel he calls us to the true faith, and to the obtaining or possession of the glory of our Lord Jesus Christ: that is to say, that we might be made the glorious and beautiful possession of our Lord Jesus Christ, a holy, innocent, and immaculate people, which might honor and worship God, and that God himself might dwell in the hearts of those who serve him. For God has not called us unto lusts and uncleanness, but to holiness and pureness, and that we might become his holy temple. These things ought to be taught to the congregations. After this manner those that are captive should be plucked out of the bondage of antichrist: and if any have not fallen into his captivity, let them here learn to give God continual thanks, and also to pray to him that he lead them not into temptation, but deliver them from that evil, sanctify them through the spirit, and by true faith to keep them in the election of salvation. COMMENTARY ON THE SECOND EPISTLE OF PAUL TO THE THESSALONIANS.[1]

THE REFUSAL TO LOVE THE TRUTH AND BE SAVED. DAVID DICKSON: Help 3. All deceivableness

---

[1] Bullinger, *Second Thessalonians*, 2:13-14*; citing Jas 2:17.

of unrighteousness, or all unjust or fraudulent deceit, such are false, counterfeits, or fawning doctrines, sophistical disputations, the enticement of riches, honors, or dignities of this world, together with threatenings and terrors, the top and height of which deceit will be in him, because he will not openly or directly fight against Christ, but he will set upon the matter secretly, and in an unhidden manner, counterfeiting himself to act the cause of the Christ, when, as much as he can, he subverts it.

"Because." Article 7. Touching the subjects of antichrist, and their perdition, and the causes thereof. The retinue of antichrist, properly called his household, and familiars, are described to be such as with obstinate minds stubbornly cleave to him, even to the end, and in whom the devil is very effectual. (1) From the property of reprobates, they perish. (2) From the meritorious cause of their perdition, because they receive not the truth offered in the Word of God, that they might be saved. . . .

They are described: (3) From the most just revenge of the Judge upon them, punishing sin with sin, and delivering them to be blinded by the devil, that they which have refused to behold light, and have renounced divine truth, should believe errors and delusions, the devices of men, most gross fables, and lies, and so should perish.

[Commenting on verse 12] They are described: (4) From their last condition, and from the meritorious cause of their condemnation, they shall be all eternally damned at that last judgment, because they have not believed the plain truth of God, laid open in the gospel, but with a full will have most unrighteously rested in the belief of lies, and obedience to their carnal desires. And this is the issue of those who obstinately cleave to the bishop of Rome, and his errors, foretold by the Spirit of God. THE SECOND EPISTLE OF PAUL TO THE THESSALONIANS.[2]

SCRIPTURE IS AN "EXTERNAL TRADITION" GOD HAS CHOSEN TO USE. JACOBUS ARMIN-

IUS: Internal tradition[†] is always and absolutely necessary to the salvation of human beings. For in no way, except by a revelation and an inward sealing of the Holy Spirit, can any person perceive, and by an assured faith apprehend the mind of God, however it may be manifested and confirmed by external signs. External tradition is necessary through the pleasure of the divine will, whether we consider that will universally; for without it he can abundantly instruct the mind of human beings. Or whether we consider it according to special modes; for it is sometimes delivered by the pronunciation of lively sounds, and at other times by writing, and at times by both methods, according to his own good pleasure, and which of them soever he has seen proper to employ. It is, from this very circumstance, necessary to human beings; and from it the inconclusiveness of this argument is apparent: "Because God formerly instructed his own church without the Scriptures by the words which he spoke himself, therefore, the Scriptures are now unnecessary." DISPUTATION 3. ON THE SUFFICIENCY AND PERFECTION OF THE HOLY SCRIPTURES IN OPPOSITION TO HUMAN TRADITIONS.[3]

THE CONFIRMATION OF THE FAITH OF THE THESSALONIANS. DAVID DICKSON: The other part of the chapter follows, wherein he confirms (three ways) the faith of the Thessalonians, lest they should be moved by this sad prophecy. (1) By thanksgiving in their behalf. (2) By an exhortation of them to constancy, and (3) by prayer for them. As for the first way in their thanksgiving he produces three arguments for the confirmation of their faith. "Brethren, beloved." Argument 1. You are our brethren, comprehended with the same love of God with us. Therefore you need not fear perishing with the antichristian sect.

---

[2]Dickson, *Exposition*, 156. Dickson is here commenting on 2 Thess 2:10-12.

[3]Arminius, *Works*, 2:106; citing 2 Cor 1:20-22; 2:10-16; 3:7-10; 2 Cor 4:6; 1 Cor 5:9; Ex 24:7; Lk 16:27-31. [†]Arminius is in this selection speaking of (1) "internal tradition" (e.g., God speaking directly to the heart, without the mediation of something like holy Scripture), and (2) "external tradition" (Holy Scripture itself).

"Chosen." Argument 2. In his decree touching the end and saving means, God has chosen you that you may obtain salvation through faith, and sanctification by the Holy Ghost, as by means, whereby you may attain salvation, freely appointed for you. . . .

Argument 3. God now effectually called you through the gospel preached by me, that you may obtain glory purchased by Christ. Therefore there is no reason that you should be moved by this sad prophecy. THE SECOND EPISTLE OF PAUL TO THE THESSALONIANS.[4]

2:15-17 Stand Firm, Hold to the Traditions

THE APOSTOLIC TRADITION IS INSCRIPTURATED TRADITION. HEINRICH BULLINGER: Now Paul brings in that which he meant in the beginning of this chapter where he said, "I beseech you by the coming of our Lord Jesus Christ, that you be not suddenly moved from your mind. . . ." And in the meantime he disputes many things to this effect. And now at last he brings this in and says, inasmuch as it is thus, abide in our ordinances that we taught you, whether it was by mouth when we were yet among you, or else by my epistles, . . . which I sent when I was absent from you. I taught you the true gospel, you need not seek any other. The papists abuse this place for the defense of human traditions. And we do grant that the traditions of the apostles ought as well to be received as their epistles written. But we do not grant that all those are the traditions of the apostles that they thrust at us under the name of the apostles. The traditions of the apostles are not contrary to their epistles written. But these human traditions are plainly contrary to the writings of the apostles. COMMENTARY ON THE SECOND EPISTLE OF PAUL TO THE THESSALONIANS.[5]

THE PERFECTION OF GOD'S WORD. MARTIN BUCER: God's law is perfect and entire, and its teaching enables us to conform the whole of life to the will of God. Wherefore Scripture is bound to contain oracles that deal definitely though not in precise detail with every aspect of public or private life that should rightly exercise the people of God. The church has instituted the practice of meeting for worship on the Lord's day, and the observance of the sacraments of Christ with greater decency and reverence. Similarly Paul too delivered to his churches definite traditions (*paradoseis* [i.e., "tradition" or "that which is handed down"]) so that their entire life should be conducted with dignity and profit, as he bears witness of himself in 1 Corinthians and elsewhere. All such practices are based upon definite though generalized oracles to the effect that all things should be reverently ordered and administered with a view to the common advantage and the increase of faith, with is the universal requirement of the law and the prophets. But all the same, Scripture contains no explicit prescription of these traditions. COMMENTARY ON ROMANS.[6]

THE WHOLE SUM OF THE GOSPEL. HEINRICH BULLINGER: After his manner he here joins to his admonition a happy and lucky wish. And he does here very cunningly bring in together the whole sum of the gospel, that is to say, that God has loved humankind, and given to them everlasting consolation, that is Jesus Christ, who is our hope, and has given it us through his grace, and not for our merits, that is to say, that we might live evermore. He wishes unto them (I say) that the same meek and loving God would comfort their hearts and establish them in all good saying and doing, that is to say, in all righteousness. For in these two things he comprehends all the offices or duties of a Christian person. COMMENTARY ON THE SECOND EPISTLE OF PAUL TO THE THESSALONIANS.[7]

---

[4]Dickson, *Exposition*, 156.
[5]Bullinger, *Second Thessalonians*, 2:15*.

[6]Bucer, *Commentary on Romans*, 303.
[7]Bullinger, *Second Thessalonians*, 2:16-17.

3:1-18 PRAYER REQUESTS, ENCOURAGEMENT, AND BENEDICTION

Finally, brothers,[a] pray for us, that the word of the Lord may speed ahead and be honored,[b] as happened among you, ²and that we may be delivered from wicked and evil men. For not all have faith. ³But the Lord is faithful. He will establish you and guard you against the evil one.[c] ⁴And we have confidence in the Lord about you, that you are doing and will do the things that we command. ⁵May the Lord direct your hearts to the love of God and to the steadfastness of Christ.

⁶Now we command you, brothers, in the name of our Lord Jesus Christ, that you keep away from any brother who is walking in idleness and not in accord with the tradition that you received from us. ⁷For you yourselves know how you ought to imitate us, because we were not idle when we were with you, ⁸nor did we eat anyone's bread without paying for it, but with toil and labor we worked night and day, that we might not be a burden to any of you. ⁹It was not because we do not have that right, but to give you in ourselves an example to imitate. ¹⁰For even when we were with you, we would give you this command: If anyone is not willing to work, let him not eat. ¹¹For we hear that some among you walk in idleness, not busy at work, but busybodies. ¹²Now such persons we command and encourage in the Lord Jesus Christ to do their work quietly and to earn their own living.[d]

¹³As for you, brothers, do not grow weary in doing good. ¹⁴If anyone does not obey what we say in this letter, take note of that person, and have nothing to do with him, that he may be ashamed. ¹⁵Do not regard him as an enemy, but warn him as a brother.

¹⁶Now may the Lord of peace himself give you peace at all times in every way. The Lord be with you all.

¹⁷I, Paul, write this greeting with my own hand. This is the sign of genuineness in every letter of mine; it is the way I write. ¹⁸The grace of our Lord Jesus Christ be with you all.

a Or *brothers and sisters*; also verses 6, 13   b Or *glorified*   c Or *evil*   d Greek *to eat their own bread*

OVERVIEW: As they examine this passage, these early modern commentators stress the vital role of prayer in remaining steadfast in the truth. At the same time, they remind their readers how unbelief makes one "a servant of wickedness." Moreover, these authors highlight the necessity of the indwelling love of God manifesting itself. Turning to practical matters, these interpreters emphasize the spiritual superiority of secular work to the monastic life, and they give considerable attention to church discipline, which they generally conceive of as serving the purpose of repentance. Notable in this regard are comments by radical authors on the use of the ban. Finally, some of the commentators discuss issues pertaining to Paul's authorship of the epistle.

3:1-5 Pray for Us

PRAYER AND STEADFAST TRUTH. HEINRICH BULLINGER: In all troubles and perils we have these two supports to bear us up: prayer and steadfast faith. Brethren, let us remember these things, I pray you, and inasmuch as our times also are most corrupt and troublesome, and that for this cause it is not possible but that saints should be vexed, let us pray to God, and constantly believe that he will never fail us, even though in the meantime many unreasonable and evil people either persecute or betray the truth. God is true and faithful, cannot deny himself, and the truth shall remain evermore invincible. Let us cleave therefore to the truth, and we shall have the victory, although when we are overthrown by the world, we seem to be overcome. COMMENTARY ON THE SECOND EPISTLE OF PAUL TO THE THESSALONIANS.[1]

THE GLORIFICATION AND HASTENING OF THE GOSPEL. CARDINAL CAJETAN: "Finally." For, "Finally, brothers, pray for us." It is worthy to look for mutual prayer in the kingdom of God, there is no doubt. Since, there is mutual judgment among the members of the kingdom of God. "That the word of God." For, "of the Lord," this word hastens. Metaphorically, "pray" signifies that the impediments to the gospel might be taken away, so that the gospel might, both in its preaching and in its hearing hasten along.

"And be made famous," or glorified. "As among you." To the extent that [the gospel was made famous] among you, thus it [might be made famous] among others, and hasten and be glorified. ON PAUL'S SECOND LETTER TO THE THESSALONIANS.[2]

ON BEING WICKED AND EVIL. VIKTORIN STRIGEL: "From wicked and perverse people," *atopōn kai ponērōn*. All heretics are ... servants of wickedness, that is, contemptuous of common doctrine and slaves of wicked opinions. Likewise, not of sane judgment, and those judgments themselves about which they contend, not understanding rightly, but fascinated with their own opinions, and having the persuasion of wisdom [considering themselves to be wise?], and admiring themselves, and raising themselves well above others. And if anyone disagrees, raging with arrogance and hatred, neither seeking truth nor the public welfare, but actually contending for their own glory, or even their own convenience, and these ones indeed are *ponēroi* [evil]. That is, fierce, malevolent, slanderous, and burning with a love of injuring others. SECOND EPISTLE TO THE THESSALONIANS.[3]

PAUL MORE ANXIOUS FOR THE THESSALONIANS THAN FOR HIMSELF. JOHN CALVIN: Influenced by unfavorable reports, it was possible that their minds, influenced, might come to entertain some doubts as to Paul's ministry. Having taught them that faith is not always found in people, he now calls them back to God, and says that he is "faithful," so as to confirm their faith against all human contrivances, by which others will endeavor to shake them. "They, indeed, are treacherous, but there is in God a support that is abundantly secure, so as to keep you from giving way." He calls the Lord "faithful," inasmuch as he adheres to his purpose of maintaining the salvation of his people to the end, seasonably aids them, and never forsakes them when they are in danger, as in 1 Corinthians 10:13, "God is faithful, who will not suffer you to be tried above what you are able to bear."

These words, however, show that Paul was more anxious about others than about himself. Malicious people directed against him the stings of their malignity; the whole violence of it fell upon him. In the meantime, he directs all his anxieties toward the Thessalonians, lest this temptation should do them any injury. COMMENTARY ON SECOND THESSALONIANS.[4]

FAITH IS A GIFT FROM GOD. PETER RIEDEMANN: True and well-founded faith is not a human attribute. It is a gift from God, given only to those who fear God. That is why Paul says that not every person has faith. Such faith is the assurance of what is not seen. It grasps the invisible, one and only, mighty God, making us close to God and at one with him, and able to partake of his nature and character. It dispels all wavering and doubt, and makes our heart hold steadfastly and firmly to God through all distress. CONFESSION OF FAITH.[5]

WAITING AND PATIENCE. JOHN CALVIN: By this preface he prepares the way to give the instruction, which we shall find him immediately afterward subjoining. The confidence he says he has about them made them much more ready to obey than if

---

[1]Bullinger, *Second Thessalonians*, 3:1-5*.
[2]Cajetan, *Epistolae Pauli*, 138 (pdf 294-95).
[3]Strigel, *Omnes Libros Novi Testamenti*, 224 (pdf 557).

[4]CTS 42:349-50* (CO 52:210).
[5]CRR 9:84; citing Eph 2:1-10; Wis 3:14-15; Heb 11:1-3; 2 Pet 1:3-4; Jas 1:5-7; Dan 3:16-25; 6:19-28.

he had required obedience from them in a way of doubt or distrust. He says, however, that this hope which he cherished in them was founded upon the Lord, inasmuch as it is his to bind their hearts to obedience and to keep them in it. It appears to me more probable that by this expression he meant to make clear that it is not his intention to enjoin anything other than the commandments of the Lord. Here, accordingly, he marks out limits for himself as to enjoining them, and for them as to obeying him—that it should be only in the Lord. Therefore all that do not observe this limitation, do not resort to Paul's example, with the view of binding the church and subjecting it to their laws. . . . And, questionably, the love of God cannot reign in us unless brotherly love is also exercised. "Waiting for Christ,"[†] on the other hand, teaches us to exercise contempt for the world, the mortification of the flesh, and the endurance of the cross. At the same time, the expression might be explained as meaning the "patience of Christ"— that which Christ's doctrine begets in us, but I prefer to understand it as referring to the hope of ultimate redemption. For this is the only thing that sustains us in the warfare of the present experience, that we wait for the Redeemer; and further, this waiting requires patient endurance amidst the continual exercises of the cross. Commentary on Second Thessalonians.[6]

Persecution Is the "Cross" That Confirms Salvation. Matthias Flacius: Paul exhorts them to constancy in what can be named "a cross"; for a cross would be an evident proof of their salvation now, and the final judgment of the wicked, because in the cross is huge consolation for the godly, and also even a fountain of true consolation. And on this account the cross of the godly is the sign of their salvation, and [a sign] of the ungodly's damnation, because this is the nature of the ungodly, that they, after the manner of their father, who is the father of lies and murders, persecute the godly. And this is the condition of all

the godly, that they bear the cross. Paul himself soon assigns another cause. Even philosophers themselves have reasoned as soundly on the basis of solid and verifiable demonstration, as in the first book of the *Tusculan Disputations*,[†] concerning the calamities of good people in this life, the immortality of the soul, and the blessedness of the good as well as the future judgment of God on the deeds of people in this life. And here, you could, make these two points, before, at the beginning, afterward, in the midst of, and above, so that you may be considered worthy; for these two things are soon explained in the following verses: those who truly suffer for the kingdom of God are afflicted for its confession and its propagation. However, one does not do this on account of worthiness of the kingdom of heaven, but rather Paul describes the heirs [of this kingdom] as the kind who are wont to, and should [endure persecution]. To this end pertains that which Christ says, "Blessed are you when you are tested, and they persecute you." Gloss on 2 Thessalonians.[7]

3:6-15 *Warning Against Idleness*

The Importance of Meaningful Labor. Heinrich Bullinger: Whoever therefore means by bodily labor or any kind of commerce to get a living and things necessary for himself and his family, let him take these godly precepts instead of treacle,[†] and other welcome medicines to strengthen his mind against the venomous force of poisoned greediness and the infecting plague of covetousness.

And when he has with his medicine against poison, compounded by the doctrine of the Evangelists and apostles, and fortified his mind against the plague, then let him immediately bend himself to some labor and kind of occupation. But let everyone pick out and choose an honest and

---

[6]CTS 42:350-51* (CO 52:210-11). [†]"Steadfastness of Christ" in the esv.

[7]Flacius, *Glossa Compendaria*, 1026; citing Mt 5:11-12. [†]*Tusculan Disputations*, written around 45 BC, is a series of books written by Cicero (106–43 BC) in which the author attempts to popularize Greek philosophy, especially Stoicism, in ancient Rome.

profitable occupation, not a needless art, or a science hurtful to any other person. And finally let all people flee idleness as a plague of contagious disease. THE EIGHT PRECEPTS OF THE TEN COMMANDMENTS.[8]

HOW TO RELATE TO THE IDLE. PILGRAM MARPECK: We are faithfully warned not to judge prematurely what is hidden, but to commit it to the Lord. This is especially the case with those who appeal to the Lord regarding their evil appearance. Paul commands us to avoid such people, but not to ban them. These are to be left to the Lord until the revealing of the fruit and are not to be separated from the congregation. JUDGMENT AND DECISION.[9]

THE NAME "CHRISTIAN" DOES NOT MAKE ONE A CHRISTIAN. JOHN JEWEL: The kingdom of God is like a net cast into the sea that gathers all kinds of things. It is like a field, in which grows both wheat and weeds. Sundry virgins went out to wait for the groom; some were wise, some were foolish; some had oil in their lamps, some had none. Many came to the marriage; some had their wedding garment, some lacked it. Many are called, but few are chosen. Some bear the name of Christians, yet live in usury, to the spoil and undoing of their brethren. Some bear the name Christians, yet live in adultery and fornication, as the heathen who do not know God. These are the ones through whom the name of God is spoken evil of. UPON THE SECOND EPISTLE TO THE THESSALONIANS.[10]

A PROPER KIND OF CHRISTIAN WITHDRAWAL. HEINRICH BULLINGER: Now he recites the commandment of Christ: that you withdraw yourselves from every person who behaves themselves inordinately, that is to say, not after the institution which they received from us. We will speak of that institution a little hereafter. Erasmus

says that those are brought into an order, which are bound to the common law, and differ in nothing from other people. And that it is contrary to this, when anyone the public laws neglect lives at their own pleasure. And that Paul should mean this, by walking inordinately, the life of monks, which is received of us against the institution of the Lord and of the apostles agrees with this in all points. But when he commands that we should withdraw ourselves from them, he commands us not to do as the Anabaptists do, who, separating themselves from the communion of saints, set up a private congregation: but that we should flee their company as much as we can, to the intent that they might be ashamed and perceive themselves to be condemned for their slothfulness, and so be converted to the Lord. COMMENTARY ON THE SECOND EPISTLE OF PAUL TO THE THESSALONIANS.[11]

STAY AWAY FROM IDLERS AND THOSE WHO DO NOT KEEP THE TRADITIONS. DAVID DICKSON: That they by ecclesiastical censures would restrain the sluggish, and drones eating up the honey, and by fit course would correct all that are employed in no honest labor or business, but coveted after other people's goods. The censure of these (the remedies of lighter censures and admonitions being premised) is excommunication. For he forbids their being familiar with them, that is, after their rejection of private admonitions, and the public sentence of the church. And that they withdraw themselves from them, nor admit them to their society, which is the consequent of excommunication. . . .

Reason 1. Because this is the will of Christ, in whose authority he commands that.

"Disorderly." Reason 2. Is contained the description of sin, because whosoever lives disorderly, and not according to the rule of the doctrine, delivered to the church by me, are to be excommunicated. THE SECOND EPISTLE OF PAUL TO THE THESSALONIANS.[12]

---

[8]Bullinger, *Fifty Godly and Learned Sermons*, 266*. †Treacle can be a syrup, often sweet, and at times could be used medicinally.
[9]CRR 2:345. Marpeck here proceeds to allude to 1 Thess 5:22. See commentary there.
[10]Jewel, *Works*, 2:938-39*.

[11]Bullinger, *Second Thessalonians*, 3:6.
[12]Dickson, *Exposition*, 157*.

PAUL DENIES HIS RIGHTS IN ORDER TO TEACH BY EXAMPLE. MATTHIAS FLACIUS: The application of his [Paul's] example with an exaggeration is that he teaches that he acted prescriptively without pay so that he would teach by his own example the rule by which it would be necessary for them to live. The amplification is in it because he says that he acted contrary to his own right when otherwise for legitimate reason he could have received support from them as though he were their teacher. In truth, for that reason he says it so that he may certainly preoccupy their thoughts so that they would not thereafter gather that it is not necessary for those who are taught to pay for obtaining it. [Paul] therefore distinguishes between a right and act in order that they may gather henceforth that if he himself, having neglected his right, labored, since he valued leisure only a little, they ought to do much more for him because at that time necessity compelled him to work. He extends his example in the same manner, but yet much more copiously in 1 Corinthians 9. GLOSS ON 2 THESSALONIANS.[13]

WHETHER "COMMAND" OR "ADVICE," WE SHOULD LISTEN TO THE LORD. MENNO SIMONS: Question 1. Is separation a command or is it a counsel of God? Answer. Let everyone weigh the words of Christ and of Paul . . . and he will discover whether it is a divine commandment or whether it is a counsel. Everything Paul says in regard to separation he generally speaks in the imperative mode, that is, in a commanding manner. "Expurgate," that is to purge. "Profligate," that is, to drive out. *Sejungere*, that is, to withdraw from. *Fuge*, that is, flee. Again: we command you, brethren, in the name of our Lord Jesus Christ. I think, brethren, these Scriptures show that it is a command; and even if it were not a command but an advice of God, should we not diligently follow such advice? If my spirit despise the counsel of the Holy Spirit, then I truly acknowledge that my spirit is not of God. And to

what end many have come who did not follow God's Spirit, but their own, may be read in many passages of sacred history and may be seen in many instances, at the present time. ON THE BAN: QUESTIONS AND ANSWERS.[14]

SHUN THE IMPURE. DIRK PHILIPS: He teaches expressly that the believers shall have nothing to do with those who allow themselves to be called brothers or sisters and are fornicators, or greedy, or servants of idols, or blasphemers, or drunkards, or robbers. With such the Christians shall not eat or have fellowship. For they must separate them and afterward shun them and this because of three principal reasons. The first is so that the congregation not become participant of the estranged one's sins, and that a little leaven not ferment the whole lump. The second reason is so that those who have sinned be shamed and disciplined in their flesh, and that their spirit be saved in the Day of the Lord Jesus. The third reason is so that the congregation of God not be blasphemed because of evil and bear no guilt before the Lord on account of them. THE BAN.[15]

WHAT A TRUE SHEPHERD IS LIKE. PILGRAM MARPECK: Certainly, the true shepherds will not drive a patient, humble, meek, and loving heart any further than the chief Shepherd, Christ has driven and abound it, but will let it go out and in, find full and sufficient pasture, and be and remain victorious over all temptation in Christ Jesus. Any who act differently are false shepherds, liars, and hirelings, who do not own the sheep. If one does not immediately agree with their understanding and concur with in their judgment, they do not spare the sheep, but rather strike and subject them to a false ban, as the pope does. Now, when Paul commands the one avoid any brother or sister who walks in a disorderly fashion, he does so

---

[14]LCC 25:263; citing 1 Cor 5:11, 7; 1 Tim 6:5; Titus 3:9.
[15]CRR 6:245-46*; citing 1 Cor 5:9-10; 2 Jn 11; 1 Cor 5:6; Gal 5:9; 1 Cor 5:5; 2 Thess 3:14; Ezek 36:20; Rom 2:24; Josh 7:20-26; 1 Jn 1:3; Deut 13:6-10; 17:7; 19:19.

---

[13]Flacius, *Glossa Compendaria*, 1035.

because of the chaos of the vices mentioned above. JUDGMENT AND DECISION.[16]

THE POPE AGAINST THE APOSTLE. WILLIAM TYNDALE: Note also how craftily he would make them owners of[†] the apostles of Christ with their wicked traditions and false ceremonies which they themselves have feigned, alleging Paul. I answer that Paul taught by mouth such things as he wrote in his epistles. And his traditions were the gospel of Christ and honest manners and living and such a good order as becomes the doctrine of Christ. As that a woman obey her husband, have her head covered, keep silence and go womanly and Christianly appareled: that children and servants be in subjection: and that the young obey their elders, that no man eat but that labors and works, and that men make an earnest thing of God's word and of his holy sacraments and to watch, fast and pray, and so on, as the Scripture commands. Which things he that would break were no Christian man. But we may well complain and cry to God for help, that it is not lawful for the pope's tyranny, to teach the people what prayer is, what fasting is, and wherefore it serves. There were also certain customs always that were not commended in pain of hell or everlasting damnation, as to watch all night, and to kiss one another: which as soon as the people abused them they break them. For which cause the bishops might break many things now in like manner. Paul also in many things which God had made free, gave pure and faithful counsel without tangling of any person's conscience and without all manner commanding under pain of cursing, pain of excommunication, pain of heresy, pain of burning, pain of deadly sin, pain of hell and pain of damnation. THE OBEDIENCE OF A CHRISTIAN MAN.[17]

INSTRUCTIONS FOR THE LORD'S SUPPER AND CHURCH DISCIPLINE. PILGRAM MARPECK: Those who take part without having rebuked, according to the order of the Spirit, any sins or vices dealing with a brother or sister are also unworthy to eat and drink Communion, because the body of Christ is not differentiated from the hatred and scorn of the devil, and the innocent participated in other's sins. Therefore, Paul says, "Root out the evildoer from your community," which means that we are to discern the body of Christ. But we are not to be like those who maintain the ban, banning people from the face of the earth, seizing life and land, forbidding place and people. Such a ban does not belong to the Christian church, nor may such a ban ever be permitted in the kingdom of Christ, according to the words of the Lord and Paul.

Christ states that they shall be regarded as the heathen. Paul says that they shall be punished not as enemies, but as friends, for other major vices as well, but only for their improvement and repentance. The Son of Man did not come to damn anyone, either, he has come to save all of humankind. THE ADMONITION OF 1542.[18]

THE NECESSITY OF LABOR. HEINRICH BULLINGER: But nowadays there are many who, having nothing of their own, spend their time in rich people's houses, from whence if they should be driven out they must either beg or steal. Also this place of Paul condemns all sturdy beggars. I need not to speak anything of monks and such sacrificers, as are unprofitable to the godly ministration of the church, seeing there can nothing be feigned that does more condemn them than this. [And now a note to princes and rulers . . .] You princes and rulers of cities take good heed, that this law of God be put in use and have place among you, if you love the health of the commonwealth. I pray you suffer not the substance of your people, to be cast unto these puttocks[†] to be devoured, like those who were bewitched under the pretense of

---

[16]CRR 2:346; citing John 10:11; Rom. 2:3; Eph 5:1; 1 Tim. 6:3. Marpeck is here clearly contrasting his understanding of the role of the shepherd with those he considers to be false shepherds, and he includes the pope in this latter group

[17]Tyndale, *Obedience*, 76-77. [†]Tyndale uses the older English term *enfeoff* here. The text follows volume editor David Daniell's suggestion for a smoother contemporary English meaning.

[18]CRR 2:275-76; citing 1 Cor 5:13; Mt 18:17; Jn 3:17.

religion, and wink not always at these crafty briers. Defend your people for God's sake, and bring the law of God again into your commonwealths. COMMENTARY ON THE SECOND EPISTLE OF PAUL TO THE THESSALONIANS.[19]

STAYING TRUE TO CHRIST. PILGRAM MARPECK: Some tempters say, if one cannot tear them from Christ's hand, neither could false teaching injure them. But Deuteronomy 6:16 speaks against this notion: "You should not tempt the Lord your God." We must employ the designated means of Christ; for instance: "Ask and you shall receive, seek and you shall find, knock and it shall be opened to you," guard yourself against the false prophets; whoever does not work, he shall not eat; whoever does not accept the teaching of Christ and follow him is not worthy of him. For the Son of God is the true door through which the sheep go in and out and find pasture, in fullness and satisfaction. He does not contradict the created nature which is created by the Father through him as a lord of nature; rather, he permits created nature to remain unbroken in its working power until the last time when all natural workings cease. The evil one works evil, and the good ones work good. A CLEAR AND USEFUL INSTRUCTION.[20]

YOUNG WOMEN MUST BE KEPT OCCUPIED. JUAN LUIS VIVES: Love sends out deep roots if you think much and often about what you love. Jerome persuades Demetrias to avoid idleness altogether. And to that end he tells her that when she has finished with her prayers, she should take her work in hand and prepare the weaving so that by this alternation of tasks the days will never seem long. He requires the unceasing activity of her not because she had need of it, for she was one of the noblest and wealthiest women of Rome, but that through this constant activity she would think nothing that did not have to do with the service of God.† . . . And so it is in very fact: A woman who is indolent and slothful or (if you please)) spends her time in amusements and pleasures is unworthy of her sustenance in the Christian church, in which Paul, Christ's chief herald, proclaims as a law: "If anyone will not work then let him not eat." The penalty inflicted by God upon the human race for that first fault is common to all people: "By the sweat of your brow you will eat your bread." ON UNMARRIED WOMEN.[21]

THE GOOD OF QUIET LABOR. HEINRICH BULLINGER: Necessary labor brings with it much quietness and utility. Those who go about their own business and work with their own hands have need of nothing. Therefore one is financially dependent to no person, but gives to those who have need. As many of you as are dependent on other people, all of those who do no work at all but go about things that are to no purpose, think that this is spoken to you also. Christ shall punish you, unless you leave your dishonest and most uncomely idleness, and get you to labor. And here is a goodly place to speak of the kinds of labors and business, and of the helping and duties to the poor also. For all things are out of order among us, but I had rather subscribe unto other better learned [persons], than to show forth my ignorance. Luis Vives† has written two books of this matter, in which if the rulers would exercise themselves continually, peradventure the commonwealth should be in better case than it is, and there should be less sloth and idleness, and more labor and quietness. COMMENTARY ON THE SECOND EPISTLE OF PAUL TO THE THESSALONIANS.[22]

---

[19]Bullinger, *Second Thessalonians*, 3:10. †A puttock is a bird of prey (e.g., a hawk). "Puttock" here could refer metaphorically to a rapacious person.
[20]CRR 2:85; citing Mt 7:7, 15; 10:37; Jn 10:7. In short, Christians should use Christ's own designated means to follow Christ. It is interesting that Marpeck feels quite free to quote Paul when listing the "designated means of Christ."
[21]Vives, *The Education of a Christian Woman*, 92; citing Gen 3:19. †Jerome, *Letters* 130, NPNF² 6:269.
[22]Bullinger, *Second Thessalonians*, 3:11-12*. †Bullinger is likely referring to Juan Luis Vives, who was born in Valentia, Spain, in 1492 and was considered one of the most learned men of his time. One of his most well-known writings is a commentary on Augustine's *City of God*.

Why Anabaptists Feed Children but Don't Baptize Them. Peter Riedemann: Now, they say, if we are not to baptize infants because they cannot believe and confess, or because we cannot teach them, then it would also follow that we should not feed them, because they do not work. For Paul says, "Whoever will not work shall not eat." So we should let the children die of hunger.

Here as in other places, Scripture is drawn upon to testify against itself. Paul does not say, "If anyone does not work, neither shall they eat," but "If anyone does not want to work, neither should they eat." He is not speaking about little children who are not able to work, but of those who are able but do not want to work. So this text does not apply. It does no more than resist the truth, as Jannes and Jambres did, striving to crush it with contrived words. Confession of Faith.[23]

The Ban and Those Who Deny Apostolic Teaching. Menno Simons: Question 8. Who, according to Scripture, should be banned or excommunicated? Answer. Christ says: "If your brother trespasses against you . . . , and will not hear you of the witnesses, nor the church, let him be unto you as a heathen man and a publican." And Paul: If any person who is called a brother be a fornicator, or covetous, or an idolater, or a railer, or a drunkard, or an extortioner; with such a one do not eat. To this class also belongs perjurers, thieves, violent persons, haters, fighters, and all those who walk in open, well-known damnable works of the flesh, of which Paul enumerates a great many. Again, disorderly persons, working not at all, but who are busybodies; such as do not abide in the doctrine of Christ and his apostles and do not walk therein, but are disobedient. On the Ban: Questions and Answers.[24]

We Should Do Good to Every Man. Heinrich Bullinger: Most of the rich people upbraid the poor for sluggishness and idleness. [These ones are] otherwise not so evil or mischievous, as wretched and miserable, and by this pretense they keep their charity from those who have need of it. Therefore St. Paul says: I will not by this means withdraw any person from well doing, or give any person an occasion for to order miserable people the more cruelly or ungently. For people ought always to do good. They should do well to every person, but specially to godly people. We would not have it God that you should be weary of our necessities! We would hope that he should receive our regular requests with a merry countenance. Therefore we should not be weary also, when his members call upon us for our help. It is a piteous thing, yes, that a very idle person should perish for hunger. Commentary on the Second Epistle of Paul to the Thessalonians.[25]

The Goal of Excommunication Is Repentance. David Dickson: [Commenting on verse 14:] That they are not stubbornly resistant, and they that do not obey the apostolic doctrine are identified, that is, that they excommunicate them. This is manifest from this passage, that he commands that they have no society with the one who is thus noted, which is the consequence of excommunication, and for this end he commands that the excommunicate person is segregated from the society of others and being ashamed might enter into themselves and repent. . . .

[Commenting now on verse 15:] He expounds the commandment, so that they should not be cruel toward the excommunicated person nor esteem them as an enemy, but instead show their hatred to the sin, that the excommunicated person may understand that through this severe correction, there is brotherly love, and so they may be return into favor with God and the church by repentance. The Second Epistle of Paul to the Thessalonians.[26]

---

[23]CRR 9:104*; citing Ex 7:9-13; 2 Tim 3:8.
[24]LCC 25:270; citing Mt 18:15-17; 1 Cor 5:11; Rom 1:29; Gal 5:19; 1 Cor 6:9; Eph 5:5.

[25]Bullinger, *Second Thessalonians*, 3:13*.
[26]Dickson, *Exposition*, 157*.

The Proper Goal of Church Discipline.
Heinrich Bullinger: For this discipline is not
ordained for the destruction of any person, but for
their health. Therefore you shall not utterly put
from you a sinner, but love them always as a
brother: but yet in the meantime you shall admonish them of their fate and correct them. And out of
this place we may learn what the discipline of the
church is, . . . and also why the apostle commands
us to flee the company of the disobedient: not that
we should abhor them as enemies and wicked, not
that we should prefer ourselves above others in
holiness, or else stand well in our own conceits, or
exercise tyranny toward the miserable people: but
that those who are guilty, being taught through our
withdrawing from them, and as it were warned of
themselves, should remember themselves, and
esteem their filthiness as it is indeed, and so being
ashamed, to amend. And if that by the means of
the evil that reigned in them they will not amend,
and by this means come to themselves and repent,
then shall the saints take deliberation among them,
by what means this mad person may be helped, lest
that either they themselves utterly perish, or else
infect others with the same disease. For they are
deceived, when the avoiding of his company avails
not, set aside all farther remedies, thinking that
after this, the churches may use no other means to
bring them into the way. But Paul says, send us
word of them by a letter. To what purpose I pray
you? That he might have the name of the one who
disobeys? But what profit should come of it? He
would therefore have knowledge of such by an
epistle, that he might take with godly people such
counsel for those unruly people, as they should
think appropriate. For we ought all of us to do our
diligence that we destroy not them for whom
Christ died, neither by our importunity or cruel-
ness, neither yet by our ignorance and negligence.
But these words of the apostle seem to some people
to be understood of the private conversation of
people: that is to say, that every person should
abstain so much as they could from the company
and familiarity, of such as are disobedient: And
many have expounded it of the open excommuni-

cation. Commentary on the Second Epistle
of Paul to the Thessalonians.[27]

**Withdrawing from Those Who Depart
from God's Word.** Menno Simons: Now
judge for yourself what kind of sin it is not to be
willing to hear and obey God's Word. Paul says:
Now we command you, brethren, in the name of
our Lord Jesus Christ, that you withdraw yourselves from every person who walks disorderly, and
not after the tradition that you received of us; again:
And if anyone does not obey our word by this
epistle, do not associate with that person, and have
no company with them, that they may be ashamed.
Inasmuch as the ban was so strictly commanded by
the Lord, and practiced by the apostles, therefore
we must also use it and obey it, since we are thus
taught and enlightened by God, or else we should
be shunned and avoided by the congregation of
God. This must be acknowledged and confessed.
On the Ban: Questions and Answers.[28]

Hope for the Shunned. Peter Riedemann:
When a person is banned, we have no fellowship
with them and nothing to do with them, so that
they may become ashamed. Yet the excluded
person is called to repentance, in the hope that the
sinner will be moved to return all the more quickly
to God. If that does not happen, the church
remains pure and innocent of their sin. It has no
guilt and earned no rebuke from God. Confession of Faith.[29]

3:16-18 Benediction

Paul Blesses the Thessalonians. Heinrich Bullinger: He concludes his epistle and
wishes them the bond of all righteousness, holy
peace, that they might keep that always and in all
their business. For Satan is the author of discord,
chiding, strife, envy, and private hatred, and God is
the author of concord, meekness, and charity. He

---

[27]Bullinger, *Second Thessalonians*, 3:15*.
[28]LCC 25:264; citing Mt 18:17.
[29]CRR 9:153*; citing 2 Cor 7:8-11; Josh 7:1-5.

dwells with all saints, so long as they live in this world in truth and righteousness. His presence is the fountain of all goodness, and his absence is the cause of all darkness, error, and eternal horror. St. Ambrose says that for fear of choppers and changers and corrupters of Scriptures Paul testifies, that he always subscribed his salutation in every one of his epistles with his own hand: to the intent that any epistle received in his name might not be allowed if it were not subscribed with his own hand. The apostles took such care, lest the congregations should be deceived by any craft or deceit. These things show of what certainty and truth the apostles' writings are. And because Paul taught constantly among all nations that humankind was saved by the grace of God, therefore he included his own signature at the end of all his epistles, this mark and seal of our faith: The grace of our Lord Jesus Christ be with you all. It appears, therefore by this that the apostle used the help of a notary or secretary to write his epistles that he sent. COMMENTARY ON THE SECOND EPISTLE OF PAUL TO THE THESSALONIANS.[30]

GOD PROVIDES FOR THE CHURCH THROUGH PAUL. JOHN CALVIN: Here again he provides against the danger of which he had previously made mention[†]—lest epistles falsely ascribed to him should find their way into the churches. For this was an old artifice of Satan—to put forward spurious writings, that he might detract from the credit of those that are genuine; and further, under pretended designations of the apostles, to disseminate wicked errors with the view of corrupting sound doctrine. By a singular kindness on the part of God, it has been brought about that, his frauds being defeated, the doctrine of Christ has come down to us sound and entire through the ministry of Paul and others. The concluding prayer explains in what manner God aids his believing people—by the presence of Christ's grace. COMMENTARY ON SECOND THESSALONIANS.[31]

---

[30]Bullinger, *Second Thessalonians*, 3:16.

[31]CTS 42:362 (CO 52:217-18). [†]Calvin is here pointing to his own comments in this commentary on 2 Thess 2:2, where Paul writes, "not to be quickly shaken in mind or alarmed, either by a spirit or a spoken word, or a letter seeming to be from us, to the effect that the day of the Lord has come."

COMMENTARY ON 1 TIMOTHY

1:1-2 INTRODUCTION TO 1 TIMOTHY
AND PAUL'S GREETING

Paul, an apostle of Christ Jesus by command of God our Savior and of Christ Jesus our hope, ²*To Timothy, my true child in the faith:* *Grace, mercy, and peace from God the Father and Christ Jesus our Lord.*

OVERVIEW: Our early modern commentators introduce this first of Paul's Pastoral Epistles by providing a preview of its contents and highlighting the apostle's main arguments. In so doing, they portray it as providing practical instruction for clergy. Notably, while discussing the provenance of the epistle, the authors interact with the exegetical work of contemporaries. Moreover, they relate the epistle directly to the ecclesiological debates of the sixteenth and seventeenth centuries, as evidenced by the debate on whether Timothy was a bishop or an evangelist. Some commentators, furthermore, appropriate this epistle to defend the doctrine of apostolic succession. As they expound on Paul's greeting, the authors stress the role of the clergy in extirpating false doctrine from the church and emphasize their utter dependence on God's grace for the faithful execution of their ministry.

Introductory Comments

HELPING BISHOPS GOVERN THE CHURCH.
WILLIAM TYNDALE: St. Paul writes this epistle to be an example to all bishops of what they should teach and how they should govern the congregation of Christ in all degrees, so that it should not

be necessary to govern Christ's flock simply with the doctrine of their own good intentions.

In the first chapter he commands that the bishop shall maintain the right faith and love, and resist false preachers who make the law and works equal with Christ and his gospel. And he makes a short summary of all Christian learning: the purpose the law serves and what the end of it is; also what the gospel is; and puts forward himself as a comforting example to all sinners and troubled consciences.

In the second chapter, he commands Timothy to pray for all people; and charges that the women shall not preach or wear costly clothing, but be obedient to the men. In the third chapter he describes what sort of people the bishop or priest and their wives should be, and also the deacons and their wives; and he commends it if anyone desires to be a bishop of that sort.

In the fourth chapter, he prophesies, and speaks in advance of the false bishops and spiritual officers that will arise among the Christian people—to be, do, and preach clean contrary to the aforementioned example; and to depart from the faith in Christ and forbid people to marry and to eat certain foods, teaching them to put trust in such things both for justifying and forgiveness of sins, and also of deserving of eternal life.

In the fifth chapter, he teaches how a bishop should behave toward young and old; and concerning widows, what is to be done and which should be funded out of the common purse; and teaches also how people should honor the virtuous bishops and priests and how to rebuke the evil.

In the sixth chapter, he exhorts the bishops to cleave to the gospel of Christ and true doctrine, and to avoid vain questions and superfluous disputes that engender strife and quench the truth, and by which also the false prophets gain authority and seek to satisfy their insatiable covetousness. New Testament. Preface to 1 Timothy.[1]

The Life and Work of a Bishop. Desiderius Erasmus:

Timothy's mother was born a Jew; nevertheless, she was a Christian, and his father was a Greek. This Timothy, being an honest young man and well learned in holy Scriptures, Paul chose to be a minister. And yet because of the Jews, he was compelled to circumcise him. Inasmuch as he had committed to Timothy (as he did also to Titus) the care of those congregations that he could not go to himself, he instituted him in the office of a bishop and in the discipline of the congregation, not admonishing him as a disciple, but as a son and as a fellow in office. . . .

Paul admonishes him to reject those who would bring in Jewish fables, and to teach those things that pertain to faith and charity. Then, since the order of a city and the tranquility of a commonwealth depends on the authority of princes and magistrates, he would not have their authority treated with contempt by the Christians, but also commands them to be prayed for. He prescribes how it is fitting both for men and for women to behave in the open congregation. He paints out what a bishop and his household should be. He addresses these things in almost all of the first three chapters.

Then he warns him not to receive any Jewish fables, and speaks of choice of foods and forbidding of marriage. And then he teaches him straightaway how he should behave toward old men, toward young men, toward old women, toward young women, toward both rich and poor widows (those that ought to be supported out of the common stock of the congregation), and toward the younger women. . . . Furthermore he prescribes to him what he must command to masters, what to servants, and what to rich men, admonishing him to reject with all possible means contentious sophistical questions that have nothing but a vain show of learning. This epistle he wrote from Laodicea by Tychicus the Deacon. Paraphrases.[2]

Establishing Church Order. Martin Luther:

I have taken up the epistle to Timothy in which Paul establishes not only the bishop but all the ecclesiastical orders. The epistle is not didactic, and it does not strive to establish basic teaching. Rather, it establishes the church and sets it in order. And yet, in the midst of this process Paul does not neglect to add very important doctrinal subjects. It was characteristic of the Christians to be daily involved with these subjects. Lectures on 1 Timothy.[3]

A Letter for All to Profit By. John Calvin:

We must not imagine that this letter was written by St. Paul for the benefit of one man only, but it is for the whole church, as we can see from the contents of it. For Timothy had no need of many of the directions that St. Paul gives here. He speaks to the situation of others rather than to him. And surely one can easily see this at first glance, in that St. Paul gives himself the title of "apostle," and confirms his vocation toward them, who would not have yielded to him such authority if he had not made himself known as such. But when he writes to the churches that already approved of him, he makes only brief mention of this word "apostle," or simply calls himself a servant of God. By this he shows that he was not pushing in on his own account but that he was appointed by God, and

---

[1] Tyndale, *The Newe Testament*, cccii*.

[2] EOO 6:924.
[3] LW 28:217 (WA 26:4).

that his charge was committed to him by our Lord Jesus Christ. And why does he do this unless he is concerned with others more than Timothy?

So then, we see that this letter was so addressed to one man that it is also addressed to all, and that it ought to profit the children of God generally. As we will see, St. Paul wants to edify all those to whom this letter comes. And indeed he shows here what the true order of the church is, how the Word of God ought to be handled, and to what use it ought to be applied. He declares every person's duty. And so we see that is not a question of one man in particular, but something everyone ought to give attention to, because God intended to direct this doctrine to his church by the mouth of St. Paul. SERMONS ON 1 TIMOTHY.[4]

WRITTEN FROM MACEDONIA IN AD 57. JOHN MAYER: When the apostle Paul was forced to leave Ephesus, by reason of the uproar made there against him, as appears in Acts 19–20, and to go into Macedonia, he left Timothy, a man of excellent parts, and with whose virtues he was well acquainted, behind him for the government of the churches and the helping forward of the gospel there, the seeds of which he had sown before his departing. So that it is not to be doubted but that he sat in Ephesus as chief of the bishops, as all the ministers of the gospel were then called, and yet no archbishop by name, as Cornelius À Lapide the Jesuit[†] would have him; for the name archbishop, and the office as it is now, was of late invention. . . .

Now Timothy being thus left, and being but a young man, it is likely that he was subject to more contempt, and therefore to add to his authority and

that he might have more sway, it seemed good to the apostle to write to him (as Calvin and Bullinger would have it), not so much for his own instruction, who was of such excellent knowledge, but for all bishops and pastors, to whom when he should urge these things as coming from Paul, it was likely that they should be regarded the more. . . .

Baronius thinks that Timothy continued as bishop of Ephesus until the year AD 109,[†] which, if it were so, would mean he was the angel of the Church of Ephesus, to whom one of the seven epistles in Revelation was directed. . . . The time of the writing of this epistle assigned by Baronius was AD 57. Touching the place from whence this epistle was sent, some are for Laodicea, according to the postscript,[††] but Baronius says it was written from Macedonia, to which place Paul went when he departed from Ephesus; Beza says it was sent from Philippi in Macedonia,[†††] affirming that one manuscript copy has it so. COMMENTARY ON PAUL'S EPISTLES.[5]

TIMOTHY AN EVANGELIST, NOT A BISHOP. THOMAS CARTWRIGHT: It is not true to say that Timothy was a bishop, for the ministry committed to him was related to the work he was commanded to execute—and it is expressly commanded him that he should execute the work of an *evangelist*. Again, he had that kind of ministry which he accomplished and exercised, but that he exercised the office of an evangelist (which is to water in

---

[4]CO 53:5. George W. Knight III, *The Pastoral Epistles: A Commentary on the Greek Text*, New International Greek Testament Commentary (Carlisle, UK: Paternoster, 1992), 277, comments that the plural "you" at the end of 1 Tim 6:21 "indicates that Paul expected this letter to be read to the believers, and it further indicates that all along he has had them, not just Timothy, in view." The word "you" was not, however, in the plural form in the Textus Receptus used by our commentators, but in the singular. See Bruce M. Metzger, *A Textual Commentary on the Greek New Testament*, 2nd ed. (Stuttgart: Deutsche Bibelgesellschaft, 1994), 577.

[5]Mayer, *Commentarie*, 484*; citing Rev 2:1. †Cornelius À Lapide (1567–1637) was a Flemish Jesuit and author of *Commentaria in Omnes Divi Pauli Epistolas* (Antwerp, 1614). T. Moseman abridged it and translated it into English as *The Great Commentary of Cornelius a Lapide* (1876), omitting much of the technical detail of the original. †Baronius is Cardinal Cesare Baronio (1538–1607), author of *Annales Ecclesiastici*, 12 vols. (1588–1607), which Lord Acton called "the greatest history of the Church ever written" in his *Lectures on Modern History* (London: Macmillan, 1930), 121. See *Epitome Annalium Ecclesiasticorum Cæsaris Baronii* (Venice, 1602), 1:40. ††The postscript (or subscription, as Cartwright calls it in the next extract) is the note added to the end of many manuscripts of the letters stating their author and provenance. The subscription to 1 Timothy in Codex Alexandrinus states that it was written to Timothy from Laodicea. †††Beza, *Novum Testamentum*, 711.

diverse and sundry places where the apostles planted) appears by diverse and sundry places and countries where he exercised his ministry: whereas the ministry of a bishop is tied, as it were, to the stake or glebe[†] of one particular church. Last of all, he is called an evangelist of the apostle, and never termed by the name of a bishop; which reason is so much the stronger, as the name of apostle and prophet is sometimes in the Scripture given to other offices . . . but this title of evangelist is communicated in the Scripture to none but those which did execute the proper office of an evangelist.

It is true that in the subscription at the end of the epistles, and in other ancient writers, Timothy is called a bishop, but that is in the sense that they call the apostles bishops, because they had the highest authority and degree of ministry in the places where they exercised their extraordinary callings, even as the bishops or pastors in the ordinary functions of their particular church are the highest officers of the ecclesiastical presbytery. . . . It is true, however, that in instructing Timothy he does also instruct bishops, because that which was his office in many places is also the bishops' in their several and particular churches. CONFUTATION OF THE RHEMISTS.[6]

Timothy a Bishop, Not an Evangelist.

ABRAHAM SCULTETUS: If any desire the examples of apostolical bishops, the books of the ancients are full of episcopal authority, of Timothy, and Titus, both of which, in some way, first performed the office of an evangelist. Yet, notwithstanding, Timothy ceased to be an evangelist after he was placed over the church of Ephesus, and Titus over the church of Crete. For evangelists only laid the foundations of faith in foreign places, and then commended the rest of the care to certain pastors; but they themselves went to other countries and nations, as Eusebius writes in his *Ecclesiastical History*.[†] But Paul taught sometimes in Ephesus

and Crete and laid the foundations of faith there; therefore he commanded Timothy to stay at Ephesus, and Titus at Crete, not as evangelists but as governors of the churches.

And indeed the epistles written to either of them reveal the same. For in these, he does not prescribe the manner of gathering together a church—which was the duty of an evangelist—but the manner of governing a church already gathered together—which is the duty of a bishop. And all the precepts in those epistles are so conformable to this, as that they are not referred only to Timothy and Titus, but in general to all bishops, and therefore in no way do they fit with the temporary power of evangelists.

Besides, that Timothy and Titus had episcopal jurisdiction, not only Eusebius, Chrysostom, Theodoret, Ambrosius, Jerome, Epiphanius, Oecumenius, Primasius, and Theophylact, but also the most ancient writers of any that write the history of the New Testament whose writings are now lost, do sufficiently declare. DIVINE RIGHT OF EPISCOPACY.[7]

Successors to the Apostles.

RICHARD HOOKER: Apostles, whether they settled in any one place, as James, or else did otherwise, as the apostle Paul, episcopal authority either at large or with restraint they had and exercised: Their episcopal power they sometimes gave to others to exercise as agents only in their stead, and as it were by commission from them. Thus Titus, and thus Timothy, at the first, though afterward endued with apostolic power of their own. . . . All bishops are, says Jerome, the apostles' successors.[†] LAWS OF ECCLESIASTICAL POLITY.[8]

The New Ceremonial Law Is Here.

LAMBERT DANEAU: The whole ceremonial law appointed by the Lord himself—what else, I pray you,

---

[6]Cartwright, *Confutation*, 536-37*; citing 2 Tim 4:5. [†]A glebe is a piece of land from which the income is set aside for the support of the clergy.

[7]Scultetus, *Divine Right of Episcopacy*, 176-177*. [†]Eusebius, *Ecclesiastical History* 3.37 (see also chap. 4).

[8]Hooker, *Ecclesiastical Polity*, 3:79-80 (bk. 7, chap. 4). [†]See Jerome, *Letter* 146 (*NPNF*[2] 6:288), which is also cited for a different reason by Edward Leigh in comments on Titus 1:5, below.

is it but a most ample and a most clear description of ecclesiastical discipline? And as the Lord was not sparing in the institution of this, under the Old Testament, so has he as largely under the new instituted the same (or rather, restored it, being fallen down and decayed) by his apostles, as being a matter altogether most necessary for the right constitution and government of his church. This appears in many places in the New Testament, and especially in the Acts of the apostles, the first epistle of Paul to the Corinthians, the first epistle to Timothy, and the epistle to Titus. In all these and similar places, whatever appertains to the right and lawful government of the church is carefully and largely set down: whether you regard the ordering of the whole church in general, or in the governing of some few in particular.

Considering this, I think it is a wonderful and an absurd case that afterward so many canons, so many decrees of synods, so many constitutions of churches, both general and particular, were written and established for the ordering of ecclesiastical government. For what need was there of this labor that only arose from the great contempt and ignorance of these precepts that the Holy Spirit had set down by the pen of the apostles? This was because people despised the ways of God, that they might establish the inventions of their own brains, and bring into the church their own traditions, which for the most part were too absurd and childish, and always clean contrary to the discipline prescribed in the Word of God. Preface to 1 Timothy.[9]

Pull Up the Weeds of False Doctrine.
Giovanni Diodati: Timothy was the son of a Greek father, who was likewise a proselyte, and of a Jewish mother, who, having learned the Christian faith, had brought up and instructed her son in it from his childhood. And both their pieties were so abundantly blessed by God that Timothy in his youth was entertained by St. Paul, who, besides the large instructions he gave him, also obtained the miraculous gift of the Holy Spirit for him in knowledge, revelation, strength, and infallible conduct, to be made capable of the office of evangelist, which was not much inferior to that of apostle: and to supply St. Paul's absence in various churches that he had newly founded. This is noted to have been always accompanied with a perfect confidence and fatherly love on the apostle's side and with an entire fidelity and humble reverence on Timothy's side.

Now among other occasions in which he was employed by the apostle, he was left at Ephesus, where St. Paul had planted a most noble church. And being by his calling led away to preach elsewhere, he left Timothy there to finish the ordering and establishing of it. And while he was executing this charge, he wrote this epistle to him to instruct, strengthen, and encourage him, and by his means to confirm that church in which the devil had already sown many weeds of false doctrines and curious questions, and especially by the means of false Christianized Jews, perpetual corrupters of the pureness of the gospel in those days.

The apostle then at the first exhorts them to root out that evil seed of false doctrine, and to maintain the truth in its purity, and the church in its integrity, touching some points necessary for the circumstance of those times and places: such as praying for all manner of persons, even for kings and princes; of the decency and modesty of women in their clothing, and of their silence in holy assemblies; but especially of qualities required of bishops and other ecclesiastical persons. Then he proceeds to foretell by divine inspiration the horrible corruptions that would befall the church in ensuing ages, in doctrine as well as in manners, exhorting Timothy to forewarn the church, and cause it to beware of those things. He also gives him various particular instructions: of sincerity and discretion in pastoral censures; and of choosing men for several degrees of ecclesiastical offices; of admonishing the rich, that they should not trust nor set their hearts upon riches, but employ them in charity and Christian fellowship; to refute false teachers and their avarice, and to endeavor to persevere in all contrary virtues.

---

[9]Daneau, *The Judgement of Danæus*, 5-6*.

Naturally this epistle is a gathering together of precepts necessary for pastors, that they should preserve a good form in the state of the church in their times as well as leave it well established after them; and, in addition, to prepare themselves for greater combats, and strengthen them against dangerous scandals until the end of the world. Annotations on the New Testament.[10]

1:1 Greetings from Paul to Timothy

Paul Establishes His Credentials. John Calvin: "Paul an apostle." If he had written to Timothy alone, it would have been unnecessary to claim this designation, and to maintain it in the manner that he does. Timothy would undoubtedly have been satisfied with having merely the name; for he knew that Paul was an apostle of Christ, and had no need of proof to convince him of it, being perfectly willing, and having been long accustomed, to acknowledge it. He has his eye, therefore, chiefly on others, who were not so ready to listen to him, or did not so easily believe his words. For the sake of such persons, that they may not treat lightly what he writes, he affirms that he is "an apostle of Christ."

"According to the appointment of God our Savior, and of the Lord Jesus Christ." He confirms his apostleship by the appointment or command of God; for no man can make himself to be an apostle, but he whom God has appointed is a true apostle, and worthy of the honor. Nor does he merely say that he owes his apostleship to God the Father, but ascribes it to Christ also; and, indeed, in the government of the church, the Father does nothing but through the Son, and therefore they both act together.

He calls God the Savior, a title that he is more frequently accustomed to assign to the Son; but it belongs to the Father also, because it is he who gave the Son to us. Justly, therefore, is the glory of our salvation ascribed to him. For how comes it that we are saved? It is because the Father loved us in such a manner that he determined to redeem and save us

through the Son. He calls Christ our hope; and this appellation is strictly applicable to him; for then do we begin to have good hope, when we look to Christ, since in him alone dwells all that on which our salvation rests. Commentary on 1 Timothy.[11]

Confirming Paul's Apostleship and Hope. David Dickson: The inscription of the epistle, wherein: (1) That he might win authority for this epistle, Paul affirms that in writing it, he fulfilled his apostolical business as an envoy for Christ. (2) He confirms his apostleship by a special command from God the Father, whom he calls the savior because he is the author of our salvation, and who had called him to the office of an apostle, and used him in the execution of his office about the present matter he had in hand. (3) He confirms his apostleship from the command of our Lord Jesus Christ, whom he calls our hope, because he is the author, the meritorious cause, the object, and the finisher of our hope. Exposition of All Paul's Epistles.[12]

Christ Alone Is Our Hope. Christian Chemnitz: Christ is called "our hope." This passage is rightly opposed to the priestly papists, who also call the saints who are reigning with Christ "their hope." For Estius says, "Every help, that they hope for from them, they do not await except through Christ's merit."† But we should reply: (1) This itself is in question, whether help from the saints is to be hoped for through Christ. For we have neither a command, nor a promise, nor a proven pattern for such a thing. (2) "The intercession of the saints" is no means of applying Christ's merit to ourselves. (3) Indeed, nor is any other creature, but God alone, the right object of our hope and faith. A Little Commentary on All Paul's Epistles.[13]

---

[10]Diodati, *Pious Annotations*, NT 37-38*.

[11]CTS 43:19-20* (CO 52:249-50).
[12]Dickson, *Exposition*, 158*.
[13]Chemnitz, *Commentariolus*, 5. †Willem Hessels van Est (1542–1613) was a Dutch Catholic theologian who taught at Leuven and Douai.

Christ's Gospel Promises. Caspar Cruciger: Paul briefly sets out the argument of his discourse, or the title of his profession, and he distinguishes the ministry of the gospel from the law, as if to say: Paul, chosen by God for the proclamation of the promise by the Savior, who is our hope. For I do not bring the law, but another kind of doctrine, in which those wonderful promises are demonstrated, freedom from sin and death, the gift of righteousness, and living with God in eternal life. It is these great things that I bring, even if the world despises us. And these are given because of Jesus the Son of God. This Jesus is powerful: he will remove sins and death, and he will join us to him in eternal life in his eternal kingdom. And these benefits begin also in us: he forgives sins, he sanctifies us by the gift of the Holy Spirit, he directs us, he defends, and he frees us many times over from death. This is the one whom the father offered; on his account he is willing to be reconciled, to give ear, and to save. For this reason I call him our hope, that is, our propitiator and our Savior, in whom we should trust that our sins are forgiven, that we are heard, that we are guided, defended, and saved. This teaching differs from the teaching of the law, which shows our sin, accuses us, demonstrates the anger of God, does not offer freely the forgiveness of sins, and so on. Therefore, this separation between the law and the gospel should be diligently studied, about which much is said elsewhere. Commentary on 1 Timothy.[14]

1:2 Grace, Mercy, and Peace

Paul's Son in the Faith. English Annotations: He calls Timothy his own son in the faith, either because he was a means and instrument whereby Christ was perfectly formed in Timothy; or because he served him as a son serves his father, namely, in the ministry; or because he resembled the apostle both in his preaching and in his life, as a natural son is like his father.

Grace is the fountain from which mercy and peace flow; for the free goodwill of God, whereby he has chosen us in Christ, procures us mercy in the forgiveness of sins; and by the apprehension of his mercy we have peace of conscience. English Annotations.[15]

Timothy Resembles Paul. David Dickson: Timothy, to whom this epistle is written, is called the son of the apostle, not *simply*, but in the faith, because he was his disciple. And as the son represents the father in face and manners, so Timothy resembled Paul in doctrine and in holy conversation. In his salutation he wishes to Timothy: first, *grace*, that is, the renovation of the image of God, from the fountain of God's free goodwill; second, *mercy*, that is, free remission of sins, because he knew that the holy young man, affected with the sense of his sins, with many tears did daily prostrate himself before God; third, *peace*, that is, quietness of conscience, and joy from the apprehension of divine favor, and finally a complete felicity in the life to come, which is comprehended under peace. Exposition of All Paul's Epistles.[16]

Bishops Especially Need Mercy. Martin Luther: "Grace, mercy, and peace." This is the forgiveness of sins, peace, joy, and the soul's freedom from care. He clearly distinguishes between these and gifts of the world. He also adds a third word, which he does not generally use in his letters to the churches—"mercy." Why does he add it here? Every theologian has been established as a bishop of the church to bear the troubles of everyone in the church. He stands on the battle line. He is the prime target of all attacks, difficulties, anxieties, disturbances of consciences, temptations, and doubts. All these hit the bishop where it hurts. Still greater trials follow. The princes of the world and the very learned seek him out. He is made a spectacle for both devils and angels. So then, it is enough to pray for two things for the

---

[14]Cruciger, *In Epistolam Pauli*, 3-4.

[15]Downame, ed., *Annotations*, s.v.
[16]Dickson, *Exposition*, 158.

rest: that they be in grace and peace; yet for a bishop one must add "mercy," not only that God would deign to give his grace that he might have forgiveness of sins and peace but that he would have constant mercy on him, that he would heap many gifts on him with which to serve his brothers; also, that God would grant him mercy because he constantly endures great tribulation. Were he to have no other temptation, it would be enough that he must battle with devilish heretics, who direct their efforts to turn away the hearers and brothers —a most troublesome situation. Satan meets him on the field and assails him in a spiritual battle.

Satan takes from him the beautiful statements of Scripture and corrupts them, just as he did with Christ in the desert: "He will give his angels charge," and "if you will worship me." The office of a bishop is a great responsibility, one that Christ first held in the church. Therefore there is need to abide in prayer; that is why one must pray for grace and peace. Each person has their own temptation. But the bishop is the womb of the Lord Jesus, in which he carries others through the Word, to comfort the sad, convince the foolish, and teach the unlearned. LECTURES ON 1 TIMOTHY.[17]

---

[17]LW 28:219 (WA 26:5-6); citing Mt 4:6, 10.

1:3-11 WARNING AGAINST FALSE TEACHERS

³As I urged you when I was going to Macedonia, remain at Ephesus so that you may charge certain persons not to teach any different doctrine, ⁴nor to devote themselves to myths and endless genealogies, which promote speculations rather than the steward-shipᵃ from God that is by faith. ⁵The aim of our charge is love that issues from a pure heart and a good conscience and a sincere faith. ⁶Certain persons, by swerving from these, have wandered away into vain discussion, ⁷desiring to be teachers of the law, without understanding either what they are saying or the things about which they make confident assertions.

⁸Now we know that the law is good, if one uses it lawfully, ⁹understanding this, that the law is not laid down for the just but for the lawless and disobedient, for the ungodly and sinners, for the unholy and profane, for those who strike their fathers and mothers, for murderers, ¹⁰the sexually immoral, men who practice homosexuality, enslavers,ᵇ liars, perjurers, and whatever else is contrary to soundᶜ doctrine, ¹¹in accordance with the gospel of the glory of the blessed God with which I have been entrusted.

a Or *good order*   b That is, those who take someone captive in order to sell him into slavery   c Or *healthy*

OVERVIEW: Throughout their expositions of this passage, these Reformation-era commentators examine the traits of heresy and provide criteria for determining sound doctrine, the principle of which is whether a given teaching edifies the church. In this regard, when discussing Paul's reference to "endless genealogies," the authors severely criticize what they perceive as the excesses of scholastic theology, which they believe only obfuscated rather than enlightened. However, this does not mean that serious theological questions should be avoided. For example, these commentators go on to explore the functions of the law and the role of love in its fulfillment. In this regard, they maintain the distinction between the law, which exposes and condemns sin, and the gospel, which promises God's grace through Christ. Generally many of the reformers assigned three functions to the law: restraint of sin in human society; confrontation of sinners with the reality of their sin, thus pointing individuals to Christ; and a guide for the living of the Christian life.

1:3-4 Edification Not Speculation

TIMOTHY NOT A PERMANENT BISHOP. DUTCH ANNOTATIONS: Here the end is expressed why Paul left Timothy at Ephesus, not to continue there always, and to be bishop there, as some think, but for a while as an evangelist and fellow laborer of the apostles, to confirm the church against those who fought to bring in perverse doctrines, as he says in Acts 20:29-30. That Timothy afterward returned to Paul appears from 2 Timothy 4:9-11. DUTCH ANNOTATIONS.[1]

THE MARK OF HERETICS. WILLIAM FULKE: The proper mark of heretics is to teach otherwise than the truth, or contrary to it. But if the teacher finds people entangled with pernicious errors, even if they enjoy great peace and agreement among themselves, they are not in the unity of the catholic church. Those who teach "different doctrine" are the ones who teach other than they learn out of the Scripture—not those who teach something

---

[1]Haak, *Annotations*, s.v.*

different to what other people are falsely persuaded by. Therefore, seeing Luther taught not otherwise than the prophets and apostles, his doctrine was not odd, singular, and new but catholic, ancient, and true. Therefore, finding many nations seduced by errors, he called them back to the true faith taught by the apostles, from which the church had made a manifest revolt and apostasy. Yet there were before him the persecuted churches of God in diverse nations that held the same true faith and religion that he preached, not only in England, but also in France, Italy, Germany, Bohemia, Moravia, and so on, with all the churches of the east and north parts of the world not agreeing with the Romish Church. They must hear nothing taught otherwise than they are persuaded they have received from the apostles. TEXT OF THE NEW TESTAMENT.[2]

THE SUBTLETIES OF AMBITIOUS SCHOLASTICS.

JOHN CALVIN: Paul judges of doctrine by the fruit; for everything that does not edify ought to be rejected,[†] although it has no other fault; and everything that is of no avail but for raising contentions ought to be doubly condemned. And such are all the subtle questions on which ambitious people exercise their faculties. Let us, therefore, remember, that all doctrines must be tried by this rule, that those which contribute to edification may be approved, and that those which give ground for unprofitable disputes may be rejected as unworthy of the church of God.

If this test had been applied during several centuries, although religion had been stained by many errors, at least that diabolical art of disputing that has obtained the appellation of "scholastic theology" would not have prevailed to so great an extent. For what does that theology contain but contentions or idle speculations, from which no advantage is derived? Accordingly, the more learned a person is in it, we ought to account them the more wretched. I am aware of the plausible excuses by which it is defended, but they will never make out that Paul has spoken falsely in condemning everything of the sort.

"Rather than godly edification." Subtleties of this description edify in pride, and edify in vanity, but not in God. He calls it "the edification of God," either because God approves of it, or because it is agreeable to the nature of God. COMMENTARY ON 1 TIMOTHY.[3]

ENDLESS GENEALOGIES. ENGLISH ANNOTA-

TIONS: Paul calls them endless genealogies, not because in the genealogies there was no end, neither upward nor downward; but because those of the Jews who embraced Christian religion were so addicted to these genealogies that they might have a pretense of claiming kindred of Christ, that they made no end of drawing down their lines of descent from David, or from Abraham; or because the questions moved concerning genealogies, by reason of the slender proof and ground they had for them, could receive no determination or end. ENGLISH ANNOTATIONS.[4]

NOT ALL QUESTIONS TO BE AVOIDED.

WILLIAM FULKE: Not all questions are to be avoided, but only such as do not pertain to godly edifying,[†] which is by faith. Those contentions and questions that have been necessarily moved to build up the ruins of the church in faith . . . have brought forth great increase of good life and true devotion in those who have embraced the faith. The wickedness that abounds is exposed by the light in most, rather than increased in any by the coming of the light. But this is condemnation (says our savior Christ), that people love darkness rather than light, because their works are evil. TEXT OF THE NEW TESTAMENT.[5]

---

[3]CTS 43:24 (CO 52:252). For Calvin's view of the *Sorbonicae scholae*, see below on verse 7. [†]Along with Erasmus and the Vulgate, Calvin's Latin of 1 Tim 1:4 reads *aedificationem Dei*, "edification of God," following the Western reading, *oikodomēn*, rather than *dispensationem Dei*, "stewardship from God" (*oikonomian theou*), which is the much-better-supported reading. See Bruce M. Metzger, *A Textual Commentary on the Greek New Testament*, 2nd ed. (Stuttgart: Deutsche Bibelgesellschaft, 1994), 571.
[4]Downame, ed., *Annotations*, s.v.
[5]Fulke, *Text of the New Testament*, 365*; citing Jn 3:19. [†]See note 3 above concerning the textual variant *aedificationem Dei* (*oikodomēn theou*) / *dispensationem Dei* (*oikonomian theou*).

---

[2]Fulke, *Text of the New Testament*, 365*.

1:5 Love from a Pure Heart

The Scope of the Law. Dutch Annota-tions: By the Greek word *parangelia*, that is, command, charge, or exhortation, which is used here and in verse 18, some understand the charge that Paul here lays on Timothy, of which the end or scope is "charity out of a pure heart." Others by this word "commandment" understand the law of God, which some fought without reason to introduce besides the gospel; of which the apostle teaches that the right end or scope under the gospel must be love to God and our neighbor out of a pure heart, not that the same law must be so taught as some perversely urged it. And this interpretation better agrees with the seventh and other following verses. Dutch Annotations.[6]

Love Is the Purpose of the Law. Geneva Bible: Because these questioners preferred their curious fables to all other knowledge, and beauti-fied them with the law, as if they had been the very law of God, Paul shows that the end of God's law is love, which cannot be without a good conscience, neither a good conscience without faith, nor faith without the word of God. So their doctrine, which is an occasion of contention, is worth nothing. Geneva Bible. Annotation on 1 Timothy 1:5.[7]

The Law's Dual Purpose. Matthias Flacius: [Paul] disputes certain perverse things [said about] the law because they do not edify; therefore, he now teaches this fourth canon on the usefulness of the law. Therefore in the second part of this chapter here, a double use of the law is indicated: first, the law of God is a pedagogue that should lead us to Christ so that through him true faith may be apprehended by our heart purified by imputed righteousness or the remission of sins, and by the regeneration of the Holy Spirit, which doctrine is fully set forth in Acts 15 and Hebrews 9–10: for which reason arises a good conscience

that simultaneously requires the earnest proposi-tion of doing well. Likewise it so rises from the purification of the heart or regeneration and flourishes perpetually in love and other virtues. To this the law of God also furthermore impels us, and his law prescribes our rules and actions. And finally, there is another use of the law, which corrects evildoers with threats and penalties so that they may cease to sin at least from the dread of punishment if they do not want to abandon it out of love for virtue: [Paul] speaks about this below. Faith that is not feigned is a true and living faith that apprehends Christ and his benefits, not hypocrisy, which alone flees to death. On purifica-tion of the heart, see Acts 15 and Hebrews 10. Gloss on 1 Timothy[8]

1:6-7 Aspiring Teachers Who Don't Understand

The Ignorance of Inventive Imagina-tions. John Calvin: When he says that this sort of people wish to be doctors of the law, and yet do not know what they are talking about, he shows that there are two contrary things in them. For if they had given over their studies to profit well in the law of God, they would have had such a certainty that those who had been taught by them could not have doubted. Those who have profited well in the school of God will not let loose the bridle to their imaginations, to invent anything whatsoever, but will have this simplicity, to hold themselves to that which God has shown to all. See then how all those who are rightly instructed in the law of God will have a certain knowledge, but those who do not know what they are talking about demonstrate perfectly that they have forged for themselves vain dreams, and wish to mix their own inventions with the truth of God. This is nothing else but to introduce corruption and bring everything to naught.

And why so? Has God spoken? Do we have the witness of holy Scripture? That is sufficient for us.

---

[6]Haak, *Annotations*, s.v.*
[7]Geneva Bible 1576, NT 92*.

[8]Flacius, *Glossa Compendaria*, 1041.

There are no more questions when we are grounded in the truth of God. If all the world rise up against us, yet we must hold fast and continue with an invincible constancy. For we know, says St. Paul in another place, he whom we have believed. For as soon as we begin to doubt the pure word of God, we cannot but be shaken, and unable to grasp what God wants to say. And what discretion and wisdom can there be in someone who cannot submit to God, and has the audacity to measure what is good by the standard of their own dreams? God has reserved such authority to himself, that he might be our only master. If people rush in to mix their own fantasies with his decrees, how can this not end up in doubt and wavering? Sermons on 1 Timothy.[9]

Curiosity Is an Adversary of Faith.

Desiderius Erasmus: Paul says to Timothy: warn some corrupt apostles there (whose names I prudently pass over at this time, lest being thereby provoked they become more shameless) not to defile or subvert the pure doctrine of the gospel that we taught to the Ephesians, with their new doctrine. And on the other hand, warn the faithful flock beforehand not to lend their ears so easily to such false apostles, to their own peril. For they do not teach those things that lead to eternal salvation and are worthy of the gospel of Christ, but throw in unfruitful Jewish fables, playing on people's superstitious natures, which is not a route to true godliness. And they talk about an intricate succession of pedigree from grandfathers, great-grandfathers, and great-great-grandfathers, as though the gift of salvation taught in the gospel came down to us by corporal lineage descending from sundry ancestors and not, rather, by heavenly goodness poured once universally on all who embrace the faith of the gospel.

And this they preach, not for the glory of Christ but partly so that they themselves may be more valued among you and be commended as noble doctors; and partly so that they may be considered much more learned, because even though the doctrine of the gospel is plain and simple they can throw in a maze of doubtful difficulties and inexplicable riddles: as though those things were not best that are most plain.

The gospel brings salvation to the believer in a straightforward way. But this kind of human doctrine brings in question on question, and not only is nothing applicable to heavenly godliness (which God bestows on us through faith) but it overturns the chief point of the religion of the gospel. Whoever believes purely does not linger on such questions. And those who tie and untie the knots of questions, what else do they teach people but to doubt? This curiosity of questioning is diametrically opposed to faith. If they believe God, why do they quarrel with his promises? If the faith and love of the gospel gives salvation without much ado, to what purpose are people's fantasies mingled into it— things such as circumcision, washing of hands, food laws, and observation of holy days? Paraphrases.[10]

The Audacity of Academic Theologians.

John Calvin: None will be found more bold in pronouncing rashly on matters unknown to them than the teachers of such fables. We see in the present day with what pride and haughtiness the schools of the Sorbonne pronounce their authoritative decisions. And on what subjects? On those which are altogether hidden from human minds— which no word of Scripture and no revelation has ever made known to us. With greater boldness do they affirm their purgatory than the resurrection of the dead. As to their contrivances about the intercession of the saints,† if we do not hold them to be an undoubted oracle, they cry out that the whole of religion is overturned. What shall I say as to their vast labyrinths about the hierarchies of heaven, relationships, and similar contrivances? It is a matter that has no end. Commentary on 1 Timothy.[11]

---

[9]CO 53:43; citing 2 Tim 1:12.

[10]Erasmus, *Paraphrases*, 14-15.

[11]CTS 43:29 (CO 52:254). In his sermons on this passage, Calvin shows that he is not against all academic study of theology per se, but against the "school doctors," particularly those of the Sorbonne in Paris, who "torment themselves with questions about which one cannot find any testimony in the holy Scriptures" (CO

Do Not Make Sin Where There Is No Sin.
Pilgram Marpeck: The enemy of truth has another trick, ... to lead people astray with hasty and uncertain judgments. By doing so, they are judging and condemning themselves, making sin where there is no sin, setting up laws, commandments, and prohibitions against the authority and sovereignty of the Spirit of the Lord Jesus Christ, who gave his own no law except the law of love. ... They seek to establish laws, and would become the masters of Scripture, but they do not know what they establish. Because of this ignorance, the enemy takes hearts and consciences captive. But to those who are in Jesus Christ and are justified through Christ, no law is given. Judgment and Decision.[12]

1:8-11 The Right Use of the Law

For Whom Is the Law? Desiderius Erasmus: We both know and acknowledge that the law is good only if it is lawfully used. And they are abusers of the law who expound it against itself. The chief purpose of the law was to lead us to Christ. So that they turn the law, which is good, into their own destruction when they, by the law, draw people away from Christ. For whom is the law good? For those who see and discern how the law (which was given for a time) must give place to the gospel, and in what way it ought to continue in its perpetual strength; and for those who understand how to apply the outward letter of the law to the spiritual doctrine of the gospel; and for those who perceive how they, whom Christ has redeemed with his blood from the tyranny of sin and do more of their own accord at the motion of love than Moses appointed in the law, have no need of the fear or admonition of the law, either to be restrained from wickedness or steered to their duty. For them indeed, the law is good.

For they understand that the law does not belong to the one who has learned by the gospel not only to hurt no one but also to do good to one's enemies. Why should a horse that thus runs well and of its own accord need a bridle or a spur? Those who are led and ordered by the Spirit of Christ run uncompelled, and do more than all the whole law requires. And having once freely attained righteousness, they flee from all unrighteousness. Therefore the law, which restrains people from doing evil by means of fear, is not given in any way to those who do willingly and gladly that which the law requires, even if they do not have the words of the law.

For whom was the law laid down? Truly it was for those who are deaf to the law of nature and, being without love and readily inclined to all mischief, are guided by their own lusts unless they are held back by the barrier of the law. And if the law suffers them to sin unpunished, they return by and by to their own inclinations, and become the same openly as they were inwardly. Paraphrases.[13]

Spiritual Affections Needed to Properly Fulfill the Law. Thomas Venatorius: We are not lacking people today who proclaim the law; but because they do not interpret the law correctly, to their own death and destruction they abuse the law, which is otherwise good for those who understand it rightly. Wherefore, those who hold the correct understanding of the law know that the law is spiritual, and they know that sufficiently spiritual affections are needed for the law to be appropriately fulfilled. For in order for the law to be fulfilled in the affection of the flesh to the greatest degree both in the eyes of the world, and certainly in the eyes of God, unless it is fulfilled in the affection of the Spirit, it will not be fulfilled. As the apostle testifies elsewhere, the affection of the flesh is death. By contrast, the affection of the Spirit is life and peace. To the contrary in the case of the affection of the flesh: it is hostility to God, nor does it submit to the law of God, if indeed it even could. Nor are those who are in the flesh able to please

---

53:25-26) and the "frivolous questions which bring forth no doctrine at all" and do not help prepare people to preach (CO 53:42-43). See also on 1 Tim 6:4. †See also the comments below on 1 Tim 2:5 concerning the prayers of the departed.
[12]CRR 2:327.

[13]Erasmus, *Paraphrases*, 17-18.

God. Those who are led by the affection of the flesh are simply not able to see the disease of their soul. They are so far from correctly understanding the office of the law that the sky is not as far from the ground as they are from a true and genuine understanding of the law. It is therefore the purpose of the law, first to frighten the conscience, rather, to condemn the judgment of the whole of the rational faculty; and utterly to put to death the strength of our flesh. However, the law is not capable of restoring consciences that have been frightened in this way and led to despair and death. Wherefore, apart from its role of pointing out sin, and apart from the fact that consciences are put in fear by the revelation of the law, it has still another function, that is, as Paul says to the Galatians, "the law was our guardian until Christ came, in order that we might be justified by faith." EXPOSITIONS OF 1 TIMOTHY.[14]

THE USES OF THE LAW. MARTIN LUTHER: The law is good, and it was not laid down for the just. . . . The two functions of the law are to reveal sinners and restrain them. The third function, however, to remove sin and to justify, is limited to this: The Lamb of God, and not the law, takes away sin. It is Christ who removes sin and justifies. Consequently, we must distinguish between the function of the law and that of Christ. It is the law's function to show good and evil, because it shows what one must do and reveals sin, which one must not commit. The law therefore is good because it shows not only evil but also the good that one must do. But beyond that it does not go. It does not kill Og and King Sihon. It merely reveals good and bad; Joshua [does the rest]. LECTURES ON 1 TIMOTHY.[15]

THE LAW IS FOR RESTRAINING THE WICKED. JOHN CALVIN: Having such adversaries, in order to restrain their haughty insolence, Paul remonstrates that the law is, as it were, the sword of God

to slay them; and that neither he nor any like him have reason for viewing the law with dread or aversion; for it is not opposed to righteous persons, that is, to the godly and to those who willingly obey God. I am well aware that some learned men draw an ingenious sense out of these words; as if Paul were treating theologically about the nature of "the law." They argue that the law has nothing to do with the sons of God, who have been regenerated by the Spirit; because it was not given for righteous persons. But the connection in which these words occur shuts me up to the necessity of giving a more simple interpretation to this statement. He takes for granted the well-known sentiment that "from bad manners have sprung good laws,"[†] and maintains that the law of God was given in order to restrain the licentiousness of wicked people; because they who are good of their own accord do not need the authoritative injunction of the law. COMMENTARY ON 1 TIMOTHY.[16]

USING THE LAW LAWFULLY. JOHN MAYER: The law is said here not to be given to the just, because not for fear of the law but out of love of virtue do such live in a righteous and holy way. But the wicked who have no love of a virtuous life are urged and threatened by the law, and so stirred up to that which of themselves they have no mind to. For they only use the law lawfully who perform what is hereby commanded but seek not justification by thus doing, but in Christ only, who is able perfectly to justify all that come to him. . . . The threatenings of the law, as it was necessary, were added to curb the wicked and ungodly who have no love of virtue. . . . The wicked use the law lawfully when they are hereby converted and made to fly to Christ to seek justification by him; but then they are no longer wicked but just, and so not under the law and thus not such as to whom the

---

[14]Venatorius, *Distributiones*, 22; citing Rom 8:6-8; Gal 3:24.
[15]LW 28:235 (WA 26:16-17); citing Num 21:21-35. See Edward A. Engelbrecht, *Friends of the Law: Luther's Use of the Law for the Christian Life* (St. Louis: Concordia, 2011).

[16]CTS 43:30-31 (CO 52:255). [†]This saying can be traced back at least as far as Macrobius in the fourth century AD, who said *uetus uerbum est leges inquit bonae ex malis moribus procreantur*, "It is an old saying: good laws, it is said, are begotten by bad manners" (*Saturnalia* 3.17.10). See also Isocrates, writing in c. 350 BC, *Areopagiticus* 7.39-40/147 (LCL 229:128-29).

law is given. The false teachers, not understanding this, abused the law by imposing it on Christians who were by faith justified. COMMENTARY ON PAUL'S EPISTLES.[17]

THE LAW SHOULD LEAD TO REPENTANCE.
THOMAS CARTWRIGHT: The meaning of the apostle is that the Jews, abusing the law to foolish and unprofitable questions, thereby handle it as if the men with whom they dealt with had been just, needing not to be convicted or reproved for sin. Whereas the law is given to people who are unjust, to lay open sin, with the filth and punishment of it, so that people might by repentance seek the remedy in the gospel. CONFUTATION OF THE RHEMISTS.[18]

THE LAW PROVES YOUR SIN. GIOVANNI DIODATI: He shows that, contrary to the opinion of those false doctors of the law, since it is composed of so many threatenings, prohibitions, and other rigors, the law carries with it a certain proof of humankind's perverseness. It is evident that humankind has no natural disposition or voluntary inclination to fulfill it, for otherwise they would apply themselves to it of their own proper motion, as believers and those who are regenerate by God's Spirit do. These have the habit of righteousness in themselves, as an inward and living law, and have no need of the law's terror. They are also justified in Christ and freed from the curse of it. . . . He names certain grievous sins here, not because the law does not condemn all others (even the least), but only to reprove those hypocrites who were so zealous of the law and its righteousness and yet were stained with most horrible vices. PIOUS ANNOTATIONS.[19]

THE IRREVERENT AND UNHOLY SHOULD BE MADE TO FEAR. AEGIDIUS HUNNIUS: With the voice of the law, which is like a hammer (to which the law is likened), they should be made to fear, so that they should be lead to heartfelt admission of sins. So they act preposterously who proclaim the

gospel and the absolution of the gospel to those who are manifestly defiled. This in truth is to put pearls before swine, and to give what is holy to dogs. By this untimely declaration of the gospel dissolute people are confirmed in their lack of repentance and their sins, and leave not better but in a worse state. And this is what the Lord condemns so many times in the false prophets, that they say to an irreverent people: "Peace, when there is no peace. . . ."

The gospel should be preached to the poor—he means of course to the poor in Spirit who hunger and thirst for righteousness, those who have a contrite heart and a troubled spirit. The rest, especially those who are manifestly irreverent, Moses addressed and struck their hearts with the thunder of the judgment of God until, worn down, they would soften. Worked over by the plow of the law, they would be prepared for receiving the seed of the gospel, so that fruit might be produced. If in truth the naked voice is not strong enough to correct them toward better virtue, let the sword be applied that the law provides to the magistrate of God, to be used against these kinds of stubborn despisers and transgressors of all laws. Just as public laws go forth from their source armed with an avenging sword so that evil can be removed from our presence, so also Moses in the law of the Decalogue, when talking of the removal of murderers, adulterers, and other defiled people, adds this counsel immediately after: that the evil should be removed from the people of God. COMMENTARY ON 1 TIMOTHY.[20]

APOSTOLIC DOCTRINE DOES NOT DETRACT FROM THE LAW. DAVID DICKSON: In verse 8 he answers an objection: "Therefore, are you against the divine law, who so earnestly rebuke the teachers of it?" The apostle answers that he did not at all detract from the law (reproving those who abuse it) but rather commends and teaches the right use

[17]Mayer, *Commentarie*, 486-87*.
[18]Cartwright, *Confutation*, 540*.
[19]Diodati, *Pious Annotations*, 38-39*.
[20]Hunnius, *Thesaurus Apostolicus*, 738; citing Jer 23:29; 8:11; Mt 11:5; 5:3, 6; Rom 13:4. On the last point, see Deut 13:5; 17:7, 12; 19:13; 21:9, 21; 22:21-22, 24; 24:7.

of the law. He confirms the answer with three reasons: The first is, from the end of the law, or the legal covenant, so far as it is opposed to the gospel. The law is established, not that the faithful, justified by faith in Christ, should be justified by the law (as the perverse teachers of the law intended) but that the unrighteous, and unbelievers, as are all wicked and profane persons condemned by the law, might acknowledge their unrighteousness and deserved condemnation, and so repent and fly to Christ. Therefore the apostle's doctrine detracts nothing from the law. He recommends and teaches the right use of the law.

He confirms the answer with three reasons:

Reason 1: From the end of the law, or the legal covenant, so far as it is opposed to the gospel, the law is established, not that the faithful, justified by faith in Christ, should be justified by the law (as the perverse teachers of the law intended), but that the unrighteous and unbelievers, as are all the wicked and profane persons condemned by the law, might acknowledge their unrighteousness, and

deserved condemnation, repent, and fly to Christ. Therefore the apostle's doctrine does not detract from the law.

Reason 2. All sins that are forbidden by the law are also prohibited by the sound doctrine of the glorious gospel; and all the duties that are commanded by the law are earnestly urged and taught in the gospel, so much as concerns the performance of our obedience to God, the demonstration of our thankfulness, and the proof of the sincerity of faith in the fruits of holiness. Therefore the doctrine of the gospel detracts nothing from the law.

Reason 3. I, an apostle, to whom the gospel of God (in himself most blessed, and the author of all blessings toward us) is committed, do no less urge this wholesome doctrine of sanctification, and all good works that are commanded in the law, than any zealot of the law, although not to the same end. Therefore the apostolic doctrine detracts nothing at all from the law. EXPOSITION OF ALL PAUL'S EPISTLES.[21]

---

[21]Dickson, *Exposition*, 159.

1:12-20 CHRIST JESUS CAME TO SAVE SINNERS

[12]*I thank him who has given me strength, Christ Jesus our Lord, because he judged me faithful, appointing me to his service, [13]though formerly I was a blasphemer, persecutor, and insolent opponent. But I received mercy because I had acted ignorantly in unbelief, [14]and the grace of our Lord overflowed for me with the faith and love that are in Christ Jesus. [15]The saying is trustworthy and deserving of full acceptance, that Christ Jesus came into the world to save sinners, of whom I am the foremost. [16]But I received mercy for this reason, that in me, as the foremost, Jesus Christ might display his perfect patience as an example to those who were to believe in him for eternal life. [17]To the King of the ages, immortal, invisible, the only God, be honor and glory forever and ever.[a] Amen.*

[18]This charge I entrust to you, Timothy, my child, in accordance with the prophecies previously made about you, that by them you may wage the good warfare, [19]holding faith and a good conscience. By rejecting this, some have made shipwreck of their faith, [20]among whom are Hymenaeus and Alexander, whom I have handed over to Satan that they may learn not to blaspheme.

a Greek *to the ages of ages*

OVERVIEW: These early modern commentators concentrate significantly on soteriological issues in their expositions of this passage. Central to their discussion is the relationship between faith and works in justification as exemplified in the contrasting positions of Martin Luther and Petrus Stevartius. This debate occurs within the larger context concerning the roles of grace and free will in human salvation. The authors also explore the nature of sins of ignorance as well as the correlation between faith and conscience. Occupying a key place in their examination of the passage is the gravity of sin as illustrated in Paul's account of his preconversion life. Another crucial subject considered is excommunication as a remedial means of discipline for lapsed Christians.

1:12-14 *Paul's Past*

GRATITUDE FOR STRENGTH TO SERVE FAITHFULLY. MARTIN LUTHER: So I thank him because he has not only given it to me but has also strengthened it in me lest I run in vain or in uncertainty, like those who teach it and do not know if it is true. Thus in our time many have kept that Word only because of novelty and because heretics have arisen. They have not received it as the Word of God. These are vainhearted people who are bound by an enthusiasm for new things. This Word wants us to adhere strongly to it. God gives it that we may be strong in it. One is strengthened by his practice in teaching, testing, battling. Earlier,[†] in the Epistle to Titus, we have "that you insist on these things." We do this to strengthen our own people, who are not strong and sure and fully persuaded but are easily misled because they have no zeal for the truth and do not take this seriously. That is, the Word makes me strong for Christ so that I have no doubts, and we should let that count for something that someone can give thanks to God. Anyone can let the spit fly in public and be considered a learned teacher. But to teach with this confidence is indeed a rarity. . . . It is the great blessing of all Christians and especially of those in the ministry that they are sure that they have the Word of God. Out of that certainty follow peace of heart, rejoicing, thanksgiving, and an entire life that becomes more bearable. On the other hand, whoever lacks this certainty is without peace and comfort. LECTURES ON 1 TIMOTHY.[1]

PAUL'S IGNORANCE. DUTCH ANNOTATIONS: Paul says mercy was shown to him, seeing he was ignorant of the divinity and truth of the gospel, wherefore he does not excuse himself, as if he had not therefore been liable to punishment before God, for he testifies the contrary of himself afterward in verses 15-16 as also in general. But he gives hereby to understand that his sin was not the sin against the Holy Ghost, done out of obstinacy and hatred of the known truth, and therefore pardonable through the grace and merits of Christ. ANNOTATIONS ON 1 TIMOTHY 1:13.[2]

JUSTIFICATION IS NOT BY FAITH ALONE. PETRUS STEVARTIUS: The Lord requires from us this superabundance of our righteousness. Of course it arises from faith, and from love, exceeding the righteousness of the scribes and the Pharisees that arises from the law of servitude. He says, "unless your righteousness abounds beyond that of the scribes and Pharisees," and so on. And so the apostle did not say "The grace of our Lord super-abounded with faith." So it is not from faith alone as on the Lutherans' misinterpretation, just as they misinterpret everything else and have done so in other places. But the apostle said, "Grace super-abounded with faith and love." With these words the apostle adequately cautioned us that what he stated in other passages of his letters on the topic of justifying faith, that is of proper faith, must be understood of a living faith that works through love.

If the grace of our Lord by which we are justified abounded beyond the righteousness from the law (this is what superabound means), then the grace of God did not abound together with faith alone beyond the righteousness that comes from the law. And thus we are not justified by faith alone, because righteousness based on faith alone does not overcome righteousness from the law. Therefore whoever attributes justifying power to faith alone and not, rather, to faith accompanied by love that at the same time produces faith, denies the grace of our Lord. COMMENTARY ON 1 TIMOTHY.[3]

PAUL NOT EXCUSING HIS SIN. EDWARD LEIGH: "Because I had acted ignorantly in unbelief." The words are rather thus to be read: "notwithstanding," or "although I did it ignorantly," not "for I did it ignorantly, or because I did it ignorantly," by way of excuse. He was not converted because he did it ignorantly; for then all those who sin ignorantly should be converted. *Hoti* is rendered "although" in Luke 23:40, and is the same Greek word that is used here.[†] The words are brought in by way of aggravation, "did it ignorantly in unbelief," an ignorance of disposition. Some say his ignorance left a capacity in the subject, not in the sin; else he had sinned, committing it so maliciously against the Holy Ghost. ANNOTATIONS.[4]

GOD'S MERCY, NOT FREE WILL ALONE, IS NECESSARY. PETRUS STEVARTIUS: Although Paul acknowledges that the power of nature and of his own life is of no value or significance, nevertheless with the help of divine grace (and Paul testifies that he is the greatest herald of grace), he does not deny that he is something or has some ability. But the beginning of every good work, in this passage, as at the end of Philippians 2, he attributes to God's mercy. And all the more so because every good that a human being can work through the free expres-

---

[1] LW 28:239-240 (WA 26:20-21); citing Gal 2:2; 1 Cor 9:26.
[†] Luther had lectured on Titus in the previous month.
[2] Haak, *Annotations*, s.v.*; citing 2 Thess 1:8; Mk 3:29.

[3] Stevartius, *Commentarius*, 78; citing Mt 5:20.
[4] Leigh, *Annotations*, 320*. Modern commentators can also be keen to show that Paul is not excusing his sin here; George W. Knight III, *The Pastoral Epistles: A Commentary on the Greek Text*, New International Greek Testament Commentary (Carlisle, UK: Paternoster, 1992), 96, comments that the *hoti* clause "does not give the reason that Paul was shown mercy, as if his ignorance made him worthy and therefore elicited the mercy, nor is it written to indicate that what is described in v. 13a is not sin." Like the *Dutch Annotations* above, Knight believes Paul is showing why his sin was neither the high-handed sin of the Old Testament (e.g., Num 15:30-31) or the sin against the Holy Spirit (Mt 12:31). [†] The ESV translates *hoti* as "since" in Lk 23:40, and as "because" in 1 Tim 1:13.

sion of the will—if he is not supported by divine power—is neither useful nor either suited to or sufficient for obtaining salvation. Thus it follows, says the apostle, that without God's help human power is not equal to accomplishing good actions; because in the things that we do there must always be an end goal for which we work. Commentary on 1 Timothy[5]

1:15-17 Christ Came for Sinners Like Me

A Gift for the Unworthy. Martin Luther: This passage has quite often been life and salvation for me. So Paul praises it with a beautiful preface. He speaks with great certainty. Oh, who else could speak with such assurance! This is a very trustworthy and certain statement. Then, "worthy of full acceptance." This we should receive.... Human reason shudders at the greatness of the gift, because I am to believe that God gives me eternal life for all my sins, as I said earlier. But this is too much! The greatness of the past gift makes possible also the gift that is yet to come. Because this has happened, because God has given his Son, therefore the other will happen. Even if I am not worthy, it is still true.... Christ did not come to judge, to destroy, but to give himself for the salvation of sinners. Therefore let no sinner lose hope. Rather let the one despair who does not want to be a sinner, as the self-righteous. The sinner has the opportunity to hope because "Christ has come." Like the devil, the law of Moses condemns. We do not need Christ to condemn us, nor was he sent to condemn; and yet we receive him thus because we have neither read nor understood Scripture. Lectures on 1 Timothy.[6]

Courageous Confidence for Sinners. John Calvin: Although God the Father a thousand times offer us salvation, and although Christ himself preaches about his own office, yet we do not on that account cease to tremble, or at

least to debate with ourselves if it is actually so. Wherefore, whenever any doubt shall arise in our mind about the forgiveness of sins, let us learn to repel it courageously with this shield, that it is an undoubted truth, and deserves to be received without controversy. "To save sinners." The word "sinners" is emphatic; for they who acknowledge that it is the office of Christ to save have difficulty in admitting this thought, that such a salvation belongs to "sinners." Our mind is always impelled to look at our worthiness; and as soon as our unworthiness is seen, our confidence sinks. Accordingly, the more any one is oppressed by their sins, let them the more courageously betake themselves to Christ, relying on this doctrine, that he came to bring salvation not to the righteous, but to "sinners." . . . And, indeed, the distrust entertained by all of us is counteracted when we thus behold in Paul a visible model of that grace which we desire to see. Commentary on 1 Timothy.[7]

The Chief of Sinners. Edward Leigh: Some say Paul calls himself the chiefest of sinners because his sins were more general than others, or because of his persecution of the whole church.... Some say he was not absolutely a greater sinner than the Pharisees, who sinned against the Holy Ghost, but the greatest sinner of all that should be saved, for he says in the same verse "Christ Jesus came to save sinners of which saved sinners I am the chief." Others interpret it thus: that Paul was so in his own apprehension; he esteemed himself the greatest sinner.... By these words we are admonished ... what a great and heinous crime infidelity is, especially where obstinacy and cruelty is joined with it. Annotations.[8]

Paul as an Example. Martin Luther: Here Paul is saying that this occurrence is not per se a miracle but a general example. As an individual thing, this passage speaks of special prerogative. Therefore all comfort is taken away. But when it is

---

[5]Stevartius, Commentarius, 71.
[6]LW 28:246-47 (WA 26:25-26).
[7]CTS 43:39, 41 (CO 52:259-61).
[8]Leigh, Annotations, 320*.

written as a comfort and example for me, then it applies to me, so that I may glory in this passage, not just Paul, who has reached his goal. "Therefore," he says, "he has had compassion on me," so that it might not have a secret and individual privilege, but that "Jesus Christ might display," that is, that all Christians, who are sinners, might know "from my example" what sort of a person Christ is: The Lord is long-suffering, patient, and so on; he can forgive and is willing to forgive our countless sins. "Therefore I have been set up as an example for the whole church that all may fix their eyes on me as an example of his long-suffering mercy." "Patience." Every kind of patience. "He could endure my murders, blasphemies, seductions, crimes of violence. I used to force people to blaspheme, revoke, and deny Christ." LECTURES ON 1 TIMOTHY.[9]

GLORY TO GOD FOREVER. JOHN CALVIN: Paul breaks out into this exclamation because he could not find words to express his gratitude; for those sudden bursts occur chiefly when we are constrained to break off the discourse, in consequence of being overpowered by the vastness of the subject. And is there anything more astonishing than Paul's conversion? Yet, at the same time, by his example he reminds us all that we ought never to think of the grace manifested in God's calling without being carried to lofty admiration.

"Immortal, invisible, the only God." This sublime praise of the grace that God had bestowed on him swallows up the remembrance of his former life. For how great a deep is the glory of God! Those attributes he ascribes to God, though they belong to him always, yet are admirably adapted to the present occasion. The apostle calls him the King eternal, not liable to any change; invisible, because he dwells in light that is inaccessible; and last, the Only Wise, because he renders foolish and condemns as vanity all human wisdom. . . .

Yet as to the last epithet "Only," it is uncertain whether he means to claim all glory for God alone, or calls him "the only wise," or says that he only is

God.[†] The second of these meanings is that which I prefer; for it was in fine harmony with his present subject to say that human understanding, whatever it may be, must bend to the secret purpose of God. And yet I do not deny that he affirms that God alone is worthy of all glory; for, while he scatters on his creatures in every direction, the sparks of his glory, still all glory belongs truly and perfectly to him alone. But either of those meanings implies that there is no glory but that which belongs to God. COMMENTARY ON 1 TIMOTHY.[10]

1:18-20 *Paul's Charge to Timothy*

TIMOTHY THE GOOD SOLDIER OF CHRIST.
WOLFGANG MUSCULUS: Paul has in mind here the prophecies that had previously been made about Timothy, so that as if by applying goads he could stimulate and excite his mind, so that he would beware, not to differ from the excellent testimonies and prophecies about him. With the same counsel he reminds him elsewhere of the sincere faith that was in his grandmother Lois, and his mother Eunice, and in himself also. He also reminds him of the excellent gift that he had received through the laying on of his own hands, that he might fan it into flame.

Therefore note how those who are adorned with some particular gift from God—whether of faith, knowledge, or intelligence—should not be free from care. The apostle judged that even his own Timothy should be so carefully warned and reminded of the prophecies and gifts from God with which he had been adorned, lest through negligence and stupidity those things that he had received from the Lord for the benefit of the faithful he should render vanities.

---

[9]LW 28:248 (WA 26:26-27).

[10]CTS 43:41-42 (CO 52:261); citing 1 Tim 6:16. [†]The Textus Receptus inserted the word for "wise" after "only" here, along with various manuscripts including most minuscules. Bruce M. Metzger, *A Textual Commentary on the Greek New Testament*, 2nd ed. (Stuttgart: Deutsche Bibelgesellschaft, 1994), 572, concludes that it is "no doubt a scribal gloss derived from Ro. 16:27" given that the shorter reading is strongly supported by good representatives of the Alexandrian and Western text types.

Next the military metaphor that he uses here should be noted. He compares the minister of Christ to a soldier, and his ministry to military service, and the gifts that he had received from God, to a soldier's weapons. For the soldier it is well known to where he has been called and taken into military service, namely, to serve his king. Next he is conscious that he strives to serve well as a soldier. And third, he knows for what purpose he has received a soldier's weapons, namely, to fight against the enemy. No soldier is so dull as to be ignorant of these things. In the same way, it is fitting that the minister of Christ should be encouraged to continually reflect on the fact that he has been taken into the military service of Christ in order that he should serve well and faithfully as a soldier for him, and that the things which have been given him by God he has received as if they were a soldier's weapons.

This thought should be repeatedly renewed in their minds, so that they may be urged on to this, namely, to fight faithfully for the Lord, not only by teaching the wandering, but also by rebuking the insolent and false teachers—as well as by keeping those in their station who are tempted to defect, with steadfast warnings and denouncements. COMMENTARY ON PAUL'S EPISTLES.[11]

THE PROPHETIC CHOICE. JOHN MAYER: Diverse expositors conjecture in different ways about the prophecies that were previously made about Timothy that are spoken of here. They also differ in referring the commandment discussed here when they ask what commandment is meant which the apostle says he gave it to him. Some refer it to the words in the same verse immediately following, "That you fight a good fight according to the prophecies that were made about you." Some see it as a reference to that which was said previously, touching the law, which was not given to the righteous but to sinners, and to the whole the gospel, which was also previously spoken of, that Christ came into the world to save sinners. These

things they say he commended to Timothy to persevere, and not to be corrupted. Last, some expound it as a return to the charge mentioned in verse 3, that he should not suffer the teaching of any other doctrine; for after other things are spoken of, a parenthesis apologizing for himself, who might be thought an unfit minister of the gospel seeing he was before a persecutor and a blasphemer, after which he returns not to his first argument again, rendering a reason why he gave him this charge when he left him at Ephesus. And this is doubtless the best exposition, the very word *parangelia* giving light into it, being the same that was used in verse 3. . . .

Touching the prophecies that he says were previously made about Timothy, some read it somewhat otherwise, "according to the prophecies, which have come even unto you." So they expound it of the doctrine here commended to him, as being the same as that in the prophecies set forth by the holy prophets of old, which, being kept from one age to another, had now come to the hands of Timothy, whose training up in the knowledge of the holy Scriptures he also elsewhere commends. Others understand by prophecies the doctrines the teaching that was committed to Timothy. . . . Others . . . understand the gifts of the Holy Ghost, with which Timothy was endued. Others again understand the prophetic conjectures of many men concerning Timothy, when he was first ordained, by reason of the grace that they saw to be in him.

Last, some understand the prophecies as revelations the apostle had concerning Timothy when he constituted him bishop of Ephesus, as it is said concerning Paul and Barnabas, "The Holy Spirit said, 'Set apart for me Barnabas and Saul.'" And these revelations some think not only Paul had, but others also, because it is said in the plural number "prophecies," as it was necessary for so eminent a man in the church as he was, being also very young when he was appointed to an episcopal function, so that he might have more authority in people's hearts, whereas otherwise he should have been, for his youth, subject to contempt. And to this last opinion do I subscribe as most agreeable

---

[11]Musculus, *In Divi Pauli Epistolas*, 348-49; citing 2 Tim 1:3-7.

to that which is reported of Timothy when Paul first took him to himself, namely, that the brethren testified well of him. . . . That which is there called their testifyings is here happily called the prophecies that were previously made about him. Commentary on Paul's Epistles.[12]

A Good Conscience. Dutch Annotations: A "conscience," that is, an upright conscience, which in all its actions orders itself according to that whereof it is informed out of the Word of God, and not according to ambition, covetousness, or other evil affections that may easily be judged of by those who compare people's words with their actions. Annotation on 1 Timothy 1:19.[13]

Faith and Conscience Together. John Trapp: A good conscience, says one, is as it were a chest in which the doctrine of faith is to be kept safe. That doctrine of faith will quickly be lost if this chest is broken. For God will give over to errors and heresies those who cast away conscience of walking after God's word. Commentary upon All the Epistles.[14]

The Mother of All Heresies. John Calvin: They who do not serve God with a sincere and a perfect heart, but give a loose rein to wicked dispositions, even though at first they had a sound understanding, come to lose it altogether. . . . We know that the treasure of sound doctrine is invaluable, and therefore there is nothing that we ought to dread more than to have it taken from us. But Paul here informs us that there is only one way of keeping it safe; and that is to secure it by the locks and bars of a good conscience. This is what we experience every day; for how comes it that there are so many who, laying aside the gospel, rush into wicked sects, or become involved in monstrous errors? It is because, by this kind of blindness, God punishes hypocrisy; as, on the other hand, a genuine fear of God gives strength

for perseverance. Hence we may learn two lessons. First, teachers and ministers of the gospel and through them all the churches are taught with what horror they ought to regard a hypocritical and deceitful profession of true doctrine, when they learn that it is so severely punished. Second, this passage removes the offense by which so many persons are greatly distressed, when they perceive that some who formerly professed their attachment to Christ and to the gospel not only fall back into their former superstitions but (which is far worse) are bewildered and captivated by monstrous errors. For by such examples God openly supports the majesty of the gospel, and openly shows that he cannot at all endure the profanation of it. And this is what experience has taught us in every age. All the errors that have existed in the Christian church from the beginning proceeded from this source: that in some persons ambition, and in others covetousness, extinguished the true fear of God. A bad conscience is, therefore, the mother of all heresies. Commentary on 1 Timothy.[15]

Making a Shipwreck of Faith. English Annotations: "Holding faith." That is, the profession or doctrine of the true faith, as appears by the opposition to the blasphemings of Hymenaeus and Alexander. "Good conscience." An upright conscience, which directs a person in all their doings to that which they have been instructed out of the Word of God. But some, for giving reins to a licentious course of life against the dictates of their own conscience, God has punished, by taking away the light of his Spirit from them, that in the midst of their course they should lose their most precious spiritual merchandise, and be drowned in error and heresy after the manner of those who in a sea tempest suffer shipwreck. English Annotations.[16]

Excommunication Is to Be Feared. William Fulke: They that do not have a good

---

[12]Mayer, *Commentarie*, 490-91*; citing Acts 13:2; Acts 16:2.
[13]Haak, *Annotations*, s.v.*
[14]Trapp, *Commentary*, 301-2*.

[15]CTS 43:45-46 (CO 52:263-64).
[16]Downame, ed., *Annotations*, s.v.

conscience with faith, may fall from faith, and make shipwreck of it. But it is not a lively faith, whereby someone is justified, but a dead faith, consisting only in knowledge of the principles of religion. But those who are justified by a lively faith can never finally fall from it, because those whom God justified he also glorified. . . . The apostles had extraordinary power to afflict the bodies of men that obstinately opposed them against the truth. But it was not ordinary in all of those who had the power of excommunication in the primitive church. But notwithstanding, just excommunication by those who have lawful authority is greatly to be feared. TEXT OF THE NEW TESTAMENT.[17]

JUDGE HARSH SAYINGS WITH REVERENCE.
THE SECOND BOOK OF HOMILIES: Whereas we read in diverse psalms how David wished the adversaries of God sometimes shame, rebuke, and confusion, sometimes the decay of their offspring and issue, sometimes that they might perish and come suddenly to destruction . . . [and] with such other manner of imprecations,[†] we ought not to be offended at such prayers of David, being a prophet as he was, singularly beloved of God and rapt in spirit, with an ardent zeal for God's glory. He spoke them not of a private hatred and in a stomach against their persons, but wished spiritually the destruction of such corrupt errors and vices that reigned in all devilish persons set against God. He was of like mind as St. Paul was, when he delivered Hymenaeus and Alexander, with the notorious fornicator, to Satan, to their temporal confusion, "that their spirit might be saved against the Day of the Lord." . . . Let us not therefore be offended, but search out the reason of such words before we are offended, that we may the more reverently judge of such sayings, though strange to our carnal understandings, yet to those who are spiritually minded, judged to be zealously and godly pronounced. THE SECOND BOOK OF HOMILIES.[18]

---

[17]Fulke, *Text of the New Testament*, 365*; citing Rom 8:30.

[18]Jewel, *Second Tome of Homilees*, 313-15*; citing 1 Cor 5:5. [†]See, e.g., Ps 6:10; 31:17-18; 35:4, 8; 40:14; 71:13; 109:6-20.

2:1-7 PRAY FOR ALL PEOPLE

First of all, then, I urge that supplications, prayers, intercessions, and thanksgivings be made for all people, ²for kings and all who are in high positions, that we may lead a peaceful and quiet life, godly and dignified in every way. ³This is good, and it is pleasing in the sight of God our Savior, ⁴who desires all people to be saved and to come to the knowledge of the truth. ⁵For there is one God, and there is one mediator between God and men, the manᵃ Christ Jesus, ⁶who gave himself as a ransom for all, which is the testimony given at the proper time. ⁷For this I was appointed a preacher and an apostle (I am telling the truth, I am not lying), a teacher of the Gentiles in faith and truth.

a *men* and *man* render the same Greek word that is translated *people* in verses 1 and 4

OVERVIEW: Having begun to deal with doctrine and church discipline, Paul now moves on to discuss the public assemblies of God's people and particularly the subject of prayer. He urges Timothy to ensure that there are public prayers for all, including the Roman authorities, since God desires all to be saved and know the truth. In a context where some radical Anabaptist groups appeared seditious and undermined good order in the state, the magisterial reformers were keen to be heard encouraging prayer for their leaders and civil obedience. Precisely how we are meant to understand God's will here in the context of the rest of the Bible's teaching on God's sovereignty was a contentious issue among our commentators, requiring some careful distinctions and discussion of the precise meaning of the word "all," which appears several times in this passage. At the same time, the uniqueness and sufficiency of Christ's mediation and intercession raised by 1 Timothy 2:5 was an issue of major disagreement between Protestants and Romans Catholics.

2:1-3 Prayers for Those in Authority

DIFFERENT KINDS OF PRAYER. ENGLISH ANNOTATIONS: Either these words are synonyms, all signifying the public devotions of the church in her service and liturgy; or they may be thus distinguished: by "supplications" are meant such prayers as we make in our necessities and distresses, to prevent and avoid evils that may befall us or that come upon us; by "prayers" are meant the prayers in which we plead for good things at God's hands, namely, spiritual and temporal blessings; by "intercessions" are meant the prayers in which we entreat God for the good of others. ENGLISH ANNOTATIONS.[1]

PRAY FOR THE POWERS THAT BE. HULDRYCH ZWINGLI: If the two brightest luminaries of our faith, Jeremiah and Paul, both command us to pray to the Lord for the powers that be, that we may be enabled to live a godly life, how much more is it the duty of all people in the different kingdoms and peoples to attempt and accomplish all that they can to safeguard Christian quietness. We teach, therefore, that tributes, taxes, dues, tithes, pledges, loans, and all kinds of obligations should be paid and that the common laws should generally be obeyed in such matters. EXPOSITION OF THE FAITH.[2]

IT IS GOOD FOR US TO PRAY FOR OUR RULERS. HEINRICH BULLINGER: Let subjects pray for their princes and magistrates, that the Lord may give them wisdom, knowledge, fortitude, temperance, justice, upright severity, clemency, and all other

---

[1]Downame, ed., *Annotations*, s.v.*
[2]LCC 24:268; citing Jer 29:7.

requisite virtues, and that he will vouchsafe to lead them in his ways, and to preserve them from all evil, that we may live under them in this world in peace and honesty. Paul requires this at the hands of subjects, in 1 Timothy 2 and in Jeremiah 29. . . . The minds of many are very slow and careless, and that is the cause many times why they feel the things that they would rather not, and rightly bear the burdens that they need not, with grief enough. For if they would but do their duty willingly, in praying for their magistrate earnestly, their case undoubtedly would be far better than it is. DECADES.[3]

PRAYER FOR THE SOVEREIGN AND COUNCIL. BOOK OF COMMON PRAYER (1552): Almighty and ever-living God, which by thy holy apostle hast taught us to make prayers and supplications, and to give thanks for all people: we humbly beseech you most mercifully to accept our alms, and to receive these our prayers that we offer to your divine majesty. . . . We beseech you also to save and defend all Christian kings, princes, and governors, and specially your servant, Edward our king, that under him we may be godly and quietly governed: and grant to his whole council, and to all put in authority under him, that they may truly and indifferently [i.e., impartially] minister justice, to the punishment of wickedness and vice, and to the maintenance of God's true religion and virtue. THE LORD'S SUPPER.[4]

WE MUST PRAY ESPECIALLY FOR MAGISTRATES. MATTHIAS FLACIUS: [Paul] sets forth such an important kind of people for whom prayer ought to be made, namely, magistrates. For at that time there was considerable doubt (so he said) concerning them. Also Satan most vehemently resists the ordinance of God; indeed, he commonly [seeks to] overturn it, and also destroy the Lord and his Christ, and in truth all founded by him so that the conversion and government of those from God may be accomplished. Observe, however, the distinction of persons, the ordinance of God, and their sins. Prayer must be made for those who govern and rule by God's ordinance, that God may preserve them. Prayer must be made for people, if they are good, that God may save them; if they are bad, that God may convert them. Prayer must be made against their wicked endeavors, or sins, particularly against the first table [of the law], that God may especially impede them. Furthermore, the first reason for this rule is summarized here as the final cause: Prayer should therefore be made especially for the government of the magistrate, who, by the administration of God, may govern more correctly according to their function; for the direction and fortune of their endeavor and duty so that there will be peace and tranquility for us, and that we may seek to live in his administration tranquilly, piously, and honestly. For when our magistrate cannot repel the enemy powerfully by his force, we will have war at home in which every kind of evil, and sin will rage, all of which must be impeded rightly by force. GLOSS ON 1 TIMOTHY.[5]

2:4 God Desires All to Be Saved

GOD'S WILL OF COMMAND. MARTIN LUTHER: Prayer for all people is acceptable, because he desires all people to be saved. Paul is not speaking about God's incomprehensible will—a topic forever secret, as here regarding the will of his command. There is a will that is hidden and reserved for himself. This he points out to us in word and deed. His other will he reveals with many signs. Therefore we take this passage to refer to the will of his command or work, not to his hidden will. LECTURES ON 1 TIMOTHY.[6]

GOD'S ANTECEDENT AND CONSEQUENT WILL. FRANÇOIS CARRIÈRE: "God wants all people to be saved and to attain the knowledge of truth." Why therefore are not all people saved? For who can resist his will? I answer that the will of God ought

---

[3] Bullinger, *Decades*, 219-20*.
[4] Ketley, ed., *Two Liturgies*, 270-71*.

[5] Flacius, *Glossa Compendaria*, 1046.
[6] LW 28:262 (WA 26:36).

to be understood differently in different contexts. For he who defines sin as a word, deed, or desire against the law of God, this person must grant that if some sin occurs, it happens contrary to God's will. For they would not be sins unless they were contrary to the will of God. Therefore, many things constantly happen contrary to God's will, and God is incited by these to exercise vengeance against such actors. Thus I say in keeping with John of Damascus,† that there is in God a twofold will of good pleasure. One is an antecedent will that of course precedes all foresight of human beings' good or evil works, and which only has its origin from God and from God's goodwill toward humankind. The other will is consequent, and when the good or evil deeds of human beings have been foreseen, it desires completely and efficaciously either to save or condemn that man in keeping with the antecedent will. The antecedent will is weighty and efficacious (because it provides everyone with the means for obtaining salvation as much as lies with it). It desires all people to be saved. Therefore in verse 5 Paul adds, "There is one mediator between God and men, the man Jesus Christ who gave himself as a redemption for all." But by the consequent will, based on a final foreseen lack of repentance or death of the person in sin, he wills to condemn a particular person and ones like him, just as also he wills to save efficaciously those whom he sees are penitent at death. The first will is not absolute, for in that case every last person would be saved. But it is hypothetical, if the very people in question also desire to be saved and show forth what is required of them, namely, keeping the commandments. This is what Chrysostom, Ambrose, Augustine, and the ecumenical councils held. COMMENTARY ON THE WHOLE OF SCRIPTURE.[7]

GOD'S DESIRE AND PREDESTINATION. MARTIN LUTHER: There are many arguments against predestination, but they proceed from the "prudence of the flesh." Therefore those who have not denied themselves and learned to subject their questions to the will of God and hold them down will always keep asking why God wills this and does that, and they will never find the reason. And very properly. Because this foolish wisdom places itself above God and judges his will as something inferior, when actually it should be judged by him. . . . The second argument is that "God desires all men to be saved," and he gave his Son for us human beings and created humankind for eternal life. . . . For these verses must always be understood as pertaining to the elect only, as the apostle says in 2 Timothy 2:10, "everything for the sake of the elect." For in an absolute sense Christ did not die for all, because he says, "This is My blood which is poured out for you" and "for many"—he does not say: for all—"for the forgiveness of sins." LECTURES ON ROMANS.[8]

PREDESTINATION UNDERMINES THIS COMMAND TO PRAY. JACOBUS ARMINIUS: This predestination† is in open hostility to the ministry of the gospel . . . because it hinders public prayers from being offered to God in a becoming and suitable manner, that is, with faith, and in confidence that they will be profitable to all the hearers of the word; when there are many among them, whom God is not only unwilling to save, but whom by his absolute, eternal, and immutable will (which is antecedent to all things and causes whatever) it is his will and pleasure to damn. In the meantime, when the apostle commands prayers and supplications to be made for all people, he adds this reason, "for this is good and acceptable in the sight of God our savior; who will have all people to be saved, and to come unto the knowledge of the truth." DECLARATION OF SENTIMENTS.[9]

---

[7]Carrière, *Commentarius in Universam Scripturam*, 777; citing Rom 9:14. †The point about the antecedent will of God, rather than the consequent will, is mentioned in this context as early as John of Damascus in the eighth century (see *De fide orthodoxa* 2.29, in NPNF² 9:42). See Richard A. Muller, *Dictionary of Latin and Greek Theological Terms Drawn Principally from Protestant Scholastic Theology*, 2nd ed. (Carlisle, UK: Paternoster, 2000), 331-33, on *voluntas Dei*.

[8]LW 25:375-76* (WA 56:385); citing Mk 14:24; Mt 26:28.
[9]Arminius, *Writings*, 1:232-33. †I.e., the doctrine of predestination, which Arminius opposed.

Christ Offers Salvation to All. Conradus Vorstius: "For all." Here the native or proper sense of the universal particle should be kept, since it is most true that God for his part offers eternal salvation in Christ for all people and, moreover, sufficient provision for salvation is set out for all in his word. "God desires"—Of course his desire is antecedent and conditional, but not consequent and absolute. . . . And it is in this way that all passages of the same kind, where it talks about the universal kindness of God, whether in the love and saving grace set forth in Christ, are to be understood. Commentary on the Epistles.[10]

How Can We Understand "All"? Peter Martyr Vermigli: First we take this to be spoken of all estates and kinds of people, namely, that God will have some of all kinds of people to be saved: which interpretation agrees excellently well with the purpose of the apostle. He had commanded that prayers and supplications should be made for all people, and especially for kings, and those who have public authority, that under them we may live a quiet life, in all godliness and chastity. And therefore to declare that no estate or kind of people is excluded, he added, "God desires all people to be saved." It is as if he should have said, "No one is hindered by the vocation and class that they are placed in—as long as it is not repugnant to the word of God—but they may come to salvation"; and therefore we ought to pray for all kinds of people. But we cannot infer from this that God endues every person particularly with grace, or predestines everyone to salvation. Similarly, as in the time of the flood, all living creatures are said to have been saved in the ark with Noah, even though there were in fact only some of every kind gathered together in it.

Or we may understand it thus: that God will have all people to be saved; for as many as are saved, are saved by his will.† As if we should say of one that teaches rhetoric in a city that they teach all people: by which kind of speech is not signified that all the citizens are hearers of rhetoric, but that as many as learn are taught by him. In the same way, if someone pointing to the gate of a house should say that "all enter in this way," we must not thereby understand that all people enter into that house, but that as many as do enter, enter in by that gate only.

Further, there are some who interpret these words of the apostle as referring to the signified will or the antecedent will—that all are invited, for preaching is set forth to all impartially. Neither is there anyone who does not in some way feel an inward spur, by which they are often stirred up to live well. So that if we respect this will of God, we easily grant that he will have all to be saved. But they will not have it to be understood of the hidden and effectual will, which they call consequent. . . .‡

All these interpretations are doubtless very likely, and also appropriate; yet there is another besides these, plain and ready to hand. The holy Scriptures set forth two societies of people: the one of the godly, and the other of the ungodly; and both of these have universal propositions ascribed to them, which the careful reader needs to rightly allocate to their kind.†† . . . But these universal sayings ought not to be extended beyond their own society. This is the distinction which Augustine referred to in his book the *City of God*, where he declares and proves that there have always been two cities, namely, the city of God and the city of the devil. So in these general propositions we must always consider to which order or fellowship of people they refer. If we do that here in 1 Timothy 2:4 then we must apply it to the saints and the elect, and by that means all manner of doubt is taken away. Commonplaces.[11]

---

[10]Vorstius, *Commentarius*, 462; citing Jn 3:16; Mk 16:15; Titus 2:11.

[11]Vermigli, *Commonplaces*, 3:31-32*; citing Gen 8–9. †This point is made by Augustine in *Enchiridion* 103 (27); see NPNF 3:270-71. ‡Vermigli's three points so far are also suggested as possible ways of understanding this verse theologically by Thomas Aquinas in *Summa theologiae* I, q. 19, a. 6, and his *Commentary* (trans. Larcher), 264-65 (using a similar illustration of the teacher). ††The examples he gives here are Jn 6:45; Jer 31:34; Jn 12:32; Joel 2:28; Is 66:23; Lk 3:6; and Ps 145:14 (of the godly); and Jn 3:32; Mt 10:22; Phil 2:21; and Ps 14:3 (of the ungodly).

ALL KINDS OF PEOPLE ARE SAVED. JOHANNES PISCATOR: Here we must reconcile an apparent contradiction about salvation. Since Paul says in this place that God wants all people to be saved, how can it be that not all are saved, since God is all powerful and thus he could easily bring to pass whatever he wants? For surely this saying of Paul's does not at all fit with those places in Scripture which attest that God wishes only the elect (that is, those whom he himself has chosen for eternal life) to be saved? As for example Romans 8:30, "Those whom he predestined, he also called, and those whom he called, he also justified; but those whom he justified, he also glorified." As if to say, "He saves only these, but not those whom he did not predestine to eternal life." John 10:26, "You do not believe, for you are not of my sheep"—that is, of the elect. And a little later in verse 28, "I give eternal life to them"—no doubt meaning "to my sheep"— as if to say, "but not to those unbelieving people, who are not of my sheep." I reply: Paul at this point does not understand by *pantas* (that is, "all"), "single individuals," as is clear from the comparison of preceding verses. But instead he understands *pantodapous*, that is, that people of every kind are chosen. COMMENTARY ON 1 TIMOTHY.[12]

UNIVERSAL GRACE IS CONDITIONAL. MOÏSE AMYRAUT: In not receiving Christ as Savior, one rejects the unique means of obtaining salvation. And besides the sin of despising so great a grace as God has presented there is, furthermore, also this crime of accusing God of lying, in not believing the testimony that he has given concerning his Son. So, if you consider the care that God has taken to procure the salvation of the human race by sending his Son into the world, and the things that he has done and suffered to this end, the grace is universal and presented to all people. But if you consider the condition that he has necessarily applied—to believe in his Son—you will again find that while this compassion of giving people a Redeemer proceeds from a marvelous love toward the human race, yet

this love does not exceed this measure—to give salvation to people, provided that they do not refuse it. If they refuse it, he deprives them of hope and they, by their unbelief, aggravate their condemnation. Consequently these words, "God desires the salvation of all people," necessarily receive this limitation—"providing that they believe." If they do not believe, he does not desire it. This will to make the grace of salvation universal and common to all people is thus conditional, that without the accomplishing of the condition, it is entirely ineffectual. BRIEF TREATISE ON PREDESTINATION.[13]

LUTHERANS AND CALVINISTS DISAGREE ON THE FOUNDATIONS OF SALVATION. CHRISTIAN CHEMNITZ: We should be on our guard against the most unwholesome particularity of the Calvinists, as if it were the abyss of despair. The statements, "God wants all men to be saved" and "God does not want all men to be saved" are contradictory. Since therefore the Lutherans embrace the former, while the Calvinists the latter, they are at variance on the foundation of salvation and faith.

You will be directed: "Lutherans believe that they are saved through Christ. Calvinists also believe they are saved through Christ. Therefore they agree on the foundation, in that they have the same causes of salvation." We reply: (1) Lutherans consider Christ the universal Redeemer, while Calvinists hold him to be the particular redeemer. Wherefore, they have the same material object, but not the same formal object. However, as the formal object, so should the material object be the universal object of faith. However, faith cannot be derived from the particular, because either the particular is greater, or the lesser seeks that which is in principle. (2) Christ is not a particular foundation, but only a universal one. Wherefore it is false to say that they have the same foundation as well as the same causes of faith and salvation. To which pertains their response, who distinguish between the object itself, and the teaching about

---

[12]Piscator, *Commentarii*, 1234; citing Jn 10:28.

[13]Amyraut, *Brief Traitté de la Prédestination*, 88-89.

the object, that is, between the real foundation, and the doctrinal. A Little Commentary on All Paul's Epistles.[14]

Christ Given for All, Not Just Jews.
Moïse Amyraut: There is only one God of all the people of the world, who, despite their revolt, always wanted to maintain this relationship with them. And there is only one Mediator between God and people—our Lord Jesus Christ—who willed to become man to demonstrate that he does not wish to exclude from his grace any of those with whom he shares that fellowship of humanity. Therefore, in the same way, he gave himself to serve as a ransom for the redemption of all of them. This was hidden and unknown in times past, which is why the Jews felt that the Redeemer would come only for their nation. And if we were to believe them, we would only offer the grace of God to those who are Jews by birth, or at least by profession. But he has given us the revelation and the testimony at the proper time, that he had determined for this effect. And it is for this reason (says Paul) that I have been appointed, to herald and preach this doctrine as an apostle of Jesus Christ. Paraphrases.[15]

Scholastic Distinctions May Help. John Davenant: If God desires to save all those to whom he sends the saving gospel, why are they not all saved, since the will of God cannot be hindered in producing its intended effect, either in itself or in the means by which it acts? The usual response is from Augustine. . . . God wills that some should be saved from every kind. But the well-received scholastic distinction between the will of God's good pleasure and his revealed will seems to me to be better suited to this passage.[†] We respond, therefore, that the will of his good pleasure is always effectually implemented, because it is formally in God, and is his absolute and practical will concerning a future good. But the revealed will

is not always implemented, because it is not formally in God, neither is it his absolute and practical will; rather, it is his declared will or will of approval (if I may be permitted to put it that way). God, therefore, is said to will with his revealed will the salvation of all to whom he proposes and offers the gospel, which is the ordinary means of effecting salvation. On the other hand, we are not to inquire into the hidden will of God; but all of our actions must be directed according to his revealed will.[†] We ought, therefore, to desire and aim at the salvation of all those to whom God is pleased to grant the saving gospel. Commentary on Colossians.[16]

This Is Not About Predestination but Preaching. John Calvin: Hence we see the childish folly of those who represent this passage to be opposed to predestination. "If God," they say, "wishes all people indiscriminately to be saved, it is false that some are predestined by his eternal purpose to salvation, and others to perdition." They might have had some ground for saying this, if Paul were speaking here about individual people; although even then we should not have wanted the means of replying to their argument; for although the will of God ought not to be judged from his secret decrees, when he reveals them to us by outward signs, yet it does not therefore follow that he has not determined with himself what he intends to do as to every individual person.

But I say nothing on that subject, because it has nothing to do with this passage; for the apostle simply means that there is no people and no rank in the world that is excluded from salvation; because God wishes that the gospel should be

---

[14]Chemnitz, *Commentariolus*, 12.
[15]Amyraut, *Paraphrase*, 14-15.

[16]Davenant, *Expositio*, 182. [†]Davenant's distinction is between *voluntas beneplaciti* (God's ultimate, effective, and hidden will) and *voluntas signi* (his will as indicated in revealed commands or precepts). See Muller, *Dictionary of Latin and Greek Theological Terms*, 331-33, on *voluntas Dei*. See also Peter Lombard, *Sentences*, 1.46.1-2 (197-98), in *The Sentences*, vol. 1, *The Mystery of the Trinity*, trans. Giulio Silano (Toronto: Pontifical Institute of Mediaeval Studies, 2007), 246-48, for its medieval scholastic use in discussing this verse. [†] Davenant is alluding here to the end of article 17 of the Thirty-Nine Articles.

proclaimed to all without exception. Now the preaching of the gospel gives life; and hence he justly concludes that God invites all equally to partake salvation. But the present discourse relates to classes of people, and not to individual persons; for his sole object is to include in this number princes and foreign nations.... The universal term "all" must always be referred to classes of people, and not to persons,[†] as if he had said that not only Jews, but Gentiles also, not only persons of humble rank, but princes also, were redeemed by the death of Christ. COMMENTARY ON 1 TIMOTHY.[17]

DISTINCTIONS WITHIN THE WILL OF GOD.
BALTHASAR HUBMAIER:
"God wants all people to be saved." "Who will now resist his will?"

There once again my friends Eliphaz, Bildad, and Zophar say, "Do you hear that God wants all people to be saved. Therefore neither to will nor not to will lies in us." Answer: Here, however, an equating and mixing of the wills is going on. For the first Scripture refers to the revealed will of God, the second to his hidden will. Therefore, since these are half-truths, one must divide the judgment and thus not swallow them undivided or unchewed, or one will eat death therein, as is said above.

Now we will let the secret will of God, which is unnecessary for us to explore, remain in its dignity. We want to take the revealed in hand and divide the same according to the order of the Scriptures into a facing and withdrawing will. The facing will of God is that God wants all people to be saved. Therefore he turns himself to all people with the offer of his grace and mercy, not saving even his only begotten Son, but giving him for us all into death so that we are not lost but receive eternal life.

God bears this salvation toward us and offers it to us joyfully.... As soon as now God turns to us, calls, and admonishes us to follow after him, and we leave wife and child, ship and tools, also everything that hinders us on the way to him, we

are already helped. That is called his facing and drawing will with which he wants and draws all people so that they be saved. Nevertheless, the choice lies with them for God wants them, unpressed, unforced, and without coercion.

Whichever people do not accept, hear, or follow after him, the same he turns himself away from and withdraws from and lets them remain as they themselves want to be. That is now called the withdrawing will of God, concerning which David gives information when he says, "O God, do not turn your face from me." So just in this way is God holy with the holy and withdrawing with the withdrawn.... The Scripture that says, "God wants all people to be saved," refers to the first revealed will of God. The second part of the Scriptures, "that God wants to harden the godless and damn them," refers to the second. The hidden will of God still remains upright and omnipotent, according to which he can do what he wants and no one need question, "Why did you do that?" His facing will is a will of mercy. His withdrawing will is a will of his justice and punishments, of which we are guilty with our vices, not God. FREEDOM OF THE WILL.[18]

2:5 Christ Jesus the Mediator

THE SAVIOR OF ALL MEDIATES FOR ALL.
CONRADUS VORSTIUS: This sentence is concise and almost elliptical, in that it requires one to understand from the preceding context that all can be saved by the grace of the one God.... As if to say: The creator of all things is one, who is at the same time the Savior of all. Compare Romans 3:30, Galatians 3:20. He is called the mediator *of God* because God avails of himself as a go-between and surety among people: but he is also *of people*, because he intercedes for people in the presence of God, and reconciles them to God by his death. He is called "the man," not because he is naked or uncovered, nor because he is a mediator only according to the human nature, but because the

[17]CTS 43:54-55, 57* (CO 52:269-270). [†]I.e., *ad hominum genera* rather than *ad personas*.

[18]CRR 5:474-76*; citing Rom 9:19; Lev 11:1-47; Rom 11:4; 8:32; Jn 3:16; Is 55:1; 1 Cor 6:20; Mt 11:28; Jn 1:35; Ps 51:11; Ex 4:21; Rom 9:20.

label "man" is particularly appropriate for this context, where it concerns encouraging us to a good hope. COMMENTARY ON THE EPISTLES.[19]

CHRIST IS MEDIATOR IN BOTH HIS NATURES.
PETER MARTYR VERMIGLI: Those who want Christ to be mediator only as regards his human nature are accustomed to put forward what is said to Timothy, "There is one mediator between God and humankind, the man Christ Jesus."[†] But it is easy to accept and interpret this passage the right way. When Paul called Christ a man, he did not at the same time deny that he is God. Neither did he insert *only*, an exclusive adverb. But there were two reasons why he mentioned the human nature: first, lest that mediator be thought to stand far off from us. He says, "He is so close that he also wanted to be a man." Ambrose testifies very clearly about this passage that Christ is mediator both as regards his divinity and as regards his human nature.[‡] The second reason is that the apostle had in view the things he wanted to weave in, namely, that this mediator gave himself up for all people. Therefore he mentioned only man, because he encountered death for our salvation according to his human nature. LETTER TO POLAND.[20]

IT IS FOOLISH TO SEEK ANOTHER INTERCESSOR. JOHN WYCLIFFE: It is a certitude of the faith that Christ Jesus is suited to be mediator between God and humankind, should something be granted from the Trinity through the prayers of any other saint. So it seems to many that whenever a particular prayer is offered to this mediating person for spiritual aid, it adds more to the church than does seeking aid from many intercessors. . . . Many think it would be helpful if Christ alone among men was worshiped, because he is the greatest mediator and intercessor, most able in any circumstance, best because of love and infinite mercy. So he would be a fool who sought some other intercessor. . . . So it is not fitting for him to mediate in company with other saints, since he is kinder, and more likely to help than any other. And praying to a multitude of the blessed is disturbing to the viator's mind because its affection for Christ is scattered and lost; being finite, its attention would be lost within the cloud of such a multitude. Afterward, cupidity and a personal feeling about the church arise that can lead to a twisted devotion in which one stupidly worships canonized demons, esteeming them as blessed. The other blessed souls provide spiritual assistance through their own worship of Christ and their service to his rule, and in whatever way they serve him, they do not give assistance to another save insofar as it is permitted by this Lord. It is madness, then, to leave this font of all ability behind in favor of a sluggish and remote rivulet, especially when the faith does not teach that such a stream has its source in this font of life. . . . The person faithful in the Lord's actions should consider why private sects beg the Roman curia with such industry and elaborate show to canonize their brothers. TRIALOGUS.[21]

ONLY ONE MEDIATOR. EDWARD LEIGH: In the Greek it is "one mediator of God and humankind," which may refer either to the two parties between whom he stands—pleading for God to human beings, and for human beings to God—or to the two natures—mediator of God, having the divine nature, and of humankind, having the human nature on him. The papists say Christ is our only mediator of redemption, but the saints are mediators of intercession. But the apostle speaks so plainly of prayer and intercession, that this

---

[19]Vorstius, *Commentarius*, 462.
[20]Donnelly, James, and McLelland, eds., *Peter Martyr Reader*, 130. [†]Some medieval and Roman Catholic authorities sought to do this. See Lombard, *Sentences* 3.19.6-7, and Aquinas, *Summa theologiae* III, q. 26, a. 2, who both rest on Augustine (e.g., *City of God* 9:15, "He is mediator as he is man"). By contrast, see Westminster Confession 8:7, "Christ, in the work of mediation, acts according to both natures, by each nature doing that which is proper to itself; yet, by reason of the unity of the person, that which is proper to one nature is sometimes in Scripture attributed to the person denominated by the other nature." [‡]He refers not to Ambrose but to Ambrosiaster, *Commentaria in Epistolas B. Pauli* (PL 17:493).

[21]Wycliffe, *Trialogus*, 188-89 (3.30).

distinction will not serve. The office of intercession pertains to Christ as part of his mediation. Annotations.[22]

The Prayers of the Departed. John Mayer: In that he calls Christ the one mediator between God and humankind, he plainly excludes all other mediators, not only of redemption but also of intercession, as is elsewhere further explained. So we may not seek the help of any other than God in our prayers, but always come in his name and by him make all our petitions, as the Lord himself expressly teaches. We may indeed and ought to pray for one another, while we live together in this world, and it is held that the saints departed out of this life do pray still for the church militant here on earth. But this is no ground to make them together with Christ our mediators, by praying to them, that by their help we may be the more accepted before God in our prayers. We do rightly indeed desire others (who live here together with us) to pray for us; but to pray to any departed to pray for us, is to ascribe omniscience to them, as to Christ. And by their mediation in heaven to seek the favor of God, as by the mediation of Christ, and to make more mediators contrary to this "There is one mediator" and to that of saint John "We have *an advocate* in heaven, Jesus Christ the righteous," not *advocates*, which would be to deprive ourselves of all benefit

of Christ's mediating and interceding for us. Commentary on Paul's Epistles.[23]

We Should Emulate the Saints, but They Are Not Intercessors. Martha Elisabeth Zitter: The other motive that moved me to leave the Roman church is that along with the trust in their own works, they place hope and confidence in the merits, help, and supplications of the saints of their church, make vows, and give similar honors to those who belong only to God, and at the same time completely presumptuously set aside the true worship service. Out of a hundred churches in Catholicism one will scarcely be found that is dedicated to the Holy Trinity or one of the persons of the Godhead. Out of a thousand people there is often not one who takes their refuge—whatever their needs or desires are—in Christ, who is the only aid and intercessor between God and humans. They all turn from him to certain saints, hoping and waiting for help. They also write that they have received help from the saints they have called on, or through their intercession. How does this fit in Scripture, where God commands in Psalm 50:15, "Call on me in your need, I will deliver you, and you shall glorify me." And in 1 Timothy 2:5, "Just as there is only one God, there is only one intercessor between God and humans, that is, the man Jesus Christ, who gave himself for us." It also then similarly pleases me that it is taught in the evangelical religion that one should that one should regard the saints as honorable and imitate their faith and blessed lives. This religion, which alone makes one sanctified, is falsely accused of teaching that one should dishonor and defame the mother of God and the saints. Reasons for Conversion to the Evangelical Religion.[24]

2:6-7 Christ Gave Himself as a Ransom for All

His Blood Was the Price of Redemption. Conradus Vorstius: From this, other very

---

[22]Leigh, *Annotations*, 321-22*. See Calvin, *Institutes* 3.20.20, against Johannes Eck, *Enchiridion of Commonplaces Against Luther and Other Enemies of the Church*, trans. Ford Lewis Battles (Grand Rapids: Baker, 1979), 14-15, and Aquinas, *Summa theologiae* II-II, q. 83, a. 11, as well as Cartwright, *Confutation*, 543-45 and Fulke, *Text of the New Testament*, 367-68, against the Rhemists on this verse. The Council of Trent, Session 25 (1563) exhorted all ministers to instruct the faithful diligently regarding the intercession of the saints, "teaching them that the saints who reign together with Christ offer up their prayers to God for men, that it is good and beneficial suppliantly to invoke them and to have recourse to their prayers, assistance, and support . . . and that they think impiously who deny that the saints who enjoy eternal happiness in heaven are to be invoked, or who assert that they do not pray for men, or that our invocation of them to pray for each of us individually is idolatry, or that it is opposed to the word of God and inconsistent with the honor of the *one mediator of God and men, Jesus Christ* (1 Timothy 2:5)." H. J. Schroeder, ed., *The Canons and Decrees of the Council of Trent* (Rockford, IL: Tan, 1978), 215.

[23]Mayer, *Commentary*, 497-98*; citing Rom 8:33; 1 Jn 2:2; Jn 14:1-31. [24]Wiesner-Hanks, ed., *Convents Confront the Reformation*, 99*.

similar passages are to be explained, where Christ is declared to have given his own life, or his own blood, or something similar, for us as the price of redemption. "For all." Here too the proper significance of the universal sign is to be kept: but this distinction should be added, one once accepted by almost everyone, that of course Christ died a sufficient death for all universally, but with effect only for the elect and the believers. COMMENTARY ON THE EPISTLES.[25]

SUFFICIENT FOR ALL, BUT NOT EFFECTUALLY. PETER MARTYR VERMIGLI: They grant also that Christ died for us all; and from this they infer that his benefit is common to all. Which we also will easily grant, if only the worthiness of the death of Christ is considered: for as touching that, it might be sufficient for all the sinners of the world. But although in itself it is sufficient, yet it neither had, nor has, nor shall have effect in all people. The schoolmen also confess this when they affirm that Christ has redeemed all people sufficiently, but not effectually.[†] For it is necessary that the death of Christ be useful to us, and that we take hold of it, which cannot be done except by faith—which faith we have before abundantly declared to be the gift of God, and not to be given to all. COMMONPLACES.[26]

THE SUFFICIENT-EFFICIENT DISTINCTION MAKES NO SENSE. JOHANNES PISCATOR: When Paul says that Christ gave himself as the price of redemption for *all*: one asks whether therefore all people *individually* are redeemed through Christ? I reply: not people individually, but only those chosen by Christ are redeemed. For Christ, as he

was about to perform the work of redemption, that is, offering himself to his Father on the cross, only prayed for those who were given to him by the Father (these are the elect), while excluding the world (that is, the reprobate). Hence also what Christ himself said, that he had come in order to give his life as the price of redemption "for many." He did not say, "for all," that is, for all people individually: but, "for many," that is, for the whole multitude of the elect. In the same way, in the institution of the Last Supper he said that his blood would be poured out for many. But when Paul says here, "for all," he does not understand it to mean for all individually, but for people of every kind and every station, as is clear from a comparison of what has gone before.

Similar are all those sayings of Scripture where redemption is ascribed to the whole world. . . . The crowd of scholastics make use of this and say that Christ is the propitiation for the sins of the whole world (that is, of all people individually), sufficiently, but not efficiently. This distinction has the appearance of learning. But in reality it is without sense, because it implies a contradiction. For the preposition *pro* (for) certainly denotes the end or the goal of Christ's offering of himself, and consequently also the accomplishment of it. For whatever Christ has ever proposed for himself to accomplish, he also in matter of fact accomplished. It follows that if he intended for himself to offer an expiatory sacrifice to his Father for the sins of people individually, certainly in matter of fact he accomplished it. And therefore it must be said that he is the propitiation for the sins of people as individuals, not only sufficiently but also efficiently. But, I say, Christ intended to offer himself for the elect only, as previously was shown from John 17, and not for the reprobate, and so not for people individually. Wherefore it should not be said that Christ died for people individually, and not efficiently. For this then is like saying, "He died for individuals, but he did not die for individuals." Which is a manifest contradiction. COMMENTARY ON 1 TIMOTHY.[27]

---

[25]Vorstius, *Commentarius*, 462. Vorstius's predecessor at Leiden, Jacobus Arminius, also accepted the sufficient-efficient distinction, though not in the way his Calvinist interlocutors did; see Arminius, *Works*, 3:345-46.

[26]Vermigli, *Commonplaces*, 3:31*. [†]See, e.g., Peter Lombard, *Sentences* 3.20.5, in *The Sentences*, vol. 3, *On the Incarnation of the Word*, trans. Giulio Silano (Toronto: Pontifical Institute of Mediaeval Studies, 2008), 86, and Thomas Aquinas's comments on 1 Tim 2:5 in his *Commentary* (Larcher trans.), 265. Cf. Lee Gatiss, "Grace Tasted Death for All: Thomas Aquinas on Hebrews 2:9," *Tyndale Bulletin* 63, no. 2 (2012): 228-31.

[27]Piscator, *Commentarii*, 1235; citing Jn 17:9, 20; 1 Jn 2:2.

2:8-15 WOMEN AND MEN IN THE CHURCH

⁸I desire then that in every place the men should pray, lifting holy hands without anger or quarreling; ⁹likewise also that women should adorn themselves in respectable apparel, with modesty and self-control, not with braided hair and gold or pearls or costly attire, ¹⁰but with what is proper for women who profess godliness—with good works. ¹¹Let a woman learn *quietly with all submissiveness. ¹²I do not permit a woman to teach or to exercise authority over a man; rather, she is to remain quiet. ¹³For Adam was formed first, then Eve; ¹⁴and Adam was not deceived, but the woman was deceived and became a transgressor. ¹⁵Yet she will be saved through childbearing—if they continue in faith and love and holiness, with self-control.*

OVERVIEW: This passage receives substantial attention from these early modern commentators. Since Paul is giving directions for the conduct of men and women in public worship, the authors vividly describe the attitudes toward God and other Christians that should accompany prayer. Moreover, they emphasize prayer as a priestly activity performed by all Christians within the context of public worship, which points to some measure of the doctrine of the "priesthood of all believers." However, the section that receives particularly extensive and sustained treatment is Paul's instructions concerning the role of women. Many of these authors argue that women should be barred from the preaching office in the church and subordinate to their husbands at home, principally on the basis of the notion that in the fall, Eve allowed herself to be deceived by Satan.

However, these same commentators endeavor to reconcile this position with sundry instances in Scripture in which women, such as Deborah and Huldah, functioned as prophets as well as examples of Paul's women coworkers, like Priscilla, who engaged in teaching. Some of these authors explore the implications of these accounts for the possession and exercise of political authority by women, especially in the case of Queen Elizabeth I. Moreover, these writers explain extensively the differences between "preaching" and "prophesying" so as to reconcile Paul's instructions in this passage with his acknowledgment of women prophesying

in 1 Corinthians 14. Of particular interest is the manner in which women interpreters interact with this passage. While acknowledging their societal status, which proscribed them from exercising the public pastoral office, as Marie Dentière explains, these women utilized their position to exhort by way of written discourse.

2:8 *Lifting Holy Hands*

PRAY IN EVERY PLACE. PETER MARTYR VERMIGLI: "In every place." Now then, having Christ with us, we may pray everywhere; especially since by our communion with him we are the temples of God.... Wherever we are, therefore, given that we are not divided from Christ, we may very well pray with this full trust, in which we doubt not but that we are the temple of God. We do not say these things as though we condemn the having of a certain place, where godly congregations may publicly be had. For this is necessary, seeing as there are so many of us who serve Christ and have need of a physical place if we are to meet together at any time. But we must understand that such places are not so fixed that they may not be changed, as it shall be convenient for the church; neither yet are they so prescribed and limited for prayer that it should be counted wicked to pray out of them. Doubtless we do greatly honor and esteem the godly meetings at places appointed and agreed on, since we understand that Christ is especially with us when we are joined together. But to the place where the ark of the covenant was, there is no need for us to come: for the old ceremonies are taken away by the benefit of Christ, and every place is open to us for prayer. Therefore, in 1 Timothy 2 it is written, "And I desire that in every place the men should lift up holy hands." Indeed, Paul himself was heard in the prison and the thief on the cross: for God holds no place in contempt, but hears believers everywhere. Commonplaces.[1]

Lifting Pure and Holy Hands to God.

Desiderius Erasmus: Paul now returns to his previous subject and says, I would have the men to pray, not only in the congregation, but also wherever occasion requires it. The Jews pray to God in no place but at Jerusalem. The Samaritans pray on mountains and in woods. But to the Christians all places are pure and holy to offer up sacrifices of prayers. They esteem every place to be a holy temple to God, and when they offer, as it were, a sacrifice, they lift up pure hands everywhere to heaven. They have no need to wish for the mercy seat or most holy place in the temple. Wherever they are, God will hear them. They do not need to pass on Jewish sin offerings, either ceremonies or sacrifices. When it comes to Christian sacrifices, every man can be a sacrificer. God does not respect the offering up of beasts or the perfume of sweet smells, for a pure earnest supplication proceeding from a pure heart is a sacrifice most acceptable to God. Let the Jews wash themselves as clean as they can, yet their oblations are unclean. God accepts the hands as clean, even if they are not washed, provided the conscience is quiet and he does no wrong, but wishes well to everyone and is not soiled with spots of filthy lust, greed, or ambition. This is the purity and cleanness that makes a Christian man's sacrifice acceptable in the eyes of God. He is delighted to be offered this kind of sacrifice. Paraphrases.[2]

Praying Without Anger or Quarreling.

John Calvin: It is true that when we pray to God we must not bring with us our grievances and fretting and fuming, as though we wanted to be at odds with him, like those who come to God when they are angry or murmuring with impatience because of the afflictions which he has sent them. For we do God no great honor when we pray to him reproachfully like this. There are many who pretend to pray, but they protest against him, they get angry with him, they fret and fume, because he does not treat them as they would like. So they come to God, but only in defiance. It is like a husband who is annoyed with his wife, "You should do this! You are not doing what you should!" Or as if a wife should ask something of her husband but first reproach him "Oh, you don't care about me!" Thus many do with God, though it would be better if they never prayed to him at all than that they should come with a heart so poisoned against him. Therefore we must pray to God with a peaceable heart....

We shall not have access to pray to God unless we are joined together. For those who separate themselves from their neighbors shut their own mouths, so that they cannot pray to God as our Lord Jesus Christ has prescribed for us. In brief, we must agree and unite together in a bond of peace before we can approach our God to present ourselves to him. Because these discords and disputes that we have spoken of were between the Jews and the Gentiles, St. Paul shows that they cannot call on God, but shall be refused and rejected, until they are reconciled with one another. And this is the reason why he says here that they must pray without anger or quarreling. That is to say, that they must not enter into such contentious brawling with each other....

All these disputes must cease (says St. Paul) and they must make a good reconciliation to show that they all have the Spirit of adoption—that is to say, that the Spirit of God governs them, even that Spirit who brings with him peace and unity. And from this we must gather this general doctrine, that before we can dispose ourselves to pray well, we must have this brotherhood which God commands

---

[1]Vermigli, *Commonplaces*, 3:306*; citing Acts 16:25; Lk 23:42.
[2]Erasmus, *Paraphrases*, 31-32.

us, and this union. For he does not want every one by themselves, but he wants there to be one harmony and one melody in the mouth of all. Although every one of us speak, although we are every one separate in their own place, and pray to God in private, yet must our good accord come to heaven as we say with all affection, and in truth, "Our Father." Sermons on 1 Timothy.[3]

2:9-10 Adorned with Good Works

The Beauty of a Christian Woman. Desiderius Erasmus: Now let the women pray, cultivating their souls not their bodies, nor enticing men's eyes to lust after the nakedness of their flesh. But let them be covered with a garment, and with such a garment as represents modesty, decency, and chastity. God forbid that Christian women should come into the holy congregation in such manner of clothing as the common sort of profane women are accustomed to wear to weddings or to the theater, having spent too much time and effort in front of a mirror first, with hair finely curled or interwoven with gold, or with pearls hanging from their ears or necks, or wearing silks or fine purple. These are designed to show off their beauty to such as gaze on them and to display their wealth to those who are poorer. But rather, let the clothing of Christian women be like their lives, appropriate for women who profess true godliness and the true worship of God—not the display of riches but of good works, which wealth alone is pleasing to God. What appears elegant, splendid, or magnificent to others in his eyes is repulsive. Paraphrases.[4]

Garments and Graces. John Trapp: Men have had their lessons. Now for women, they are taught modesty in their attire (such as may neither argue wantonness nor wastefulness), silence in the church, subjection in the family. [Of costly array] which yet great ones may wear; but they may not buy it with extortion, and line it with pride. Since clothes are the ensigns of our shame, our fineness is our filthiness, and our neatness our nastiness. . . .

[But that which becomes women . . .] Our common conversation should be as becomes the gospel of Christ. And it is a sure sign of a base mind to think that one can make himself great with any thing that is less than himself, or that he can win more credit by his garments than by his graces. The worst apparel, says one, is nature's garment; the best, but folly's garnish. A Commentary.[5]

Renouncing the Vanity and Pomp of the World. David Dickson: [Paul lays down a] precept that women, while they pray together with the assembly, and are present in other sacred performances, in their clothes and other habits, compose themselves to honesty and modesty, which will prove a greater ornament to them than if they should come into public with broidered hair, or gold, or pearls, or costly apparel: in which, if there be superfluity, the adorning is unlawful, and forbidden in this place. He requires further to the adorning of women, both public and private, that they be eminent in good works: the reason whereof is given from their Christian profession, whereby in baptism they promised to renounce the vanity and pomp of the world. An Exposition of All Paul's Epistles.[6]

2:11-12 The Role of Women

We May Not Be Able to Teach, but We Can Write. Marie Dentière: However, my most honored lady, I wanted to write to you not to teach you, but so that you might take pains with the king, your brother, to obviate all these divisions that reign in the places and among the people over whom God commissioned him to rule and govern. And also over your people, whom God gave you to provide for and to keep in order. For what God has given you and revealed to us women, no more than men should we hide it and

[3]CO 53:189-91.
[4]Erasmus, *Paraphrases*, 32-33.
[5]Trapp, *Commentary*, 304*.
[6]Dickson, *Exposition*, 161-62.

bury it in the earth. And even though we are not permitted to preach in public in congregations and churches, we are not forbidden to write and admonish one another in all charity. . . . Not only will certain slanderers and adversaries of truth try to accuse us of excessive audacity and temerity, but so will certain of the faithful, saying that it is too bold for women to write one another about matters of Scripture. We may answer them by saying that all those women who have written and have been named and praised in holy Scripture should not be considered too bold. Several women are named and praised in holy Scripture, as much for their good conduct, actions, demeanor, and example as for their faith and teaching: Sarah and Rebecca, for example, and first among all the others in the Old Testament; the mother of Moses, who, in spite of the king's edict, dared to keep her son from death and saw that he was cared for in Pharaoh's house . . . , and Deborah, who judged the people of Israel in the time of the Judges, is not to be scorned. Must we condemn Ruth, who, even though she was of the female sex, had her story told in the book that bears her name? I do not think so, seeing that she is numbered among the genealogy of Jesus Christ. What wisdom had the queen of Sheba, who is not only named in the Old Testament, but whom Jesus dared to name among the other sages! If we are speaking of the graces that have been given to women, what greater grace has come to a creature on earth than to the Virgin Mary, mother of Jesus, to have carried the son of God? It was no small grace that allowed Elizabeth, mother of John the Baptist, to have born a son miraculously after having been sterile. What woman was a greater preacher than the Samaritan woman, who was not ashamed to preach Jesus and his word, confessing him openly before everyone, as soon as she heard Jesus say that we must adore God in spirit and truth? Who can boast of having the first manifestation of the great mystery of the resurrection of Jesus, if not Mary Magdalene, from whom he had thrown out the seven devils, and the other women, to whom, rather than to men, he had earlier declared himself

through his angel and commended them to tell, preach, and declare it to others?

Even though in all women there has been imperfection, men have not been exempt from it. Why is it necessary to criticize women so much, seeing that no woman ever sold or betrayed Jesus, but a man named Judas? Who are they, I pray you, who have invented and contrived so many ceremonies, heresies, and false doctrines on earth if not men? And the poor women have been seduced by them. Never was a woman found to be a false prophet, but women have been misled by them. While I do not wish to excuse the excessively great malice of some women that goes far beyond measure, neither is there any reason to make a general rule of it, without exception, as some do on a daily basis. . . . Therefore, if God has given grace to some good women, revealing to them by his holy Scriptures something holy and good, should they hesitate to write, speak, and declare it to one another because of the defamers of truth? Ah, it would be too bold to try and stop them, and it would be too foolish for us to hide the talent God has given us, God who will give us the grace to persevere to the end. Amen. EPISTLE TO MARGUE- RITE DE NAVARRE.[7]

COMPELLED TO SPEAK. ARGULA VON GRUM- BACH: I had to listen for ages to your decretal preacher crying out in the Church of Our Lady: *Ketzer/ketzer*, "Heretic, heretic!" Poor Latin, that! I could say as much myself, no doubt; and I have never been to university. But if they are to prove their case they'll have to do better than that. I always meant to write to him, to ask him to show me which heretical articles the loyal worker for the gospel Martin Luther is supposed to have taught.

However I suppressed my inclinations; heavy of heart, I did nothing. Because Paul says in 1 Timothy 2: "The women should keep silence, and should not speak in church." But now that I cannot

---

[7]Dentière, *Epistle to Marguerite de Navarre*, 52-56; citing Gen 11:27–23:20; 24:1–28:22; Ex 2:1-10; Judg 4:1–5:31; Mt 1:1-25; 1 Kings 10:1-29; Mt 12:42; Lk 1:1-80; Jn 4:1-54; Lk 23:1–24:50; Mt 28:1-10; Mk 16:9; Jn 20:1-18.

see any man who is up to it, who is either willing or able to speak, I am constrained by the saying: "Whoever confesses me." And I claim for myself Isaiah 3: "I will send children to be their princes; and women, or those who are womanish, shall rule over them." And Isaiah 29: "Those who err will know knowledge in their spirit, and those who mutter will teach the law." And Ezekiel 20: "I raise up my hand against them to scatter them. They never followed my judgments, they rejected my commandments, and their eyes were on the idols of their fathers. Therefore I gave them command-ments, but no good ones; and judgments by which they could never live." And Psalm 8: "You have ordained praise out of the mouth of children and infants at the breast on account of your enemies." And Luke 10: "Jesus rejoiced in the Spirit, and said 'Father, I give you thanks that you have hidden these things from the wise, and revealed them to the little ones.'" Jeremiah 31: "They will all know God, from the least to the greatest." John 6, and Isaiah 54: "They will all be taught of God." Paul in 1 Corinthians 12: "No one can say 'Jesus' without the spirit of God." Just as the Lord says of the confession of Peter in Matthew 16: "Flesh and blood has not revealed this to you, but my heavenly Father." To the University of Ingolstadt.[8]

WOMEN SHOULD BE SILENT, UNLESS MEN ARE AFRAID. BALTHASAR HUBMAIER: In this gathering women shall be silent and at home they should learn from their husbands, so that every-thing might take place properly and in order. But where men are afraid and have become women, then the women should speak up and become manly, like Deborah, Hulda, Anna the prophetess, the four daughters of the evangelist Philip, and in our times Argula. THESES AGAINST ECK.[9]

WIVES SHOULDN'T TEACH CONTRARY TO THEIR HUSBAND'S AUTHORITY. MARTIN LUTHER: I believe that Paul is still speaking about public matters. I also want it to refer to the public ministry, which occurs in the public assembly of the church. There a woman must be completely quiet, because she should remain a hearer and not become a teacher. She is not to be the spokesman among the people. She should refrain from teaching, from praying in public. She has the command to speak at home. This passage makes a woman subject. It takes from her all public office and authority. On the other side is the passage in Acts about Queen Candace. We read many such examples in sacred literature—that women have been very good at management: Huldah, Deborah, Jael, the wife of the Kenite, who killed Sisera. Why, then, does Paul say here that he deprives them of the administration of the Word as well as of work? You should solve that argument in this way. Here we properly take "woman" to mean wife, as he reveals from his correlative phrase "to have author-ity over man," that is, over her husband. As he calls the husband "man," so he calls the wife "woman." Where men and women have been joined together, there the men, not the women, ought to have authority. An exceptional example is the case where they are without husbands, like Huldah and Deborah, who had no authority over husbands. . . . He forbids teaching contrary to a man or to the authority of a man. Where there is a man, there no woman should teach or have authority. Where there is no man, Paul has allowed that they can do this, because it happens by a man's command. He wants to save the order preserved by the world—that a man be the head of the woman, as 1 Corin-thians 11:3 tells us. Where there are men, she should neither teach nor rule. . . . Paul does not entrust the ministry of the Word to her. He considers this the greatest thing that goes on in the church. You must always understand this with the condition that men are present. Paul says this that there may be peace and harmony in the churches when the Word is taught and people pray. There would be a disturbance if some woman wished to

[8]Grumbach, *A Woman's Voice in the Reformation*, 79-80*; citing Mt 10:32; 1 Tim 2:12; Is 3:4, 12; 29:24; Ezek 20:23-26; Ps 8:2; Lk 10:21; Jer 31:34; Jn 6:45; Is 54:13; 1 Cor 12:3; Mt 16:17.
[9]CRR 5:56*; citing 1 Cor 14:34; Joel 2:1-32; 1 Cor 11:1-34; Judg 4:1–5:31; 2 Chron 34:22; Lk 2:36; Acts 21:9, 18; Deut 1:28. The Argula that Hubmaier refers to is Argula von Grumbach*.

argue against the doctrine that is being taught by a man. The method of 1 Corinthians 14 has now perished. I could wish it were still in effect, but it causes great strife. Where a man teaches, there is a well-rounded argument against a man. If she wishes to be wise, let her argue with her husband at home.[†]

"To have authority." That is, she ought not take over for herself the heritage which belongs to a man so that a man says to her, "My lord." She wants her own wisdom to have priority, that whatever she has said should prevail and whatever the man says should not. We say: Paul is saying with power what is to be said. He is not speaking about real physical domination, but about the authority of the word, that she should be right and have the last word, that in the church her word ought to appear wiser and more learned and thus of greater authority than that of her husband. So also in the home. LECTURES ON 1 TIMOTHY.[10]

PROPHESYING BUT NOT TEACHING. PETER MARTYR VERMIGLI: In the beginning of the primitive church, the daughters of Philip, and other godly women, prophesied. And Paul says that a woman praying or prophesying should cover her head. But here, by the way, arises no small doubt. For if at that time it was lawful for a woman to pray and prophesy openly, why does Paul, writing to the Corinthians and to Timothy, admonish that a woman should not speak in the church? These two sayings, although they may seem somewhat repugnant, yet they may be reconciled in several ways.

Some think that Paul means that a woman prays and prophesies when she is present and hears public prayers and prophesyings in the church, directed by some godly and learned man. Others suppose that two errors crept into the church of

the Corinthians, even as soon as the same church began: the one, that women should prophesy openly; and the other, that they should do it bare-headed. And they think that Paul confuted the first error in 1 Corinthians 11:5, and the other in 1 Corinthians 14:33-35 and 1 Timothy 2:12: and that Paul thus altogether forbids that either of them should be done in the congregation.

Some others understand those words of Paul as touching the ordinary ministry, which by no means must be permitted to a woman: but that by an extraordinary means it is lawful for women sometimes to prophesy, as it was for Mary, Deborah, Huldah, and others, of whom we spoke before. If this happens at any time, they say that Paul warns that a woman should have her head covered. Others think that women are quite forbidden by Paul to prophesy openly, but that it is lawful for them to do it privately, as long as they cover their heads. COMMONPLACES.[11]

THREE REASONS WOMEN MUST NOT TEACH IN CHURCH. EDWARD LEIGH: The apostle here speaks of the order and comeliness of public ecclesiastical assemblies, in which women were not allowed to take upon them any power, or function of teaching, for three reasons here propounded. First, from their condition, which is to be obedient to man; and therefore in man's presence they must not usurp the authority of teachers. Second, their function, which is to serve men; for Adam was created first, and Eve for Adam. Third, from the weakness of their sex, which lies more open to Satan's seduction. ANNOTATIONS.[12]

UNUSUAL PRIVILEGES DO NOT SET REGULAR EXAMPLES. PETER MARTYR VERMIGLI: When God chose Deborah for the ministry of judging, being of the weaker sex, he straightway made her very famous and honorable through the gift of prophesying. By which grace, and perhaps many other miracles more, she was constituted by God

---

[10]LW 28:276–277 (WA 26:46-47); citing Acts 8:27. [†]Luther said elsewhere that "if it happened . . . that no man could be secured for [a teaching] office, then a woman might step up and preach to others as best she could; but in no other instance." *Complete Sermons of Martin Luther,* ed. John Nicholas Lenker (Grand Rapids: Baker, 2000), 3:375.

[11]Vermigli, *Commonplaces,* 1:20*; citing 1 Cor 11:5.
[12]Leigh, *Annotations,* 322*.

and confirmed by miracles as a woman chosen to so great an office. Neither was she the only woman endued with the spirit of prophecy: for in the holy Scripture we read of other women also who were in such a way instructed by the Holy Spirit.... I do not think it ought to be denied that some of those women, endued with the gift of prophecy, did openly teach the people, in declaring of those things to them which had been shown to them by God—seeing that the gifts of God are not therefore given that they should lie hidden, but to the intent that they should further the common edifying of the church.

And yet it does not follow that what God does by some peculiar privilege we should forthwith draw it into an example for us. Because according to the rule of the apostle, we are bound to an ordinary law, whereby both in the first epistle to Timothy and in the first epistle to the Corinthians, he commands that a woman should keep silence in the church. And of the silence commanded, he assigns causes, namely, because they ought to be subject to their husbands, but the office of a teacher declares a certain authority over those who are taught, which must not be attributed to a woman over men. For she was made for man, whom to obey she ought always to have a respect, which thing is also appointed her by the judgment of God, whereby he said to the woman after sin was committed, "Your disposition shall be toward your husband."

Further, the apostle derived a reason from the first fault, wherein he says that Eve was seduced, and not Adam. So if women should ordinarily be admitted to the holy ministry in the church, men might easily suspect that the devil, by his accustomed instrument, would deceive the people. And for that reason they would esteem the ecclesiastical function less, if it should be committed to women. Wherefore by the ordinary right, and by the apostolical rule, it ought to be appointed to men. However, if God sometimes does otherwise, yet he cannot be justly accused, forasmuch as all laws are in his power. If then sometime he send a prophetess, and adorns her with heavenly gifts, the same

woman speaking in the church must undoubtedly be listened to, but yet so as her state be not forgotten. COMMONPLACES.[13]

WOMEN HAVE ALWAYS BEEN DENIED THE TEACHING OFFICE. HUGO GROTIUS: A woman is not permitted to speak in the church, nor should they teach, baptize, dedicate, or arrogate to themselves the lot of any male function, still less the priestly office. ANNOTATIONS.[14]

TO TEACH WOULD GIVE AUTHORITY. DAVID DICKSON: He explains the special precept and according to his authority forbids women to teach in public. The first reason for this prohibition is contained in the latter part of the prohibition, because should a woman teach publicly, the woman would have authority over the man: she would be over, and instruct the man, when she ought with silence to be in subjection to her own husband. EXPOSITION OF ALL PAUL'S EPISTLES.[15]

EVEN A LEARNED AND GODLY WOMAN IS NOT TO TEACH PUBLICLY. JOHN TRAPP: Let a woman learn. Not to teach, to wit, in the public assemblies, be she never so learned or godly.... Nor to usurp authority (*authentein*, to have what she will), as they will easily do if suffered to preach. Preachers are rulers, guides, captains. If the hen be suffered to crow once, and so on. A prudent wife commands her husband by obeying him, as Sarah, Livia. COMMENTARY UPON ALL THE EPISTLES.[16]

WOMEN ARE PROHIBITED FROM SPEAKING PUBLICLY IN THE CHURCH ASSEMBLY. FRANÇOIS CARRIÈRE: "I do not permit a woman to teach." But in Titus 2:3-4 we read, "Old women, teaching well, let them teach the young women

---

[13]Vermigli, *Commonplaces*, 4:7*; citing Judg 4:4; 1 Cor 14:33-35; Gen 3:16.

[14]Grotius, *Annotationes*, 7:226-27.

[15]Dickson, *Exposition*, 162*.

[16]Trapp, *Commentary*, 304-5*; citing Heb 13:7, 17. Trapp refers to Abraham's wife, Sarah (1 Pet 3:6), and the wife of the emperor Augustus, Livia Drusilla (58 BC–AD 29), who was known for her modesty of apparel and her faithfulness as a wife and advisor.

wisdom." I reply that here we are dealing with a prohibition in the church or public assembly, even if a woman has received the gift of prophecy.... Thus in 1 Corinthians 14, "Women must keep silent in church. For they are not permitted to speak, but must be in submission just as the law says." The prohibition against a woman speaking in church results from feminine propriety, modesty, weakness, and talkativeness, according to Chrysostom. Then, it comes from a zeal for reverence and subjection toward her husband, which requires a woman to keep silent in his presence and while he is speaking, especially in the church and in sacred matters. For Priscilla taught the faith of Christ privately at home to the eloquent man Apollos. And in Titus, Paul wants the mistress of the home to teach the female side of the household privately. In 1 Corinthians 7:16 the believing woman is ordered to instruct and convert her unbelieving husband. So St. Cecilia taught her husband Valerian the faith of Christ; St. Natalie taught Adrian; St. Monica, Patrick; St. Martha taught Mary; Theodelinda instructed the Lombard king Agilulf; Clotilde taught Clovis king of the Franks; and Flavia Domatilla instructed Flavius Clemens. For as Chrysostom taught in *Homily* 60 on John, nothing is more powerful for teaching and shaping a man however she wants than a good woman.

Observe that Paul here not only forbids a woman to teach publicly, but he also does not permit her to teach privately—if she wants to do so—as though from an office or with authority. Thus this follows, "nor can she rule over a man but she must be silent." Someone will object, "In Christ there is neither male nor female, therefore it is a matter of indifference that woman is able just like a man to know and teach the Scriptures. For we know that the blessed Catherine of Siena once taught and gave many lectures, to some acclaim, in the public consistory of the pope." I answer that the objection is true as regards the goal, because there is no distinction between a man and a woman when it comes to the ability to strive in Christ for blessedness. At the same time, however, in whatever position and state one is, he must

remain there until that day arrives when they neither will marry nor be given in marriage. In addition, when it comes to the example of the blessed Catherine, this happened with the full approval of the pontiff, or actually at his command, because he recognized that the Spirit of God was in her, and that the fervent pursuit of love had been given to her for the building up of the church in troubling times of schism. COMMENTARY ON THE WHOLE OF SCRIPTURE.[17]

WOMEN SHOULD FOLLOW THEIR HUSBANDS. JUAN LUIS VIVES: This law clearly seems to me to mean that a wife should learn from her husband and in matters of doubt should follow his opinion and believe the same things he does. If the husband should err, he is solely to blame, the wife is innocent, unless his errors are so manifest that they could not be ignored without blame, or are contrary to the teachings of those in whom her husband should have put his faith. Acts of impiety should never be committed, no matter how much her husband orders or demands it of you, if you know them to be such. One person must be acknowledged as superior and dearer than your husband, and that is Christ. ON MARRIED WOMEN.[18]

WOMEN ARE NOT BANNED FROM SPEAKING IN CHURCH. MARGARET FELL: Here the apostle speaks particularly to a woman in relation to her husband, to be in subjection to him, and not to teach, nor usurp authority over him, and therefore he mentions Adam and Eve. But let it be strained to the utmost, as the opposers of women's speaking would have it, that is, that they should not preach nor speak in the church, of which there is nothing here. Yet the apostle is speaking to such as he is teaching to wear their apparel, what to wear, and what not to wear; such as were not come to wear modest apparel, and such as were not come to

---

[17]Carrière, *Commentarius in Universam Scripturam*, 777-78; citing Acts 18:26; 1 Cor 7:20.
[18]Vives, *The Education of a Christian Woman*, 208; citing 1 Cor 14:34-35.

shamefastness and sobriety, but he was exhorting them from broidered hair, gold, and pearls, and costly array; and such are not to usurp authority over the man, but to learn in silence with all subjection, as it becomes women professing godliness with good works.

And what is all this to such as have the power and Spirit of the Lord Jesus poured upon them, and have the message of the Lord Jesus given unto them? Must not they speak the word of the Lord because of these indecent and irreverent women that the Apostle speaks of, and to, in these two scriptures? And how are the men of this generation blinded, that bring these Scriptures, and pervert the Apostle's words, and corrupt his intent in speaking of them, and by these Scriptures, endeavour to stop the message and word of the Lord God in women, by condemning and despising of them? If the Apostle would have had women's speaking stopped, and did not allow of them, why did he entreat his true yokefellow to help those women who laboured with him in the gospel (Philippians 4:3)? And why did the Apostles join together in prayer and supplication with the women, and Mary the Mother of Jesus, and with his brethren (Acts 1:14), if they had not allowed, and had union and fellowship with the Spirit of God, wherever it was, revealed in women as well as others? But all this opposing and gainsaying of women's speaking has risen out of the bottomless pit, and spirit of darkness that has spoken for these many hundred years together in this night of apostasy, since the revelations have ceased and been hid, and so that spirit has limited and bound all up within its bond and compass, and so would suffer none to speak, but such as that spirit of darkness approved of, man or woman. WOMEN'S SPEAKING JUSTIFIED, PROVED AND ALLOWED OF BY THE SCRIPTURES.[19]

GOD CAN SPEAK THROUGH A WOMAN. KATH-ARINA SCHÜTZ ZELL: If someone says, "This is none of your business, it belongs to other folk than you." Answer: A donkey once spoke and saw the angel whom the prophet did not want to see. Is it then a wonder if I speak the truth, since I am indeed a human being? And God says through the prophet Ezekiel in the twenty-second chapter, "You child of man, will you not judge the city for its sins and point out to all its accused works?" That chapter tells very shockingly how the spiritual and the worldly are spilling innocent blood and how the princes do that in their lands; therefore God will send evil on them. And Ezekiel also points out how they despise his law and make no distinction between holy people (saints) and the outlaws; therefore in the previous chapter he calls such a person a wicked, base leader of his people....

If one wishes to say, "What is in the Ezekiel passage is 'you son of man'"—that it is not said to you but to learned men. Paul says that women should keep silent. I answer, do you not know, however, that Paul also says in Galatians 3, "In Christ, there is no man nor woman"? And God in the prophet Joel says in chapter 2, "I will pour out my Spirit over all flesh, and your sons and daughters will prophesy." And you know also that Zechariah became dumb, so that Elizabeth blessed the Virgin Mary. So may you also receive me in good part. I do not seek to be heard as if I were Elizabeth, or John the Baptist, or Nathan the prophet who pointed out his sin to David, or as any of the prophets, but only as the donkey whom the false prophet Balaam heard. For I seek nothing other than that we might be saved together with each other. May God help us do that, through Christ his beloved son. Amen. APOLOGY FOR MATTHEW ZELL.[20]

---

[19]Fell, *Women's Speaking*, 9-10*.

[20]Zell, *Church Mother*, 81-82*; citing Num 22:23-30; Ezek 22:2-26; 21:25; 1 Cor 14:34; Gal 3:28; Joel 2:28; Acts 2:17; Lk 1:22, 42-45; Mt 3:7; 2 Sam 12:1; Num 22:28, 30. †St. Thecla was an early follower of Paul whose life is reported in the apocryphal Acts of Paul and Thecla. St. Petronilla was a martyr of the early church reported to be a daughter or convert of the apostle Peter. There is an ancient tradition that holds Mary Magdalene spent the last thirty-three years of her life in penance and contemplation at Sainte-Baume near Marseilles. See Katherine Ludwig Jansen, *The Making of Mary Magdalene: Preaching and Popular Devotion in the Later Middle Ages* (Princeton, NJ: Princeton University Press, 2000). Sibyls were female prophets of the ancient world.

Women Have Ministered Since the Apostolic Church.

Marie le Jars de Gournay: If St. Paul, to follow my trail of testimonies from the saints, forbids them the ministry and commands them to keep silent in church? It is plain that this is not all out of contempt but rather, indeed, only for fear lest they should arouse temptations by that display, so plain and public, that must be made in the course of ministering and preaching, since they are of greater grace and beauty than men. It is clear as day, I affirm, that contempt has nothing to do with it, since that apostle speaks of Phoebe as his cohelper in the work of the Lord—apart from the fact that St. Thecla and Apphia have a place among his dearest children and disciples, not to mention the great credit of St. Petronilla with respect to St. Peter— or to add that Mary Magdalene is names in the church as equal to the apostles, among other places in the calendar of the Greeks named by Génébrard. Indeed, the church and those very apostles allowed an exception to that rule of silence for her, who preached thirty years in the Baume of Marseilles, let them be asked what else the Sibyls were doing but preaching about God's universe by divine inspiration, in anticipation of the future coming of Jesus Christ?† The Equality of Men and Women.[21]

Equal Admission, but Not Leadership, with Exceptions.

Gisbertus Voetius:

Question 5: Whether women should be admitted equally with men to religious exercise—public, private, and semiprivate.

The response is in the affirmative, since all those things are theirs and they are Christ's. And communion of the members with Christ, their head, and with each other belongs to women no less than men.... There is only the exception that they may not speak in church; that is, they may not perform a public office of teaching; nor may they cast votes together with men in the exercise of government and discipline in the church. The fact that God in extra ordinary circumstances made use of the deeds of certain women (such as Deborah, Hulda . . .) does not make this a rule or order, nor is it for anyone to imitate. At the same time, as overseers and mothers, women are not only permitted within their own family to teach their children, maidservants, and other domestics and to lead them in prayers and other household devotional exercises, they are also required to do this in cases where the father of the family is either absent or clearly unsuited for such tasks or estranged from the true religion or the practice of piety. Not only in their homes but also elsewhere in gatherings and occasional religious or devotional exercises or in private discussions and deliberations, where a certain woman excels by virtue of learning and capacity for interpretation, she may lead in a women's meeting of the subject and occasion comes about in this way. These kinds of private discussions, deliberations, and gatherings of the faithful are treated here and there. Concerning Women.[22]

Women's Experience and Learning Matter.

Katharina Schütz Zell: For I also am no longer a young schoolchild who is still drinking and learning the ABC's; but I am an old student who has studied a long time, when you were still children and played in the sand. I ought now to be a master, while you would be a student who lights the fires. (Please accept my little joke well.) I have exercised myself in the holy Scriptures and godly matters more than forty-eight years now and have never abandoned the grace of God; I have heard the old teachers and let them be my counselors and made the wine new (to put in new skins) since I was ten years old. I never got bogged down hearing, learning, and following until the day (sad to me but happy to him) of the death of my dear and good husband. I could not teach others and with the elderly Anna prophesy about Christ to those who are waiting for redemption and praise the Lord. But

---

[21]Gournay, *Apology for the Woman Writing*, 89-90*; citing Rom 16:1-2; Philem 2; 1 Cor 16:19.

[22]Schurman, *Whether a Christian Woman Should Be Educated*, 134-35; citing Gal 3:28; 1 Cor 15:34; 1 Thess 4:11-14; Rom 15:14; Heb 3:13; Acts 12:12; 16:13; Mt 18:20.

considering that I must appropriately be submissive under the man's office, according to the teaching of St. Paul, I myself seek to hear others and be exhorted, as far as they speak the truth. But where that is not so, then I would tell you and not keep silent, but speak, point out, and answer your wrong preaching and insulting words about the innocent. AUTOBIOGRAPHY AND POLEMIC.[23]

THE LEGITIMACY AND LIMITS OF FEMALE RULERS. GISBERTUS VOETIUS: Some may perhaps object that women have presided over public governance of the church among Protestants: as the papists often charge us. Supremacy was attributed to Queen Elizabeth; that is to say, she was said to be supreme head under Christ and governor of the Anglican church. *Response:* What was attributed to her and what she claimed was not formally ecclesiastical power but political power that also had to do with the church and ecclesiastical matters. And such power is fitting for every legitimate magistrate not only supreme but also subaltern, of whichever sex, such that, if the fortunes of the whole state belong to a woman, power with regard to the church and ecclesiastical matters must not be denied the same. But that a woman may call or choose ministers of the Word, administer the keys to the kingdom of heaven, exercise discipline, and this teach the church, neither the Word of God nor the order of reformed churches permits. CONCERNING WOMEN.[24]

ON FEMALE RULERS. THE THIRTY-NINE ARTICLES: The queen's majesty has the chief power in this realm of England, and other her dominions, unto whom the chief government of all estates of this realm, whether they be ecclesiastical or civil, in all causes does appertain, and is not, nor ought to be, subject to any foreign jurisdiction. Where we attribute to the queen's majesty the chief government, by which titles we understand the minds of

some slanderous folks to be offended; we give not to our princes the ministering either of God's Word, or of the sacraments, the which thing the injunctions also lately set forth by Elizabeth our queen do most plainly testify; but that only prerogative, which we see to have been given always to all godly princes in the holy Scriptures by God himself; that is, that they should rule all estates and degrees committed to their charge by God, whether they be ecclesiastical or temporal, and restrain with the civil sword the stubborn and evildoers. ARTICLE 37 OF THE THIRTY-NINE ARTICLES.[25]

2:13-15 *The Deception and Salvation of Woman*

THE DEVIL WORKS BY DECEPTION. JOHN OWEN: Further to manifest the strength and advantage that sin has by its deceit, we may observe that the Scripture places it for the most part as the head and spring of every sin, even as though there were no sin followed after but where deceit went before. The reason the apostle gives why Adam, though he was "first formed," was not "first in the transgression," is because he was not "first deceived." The woman, though made last, yet being first deceived, was first in the sin. Even that first sin began in deceit, and until the mind was deceived the soul was safe. Eve, therefore, truly expressed the matter, though she did it not to a good end. "The serpent beguiled me," she says, "and I ate." She thought to extenuate her own crime by charging the serpent; and this was a new fruit of the sin she had cast herself into. But the matter of fact was true—she was beguiled before she ate; deceit went before the transgression. And the apostle shows that sin and Satan still take the same course. "There is," he says, "the same way of working toward actual sin as was of old: beguiling, deceiving goes before; and sin, that is, the actual accomplishment of it, follows after." Hence, all the great works that the devil does in the world to stir people up to an opposition to

[23]Zell, *Church Mother*, 196-97*; citing Mt 9:16-17; Mk 2:22; Lk 2:36-38; 1 Cor 14:34.
[24]Schurman, *Whether a Christian Woman Should Be Educated*, 135.
[25]The Thirty-Nine Articles of Religion (1571).

the Lord Jesus Christ and his kingdom, he does them by deceit: "The devil, who deceives the whole world." It is utterly impossible that men should be prevailed on to abide in his service, acting his designs to their eternal, and sometimes their temporal ruin, were they not exceedingly deceived. Indwelling Sin in Believers.[26]

An Instrument Fit to Deceive. Peter Martyr Vermigli: Although both those two first parents sinned, there was not one manner of transgression in them both: for he says that Adam was not deceived, which is seen in the answers they gave to God when he reproved them: for the woman, being asked what she had done, accused the serpent: "The serpent," she said, "deceived me." But Adam, when he was asked the same question, did not say that he was deceived, but that "the woman, whom you have given me, delivered me an apple, and I ate." These things must not be so understood as though we affirmed that no error happened to the man when he transgressed. . . . This only we are taught, that man was not seduced by so gross a guile as the women was.

And this did very much further Paul's reason; for in the same place, he willed the woman to keep silence in the church because she was an instrument fit to deceive. And this he confirmed by the example of the first parents: for she who persuaded man to sin, it is not likely that she can rightly instruct him; and she who could be seduced by the devil, and deceived by the serpent, it is not appropriate for her to bear office in the church. Commonplaces.[27]

Adam's Sin Was Greater. Edward Leigh: To be deceived is to err and mistake in judging. Adam did not eat out of error as did Eve; for he did not persuade himself that he should get more knowledge by it, but was only drawn to follow his wife by her entreaty, as not thinking death could follow the eating of the fruit when he saw that his wife (who

had eaten already) was not dead, but as healthy as before. Yet Adam sinned more than Eve, because he received the commandment from the Lord, he had more wisdom and strength, and had a greater measure of knowledge. Therefore this place here . . . is to be understood of the weakness of women, not of the greatness of the sin. Annotations.[28]

Punishment for Sin Does Not Hinder Salvation. Giovanni Diodati: In the bringing forth of children, and in the subjection to the husband, God has imprinted the marks of the punishment imposed on the woman. It might seem from this that among women there is no salvation, but only for those who are married; yet by Christ all condemnation is taken away, and these corporal evils in no way hinder the work of grace. Annotations.[29]

Saved Through the Childbearing. John Mayer: Since the apostle seems to ascribe salvation to the bearing of children here, diverse expositors have conjectured diversely of the meaning. Some by "the bearing of children" will have the bearing of Christ to be understood, so that it is as much as if he had said, "Woman, despite her being in the transgression and offering that to the man whereby he also was drawn to transgress, has brought forth one child—the Lord Jesus Christ—by whom all faithful, loving, and modest women shall be saved."[†]

Some again by "the bearing of children" understand "in the married and childbearing estate." . . . And so they will have the meaning to be that . . . though she does better who continues a virgin, as is taught in 1 Corinthians 7, yet even the married and childbearing woman shall be saved, if she is a pursuer of such virtues and graces as are here set forth. And being subjected to the sorrows of childbearing, this is yet her comfort, that she shall be saved.

Others understand the childbearing here spoken of as a means to bring her to salvation, taking childbearing not only for conceiving and

---

[26]Owen, *Works*, 6:212-13*; citing 1 Tim 2:13-14; Gen 3:13; 2 Cor 11:3; Rev 12:9.

[27]Vermigli, *Commonplaces*, 2:242*; Gen 3:13, 12.

[28]Leigh, *Annotations*, 322*.

[29]Diodati, *Pious Annotations*, 40*.

bringing forth but also for the bringing up of her children in the fear and instruction of the Lord, so that such good impressions are made in them in their tender age that they continue when they are grown up in faith, in love, holiness, and sobriety. . . .

Others by being saved understand nothing else but being delivered from the brand of disgrace, with which she was marked by being the author of sin to her husband. For if she breeds and brings up her children well she shall not be infamous for that sin anymore, but be honored for performing her duty toward her children, if she be faithful and loving to her husband.

There is also another exposition . . . understanding the bearing of children here mystically, of the bringing forth of good works. But this is not to the purpose and therefore may be passed over, as strained. . . .

Note, against that fond imagination of some who say women have no souls, that they both have souls and are partakers of the same salvation with men, through the seed of the woman, the Lord Jesus Christ. Always provided that both men and women be faithful, loving, holy, and sober. It is not bare faith that will save the soul, but when it is accompanied with all other Christian graces and virtues. If Mary had not borne Christ in her heart as well as in her womb, she would not have been saved.

Note again how careful the apostle is in speaking against the woman, that she is not overwhelmed with despair, or left in disgrace to her discouragement. He immediately adds something to comfort and to grace her, when he had discomforted and debased her in regard of her sin. So that it is not the part of a preacher of the word of God to put any to confusion, and so to leave them, as the end aimed at in their preaching; but so to shame sinners that they may thus make way to the converting of them, always immediately annexing the comforts that belong to the penitent. COMMENTARY ON PAUL'S EPISTLES.[30]

CHRIST RULES OVER HUSBANDS, HUSBANDS RULE OVER WIVES. DAVID JORIS: Make captive your understanding, you women, under the obedience of the Christian husband. Assent to his wise speech, which has been spoken from fear of the Spirit. Quarrel not against him, but bow your understanding under his. Be obedient from the fear of the Lord. And you shall rise as a great light, shine as a great salvation. God will punish the evil and unrighteous ones. Fulfill the will of the Almighty. Do not look after the husband to see that he fears for the Lord, but let him look after you, for he was made first, then the woman. He is also her head, but Christ is before and above all of these. Therefore, he has the preeminence in all things. He precedes us in a legal and human fashion. Behind him follows the man, then the woman must follow the man. But she must attend to the children, so they will learn correctly and properly from her and be maintained and taught to virtue in the fear of the Lord. But Christ attends to the man and the man to the woman, who is his concern. Pay attention to what I say to you. OF THE WONDERFUL WORKING OF GOD.[31]

CONSOLATION AND THE WAY OF FAITH. JOHN CALVIN: It might have the effect (as I have already said) of striking terror into the minds of women, when they were informed that the destruction of the whole human race was attributed to them; for what will be this condemnation? Especially when their subjection, as a testimony of the wrath of God, is constantly placed before their eyes. Accordingly, Paul, in order to comfort them and render their condition tolerable, informs them that they continue to enjoy the hope of salvation, though they suffer a temporal punishment. It is proper to observe that the good effect of this consolation is twofold. First, by the hope of salvation held out to them, they are prevented from falling into despair through alarm at the mention of their guilt. Second, they become accustomed to endure calmly and patiently the necessity of servitude, so as to

[30]Mayer, *Commentary*, 498*. †This he eventually argues is his preferred interpretation, because others are either strained or attribute too much to being married (whereas Paul is very positive about singleness), though some of the other options are not without merit.

[31]CRR 7:116*; citing Eph 5:22-24; Is 58:8; 62:1; 1 Cor 11:8.

submit willingly to their husbands, when they are informed that this kind of obedience is both profitable to themselves and acceptable to God. If this passage be tortured, as papists are wont to do, to support the righteousness of works, the answer is easy. The apostle does not argue here about the cause of salvation, and therefore we cannot and must not infer from these words what works deserve; but they only show in what way God conducts us to salvation, to which he has appointed us through his grace.

"Through childbearing." To censorious men it might appear absurd for an apostle of Christ not only to exhort women to give attention to the birth of offspring but also to press this work as religious and holy to such an extent as to represent it in the light of the means of procuring salvation. Nay, we even see with what reproaches the conjugal bed has been slandered by hypocrites, who wished to be thought more holy than all other men. But there is no difficulty in replying to these sneers of the ungodly. First, here the apostle does not speak merely about having children, but about enduring all the distresses, which are manifold and severe, both in the birth and in the rearing of children. Second, whatever hypocrites or wise men of the world may think of it, when a woman, considering to what she has been called, submits to the condition that God has assigned to her, and does not refuse to endure the pains, or rather the fearful anguish of childbirth, or anxiety about her offspring, or anything else that belongs to her duty,

God values this obedience more highly than if, in some other manner, she made a great display of heroic virtues, while she refused to obey the calling of God. To this must be added, that no consolation could be more appropriate or more efficacious than to show that the very means (so to speak) of procuring salvation are found in the punishment itself. COMMENTARY ON 1 TIMOTHY.[32]

Adam Disobeyed God to Not Upset Eve.

BALTHASAR HUBMAIER: That the fall of the soul is reparable and harmless here on earth, while that of the flesh irreparable and even deadly, is due to the following: Adam, a figure of the soul—as Eve is a figure of the flesh—would have preferred not to eat of the forbidden tree. He was not seduced by the snake but Eve was. Adam knew well that the word of the serpent contradicted the word of God. Nevertheless he willed to eat of this fruit against his own conscience in order not to grieve or anger his rib and flesh, Eve. He would have preferred not to do it. This, since he was more obedient to Eve than to God, he lost the knowledge of good and evil. So he cannot will or choose good, nor can he not will or flee something evil, for he does not know what is truly good or evil before God. Nothing tastes good to him but that which tastes and seems good to his Eve, that is, his flesh. For he has lost the right sense of taste. FREEDOM OF THE WILL.[33]

---

[32]CTS 43:70-71* (CO 52:277-78).
[33]CRR 5:435-36*; citing Gen 3:6; Ps 14:3; 32:5; 53:2.

3:1-13 QUALIFICATIONS FOR OVERSEERS AND DEACONS

The saying is trustworthy: If anyone aspires to the office of overseer, he desires a noble task. ²Therefore an overseer[a] *must be above reproach, the husband of one wife,*[b] *sober-minded, self-controlled, respectable, hospitable, able to teach, ³not a drunkard, not violent but gentle, not quarrelsome, not a lover of money. ⁴He must manage his own household well, with all dignity keeping his children submissive, ⁵for if someone does not know how to manage his own household, how will he care for God's church? ⁶He must not be a recent convert, or he may become puffed up with conceit and fall into the condemnation of the devil. ⁷Moreover, he must be well thought of by outsiders, so that he may not fall into disgrace, into a snare of the devil.*

⁸Deacons likewise must be dignified, not double-tongued,[c] *not addicted to much wine, not greedy for dishonest gain. ⁹They must hold the mystery of the faith with a clear conscience. ¹⁰And let them also be tested first; then let them serve as deacons if they prove themselves blameless. ¹¹Their wives likewise*[d] *must be dignified, not slanderers, but sober-minded, faithful in all things. ¹²Let deacons each be the husband of one wife, managing their children and their own households well. ¹³For those who serve well as deacons gain a good standing for themselves and also great confidence in the faith that is in Christ Jesus.*

a Or *bishop;* Greek *episkopos;* a similar term occurs in verse 1   b Or *a man of one woman;* also verse 12   c Or *devious in speech*   d Or *Wives likewise,* or *Women likewise*

OVERVIEW: The government of the late medieval church was highly stratified. At the top of the hierarchy sat the pope, who ruled the universal church as the vicar of Christ. Beneath the pope were the cardinals, who advised and elected the pontiff. Many cardinals functioned as archbishops, who governed ecclesiastical provinces, which in turn were divided into dioceses, each of which was ruled by a bishop. Each diocese consisted of multiple parishes whose churches were overseen by priests. Other orders below that of priest were deacon, subdeacon, acolyte, reader, and some others. During this period, the order of deacon was viewed as preparatory for the priesthood.

Our early modern commentators interacted with various aspects of this ecclesiastical structure throughout their expositions of this passage. In response to the reputed abuses by the clergy, these authors highlight the moral and ethical requirements outlined by Paul for the office of bishop. By stressing these qualifications, some of the authors nullify the alleged bodily impediments to holy orders defined by canon law. Their treatments reveal an effort to recover the spiritual nature of clerical office. A central subject of discussion throughout these expositions is clerical celibacy. While Catholic exegetes argue for retaining this canonical practice on the grounds that marriage would defile their administration of the Eucharist, Protestant authors contend on the basis of the Pauline requirements for both the legitimacy and the benefits of clerical marriage. Turning to the subject of the diaconate, these authors portray it as a ministry in itself rather than just a preparatory step for the priesthood. The commentators stress care for the poor as the prime responsibility of the diaconate.

3:1-7 Qualifications for Overseers

IT USED TO BE HARD TO FIND MEN WILLING TO BE BISHOPS. JAN HUS: Perhaps you reply that since the clerical office is so hemmed in on every side, it is not wise to seek priesthood or episcopacy.

But that is contrary to reason, which shows the preeminent worth of that estate which no one can rightfully occupy or enjoy unless they deliberately seek after it. For St. Paul says, "He who seeks episcopacy, desires a good work." . . . But because bishops nowadays have undertaken the management of property, they seek property, and episcopacy on account of property. Furthermore, since bishops no longer fear martyrdom, they eagerly run after episcopacy. Formerly it was hardly possible to find a man willing to be a bishop; for it involved being poor and ready for martyrdom. . . . Take care, therefore, if you wish to seek priesthood or episcopacy, that first of all you examine your conscience. . . . Then if you enter the office, beware that simony,[†] pride, self-indulgence, and avarice, and above all hypocrisy, do not gain sway over you. ON SIMONY.[1]

THE CHURCH STRUGGLES WITHOUT COMPETENT PASTORS. THOMAS CRANMER: Just as the condition of the state is ruined when it is governed by people who are stupid, demanding, and burning with ambition, so in these times the church of God is struggling, since it is committed to the care of those who are totally incompetent to assume so important a task, in which respect it has fallen very far short indeed of those rules of the blessed Paul, which he prescribed to Timothy and Titus. Therefore we must find an appropriate remedy for so serious a plague on our churches. Everyone who obtains [an ecclesiastical] living in any way whatsoever shall be most carefully tested and examined according to the form and procedure of our laws, lest a bishop lay his hand suddenly on someone and so become a partner in the crimes of others. Nor shall anyone be allowed to run a church, unless he has been duly examined beforehand. . . .

In a presbyter, there shall shine those qualities described by the Lord Paul in 1 Timothy 3 and in Titus 1. They shall regularly feed the flock of God committed to them with the word of life, and they shall constantly nurture all Christians in a sincere obedience both to God, and to the magistrates, and to those placed in a higher dignity, and earnestly encourage them to love one another. They shall not be drunkards, gamblers, fowlers, hunters, hypocrites, sluggards, or weaklings, but they shall devote themselves to the study of sacred letters, to the preaching of the Word, and to prayers to the Lord for the church. No single man shall allow a woman of less than sixty years of age to dwell in his house unless she is his mother, his father's sister, his mother's sister, or his own sister. Every presbyter shall have his own Holy Bible, not only in English but also in Latin. His attire shall be decent and sober, as befits a minister, not a soldier, as the bishop shall appoint. REFORMATION OF CHURCH LAW.[2]

THE HONORABLE TASK OF BIBLICAL EPISCOPACY. WOLFGANG MUSCULUS: He could simply have said, "He desires an honorable task, whoever seeks the position of bishop"; but he wanted to take up the theme of relating the dignity of the position of bishop—of what it consisted, and how not just anyone is suitable for bearing its burden. They would allege that to be the overseer was a good and noble task, and that they for that reason sought it in the church, as if they were seeking to engage in good and noble deeds in the church. So when he had laid down this duty of appointing elders and overseers, he determined that he should remind Timothy that the reward of the work is from the thing itself, and inform him with a particular list, according to which he would conduct the election of the bishops in the churches.

---

[1]LCC 14:256-57. [†]Simony is the buying or selling of church benefices or ecclesiastical privileges and pardons.

[2]Bray, ed., *Reformatio Legum Ecclesiasticarum*, 11.1-2 and 20.4. The *Reformatio Legum Ecclesiasticarum* (The reformation of church law) was drafted by a legal committee appointed and overseen by Archbishop Thomas Cranmer* for the purpose of producing a reformed canon law for the evangelical Church of England during the reign of Edward VI*. However, in 1553, due to opposition by the Duke of Northumberland, the regent for the young monarch, the document never received statutory approval by Parliament, and thus remained only a proposed draft. A 1571 attempt in Parliament to enact this code also failed. The martyriologist John Foxe (1516–1587), who published the code in the same year, gave it its title.

And in order that he might at once forestall the pretexts of the ambitious, lest he allow himself to be imposed upon, he says, "It is a sure saying that if someone seeks the position of bishop, he desires a noble task." As if to say: for sure, the position of bishop is a good and noble task. About this matter there is no doubt in the churches. But in the judgment of unbelievers, to whom the whole of Christendom is an abomination, the fact that one among the believers has precedence over the rest makes it even more detestable. And for that reason the ministers of the Word and the elders are considered to be in favor of removing impostors in the world.

Assuredly among the churches may the task of the bishop be noble and honorable by the consensus of all the faithful, nor let there be anyone who calls this into doubt. Wherefore it is in itself true that anyone who desires the position of bishop desires an honorable task. But it should be brought to mind what kind of a man the eminence and nobility of the episcopate demands. Manifestly, the person chosen cannot be just anyone, but should match the honor of the task itself, and once engaged in it should perform it honorably. . . . In truth this saying is not only called into doubt, but by a great many is rejected, as being the greatest falsehood of them all. Nay it should rather now be formulated as follows: "It is a sure saying, that if anyone seeks the position of bishop, he seeks after the royal eminence, wealth, and domination of others by the reign of Christ." In no way at any time would the apostle have called such an episcopate as the pope has an honorable task. Commentary on Paul's Epistles.[3]

Bodily Defects No Longer a Barrier to Ministry. Friedrich Balduin: As far as public life is concerned, Paul has two requirements: First, he says, a bishop should be blameless. It is not a matter here of any censure; accordingly, we need first to remove from consideration that which the matter does not concern: he is not talking about that kind of censure that may be the product of the defects of the body. It is disputed in the papacy whether those who labor under defects of the body, such as those who are lame, maimed, crippled, and similar, are in a position to be admitted into the ministry. On which question, that we may speak briefly, we should know that those who are stricken by this kind of blemish were at one time in the Old Testament simply excluded from the ministry, as is clear from Leviticus 20:17-21. However, this was the ordinance as it contained a type of the highest priest of the New Testament, Jesus Christ, who had to be whole and spotless. Brief Foundations for Ministers of the Word.[4]

Overseers of Flocks or of Pastors Too. English Annotations: "If a man desire." . . . Not ambitiously affect, but finds in himself a fitness and willingness to take on that office, moved by a holy and sincere affection to consecrate himself to God in the service of the church, and to employ and improve there those gifts he has received of him for the edification of God's people.

"A bishop." . . . That is, the office of an overseer, which word may either have relation to the flock of Christ only, and in that sense it belongs to all pastors who have cure of souls; or, to the pastors themselves also, as well as the flock. In that latter sense, antiquity has appropriated the word to signify the chief presbyter or minister, who has superintendence over a whole church comprised within a city or diocese, in which there were diverse "inferior" pastors. English Annotations.[5]

Marriage Pollutes the Unbloodied Sacrifice of the Mass. Petrus Stevartius: In their typical fashion the Lutherans rave against the tyranny of the pontiffs, on the grounds that they have joined celibacy to the priesthood and have forbidden priests from having children. As though the pontiffs ever compelled anyone into the priesthood or into a bishopric! But they have, for

---

[3]Musculus, *In Divi Pauli Epistolas*, 366.

[4]Balduin, *Brevis Institutio Ministrorum Verbi*, 252; citing Heb 7:1.
[5]Downame, ed., *Annotations*, s.v.*

good reasons, demanded this condition from those who voluntarily wanted to pledge themselves to sacred ministry: they must abstain from women in order to be able to carry the vessels of the Lord in a more pure and holy fashion, and to assist at the holy altars. For marriage is the greatest obstacle to prevent priests from fulfilling the ecclesiastical duties proper to that order. The unique and special office of a priest, which consists in sacrificing and offering to God the Father an unbloodied sacrifice for the salvation of the living and the dead, occupies them, just as Jerome teaches in book one *Against Jovinian*.[†] For in marriage there is an admixture, not indeed a sinful one, but a certain kind of impurity born from sin and a pollution, which very much undermines the purity required in the one making sacrifice. COMMENTARY ON 1 TIMOTHY.[6]

MINISTERS MUST RENOUNCE FLESHLY LUSTS. MARTIN BUCER: In the first place it is the will of the Holy Spirit that the church's ministers should each be the husband of only one wife, temperate, virtuous, well-mannered, self-controlled, pure, not addicted to wine. They should be able to maintain discipline, so that no charge of indiscipline can be laid against their own children and servants. In other words, it is the will of the Holy Spirit that such people should demonstrate in themselves and in those who belong to them the highest degree of discipline and holiness, and complete renunciation of all fleshly lusts and concerns.

This is because if they are to teach the whole church to renounce all fleshly desires and lusts it is necessary for them to furnish the highest example of this in themselves and those who belong to them. And those who do not stand earnestly and firmly against things of this nature will easily be overtaken by evil lusts and desires, with the result that they will be careless in the things of God for themselves, and will be despised and shunned by others as unfit. CONCERNING THE TRUE CARE OF SOULS.[7]

MARRIED BISHOPS WERE COMPELLED TO REFRAIN FROM SEX. LIBERT FROIDMONT: "Husband of one wife." This means monogamy, that is, that one may not marry many wives in succession. For the union of husband and wife is a figure for the conjunction of Christ the one bridegroom with his one bride the church. Consequently, those men who divide their own flesh into many, as the canons say, are out of order. But in the time of the apostles, because few virgins were found suitable for the bishopric, sometimes married men were admitted to the office. Nevertheless, they were compelled to refrain from the marriage bed of their wife by mutual consent. Therefore the apostle does not command a bishop to have a wife (as the heretics jest). "For otherwise neither Paul nor John would have been bishops," as Jerome says. Nor does he also command, as Calvin holds, that they not have multiple wives at the same time, because there was no need to give such an order since no Christians ever had two wives at the same time. There was once an argument between Augustine and Jerome as to whether that kind of bigamy in which a man who had married one wife before and another after baptism was out of order. Or even if he had two wives before baptism. Jerome denies that this is an irregular sort of bigamy; Augustine states that it is. The church follows Augustine. COMMENTARIES ON THE EPISTLES.[8]

CLERICAL CELIBACY IS NOT HERE REFUTED. PETRUS STEVARTIUS: In the first place, then, after the requirement of a blameless life he wants a bishop to be the husband of one wife. This is not because he means that no one ought to be a bishop unless he is a husband (as the Lutherans interpret the passage), since for the fulfillment of the office of bishop the man without a wife is far more suited than someone else. But Paul makes this requirement so that a future bishop, once his first wife has died, does not take a second. For although Paul desires that all Christians be like he was, that is, celibate, and free from the worries and cares of the

---

[6]Stevartius, *Commentarius*, 205. [†]Jerome, *Against Jovinianus*, NPNF[2] 6:371-72.
[7]Bucer, *Concerning the True Care of Souls*, 47.

[8]Froidmont, *Commentaria*, 368.

present life, he desired this quality far more in bishops. For they care for the souls of countless people. Therefore he instructed that if possible continent men be chosen, as is evident in the case of Timothy, Titus, Evodius,[†] and Clement,[‡] who led their lives in purity and virginity. But because it was not possible in those times, the apostle at least in this passage wants the selection of bishops to be from those who were married only once, or who by the intervention of death had been made free from the chains of a wife, or who were going to be victorious later in a more perfect chastity by mutual consent. . . . The Lutherans so shamelessly attack what the apostles taught and antiquity itself has preserved (as the fathers speak in the Second Council of Carthage). They attach to this passage the following meaning: a bishop must be the husband of one wife, that is, one who does not have multiple wives at the same time. But these men, no less ignorant than wicked, do not see that in Paul's time, not even in that time of Christ, was there any sort of Jewish custom of taking to oneself in marriage two wives at once. When the Scripture of the New Testament speaks of marriage, it is always in the singular, for example. COMMENTARY ON 1 TIMOTHY.[9]

An Overseer's Household Is a Model.

MATTHIAS FLACIUS: The fourth rule is affirmatively describing the character of the pastor based on his experience in managing his house. For it requires as a stipulation, and by additional reason from the contrary, for a bishop/overseer to govern his house rightly. It is therefore his description first here in the affirmative, and afterward in the negative because [an overseer/bishop] acts from a double cause: now if his household is not a bad example, or scandal to others, then he could be seen to be placed over the Lord's house as one who desires to rule his own house well. He therefore wants him to order his household so

that he may then teach it to be now obedient, and then by all means honest, and also for his character and manners to be seen as industrious. GLOSS ON 1 TIMOTHY[10]

Polity for the Church.

BELGIC CONFESSION: We believe that this true church must be governed by the spiritual polity that our Lord has taught us in his Word—namely, that there must be ministers or pastors to preach the Word of God, and to administer the sacraments; also elders and deacons, who, together with the pastors, form the council of the church; that by these means the true religion may be preserved, and the true doctrine every where propagated, likewise transgressors punished and restrained by spiritual means; also that the poor and distressed may be relieved and comforted, according to their necessities. By these means every thing will be carried on in the church with good order and decency, when faithful men are chosen, according to the rule prescribed by St. Paul to Timothy. BELGIC CONFESSION.[11]

Reverent Estimation of Qualified Ministers.

THE ORDINAL: It is evident to all those diligently reading holy Scripture and ancient authors that from the apostles' time there have been these orders of ministers in Christ's church: bishops, priests, and deacons.[†] Which offices were evermore had in such reverent estimation that no man by his own private authority might presume to execute any of them, except he were first called, tried, examined, and known to have such qualities as were requisite for the same; and also by public prayer, with imposition of hands, were approved and admitted to it. And therefore, to the intent these orders should be continued, and reverently used and esteemed in this Church of England, it is requisite that no man (not being at this present time bishop, priest, nor deacon) shall execute any of them except he be called, tried, examined, and admitted, according to the form hereafter following.

---

[9]Stevartius, *Commentarius*, 201-2; citing 1 Cor 7; Titus 1. [†]Evodius, or Euodias (died AD 69), was bishop of Antioch. [‡]Clement (died AD 97) was bishop of Rome.

[10]Flacius, *Glossa Compendaria*, 1168.
[11]Schaff 3:421-22.

And none shall be admitted a deacon, except he be twenty-one years of age at the least. And every man who is to be admitted a priest shall be full four and twenty years old. And every man who is to be consecrated a bishop shall be fully thirty years of age.[†] And the bishop, knowing either by himself or by sufficient testimony, any person to be a man of virtuous conversation and without crime, and after examination and trial, finding him learned in the Latin tongue and sufficiently instructed in holy Scripture, may upon a Sunday or holy day, in the face of the church, admit him a deacon, in such manner and form as hereafter follows. THE ORDINAL (1549).[12]

PRAYER FOR BISHOPS. THE ORDINAL: Almighty God, giver of all good things, who by your Holy Spirit has appointed diverse orders of ministers in your church: mercifully behold this your servant now called to the work and ministry of a bishop, and replenish him so with the truth of thy doctrine and innocence of life, that both by word and deed he may faithfully serve you in this office, to the glory of your name and profit of your congregation,[†] through the merits of our Savior Jesus Christ, who lives and reigns with you and the Holy Ghost, world without end. Amen. THE ORDINAL (1549).[13]

THE MARRIAGE OF MINISTERS. MARTIN BUCER: The fact that on the subject of wives the Holy Spirit defines discipline and holiness in terms of each one being the husband of only one wife, that is, that no one should have more than one wife (since then at the commencement of the church there were those who came to Christ, both Jews and Gentiles, who perhaps had more than one wife) indicates and proves that the Holy Spirit does not frown on the marriage of ministers, but officially recognizes that elders may live in the state of marriage without blame or guilt. For in both places, writing to Timothy and to Titus, where he writes: "above reproach, blameless," the apostle goes on immediately to add: "the husband of one wife."

For although marriage involves temporal concerns, troubles, and affairs that might be a hindrance to the work of the ministry, it also has many advantages in enabling the minister not only to live a disciplined and blameless life, but also to be more free of temporal cares and affairs and to serve the Lord more faithfully, zealously, and without hindrances; and especially at this time when the faithful and industrious ministers of the church are so few in number, since the ministers of antichrist are still in a position to squander the inheritance of Christ in large amounts. . . .

But this is how it must turn out when people want to be wiser and more holy than the Holy Spirit; for nowhere in the whole of Scripture by one single word has he indicated that marriage is to be avoided by ministers of the church, stating rather that he desires marriage to have the same status with ministers as with all those whom he has not appointed to live outside the married state, of whom there are not many. And this is why the first and better churches have been greatly blessed as they have not excluded the marriage of ministers; and as soon as it was excluded, it led to such unholy offenses in the churches as are sadly

---

[12]*Forme and Maner*, preface*. [†]Philip H. Towner, *The Letters to Timothy and Titus*, New International Commentary on the New Testament (Grand Rapids: Eerdmans, 2006), 242, comments, "Often the developed three-tiered ecclesiastical organization found in Ignatius's letters (c. 110 C.E.: a single bishop presiding over elders and deacons) has been the benchmark by which [1 Timothy and Titus] have been assessed. Simply put, however, there is very little indication in them of a degree of church organization that comes very close to the scenario depicted in Ignatius. But it has been common to place them in the line leading from charismatic (non-official) leadership to the later monepiscopal model." [‡]The appropriate ages for ordination candidates have often varied. In the Church of England, the Canons of 1604 increased the normal minimum age of Anglican deacons to twenty-three, while the Council of Trent (session 23, chapter 12) required Roman Catholic deacons and priests to be at least twenty-three and twenty-five respectively.

[13]*Forme and Maner*, Consecrating of a Bishop*. The Ordinal (the rite for ordination of deacons and priests, and for the consecration of bishops) was published by Archbishop Thomas Cranmer* in 1549. Having been subject to significant critique

by Martin Bucer,* a more reformed version of the Ordinal became part of the 1552 Book of Common Prayer. [†]1549: "profit of thy congregation." 1662: "the edifying and well governing of thy Church."

testified to by the situation today. CONCERNING THE TRUE CARE OF SOULS.[14]

MONOGAMOUS AND NOT DIVORCED. DUTCH ANNOTATIONS: "The husband of one wife." . . . Not that he must necessarily be married, seeing Paul himself was not married, but because he might not have many wives together, or one after another by divorce, as was a long time usual with the Jews and Greeks, and especially in those Oriental countries; which seems indeed for a while to have been tolerated in others, but might not be tolerated in teachers. DUTCH ANNOTATIONS.[15]

MINISTERS SHOULD MARRY HONORABLE AND DEVOUT PARTNERS. FRIEDRICH BALDUIN: There is, therefore, no reason why he should debar ministers from this, to whom elsewhere, as is established from the foregoing, he has not forbidden marriage itself. For the fact that the papists assert that a second marriage is a sign of lack of self-control is of no value. For in many cases it shows nothing other than care for one's household, while at other times it is the need to avoid scandal and suspicion that leads one to a second marriage, and if a lack of self-control were indeed to vehemently demand a second marriage, it would be better to marry than to burn, according to the rule.

Ministers' wives should be honorable, and eager for many virtues, as Paul teaches in 1 Timothy 3:11. At one time the Lord was not willing to make a harlot or a prostitute priest, or indeed anyone of ill repute. For just as in the whole of their lives there should be nothing vulgar, so also he desired their marriages to be pure and chaste, lest slanderers find a way to reproach them. Julius Caesar also wanted his wife to be free from slander. The same view is to be held in regard to the wife of a minister of the church, whose marriage should be all the purer and more chaste the more enemies it has, and distinguished by the sum of its virtues. A minister of the word should therefore choose a life partner of the

following kind: let not a woman habituated to the delights of the world, that is, pride, extravagance, pleasure, and similar vices, dishonor the holy order, but let her be well brought up from youth, one who is devout, moderate, temperate, and discrete, and altogether, as far as it is within her power, let her be a mark of her husband's honor. This, then, is the first requirement of the minister, as far as his private affairs are concerned. BRIEF FOUNDATIONS FOR MINISTERS OF THE WORD.[16]

HONORABLE MARRIAGE BETTER THAN CLERICAL VICE. KATHARINA SCHÜTZ ZELL: Another reason they resist clerical marriage is that, should priests have (legal) wives, they would have to choose one and give up the others. They will not be able to behave as they do with the prostitutes, throwing one out, taking in another. For Paul says, "A bishop should be the husband of one wife." Therefore they must each live honorably, and if having the same woman does not please the man, he may not exchange her. For in marriage the couple must have and bear many griefs with each other (on which account these priests do not wish to be bound to any marriage). Still, one often suffers more from a harlot—he would not suffer half of that from an honest (legal) wife!

However, if they want to treat clerical marriage honorably, they would then need to punish adultery in the pulpit more strictly. Otherwise, how can they punish it when they are mixed up in it? In such a case (when they are mixed up in it also) the going thing is a mutual blind eye: "If you overlook my fault, I will overlook yours." If, however, a priest had a (legal) wife and then did evil, one would know how to punish him. But this way the clergy always have an excuse to say nothing else than, "You worldly folk can talk about this easily; you have your wives. So I also am a man; how can I behave like an angel?" and so forth. And that is also true. Oh, then why not leave things the way God made them?! "Let each one

---

[14]Bucer, *Concerning the True Care of Souls*, 48-49; citing Titus 1:6.
[15]Haak, *Annotations*, s.v.*; citing 1 Cor 7:7.

[16]Balduin, *Brevis Institutio Ministrorum Verbi*, 284-85; citing 1 Cor 7:9; Lev 21:7.

have his wife, on account of harlotry." Does God not know better than the devil what is good? For the prohibition of marriage comes only from the devil and marriage comes from God, says the Holy Spirit himself in the epistle to Timothy. APOLOGIA FOR MATTHEW ZELL.[17]

IMPETUOUS OVERCONFIDENT NOVICES NEED NOT APPLY. JOHN CALVIN: "Not a recent convert." . . . There being many men of distinguished ability and learning who at that time were brought to the faith, Paul forbids that such persons shall be admitted to the office of a bishop as soon as they have made profession of Christianity. And he shows how great would be the danger; for it is evident that they are commonly vain, and full of ostentation, and in consequence of this haughtiness and ambition will drive them headlong. What Paul says we experience; for "novices" have not only impetuous fervor and bold daring, but are also puffed up with foolish confidence, as if they could fly beyond the clouds. Consequently, it is not without reason that they are excluded from the honor of a bishopric, till in process of time their proud temper shall be subdued. COMMENTARY ON 1 TIMOTHY.[18]

GOOD REPUTATION, NOT DESIRE FOR PRE-EMINENCE. DESIDERIUS ERASMUS: It is dangerous if someone who is but raw and not yet sufficiently confirmed in religion is advanced to an honor that they did not have before. They will be puffed up with pride and perniciously begin to stand in their own conceit, as though they were elected into the company of religion in order to have preeminence over religion. In that way he will be caught in the devil's snares—many of which he lays, but none more deceitfully than the snares of ambition. Behaving in too stately a manner because of the honor committed to him, he will not escape the slander of evil speakers. They will surmise that he converted to the Christian religion for this

reason: that whereas he was of low estate among his previous companions, he might have authority and honor among the Christians. "He left us at just the right time," they will say, "and changed his religion for his own advantage. He would rather be a Christian bishop than live like a private person among us." But the one who for a long season has displayed special tokens of true godliness and soberness in himself shall be saved from this sort of suspicion.

I will not hear this objection, which some bring, saying, "Why should it matter to me if outsiders say bad things about me? It is enough for me to be well thought of by my own people." For me, this is not sufficient respect for a bishop, for his reputation ought to be so pure and clear from all suspicion that it should be a small matter to be well thought of by his own people to whom he is more intimately known. He should also have the testimony of those outside, who cannot see his true godliness as perfectly as it is but only judge whether he appears outwardly evil. So great care must be taken in every way that no occasion for slander be given to those who are strangers from our profession of faith. PARAPHRASES.[19]

THOSE WITH INTEGRITY RECOGNIZED EVEN BY UNBELIEVERS. JOHN CALVIN: "Well thought of by outsiders." . . . This appears to be very difficult, that a religious man should have, as witnesses of his integrity, infidels themselves, who are furiously mad to tell lies against us. But the apostle means that, so far as relates to external behavior, even unbelievers themselves shall be constrained to acknowledge him to be a good man; for, although they groundlessly slander all the children of God, yet they cannot pronounce him to be a wicked man who leads a good and inoffensive life among them. Such is that acknowledgment of uprightness which Paul here describes. COMMENTARY ON 1 TIMOTHY.[20]

---

[17]Zell, *Church Mother*, 75*; citing 1 Cor 7:2; 1 Tim 4:3.
[18]CTS 43:83-84 (CO 52:284).

[19]Erasmus, *Paraphrases*, 41.
[20]CTS 43:84 (CO 52:285).

The Virtues Required of Ministers, Especially Discretion.

The Virtues Required of Ministers, Especially Discretion. Friedrich Balduin: It is not to be doubted that a minister of the word should shine with as many stars of virtue as is possible. For, insofar as they are *anepilēptos*, "without censure," and *typos*, "a type," of the faithful, we should seek all virtues that Scripture asks of the faithful in them. Among these the foremost are devotion, faith, hope, patience, zeal, grace, kindness, gentleness, moderation, and self-control, which Paul calls fruit of the Spirit. Here, however, we will not consider those that they have in common with many others, but those which are particularly needed by ministers on account of their ministry, without which they will very often dash themselves to pieces. Of these, our Paul enumerates six at 1 Timothy 3:2-3.

The first is discretion. For he desires the overseer to be *nēphalion kai sōphrona*, that is, watchful and sensible, since *sōphrosynē* is discretion [*prudentia*], that is, *sōzousa tēn phronēsin*, "maintaining sense," according to Aristotle's *Ethics*.[†] Formerly they said that discretion was the charioteer of all the virtues, and Aristotle's *Ethics*[‡] taught that all virtues were brought together in discretion. Socrates too said that all the virtues were certain discretions, in that they are directed by discretion, which commands what is to be done, and what is to be avoided. First, Chrysostom[††] judged this virtue to be so needful for the minister of the word that he considered that no one, even if they have given much proof of piety in themselves, was worthy of ministry, unless alongside the greatest degree of holiness, they also abounded in discretion. Brief Foundations for Ministers of the Word.[21]

Pastors Must Meet Paul's Standard.

Pastors Must Meet Paul's Standard. Michael Sattler: We have been united as follows concerning shepherds in the church of God. The shepherd in the church shall be a person according to the rule of Paul, fully and completely, who has a good report of those who are outside the faith. The office of such a person shall be to read and exhort and teach, warn, admonish, or ban in the congregation and properly to preside among the sisters and brothers in prayer and in the breaking of bread, and in all things to take care of the body of Christ, that it may be built up and developed, so that the name of God might be praised and honored through us, and the mouth of the mocker be stopped. Schleitheim Articles.[22]

3:8-13 Qualifications for Deacons

Occasional Preachers Assisting with Practicalities.

Occasional Preachers Assisting with Practicalities. Martin Luther: Deacons were men who also preached occasionally. We read in Acts 6:1-6 that they chose seven men in the church to be in charge of providing for the poor and the widows. Those deacons also at times preached, as did Stephen, and they were admitted to other duties of the church, although their principal responsibility was to care for the poor and the widows. That custom has long ceased to exist. . . . There ought to be deacons for the church—men who should be of service to the bishop and at his recommendations have control in the church in external matters. "Serious" is honorable. That is, let them walk in seemly clothes and behavior. Let them use seemly language and act the same way. Let everything about them be honorable, because this befits the propriety of their persons. Lectures on 1 Timothy.[23]

Deacons Take Charge of Alms.

Deacons Take Charge of Alms. Martin Bucer: The office of the deacons is the providing of alms. What this office and ministry was and should still be is this: to take faithful charge, both at home and on the move, of what Christians bring and offer for the care of the poor at their assemblies on Sundays and at other times, and also what particular people, whether of high or

---

[21]Balduin, *Brevis Institutio Ministrorum Verbi*, 264-65; citing Gal 5:23. [†]Aristotle, *Ethics* 3.10. [‡]Aristotle, *Ethics* 6.3. [††]John Chrysostom, *De sacerdotali dignitate* 15.

[22]CRR 1:38-39.
[23]LW 28:295-96 (WA 26:59).

low standing, give to the church for this work of God; and to distribute it to all the needy in the congregation, both local people and visitors, according to the general rule of the church and also the particular instructions of the elders and especially of the chief pastor, namely, the bishop. This is because the bishop, as the chief overseer of all need in the church, and the elders as his fellow overseers, are aware of the daily occurring need of Christians, strangers and local alike, and observe the help that can be given to them according to the church's resources. And these ministers of the church have always kept faithful account of the income and expenditure of the church's assets, as can be clearly seen from the ancient holy fathers and the church law or canons. CONCERNING THE TRUE CARE OF SOULS.[24]

GOSPEL ORDER DEMANDS THE CARE OF THE POOR.

JOHN CALVIN: It is certain that God wants this rule to be observed and kept in his church, that is to say, that the poor be cared for. And not only that every private person on their own behalf by themselves should help those who are poor, but that there should be a public office, and people appointed to have care of those who are in need, that things may be ordered as they ought. And if it is not so, it is certain that we cannot boast that we have a church well ordered according to the doctrine of the gospel, but only so much confusion. SERMONS ON 1 TIMOTHY.[25]

COMFORTING PEOPLE WITH DIVINE REVELATION.

DUTCH ANNOTATIONS: Deacons must be those holding (Gk., "having," that is, preserving or keeping) the mystery of the faith, that is, the doctrine or the profession of the doctrine of the gospel, which is everywhere called a mystery because it was made known to us not by nature but by divine revelation.... For though the office of deacons was not to teach publicly in the assemblies, nevertheless their office involved them conversing

with many sorts of people, whom they ought also to instruct and comfort, and sometimes also gainsay, as there is an example in Stephen. That Philip instructed and baptized the Ethiopian was done by an extraordinary call, when he was now made an evangelist. DUTCH ANNOTATIONS.[26]

THE ROLE OF THE DEACON.

THE ORDINAL: It appertains to the office of a deacon to assist the priest in divine service, and especially when he ministers the holy Communion, and help him in the distribution thereof, and to read holy Scriptures and homilies in the congregation, and instruct the youth in the catechism, and also to baptize and preach if he be commanded by the bishop. And furthermore, it is his office to search for the sick, poor, and impotent people of the parish and to intimate their estates, names, and places where they dwell to the curate, that by his exhortation they may be relieved by the parish or other convenient alms. THE ORDINAL (1549).[27]

DEACONS MUST BE TESTED FOR STABILITY OF CHARACTER AND HONESTY.

PETRUS STEVARTIUS: "Moreover, these men also should first be tested, and thus let them serve if they have no charge against them." Before anyone is promoted to the rank of deacon or other ministry in the church, the apostle requires that the leaders in the church conduct a thorough review of his previous life and morals. This is done lest perhaps it reveal a previous accusation against the same man. For this the man called to public service, not without loss of reputation and disadvantage to the public welfare, should be punished. Therefore, before they are admitted to this rank of honor, the apostle wants the same to have been tested, namely, for the consistency and stability of their character and honesty. He wants those men to whom responsibility for testing belongs to make a trial of these candidates. COMMENTARY ON 1 TIMOTHY.[28]

---

[24]Bucer, *Concerning the True Care of Souls*, 30-31.
[25]CO 53:293.

[26]Haak, *Annotations*, s.v.*; citing Acts 7:1-60; Acts 8:29; 21:8.
[27]*Forme and Maner, Making of Deacons*.
[28]Stevartius, *Commentarius*, 260.

DEACONS AND THEIR WIVES. SEBASTIAN SCHMIDT: Let me now turn from their bishops to their deacons: Deacons should be similarly disposed toward seriousness, not double-tongued, not given to much wine, and not desirous of dishonourable gain. "Holding the mystery of the faith with a pure conscience." For they should be those who should take the place of their bishops in respect of their service of teaching from time to time. And lest neither the church nor you be deceived headlong in this matter, first they are tested; then, if they are found to be upright, blameless and capable for the service of the diaconate, at that point they should be received into the order, so that, in their capacity as those belonging to the order, they be in a position to dispense their office, in the hope that they perform their office faithfully.

Similarly their wives, serving as they do in the temple or in the assembly of the church, not in word, but rather in toil for the provision of the church and of the divine service, or in service of the saints, should also be serious in their behavior and in the morals, not slanderers of other people. They should be temperate and faithful in all things that are entrusted to them.

In addition, I advise this too, that deacons should be the husbands of one wife in total, and not more, that they may also lead their children, if they have any, and their families well and with devotion. For those who by this reasoning in the aforementioned domains discharge the diaconate well, gain for themselves good station in the church, so that they can also move on to the episcopate. They have great confidence in speaking about the faith, both in the presence of the faithful and outsiders, for they know that they cannot be reproached for any evil or scandal. PARAPHRASE OF 1 TIMOTHY.[29]

PRAYER FOR DEACONS. THE ORDINAL: Almighty God, giver of all good things, which of thy great goodness hast vouchsafed to accept and take these thy servants unto the office of deacons in thy church: make them, we beseech thee O Lord, to be modest, humble, and constant in their ministration, and to have a ready will to observe all spiritual discipline, that they having always the testimony of a good conscience, and continuing ever stable and strong in thy Son Christ, may so well behave themselves in this inferior office,[†] that they may be found worthy to be called unto the higher ministries in thy church: through the same thy Son our Savior Christ, to whom be glory, and honor, world without end. Amen. THE ORDINAL (1549).[30]

THE OFFICE OF DEACONS IS TO ASSIST THE PRIESTS. PETRUS STEVARTIUS: All the ancient fathers have handed down to us that the office of deacon consists in assisting the priests and serving in all things that are done, in sacraments of course, in baptism, in chrisms, in the patina and chalice. Likewise they serve also in carrying oblations and placing them on the altar, in setting up the table of the Lord, reading the gospel publicly in church, and so on. It was also formerly permissible to entrust to deacons activities that properly belong to bishops and to priests for their administration according to their own duties, that is, both the procurement and the distribution of alms and of the common possessions of the church. COMMENTARY ON 1 TIMOTHY.[31]

ALL MINISTERS MUST BE WELL TESTED. MARTIN BUCER: This is why the apostle states concerning deacons something that is also to be diligently observed in the case of all ministers: "They must first be tested; and then if there is nothing against them, let them serve." It is shown by the fact that he does not wish a novice to be chosen, who is not yet sufficiently well known. In addition the ancients did not allow a bishop to be chosen from another church when there was a suitable person to be found in that church who

---

[29]Schmidt, *Paraphrasi*, 902.

[30]*Forme and Maner, Making of Deacons**. [†]1549: "use themselves." 1662: "behave themselves."
[31]Stevartius, *Commentarius*, 252.

could be appointed as bishop. Similarly, that no one should be elected to the higher ministry of the church who had not previously been experienced and proved in all the other orders of ministry.

All this shows what great diligence the churches, after they have faithfully prayed to the Lord for his guidance, are to exercise, how seriously they are to inquire, investigate and find out about everything, so that they are not deceived by false appearances and may discern and discover the true guidance of the Holy Spirit as to those whom they are to call and appoint to this ministry. Concerning the True Care of Souls.[32]

An Honorable Foundation for a Higher Degree. David Dickson: Lest anyone should despise the deaconship as a mean office, Paul teaches that they who have well discharged this office are worthy of honor while they manage it, and lay a foundation to a higher degree in the church.[†] They finally gain a large opportunity for the confirming of their boldness toward God, by faith in Christ, which the faithful administration of their deaconship (as a testimony of the sincerity of their faith) ought to confirm. Exposition of All Paul's Epistles.[33]

The Diaconate Is Not Just the Nursery for Presbyters. John Calvin: It is certain that the apostle speaks of those who hold a public office in the church; and this refutes the opinion of those who think that domestic servants are

here meant. As to the view given by others, that it denotes presbyters who are inferior to the bishop, that is without foundation; for it is manifest from other passages that the term bishop belongs alike to all presbyters. All are constrained to acknowledge this; and more especially a passage in the first chapter of the epistle to Titus proves clearly that this is the meaning. It remains to be stated that we understand "the deacons" to be those who are mentioned by Luke and who had the charge of the poor.[†]

. . . Owing to a practice that came into use one or two centuries after the death of the apostles, of choosing presbyters from the order of deacons, this passage has been commonly interpreted as describing elevation to a higher rank, as if the apostle called to the honor of being presbyters those who had faithfully discharged the office of a deacon. For my own part, though I do not deny that the order of deacons might sometimes be the nursery out of which presbyters were taken, yet I take Paul's words as meaning, more simply, that they who have discharged this ministry in a proper manner are worthy of no small honor; because it is not a mean employment, but a highly honorable office. Now by this expression he intimates how much it is for the advantage of the church to have this office discharged by choice men; because the holy discharge of it procures esteem and reverence. . . . Yet not a single deacon has been made, during the last five hundred years, except that, after taking this step, he may immediately rise to the priesthood. Commentary on 1 Timothy.[34]

---

[32]Bucer, *Concerning the True Care of Souls*, 62.
[33]Dickson, *Exposition*, 163*. [†]Trapp, *Commentary*, 307, also adds here that the good standing or "good degree" gained is "a fair step to a higher order, i.e., to a bishopric or presbytership."

[34]CTS 43: 85, 87-88 (CO 52:285-87); citing Titus 1:7; Acts 6:3. [†]See also Calvin, *Institutes*, 4.3.9, for his fuller account of the duties of deacons.

3:14-16 THE MYSTERY OF GODLINESS

¹⁴I hope to come to you soon, but I am writing these things to you so that, ¹⁵if I delay, you may know how one ought to behave in the household of God, which is the church of the living God, a pillar and buttress of the truth. ¹⁶Great indeed, we confess, is the mystery of godliness:

Heᵃ was manifested in the flesh,
vindicatedᵇ by the Spirit,ᶜ
seen by angels,
proclaimed among the nations,
believed on in the world,
taken up in glory.

a Greek *Who*; some manuscripts *God*; others *Which* b Or *justified* c Or *vindicated in spirit*

OVERVIEW: Throughout their expositions of this passage, our early modern commentators discuss the meaning of Paul's reference to the church as the "pillar and buttress of the truth." Catholic authors understand this to mean that the Roman Church is the infallible interpreter of Scripture, while Protestant exegetes take it to refer to the church more generally as the place where revealed truth is preserved. The commentators also discuss at length the truth of the incarnation and its myriad implications.

3:14-15 *The Dignity of the Church*

TIMOTHY ENCOURAGED BY THE DIGNITY OF THE CHURCH. RICHARD SIBBES: There are two things that God values more than all the world—the church and the truth. The church, that is the "pillar and ground of truth," as mentioned in the previous verse. The truth of religion is the seed of the church. Now the blessed apostle St. Paul prepares his student Timothy for the ministerial office on two grounds: the dignity of the church that he was to instruct, and the excellent mysteries of the gospel, that excellent soul-saving truth. He therefore seriously exhorts Timothy to take heed as to how he behaves in the church of God while teaching the truth of God. The church of God is the "household of God," a company of people that God cares for more than all humankind for whom the world stands, and for whom all things are. THE FOUNTAIN OPENED.[1]

THE CHURCH AS WITNESS TO THE TRUTH. JACOBUS ARMINIUS: The church is indeed the pillar of the truth, but it is built on that truth as on a foundation, and thus directs to the truth, and brings it forward into the sight of human beings. In this way the church performs the part of a director and a witness to this truth, and its guardian, herald, and interpreter. But in her acts of interpretation, the church is confined to the sense of the word itself, and is tied down to the expressions of Scripture: for, according to the prohibition of St. Paul, it neither becomes her to be wise "above that which is written," nor is it possible for her to be so, since she is hindered both by her own imbecility, and the depth of things divine. ORATION ON THE CERTAINTY OF SACRED THEOLOGY.[2]

A FIRM PILLAR OF THE TRUTH IN CHRIST. HEINRICH BULLINGER: But the church is the pillar and ground of truth, because being established on the foundation of the prophets and apostles— Christ himself, who is the everlasting truth of God and the only strength of the church—it receives this by the fellowship that it has with him, that she also might be the pillar and foundation of the truth. For the truth of God is in the church, and it is spread abroad through the ministry of the church. And although it is assaulted and warred against by its enemies, it stands firm and is not overcome, in

---

[1] Sibbes, *Works*, 5:459*.

[2] Arminius, *Writings*, 1:138-39; citing 1 Cor 4:6.

that being made one body with Christ, she perseveres in the fellowship of Christ, without whom she can do nothing. Decades.[3]

Using the Word of God. Peter Martyr Vermigli: The church is for no other cause said to be the pillar and ground of truth, but because it has the Word of God, and uses the same perpetually in her opinions and definitions. When it does not do that, it is not operating as the church of Christ should do. Commonplaces.[4]

Rome Is Not an Infallible Interpreter of Truth. John Preston: They say it belongs to the Church of Rome to declare what books of Scripture are canonical, what translation is authentic, what interpretation must be the sense of Scripture, and in effect they will be only judged by themselves. And whatsoever we say, they choke us with these principles: theirs is the only church, and the church can never err.[†] Now of all places of Scripture whereby they would vindicate to themselves this privilege, this verse . . . is one of the chiefest. But how justly, we are now to consider.

Says the apostle to Timothy, "I am writing these things to you so that you may know how one ought to behave in the household of God," as if he should say, "It is of much moment that the house of God be ordered and kept aright, be swept continually and purged, because it is the 'pillar and ground of truth,' that is, the ground and place where truth (which is the household's food) is nourished and grows, into which if falsehood creep their food will soon be poisoned and so not nourish but corrupt, nor fit them to salvation but destruction." . . .

The papists indeed say that the church is so the pillar and ground of truth that there is no truth but what comes from the church, and that whatsoever comes from the church is true infallibly and not subject to error. But this cannot be the apostle's meaning here. . . . By "truth" here is meant divine and sacred truth, a plant of God's own garden, not

growing in the wilderness and waste. As some truths may be found without the church, so some errors may be found within the church. . . .

Again, when he says, "the church is the pillar and ground of truth," his meaning is that in the church of God the truth ought always to be preserved and kept; that is, those that profess themselves to be the church ought to maintain the truth; that it is their duty, which they are bound at all times to perform. . . .

Last, it is to be marked that the apostle says in general terms, "The church is the pillar and ground of truth," not this or that particular people—of Ephesus, or Corinth, or Rome, or any other city of country . . . the apostle in this place speaks of a pillar . . . on which tables and proclamations and such things were wont to hang; and from such pillars such things may soon be separated. Such a pillar was this people of Ephesus, which stood long after the truth was taken down and Islam hanged up instead of it. . . . The church is the ground of truth as the garden is the ground of herbs, which we know may be plucked up and planted in another place. The Pillar and Ground of Truth.[5]

The Excellency of the Church. David Dickson: This verse contains the doctrine touching the excellency of the church. (1) That it is the "house of God," wherein he dwells, and feeds his family, and wherein he is worshiped. (2) That it is the church of the living God, or a company called out of the world by the living God, besides whom all the gods which the heathens worship are dead idols. (3) That as the church is called out of the world, begotten, nourished, and preserved of God by the truth, that it should be the church of the living God; so the truth is sustained as with a

---

[3]Bullinger, *Decades*, 833*; citing Eph 2:20.
[4]Vermigli, *Commonplaces*, 1:40*.

[5]Preston, *Sermons Preached Before His Majesty*, 3-7*. [†]Luther's opponent Johannes Eck quotes this verse and asks if the church is the pillar of the truth "How then can it err?" See his *Enchiridion of Commonplaces Against Luther and Other Enemies of the Church*, trans. Ford Lewis Battles (Grand Rapids: Baker, 1979), 9. Similarly, Cardinal Bellarmine cites this verse in his argument that the visible church cannot defect. See Bellarmine, *De Controversiis Fidei Christiani: De Ecclesia Militante* (Ingolstadt: David Satori, 1588), chap. 13.

pillar, and certain buttress, by the church. Because the church preserves the truth as it were in a treasury: in the church only, divine truth is held forth to the world and there has its seat and abiding. And the church alone it is, that by her ministers takes care that this truth be everywhere preached, proclaimed, and communicated, and defends it against all adversaries, and that with weapons properly appertaining to the truth. EXPOSITION OF ALL PAUL'S EPISTLES.[6]

A SPUR TO MINISTERIAL INDUSTRY. JOHN CALVIN: We ought to see why Paul adorns the church with so magnificent a title. By holding out to pastors the greatness of the office, he undoubtedly intended to remind them with what fidelity, and industry, and reverence they ought to discharge it. How dreadful is the vengeance that awaits them, if, through their fault, that truth which is the image of the divine glory, the light of the world, and the salvation of humankind, shall be allowed to fall! This consideration ought undoubtedly to lead pastors to tremble continually, not to deprive them of all energy, but to excite them to greater vigilance. COMMENTARY ON 1 TIMOTHY.[7]

3:16 The Mystery of Godliness

THE INCARNATION IS THE MARROW OF THE GOSPEL. RICHARD SIBBES: We cannot too often meditate on these things. It is the life and soul of a Christian. It is the marrow of the gospel. It is the wonder of wonders. We need not wonder at anything after this. It is no wonder that our bodies shall rise again; that mortals should become afterward immortal in heaven, since the immortal God has taken human nature and died in it. All the articles of our faith and all miracles yield to this grand thing: "God manifest in the flesh."[†] Believe this, and believe all other. Therefore, let us often have these sweet cherishing notions of God in our flesh, that it may strengthen, and feed, and nourish

our faith, especially in the time of temptation. THE FOUNTAIN OPENED.[8]

THE GOSPEL SHOULD MOTIVATE TIMOTHY'S GODLY LEADERSHIP. PETER MOFFETT: The point of the apostle Paul in this most precious sentence is to move Timothy to behave himself very religiously and reverently in the church of God. . . . He makes a similar argument for the same reason and purpose in the previous sentence, which makes this point: seeing that the house or church of God in which you are a minister is not a synagogue of error or a temple of types and figures, but a real pillar of truth, you are, as a pastor of the Christian flock, to walk very orderly, religiously, and righteously in all respects. Another reason implying the same purpose is stated in this conclusion of the chapter, which is a summary: Just as the gospel is a most excellent mystery, it behooves you, a steward of secrets, to show all wisdom and faithfulness in the course of your conduct and the discharge of your ministry. . . .

For the purpose therefore that all the faithful may in all times and places, and among all people, know which is the Lord's camp, go to it, and remain it—the apostle shows there that it can always be discerned by this banner or emblem of the mystery of the gospel. Those congregations then are undoubtedly the true churches of God, which firmly hold the articles of faith, and soundly acknowledge Christ Jesus to be the Son of God and the only foundation of salvation, even if in other respects they may be far from spotless perfection. . . .

The third point in this commendation of the gospel by us to be observed, is, that it is a mystery. This word in the Greek tongue signifies a secret or a hidden matter. It is also usually applied to note out those precepts and things that are sacred and chiefly to be regarded. But although the gospel is here termed a mystery, yet the apostle's meaning is

---

[6]Dickson, *Exposition*, 163.
[7]CTS 43:90 (CO 52:288).

[8]Sibbes, *Works*, 5:485*. [†]The Textus Receptus reads *theos*, "God," but the more likely original reading is the relative pronoun *hos*, "who." See Bruce M. Metzger, *A Textual Commentary on the Greek New Testament*, 2nd ed. (Stuttgart: Deutsche Bibelgesellschaft, 1994), 573-74.

not that it is such a secret as ought not to be communicated to the common multitude. For the Lord, enjoining his disciples to teach all nations, and to preach the gospel unto every creature—whether male or female, learned or unlearned, young or old—in them wills and warrants all his ministers to impart this doctrine to all sorts of people. Neither is the doctrine of the New Testament in any such sort here termed a mystery as if it were after a more dark manner set down and delivered unto us than the book of the law or the old covenant. For as one says very well, the Old Testament is the New enclosed in obscurity, and the New is the Old unfolded in the light. The Excellency of the Mystery of Christ Jesus.[9]

The Double Justification of Christ. Richard Sibbes: He was "justified" in a double regard.

1. "In regard of God," he was justified and cleared from our sins that he took upon himself. He "bore our sins upon the tree," and bore them away that they should never appear again to our discomfort. He was made "a curse for us." How came Christ to be cleared of our sins that lay upon him? When by the Spirit, by his divine nature, he raised himself from the dead. So he was "justified" from that that God laid on him, for he was our surety. Now the Spirit raising him from the dead showed that the debt was fully discharged, because our surety was out of prison. All things are first in Christ and then in us. He was acquitted and justified from our sins, and then we.

2. And then he was justified by the Spirit "from all the imputations of people, from the faulty notions that the world had of him." They thought him to be a mere man, or a sinful man. No. He was more than a mere man; nay, more than a holy man; he was God-man. . . . In those excellent miracles he was "justified," and declared to be the Son of God, especially in his resurrection and ascension, and

daily converting of souls by his ministry; all being done by the Spirit, which is his vicar in the world, ruling his church and subduing his enemies. So that he was every way "justified in the Spirit" to be God, to be true Messiah prophesied of and promised to the church. The Fountain Opened.[10]

The Fundamental Doctrines of the Gospel. David Dickson: The fundamental doctrines that are comprehended in this verse, and that are necessary to be acknowledged with the unanimous consent of all true Christians, are seven:

1. The sum of the gospel is the mystery of godliness, and that indeed is great. The gospel is called a mystery because it is hid from natural reason, nor can it ever be understood by anyone without divine manifestation and supernatural revelation. . . . And that we may understand the word of God, we must beg the illumination of the Spirit. It is called the mystery of godliness because it has for its end Christian piety, which consists in faith and obedience to the commands of Christ, or in faith which works by love. . . .

2. The second fundamental doctrine is this: in the person of Christ, God was manifested in the flesh. . . . In the human nature, even mortal and frail, but free from sin, he showed forth himself the true Immanuel, and God with us. And here the two natures are pointed out, the divine, which assumed, and the human, which was assumed. And the whole debasement of Christ in the flesh is herein contained.

3. "Vindicated by the Spirit . . ." Christ by his divine power (which showed itself forth in his doctrine and life, also in his miracles, especially in his glorious resurrection from the dead) was not only just and true, but also abundantly declared the only begotten Son of God and the supreme prophet of the church, and king and priest eternal; and acquitted from all the calumnies and reproaches of the Jews, and all his enemies.

4. "Seen by angels . . ." He was acknowledged by the angels, and by the clearer manifestation of his

---

[9]Moffett, *The Excellencie of the Mysterie of Christ Jesus*, 1, 3, 10-11*. He appears at the end to be alluding to the famous saying of Augustine: *In Vetere Novum lateat, et in Novo Vetus pateat*, "In the Old the New is concealed, and in the New the Old is revealed," from *Quaestionum in Pentateuchum* 2.73 (on Ex 20:19) in PL 34:623.

[10]Sibbes, *Works*, 5:489*.

majesty and also of the divine will, Christ (God incarnate) was more apparently seen. And therefore the angels are made use of by God as fit witnesses of the conception, birth, suffering, and resurrection of Christ, who hitherto admire this mystery, amazed with the excellency of the matter, desire to look further into it, stooping down to behold things that are revealed to the church by the Spirit. For touching the manner of our redemption, it was thought meet to conceal it from the angels for a time, that the goodness of God might be the more admired.

5. "Proclaimed among the nations . . ." It is a wonderful thing that the Gentiles (who as yet wandered in the blindness of their minds) should have the revelation of the Son of God; which doctrine was at first concealed from the apostles themselves, as also the angels of heaven.

6. "Believed on in the world . . ." It is no small part of this mystery that the efficacy of the gospel should be such in the world (which lies in evil and is contrary to God) by the labor of lowly humans and no ways garnished with human splendor, when all passages were stopped and locked up, the faith of Christ conquering all difficulties, should be entertained and gain the victory after an incredible manner, so that the name of Christ is believed in, and acknowledged in the world, whichever way the preaching of the gospel spreads itself.

7. "Taken up in glory . . ." The mystery is great and worthy of admiration, that Christ, who in the infirmity of the flesh, in the most abject condition of a servant, lay hid so many years in the world, and at length crucified, seeming to end his life most miserably, yet notwithstanding should be received up into glory. From whence sending the Holy Ghost, and giving gifts to human beings, to this very day he manifests the glory of his deity,

showing what power he has in heaven and earth, that all things are put under his feet. These are the doctrines that he wills the churches to hold fast. EXPOSITION OF ALL PAUL'S EPISTLES.[11]

FROM CONCEPTION TO ASCENSION THE ANGELS SAW HIM. RICHARD SIBBES: The angels knew of Christ's coming in the flesh before it was, for what the church knew the angels knew in some measure. When God made the promise of the promised seed, the angels knew of it. . . . They knew of the incarnation of Christ before. You know the angel brought the news of it beforehand to the Virgin Mary. The angels attended on Christ from his very infancy. The angels ministered to him in his temptation. Before his death they comforted him in the garden. . . . Then they saw when he was buried; they "rolled away the stone." . . . Then when he rose there were angels, one at the head and another at the feet; and they told Mary that he was risen. And then at his ascension the angels told the disciples that Christ should come again. You have the story of it at large in the Gospel, how from the annunciation of his conception to his ascension they saw him, and attended on him, and witnessed of him. THE FOUNTAIN OPENED.[12]

A BRIEF HISTORY OF REDEMPTION. DIRK PHILIPS: In summary, God is revealed in the flesh, and has allowed himself to be seen on earth, the Lord God Sabaoth has come from his holy place in order to redeem Zion and has his dwelling with her. CONCERNING THE TRUE KNOWLEDGE OF JESUS CHRIST.[13]

---

[11]Dickson, *Exposition*, 164*; citing 1 Pet 1:12; Eph 3:10.
[12]Sibbes, *Works*, 5:496-97*; citing Mt 4:11; Lk 22:43; Mt 28:2.
[13]CRR 6:161*; citing Bar 3:37; Zech 2:10.

4:1-5 SOME WILL DEPART FROM THE FAITH

Now the Spirit expressly says that in later times some will depart from the faith by devoting themselves to deceitful spirits and teachings of demons, ²through the insincerity of liars whose consciences are seared, ³who forbid marriage and require abstinence from foods that God created to be received with thanksgiving by those who believe and know the truth. ⁴For everything created by God is good, and nothing is to be rejected if it is received with thanksgiving, ⁵for it is made holy by the word of God and prayer.

Overview: While commenting on this passage, many early modern authors draw parallels between the heresies that Paul condemns and contemporary practices imposed by the Roman Church on its adherents. Principal among these practices are clerical celibacy and the prohibition of certain foods on prescribed feast days. In their view, by imposing such rules, the Roman Church continues ancient heresies that had been condemned. Throughout their discussions, these commentators generally respond to these regulations by affirming the goodness of marriage, food, and so on as God's gifts to be received with thanksgiving and used wisely.

4:1-3 Seared Consciences Forbid Marriage and Meats

Binding Consciences Is Godless Teaching. Philipp Melanchthon: First, ministers are bishops, not rulers or magistrates. Second, bishops do not have the right to establish laws, since they have been commanded to preach only the Word of God, not the word of human beings. . . . If they have issued anything outside of Scripture so as to bind consciences, they should not be heard. For nothing obligates the conscience except God's law [*ius divinum*]. Paul was speaking of this in 1 Timothy 4, where he calls the law of celibacy and the banning of certain foods "doctrines of demons." Although they may not seem contrary to Scripture and although they are not of themselves evil (for neither celibacy nor abstaining from meat is evil), still they are godless if you think that you are sinning by doing differently. Those who think that a person sins if they do not observe the canonical hours or eat meat on the sixth or seventh day, and so on, are teaching godless things. For a bishop cannot bind the Christian conscience. Commonplaces.[1]

Prophecy of Apostasy and Seared Consciences. English Annotations: The Spirit speaks expressly in the Scriptures concerning apostasy from the faith in general, and seduction by false teachers. . . . But he also speaks through me, Paul, by special revelation, that the false prophets shall broach such false and damnable doctrines in particular as are afterward mentioned. By "seducing spirits" he either means devils, who are lying spirits, or wicked and ungodly people, who are the devil's instruments to spread errors and heresies, as the word is taken to mean in 1 John 4:1.

Their consciences are seared as with a hot iron. This means either branded consciences, or stigmatized with the marks of many foul and enormous crimes; a metaphor taken from rogues who are burnt in the hand or some other part of the body. Or it means consciences so insensible of their own dangerous estate, and of the fearful judgments of God, like dead and hard flesh seared with a hot iron whereby physicians consume rotten flesh to save the sounder parts. English Annotations.[2]

---

[1] Melanchthon, *Commonplaces*, 188.
[2] Downame, ed., *Annotations*, s.v.*; citing Mt 24:23-24; Lk 18:8.

The Causes of Apostasy. David Dickson: As to what concerns the prophecy of the future apostasy from the faith or sound doctrine of the gospel, he premises four things. The first concerns the certainty of the defection, because the Holy Spirit not obscurely or darkly but expressly forewarned them of this apostasy, and foretold them of the times immediately following when the defection from the faith should begin and should prevail in the visible church.

The second point contains three causes of their defection: (1) Deceiving spirits, that is, devils, authors of all kinds of errors, and impostures. (2) False teachers who taught and propagated by the inspiration of the devil, false doctrines or doctrines of devils, invented by him in the church. (3) Attention, hearkening to and—miserable people—giving credit to those teachers and devils.

In the third place, he describes those diabolical teachers or instruments of the devil by whom the devils bring in those false doctrines into the church. They have two properties: (1) There shall be hypocrites, counterfeiting themselves lovers of the truth in all things, even when they obtrude their false opinions on the church. They shall dissemble holiness and sanctity, while they cry up their fictions as the worship of God. (2) They shall have consciences seared with a hot iron, because they shall speak and do many things against the dictates of conscience, nor shall they be affected with any sorrow after they have offended God and destroyed the souls of people by their sacrileges, heinous wickednesses, and false doctrines.

In the fourth place, he propounds two examples of these diabolical doctrines in things indifferent, by which doctrines, as by certain marks, we may know those diabolical teachers with their apostate followers. The first is forbidding to marry; and it matters not what authors this error has besides the devil; it has the pope's patronage, with whom it has for a long time been favored and still is, since all their clergy are enjoined to singleness of life. Another doctrine of devils is about the choice of meats, and abstaining from some as impure, which error among the Romanists is urged, observed, and defended with more religion than most exercises of piety and justice prescribed by God. Exposition of All Paul's Epistles.[3]

The Evil Origin of Clerical Celibacy. Huldrych Zwingli: We have been so on fire from passion—with shame be it said!—that we have done many unseemly things, yet whether this should not be laid on those to some extent who have forbidden marriage we refrain from saying now....

Here we would have those prick up their ears who make a fine show of chastity and keep it ill; for what they do secretly is wicked even to think of. The Spirit speaking in Paul says that in the latter days, in which we are no doubt also included, it shall come to pass that some will turn away from the faith to their own works that are not of God. Also that this shall happen at the instigation of evil spirits who shall speak things good in appearance only, and shall commend them especially by the mouths of those who go about in sheep's clothing raging like wolves, and therefore they have ever been singed in their own eyes and condemned by their own judgment. And they shall forbid marriage. Behold, Most Reverend Father, the origin of their feigned chastity!

... For the sake of Christ the Lord of all of us, therefore, by the liberty won by his blood, by the fatherly affection that you owe to us, by your pity of our feeble souls, by the wounds of our consciences, by all that is divine and all that is human, we beseech you mercifully to regard our petition and to grant that which was thoughtlessly built up be thoughtfully torn down, lest the pile constructed not in accordance with the will of our heavenly Father fall some time with a far more destructive crash. Petition of Certain Preachers.[4]

Catholics Do Not Forbid Marriage or Certain Foods to Everyone. Petrus Stevartius: Although I have now thoroughly explained what are the heresies and sects that the

---

[3]Dickson, *Exposition*, 164-65*.
[4]Jackson, ed., *Selected Works*, 34-37.

apostle, with the Holy Spirit's guidance, condemns in this passage, the innovators of our time, the Lutherans, abuse these words of the apostle as an insult to Catholic truth. Catholic truth prefers celibacy to marriage and praises abstinence from foods. For the Catholic Church does not, as the Lutherans imagine, forbid legitimate marriage and the undefiled bed. For it knows that these are honorable according to the Word of God, and in keeping with the apostolic injunction regularly urges toward such those to whom it is permitted, if they cannot remain chaste. More than that, in the apostolic constitutions elders are warned to take care to contract marriages readily when they are young men, in order to circumvent the snares of youthful lust. COMMENTARY ON 1 TIMOTHY.[5]

THE REASON SOME FOODS WERE PROHIBITED BY HERETICS. FRANÇOIS CARRIÈRE: "Abstaining from the foods which God created is the teaching of demons." But Acts 15:29 says, "It seemed good to the Holy Spirit that you abstain from sacrifices of images, and from blood and from what has been strangled." And Mark 1, "John the Baptist came not eating anything but locusts and honey from the forest." I answer that this passage is identifying a sect of heretics that was about to appear, prohibiting marriage, and commanding abstention from unclean foods, like the Jews do, or from foods that were wicked per se, so to speak, and generated by a wicked god. I mean the Simonians, Ebionites, Marcionites, Manichees, and Encratites. They taught abstention from every kind of animal flesh, as though all animals were endowed with a rational or at least immortal soul, and they forbade marriage as though it had been instituted by a wicked god or demon.... Therefore, this passage does not speak at all against the celibacy of priests or of church fastings wherein the eating of flesh and marriage are forbidden. Not as though these practices were in themselves or per se wicked, but they exist only to rein in concupiscence, to practice obedience, penitence, and zeal for prayer, according

to the example of John the Baptist, Christ himself, and the saints of the primitive church. These innovators therefore argue absurdly against Catholics when, from the statement that simply says, "Pontiffs forbid clergy to marry," they conclude that therefore Catholics forbid the marriage that Paul here singles out. Why then does Paul himself in chapter 5 verse 12 condemn union of widows' who marry after taking a vow of chastity? "Because," he says "they have rendered their first faith void." Surely then he does not condemn it in itself? This also applies concerning the decree of the church with respect to those who have freely practiced celibacy. COMMENTARY ON THE WHOLE OF SCRIPTURE.[6]

BE THANKFUL FOR GOD'S GIFTS. OLYMPIA MORATA: Most base, then, for a preacher, who shows others the way but does not know the right way himself. For if a philosopher who sins in his way of life is the more base, in that he fails in the office of which he wishes to be master, surely a preacher is the most base if he tells others how to lead their lives but leads his own life most scandalously. Or is it not a great scandal to drink all the time, to be drunk, to abuse the wonderful gift of God, which was given to us that we might enjoy it with an expression of thanks, not that we might abuse it. LETTER 39 TO A CERTAIN GERMAN PREACHER.[7]

PAUL'S WORDS ARE NOT JUST APPLICABLE TO ANCIENT HERESIES. JOHN CALVIN: To no purpose do the papists point to the ancient heretics, as if they alone were censured here; we must always see if they are not guilty in the same manner. They object that they do not resemble the Encratites and Manichaeans because they do not absolutely forbid the use of marriage and of flesh,[†] but only on certain days constrain to abstinence from flesh, and make the vow of celibacy compulsory on

---

[5]Stevartius, *Commentarius*, 316-17. Cf. 1 Cor 7:36.

[6]Carrière, *Commentarius in Universam Scripturam*, 778; citing Mark 1:4-6.
[7]Morata, *Complete Writings*, 134.

none but monks and priests and nuns. But this excuse also is excessively frivolous; for, first, they nevertheless make holiness to consist in these things; next, they set up a false and spurious worship of God; and last, they bind consciences by a necessity from which they ought to have been free. Commentary on 1 Timothy.[8]

False Teachers Propagate Jewish Falsehoods. Desiderius Erasmus: The Spirit himself, foreknowing things to come, clearly and certainly signifies by those whom he has inspired that in the latter times some shall spring up who shall depart from the sincerity of the faith that the gospel teaches and slide back into a certain Jewishness. They will rest the chief principle of godliness in those things that not only do nothing for our godliness but that in fact often hurt us. And being rebels against the Spirit of Christ, they shall instead take heed of deceiving spirits, and being turned away from the doctrine of the true God they shall give their ears and minds to the doctrine of devils. In outward show of feigned godliness they shall speak things that are absolutely contrary to the truth of the gospel. In the sight of the simple people they will present themselves in an outward appearance of holiness, whereas in the sight of God they have an unclean conscience, defiled and marked and printed with many marks of worldly lusts. Those kinds of people swim inwardly in malicious bitterness, hatred, greed,

ambition, and other diseases that are absolutely repugnant to true godliness.

They shall (after the example of the Essenes) forbid lawful marriage,[†] as if wedlock chastely kept was not honorable before God and the bed undefiled. They want to be esteemed as holy because they live single, unmarried lives, but are nevertheless infected with innumerable pestilential vices. They are free from wives, but not from filthy lusts.

They shall also attempt to draw people back again into making distinctions about meats, after the manner of the Jews, as though meat itself had some impurity in it, whereas God has ordained all kinds of meats that we might use them moderately for the necessary relief of our bodies and to keep up our strength, thanking him for his kindness. Those who have embraced the faith of the gospel in place of Moses' law and have wiped away the mists of Jewish superstitions are brought to the light of truth, knowing that whatever is created by almighty God is of its own nature good if we use it as it ought to be used and to the purpose for which it was created. There is no kind of meat to be abhorred or refused if it is received with thanksgiving as God's bountiful gift. This is a Jewish manner of saying, not a Christian one: "Do not eat this meat! Do not touch this body! Do not wear this garment! Today do not do this thing or that thing." There is nothing impure or unclean if the conscience of the user is pure and clean. Paraphrases.[9]

4:4-5 Everything Created by God Is Good

Using Creation Wisely. Peter Martyr Vermigli: It is our duty to use God's creation wisely and justly, for one another's comfort and

---

[8]CTS 43:102 (CO 52:295). An example of Roman Catholic apologetic here can be seen in Martin, *New Testament*, 574-75, who argues that Paul has in mind certain ancient heretics whose "heresy about marriage was that to marry or to use the act of matrimony, is of Satan . . . and that the distinction of male and female and the creation of man and woman for generation came of an ill God. . . . Is it not now an intolerable impudence of the Protestants, who for a small similitude of words in the ears of the simple, apply this text to the fasts of the Church, and the chastity of Priests and Religious?" [†]The Encratites were a second-century sect of ascetics who proclaimed abstinence from sex and marriage. See Irenaeus, *Against Heresies* 1.28 (ANF 1:353) and Eusebius, *Ecclesiastical History* 4.28-29 (NPNF[2] 1:207-9). The Manichaeans were a dualistic group with both Christian and Gnostic elements; Augustine had been a Manichaean before he was a Christian, and he refutes their basic beliefs in *Against the Epistle of Manichaeus Called Fundamental* (NPNF 4:129-50).

[9]Erasmus, *Paraphrases*, 47-49; citing Heb 13:4; Col 2:20-23. [†]I. Howard Marshall, *The Pastoral Epistles*, International Critical Commentary (London: T&T Clark, 2004), 533, also mentions the Essenes, a Jewish ascetic sect, as one possible background influence at work here, citing Josephus and Philo for evidence of celibacy. Pliny, *Historia naturalis* 5.15 (73), describes the Essenes as *sine ulla femina, omni venere abdicata*, "without any women, renouncing everything to do with Venus," though Josephus, *The Jewish War* 2.18.13 (160) claims that some of them did marry, but only for the sake of posterity (LCL 203:384-85).

benefit, giving praise and thanksgiving to the divine goodness for allowing us to use created things, and for its bounty. As Paul wrote in his first letter to Timothy, God created all good things so that the faithful might enjoy them with due gratitude. None of these things should be rejected as inherently evil. Even if they were to be tainted, they can be sanctified by the Word and prayer. Furthermore, creation not only serves to sustain our earthly existence but also bears strong witness to the perfection, skill, and unique goodness of our blessed Father, a witness not to be despised since it is absolutely true. Commentary on the Apostles' Creed.[10]

Everything God Made Is Good. Matthias Flacius: [Paul] opposes all those doctrines, canonical regulations, and most meritorious observances of demons both affirmatively and negatively by also adding a fourth condition, which is the fourth rule. Affirmatively he says that every creature of God is good, and therefore lawful and useful. Afterward, he states this negatively by rejecting none. The manifest reason [for this] is because the good author produced all good things, and for good use. The condition of good use is also added so that it may be taken up with thanksgiving, and so that also the petition of good things from

God may also be fulfilled by their moderate use. Gloss on 1 Timothy[11]

We Are Lords of the World in Christ. John Calvin: Common sense, indeed, pronounces that the wealth of the world is naturally intended for our use; but since dominion over the world was taken from us in Adam everything that we touch of the gifts of God is defiled by our pollution; and, on the other hand, it is unclean to us, until God graciously comes to our aid and, by ingrafting us into his Son, constitutes us anew to be lords of the world, that we may lawfully use as our own all the wealth with that he supplies us.

Justly, therefore, does Paul connect lawful enjoyment with "the word," by which alone we regain what was lost in Adam; for we must acknowledge God as our Father, that we may be his heirs, and Christ as our Head, that those things that are his may become ours. Hence it ought to be inferred that the use of all the gifts of God is unclean, unless it be accompanied by true knowledge and calling on the name of God; and that it is a beastly way of eating, when we sit down at table without any prayer; and when we have eaten to the full, depart in utter forgetfulness of God. Commentary on 1 Timothy.[12]

---

[10]Donnelly, James, and McLelland, eds., *Peter Martyr Reader*, 10.

[11]Flacius, *Glossa Compendaria*, 1062.
[12]CTS 43:105 (CO 52:297).

4:6-16 A GOOD SERVANT
OF CHRIST JESUS

⁶If you put these things before the brothers,ᵃ you will be a good servant of Christ Jesus, being trained in the words of the faith and of the good doctrine that you have followed. ⁷Have nothing to do with irreverent, silly myths. Rather train yourself for godliness; ⁸for while bodily training is of some value, godliness is of value in every way, as it holds promise for the present life and also for the life to come. ⁹The saying is trustworthy and deserving of full acceptance. ¹⁰For to this end we toil and strive,ᵇ because we have our hope set on the living God, who is the Savior of all people, especially of those who believe.

¹¹Command and teach these things. ¹²Let no one despise you for your youth, but set the believers an example in speech, in conduct, in love, in faith, in purity. ¹³Until I come, devote yourself to the public reading of Scripture, to exhortation, to teaching. ¹⁴Do not neglect the gift you have, which was given you by prophecy when the council of elders laid their hands on you. ¹⁵Practice these things, immerse yourself in them,ᶜ so that all may see your progress. ¹⁶Keep a close watch on yourself and on the teaching. Persist in this, for by so doing you will save both yourself and your hearers.

a Or *brothers and sisters.* In New Testament usage, depending on the context, the plural Greek word *adelphoi* (translated "brothers") may refer either to *brothers* or to *brothers and sisters* b Some manuscripts and *suffer reproach* c Greek *be in them*

OVERVIEW: In commenting on this passage, these Reformation-era authors contend that true holiness is not obtained by either taking monastic vows or undertaking acts of mortification. Moreover, the commentators allege that the pursuit of holiness is not only an individual, but also a communal endeavor. They further speak of God's general preserving of all human beings, both believers and unbelievers. The interpreters also discuss the various ways in which Christ should be understood as the "Savior of all," and they stress the importance of both reading and teaching the Scriptures for the edification of the church. Finally, they emphasize the importance of ordination as the church's means of setting apart those given the responsibility of preaching the Word.

4:6-8 Training in Godliness

PUTTING TOGETHER THE TEACHING OF THIS EPISTLE. MARTIN LUTHER: Verse 6 ties together everything that Paul teaches in this epistle. First, he teaches the fundamentals of redemption. Next

come the orders and ranks of the church, as those of bishops and deacons. Then he speaks of husbands and wives in general. He also teaches us to beware of erring spirits and doctrine, and so on. Now he ties them all together: "If you put forth these instructions, . . . you will be a good minister of Christ," not only a good one but also one who pleases God and has the favor of human beings. LECTURES ON 1 TIMOTHY.[1]

THE THINGS THAT PURIFY THE HEART. ENGLISH ANNOTATIONS: Some hereby understand the exercises of those that strived for prizes, by wrestling, running, or the like; of which the apostle speaks in 1 Corinthians 9:25. But since the apostle is here treating of good works, others do more fitly understand this of external exercises of mortification whereby the body is tamed and kept under; as watching, abstinence from such and such meats, lying hard, and the like; which are otherwise lawful in themselves, and indeed may have

---

[1]LW 28:319 (WA 26:75).

some use,[†] but little in comparison to godliness. . . . They are in no way able to purify the heart. English Annotations.[2]

Holiness Is Not Found in Outward Austerity.
Giovanni Diodati: The "silly myths" here are vain human imaginations, as if our true holiness before God consisted in outward austerity, abstinences, fasts, and so on (which he calls disciplines and exercises of the body). By "godliness" he means all spiritual service to God, which lies in a good conscience. "Bodily training" means all that people do outwardly in devotion or religion. This can do little, seeing all the good that it can do is but to tame the members of the body and their external motions without sanctifying the heart and the inward part of the person, as lively faith and the love and fear of God do. Pious Annotations.[3]

Monastic Vows, Rightly Understood, Can Be Used.
Philipp Melanchthon: Obedience, poverty, and celibacy, provided they are not impure, are nonobligatory forms of discipline. Hence the saints can use them without sinning, as did Bernard, Francis, and other holy people. They used them for their physical advantage, to have more leisure for teaching and other pious duties, not because the works themselves are services that justify or merit eternal life. Finally, they belong to the class of which Paul says, "Bodily training is of little value." It is likely that here and there in the monasteries there are still some good men serving the ministry of the Word who follow these observances without wicked ideas. But the notion that these observances are services because of which we are accounted righteous before God and through which we merit eternal life conflicts with the gospel of the righteousness of faith, which

teaches that for Christ's sake righteousness and eternal life are given to us. Apology of the Augsburg Confession.[4]

Godliness Underrated by the World, but Ultimately Profitable.
Charles Pinner: We need go no further for weapons to slay the madness of atheism, that is, ungodliness of life, which sets godliness at naught and teaches people to mock at it as a thing of nothing. . . . *O tempora, o mores*—O times, O manners, says he who saw the discipline of the city of Rome so weak that Catiline, a seditious villain, could sit and be seen in the senate among them.[†] And we must swallow our grief and say nothing, to see the church of God defiled with thousands of those (sitting almost in the senate and chiefest rooms among us) who not only secretly undermine, but even bid open battle (almost) to the name of godliness. . . . But the vomit of these people is loathsome, and we will leave it. And for the praise and prize of godliness we will come to the proof of that which the apostle has said of it . . . that "godliness is profitable unto all things." . . . For "all things" are contained in this life and in that which is to come. Sermon upon 1 Timothy 4:8.[5]

Godliness Profits a Nation.
John Owen: Wherever the gospel is by any nation owned, received, embraced, it is the blessing, benefit, prosperity, and advantage of that nation. They that love Zion shall prosper. Godliness has the promise of this life, and is profitable unto all things. The reception of the word of truth, and subjection to Christ therein, causing a people to become willing in the day of his power, entitle that people to all the promises that ever God made to his church. They shall be established in righteousness; they shall be far from oppression; and for fear and terror, they shall not draw nigh to them: whosoever contends against such a people shall fall

---

[2]Downame, ed., *Annotations*, s.v.* [†]I. Howard Marshall, *The Pastoral Epistles*, International Critical Commentary (London: T&T Clark, 2004), 552, comments that there is no evidence that the word *gymnasia* can have this meaning. "It is unattested," he says, and, "The asceticism in 4.3 is so thoroughly rejected that even a limited approbation of it here is very unlikely."
[3]Diodati, *Pious Annotations*, 326*; citing 1 Cor 9:27.

[4]Tappert, ed., *Book of Concord*, 272-73.
[5]Pinner, *Sermon upon the Words of Paul the Apostle unto Timothie*, 12-15*. [†]An allusion to Cicero's first oration against Catiline, *In Catilinam* 1.2 (LCL 324:32-33).

thereby. No weapon that is formed against them shall prosper; every tongue that shall rise against them in judgment, they shall condemn. For this is the inheritance of the servants of the Lord. SERMON ON CHRIST'S KINGDOM AND THE MAGISTRATE'S POWER.[6]

4:9-10 *The Savior of All*

GOD DEFENDS AND SUSTAINS EVEN UN-BELIEVERS. JOHN CALVIN: God maintains all creatures, although they are not as precious to him as his children who he has adopted. For this word "Savior" is not taken here in its proper and narrow signification, that is, in respect of everlasting salvation which God promises to his elect, but in the sense of deliverer or defender. So we see that God defends even unbelievers when it says that he makes the sun shine on both the good and the evil, and all are fed by his goodness, and delivered out of many dangers. And thus he is called here a savior of all, not in respect of spiritual salvation of souls, but because he maintains all his creatures. . . . Thus is our Lord a Savior of all, that is to say, because his goodness stretches even to those who are furthest away from him and deserve to have no acquaintance with him but should rather be cut off from among the creatures of God and utterly cast away. And yet we see how God stretches out his grace even this far, for the life that is given to them is a testimony of his goodness. And therefore seeing God has such a great care over those who are strangers to him, what shall we think of ourselves, who are of his household? SERMONS ON 1 TIMOTHY.[7]

GOD CONSERVES BELIEVERS BOTH PHYSI-CALLY AND SPIRITUALLY. ENGLISH ANNOTA-TIONS: God in general not only saves all people, but beasts also. "Savior" here is taken for protector or preserver, because he conserves all people in their natural and temporal being in general. But he is said to be the Savior especially of those who believe because he is the conserver of them in their eternal and spiritual being. He conserves all creatures in their estate, people in their ways and callings, but the faithful in the state of grace. He preserves all creatures from disorder and utter confusion, all people from manifold calamities and miseries, but the faithful from the power of sin and death. ENGLISH ANNOTATIONS.[8]

THE SENSES IN WHICH CHRIST IS THE SAVIOR OF ALL. LIBERT FROIDMONT: Psalm 35:10, "Who is the Savior" (as regards salvation in temporal life so also of eternal life for those to whom it applies) "of all people." So also of carnal and reprobate humankind. But the salvation of those people is carnal and is like the salvation of beasts, as Augustine says in his commentary on Psalm 35. Lord you will save humans and beasts. "And especially of those who believe." This means, of the elect, the portion of the faithful who are more deserving, whom God saves not only by a temporal salvation but by an eternal. Because of this difference in salvation and blessings, God is only said to be mindful of the reprobate as though they were placed far away from him, says Augustine. But he is said to visit the elect, whom he illuminates with the light of his countenance, according to the expression, "Lord, what is man that you are mindful of him?" From this it is obvious, says van Est,[†] that some people wrongly apply this passage of the apostle to approve of their own doctrine of grace sufficient for salvation, which they claim is offered to all. . . . Because he is only speaking about the general goodness of God by which he makes the sun to rise on the good and the evil and bestows very many blessings on all, especially external ones. Yet he does not grant to all of them the particular internal grace that is sufficient for salvation. COMMENTARIES ON THE EPISTLES.[9]

---

[6]Owen, *Works*, 8:390-91; citing Ps 122:6; Is 54:14-15, 17.
[7]CO 53:400-401; citing Mt 5:45.
[8]Downame, ed., *Annotations*, s.v.*; citing Ps 36:6.
[9]Froidmont, *Commentaria*, 374; citing Ps 8:5. [†]Willem Hessels van Est (1542–1613) was a Roman Catholic biblical scholar whose most notable work was a commentary on the Pauline letters.

Some Say Christ Is the Means of Salvation for All. John Mayer: This verse may seem to be on the side of those who think it shall go well with all. But all expositors understand the word "Savior" here used more generally than when it is put for saving the soul. Some indeed interpret it of a Savior in this sense, but then they render this to be the meaning: he is the Savior of all, that is, because he sends the means of salvation, Christ Jesus and the gospel, to all. "Especially of those that believe"—for they have not only the means but also grace through the means actually wrought in their hearts and afterward everlasting life. But others better understand it of saving in this life, and delivering out of deadly and apparent dangers. Commentary on Paul's Epistles.[10]

Christ Came for All Who Have Not Made Themselves Unworthy. Heinrich Bullinger: He confirms what he said, namely, that holiness is useful for all things, inasmuch as it is that which holds promises of present and future life. So what I related he said about holiness is true, devoid of doubt and clearly worthy of being received by all. But that which we inculcate to so great an extent with words, and bandy about as doubtless truth in the presence of all, this very thing we show to be certain in the actual fact in our body and our afflictions. For unless it is most persuasive to me that salvation is only in the one living God, which salvation the merit of Christ has conferred on us, it is certain that I will not with such single-mindedness steadfastly endure the troubles of this life, the prisons, and the various deaths. But now, he says, by esteeming bodily exercise less, by neglecting ceremonies and Jewish shadows, indeed at once rejecting all external things that the world admires, I preach only the holiness of the gospel, teaching that Christ the Lord has come, not for one people, but to save all those who have not made themselves unworthy of this salvation by faithlessness. For this is only grasped by faith, and is expressed in love. "For the sake of this teaching I endure much," says Paul, "yet willingly and readily, thus at the same time testifying that what I teach is true." Clearly the teaching of holiness is so sure that whatever is produced by the exercise of the body by superstitious people will yield to this merit. For these things are sure, indeed doubtless, and for that reason he worthily adds them here. Commentary on All the Apostolic Epistles.[11]

Protector of All Human Life. Peter Martyr Vermigli: But that place, written to Timothy, where God is called the Savior of all, and especially of the faithful, seems to be more difficult. This word *sōtēr*, that is Savior, is to be taken not as though God gives to all people eternal salvation, but that he preserves and defends all people from many evils, which otherwise the devil practices against them. For so great is his rage against humankind that if he were not restrained by God he would destroy all things. He would permit no commonwealth or church, but would bring to naught both goods and all things that pertain to human life. So, therefore, God is the Savior of all people, in that he drives away such great evils from us. But as touching eternal salvation, that is to be understood of the elect only, and therefore it is added "and especially of those who believe."[†] For seeing they are predestined, they above all others attain to this benefit. Commonplaces.[12]

4:11-12 Let No One Despise You

Act Above Your Age. John Calvin: He says this, both in regard to others, and to Timothy

---

[10]Mayer, *Commentary*, 514*.

[11]Bullinger, *Apostolicas Epistolas*, 583.

[12]Vermigli, *Commonplaces*, 3:33*. Aquinas, *Commentary* (Larcher trans.), 301, also understands this verse to speak of a bodily salvation (*salute corporali*) for all, alongside a spiritual salvation that is only for believers. [†]Based on its use elsewhere in the Pastorals, and in papyrus letters, George W. Knight III, *The Pastoral Epistles: A Commentary on the Greek Text*, New International Greek Testament Commentary (Carlisle, UK: Paternoster, 1992), 203-4, thinks it most likely that the Greek word *malista* (translated in the esv as "especially") is better understood as "that is" or "namely." See also in 1 Tim 5:17; 2 Tim 4:13; Titus 1:10.

himself. As to others, he does not wish that the age of Timothy should prevent him from obtaining that reverence which he deserves, provided that, in other respects, he conduct himself as becomes a minister of Christ. And at the same time he instructs Timothy to supply by gravity of demeanor what is wanting in his age. As if he had said, "Take care that, by gravity of demeanor, you procure for yourself so great reverence that your youthful age, which, in other respects lays one open to contempt, may take nothing from your authority." Hence we learn that Timothy was still young, though he held a place of distinguished excellence among many pastors; and that it is a grievous mistake to estimate by the number of years how much is due to a person. . . .

He next informs him what are the true ornaments; not external marks, such as the crosier, the ring, the cloak, and similar trifles, or children's rattles; but soundness of doctrine and holiness of life. When he says, by speech and conversation, the meaning is the same as if he had said, "by words and actions," and therefore by the whole life. COMMENTARY ON 1 TIMOTHY.[13]

4:13 *The Public Reading of Scripture*

SHAME ON THOSE WHO ARE LAZY IN READING SCRIPTURE. HEINRICH BULLINGER: Paul requires of Timothy a diligent reading, that is to say, a continual study, whereby he may more perfectly exhort and teach. But Paul requires this continual study of the Scriptures of one who has been brought up in the knowledge of the Scriptures from infancy, as he writes elsewhere. What great diligence then does the apostle require of those who have neither known the Scriptures from infancy nor obtained such plentiful gifts of the Spirit, as Timothy had? Let them therefore be ashamed of their unskillfulness: let them be ashamed of their leisurely illiteracy and idleness. For as many read nothing at all but continually live idly and, as it were, rot away in idleness: so a number of innumer-

able others are busied in those things that are inappropriate for bishops. DECADES.[14]

EDIFYING GOD'S DEPENDENT PEOPLE. WESTMINSTER DIRECTORY: Reading of the Word in the congregation being part of the public worship of God (wherein we acknowledge out dependence on him and subjection to him), and one means sanctified by him for the edifying of his people, is to be performed by pastors and teachers. However, such as intend the ministry may occasionally both read the word and exercise their gift in preaching in the congregation, if allowed by the Presbytery thereunto.

All the canonical books of the Old and New Testament (but none of those which are commonly called Apocrypha) shall be publicly read in the vulgar tongue, out of the best allowed translation, distinctly, that all may hear and understand. How large a portion shall be read at once is left to the wisdom of the minister. But it is convenient that ordinarily one chapter of each Testament be read at every meeting, and sometimes more where the chapters be short or the coherence of matter requires it. It is requisite that all the canonical books be read over in order, that the people may be better acquainted with the whole body of the Scriptures. And ordinarily, where the reading in either Testament ends on one Lord's day, it is to begin the next.

We commend also the more frequent reading of such Scriptures as he that reads shall think best for edification of his hearers, as the book of Psalms and others. When the minister, who reads, shall judge it necessary to expound any part of what is read, let it not be done until the whole chapter or psalm be ended; and regard is always to be had unto the time, that neither preaching nor other ordinance be strained or rendered tedious. Which rule is to be observed in all other public performances.

Beside public reading of the holy Scriptures, every person who can read is to be exhorted to read the Scriptures privately (and all others that cannot

---

[13]CTS 43:113-14 (CO 52:301-2).

[14]Bullinger, *Decades*, 911*. Cf. *Sermonum Decas Quinta*, 53; citing 2 Tim 3:15.

read, if not disabled by age or otherwise, are likewise to be exhorted to learn to read) and to have a Bible. Westminster Directory. Of Public Reading of the Holy Scriptures.[15]

4:14-15 Do Not Neglect the Gift

A Power to Teach and Exhort. Martin Luther: This is a free gift. What kind of gift this was he does not say, but I think it is a power in doctrine and exhortation. We say that it is a singular gift to interpret Scripture soundly. What another person cannot interpret in Scripture he must do. "The Lord has bestowed on you an outstanding gift, which another person cannot have. See to it that you attend to . . . that you do not let this gift lie idle. After all, it was not given you to waste but to train and enrich the brethren." "Which was given you by prophetic utterance." Here he is treating some ritual. . . . He has this gift because of the laying on of hands. At that time the Holy Spirit used to be given also visibly when they would lay on hands, as in the primitive church, according to Acts. That laying on of hands was nothing else but the receiving and assigning of those things for which some duty was being committed, as in Acts 13. The same thing was applied to Timothy. Lectures on 1 Timothy.[16]

Named by the Spirit, and Ordained, Use Your Gift. John Calvin: The apostle exhorts Timothy to employ for the edification of the church that grace with which he was endued. God does not wish that talents—which he has bestowed on anyone, that they may bring gain—should either be lost, or be hidden in the earth without advantage. To neglect a gift is carelessly to keep it unemployed through slothfulness, so that, having contracted rust, it is worn away without yielding any profit. Let each of us, therefore, consider what gift they possess, that they may diligently apply it to use.

He says that grace was given to him by prophecy. How was this? It was because, as we have already said, the Holy Spirit marked out Timothy by revelation, that he might be admitted into the rank of pastors; for he had not only been chosen by the judgment of men, in the ordinary way, but had previously been named by the Spirit.

"With the laying on of the hands of the presbytery." He says that it was conferred "with the laying on of hands"; by which he means that, along with the ministry, he was also adorned with the necessary gifts. It was the custom and ordinary practice of the apostles to ordain ministers "by the laying on of hands."[†]

They who think that "presbytery" is here used as a collective noun for "the college of presbyters or elders" are, I think, correct in their opinion; although, after weighing the whole matter, I acknowledge that a different meaning is not inapplicable, that is, that presbytery or eldership—is the name of an office. He put the ceremony for the very act of ordination; and therefore the meaning is that Timothy—having been called to the ministry by the voice of the prophets, and having afterward been solemnly ordained—was, at the same time, endued with the grace of the Holy Spirit for the discharge of his office. Hence we infer that it was not a useless ceremony, because God by his Spirit accomplished that consecration which men expressed symbolically "by the laying on of hands." Commentary on 1 Timothy.[17]

Be a Diligent Evangelist. Giovanni Diodati: Exercise carefully your calling of evangelist; revive, mature, and strengthen the gifts that you have received therefore, namely, God having declared your vocation not by votes of human or ordinary election, but by prophetic revelation and express oracle, signified to the church by the prophets. "With the laying on of hands," not to add by human means any weight to

---

[15]*Directory*, 6-7*.
[16]LW 28:330 (WA 26:82-83).

[17]CTS 43:115-16 (CO 52:302-3); citing Mt 25:18, 25. [†]See Calvin's explanation of the origin and meaning of this ceremony in *Institutes* 4.3.16.

the divine calling, but only for a sign of consecration and blessing. PIOUS ANNOTATIONS.[18]

ORDINATION BY THE ELDERS THROUGH LAYING ON OF HANDS. ENGLISH ANNOTATIONS: Some by "presbytery" understand the office of presbyter, which Timothy received by the imposition of hands. But the word *presbyteriou* is never taken in the Scripture for the office of a presbyter, but for the company of the elders, who here laid hands on Timothy when he was ordained. For although he was ordained by St. Paul, this ordination was performed in the assembly of elders, and with the laying on of their hands also. Agreeable to this is the canon of the Fourth Council of Carthage,[†] and the practice of the Church of England and other reformed churches at this day. ENGLISH ANNOTATIONS.[19]

GRACE IS NOT CONFERRED BY THE VERY ACT OF IMPOSITION. THOMAS CARTWRIGHT: That grace is given *by* and with the ordination of the ministers, when it is duly given and received, we willingly yield, because the words of the Scripture bear it. But that it is given *in* either imposition of hands or *in* any sacraments is a dream. As also it is a frantic device to imagine that by the very work of imposition of hands grace is given, which is only the instrumental means whereby it is given. . . . The preposition *dia*, construed with a genitive case, notes an instrumental working only, unless it be in very few cases as when it is applied to the Son, the Father, or such like, where the thing itself is such as will not admit that signification. CONFUTATION OF THE RHEMISTS.[20]

4:16 *Keep a Close Watch on Yourself*

BEHAVE WELL AS A PUBLIC FIGURE. MARTIN LUTHER: "Keep on; take care of yourself; have

regard for yourself. Don't do this because it is most ennobling for your body, but see what sort of office you have and what sort of man you are. You have the gift. As a bishop, you are a public figure. Everybody will depend on you. See to it that you conduct yourself as you have been established, lest you be a source of scandal. Rather be a cause for salvation, that you may edify, lead all people, harm no one." This is noble for him. . . . You see, if there is anyone in office and he works only for his own advantage, as I said earlier, he is not fit for the office. Public offices change one's habits, but rarely for the better. . . . "When you were still a private citizen, you had other habits. Now watch yourself. Do the things that befit your calling and station. Also carefully consider which is your chief responsibility. Teach the things that befit doctrine, so that you may not be misled. Satan will keep his eye on you." LECTURES ON 1 TIMOTHY.[21]

LIVE OUT WHAT YOU TEACH TO OTHERS. THOMAS VENATORIUS: Paul says that the bishop will enter the sum of fruitfulness twofold, if they keep both careful and constant watch on the elements of their office. Since where sincere conduct commends the truth of teaching, it cannot be otherwise than that bishops serve both themselves and their hearers. For the one who does not seek after their own interests, but those of Jesus Christ, who is not mixed with any hypocrisy in the office that has been given to them, who keeps their mind a stranger to envy, greed, and ambition, who both teaches and does all things truly and from their heart, always taking care that they do not admonish others, yet render themselves false; these, I say, will easily serve both themselves and the rest of the multitude. For how could someone who teaches rightly, and who no less lives rightly, lead others into destruction? Fit for double renown is the one who lives out what they teach to others. For they first satisfy their own conscience, in that the whole rationale of human salvation is in accord with it, and second they encourage others into the

---

[18]Diodati, *Pious Annotations*, 326*; citing Acts 13:1-2; 1 Tim 1:18.
[19]Downame, ed., *Annotations*, s.v.*; citing 2 Tim 1:6. [†]See NPNF[2] 14:437-510, presumably canons 13 and 49 concerning bishops being consecrated by three or twelve others.
[20]Cartwright, *Confutation*, 564*.

[21]LW 28:330-31 (WA 26:83).

hope of the safety that follows, through Jesus Christ our Savior, who is God blessed for ever. EXPOSITIONS OF 1 TIMOTHY.[22]

THE DEVIL STRIVES TO PREVAIL AGAINST OUR FAITH. CHARLES PINNER: Timothy must take heed to himself and to his doctrine, which implies this much: that doubtless there is danger to both. . . . We daily see and feel too well that the devil and the world labor for nothing more than to remove or reprove both the minister and his doctrine. . . . Look therefore how much our adversary the devil—in the rage of his desire and diligence to destroy—prevails against the preacher, that is, the minister and his doctrine. As he prevails here, he prevails against our faith. And therefore here he fights and strives, and here he spends shot and powder to make a breach, where most assuredly he may enter the fort of our souls. The malice he bears to the church and the whole body of the people of God, here he unloads it to the full. SERMON ON 1 TIMOTHY 4:16.[23]

STUDY TO SAVE YOURSELF AND YOUR HEARERS. RICHARD BAXTER: The ministerial work must be carried on purely for God and the salvation of souls, not for any private ends of our own. A wrong end makes all the work bad as from us, however good it may be in its own nature. It is not serving God, but ourselves, if we do it not for God, but ourselves. They who engage in this as a common work, to make a trade of it for their worldly livelihood, will find that they have chosen a bad trade, though a good employment. Self-denial is of absolute necessity in every Christian, but it is doubly necessary in a minister, as without it he cannot do God an hour's faithful service. Hard studies, much knowledge, and excellent preaching, if the ends be not right, is but more glorious hypocritical sinning. The saying of Bernard is commonly known: "Some desire to know merely for the sake of knowing, and that is shameful curiosity. Some desire to know that they may sell their knowledge, and that too is shameful. Some desire to know for reputation's sake, and that is shameful vanity. But there are some who desire to know that they may edify others, and that is praiseworthy; and there are some who desire to know that they themselves may be edified, and that is wise." REFORMED PASTOR.[24]

---

[22]Venatorius, *Distributiones*, 93; citing Phil 2:21.
[23]Pinner, *A Sermon . . . on 1 Tim. 4:16*, 6-7*.
[24]Baxter, *Reformed Pastor*, 111-12.

5:1-16 INSTRUCTIONS FOR THE CHURCH

Do not rebuke an older man but encourage him as you would a father, younger men as brothers, ²older women as mothers, younger women as sisters, in all purity.

³Honor widows who are truly widows. ⁴But if a widow has children or grandchildren, let them first learn to show godliness to their own household and to make some return to their parents, for this is pleasing in the sight of God. ⁵She who is truly a widow, left all alone, has set her hope on God and continues in supplications and prayers night and day, ⁶but she who is self-indulgent is dead even while she lives. ⁷Command these things as well, so that they may be without reproach. ⁸But if anyone does not provide for his relatives, and especially for members of his household, he has denied the faith and is worse than an unbeliever.

⁹Let a widow be enrolled if she is not less than sixty years of age, having been the wife of one husband,ᵃ

¹⁰and having a reputation for good works: if she has brought up children, has shown hospitality, has washed the feet of the saints, has cared for the afflicted, and has devoted herself to every good work. ¹¹But refuse to enroll younger widows, for when their passions draw them away from Christ, they desire to marry ¹²and so incur condemnation for having abandoned their former faith. ¹³Besides that, they learn to be idlers, going about from house to house, and not only idlers, but also gossips and busybodies, saying what they should not. ¹⁴So I would have younger widows marry, bear children, manage their households, and give the adversary no occasion for slander. ¹⁵For some have already strayed after Satan. ¹⁶If any believing woman has relatives who are widows, let her care for them. Let the church not be burdened, so that it may care for those who are truly widows.

a Or *a woman of one man*

OVERVIEW: As they interact with this passage, these early modern commentators discuss the manner in which pastors are to interact with different types of people within the church. The authors urge pastors to reprove and encourage older believers respectfully with gentleness. Generally, they are to temper their corrections with the utmost care. Moreover, pastors are to relate to the opposite sex with integrity. One of the most notable aspects of these expositions concerns Paul's references to widows. The commentators mainly regard the widows mentioned in the passage as deaconesses who served the church in return for its support. However, they clearly point out that in order to occupy such an office, a woman had to at least be sixty years old. They further observed that younger women were barred from the position because it would prove spiritually harmful for them. In highlighting this, the authors imply that

disregard of this Pauline prohibition ultimately led to young women pursuing the monastic vocation as nuns. Finally, the commentators consider the necessity of Christians supporting their families on pain of excommunication.

5:1-2 Respect and Encouragement

SPEAK TO OLDER MEN RESPECTFULLY.

MARTIN LUTHER: Up to now Paul has established for Timothy how he ought to conduct himself in his associations and in his person. Now he explains how Timothy ought to behave toward various persons. . . . Now Paul wants Timothy to have particular regard for his elder. There is no agreement as to whether with this word he means an older man or one who holds an office. I lean more toward the idea that he is speaking in general terms about older men. . . . Moses demands reverence toward old men. We must respect their age and, as the text says, their gray hair.[†] That discipline is necessary not only in the church but in every political unit. It is a disgraceful situation when the young lack such respect.... Therefore a teacher of the church ought to respect older men. "You should not snap at old people the way you do at younger people and those similar to you in age." You see that Paul established the congregation with very gentle conversation.... You should exhort a pious man if you have seen that he is not doing what he ought. You should direct the exhortation to those who know they should be doing the things of faith, love, and Christ. Don't be sarcastic. Don't assail them publicly. Rather, admonish them. Yet one ought not grow old in his responsibility. He should go forward, sparing no one. Look at Christ. His disciples often slipped. He bore it. He corrected them both gently and sweetly.... If you hold a person on the level of your father, you will not snap at him but will exhort him with sweet language. Nature teaches this—that you not rebuke. All the less is this bearable in the church. LECTURES ON 1 TIMOTHY.[1]

LOVING REBUKES MUST BE APPROPRIATELY TEMPERED. DESIDERIUS ERASMUS: A pastor must never shrink from upright sincerity of doctrine. Yet to heal things that are amiss in someone it is not always possible for a teacher or an admonisher to use a soft approach. For the authority of a bishop must be held up in such a way that they may be quite without appearance of tyranny and that it might appear in every situation that they act as they do out of an intent to do good and not because they are displeased. Therefore, it is not expedient to enforce discipline with rigorous sharpness if people can be brought to amendment with leniency and gentleness. For people are more likely to respond well if they perceive that they are loved by the one rebuking them. It is human nature

to prefer coaxing to compulsion; and it is not unusual for persuasion to obtain what would be impossible to accomplish with severity. So the medicine of reprimand must be tempered according to the age and state of each person. PARAPHRASES.[2]

BE SEEN TO BEHAVE PROPERLY WITH WOMEN. JOHN CALVIN: When St. Paul says to Timothy that he should behave with all purity with regard to the young women, he is not saying so much that Timothy should abstain from all dissolute manners, for he was a man of great holiness. But again, he wants to prevent such suspicions as might arise (since the world is wicked) because so soon as one sees a man speak with a young woman, even if it is for her salvation, straightaway they talk of it and murmur. And therefore St. Paul, seeing Timothy might be subject to false reports, warns him to be prudent about this, and if he needs to communicate with young women, to warn them of their duty, that he does it in such fear and reverence that the mouths of the wicked may be stopped, and that the weak are not scandalized, that they may conceive no evil opinion to trouble them. And this is a verse well worth noting. For we know that the devil seeks nothing but to make the word of God odious and uses such craft, especially to hinder us, that we may not exercise the charge which God has committed to us. SERMONS ON 1 TIMOTHY.[3]

REBUKE OLDER BELIEVERS RESPECTFULLY. CARDINAL CAJETAN: "Do not rebuke an older man but, please, exhort him as a father." It is evident from other attending words dealing with age that the word "older" in this passage refers to age.[†] And because of the joining of other words dealing with age to this one, the word "exhort" seems more regular than "please," since the same word applies to all the following instructions. And so Paul commands that an old man who is sinning should not be rebuked but exhorted, that one would use toward him the respect of a son. For this is an

---

[1]LW 28:332-333 (WA 26:83-84). [†]Luther is thinking of Lev 19:32, "You shall stand up before the gray head and honor the face of an old man."

[2]Erasmus, *Paraphrases*, 54.
[3]CO 53:445.

easier way to correct an old man. "Try to encourage young men as brothers, old women as mothers, young women as sisters in all purity." It was necessary to add this when it comes to exhorting young women because of the danger of their age. And he says "in all," so that purity is present in looks, in gestures, in words, and so on. The Epistles of Paul and the Other Apostles.[4]

Ministers Should Not Be Intemperate in Their Corrections. Thomas Venatorius: So far from propriety is it for bishops to have the right to exercise tyranny over their subjects that the apostle also wishes them to be strangers to absolutely any immoderate reproof. For the one who rises up against those who fail in a rather immoderate way, with harsh words, quite apart from the fact that they will incur hatred for themselves on account of their inconsiderate bitterness, has also not infrequently been seen to incur the suspicion of tyranny. Here we see that we come up against an immoderate kind of healing, with human faults, and sharper words, though sinners are from time to time restored to innocence even by this kind of rather intemperate remedy. For just as those who apply cuttings and burnings in the case of dangerous diseases, lest the whole body perish, do not do this that they would die, so as to pile evil on evil, but in order, by the severity of pain, either to lessen or to remove that which, when touched by mildness, showed no signs of cure. Thus no other way is to be considered for the correction of people's errors; for either the sinner is brought to a state of peace through holy correction, and is then received into the bosom of the church with joy, or they disdain to return to good fruit, and the church of Christ proves the authority of the divine word in punishing the one who is so disdainful, at once for the fear and the comfort of others.

In these matters, ministers eager to avoid all adverse suspicion will never contrive anything either by hate or perverse love against offenders. Instead, mindful of Christian instruction, and everywhere preserving all charity (without which the fruit of holy admonition is never attained), they will always accommodate the remedy of reproof. For since they are called doctors of souls, they should heal and not harm. For authority has been given to them by the Lord for building up, not for tearing down. Expositions of 1 Timothy.[5]

5:3-7 Godly Widows

Qualifications of a True Widow. David Dickson: Paul charges Timothy that he observe in the choice of widows that she who is chosen is not without the qualifications of a true widow, or Christian widow, to be provided for by the church. Here he sets down four qualifications. (1) It is required that she be alone, that is, destitute of children and nephews, and all human supply. (2) That she be faithful, trusting in God, not getting her living by evil courses but relying on God. (3) That she be daily given to the exercises of piety. (4) That she be not of the number of wanton widows, who indulge themselves in idleness and pleasures, not regarding the exercises of godliness. The reason of this qualification is given, because those unprofitable women are as it were dead while they live, both in respect to God, whom they do not serve, and in respect of human society, whom they no ways endeavor to benefit by their work. Exposition of All Paul's Epistles.[6]

Training in the Home. John Calvin: "If any widow . . ." There are various ways of explaining this passage; and the ambiguity arises from this circumstance that the latter clause may refer either to widows or to their children. Nor is this consistent with the verb ("let them learn") being plural, while Paul spoke of a widow in the singular number; for a change of number is very customary in a general discourse, that is, when the writer

---

[4]Cajetan, *Epistolae Pauli et Aliorum Apostolorum*, 144. †I.e., *seniorem* could refer to hierarchical status, regardless of age.

[5]Venatorius, *Distributiones*, 94-95.
[6]Dickson, *Exposition*, 166*.

speaks of a whole class, and not of an individual. They who think that it relates to widows are of the opinion that the meaning is, "let them learn, by the pious government of their family, to repay to their successors the education that they received from their ancestors." This is the explanation given by Chrysostom and some others.† But others think that it is more natural to interpret it as relating to children and grandchildren. Accordingly, in their opinion, the apostle teaches that the mother or grandmother is the person toward whom they should exercise their piety; for nothing is more natural than the return of filial for parental affection; and it is very unreasonable that it should be excluded from the church. Before the church is burdened with them, let them do their duty.

Hereto I have related the opinion of others. But I wish my readers to consider if it would not agree better with the context in this manner: "Let them learn to conduct themselves in a godly manner at home." As if he had said that it would be valuable as a preparatory instruction that they should train themselves to the worship of God by performing godly offices at home toward their relatives. For nature commands us to love our parents next to God; that this secondary piety leads to the highest piety. And as Paul saw that the very rights of nature were violated under the pretense of religion, in order to correct this fault, he commanded that widows should be trained by domestic apprenticeship to the worship of God. COMMENTARY ON 1 TIMOTHY.[7]

5:8 Caring for One's Own Family

FAMILY IS GIVEN TO STIR US UP TO LOVE. PETER MARTYR VERMIGLI: Now, as touching the degrees in charity, often the kindred of the flesh is the cause of loving our neighbor, and that according to charity. Paul says to Timothy, "If anyone does not provide for his relatives, and especially for members of his household, he has denied the faith

and is worse than an unbeliever." This is because, under pretense of religion, they live worse than infidels, who by the guide of nature alone show benevolence toward their own kindred, and provide necessary things for them. So then, we must judge that the joining of flesh and kindred is given to us by God, to stir us up to charity; not to have respect to those things as our own, but as joined to us by God. For otherwise there is none that shall make a choice for himself of parents, brothers, or country. We ought therefore to care for those things that are given to us by God; and not to spend our labor pursuing our own pleasure, without looking to them. Not that we should not extend our goodwill and charity to all, whoever they are: but we are now only speaking of the degrees of ordinary and usual charity, where we ought to begin, unless some other occasion draw us to that which is more needful. COMMONPLACES.[8]

EXCOMMUNICATION FOR THOSE WHO REFUSE TO PROVIDE FOR FAMILY. DAVID DICKSON: He censures those who refuse to provide for widows, their mothers or grandmothers, as it is prescribed earlier, that is, that they should be excommunicated by the church, and accounted deserters of the Christian doctrine, for heathens or infidels, until they repent, which is the consequence of excommunication. EXPOSITION OF ALL PAUL'S EPISTLES.[9]

5:9-16 Older and Younger Widows

WIDOWS CHOSEN AS DEACONESSES. DUTCH ANNOTATIONS: "Let a widow be enrolled . . ." Namely, to the office of a deaconess, which in the primitive church served the church among sick strangers, and poor people, and who for that cause, need so requiring, were maintained by the church. . . . "But refuse to enroll younger widows." Namely to choose them into the office of deaconesses: for otherwise they were not rejected from the number of the members of the church, when they were of

---

[7]CTS 43:121-22 (CO 52:305-6). †For Chrysostom's explanation see NPNF 13:450.

[8]Vermigli, *Commonplaces*, 2:558-59*.
[9]Dickson, *Exposition*, 167*.

a good life, as appears from verse 14 and also from Romans 7:3 and 1 Corinthians 7:39. . . . No, nor yet from the help of the church, when they had need of it, and had no children or friends who could help them, as Paul concludes in verse 16. DUTCH ANNOTATIONS.[10]

OLDER AND YOUNGER WIDOWS. DAVID DICKSON: Paul observes three other qualifications requisite in the admission of widows to the common table, that they be sustained by the public charges. (1) That she be a widow of sixty years old at the least, at which age the desires of the flesh begin to abate, and are unable by the labor of their hands to get their living. (2) That she has been the wife of one husband, or has not violated the laws of marriage, whereupon it may be hoped she is a chaste and self-controlled woman. (3) That she have a testimonial of her piety, declared in her deeds and works, especially in these five which may demonstrate that she is appropriate to serve the poor when they are sick: (i) If she brought up her children honestly. (ii) If she has been given to hospitality. (iii) That she has submitted to the lowest offices of charity, or was ready to submit, even to wash the saints' feet if need required. (iv) If she has succored those who were afflicted. Finally, (v) if she has exercised herself in all sorts of good works.

But they must not admit into the college of widows those that are younger widows. He gives two reasons. (1) Because there is danger, lest being pampered with the church's bread they begin to wax wanton against Christ (as some younger widow have done already), and despairing of marriage in the church they think of falling away from the faith of Christ and afterward openly revolt, that they may marry some infidel out of the church. He seems to point at some widows of this sort, whose condition he shows to be damnable and miserable, upon this that they have rejected the profession of their faith, which they first made in baptism. (2) Because the younger widows (as it

seems to be evident upon experience) will become idle, wanderers, triflers, busybodies, tattlers, wandering from house to house, curiously inquisitive into other people's matters, and speaking things which they ought not. EXPOSITION OF ALL PAUL'S EPISTLES.[11]

THE CONDEMNATION OF THOSE WHOSE PASSIONS DRAW THEM AWAY. THOMAS CARTWRIGHT: The word "damnation" here does not yield this signification of damnation so pressingly and pregnantly as the Jesuits ignorantly say.[†] For it is used before in a softer and milder signification, and is there the same with another word noting reproach or blame. There wanted not another word used elsewhere by the apostle that carries with it a stronger and sharper process against them than this. Nevertheless, the truth is that the word having in itself a more general signification seems by circumstance of place (noting the word and wages of a heinous sin) to force this particular signification of "damnation." Make it as heavy as you like, yet it has already, and shall further appear that it makes nothing for condemnation of marriage after vows. CONFUTATION OF THE RHEMISTS.[12]

CELIBACY PROMOTES SIN. MATTHIAS FLACIUS: [Paul] continues to describe many reasons by enumerating bad things that arise from young, unmarried celibates, and also from anger to advise the bishop that those intended for the diaconate do not undertake celibacy. He says that they, for the sake of the dispatching of the business of their function (for indeed it was to

---

[10]Haak, *Annotations*, s.v.

[11]Dickson, *Exposition*, 167*.

[12]Cartwright, *Confutation*, 569*; citing 1 Tim 3:6-7. The Greek word used by Paul in 1 Tim 3:6 and 1 Tim 5:12 is *krima*. Knight, *The Pastoral Epistles*, 226, translates it as "censure" rather than condemnation. [†]See Martin, *New Testament*, 580, who says, "It signifies not blame, check, or reprehension of men, as some, to make the fault seem less, would have it. But judgment or eternal damnation, which is a heavy sentence. God grant all married Priests and Religious may consider their lamentable case." The idea is that monks or nuns who deny their monastic vows in order to get married are condemned because of this.

swear poverty of every sort that monks sought alms from those who were destitute, but alas, they were given the name of "pastors"), are wont to wander about through strange homes with the desire of exploring, by certain babblings, either indeed from gluttony, while lying in wait for little gifts, or from lust by hunting [others'] wives, or similarly by doing anything perversely, for which reason they do not sin only, but draw others into sin, and excite all other kinds of scandals. Gloss on 1 Timothy[13]

Widows Serve for the Benefit of the Church. Sebastian Schmidt: Verse 9: Paul says if a widow is to be chosen for the care and subvention of the church, in order that she can serve for the benefit also of the church, insofar as she is able, a woman should be chosen who is not less than sixty years old, who is of good repute, and who was the wife of one man, while she lived in matrimony, and without accusation of adultery or of licentious company.

Verse 10: In addition, she ought to have evidence that she has been involved in good works, that she has brought up her children well and with devotion, that she has been hospitable, that she has washed the feet of the saints, that she has ministered to the afflicted as much as she could, and that she has been occupied in every other good work. For such as these are deserving of mercy and whatever is like it. And they should also know how to serve in the church among such people.

Verse 11: But reject younger widows who are below this age, and do not admit them to the maintenance of the church and the service of the faithful. This is mainly because when they become wanton against the holy teaching and faith of Christ, and against the chastity that is becoming of Christian women, they seek matrimony of such a kind that they can sate their wantonness.

Verse 12: How they have the reproach of condemnation in that they reject saving faith for that wantonness that opposes the Christian faith that they formerly held, and render it void.

Verse 13: Truly in part they also become lazy, and from their sluggishness in regard to doing anything good, they learn to go round among houses in order to spend their time in leisure. However, they do not only become lazy, but they also become talkative and meddlesome, saying those things that are neither fitting nor beneficial.

Verse 14: So for these reasons I desire younger widows to marry, bear children from a chaste bed, administer their household with industry, and in this way provide no opportunity to the enemy, through wantonness and other vices, for us to be slandered.

Verse 15: I desire all the more that these things take place, since experience has taught me that certain women, in order to satisfy their wantonness, have gone off track to such a degree that in their pursuit of Satan on account of marriage they have departed again from the faith.

Verse 16: In order to obviate such evils, I desire the following to happen: a person of faith, or any person of faith who has widows, should support them until they are married once again; nor should the church be burdened in supporting them, so that those resources that are given in common by the church can suffice for those who are truly widows, about whom I wrote above. Paraphrase of 1 Timothy.[14]

Withhold Vows from the Young. Andreas Bodenstein von Karlstadt: Anyone who is inclined to chastity ought to remain chaste, but without making any vows until after the sixtieth year, for under that age he does what is wrong and the pastor must declare his vow inadmissible. Refuse those who are younger than sixty. Regarding Vows.[15]

[13]Flacius, *Glossa Compendaria*, 1062.

[14]Schmidt, *Paraphrasi*, 905-6.
[15]CRR 8:80.

5:17-25 HONORING ELDERS

[17]Let the elders who rule well be considered worthy of double honor, especially those who labor in preaching and teaching. [18]For the Scripture says, "You shall not muzzle an ox when it treads out the grain," and, "The laborer deserves his wages." [19]Do not admit a charge against an elder except on the evidence of two or three witnesses. [20]As for those who persist in sin, rebuke them in the presence of all, so that the rest may stand in fear. [21]In the presence of God and of Christ Jesus and of the elect angels I charge you to keep these rules without prejudging, doing nothing from partiality. [22]Do not be hasty in the laying on of hands, nor take part in the sins of others; keep yourself pure. [23](No longer drink only water, but use a little wine for the sake of your stomach and your frequent ailments.) [24]The sins of some people are conspicuous, going before them to judgment, but the sins of others appear later. [25]So also good works are conspicuous, and even those that are not cannot remain hidden.

OVERVIEW: Throughout their expositions of this passage, these early modern commentators devote considerable attention to the treatment of pastors. Generally, they interpret Paul's reference to those worthy of double honor as instruction to compensate pastors fairly for their labor in the Word. The authors further infer from Paul's directive that the minister's chief responsibility is to preach and teach the Word. Furthermore, a frequent subject of their reflection is the distinction that some reformers made between "ruling" and "teaching" elders. In addition, they caution their readers concerning the seriousness of making charges against elders.

5:17-18 Double Honor

ELDERS WORTHY OF DOUBLE THE HONOR OF WIDOWS. JOHN CALVIN: Chrysostom interprets "double honor" as meaning "support and reverence."[†] I do not oppose his opinion; let it be adopted by anyone who chooses. But for my own part, I think it is more probable that a comparison is here drawn between widows and elders. Paul had formerly enjoined that honor should be paid—to widows; but elders are more worthy of being honored than widows, and, with respect to them, ought therefore to receive double honor. COMMENTARY ON 1 TIMOTHY.[1]

TEACHING ELDERS AND RULING ELDERS. DAVID DICKSON: He makes two orders of these elders: one that labors in the word and doctrine, such are pastor and doctors; another, of those that rule well, namely, who endeavor to govern the church in life and manners, but labor not in the Word and doctrine, such are elders which are called rulers. He would have both these kinds of elders rightly managing their offices, accounted worthy of double honor, but especially those who labor in the word and doctrine, because they are wholly set apart to the word and prayer; therefore it is fitting that they should be liberally maintained. He calls the stipend given them by the name of "honor," because of such moment is their work that it cannot be valued, at any rate, and because the stipend that is allowed them is to be given not on the account of wages, but an honorary or an honorable reward. EXPOSITION OF ALL PAUL'S EPISTLES.[2]

TWO KINDS OF ELDERS: RULING AND TEACHING. JOHN CALVIN: We may learn from this that there were at that time two kinds of elders; for all were not ordained to teach. The words plainly mean that there were some who "ruled well" and honorably, but who did not hold the office of

---

[1]CTS 43:137-38 (CO 52:315). [†]See NPNF 13:460.

[2]Dickson, *Exposition*, 167*; citing 1 Cor 12:28; Rom 12:8.

teachers.[†] And, indeed, there were chosen from among the people men of worth and of good character, who, united with the pastors in a common council and authority, administered the discipline of the church, and were a kind of censor for the correction of morals. Ambrose complains that this custom had gone into disuse, through the carelessness, or rather through the pride, of the doctors, who wish to possess undivided power.[†]

To return to Paul, he enjoins that support shall be provided chiefly for pastors who are employed in teaching. Such is the ingratitude of the world that very little care is taken about supporting the ministers of the Word; and Satan, by this trick, endeavors to deprive the church of instruction, by terrifying many, through the dread of poverty and hunger, from bearing that burden. COMMENTARY ON 1 TIMOTHY.[3]

BISHOPS MUST BE ABLE TO TEACH. THOMAS CARTWRIGHT: Every bishop and pastor administering the sacraments cannot preach in like ability, either of knowledge or utterance, yet we utterly both contemn and condemn those bishops who having no tolerable gift of teaching are (like idols in their cases, or rather coffins) set up in the church's chair. For to be able to teach and not to be a novice are placed before as the essential points required in every lawful pastor and doctor of the church, whereby he differs from the rest of the church, which in every member of it ought have the other qualities there required of a bishop. And therefore we never read in Scripture of any to whom the administration of sacraments was committed

which were not trusted with the preaching of the Word. CONFUTATION OF THE RHEMISTS.[4]

EJECTING NEGLIGENT PASTORS. RICHARD BAXTER: I confess, if I had my will, that man should be ejected as a negligent pastor who will not rule his people by discipline, and well as he is ejected as a negligent preacher who will not preach; for ruling I am sure is as essential a part of the pastor's office as preaching. REFORMED PASTOR.[5]

NOT TWO KINDS OF PRESBYTERS. EDWARD LEIGH: Some learned and late writers conceive that this place allows for lay presbyters. Others say here are not two sorts of elders—one to govern, the other to teach—but two duties of each presbyter, namely, to teach and govern. The conclusion of the former is this: there were elders who ruled well and labored in the Word of God; therefore there were elders that did not rule and labor well.... Here two elders are mentioned, but the difference, whether official or personal, is very doubtful. One office may comprehend both these duties, and the comparison may be in their personal excellencies. One may excel in the governing part of the office, and the other in the doctrinal part....

It is imagined that two kinds of presbyters as well as two parts of their office are expressed: one of ministers of the church, another of the people; one perpetual, the other temporary for their time; both interested in the government of the church, although the office of preaching charged upon the one. How little of this is set down in the words of the apostle, were the sense of them that which is pretended, let all the world judge. ANNOTATIONS.[6]

---

[3]CTS 43:138-39 (CO 52:315-316). [†]Others dispute this idea, below, but the words themselves are not as obvious as Calvin appears to think if the Greek word *malista* (translated in the ESV as "especially") is better understood as "that is" or "namely," which some have concluded on the basis of its use elsewhere in the Pastorals, and in papyrus letters. See T. C. Skeat, "'Especially the Parchments': A Note on 2 Timothy IV.13," *Journal of Theological Studies* 30 (1979): 173-77, and 1 Tim 4:10; 2 Tim 4:13; Titus 1:10. [†]See Ambrosiaster on 1 Tim 5:2 in *Commentaries on Galatians–Philemon*, ed. and trans. Gerald L. Bray, Ancient Christian Texts (Downers Grove, IL: IVP Academic, 2009), 133.

[4]Cartwright, *Confutation*, 573*; citing 1 Tim 3:2, 6; Titus 1:9. This should not be read as Cartwright disagreeing with the idea that there are two kinds of elders described here. He says on the next page that "if there be but one kind of church officers here noted, then the words 'especially those that labor' do not cause the apostle's speech to rise, but to fall; not to go forward, but to go backward." [5]Baxter, *Reformed Pastor*, 171. [6]Leigh, *Annotations*, 327*.

One Kind of Elder, with Two Functions.
Thomas Bilson: It is resolutely inferred, *ergo*,
there were some elders that labored not in the
word and doctrine; and those by comparison of
other places are supposed to be "governors," which
office Paul names among the spiritual functions of
the church when he says, "He who rules, (let him
do it) with diligence." It is a matter of no small
weight to give laymen power in every parish to
impose hands and use the keys, yea, to have the full
and whole government of the church above and
against the pastors by number of voices, if they
differ in judgment; and therefore the ground that
shall bear the frame of the lay presbytery had need
be sure, especially when it is urged as a part of
Christ's spiritual kingdom, without which no
church can be Christ's, any more than it may
without the truth of his doctrine. . . .

The first reason I have of the weakness of this
place to uphold lay presbytery is that many learned
and ancient fathers have debated and sifted the force
of these words, and not one of them ever so much
as surmised any such thing to be contained in this
text.[†] . . . Now that lay judges and censors of
manners were in the apostles' time found at the
expenses of the church, or by God's law ought to
have their maintenance at the people's hands, is a
thing to me so strange and unheard of, that until I
see it justly proved, I cannot possibly believe it. . . .
And so not two sorts of elders, but two parts of the
pastoral charge and function are implied in these
words. . . . It is then no consequent out of this place,
ergo, some elders did not teach, but govern; this
rather is inferred, *ergo*, more is expected of an elder
than teaching, to wit, good example of life, and
watchfulness over his charge. . . . Set this place aside,
in which I see utterly nothing for lay elders, and
where else in the New Testament shall we find, I say
not a sentence, but a syllable, sounding for them?
Perpetual Government of the Church.[7]

Remuneration and Respect for Ministers.
Conradus Vorstius: Those who
faithfully perform the holy ministry are to be
deemed worth of a double honor: think first of
an honest maintenance, then of reverence or a
certain regard, together with imitation of the
virtues. On the first kind of honor, see the whole
of 1 Corinthians 9 concerning the rightful
salaries of ministers. On the second, see Hebrews 13:17. And here it is to be noted, inciden-
tally, that this passage can be read in two ways.
According to the first interpretation, he is
speaking about two ranks of presbyters, where
one is in charge of the ministry of the word,
while the other is in charge of the exercise of
discipline. According to the second interpretation, he is speaking about one and the same rank
of ministers of the Word, but in which some are
more diligent than others. For there is good
reason to doubt whether there was once one
kind of presbyter, who abstained completely
from the ministry of the Word. . . .

Among other kinds of honor that are due to
the sacred ministry, and likewise to the ministry
of the presbyter, this is not to be considered the
least: namely, that accusations of any old kind
against ministers and presbyters should not be
admitted rashly. Rather two or three witness
worthy of trust should be examined before
everything else, under whose deposition the
ministers should finally be judged or condemned.
The rationale for this caution, among others, is
that the ministry should not easily be defiled,
especially since it is most hateful to Satan and is
therefore liable everywhere to malicious allegations from people of ill-intent.

In passing, it should be noted in this connection,
against followers of the pope, that there is here set
up no episcopal forum, or judgment seat of officials.
As if one bishop or one of his officials, or an
archdeacon, should have authority of deciding
cases of controversy involving individual ministers
of the church, and this not only in spiritual matters,
but also secular. For even if Timothy is the only
one nominated here, yet it is not the case that every

---

[7]Bilson, *Perpetual Government*, 183-93; citing 1 Cor 12:28; Rom 12:8.
The whole of chapter 10 is given over to disproving the idea seen
in Calvin, Dickson, and others that the text implies two kinds of
elders. [†]He names Chrysostom, Jerome, Ambrose, Theodoret,
Primasius, Oecumenius, Theophylact, "and divers others."

trial or judgment is attributed to him alone. Especially since elsewhere the whole presbytery, indeed the whole church, is commended. In any case, Timothy was an evangelist, and therefore could exercise a certain extraordinary power. COMMENTARY ON THE EPISTLES.[8]

DO NOT MUZZLE THE OX. GIOVANNI DIODATI: It was the custom of the eastern countries, and many others also, to tread out the corn with the feet of oxen or horses, and because they being far in among the sheaves on the floor of the barn, always got a mouthful, therefore they muzzled them, and reason requires that they should feed with the fruits of their own labors. PIOUS ANNOTATIONS.[9]

HEED GOD'S MINISTERS. DAVID JORIS: If you believe God, then believe also his prophets, so that it be well with you. Fear God with all your soul and keep his ministers in great worth. Therefore, love with all your strength those who have made you, and do not abandon his ministers. Fear the Lord with all your heart and soul, and honor the priests, and purify yourselves with the poor. THE BUILDING OF THE CHURCH.[10]

5:19-25 Charges Against Elders

CHARGES BROUGHT TO TIMOTHY. DAVID DICKSON: Paul affirms that an accusation against an elder should not be received or taken for true unless upon the testimony of three witnesses, or at the least two (worthy of credit). And that which is here spoken to Timothy alone is spoken to all that sit in the presbytery, because elsewhere judgment is committed to the whole presbytery; yea, what is spoken here to Timothy is spoken to the whole presbytery at Ephesus, touching the administration of the whole discipline of the church. Timothy the evangelist, in the meantime,

might exercise extraordinary power, as he was an evangelist and the apostle's legate. EXPOSITION OF ALL PAUL'S EPISTLES.[11]

DO NOT RECEIVE ACCUSATIONS AGAINST ELDERS EASILY. DUTCH ANNOTATIONS: Not only do not condemn him alone without sufficient witness, which might not be done to any according to the law of Moses, but do not so much as receive any accusation to judge thereof. The reason is because such as are in this public service of the governing of the church, seeing they must admonish every one and rebuke the unruly, may easily stir up displeasures and ill will against themselves; and because the very receiving of accusations to judge of them makes a man suspected, and therefore tends to the offense of the church, and to the reproach of the same. DUTCH ANNOTATIONS.[12]

YOU HAVE THOUSANDS OF WITNESSES TO YOUR ACTIONS. JOHN OWEN: If we are the church and tabernacle of God, God walks among us this day; Christ is among us by his special presence. "Where two or three are gathered together in my name, there am I in the midst of them." And much more may his presence be expected in so great a transaction of his authority as this we are now engaged in. The holy and elect angels are present with us, to give glory to the solemnity. Hence our apostle charges Timothy, "I charge you before God, and the Lord Jesus Christ, and the elect angels, that you observe these things." Why before the elect angels? Because they are present as *witnesses* in the collation of authority from Christ. You have thousands of witnesses more than you see; there are more eyes on you than you take notice of. God is present, Christ is present, the elect angels are present. These things are the true and faithful sayings of God. SERMON ON EPHESIANS 4:8.[13]

---

[8]Vorstius, *Commentarius*, 494; citing Mt 18:15.
[9]Diodati, *Pious Annotations*, 327; citing Deut 25:4.
[10]CRR 7:178.

[11]Dickson, *Exposition*, 167*; citing Acts 20:28.
[12]Haak, *Annotations*, s.v.; citing Deut 19:15.
[13]Owen, *Works*, 9:439-40*; citing Mt 18:20.

Do Not Be Hasty in Laying On Hands.

Martin Luther: He who has a conscience does not lay on hands hastily. Trust no one easily in regard to his knowledge, learning, or piety. There, too, insist on witnesses who consistently speak about his integrity and circumstances. Then you can say, "I do not believe myself but the two witnesses. I have done this because You have sent it, O God." Lectures on 1 Timothy.[14]

Angels Are Witnesses of Your Faithfulness in Ministry.

John Owen: Paul tells us that the apostles in their preaching and sufferings were made "a spectacle unto angels." The holy angels of God looked on, rejoicing to behold how gloriously they acquitted themselves in the work and ministry committed to them. And to this end he charges Timothy before "the elect angels" to look to and discharge aright the work of an evangelist, because they were appointed by God to be witnesses of his faithfulness and diligence therein. And it is not improbable but he has respect unto the presence of angels in the assemblies of the saints for the worship of God, where he enjoins modesty and sobriety to women in them on their account. And from that particular instance a general rule may be drawn for the observation of comeliness and order in all our assemblies—namely, from the presence of these holy witnesses at all our solemn worship; for church assemblies are the court, the dwelling place, the throne of Jesus Christ, and therefore in them he is in an especial manner attended by these glorious ministers of his presence. Commentary on Hebrews.[15]

The Sins of Candidates for Ministry.

Dutch Annotations: Lay hands suddenly on no man. That is, without having made due and sufficient trial of the person, his life, and his doctrine. Neither have any communion with the sins of others: this may be understood either of those who would choose an unfit person to the ministry, or of the person who chosen, being unfit. . . . Some sins are manifest before, namely, before they are chosen to the ministry . . . and in some also they follow after. This some understand thus: that some men's scandalous life or evil doctrine is sufficiently known before, yea even before trial is made thereof, and therefore, they may be passed by without difficulty. But some men's sins follow after, that is, are not known until search is made thereof, and therefore men should make diligent search before they choose. Other stake it for being known after that they are chosen, seeing beforehand, as hypocrites are wont to do, they carried themselves well for a while, and that therefore they that choose them are not guilty of those secret sins, if there were but due search made. Dutch Annotations.[16]

Taking Part in the Sins of Others.

Edward Leigh: This is diversely interpreted. First, as if this were the meaning: there are many who will ordain rashly; don't you fall into such men's sins, so as to be like them. Second, there are many who will importunately desire such to be ordained, who may please their humors; but don't you yield to such importunity, lest you partake of their sins. But third, it may have reference to their doctrine and conversation; all the wickedness these ministers should afterward commit in the discharge of their duty would be accounted as his, and he should answer for them. Annotations.[17]

Timothy's Health.

David Dickson: As to the latter part of the precept of keeping himself pure—because the apostle knew that Timothy, by reason of his earnest endeavors after purity and chastity, had been injurious to his own health, therefore by the way he advises him that he

---

[14]LW 28:354 (WA 26:99).
[15]Owen, *Works*, 20:252-53* (commenting on Heb 1:14); citing 1 Cor 4:9; 11:10.
[16]Haak, *Annotations*, s.v.
[17]Leigh, *Annotations*, 328*.

should not so understand the precept of keeping himself pure as to neglect his health and render himself unfit for the works of his calling, but use a holy prudence. And in subduing his body, by drinking of water, to use a little wine as it were physically, and of the necessity of health, lest if he should proceed in not favoring his weak stomach, and his body laboring under regular infirmities,[†] immediately the tabernacle of his body should fall to decay, and the church should be deprived of so profitable an instrument. EXPOSITION OF ALL PAUL'S EPISTLES.[18]

[18]Dickson, Exposition, 168*. [†]Gordon D. Fee, 1 and 2 Timothy, Titus, New International Biblical Commentary (Carlisle, UK: Paternoster, 1995), 132, thinks that "the mention of Timothy's frequent illnesses helps to contribute to the picture of timidity that emerges in the various texts." William D. Mounce, Pastoral Epistles, Word Biblical Commentary 46 (Nashville: Thomas Nelson, 2000), 319, counters that "physical weakness has no necessary connection with personal timidity, and it is hard to see Paul sending a timid person into the problems that existed in Ephesus."

6:1-10 TRUE CONTENTMENT

Let all who are under a yoke as bondservants[a] regard their own masters as worthy of all honor, so that the name of God and the teaching may not be reviled. [2]Those who have believing masters must not be disrespectful on the ground that they are brothers; rather they must serve all the better since those who benefit by their good service are believers and beloved.

Teach and urge these things. [3]If anyone teaches a different doctrine and does not agree with the sound[b] words of our Lord Jesus Christ and the teaching that accords with godliness, [4]he is puffed up with conceit and understands nothing. He has an unhealthy craving for controversy and for quarrels about words, which produce envy, dissension, slander, evil suspi- *cions, [5]and constant friction among people who are depraved in mind and deprived of the truth, imagining that godliness is a means of gain. [6]But godliness with contentment is great gain, [7]for we brought nothing into the world, and[c] we cannot take anything out of the world. [8]But if we have food and clothing, with these we will be content. [9]But those who desire to be rich fall into temptation, into a snare, into many senseless and harmful desires that plunge people into ruin and destruction. [10]For the love of money is a root of all kinds of evils. It is through this craving that some have wandered away from the faith and pierced themselves with many pangs.*

a For the contextual rendering of the Greek word *doulos*, see Preface b Or *healthy* c Greek *for*; some manuscripts insert [it is] *certain* [that]

OVERVIEW: Throughout their expositions of this passage, these Reformation commentators bring Paul's instructions concerning the relations between masters and slaves to bear on contemporary relationships of servitude. In so doing, they point out that the Scriptures did not condemn slavery, but rather prescribe the manner in which masters and servants were to interact with each other according to their respective roles. Though they function in these societal roles, the servant and master were brothers and sisters in Christ. Equality in Christ does not completely dissolve the social distinctions, but it does alter societal relations and institutions of the commonwealth. The authors therefore urge their readers to be content with their social stations and honor God within them. From here the commentators explore the nature and causes of covetousness as the prime motive of false teachers. They also warn their readers to avoid greed as inimical to faith.

6:1-2a *Honor Your Masters*

THE GOSPEL DOES NOT STIR US UP TO REBELLION. GENEVA BIBLE: He adds also rules for the servant's duty toward their masters. Whereupon no doubt there were many questions then moved by those who took occasion by the gospel to trouble the common state. And this is the first rule: let servants who have come to the faith and have infidels as masters serve them notwithstanding with great fidelity. The reason: lest God should seem by the doctrine of the gospel to stir people up to rebellion and all wickedness. The second rule is: let not servants who have come to the faith, and also have masters of the same profession and religion, abuse the name of brotherhood, but let them so much the rather obey them. Let this be sufficient, that as touching those things which pertain to everlasting life, they are partakers of the same goodwill and love of God as their masters themselves are. A general conclusion: that these things ought not only to be simply taught, but must with exhortations be diligently beaten into their heads. GENEVA BIBLE.[1]

DILIGENT SERVANTS INSPIRE INTEREST IN THE GOSPEL. DESIDERIUS ERASMUS: It is not our role to attack the lives of those who are strangers to the profession of Christ. It is necessary for us to provoke them to a better mind by our good works, rather than to provoke them with reproachful rebukes. Religion ought to be so ordered that it does not seem to be an occasion for or the sowing of sedition. When it is necessary for us to deal with pagans, let them perceive from us that we have become more diligent to do good, because of religion, and not more unprofitable nor more impudent. For by that means they shall be more easily allured into our fellowship of religion.

Therefore, those bondservants who have been baptized should remember that they are redeemed from the lordship of sin and not liberated from their master's authority. And therefore it is not seemly that upon professing faith they should bristle against their masters, as too wicked and unworthy for a Christian to serve. But let them remember that they are their masters, and therefore let them esteem them worthy of all honor, that the name of God and the doctrine of the gospel might not be defamed and despised, as they would be if it was perceived that they had become more troublesome and intractable. But let them rather be more diligent in serving than they were before, and more glad to obey, serving from the heart, that their masters might be inspired by this to more easily receive the preaching of the gospel. PARAPHRASES.[2]

DOMESTIC SLAVERY IS NOT ABOLISHED BY THE GOSPEL. CASPAR CRUCIGER: "All who are under the yoke . . ." In order to instruct people of all callings, he hands down precepts to his servants. And here let us first learn that in the gospel the ordinance concerning domestic slavery is not abolished, nor is the distinction between slave and free. On the contrary, just as the gospel confirms other secular matters, such as freedom and property, it also confirms slavery. Many similar testimonies concerning masters and slaves in Paul can be adapted for this purpose, namely for the refutation of fanatical spirits, which remove property, ownership, slavery, or like political ordinances. Indeed doubtless at the Church's beginning, some ill-taught persons had similar persuasions, as though people were not to be burdened by slavery. For this reason slaves started to be insolent. COMMENTARY ON 1 TIMOTHY.[3]

DON'T PONDER YOUR SUPERIORITY—OBEY! JOHN CALVIN: Let us compare ourselves with those who were slaves in St. Paul's time. It was distressing to see how rigorously they were treated, and yet God did not exempt them from that yoke. When we are so delicate nowadays that we cannot suffer a little subjection, but will play the rebels, is this not great ingratitude and in no way tolerable? So then we see in summary that when it pleases God to make us subject, he wants us then to have a quiet heart, gentle and meek, and that we seek nothing but to do what he requires of us.

But because people presume to stand on their dignity and think no one worthy to have preeminence above their fellows, and seeing there is nothing more contrary to our nature than to humble ourselves, for this reason St. Paul, to cut off all objections, says, "let servants who are under the yoke regard their masters." He means by this that when someone is subject to another, they must not ruminate within themselves whether they are wiser than the one who is above them, or have more excellent virtues than they do, or be of superior parentage, or have any other conditions in them whereby they ought to rule rather than obey. None of these things should enter our fantasies. . . . We must be subject and obey our superiors. SERMONS ON 1 TIMOTHY.[4]

---

[1]Geneva Bible 1599, NT 94*.
[2]Erasmus, Paraphrases, 67-68.
[3]Cruciger, Commentarius, 257.
[4]CO 53:547.

EQUALITY IN THE CHURCH AND STATE ARE DISTINCT. SEBASTIAN SCHMIDT: Paul says, I go on now to other kinds of people. I take up first the case of slaves. As many as are under a human master's yoke among the gentiles should consider their own masters worthy of their honor, and let them show them the same (viz., honor), even if they are Gentiles, lest the name of our God and the holy teaching of the gospel be blasphemed for disrupting human laws, or for despising them and considering them null and void.

But first let not those slaves with masters belonging to the Christian faith despise their masters, on the pretext that in Christ they are brothers, and to that degree equal in all things, as if equality in the church and equality in the state or the home were not distinct. Rather to the contrary, since the order of masters and slaves is not abolished by the gospel, they should serve much more and more willingly, on the grounds that they are faithful and beloved of their master, and giving thanks in their hearts for such masters, as have done them any good in their slavery, let them acknowledge their masters and they will be repaid. Once again, teach these things and remind your people of them. PARAPHRASE OF 1 TIMOTHY.[5]

6:2b-5 The Unhealthy Cravings of False Teachers

THE OSTENTATION OF HIGHER SPECULATIONS. DUTCH ANNOTATIONS: "He is puffed up . . ." Namely, although he accounts himself wise, or would gladly be accounted wise, "he rages" (Gk., "is sick or diseased"), namely, in his wits or understanding, as fanatic persons and seducing teachers used to be, who esteem the simple doctrine of godliness too mean, and therefore seek to make ostentation of higher speculations or new doctrines before the church; whom the apostle declares to be unsound in their understanding, because they reject or pass by sound doctrine. DUTCH ANNOTATIONS.[6]

THE SWELLING UP OF PRIDE IN THE HEART. JOHN TRAPP: Swelling is a dangerous symptom in the body, but much more in the soul. Pride and self-conceit is a bastard (says one) begotten between a learned head and an unsanctified heart, which being once conceived in the soul, causes it to swell till it burst asunder with unthankfulness to God for the bestowing, with envy, scorn, and disdain of human beings in the imparting of such gifts as may be to them beneficial. COMMENTARY UPON ALL THE EPISTLES.[7]

FALSE TEACHERS MOVED BY VANITY NOT CLARITY. JOHN CALVIN: False teachers are puffed up, knowing nothing. Such persons Paul first charges with pride, foolish and empty pride. Next, because no punishment can be imagined that is better adapted to chastise ambitious persons than to declare that all that they delight in proves their ignorance, Paul pronounces that they know nothing, though they are swelled with many subtleties; for they have nothing that is solid, but mere wind. At the same time, he instructs all believers not to be carried away by that windy ostentation, but to remain steadfast in the simplicity of the gospel.

"But languishing after questions and debates of words." There is an indirect contrast between "the soundness of the doctrine of Christ," and that "languishing"; for when they have wearied themselves much and long with ingenious questions, what advantage do they reap from their labor, but that the disease continually grows? Thus not only do they consume their strength to no purpose, but their foolish curiosity begets this languishing; and hence it follows, that they are very far from profiting aright, as the disciples of Christ ought to do.

Not without reason does the apostle connect "questions and disputes of words"; for by the former term he does not mean every kind of questions, which either arise from a sober and moderate desire to learn, or contribute to clear explanation of useful things, but to such questions as are agitated,

---

[5]Schmidt, *Paraphrasi*, 907.
[6]Haak, *Annotations*, s.v.*

[7]Trapp, *Commentary*, 317-18*.

in the present day, in the schools of the Sorbonne, for displaying acuteness of intellect. There one question gives rise to another; for there is no limit to them, when every person, desiring to know more than is proper, indulges their vanity; and hence, there afterward arise innumerable quarrels. As the thick clouds, during hot weather, are not dispelled without thunder, so those thorny questions must burst into disputes.

He gives the name *logomachias* to contentious disputes about words rather than things, or, as it is commonly expressed, without substance or foundation; for if anyone carefully inquires what sort of contentions are burning among the sophists, they will perceive that they do not arise from realities, but are framed out of nothing. In a word, Paul intended to condemn all questions which sharpen us for disputes that are of no value.

"From which arises envy." He demonstrates from the effects how much an ambitious desire of knowledge ought to be avoided; for ambition is the mother of envy. Where envy reigns, there also rage brawlings, contentions, and other evils, which are here enumerated by Paul. COMMENTARY ON 1 TIMOTHY.[8]

WHEN TO FIGHT FOR THE FAITH. TILEMANN HESSHUS: The world is full of unprofitable questions. Meanwhile in truth the chief Christian teachings are carelessly neglected: regarding the recognition of the true God, of faith, of the benefits of the mediator, of the distinction of law and gospel, of the true exercise of penitence, of true prayer. Therefore Paul severely censures this absurd fondness for the heretics. And he warns us to distinguish what is needful from what is not.

If someone at this point asks, "How it can be known what chief points are needful?" I respond that this can be known without difficulty: those things that point to the glory of God, that build the church, that cheer up our consciences, that protect our faith, that encourage us to prayer, that offer us consolation in affliction, that increase the love of God and the zeal for holiness in us, these things pertain to the foundation. In addition: all things that are revealed in the writings of the prophets and the apostles.

It follows then that those things which are not expounded in Scripture, which neither point to the glory of God, nor either instruct our faith, or increase it—these things are to be passed over in silence. In those matters, faithful ignorance is far safer than inconsiderate knowledge. For there is such a thing as a learned and careful ignorance. But when false teachers do not desist from those unprofitable things, but persist in pressing on those points, then we must realize that these people are fanatics, and that they are neither led by the Spirit of God, nor do they themselves seek after the truth. Rather, with subtleties and sophistry they seek praise for their genius.

Logomachias are arguments about words, where about the matters themselves there is consensus. The needful battles are to be carefully distinguished from *logomachias* that are not necessary. For the truth of the articles of faith, and for the conservation of the purity of heavenly teaching, it is necessary to fight. For this is the salvation of the church. For the salvation of the whole church depends on the purity of the teaching of Christ. COMMENTARY ON 1 TIMOTHY.[9]

REASONS TO AVOID PERVERSE TEACHERS. DAVID DICKSON: The second precept here (after the one addressed to servants) concerns avoiding perverse teachers, namely, to eject them from the ministry, or to excommunicate them from the church.[†] There were many in those times who taught otherwise, who departed either from the apostolic verity in the matter of their word, or from the apostolic simplicity in the manner of their teaching other things, or other than what the apostles were teaching, being discontent with the simplicity of Christian piety. He gives five reasons for their chastisement:

---

[8]CTS 43:154-55* (CO 52:324-25). See also Calvin's earlier comments on 1 Tim 1:6-7.

[9]Hesshus, *Commentarius*, 303-4.

1. They are obstinate who submit not themselves to the wholesome words of Christ, or to sound doctrine, which in the matter and manner of teaching is after godliness.

2. Because they are proud, puffed up with a vain opinion of their own knowledge, whereas they know nothing solidly in the mystery of the gospel.

3. They are of such a contentious disposition that they dote about foolish questions, and strife of words.

4. Because by these evil cavillations they stir up envy, contention, railing, evil surmizings.

5. Because by their perverse disputing they reveal themselves to be of a perverse and corrupt mind, destitute of the truth, and more studious of gain than of godliness; yea to be such who make a gain of godliness. Whereupon he infers the censure of withdrawing from them, which is the consequence of excommunication. EXPOSITION OF ALL PAUL'S EPISTLES.[10]

THE MARKS OF DECEIVERS. MATTHIAS FLACIUS: [Paul] proceeds to depict that sophistical logical construct with one of its own deceivers. He says that he distinguishes those [who provoke] certain perverse and injurious conflicts and disputes indeed by three marks because they are of corrupt mind, that is, by preaching from depraved judgment, and desire of unprofitable disputes: Because they are deprived of all sound and wholesome truth although they possess Christian religion and piety for profit. This is the last rule. For after he describes the seducers, with their own depraved futility, and what he thence proves about the wicked, he now commands that they must be shunned, to be sure, not only by Timothy, but by the whole church. For this is the same as being excommunicated. GLOSS ON 1 TIMOTHY.[11]

---

[10]Dickson, *Exposition*, 169*. †The KJV (following the Textus Receptus) adds the words "from such withdraw thyself" at the end of 1 Tim 6:5. This has some manuscript and patristic testimony but is not well supported by the best manuscripts of the Alexandrian and Western text types. See Bruce M. Metzger, *A Textual Commentary on the Greek New Testament*, 2nd ed. (Stuttgart: Deutsche Bibelgesellschaft, 1994), 575-76, who dismisses the addition as "a pious but banal gloss."
[11]Flacius, *Glossa Compendaria*, 1066.

6:6-8 Godliness with Contentment

TRUE PIETY HAS TRUE PLENTY. JOHN TRAPP: True piety has true plenty, and is never without a well-contenting sufficiency, a full sufficiency. The wicked in the fulness of their sufficiency is in straits. On the other hand, the godly in the fulness of their straits are in an all-sufficiency. COMMENTARY UPON ALL THE EPISTLES.[12]

GODLINESS WITH CONTENTMENT IS GREAT GAIN. EDWARD LEIGH: Godliness with self-sufficiency, for so it is word for word in the original. It restores us our primitive right and interest in the creatures. A godly person in their wants may claim the promise and live upon God. They are sure of the best supply, and in the best way. Every creature and blessing shall be sanctified to them. It produces gracious effects: (1) True contentment of mind. (2) Makes them thankful in the want of these things (as in Job). (3) They look on common favors as fruits of special love and down payments of a heavenly inheritance. (4) It makes such an impression on their hearts, as was in God in the bestowing of them; as God has showed love to them, so will they to the saints. ANNOTATIONS.[13]

THE FOOLISH HURTFUL LUSTS OF COVETOUSNESS. JOHN MAYER: Godliness is great gain, having always by God's providence that which is sufficient for food and clothing: for God will not suffer his people to want as is promised in Matthew 6:25-34 and as is prayed in Proverbs 30:8, and to this the next words seem to agree, "We brought nothing into the world. . . ." for if it be so, to have that which is sufficient here is gain enough. . . .

The foolish and hurtful lusts of those that set their hearts on riches are declared in the parable of him that thought to build his barns greater and thereinto to gather all his fruits and then to live at ease, to eat, drink, and to be merry. For such thoughts are foolish, because life is uncertain and

---

[12]Trapp, *Commentary*, 318*; citing Job 20:22.
[13]Leigh, *Annotations*, 328-29*; citing Ps 37.

when death comes there is a disappointment of the expected fruition of these things. And they are hurtful because the mind being exercised with such thoughts and desires is both distracted and troubled, having no such quiet as the minds of others, and better meditations are kept out, or choked, as the corn with briars and thorns. There is no greater hurt than this because where the word cannot work in the heart, it is most foul and corrupt, and so that soul cannot enter into God's kingdom, from which all unclean things shall be excluded; and therefore these lusts are said to drown people in perdition and destruction, that is, of soul and body....

And I think that no particular sin can be named, but covetousness may be said to be the root of it.... Covetousness, that it may fulfil its desires, commits witchcraft, murder, obscenity, or any wickedness. From hence also comes pride, said to be the beginning of all wickedness, because riches being gotten, pride follows and by riches luxury is maintained....

Apostasy comes from covetousness, whilst either for rewards or for worldly gain people forsake the faith.... And Prosper[†] notably in a few words sets forth all the miseries of the covetous, saying those who will have riches seek them not without labor, find them not without difficulty, keep them not without care, possess them not without hurtful delight, and lose them not without sorrow. Commentary on Paul's Epistles.[14]

6:9-10 The Love of Money

Riches Are an Obstruction to Faith. John Owen: Nothing but the exceeding greatness of the power of God and his grace can carry a rich man safely, in a time of suffering, unto heaven and glory. And it is confirmed by the apostle, "But they that will be rich fall into temptation, and a snare, and into

many foolish and hurtful lusts, which drown men in destruction and perdition." The riches of this world, and the love of them, are a peculiar obstruction unto constancy in the profession of the gospel, on many accounts. These, therefore, seem to be a burden, hindering us in our race in an especial manner. Commentary on Hebrews.[15]

Greed Seduces Our Minds. Marie Dentière: We are so blind because of our avarice, which is the root of all evil, that we do not know how to recognize the truth of his words. If it is pointed out to us well enough, then we can recognize it, but by false doctrines and long orations, false prophets have seduced and tricked the poor people, letting it be understood that they are christs and saviors of the people. They walk about in long robes and sheep's clothing, but inside are ravishing wolves. They forbid marriage and foods, which we should accept with thanks, or they say that Christ is here or there, which is a very strange and new doctrine. Even if Jesus Christ had not warned us to be on our guard against them, we should not believe them. For the kingdom of God does not consist in such things, not in any external or visible observation, but it is within us; it is peace, justice, and joy in the Holy Spirit. Epistle to Marguerite de Navarre.[16]

Covetousness Is an Inordinate Desire. John Owen: Covetousness is an inordinate desire, with a suitable endeavor, after the enjoyment of more riches than we have, or than God is pleased to give unto us; proceeding from an undue valuation of them, or love unto them. So it is described by our apostle. Commentary on Hebrews.[17]

Greed Worships Money, but Godliness Worships God. Martin Luther: The eagerness, or desire, for money extends more widely than greed. It extends to all other things,

---

[14]Mayer, *Commentary*, 526-27*; citing Lk 12:13-21; Mt 13:1-23. [†]He cites Prosper, *De vita contemplativa* 2.13, which is now considered a work of Julianus Pomerius; see Josephine Suelzer, *Julianus Pomerius: The Contemplative Life* (Westminster, MA: Newman, 1947), 3, 79. Cf. PL 51:47 and 59:457.

[15]Owen, *Works*, 24:226; commenting on Heb 12:1.
[16]Dentière, *Epistle to Marguerite de Navarre*, 57-58; citing Mt 7; Lk 20; 2 Pet 2; Acts 20; Mt 24; 1 Tim 4.
[17]Owen, *Works*, 24:410; commenting on Heb 13:5-6.

to the desire for power, pleasure, gold, or silver. . . .
The man who is involved with greed has the
source of every evil. One evil after another wells
up for him. . . . Those who are immersed in the
pursuits of money cannot pray, give thanks, or
hear the Word of God if so much as a penny is
taken from them. These desires are senseless
because they bring no benefit. They are hurtful
because they bring great harm. Therefore he says
it well, of all evils. On the other hand, "there is
great gain in godliness with contentment." Also,
an enthusiasm for generosity is the source of all
good things.

We have heard Paul's admonition against greed,
which he describes as the "root of all evils." He
means of this life, so that we say nothing about the
life which is to come. You see, the greedy man
deprives himself of eternal life, because his heart is
swollen with many concerns. Because he has all
these worries, he is forced to fear the dangers of fire
and of water. As many worries threaten him as
there are grains of sand on the seashore. Thus he
destroys this life as well as that which is to come,
just as "godliness has the promise." Greed is the
worship of idols. You see, greed worships money,
but godliness worships God. The greedy person is
uncertain and is deprived both of this life and that
which is to come. LECTURES ON 1 TIMOTHY.[18]

CRAVING IS AN EARNEST, ACTIVE DESIRE.
JOHN OWEN: The word for craving here is twice
used by our apostle in his first epistle to Timothy,
and nowhere else. In the one place it is applied to
the desire of episcopacy; and in the other unto that
of money—which usually are vehement. In the
latter place we render it by "coveted," a craving
desire. They had an earnest, active desire, which
put them on all due ways and means of attaining it.
Slothful, inactive desires after things spiritual and
heavenly, are of little use in or unto the souls of
men. COMMENTARY ON HEBREWS.[19]

THE PAINFUL PANGS OF THE COVETOUS.
JOHN TRAPP: They have galled and gored
themselves. The covetous person has their name
in Hebrew from a word that signifies sometimes
to pierce or wound. Those who will be rich take
no more rest than one upon a rack or a bed of
thorns: when they grasp earthly things most
greedily, they embrace nothing but smoke, which
wrings tears from their eyes and vanishes into
nothing. They have three vultures always feeding
on their heart: Care in getting, fear in keeping,
grief in spending and parting with what they
have. So they are in hell ahead of time. COMMEN-
TARY UPON ALL THE EPISTLES.[20]

---

[19]Owen, *Works*, 24:95-96* (commenting on Heb 11:16); citing
1 Tim 3:1.
[20]Trapp, *Commentary*, 320*; citing Ps 10:3; Joel 2:8.

---

[18]LW 28:371 (WA 26:111-12); citing 1 Tim 4:8.

6:11-21 FIGHT THE GOOD FIGHT OF FAITH

But as for you, O man of God, flee these things. Pursue righteousness, godliness, faith, love, steadfastness, gentleness. [12]Fight the good fight of the faith. Take hold of the eternal life to which you were called and about which you made the good confession in the presence of many witnesses. [13]I charge you in the presence of God, who gives life to all things, and of Christ Jesus, who in his testimony before[a] Pontius Pilate made the good confession, [14]to keep the commandment unstained and free from reproach until the appearing of our Lord Jesus Christ, [15]which he will display at the proper time—he who is the blessed and only Sovereign, the King of kings and Lord of lords, [16]who alone has immortality, who dwells in unapproachable light, whom no one has ever seen or can see. To him be honor and eternal dominion. Amen.

[17]As for the rich in this present age, charge them not to be haughty, nor to set their hopes on the uncertainty of riches, but on God, who richly provides us with everything to enjoy. [18]They are to do good, to be rich in good works, to be generous and ready to share, [19]thus storing up treasure for themselves as a good foundation for the future, so that they may take hold of that which is truly life.

[20]O Timothy, guard the deposit entrusted to you. Avoid the irreverent babble and contradictions of what is falsely called "knowledge," [21]for by professing it some have swerved from the faith.

Grace be with you.[b]

a Or in the time of b The Greek for you is plural

OVERVIEW: As they interpret this final passage, these Reformation-era interpreters describe the manner in which Christians "fight the good fight of faith." One wages this sustained spiritual combat by eschewing greed for earthly riches and contending against Satan and one's fallen nature. Furthermore the Christian conducts this war by steadfastly confessing the faith over and against the world's most strident opposition. The essence of confessing and living one's faith, they contend, is obedience to God. Our commentators also discuss God's attributes in order to provide motivation for obedience, and they admonish their readers to guard the faith against false teaching.

6:11-12 Fight the Good Fight

O MAN OF GOD. ENGLISH ANNOTATIONS: All righteous men are the servants of God, but the title of "man of God" implies more: for in Scripture it is attributed only to men of eminent sanctity, who had more familiarity and inwardness with God, such as Moses, Samuel, David, Elijah, Elisha, and here Timothy. A man of God is he who is wholly devoted unto God, and his chief employment is to bring messages from God, as prophets do, and bring people unto God, as the faithful ministers of the gospel do. ENGLISH ANNOTATIONS.[1]

FLEE WORLDLY CRAVINGS FOR RICHES. JAN HUS: How difficult it is for some sons of mammon to receive this instruction! For they have fallen away from Christ's command . . . and from the statement of St. Paul, who says, "But you, O man, beware of these things." . . . But a poor priest [i.e., a chaplain] says, "I am serving a parish priest and am earning nothing but my food: how shall I clothe myself and buy books to help me in preaching?" To that the prophet David replies, "I have not seen the righteous forsaken nor his seed begging bread." And the Savior replies to him, saying, "Seek first the kingdom of God and all these things"—that is, food and clothing—"shall be added unto you."

---

[1]Downame, ed., Annotations, s.v.*

Therefore, my dear priest, man of God, if you observe that you are benefiting the people, trust in his holy mercy that he will not leave you naked. ON SIMONY.[2]

THE FIGHT OF FAITH. MARTIN LUTHER: You know what the fight of faith is. After all, those who are in Christ and who have the ministry of the Word are attacked not only by impatience and wrath. Satan also attacks us especially in our greatest good, which is faith and the Word. Those who are involved in the fight of faith bear the attacks of the fear of death, hell, and despair. They ought to be exposed to others in their work. They should be patient and gentle. They should not be self-seekers. For them there remains the final battle with the demons, which Paul describes in Ephesians 6:12. . . . It is easy to fight against tyrants, because we can understand their insidious strategy. Their object here is understandable. But then Satan comes and transforms himself into the appearance of majesty or of an angel. This he does by various means.

. . . [Paul] speaks to a Timothy who is secure in the Word, to a Timothy whom Satan assaults with mental dejection, the weakness and temptation under which Job labored, so that he may [mislead] him. . . . Whatever God says Satan turns into something worthless. Thus he can convert the greatest goodness into evil, mercy into poison, so that nothing except wrath appears in God. The contrary takes place in destructive doctrines, so that nothing except goodness . . . appears in God. . . .

That battle no one understands unless he experiences it. We hear about it from the words and statements of others, but we do not understand its mood and sense. The gross temptations of anger assault us, or, at best, the anger allows us to be burned up. But this we overcome more easily than we win the fight of faith. If the fight of faith—that is, the battle that Timothy was having with heretics and all his adversaries, that is, on behalf of faith or in the cause of faith—had been overcome, it would be the smallest temptation. LECTURES ON 1 TIMOTHY.[3]

6:13-16 *Honor the King of Kings*

WHY PAUL GIVES SUCH A WEIGHTY CHARGE. JOHN FORBES: It may be asked what should move the apostle to add this heavy charge to his former precept, especially to Timothy whom he so much commended, that he found no man so similar to himself. What is the reason he, knowing him to be such a man, gives a severe charge to Timothy, and in his person to all pastors and teachers?

The reason I take to be twofold. First, that people might not dally with his doctrine, as though it might be alterable by his church, or changed at the appointment of princes. Therefore he will have them to know this is not so, but it is of divine authority, which none dare to change, as he will be answerable to God and to Christ in whose name he charges him. So neither Timothy nor any other potentate should think these precepts to be the precepts of people, or such as his church might alter at their discretion This charge is given us to this end, to force us all, and most chiefly for pastors to observe, as we will answer it before God at his most dreadful judgment. Therefore no command of princes, nor the fear of the loss of our lives might cause us to violate this truth.

The second reason why the apostle gives this weighty charge to Timothy, who was so rare a man of whole steadfastness the apostle so well approved, is this: to show that it is not an easy matter to perform this charge, but that all the grace that was in Timothy, was little enough to enable him with constancy and courage to keep it inviolably. The reason of it is this, because there is nothing in this world which Satan more opposes, nor that people set themselves against, neither anything so contrary to flesh and blood, as the truth of God's worship and the sincerity of preaching. The devil labors to corrupt the purity of doctrine and the service of God in his church above all things in the world. . . .

---

[2]Spinka, ed., *Advocates of Reform*, LCC 14:246-47; citing Ps 37:22; Mt 6:33.

[3]LW 28:373-74 (WA 26:112-13).

Therefore he gives this straight charge unto his church, that they should lay God and Christ continually before their eyes, for otherwise the terrors of people and the world will shake them and cause them to corrupt the ways of God. People always stand in danger of being overcome, either by enticement of riches or by the terror of persecution and of imprisonment. Therefore the Spirit gives us this strait charge to bind us more strongly to this doctrine. SERMON ON 1 TIMOTHY 6:13-16.[4]

CONFESSING IN DANGEROUS TIMES. JOHN OWEN: *Homologia* is the "profession" that we make of our faith and hope. And it is applied unto the witness that the Lord Christ gave unto himself and his doctrine. So is the verb *homologeō* constantly used, "to avow publicly," "to profess openly" what is our faith and hope, especially when we meet with danger on the account of it. That, therefore, which is ascribed unto these believers [in Hebrews 11:13] is, that on all occasions they avowedly professed that their interest was not in nor of this world; but they had such a satisfactory portion in the promises which they embraced, as that they publicly renounced a concernment in the world like that of other people, whose portion is in this life. COMMENTARY ON HEBREWS.[5]

WE SHOULD OBEY GOD BECAUSE OF WHO HE IS. DAVID DICKSON: Because eternal life is in the hand of Christ, who is one God with the Father and the Holy Spirit; because he only is of himself immortal and alone has immortality in his power, that he may communicate it to whom he will: therefore the former commands are to be observed. Although the reasons of his commands may not be manifest to us, yet for our obedience and faith it is sufficient to know that God in himself is a light that cannot be approached, and a hidden majesty, having his peculiar and proper essence, which our understanding cannot comprehend, nor see with a beatific vision in this mortal life: therefore it becomes us to adore, observe, and extol the pleasure of his will, rather than curiously to search into it. To him be honor and power forever. EXPOSITION OF ALL PAUL'S EPISTLES.[6]

CHRIST, THE SUPREME SOVEREIGN. GIOVANNI DIODATI: These words signify that all sovereignty and power belong to him, and that all such who have any dominion or government ought to have no authority but under him. And that we should learn to oppose his power to that of the whole world, which would withdraw us from his service. PIOUS ANNOTATIONS.[7]

GOD ALONE IS INDEPENDENTLY IMMORTAL. CHRISTIAN CHEMNITZ: In what sense is it said in verse 16 that God alone has immortality? For even the angels and the rational souls are said to be immortal. Jerome gives an answer in *Against Pelagius* book 2; and John of Damascus, in book 2 of *On the Orthodox Faith*, chapters 3 and 12. God alone has *athanasia*, "immortality" from himself and out of himself; the angels and the souls of men have it from God. Thus God is immortal independently; the angels and the souls are immortal dependently. For it should be noted that it would be possible for something to be called incorruptible and immortal, either in respect to created ability and physical corruption—whereby angelic souls are incorruptible and immortal, and this indeed by nature, since their nature was so created that it would not be able to be corrupted by any created power or physical corruption—or in respect of the absolute power of God, whereby, since the angels can be brought to nothing, they are neither incorruptible, nor are they immortal. But God alone has immortality. A LITTLE COMMENTARY ON ALL PAUL'S EPISTLES.[8]

GOD DWELLS IN UNAPPROACHABLE LIGHT. JACOBUS ARMINIUS: For since God is the Author

---

[4]Forbes, *Four Sermons*, 3-5*; citing Phil 2:20-22.
[5]Owen, *Works*, 24:89 (commenting on Heb 11:13); citing 2 Cor 9:13; Heb 3:1; 4:14; 10:23; Mt 10:32; Lk 12:8; Rom 10:9-10. Owen understands Christ's "good confession" here to be that made to Pilate when he said his kingdom was "not of this world" (Jn 18:36).

[6]Dickson, *Exposition*, 170*.
[7]Diodati, *Pious Annotations*, 328.
[8]Chemnitz, *Commentariolus*, 37.

of the universe (and that, not by a natural and internal operation, but by one that is voluntary and external, and that imparts to the work as much as he chooses of his own, and as much as the nothing, from which it is produced, will permit), his excellence and dignity must necessarily far exceed the capacity of the universe, and, for the same reason, that of mankind. On this account, he is said in Scripture "to dwell in the light unto which no one can approach," which strains even the most acute sight of any creature, by a brightness so great and dazzling, that the eye is blunted and overpowered, and would soon be blinded unless God, by some admirable process of tempering that blaze of light, should offer himself to the view of his creatures. This is the very manifestation before which darkness is said to have fixed its habitation. ORATION ON THE AUTHOR AND END OF THEOLOGY.[9]

KNOWING WHAT GOD IS NOT. JOHN OWEN: We know so little of God, because it is God who is thus to be known—that is, he who has described himself to us very much by this, that we cannot know him. What else does he intend where he calls himself invisible, incomprehensible, and the like?—that is, he whom we do not, cannot, know as he is. And our further progress consists more in knowing what he is not, than what he is. Thus is he described to be immortal, infinite—that is, he is not, as we are, mortal, finite, and limited. Hence is that glorious description of him, "Who alone has immortality, dwelling in the light which no one can approach; whom no one has seen, nor can see." His light is such as no creature can approach. He is not seen, not because he cannot be seen, but because we cannot bear the sight of him. The light of God, in whom is no darkness, forbids all access to him by any creature whatever. We who cannot behold the sun in its glory are too weak to bear the beams of infinite brightness. OF THE MORTIFICATION OF SIN IN BELIEVERS.[10]

6:17-19 The Rich Should Not Be Haughty

THE RIGHT WAY TO BE RICH. PETER MARTYR VERMIGLI: That riches may be lawfully retained by those who are just, certain conditions are required. First, that they be acquired by just means: that is, not by arts which of themselves are evil, or of themselves good yet forbidden and unsuitable for that person; for none ought to withdraw himself from teaching of the word of God to practice shoemaking, and thereby to enrich himself.

Second, let them not abuse riches, to maintain riot and pleasure. Third, let not the mind of those that procure them be drawn away from confidence in God, from their vocation, or from the worshiping of God. Fourth, let them not hoard them up, but distribute them to the poor when need shall require. Fifth, let them put no trust in them, as Paul in 1 Timothy 6 has admonished, "Command the rich of this world, that they put not their trust in the uncertainty of riches." Sixth, let not rich people become proud, advancing themselves and treating the poor with contempt.

Seventh, let them weigh that riches are unstable, and may easily be taken from them. Wherefore, let them not set their hearts on them, and when the Lord shall take them away from them, let them say, "The Lord has given, and the Lord has taken away; even as it pleases the Lord, so let it be." Eighth, let them acknowledge that they have gained these riches from the Lord, and not by their own power. Ninth, and let them every day more and more mortify the desire to possess; lest that desire should grow along with their wealth and riches. COMMONPLACES.[11]

THEY ARE ONLY RICH IN THIS WORLD. GEORGE GIFFORD: Now if we could see how far those who are rich to God excel those who are only rich in this world, it would take them down a little, and it would correct that perverse respecting of persons and blind judgment which is in us. For when he says "in this present age" opposing it to the

---

[9]Arminius, *Writings*, 1:86*.
[10]Owen, *Works*, 6:66.
[11]Vermigli, *Commonplaces*, 3:268*; citing Job 1:21.

world to come, he notes the vanity and the baseness of earthly riches, that there is no cause why any should be puffed up by them, if they were not more than blinded.

It is strange and wonderful that rich people cannot be brought to see this, and to use their riches to their best advantage, but do indeed let slip their happiness. They can willingly bestow great cost in building fair houses; it does not grieve them to bestow a great deal also in gorgeous apparel; and they reckon not what they lay out in delicate fare, both upon themselves and upon others that are wealthy. But to bestow a little more than ordinary upon those who are poor and in misery is very grievous, because they do account that to be lost or cast away. Whereas in very deed there is nothing which can be laid out to any great profit but that which is spent upon the poor: for houses, apparel, and meats do perish with their use; they are transitory and vain. But the reward promised by the Lord is a treasure that shall never come to an end.

Those former things do appertain but unto the satisfying of carnal lusts; but mercy shown to the needy heaps up glory in the heavens.... But to be rich in good works, and to lay up a good foundation against the time to come, that they may attain eternal life—this is not perceived by sense, and they cannot imagine it, and therefore they do little trouble themselves about it. At the day of judgment, this time to come ... this invisible foundation shall be seen. Four Sermons.[12]

Nourishment Is a Kindness of God.
Caspar Cruciger: By this testimony faith is strengthened in two ways. First, to know that nourishment is a kindness of God. Second, let us also add, to know that he wishes to impart these kindnesses, and for that reason that sustenance is to be sought and expected from him. In order that we do this, we need to gather testimonies like this one; as, first seek the kingdom of God, and the rest will be added to you. Again, Christ asks us to seek our daily bread. Therefore Scripture teaches, in this

testing in the matter of sustenance, that faith and invocation are to be practiced, just as also in Deuteronomy 8 it is written: I have afflicted you with want, and I gave you the food called manna, that I would be able to show, that human beings do not live on bread alone, but on every word that comes from the mouth of God. Commentary on 1 Timothy.[13]

6:20-21 *Avoiding Irreverent Babble*

Guard Sound Doctrine Against False Science. English Annotations: "Keep that which is committed ..." The precious treasure of sound or wholesome doctrine that is committed to you, as a pledge, to keep it safely yourself, and carefully transmit it to posterity, and withal the talent of those gifts which appertain unto the preaching of the same.

"Oppositions of science falsely so called ..." Opposition is made against sound doctrine out of erroneous grounds and principles of "sciences" so termed, but falsely. In which words the Greek fathers conceive that he points at the Gnostics,[†] a certain sort of heretics, who get their name from science and profound knowledge, which they arrogated to themselves. English Annotations.[14]

Defend the Gospel Against All Opposition. John Owen: It is incumbent on those who are pastors and teachers of churches "to preserve the truth" and doctrine of the gospel, that is

---

[12]Gifford, *Foure Sermons*, fourth sermon, 26-27*.

[13]Cruciger, *Commentarius*, 265-66; citing Mt 6:33; Deut 8:3.
[14]Downame, ed., *Annotations*, s.v.* †Although the Greek fathers could see linguistic and conceptual parallels between the battles of Paul's day and those against later heresies, William D. Mounce, *The Pastoral Epistles*, Word Biblical Commentary (Nashville: Thomas Nelson, 2000), 372, comments that "there is nothing in the PE [Pastoral Epistles] that gives evidence of second-century Gnosticism." Gordon D. Fee, *1 and 2 Timothy, Titus*, New International Biblical Commentary (Carlisle, UK: Paternoster, 1995), 161, adds that "Paul has previously had trouble with those who opposed his gospel in the name of wisdom and *gnōsis* (1 Cor 1:10–4:21; 8:1-13), which had become a semi-technical term for philosophy. Furthermore, deviations from the gospel in the name of philosophy had already plagued the churches in this area just a few years earlier (see esp. Col 2:1-10)."

committed to the church—to keep it entire, and defend it against all opposition. See the weighty words wherewith the apostle gives this in charge to Timothy: "O Timothy, keep that which is committed to your trust." . . . This charge is given to all of us who are ministers. "It is," says the apostle, "the glorious gospel of the blessed God, which was committed to my trust." And it is committed to *all* our trust; and we are to keep it against all opposition. The church is the ground and pillar of truth, to hold up and declare the truth, in and by its ministers. But is that all? No; the church "is like the tower of David built for an armory, whereon there hang a thousand bucklers, all shields of mighty men." The ministers of the gospel are shields and bucklers to defend the truth against all adversaries and opposers. The church has had thousands of bucklers and shields of mighty men, or else the truth had been lost. They are not only to *declare* it in the preaching of the gospel; but to *defend* and preserve it against all opposition—to hold up the shield and buckler of faith against all opposers. SERMON ON JEREMIAH 3:15.[15]

GUARD THE TREASURE BY AVOIDING IRREVERENT BABBLE. JOHN MAYER: The apostle here requires Timothy to keep the treasure of knowledge committed to him by God and himself, that as a talent he might return it multiplied and not suffer anyone to steal it from him, by the new inductions of words. And to awaken him the more, he calls him by his proper name ("O Timothy"). . . . However others expound the word *deposit* here, yet I think that it simply means the grace bestowed upon Timothy whereby he was enabled for his episcopal function. The meaning then is that he should use this with a good conscience to benefit

the church and not, by doing otherwise, corrupt it or provoke God to deprive him of it, as he did the evil servant of his talent, for this deposit and that talent are all one.

And to this end he bids him to avoid profane vain speeches, which some have expounded of words, such as fate or fortune. . . . But he means words of ostentation; those who are addicted to these, let go the study of edification. For vain speeches are not in words, but in a continued resonance which ambitious men do foam out, aiming rather at the applause of people than the profiting of the church. And therefore it is a grandiloquence, there being herein a great sound but no substance. And it is also called profane, because the force of the Spirit is absent as soon as people thus blow the pipes of their own eloquence. COMMENTARY ON PAUL'S EPISTLES.[16]

THOSE WITH FALSE KNOWLEDGE DO NOT LOVE GOD. JOHN OWEN: it is certain that those who put not their trust in God have not the knowledge of him. There is a "knowledge falsely so called," which has nothing of real spiritual knowledge but the name; and it is generally much given to disputing, or the maintaining of antitheses, or oppositions unto the truth. But it is falsely called knowledge, inasmuch as those in whom it is do neither trust in God nor adhere unto him in love. And we shall not much inquire by what means such a knowledge may be acquired. It remains, therefore, notwithstanding this objection, that all real useful knowledge of the "wonderful things" that are in the Scripture is an effect of God's opening our eyes by the illuminating grace of his Holy Spirit. THE CAUSES, WAYS, AND MEANS OF UNDERSTANDING THE MIND OF GOD.[17]

---

[15]Owen, *Works*, 9:458*; citing 1 Tim 1:11; Song 4:4.

[16]Mayer, *Commentary*, 528-29*; citing Mt 25:24-30.
[17]Owen, *Works*, 4:158*.

COMMENTARY ON 2 TIMOTHY

1:1-2 INTRODUCTION TO 2 TIMOTHY AND PAUL'S GREETING

Paul, an apostle of Christ Jesus by the will of God according to the promise of the life that is in Christ Jesus,

²To Timothy, my beloved child: Grace, mercy, and peace from God the Father and Christ Jesus our Lord.

OVERVIEW: While some demur, our commentators largely agree that Paul composed his second epistle to Timothy while imprisoned in Rome, awaiting death at the command of Emperor Nero. They find in his letter a mix of exhortation and encouragement to his younger charge, as the apostle calls on Timothy to continue in the sound doctrine that had been passed down to him, to reject false teachings and fake spiritualities, and to avoid vain speculations and contentious disputes. Further, as Paul faces martyrdom, they also draw attention to the apostle's calls for Timothy to persevere despite opposition, and recognize that like Paul and Timothy, all messengers of the gospel should be prepared to face affliction as they carry out their ministry. Some also note in Paul's greeting of Timothy as his "beloved child" the strength of the bond and depth of affection between the two, recognizing their shared love and compassion, viewing this relationship as a model for believers to follow.

Introductory Comments

WATCH OUT FOR FALSE SPIRITUALITY. WILLIAM TYNDALE: In this epistle, Paul exhorts Timothy to go forward as he had begun, and to preach the gospel with all diligence, as it needed to be, seeing many had fallen away and many false spirits and teachers had sprung up already. Therefore a bishop's role is ever to watch and to labor in the gospel. In the third and fourth chapters he prophesies, notably of the jeopardous time toward the end of the world, in which a false spiritual living should deceive the whole world with outward hypocrisy and appearance of holiness, under which all abominations should have their true passage and course—as we (alas!) have seen this prophecy of St. Paul fulfilled in our spirituality unto the uttermost jot. NEW TESTAMENT. PREFACE TO 2 TIMOTHY.[1]

PREPARE FOR MARTYRDOM. DESIDERIUS ERASMUS: In the former epistle, Paul wrote to Timothy in Ephesus, in the hope of returning again to him. Since he could not do so because he was held in bonds at Rome, he encourages him with letters, not to be discouraged with storms of persecutions but, after his example, to prepare his mind for martyrdom. For there are perilous times at hand because of some who, under pretense of

---

[1] Tyndale, *The Newe Testament*, cccvii*.

godliness, turn true godliness upside down, and so boast of themselves, as though the Christian religion consisted in words and not rather in pureness of heart. Then, testifying that the day of his death draws near, and that most people have now forsaken him, he bids Timothy and Marcus to come speedily to him at Rome. This epistle he wrote at Rome, when he was again presented at Nero's tribunal. PARAPHRASES.[2]

DO NOT SHRINK FROM AFFLICTIONS. GENEVA BIBLE: The apostle is now ready to confirm with his blood that doctrine which he had professed and taught. He encourages Timothy (and in him, all the faithful) in the faith of the gospel, and in the constant and sincere confession of it, willing him not to shrink for fear of afflictions, but patiently to attend to his task as farmers do (who at length receive the fruits of their labors), and to cast off all fear and care as soldiers do (who seek only to please their captain). He shows him briefly the sum of the gospel he preached, commanding him to preach the same to others, diligently taking heed of contentions, curious distractions, and vain questions to the intent that his doctrine may altogether edify. The examples of Hymenaeus and Philetus, which subverted the true doctrine of the resurrection, were so horrible; yet because they were men of authority and held in high estimation he did not want anyone to be offended at their fall, so he shows that not all who profess Christ are truly his, and that the church is subject to this calamity that the evil must dwell among the good until God's judgment comes. Yet he reserves those whom he has elected, even to the end. And that Timothy should not be discouraged by the wicked, he declares what abominable people and dangerous times shall follow, willing him to arm himself with the hope of the good results that God will give to his own, and to exercise himself diligently in the scriptures both against the adversaries and for the benefit of the church, desiring him to come to him for certain necessary affairs. He ends with

his own and others' salutations. GENEVA BIBLE. NEW TESTAMENT.[3]

WRITTEN IN PAUL'S OWN BLOOD. JOHN CALVIN: The chief point on which this epistle turns is to confirm Timothy both in the faith of the gospel and in the pure and constant preaching of it. But yet these exhortations derive no small weight from the consideration of the time when he wrote them. Paul had before his eyes the death which he was prepared to endure for the testimony of the gospel. All that we read here, therefore, concerning the kingdom of Christ, the hope of eternal life, the Christian warfare, confidence in confessing Christ, and the certainty of doctrine, ought to be viewed by us as written not with ink but with Paul's own blood; for nothing is asserted by him for which he does not offer the pledge of his death; and therefore this epistle may be regarded as a solemn subscription and ratification of Paul's doctrine. . . .

Having praised the faith of Timothy, in which he had been educated from his childhood, he exhorts him to persevere faithfully in the doctrine he had learned, and in the office entrusted to him; and, at the same time, lest Timothy should be discouraged on account of Paul's imprisonment, or the apostasy of others, he boasts of his apostleship and of the reward laid up for him. He likewise praises Onesiphorus, in order to encourage others by his example; and because the condition of those who serve Christ is painful and difficult, he borrows comparisons both from farmers and from soldiers, the former of whom do not hesitate to bestow much labor on the cultivation of the soil before any fruit is seen, while the latter lay aside all cares and employments, in order to devote themselves entirely to the life of a soldier and to the command of their general.

Next, he gives a brief summary of his gospel, and commands Timothy to hand it down to others, and to take care that it shall be transmitted to posterity. Having taken occasion from this to

---

[2]EOO 6:950.

[3]Geneva Bible 1560, NT 99v*.

mention again his own imprisonment, he rises to holy boldness, for the purpose of animating others by his noble courage; for he invites us all to contemplate, along with him, that crown which awaits him in heaven.

He bids him also abstain from contentious disputes and vain questions, recommending to him, on the contrary, to promote edification; and in order to show more clearly how enormous an evil it is, he relates that some have been ruined by it, and particularly mentions two, Hymenaeus and Philetus, who, having fallen into monstrous absurdity so as to overturn the faith of the resurrection, suffered the horrible punishment of their vanity. . . .

He afterward returns to exhort Timothy to persevere faithfully in the discharge of his ministry; and in order to make him more careful, he foretells what dangerous times await the good and the pious, and what destructive men shall afterward arise; but, in opposition to all this, he confirms him by the hope of a good and successful result. More especially, he recommends to him to be constantly employed in teaching sound doctrine, pointing out the proper use of Scripture that he may know that he will find in it everything that is necessary for the solid edification of the church.

Next, he mentions that his own death is at hand, but he does so in the manner of a conqueror hastening to a glorious triumph, which is a clear testimony of wonderful confidence. Last, after having besought Timothy to come to him as soon as possible, he points out the necessity arising from his present condition. This is the principal subject in the conclusion of the epistle. Commentary on 2 Timothy.[4]

To Strengthen Timothy Against Enemies. Thomas Cartwright: The chief scope of this epistle is to strengthen the hands of Timothy to a full performance of his office as an evangelist, committed to him against the difficulties that might either prevent or hinder the good course

that he had entered and set forward in. The hindrances of his ministry consist partly in the opposition of contrary doctrine by secret enemies of the gospel, and partly in fear of persecution from open enemies of it. The apostle, to hearten Timothy against the latter, puts forward his own example wherein, as in a clear glass, he might see both God's assistance and an example of Christian courage and valor, to continue under whatever trial the Lord should draw him to. Confutation of the Rhemists.[5]

Paul Not Necessarily About to Die. John Mayer: Paul did not write the exhortations contained here to constancy in the truth, and to be armed with patience against all sufferings for Timothy's sake only, who was shortly to come to him, but for the instruction of all bishops and Christian people, as Calvin notes. The time when this was written is generally agreed to have been when Paul was in prison at Rome, but whether in the two first years of his imprisonment mentioned in Acts 28, or when afterward he was taken by Nero and imprisoned again (which was nine or ten years after) and finally crowned with martyrdom, it is not agreed. . . .

That saying in 2 Timothy 4:6 ("I am already being poured out as a drink offering") does not so necessarily imply his suffering was so near at hand, since he expected still to be preserved, as appears in verse 18, and in that he willed Timothy to come to him and to bring the cloak he left at Troas and the books and parchments—which do not seem to be the words of one that expected to die by and by.[†] But being in hold, and there being such great enemies of the doctrine that he taught, he stood always ready prepared. . . .

Touching the matter handled, he urges Timothy again and again, as in the first epistle, to oppose false teachers with all constancy, to cleave to the truth, and by all means to uphold it, and with all diligence to set it forth, if those times were dangerous—prophesying yet of more dangerous

---

[4]CTS 43:179-81*. CO 52:341-44.

[5]Cartwright, *Confutation*, 578*.

times to come, against which therefore there was need to arm the faithful by diligent preaching. COMMENTARY ON PAUL'S EPISTLES.[6]

PAUL'S WILL. DAVID DICKSON: The intent of this epistle is the same with the former, not only that Timothy may be instructed and confirmed in the preaching of the gospel, but also that in his person, all teachers may learn how they ought to duly discharge the ministry of the gospel. To which end, having assured Timothy of his good will toward him, he subjoins four admonitions in chapter 1, and as many in the second chapter. Furthermore, he confirms and comforts Timothy against false brethren and afflictions, which he must suffer for the defense of the gospel, in chapter 3. Last, making his will, as it were, he most gravely charges Timothy that he faithfully discharge the parts of his duty, putting forth various reasons to this end in chapter 4. EXPOSITION OF ALL PAUL'S EPISTLES.[7]

PREPARING FOR THE CROSS. GIOVANNI DIODATI: This epistle is almost on the same subject as the former. For St. Paul being a prisoner at Rome, ready to suffer martyrdom, writes again to Timothy to seal and confirm, as he did before, his former doctrine, admonitions, and exhortation, and strengthen him against the temptation and scandal of his approaching end. Having then in the beginning born witness to his faith, in which he been brought up since childhood, he exhorts him in a lively way to persevere in it, and likewise in the exercising of his pastoral charge. And because he should not be troubled at the apostle's afflictions, he declares what his faith, comfort, victory, glory, and triumph was in them.

He recommends and blesses Onesiphorus, from whom he had received relief. He admonishes Timothy to appoint faithful pastors in the churches,

to prepare himself for the cross, showing what was the happy result and most excellent fruit of it. He exhorts him to observe purity and righteousness in teaching of God's truth, avoiding profane questions and vicious disputations, from whence heresies did spring—such as that of Hymenaeus and Philetus, who denied the last resurrection of the dead. Against this danger he heartens believers through their election, confirmed by their sanctification, for which they must all endeavor continually, and likewise exhorts Timothy to this and also to meekness and gentleness.

Then he foretells the great depravations which will happen in the church, and forearms him against them by his doctrine and example. He encourages him to the faithful exercising of his ministry and commends God's church to him—from which his presence will shortly be taken away by his glorious martyrdom, before which time he appoints Timothy to come to him, and gives him notice how his estate stands. PIOUS ANNOTATIONS.[8]

1:1-2 Greetings from Paul

THE LOVE AND COMPASSION OF GOD AND OF PAUL. JOHN CALVIN: First, according to his custom, he calls himself an "apostle of Christ." Hence it follows that he does not speak as a private person, and must not be heard slightly, and for form's sake, like a man, but as one who is a representative of Christ. . . . That his calling may be the more certain, he connects it with the promises of eternal life. . . . Thus also he points out the design of his apostleship, namely, to bring men to Christ, that in him they may find life. . . .

"My beloved son." By this designation he not only testifies his love of Timothy but also procures respect and submission to him; because he wishes to be acknowledged in him as one who may justly be called his son. The reason of the appellation is that he had begotten him in Christ; for, although this honor belongs to God alone, yet it is also transferred to ministers, whose agency he employs for regenerating us.

[6]Mayer, *Commentarie*, 531-32*; citing 2 Tim 4:18, 13. †Gordon D. Fee, *1 and 2 Timothy, Titus*, New International Biblical Commentary (Carlisle, UK: Paternoster, 1995), 289, makes the same point that this language alongside 2 Tim 4:13, 21 "does not necessarily imply an immediate death."
[7]Dickson, *Exposition*, 170* (*Expositio*, 543).

[8]Diodati, *Pious Annotations*, 44*.

"Grace, mercy" etc. The word "mercy," which he employs here, is commonly left out by him in his ordinary salutations. I think that he introduced it when he poured out his feelings with more than ordinary vehemence. Moreover, he appears to have inverted the order; for since "mercy" is the cause of "grace," it ought to have come before it in this passage. But still it is not unsuitable that it should be put after "grace," in order to express more clearly what is the nature of that grace, and whence it proceeds; as if he had added, in the form of a declaration, that the reason why we are loved by God is that he is merciful. Yet this may also be explained as relating to God's daily benefits, which are so many testimonies of his "mercy"; for whenever he assists us, whenever he delivers us from evils, pardons our sins, and bears with our weakness, he does so because he has compassion on us. COMMENTARY ON 2 TIMOTHY.[9]

TIMOTHY RESEMBLES PAUL. DAVID DICKSON: That Paul might commend Timothy (to whom he writes) to all the churches, he calls him "beloved son," most especially because he faithfully preached the doctrine which he had learned from Paul, as Paul himself, and resembled him as a father in the whole course of his life. Therefore he was beloved of Paul and had in estimation by him as a son, to whom he wishes all excellent things from God, as he had done in the former epistle. EXPOSITION OF ALL PAUL'S EPISTLES.[10]

THE GOSPEL IS A PROMISE. GIOVANNI DIODATI: "According to the promise of life" means that Paul is the apostle of the gospel, whose whole subject is not a word of plain command or narration, as the law is, but of a promise of grace and everlasting life . . . the whole foundation and root of which is Christ; and from him alone it derives upon his members by means of faith. PIOUS ANNOTATIONS.[11]

WE MUST SHOW OUR AFFECTION TO OTHERS AS PAUL DID. JOHN MAYER: Paul says, "I never praise God or pray unto him but I think upon you, or as soon as I think upon you at any time, I praise God, which argues my exceeding great love toward you, and the high esteem that I have you in. And I mention the purity of my conscience, that you may not suspect any dissimulation in my thus protesting." And thus should all preachers labor, that both their brethren in the ministry, and the people to whom they preach, might be persuaded of their sincere hearty affection toward them, that having their hearts they may the rather win them to God. COMMENTARY.[12]

---

[9]CTS 43:183-84 (CO 52:345-46).
[10]Dickson, *Exposition*, 170-71*.
[11]Diodati, *Pious Annotations*, 337*.
[12]Mayer, *Commentarie*, 535.

1:3-18 GUARD THE GOOD DEPOSIT
ENTRUSTED TO YOU

[3]I thank God whom I serve, as did my ancestors, with a clear conscience, as I remember you constantly in my prayers night and day. [4]As I remember your tears, I long to see you, that I may be filled with joy. [5]I am reminded of your sincere faith, a faith that dwelt first in your grandmother Lois and your mother Eunice and now, I am sure, dwells in you as well. [6]For this reason I remind you to fan into flame the gift of God, which is in you through the laying on of my hands, [7]for God gave us a spirit not of fear but of power and love and self-control.

[8]Therefore do not be ashamed of the testimony about our Lord, nor of me his prisoner, but share in suffering for the gospel by the power of God, [9]who saved us and called us to[a] a holy calling, not because of our works but because of his own purpose and grace, which he gave us in Christ Jesus before the ages began,[b] [10]and which now has been manifested through the appearing of our Savior Christ Jesus, who abolished death and brought life and immortality to light through the gospel, [11]for which I was appointed a preacher and apostle and teacher, [12]which is why I suffer as I do. But I am not ashamed, for I know whom I have believed, and I am convinced that he is able to guard until that day what has been entrusted to me.[c] [13]Follow the pattern of the sound[d] words that you have heard from me, in the faith and love that are in Christ Jesus. [14]By the Holy Spirit who dwells within us, guard the good deposit entrusted to you.

[15]You are aware that all who are in Asia turned away from me, among whom are Phygelus and Hermogenes. [16]May the Lord grant mercy to the household of Onesiphorus, for he often refreshed me and was not ashamed of my chains, [17]but when he arrived in Rome he searched for me earnestly and found me— [18]may the Lord grant him to find mercy from the Lord on that day!—and you well know all the service he rendered at Ephesus.

a Or with   b Greek before times eternal   c Or what I have entrusted to him; Greek my deposit   d Or healthy

OVERVIEW: Our Reformation commentators recognize that Paul begins on a personal note by urging Timothy to be loyal to both the message he has taught and to him as an apostle and friend, looking back to the faith of Timothy's grandmother and mother as well as to the special anointing he gave to Timothy. While the nature of Timothy's gifts and ordination generate some differences in interpretation, there is general agreement on the need for Timothy to continue his ministry with passion and diligence, a charge that is generalized to other officers of the church. Similarly, as they unpack Paul's turn to the "testimony about the Lord," the "good deposit" that is entrusted to Timothy, there are also some differences of doctrine and emphasis evident among our exegetes, as some prioritize election, others grace, and others faith. Nevertheless, they again conclude in unison that Timothy and the church are to stand firm in the lessons handed down to them, without fear or shame.

1:3-7 Fan into Flame the Gift of God

PAUL'S CONSTANT PRAYERS. JOHN CALVIN: "In my prayers night and day." Hence we see how great was his constancy in prayer; and yet he affirms nothing about himself but what Christ recommends to all his followers. We ought, therefore, to be moved and inflamed by such examples to imitate them, so far, at least, that an exercise so necessary may be more frequent among us. If any one understand this to mean the daily and nightly prayers which Paul was wont to offer at stated hours, there will be no impropriety in that view; though I give a more simple interpretation, that there was no time when he was not employed in prayer. Commentary on 2 Timothy.[1]

Paul Served the God of His Ancestors. Peter Martyr Vermigli: These words . . . were spoken by the apostle to the end he might purge and defend himself. For other adversaries laid to his charge that he had departed from the law, and had alienated himself from the God of Israel; and that therefore people should beware of the Jews, as of deceivers. But he answered that he worshiped the living God, whom his forefathers had also worshiped; and that in preaching of the Son of God, as he did, he did not do so deceitfully or by fraud, but with a pure and faithful conscience. But it cannot be gathered from this that he boasted of a full and perfect observation of the commandments of the law. Commonplaces.[2]

The Faith of Timothy's Mother and Grandmother. John Calvin: It is uncertain whether, on the one hand, these women were converted to Christ, and what Paul here applauds was the commencement of faith, or whether, on the other hand, faith is attributed to them apart from Christianity. The latter appears to me more probable; for although at that time everything abounded with many superstitions and corruptions, God had always his own people, whom he did not suffer to be corrupted with the multitude, but whom he sanctified and separated to himself, that there might always exist among the Jews a pledge of this grace, which he had promised to the seed of Abraham. There is, therefore, no absurdity in saying that they lived and died in the faith of the Mediator, although Christ had not yet been revealed to them. Commentary on 2 Timothy.[3]

Paul Conveyed Special, Unrepeatable Gifts on Timothy. John Lightfoot: The apostles had a power of imparting these gifts, but even they had not a power of enabling another to impart them. Paul by laying hands on Timothy could endow him with the gifts of tongues and prophecy, but he could not so endow him that he should be capable of conveying those gifts to another. This was purely apostolical to dispense these gifts; and when they died, this power and privilege died with them. Hebrew and Talmudical Exercitations.[4]

Timothy's Ordination by Paul. John Calvin: There can be no doubt that Timothy was invited by the general voice of the church, and was not elected by the private wish of Paul alone; but there is no absurdity in saying that Paul ascribes the election to himself personally, because he was the chief actor in it. Yet here he speaks of ordination, that is, of the solemn act of conferring the office of the ministry, and not of election. Besides, it is not perfectly clear whether it was the custom, when any minister was to be set apart, that all laid their hands on his head, or that one only did so, in the room and name of all. I am more inclined to the conjecture that it was only one person who laid on his hands.

So far as relates to the ceremony, the apostles borrowed it from an ancient custom of their nation; or rather, in consequence of its being in use, they retained it; for this is a part of that decent and orderly procedure which Paul elsewhere recommends . . . whenever ministers were ordained, they were recommended to God by the prayers of the whole church, and in this manner grace from God was obtained for them by prayer, and was not given to them by virtue of the sign, although the sign was not uselessly or unprofitably employed, but was a sure pledge of that grace which they received from God's own hand. . . . It does not therefore follow that Timothy had not formerly any gift, but it shone forth the more when the duty of teaching was laid upon him. Commentary on 2 Timothy.[5]

---

[1]CTS 43:186-87 (CO 52:348).
[2]Vermigli, *Commonplaces*, 2:567.
[3]CTS 43:187 (CO 52:348).

[4]Lightfoot, *Horae Hebraicæ et Talmudicæ*, 4:97, in comments on Acts 8:19.
[5]CTS 43:189-90 (CO 52:349-50); citing 1 Cor 14:40.

Timothy's Gifts and Ordination. John Mayer: When the apostle ascribes the gift of God to the imposition of hands, he speaks by a synecdoche,[†] meaning hereby the whole act of praying and imposing of hands then performed. Neither are we so to understand that gifts were given to Timothy then, as if he had before lacked them altogether, for he was even before this a man of excellent parts, and therefore was thought fit to be ordained to this office; but then it is likely that his ability and gifts were greatly increased. Commentary.[6]

Timothy Should Not Neglect His Particular Gifts. Edward Leigh: As a person preserves the fire by blowing, so by our diligence we must kindle and revive the gifts and graces of God bestowed on us. Therefore some think this is a metaphor taken from a spark kept in ashes, which by gentle blowing is stirred up until it takes a flame. . . . But it is better . . . to refer it to the type of the priests of the Old Testament, by whose daily and continual ministry the fire coming from heaven was maintained. So Timothy is commanded to stir up and preserve the gifts of the Holy Spirit received, and cause them to flame and burn in him. Not those gifts common to all the faithful—faith, hope, and charity—but the particular gifts of the Spirit, such as the gift of teaching in the schools, the gift of exhorting in the church, and persuading others of the faith of Christ, the gift of tongues. In calling it a gift, he signifies an extraordinary grace of that time; but in willing him to stir it up and not to neglect it, he shows that it was in him to procure it at God's hands, by reading, teaching, and praying, and the like means. Annotations.[7]

Bishops Must Not Be Sluggish or Sleepy but Brave. François Carrière: "For God has not given us a spirit of fear." But Isaiah 11:3 says, "And a spirit of the fear of the Lord will fill him." I respond that Paul here is warning Timothy not to hold on to the grace of his bishop's rank in a sleepy or lazy fashion. Because God has not given a spirit of sluggishness and timidity, as the Greek word *doulias* means. But he has given a spirit of power, in Greek *dynameōs*, of boldness and of strength, so that they may surpass others as an example of the bravest leaders for the expansion of the church and of faith, as Chrysostom says. But Isaiah is speaking of the fear of God that is given to Messiah. Commentary on the Whole of Scripture.[8]

Keep the Fire of Your Spiritual Office Burning. English Annotations: To stir up. Greek: kindle again, or quicken, as fire burns under ashes, signifies to rekindle or revive; for the gift of God is as it were a certain lively flame kindled in our hearts, which the flesh and the devil go about to put out; and therefore we on the contrary must labor, as much as we can, to foster and keep it burning. In the metaphor, the apostle seems to allude to the type of the priests in the Old Testament, by whose ministry the holy fire on the altar was cherished (that it might not go out) and . . . blown to a brighter flame.

Some by this gift understand the gift of miracles, which Timothy received by the imposition of the apostle's hands, and that by the laying hands of the Presbytery he was admitted into the holy ministry. But because there is no proof in Scripture, or undoubted antiquity, that Timothy had the gift of miracles, it is more probable that by gift is here meant that spiritual power or office which Timothy received at his ordination, by the laying on of the apostle's hands on him, in the presence of the Presbytery, who all gave consent thereunto and testified it by putting their hands upon him also. English Annotations.[9]

Empowered by the Spirit for Ministry. John Calvin: We are taught, first, that not one of us possesses that firmness and unshaken constancy

---

[6]Mayer, *Commentarie*, 535*. [†]Synecdoche is a figure of speech in which a part is made to represent the whole or vice versa.
[7]Leigh, *Annotations*, 331*; citing Lev 6:9-13; 1 Thess 5:19; 1 Tim 4:14.

[8]Carrière, *Commentarius in Universam Scripturam*, 778.
[9]Downame, ed., *Annotations*, s.v.*; citing Lev 6:9-13; 1 Tim 4:14.

of the Spirit, which is requisite for fulfilling our ministry, until we are endued from heaven with a new power. And indeed the obstructions are so many and so great, that no human courage will be able to overcome them. It is God, therefore, who endues us with "the spirit of power"; for they who, in other respects, give tokens of much strength, fall down in a moment, when they are not upheld by the power of the divine Spirit.

Second, we gather from it, that they who have slavish meanness and cowardice, so that they do not venture to do anything in defense of the truth when it is necessary, are not governed by that Spirit by whom the servants of Christ are guided. COMMENTARY ON 2 TIMOTHY.[10]

GOD DID NOT GIVE US THE SPIRIT OF FEAR. GIOVANNI DIODATI: "God gave us . . ." The meaning is, kindle up God's gift, and do not let it go out, nor be smothered up through carnal fear. For such a kind of fear is in no way the motion of God's Spirit, but an effect of the world and the devil's spirit. Which is here said because, perhaps, the church's afflictions, and especially St. Paul's, had somewhat terrified and affrighted Timothy. God gave us a "Spirit of love," namely, a holy love of God and Christ with which the believer, being enflamed in a lively way, freely suffers all manner of adversities. He also gave us a spirit of a sound mind, namely, by which the Holy Spirit restores the troubled soul to tranquility, and keeps away such turbulent passions as fear it. PIOUS ANNOTATIONS.[11]

A SOUND MIND IS A GIFT OF THE SPIRIT. MATTHIAS FLACIUS: The first reason for the exhortation, by itself a gift of the Holy Spirit, who himself is given to the godly for this purpose so that he may excite them for courageous and steadfast service for the glory of God, and true religion. A kind of heroic, or preferably a divine motion/movement, especially for the godly, particularly for teachers during adversities and

persecutions is necessary. Furthermore, so that he may excite them for an ardent love for their neighbor, and for sobriety, not so much corporally, but spiritually; that is, for a certain soundness of mind, which is opposed to the most fanatic spirit now stirring as well as disturbances of depraved affections, which spiritually affects every human mind as if drunk, just as in the New Testament sobriety is received by others against drunkenness as Isaiah 28 describes. GLOSS ON 2 TIMOTHY[12]

DO NOT FEAR THE FROWNS OF THE MIGHTY. JOHN MAYER: Paul would have Timothy stir up the gift of God in him, namely, by putting away fearfulness in the executing of his office, which would make anyone languish in their gifts and to do so as if the Spirit were idle and of no virtue in them. This is not the fear spoken of in Romans 8:15 but that fear of those who are mighty in this world, when they frown or take indignation at the preacher of the word for impugning of their wickedness, and the fear of being maligned by any for their faithful and free executing of their office. It is not thus with those who have the Spirit, but contrariwise, they act like people of power boldly and freely going on to do their office in speaking against error and vice in whomsoever. Wherefore if any minister through timidity does otherwise, they have not the Spirit in them. "Love" and "sobriety" are added to distinguish the Spirit of power from the distemper of fanatical persons, who rush on with a turbulent force and boast stoutly of the Spirit of God in them, whilst the true minister of God is sober and temperate in their proceedings, in all things showing love and a studious desire to do good. COMMENTARY.[13]

1:8-14 Guard the Good Deposit

SUFFERING BY THE POWER OF GOD. DAVID DICKSON: If anything is laid on us to be borne for Christ above our strength, the power of God will

---

[10]CTS 43:191 (CO 52:350).
[11]Diodati, *Pious Annotations*, 337*.

[12]Flacius, *Glossa Compendaria*, 1072.
[13]Mayer, *Commentarie*, 536*.

be present to help and deliver us. Trusting in his power and supported by his aid we are bound to be confident and rely upon him above our own strength. Exposition of All Paul's Epistles.[14]

Effectual Calling by Grace. Peter Martyr Vermigli: "Called us with a holy calling." Here he speaks of the effectual calling whereby we are justified, and not of the common calling, which is by the preaching of the Word of God, that is laid open to all people. And since this does not consist (as Paul says) of merits or works, neither can justification also come from them. Commonplaces.[15]

A Perfect Expression of Free Grace. Heinrich Bullinger: I truly think that if someone had set themselves to say something in defense of this matter, they could not have framed any sentence so fit and evident as these words are. So now it is manifest that the grace of God is altogether free, as that which excludes all our works and merits. And this free love of God is the only cause and true beginning of the gospel, which is why Paul calls the gospel the preaching of grace. Decades.[16]

Grace Given to Us Through the Covenant. David Dickson: Grace is given to us in Christ, before the world began, before we or our works could have any being, that is, before all time. Therefore it is not meet that we should be ashamed of the testimony or cross of Christ. It is called "grace given to us in Christ" because although we had not any being, yet Christ the designed mediator, the second person of the Trinity, subsisted from eternity and covenanted with his Father for us, his elect, before all time, and afterward in time paid the price of our redemption, and in our name received the grace assigned to us by which in time we should be called, justified, and freely saved in due season. Exposition of All Paul's Epistles.[17]

The Simplicity of Scripture on Election. Synod of Dordrecht: The synod rejects the errors of those who teach that "the good pleasure and purpose of God, which Scripture mentions in the doctrine of election, does not consist in this—that God elected some certain people rather than others—but in this: that God chose, from among all possible conditions (included in which are the works of the law) or out of the whole order of things, as a condition of salvation, the act of faith (which in itself is unworthy), and the imperfect obedience of faith. God was graciously pleased (they say) to count this as perfect obedience, and assess it worthy of the reward of eternal life." For by this pernicious error, the good pleasure of God and the merit of Christ are weakened, and people are called away from the truth of justification by grace and the simplicity of Scripture by unprofitable questions. Plus, that saying of the apostle that "God has called us with a holy calling, not by works, but by his own purpose and grace, which he gave us in Christ Jesus before the ages began" is made out by this error to be false. Canons of Dordrecht.[18]

He Brought Life and Immortality to Light. John Trapp: He brought life and immorality to light, as he drew light out of darkness at the creation. And as he then made light on the first day of the week, so on the same day he abolished death by his resurrection from the dead. A Commentary.[19]

God's Love Not Withdrawn from Christ. John Barlow: Death by Christ is destroyed.... For he only it is who has borne our infirmities and the burden of our sins ... and satisfied the justice of the Father for the first and second death....[†] Yet this is warily to be understood. We may not in any way so much as think that God the Father did ever wholly withdraw his love from Christ Jesus or

---

[14]Dickson, *Exposition*, 171*.
[15]Vermigli, *Commonplaces*, 3:101*.
[16]Bullinger, *Decades*, 530*.
[17]Dickson, *Exposition*, 171*.

[18]*Acta Synodi Nationalis*, 1:245-46 (*Rejectio Errorum*, 1:3). See also Westminster Confession 3.5.
[19]Trapp, *Commentary*, 324.

separate his affection from him; the second death so accepted is to undergo the full justice and implacable anger of God for all eternity, the which may not here in that sense be admitted. For the Father did never withdraw his love from his Son indeed: Though for the present, he looked on him as he was our surety and a sinner by imputation, with the strict eye of a severe judge and creditor, who would not remit one farthing of his due debt but exact a full and perfect satisfaction. At which time Christ felt the most bitter pangs in his passion, and that torment, the which was equivalent to the second death.... This may comfort every Christian heart in its greatest troubles.... And the reason we are so often astonished is because we do not mind or believe this thing. For if we did, we would cry out with joy, "O death, where is your sting? O grave, where is your victory?"... Wherefore in your greatest fear, call to mind that death by Christ is abolished. EXPOSITION OF 2 Timothy 1-2.[20]

WE MUST WHOLLY ENTRUST OURSELVES TO GOD. JOHN TRAPP: A child who has any precious thing given to them cannot better secure it than by putting it into their father's hands to keep. So neither can we better provide for our soul's safety than by committing them to God.... We shall be sure to be safest if we commit ourselves wholly to God, and seek not to part with him. The ship that is part in the water and part in the mud is soon beaten to pieces. A COMMENTARY.[21]

THE CERTAINTY OF FAITH. JOHN CALVIN: This is the only place of refuge, to which all believers ought to resort, whenever the world reckons them to be condemned and ruined people; namely, to reckon it enough that God approves of them; for what would be the result, if they depended on people? And hence we ought to infer how widely faith differs from opinion; because, when Paul says,

"I know whom I have believed," he means that it is not enough if you believe, unless you have the testimony of God, and unless you have full certainty of it. Faith, therefore, neither leans on the authority of people, nor rests on God, in such a manner as to hesitate, but must be joined with knowledge; otherwise it would not be sufficiently strong against the innumerable assaults of Satan.... This passage is highly worthy of attention; because it expresses admirably the power of faith, when it shows that, even in desperate affairs, we ought to give to God such glory as not to doubt that he will be true and faithful; and when it likewise shows that we ought to rely on the word as fully as if God had manifested himself to us from heaven; for he who has not this conviction understands nothing. Let us always remember that Paul does not pursue philosophical speculations in the shade, but, having the reality before his eyes, solemnly declares, how highly valuable is a confident hope of eternal life. COMMENTARY ON 2 TIMOTHY.[22]

HEAVENLY EXPECTATION DRIVES AWAY FEAR AND SHAME. JOHN MAYER: Note that the assured expectation of everlasting life drives away all fear and shame in well doing, and seeking to promote the holy gospel of Jesus Christ. And sure hereof we cannot but be, if this be our course, because God is of all power, and therefore his servants must needs be brought safely through all danger to the inheritance prepared for them. COMMENTARY.[23]

GUARDING THE DEPOSIT. THOMAS CARTWRIGHT: The doctrine of the reward of good works at the later day is true, but does not grow out of this ground, where the apostle speaks not of the reward that shall then be given, but of the preservation and continuance of himself in the fear and service of God until that day.... And it is finely said of the apostle that by faith he had commended himself to be kept in the hands of God as a precious pledge to be preserved, that no

[20]Barlow, *Exposition*, 147-48; citing 1 Cor 15:55. †On second death see Rev 2:11; 20:6, 14; 21:8, understood here as eternal condemnation.
[21]Trapp, *Commentary*, 325*.
[22]CTS 43:199-200 (CO 52:355).
[23]Mayer, *Commentarie*, 538*.

affliction nor other thing, high or low, present or to come, should be able to take him out of his hand. He exhorts Timothy that since God so faithfully and safely keeps the ministers that by a lively faith lay themselves down in his hand, that he also would keep the doctrine faithfully and carefully which God had laid up with him as a treasure of special trust. So that herein there is a kind of mutual indenture: of the Lord's part to keep us trusting in him; of our part to keep the holy faith and doctrine that he has put us in trust with. CONFUTATION OF THE RHEMISTS.[24]

OUR SALVATION IS IN GOD'S HANDS. JOHN CALVIN: Observe that he employs this phrase ("what I have entrusted to him") to denote eternal life; for hence we conclude, that our salvation is in the hand of God, in the same manner as there are in the hand of a depository those things which we deliver to him to keep, relying on his fidelity. If our salvation depended on ourselves, to how many dangers would it be continually exposed? But now it is well that, having been committed to such a guardian, it is out of all danger. COMMENTARY ON 2 TIMOTHY.[25]

THE PATTERN OF TRUE AND USEFUL SOUND WORDS. JOHN STOUGHTON: There may be no words, no doctrines, no principles delivered in the church of God but such as may be full of certain, and holy, and pious truths, such as are agreeable with truth, according to the Word of God, according to the analogy of faith; that is the first kind of soundness, the soundness of *truth*.

But the other kind of soundness, or a second branch of it, may be a soundness of *use*, that their words may be such as are fit for edification. There may be many things true, but there may be so little

substantiality, so little solidity, so little materialness for any use, so frivolous and so low, that there may be no great advantage or benefit that can come to the church by hearing or receiving them. Therefore the apostle includes this, that as there should be a care that nothing but the sound and wholesome truth of God should be delivered, so that it might be such solid and substantial truth as may be very conductible for the building up and edifying of the church of God, not frivolous and vain and curious disputes and questions, which rather make people swell and puff up, and rather make contention and jangling, but such as are solid and substantial, necessary and profitable truth for edification. A FORM OF WHOLESOME WORDS.[26]

KEEP IN MIND THE SUM OF SOUND DOCTRINE. DUTCH ANNOTATIONS: Hold the pattern of sound words. That is, keep always in your mind a brief sum of sound doctrine, wherein the principal articles of the same are as it were briefly drawn and represented, according to which you may frame your doctrines. Or as some interpret, let the sound words, that is, the sound doctrine that you have heard from me, and the manner which I observe in teaching, be a prescript unto you which you may follow in teaching. The things "which you have heard from me in faith and love": these are two principal heads whereunto all the articles or points of sound doctrine may be referred, and wherein the same are contained. DUTCH ANNOTATIONS.[27]

THE FOUNDATION OF RELIGION IS A LIVELY FAITH WORKING BY LOVE. JOHN STOUGHTON: Those truths are most properly fundamental without which we cannot be made partakers of Christ, nor be enabled to do that by which we may be made partakers of God in him. And so the sum of all is particularly mentioned in this phrase "by faith and love which is in Christ Jesus" ... which is an intimation that the main part, the principal part of the foundation of the principles

[24]Cartwright, *Confutation*, 580*.

[25]CTS 43:201 (CO 52:356). Calvin interprets "my deposit" here to mean something Paul has entrusted to God. Others take it to mean something God has entrusted to him, i.e., the gospel, which is how the word is understood in 2 Tim 1:14 and 1 Tim 6:20. See William D. Mounce, *The Pastoral Epistles*, Word Biblical Commentary (Nashville: Thomas Nelson, 2000), 487-88.

[26]Stoughton, *A Forme of Wholsome Words*, 24-25*.
[27]Haak, *Annotations*, s.v.*

of religion, yea, all the whole truth and foundation of religion, may be reduced to matters of *faith*, and matters of *practice*; to a *lively faith, working by love*: All that is requisite and required may be brought within the compass of these two. A Form of Wholesome Words.[28]

Hold Fast and Do Not Be Ashamed. David Dickson: I, Paul, have committed my body and soul to God, who is faithful and powerful, to keep what I have entrusted to him until the day of judgment. And I am persuaded that I shall be kept. Therefore neither ought I to be ashamed, nor you, O Timothy, whatever befalls us for the testimony of the gospel.... Although your own strength should fail you in the defense of your doctrine, yet the assistance of the Holy Spirit dwelling in you will be at hand for the upholding of his sincere servant, if you implore his aid. Therefore this form of sound doctrine is to be held fast. Exposition of All Paul's Epistles.[29]

The Sacred Deposit of Divine Truths Committed to Us. John Stoughton: Divine truths are a sacred deposit. We are not proprietors but depositors; they are not our own to do what we will with them, to squander them away as we wish, but they are God's, and he deposits them with us, lays them up in us, as committing of them to our custody and requiring them again of us, that so we should not see them embezzled or corrupted or abused because God has committed them to us as a sacred deposit....

Paul must have a care of it, of keeping it himself and committing it to the care of others and stirring up and provoking others.... All Timothys, all the ministers of God's word, who are God's dispensers, his stewards, and whom God has reposed special trust in: it is committed to their care in an especial manner, and they should look into it.... And divine truths and the integrity and purity and soundness of them is a thing that concerns not only (though chiefly) the ministers, but it concerns the whole church of God, and all God's people, that they should be preserved without violation, without contamination, being given for a public good, and the public good of all and every one in particular depending on it....

It has been more publicly observed in their creeds and confessions. Hence it was that the church of God did gather together and compile, as it were in a bundle, in the short compass of the creed, the sum of faith, as the epitome of those things they believed, and the groundwork of those things that are to be believed as necessary to salvation....

More privately it has been the care of people (and a commendable care) according to this rule to deliver a form of sound words, both to unlearned and beginners in a way of catechism, expressing the fundamental things of religion to the unlearned, and in a systematical way for the learned proficients to compose a body of divinity, in as narrow a compass of substantial and pithy principles from the top to the bottom as they could. This has been the care of all the churches publicly and privately that have discharged their fidelity in this charge, by their faithful care, that there might be still preserved and kept in the church of God a form of sound and wholesome words. A Form of Wholesome Words.[30]

The Good Deposit. Giovanni Diodati: He calls the graces of the Holy Spirit a thing committed, to show that an account must be given of them. And what God has entrusted us with, we must faithfully distribute. "By the Holy Spirit"—namely, by his power and grace, which you ought carefully to employ to this effect. "Who dwells within us"— he shows that the Holy Spirit is ready and prepared to succor and assist believers, provided they waive not the receiving of his grace which it is proffered them. Pious Annotations.[31]

---

[28]Stoughton, *A Forme of Wholsome Words*, 30-31*.
[29]Dickson, *Exposition*, 172*.
[30]Stoughton, *A Forme of Wholsome Words*, 38-41, 57-58*.
[31]Diodati, *Pious Annotations*, 338*.

1:15-18 Onesiphorus Was Not Ashamed of Paul

THE TREACHERY OF THOSE WHO DESERT CHRIST. JOHN CALVIN: Those apostasies he mentions might have shaken the hearts of many, and given rise, at the same time, to many suspicions; as we commonly look at everything in the worst light. Paul meets scandals of this kind with courage and heroism, that all good people may learn to abhor the treachery of those who had thus deserted the servant of Christ, when he alone, at the peril of his life, was upholding the common cause; and that they may not on that account give way, when they learn that Paul is not left destitute of divine assistance. COMMENTARY ON 2 TIMOTHY.[32]

ONESIPHORUS WAS NOT ASHAMED OF THE GOSPEL. JOHN OWEN: Onesiphorus was a man of some credit and repute in the world; poor Paul was a prisoner bound with a chain, that he might have been ashamed to own him: but, instead of that, he sought him out; he was not ashamed of his chain. To be ashamed of the poor professors of the gospel—so in themselves, or made so by the power of oppressors—is to be ashamed of the gospel of Christ, his truths, his worship, and his people. SERMON ON ROMANS 1:16.[33]

THIS IS NOT A PRAYER FOR THE DEAD. HENRY HAMMOND: What "the household of Onesiphorus" here signifies is thought fit to be examined by some in order to [prove] the doctrine of praying for the dead.[†] For because the prayer is here for the household, and not for the master of it, Onesiphorus himself, it is by some presently concluded that Onesiphorus was dead at that time.[‡] And then that being supposed, it appears that St. Paul prays for him that he may find mercy in that day. How far it may be fit to pray for those who are departed this life needs not to be disputed here. It is certain that some measure of bliss, which shall at the day of

judgment be vouchsafed the saints when their bodies and souls shall be reunited, is not till then enjoyed by them, and therefore may safely and fitly be prayed for them (in the same manner as Christ prays to his Father to glorify him with that glory which he had before the world was). And this is a very distant thing from that prayer which is now used in the Romish Church for deliverance from temporal pains, founded in their doctrine of purgatory,[††] which would no way be deducible from hence, though Onesiphorus for whom St. Paul here prays for mercy had been now dead.... But neither is there any evidence of Onesiphorus being then dead, nor probability of it here. A PARAPHRASE AND ANNOTATIONS.[34]

A PRAYER FOR MERCY. JOHN CALVIN: This prayer shows us how much richer a recompense awaits those who, without the expectation of an earthly reward, perform kind offices to the saints, than if they received it immediately from the hand of human beings. And what does he pray for? "That he may find mercy"; for he who hath been

---

[32]CTS 43:204-5 (CO 52:358).
[33]Owen, *Works*, 9:229.

[34]Hammond, *A Paraphrase and Annotations*, 707*; citing Jn 17:5.
[†]See Martin, *New Testament*, 589, who speaks of such prayers giving "the greatest hope at the day of our death or general judgment that can be," and of how "it is worth all the lands, honors, and riches of the world" to have such prayers. Fulke, *Text of the New Testament*, 386, responds to this, saying God's mercy is our only hope and "with popish priests it has always been a true proverb, *No penny, No Pater Noster.*" Luther says, "They have made an article of faith of purgatory because it has brought them the world's riches" (LW 52:180). [‡]Jerome D. Quinn and William C. Wacker, *The First and Second Letters to Timothy: A New Translation with Notes and Commentary*, Eerdmans Critical Commentary (Grand Rapids: Eerdmans, 2000), 614, suggest (as modern Roman Catholic commentators) that "the most plausible reason" for the prayer wishes being expressed here "is that Onesiphorus had died unexpectedly and that these sentences transmit that news in as delicate a manner as possible." See Mounce, *Pastoral Epistles*, 497-98, for a recent Protestant response. [††]See the 25th session of the Council of Trent (1563), which proclaimed, "The Catholic Church, instructed by the Holy Ghost, has, following the sacred writings and the ancient tradition of the Fathers, taught in sacred councils and very recently in this ecumenical council that there is a purgatory, and that the souls there detained are aided by the suffrages [intercessory petitions] of the faithful and chiefly by the acceptable sacrifice of the altar." H. J. Schroeder, ed., *The Canons and Decrees of the Council of Trent* (Rockford, IL: Tan, 1978), 214.

merciful to his neighbors will receive such mercy from God to himself. And if this promise does not powerfully animate and encourage us to the exercise of kindness, we are worse than stupid. Hence it follows, also, that when God rewards us, it is not on account of our merits or of any excellence that is in us; but that the best and most valuable reward which he bestows upon us is, when he pardons us, and shows himself to be, not a stern judge, but a kind and indulgent Father. COMMENTARY ON 2 TIMOTHY.[35]

---

[35]CTS 43:206-7 (CO 52:359).

2:1-13 A GOOD SOLIDER OF CHRIST JESUS

You then, my child, be strengthened by the grace that is in Christ Jesus, ²and what you have heard from me in the presence of many witnesses entrust to faithful men,ᵃ who will be able to teach others also. ³Share in suffering as a good soldier of Christ Jesus. ⁴No soldier gets entangled in civilian pursuits, since his aim is to please the one who enlisted him. ⁵An athlete is not crowned unless he competes according to the rules. ⁶It is the hard-working farmer who ought to have the first share of the crops. ⁷Think over what I say, for the Lord will give you understanding in everything.

⁸Remember Jesus Christ, risen from the dead, the offspring of David, as preached in my gospel, ⁹for which I am suffering, bound with chains as a criminal. But the word of God is not bound! ¹⁰Therefore I endure everything for the sake of the elect, that they also may obtain the salvation that is in Christ Jesus with eternal glory. ¹¹The saying is trustworthy, for:

If we have died with him, we will also live with him;
¹²if we endure, we will also reign with him;
if we deny him, he also will deny us;
¹³if we are faithless, he remains faithful—
for he cannot deny himself.

a The Greek word *anthropoi* can refer to both men and women, depending on the context

OVERVIEW: Our sixteenth-century commentators find much to discuss in Paul's exhortation to Timothy to endure the difficulties of ministry and to pass on the baton to faithful people who can also teach others, just as he has done. The need for courage is highlighted, as is the need to recognize and raise up other leaders to continue the work of spreading the gospel. Numerous applications are found in Paul's evocation of the soldier, farmer, and athlete as metaphors for the work of ministry, with these examples found to demonstrate the need for courage, discipline, and perseverance. Dwelling at length on Paul's call on Timothy to remember Christ and endure in him, our exegetes find a number of important themes: the primacy of the gospel, the power and supremacy of the Lord, the need for perseverance and faithfulness, and the blessing contained in the promises and hope toward which we strive.

2:1-3 Strengthened by Grace

LIKE PAUL, TIMOTHY SHOULD BE COURA-GEOUS. DAVID DICKSON: Paul admonishes Timothy that he endeavor in the propagation of the gospel, not only by himself but also by others that were to succeed him in the ministry, standing upon no pains that were requisite for the promoting of it. . . . He should arm himself with strength for the work of the ministry, and put on courage, and address himself to manage his affairs well . . . because it becomes Paul's "son" to put on courage and be valiant, and because the grace that is in Jesus Christ alone will not be wanting to you, when you prepare yourself for your work. EXPOSITION OF ALL PAUL'S EPISTLES.[1]

WE MUST SHARE THE GOOD NEWS WITH OTHERS. GENEVA BIBLE: They do not keep that worthy thing that is committed to those who keep it to themselves. Rather they most freely communicate it with others, to the end that many may be partakers of it without anyone's loss or hindrance. GENEVA BIBLE.[2]

RECOGNIZING THOSE WHOM GOD HAS GIFTED. MARTIN BUCER: Here the apostle

[1]Dickson, *Exposition*, 172*.
[2]Geneva Bible 1599, NT 94*.

instructs Timothy to be diligent in discerning and recognizing those whom the Lord has gifted to be reliable and suitable for this work. This diligence and knowledge he also requires of him as he warns him not to be hasty in laying hands on anyone, that is, before the people have been well tested.

Thus, when he orders Titus to appoint elders in the towns and immediately describes to him what they are to be like, "one who is blameless, the husband of one wife," and so on, he similarly indicates that those who should choose and appoint the ministers of the church must themselves diligently discern and, according to the common sense which God has given to them, faithfully decide who those are who show the most signs of the Holy Spirit, namely, those who are best gifted, fitted, and skilled for this ministry. CONCERNING THE TRUE CARE OF SOULS.[3]

2:4-7 The Soldier, the Athlete, and the Farmer

FINDING GOD IS NOT EASY. JOHN TRAPP: Never dream of a delicacy. You should not expect to find God in the gardens of Egypt, whom Moses found, but in the burning bush. Many love Canaan but loath the wilderness, and commend the country but look upon the conquest as impossible. They would sit in the seat of honor with Zebedee's children but not drink the cup of affliction. These deceive themselves. A COMMENTARY.[4]

LESSONS FROM THE SOLDIER, ATHLETE, AND FARMER. DUTCH ANNOTATIONS: Even as soldiers cannot trouble themselves with merchandise, trades, or husbandry whereby we commonly get a living or sustenance, but must always attend upon their watches, marches, and other services concerning the war, according to the order of their commanders: so also must a faithful teacher of the gospel do the like, and not trouble themselves with any other worldly things, to administer their office

faithfully, that they may be acceptable unto God.

And if anyone strive also—namely with wrestling, running, or other similar games, which are set up for a prize . . . they are not crowned, that is, receive not the prize which was commonly a wreathed crown, if they have not striven lawfully, that is according to the laws made for such exercises, if they have not duly fulfilled them.

The husbandman laboring must first enjoy the fruits. That is, as a farmer must first plow, harrow, sow, weed, reap, plant, water, and so on before they can receive the fruits: so also a teacher of the gospel must first put forth diligent labor before they can receive any fruit either for the church or for themselves. . . .

Apply these similitudes to yourself in your ministry. . . . But seeing by nature we cannot comprehend those things which are of the Spirit of God and are spiritually discerned, I pray to God (says Paul) that he would enlighten your understanding both in these and all other things concerning salvation and your office, to comprehend all things rightly and perfectly. DUTCH ANNOTATIONS.[5]

CHARACTERISTICS OF VIGOROUS SERVICE. MATTHIAS FLACIUS: [Paul] illustrates by these three elegant characteristics the vigorous service of Christians that he wants to arouse in bishops. This first is taken from a military camp, whose three properties indicate: first, to neglect all depraved favors for money and merchandise, to apply themselves totally to that service, and finally, for one's highest desire to be led by approval for his vigorous service.

Similarly he wishes to admonish that they add those same qualities and many others, certainly such as endurance of labors and dangers, and to be most constant in spiritual service. He looks at the same according to the parable of Christ about having taken the hand to the plow, and denying oneself in all things, and taking up his cross. GLOSS ON 2 TIMOTHY.[6]

---

[3]Bucer, *Concerning the True Care of Souls*, 61; citing 1 Tim 5:22; Titus 1:6.
[4]Trapp, *Commentary*, 326. Cf. Ex 3:1–4:31; Num 13:1–14:45; Mk 10:35-40.

[5]Haak, *Annotations*, s.v.*; citing 1 Cor 2:14.
[6]Flacius, *Glossa Compendaria*, 1076.

Ministry Incompatible with Civilian Pursuits. Thomas Cartwright: If the Scriptures had not plainly set down that ministers may not meddle with civil offices, thereby to have one foot in the church and another in the commonwealth, yet the very consideration of the bare weight and difficulty of the charges that fall into the estate of a minister on the one hand, and the regard of the small strength and sufficiency that is in a man (however sufficient) on the other hand, could shut and close up all hands from embracing both, since they cannot lodge under one roof, and are in one and the same person incompatible....

Next in sufficiency of gifts unto our Savior Christ were the apostles, yet they found the charge of preaching and prayer so great that they could not attend upon the provision of the poor. So they do evidently declare that the ministry of the word has a jealous eye that cannot abide the association of any other office with it as that which will defraud it of all that is lent unto another. And if the office of provision for the poor—for use necessary, for credit honorable, an office so close to the ministry of the word—cannot be joined with the ministry of the word (wherewith it has the nearest conjunction) much less can other offices (which touch it not so near) have any good correspondence with it. It is untrue in any person's mouth to affirm that the civil and ecclesiastical offices may meet together. Confutation of the Rhemists.[7]

Serving God and Not Mammon. John Mayer: No one can serve God and mammon. Clergy ought not to make merchandise of intercessions and of the offerings of widows, but be content to live of the altar. They ought not to entangle themselves for gain with cares and actions of the world, knowing that therein are many snares of sin hidden, and therefore they ought freely to be devoted to divine things only. And as soldiers and champions they must not fear but rejoice at the encounter of adversities. The greatness of rewards should delight their mind, but the strife of labors should not deter them, because they cannot attain to great rewards but by great labors. They shall not be crowned unless they overcome; overcome they cannot unless they strive; and strive they cannot, but having an enemy and resisting him. Yet those that labor in the spiritual husbandry, must first before all others receive of the fruits of the field wherein they labor, that is, of the carnal goods of the church. Commentary.[8]

2:8-13 Remember Our Union with Jesus Christ

Keep in Mind the Gospel Itself. David Dickson: Because Christ, the general and captain of the army, has conquered all adverse power and death itself by the virtue of his deity, rising again from the dead for us in the same flesh which he assumed from the seed of David, as I have preached: therefore, O Timothy, you may hope to be delivered from all evils and from death itself by the power of Christ, very God and very man. To which end also, he commands Timothy to remember and keep in mind this doctrine, because this is the chief foundation of faith, hope, and Christian consolation. Exposition of All Paul's Epistles.[9]

The Word of God Is Not Bound. English Annotations: Though they may confine me, says Paul, and bind me fast yet they cannot bind and fetter the gospel of Christ. That word of his ever is and shall be free, not only preached by those who are at liberty, but even by me and other servant of Christ who are restrained and in prison. English Annotations.[10]

Christ Will Defend His Truth. David Dickson: Whoever, being deceived by the terrors of persecution and the allurements of the world, casts off the profession of the name of Christ, shall also be cast off by Christ and perish.... Those who

---

[7]Cartwright, *Confutation*, 581-82*.

[8]Mayer, *Commentarie*, 542*; citing 1 Cor 10:18.
[9]Dickson, *Exposition*, 173*.
[10]Downame, ed., *Annotations*, s.v.*

are unfaithful, although they bring destruction upon themselves, yet shall they detract nothing from the truth or glory of Christ, who will defend his truth against the power of adversaries and the perfidiousness of apostates, and will establish whatever he has said for his servants, and against their enemies. EXPOSITION OF ALL PAUL'S EPISTLES.[11]

ENDURING AFFLICTIONS TO BE CROWNED WITH CHRIST. JOHN BARLOW: Seeing that to suffer afflictions is a burden not easy to be undergone, consider that the issue thereof will be of great worth, no less than to be crowned with Christ Jesus. But if this motive shall not prevail, be it known that they who deny him, must also be denied by him. EXPOSITION OF 2 TIMOTHY 1–2.[12]

IF WE ARE FAITHLESS, HE REMAINS FAITHFUL. JOHN MAYER: It may seem at the first by these words that whether we stand to Christ being strong in the faith, or deny him thus falling from faith, yet he will not deny us; but being constant and immutable he will perform to us the good which he has promised. But then these words would be contradictory to the former, verse 12, "If we deny him, he also will deny us." The meaning therefore is: if we are so weak in the faith that we cannot so fully be persuaded of that happiness which he has promised, yea, although there are some among us that believe it not, and if we should all be distrustful, yet the thing is most certain—the glory that he has promised he will perform to all his in the end. Our infidelity cannot make, but that the Lord will still be faithful of his word. For it shall at the last appear how constant he is in his love toward his chosen, who indeed cannot but believe with what diffidence soever others labor. . . . Note, that the happiness of the children of God to come when they have for a time been in misery here, is most certain. God shall as soon cease to be God as he will fail them herein. COMMENTARY.[13]

WILLINGLY ENDURE LIKE CHRIST FOR THE SALVATION OF OTHERS. DESIDERIUS ERASMUS: Paul says: I allure as many as I can to Christ, whoever they may be. It does not matter to me what I suffer, as long as I may increase the profit of the gospel of Christ. For this reason, I suffer all things willingly, being assured of my own salvation and that they also shall attain salvation through the preaching of the gospel, whom God has appointed to this happiness. This salvation is offered to all, not through the law of Moses but though Jesus Christ, and just as he has suffered for us so also it is fitting that we suffer for the sake of his gospel and for the salvation of our brethren. Just as he, through various ignominious afflictions was exalted to the glory of heaven, even so must we endure the same things on that same way.

This may seem hard and incredible to some, but it ought not to be doubted by us. For if we, through baptism, died together with Christ to the lusts of this world, or if we persevere in the profession of baptism and are caught up in the sorrows of this world, then we shall also live with Christ. That is to say, we who were companions of death with him shall also be companions of immortality with him. And if we suffer with him and for his glory, we shall undoubtedly reign with him too. For God is perfectly fair and will not suffer those to be shut out from the fellowship of reigning those whom he would have to be fellows in suffering sorrows. If we profess him boldly in this world before others, he will acknowledge us also in his majesty. But if we deny him (for they deny him who refuse his cross) it shall come to pass that we shall hear that terrible voice, "I do not know you." If we put our trust in him, we do it for our own prosperity; but if we distrust him, he shall not lose out. . . . Whether we believe or not, what he has promised to the godly shall come to pass— everlasting life—and to the ungodly, everlasting death. This is the foundation of the doctrine of the gospel. PARAPHRASES.[14]

[11]Dickson, *Exposition*, 173*.
[12]Barlow, *Exposition*, 87*.
[13]Mayer, *Commentarie*, 544*.
[14]Erasmus, *Paraphrases*, 88-89.

God's Promise Sweetens the Cross. John Calvin: We shall not be partakers of the life and glory of Christ, unless we have previously died and been humbled with him; as he says, that all the elect were "predestined that they might be conformed to his image." This is said both for exhorting and comforting believers. Who is not excited by this exhortation, that we ought not to be distressed on account of our afflictions, which shall have so happy a result? The same consideration abates and sweetens all that is bitter in the cross; because neither pains, nor tortures, nor reproaches, nor death ought to be received by us with horror, since in these we share with Christ; more especially seeing that all these things are the forerunners of a triumph. Commentary on 2 Timothy.[15]

God Can Do Anything His Holy Will Desires. Christian Chemnitz: It is sometimes asked whether God can be omnipotent if, as it says here, he cannot deny himself. We respond: To deny oneself, to die, to err, to spoil what has been done, to lie, are imperfections, laying waste to the perfection of God and to truth. But they pertain more to impotence than to power. Wherefore it can rightly be said, God can do all things, namely, those that are not opposed to his holy being and will. We should, however, add a note of caution: it is certain that those matters which imply a contradiction do not fall under divine omnipotence. In turn, however, it is also certain that many things seem to us to imply a contradiction according to our finite intellect, but which do not according to the infinite intellect of God. For example, anyone would consider the two statements that the substance of human nature is separable from nature, and that the substance of one nature can be shared with another nature, to imply a contradiction; but the mystery of the incarnation teaches that it does not imply this. Hence Paul says that God is able to do things greater than anything that we ask, or understand.

We should therefore add that God cannot do those things which imply a contradiction, truly. And this only applies where there is a contradiction in God's eyes, and not in the case of those things which appear to imply a contradiction according to our finite intellect alone. A Little Commentary on All Paul's Epistles.[16]

Those Blinded by the Allurements of the World Will Be Rejected. John Calvin: A threatening is likewise added for the purpose of shaking off sloth; for he threatens that those who, through the dread of persecution, leave off the confession of his name, have no part or lot with Christ. How unreasonable is it, that we should esteem more highly the transitory life of this world than the holy and sacred name of the Son of God! And why should he reckon among his people those who treacherously reject him? . . . Their base denial of Christ proceeds not only from weakness, but from unbelief; because it is in consequence of being blinded by the allurement of the world, that they do not at all perceive the life which is in the kingdom of God. But this doctrine has more need of being meditated on than of being explained; for the words of Christ are perfectly clear: "Whoever shall deny me, him will I also deny." Commentary on 2 Timothy.[17]

---

[16]Chemnitz, *Commentariolus*, 54; citing Eph 3:20.
[17]CTS 43:218* (CO 52:365); citing Mt 10:33. Philip H. Towner, *The Letters to Timothy and Titus*, New International Commentary on the New Testament (Grand Rapids: Eerdmans, 2006), 514, points out that "some commentators think that Christ's faithfulness is to a standard of holiness that requires him to execute judgment on deserters and apostates (unbelievers) without mercy. Others see it as a general statement of Christ's faithfulness that is meant to be taken as a note of encouragement for believers (such as Timothy) who face rejection for the faith and struggles with apostates that whatever befalls the church, Christ will remain faithful to it." I. Howard Marshall, *The Pastoral Epistles*, International Critical Commentary (London: T&T Clark, 2004), 741-42, outlines three options: that Christ is faithful to the faithless and does not reject them; that because he is faithful he must act in accordance with his warnings and judge the faithless; or, finally, the statement is a general one about Christ remaining faithful to his cause despite the apostasy of some.

---

[15]CTS 43:217 (CO 52:364-65); citing Rom 8:29.

The Unchangeable God Will Punish as He Says. Cardinal Cajetan: "He remains faithful" in the punishments he has threatened. "He cannot deny himself." Just as God cannot sin and nevertheless is all-powerful (because the "ability to sin" is not an ability but the lack of power), so the fact that he cannot deny himself is consistent with his omnipotence. For the ability to deny oneself is not an ability but a lack of power, because it is a characteristic of mutability. Everyone who can deny himself is mutable, moving from an initial consideration to a different one. Therefore, as he has decreed, he will punish unbelievers. The Epistles of Paul and the Other Apostles.[18]

---

[18]Cajetan, *Epistolae Pauli*, 149.

2:14-26 A WORKER APPROVED BY GOD

Remind them of these things, and charge them before God[a] not to quarrel about words, which does no good, but only ruins the hearers. [15]Do your best to present yourself to God as one approved,[b] a worker who has no need to be ashamed, rightly handling the word of truth. [16]But avoid irreverent babble, for it will lead people into more and more ungodliness, [17]and their talk will spread like gangrene. Among them are Hymenaeus and Philetus, [18]who have swerved from the truth, saying that the resurrection has already happened. They are upsetting the faith of some. [19]But God's firm foundation stands, bearing this seal: "The Lord knows those who are his," and, "Let everyone who names the name of the Lord depart from iniquity."

[20]Now in a great house there are not only vessels of gold and silver but also of wood and clay, some for honorable use, some for dishonorable. [21]Therefore, if anyone cleanses himself from what is dishonorable,[c] he will be a vessel for honorable use, set apart as holy, useful to the master of the house, ready for every good work.

[22]So flee youthful passions and pursue righteousness, faith, love, and peace, along with those who call on the Lord from a pure heart. [23]Have nothing to do with foolish, ignorant controversies; you know that they breed quarrels. [24]And the Lord's servant[d] must not be quarrelsome but kind to everyone, able to teach, patiently enduring evil, [25]correcting his opponents with gentleness. God may perhaps grant them repentance leading to a knowledge of the truth, [26]and they may come to their senses and escape from the snare of the devil, after being captured by him to do his will.

a Some manuscripts the Lord   b That is, one approved after being tested   c Greek from these things   d For the contextual rendering of the Greek word doulos, see Preface

---

OVERVIEW: As Paul advises Timothy on how to be a divinely approved minister in the context of false teaching, the commentary from our sixteenth-century exegetes coalesces around a number of important themes. First, they examine the need for ministers to rightly divide the Word of truth, a task that requires not only a knowledge of the text but also an examination of oneself and one's own motivations, skills, and sins before the Word can be properly examined and brought before an audience. Our exegetes also dwell on the significance of Paul's use of the metaphor of a great house. The house is understood to symbolize either the world or the visible church, where the saved and unsaved mix together and cannot be discerned by human eyes. Some have found in the text a suggestion that human works are the cause of salvation, leading some commentators to assert and defend the doctrine of predestination. Finally, as Paul looks to Timothy's interaction with his opponents, the reformers find exhortations for ministers to embrace maturity, to minister with patience and gentleness, and to bring correction from the Word of God.

2:14-19 Rightly Handling the Word of Truth

RIGHTLY DRAWING THE WORD. GIOVANNI DIODATI: The Greek term for "rightly handling" is taken from laying straight highways, or from drawing the lines on geographical maps. And as God's word is called a way, so pastors ought not to draw it awry, but to set it straight and well-dedicated. Others derive it from the distribution of food at a table or in a house, by a father of a family, to signify the faithful and wise dispensation or distribution of God's word. PIOUS ANNOTATIONS.[1]

---

[1]Diodati, Pious Annotations, 339*; citing Lk 12:42.

Rightly Handling the Word for Different Audiences. John Owen: It is . . . the duty of stewards in the house of God to give unto his household their proper portion. This is the blessed advice our apostle gives to Timothy: "Study to show yourself approved to God, a worker who needs not to be ashamed, rightly cutting out the word of truth." This is that whereby a minister may evince himself to be "a worker who needs not to be ashamed." If as, when the beasts that were sacrificed were cut into pieces, the priest according to the law disposed of the parts of them, to the altar, himself, and those who brought them, that each in the division might have his proper and legal portion; so he give out a due and proper part unto his hearers, he is an approved worker. Others cast all things into confusion and disorder; which will at length result in their own shame.

Now, whereas in all churches, auditories, or congregations, there is so great a variety of hearers, with respect to their present attainments, knowledge, and capacities, so that it is impossible that anyone should always, or indeed very frequently, accommodate his matter and way of instruction to them all; it were greatly to be desired that there might be, as there was in the primitive church, a distribution made of hearers into several orders or ranks, according as their age or means of knowledge do sort them, that so the edification of all might be distinctly provided for. So would it be if it were the work of some separately to instruct those who yet stand in need to be taught the first principles of the oracles of God, and of others to build up toward perfection those who have already made some progress in the knowledge of the gospel; or the same work may be done by the same persons at several seasons. Nor does any thing hinder but that those who are strong may be occasionally present at the instructions of the weak, and the latter at the teachings of the former, both to their great advantage.

In the meantime, until this can be attained, it is the duty and wisdom of a minister to apply himself, in the doctrine he preaches, and the manner of his delivery, unto the more general state of his hearers, as by him it is apprehended or known. And as it will be a trouble unto him who esteems it his duty to go forward in the declaration of the mysteries of the gospel, to fear that many stay behind, as being unable to receive and digest the food he hath provided; so it should be a shame to them who can make no provision but of things trite, ordinary, and common, when many, perhaps, among their hearers are capable of feeding on better or more solid provision. Commentary on Hebrews.[2]

Not Mangling or Twisting the Word of God. English Annotations: "Rightly dividing": by adding nothing to it, neither skipping over anything, neither mangling it, nor renting it in sunder, nor wresting of it; but marking diligently what the hearers are able to bear, and what is fit for edification. English Annotations.[3]

Skills Needed to Divide the Word Rightly. John Owen: With respect to the doctrine of the gospel, there is required unto the ministry of the church skill to divide the word aright; which is also a peculiar gift of the Holy Ghost. . . . If a minister would be accepted with God in his work, if he would be found at the last day "a worker who needs not to be ashamed"—that is, such a builder of the house of God as whose work is meet, proper, and useful—he must take care to "divide the word of truth," which is committed unto his dispensation, "rightly," or in a due manner. . . . It is the taking out from those great stores of it in the Scripture, and, as it were, cutting off a portion suitable unto the various conditions of those in the family. Herein consists the principal skill of a scribe furnished for the kingdom of heaven with the wisdom before described; and without this, a common course of dispensing or preaching the word, without differencing of persons and truths, however it may be gilded over with a flourish of words and oratory, is shameful work in the house of God.

---

[2]Owen, *Works*, 22:7-8*; commenting on Heb 6:1.
[3]Downame, ed., *Annotations*, s.v.*

Now, to this skill sundry things are required: (1) A sound judgment in general concerning the state and condition of those unto whom any one is so dispensing the word. It is the duty of a shepherd to know the state of his flock; and unless he do so he will never feed them profitably. He must know whether they are babes, or young men, or old; whether they need milk or strong meat; whether they are skillful or unskillful in the word of righteousness . . . what probably are their principal temptations, their hinderances and furtherances; what is their growth or decay in religion. He that is not able to make a competent judgment concerning these things, and the other circumstances of the flock, so as to be steered thereby in his work, will never evidence himself to be "a worker who needs not to be ashamed."

(2) An acquaintance with the ways and methods of the work of God's grace on the minds and hearts of people, that he may pursue and comply with its design in the ministry of the word. . . . (3) An acquaintance with the nature of temptation, with the especial, hinderances of faith and obedience, which may befall those unto whom the word is dispensed, is in like manner required hereunto. Many things might be added on this head, seeing a principal part of ministerial skill consists in this. (4) A right understanding of the nature of spiritual diseases, distempers, and sicknesses, with their proper cures and remedies, belongs hereunto. For the want hereof the hearts of the wicked are oftentimes made glad in the preaching of the word, and those of the righteous filled with sorrow; the hands of sinners are strengthened, and those who are looking toward God are discouraged or turned out of the way. And where people either do not know these things, or do not or cannot apply themselves skillfully to distribute the word according to this variety of occasion, they cannot give the household its portion of meat in due season. And those who want this spiritual gift will never divide the word rightly, toward its proper ends. A DISCOURSE OF SPIRITUAL GIFTS.[4]

REFORMERS SHOULD MODEL PAUL'S DEFINITION OF APPROVED WORKERS. CARITAS PIRCKHEIMER: So many highly educated people are in opposition to each other in many matters. Each claims to be right and yet nobody knows how he stand, not just against those who call themselves evangelical and the papists, but also the evangelicals among themselves. And we poor females are supposed to follow what every single one of them is saying. We should not recall that St. Paul taught us that we should test the spirits and accept the best. In my opinion in many hundreds of years it has never been more necessary to be cautious in accordance with Christ's warning, "Be as clever as the serpents and simple as the doves." There are so many errors about. . . .

Yes, it is said, follow those who speak the truth. But they all claim to be right and each maintains he is telling the truth. And thus we are too lowly to decide the controversy. God knows our heart. He knows we are not so stubborn that we really would not want to believe correctly, but to believe everything is folly. . . . If the good man is doing it with the best of intentions, then God will thank him. He must not hold it against us if we do not believe everything he says immediately. Without doubt he also occupied himself with it for a long time until he arrived at his present opinion and who knows whether he is still free in his conscience. I hope he will conduct himself toward us as St. Paul teaches his Timothy. A servant of the Lord should not argue, but should be gentle toward everyone, a clever and patient teacher who corrects with kindness those who stubbornly oppose him so that with time God will give them the realization of truth. But now everyone wants to force the other person to believe and do what he wants. If that does not happen, he gets angry and criticizes and ascribes guilt to the other person and harms the people. Is this the correct evangelical way? I will leave that up to God. JOURNAL.[5]

---

unto these things, people preach at random, uncertainly fighting, like those that beat the air." This, he says, "will make people weary of preaching."

[4]Owen, *Works*, 4:510-12*; citing 2 Tim 3:16-17. Cf. a similar passage in *Works*, 16:76-77, where Owen says that "without a due regard

[5]Pirckheimer, *Journal of the Reformation Years*, 134-35*; citing 1 Thess 5:21; Mt 10:16.

THE GANGRENOUS SPREAD OF HERESY. JOHN TRAPP: Gangrene presently overruns the parts, and takes the brain, piercing into the very bones, and if not suddenly cured by cutting off the part infected, kills the patient. Lo! Such is heresy and error. A COMMENTARY.[6]

THE RESURRECTION HAS ALREADY HAPPENED. GIOVANNI DIODATI: It is likely that the doctrine of Hymenaeus and Philetus was that there is no other resurrection but the spiritual resurrection of the soul, from the death of sin; or the renewing of the state of the world under the gospel (the Scripture using this word oftentimes in this sense). PIOUS ANNOTATIONS.[7]

AN ALLEGORICAL RESURRECTION OVERTHROWS FAITH. DAVID DICKSON: Experience has demonstrated this evil in the persons of two heretics (whom Paul names to their disgrace, that they may be avoided as rocks). They only acknowledge an allegorical resurrection, erring from the doctrine of truth and overthrowing the faith of some. And while they insinuated their perverse opinion into others, they gave occasion to some not well settled in the faith to renounce the profession of the Christian religion. EXPOSITION OF ALL PAUL'S EPISTLES.[8]

HERETICS ARE UPSETTING SOME PEOPLE'S FAITH. EDWARD LEIGH: They overthrow not the grace, but the profession of faith, or else the doctrine of faith which these did hold. They had run into errors and heresies. The word "upsetting" is in the present tense in the Greek, by which the apostle signifies that they not only persist in their error, but also in a perverse study of propagating it. There is an emphasis in the word "subvert" or "overthrow," because the faith of the resurrection being taken away (as the fountain of all Christian

religion) presently the whole fabric of Christian religion falls to the ground. ANNOTATIONS.[9]

ONLY GOD KNOWS THE ELECT. MOÏSE AMYRAUT: God has elected some and forsaken the others, but he has not revealed to us who these are in particular, or shown their names written in his register. So no one can be fully assured that his neighbor is saved, since one does not know if they are among those to whom it will be given to truly believe. This follows the saying of the apostle that "God knows those who are his." BRIEF TREATISE ON PREDESTINATION.[10]

THE PERSEVERANCE OF TRUE BELIEVERS. DAVID DICKSON: Paul admonishes Timothy to hold fast the doctrine of the perseverance of true believers, although the faith of some was overthrown. This admonition is propounded by way of consolation and confirmation of faith, against the scandal of apostates, especially of the famous doctors [Hymenaeus and Philetus] whose levity and perfidiousness ought indeed to stir up all to watchfulness, but it ought not in any way to weaken the assurance of faith in the saints. The doctrine to be maintained by Timothy is this: although the faith of some is overthrown, yet the building of the salvation of the elect or true believers abides. . . .

The building of the faith and salvation of the elect has a sure foundation laid by God, which stands unmovable—the free election of God—the constancy and stability whereof he compares to a foundation laid upon a rock. Therefore the perseverance of the saints is certain.

The salvation of the elect is kept in the secret custody of God, as with a signet, so that although it appears not to the world who they are who are elected, yet it is certain that they were not of us, or the number of true believers, who went out from us that truly believed, or revolted from our society. Therefore the perseverance of the saints is certain.

---

[6]Trapp, *Commentary*, 328.
[7]Diodati, *Pious Annotations*, 339*; citing 1 Cor 15:12.
[8]Dickson, *Exposition*, 174*.

[9]Leigh, *Annotations*, 333*; citing 1 Cor 15:13.
[10]Amyraut, *Traité de la Prédestination*, 134.

Those are known unto God who in a special manner are his or belong to him as his peculiar ones. He knows them and their names and number, and embraces them with special favor that he will not suffer them to be pulled from him. To know them as his own is to acquiesce in them by his special love as his peculiar ones. Therefore the perseverance of the saints is certain. EXPOSITION OF ALL PAUL'S EPISTLES.[11]

DO NOT BE SURPRISED WHEN SOME FALL AWAY. JOHN MAYER: Note that all are not as they appear and seem to be in the light and esteem of others. For they which make a glorious show, as Hymenaeus and Philetus did, may notwithstanding be none of God's foundation, but unstable and in time fall away and perish. And therefore let us not be offended, when any that have seemed very godly, prove otherwise, as though there were no solidity in any such, for in those that are known to God it is not so, but they shall stand firm unto the end and be made vessels of honor for ever. Let us therefore, that we may not become like these fickle and unstable persons, seal up our state by departing in heart and full purpose of mind from all iniquity. COMMENTARY.[12]

THE ELECT MUST SHUN ALL MANNER OF SIN. ENGLISH ANNOTATIONS: Though the Lord has eternally foreknown those who are his, yet it is not so that we presuming upon that decree should cast away all care of our salvation, and let loose the reins to all carnal liberty. For on our parts who are thus mercifully foreknown and elected to salvation, there is required a holy and a conscionable obedience, and a careful endeavor to please God in all things, and shun all manner of sin. ENGLISH ANNOTATIONS.[13]

2:20-21 Be Useful to the Master of the House

THE VISIBLE CHURCH. DUTCH ANNOTATIONS: Even as is a great house or palace that is inhabited by a rich or mighty person, there are all kinds of vessels of diverse matter, worth, and use, so also in the outward and visible church, which is the house of God are found not only true believers, chosen by God for his honor, but also hypocrites, who were never by God acknowledged for his, and in his time are discovered.... There are vessels used for honorable or excellent services, to which the elect are compared. There are some dishonorable, which are used for mean and base services: to these, hypocrites and reprobates are compared. DUTCH ANNOTATIONS.[14]

PREDESTINATION IS NOT BASED ON CLEANSING OURSELVES. PETER MARTYR VERMIGLI: We deny that good works foreseen are the causes of predestination. First, because the Scriptures nowhere teach this and we ought to affirm nothing in so weighty a matter without the holy Scriptures. However, I know that certain people have gone about to gather this sentence out of the second epistle to Timothy, where it is thus written, "In a great house are vessels of gold, silver, and wood: and if anyone shall cleanse themselves from these, they shall be a vessel to honor, and fit for every good work." From this, they conclude that certain people are therefore destined to be vessels of honor *because* they have cleansed themselves from the filthiness of sin, and from corrupt doctrine. And because they are here said to have power to perform this, they say that it lies in everyone's power to be predestined by God to felicity.

But these people do not draw a valid conclusion; for the meaning of Paul in that place is to be taken thus: He had said before that "the foundation stands firm, 'The Lord knows those who are his.'" It is as if he should have said that people may sometimes be deceived, for they often judge those to be godly who are furthest away from godliness—in which words he reproved Hymenaeus and Philetus. For a little before he had spoken of their perverse doctrine: for they taught that the resurrection had already happened. So Paul would not have it that people should be judged as they appear

[11]Dickson, *Exposition*, 174*.
[12]Mayer, *Commentarie*, 548*.
[13]Downame, ed., *Annotations*, s.v.*

[14]Haak, *Annotations*, s.v.*; citing 1 Tim 3:15; Rom 9:21.

to be at first sight. For God has in this world—in a great house, as it were—vessels, some of gold, some of silver, some of wood, and some of clay. And he knows best which of these are for honor and which are for dishonor. But we, who do not know or understand the hiddenness of his will, can only judge them by the effects—so whoever is clean from corrupt doctrine, and lives in a godly way, is a vessel made for honor.

Neither does this place prove that people can cleanse themselves, or make themselves vessels for honor. . . . And therefore, we ought not to gather more from those words of Paul than that such cleansing is a token, whereby we judge of the worthiness, or of the unworthiness, of the vessels in the church. It is God who knows truly what kind of vessel every person is, and his foundation stands firm. . . .

Neither do they rightly understand the apostle who conclude from this verse that it lies in our will to make ourselves vessels of honor. For the strength of our free will is not proved by conditional propositions, so that we should thus infer: "The holy Scriptures teach that if you shall do this or that, or if you shall believe, you shall have salvation: therefore we can of ourselves believe or live in a godly way." Such conclusions are weak: for God, in another place teaches that "he will make us able to walk in his ways."

Therefore, we ought not to gather out of these places what our own power and strength is able to do. But it is easy to declare why people who are purged by God are also said to purge themselves. For God does not work in people as if they were tree trunks or stones; for stones are moved without having sense and will. But God, when he regenerates people, so cleanses and renews those who themselves both understand what they do, and also above all things why they desire and will the same, after they have once received a heart of flesh in place of their heart of stone. So then, after they are once regenerated, they are made workers together with God; and of their own accord they bend themselves to holiness and to purity of life. COMMONPLACES.[15]

THIS DOES NOT ESTABLISH FREE WILL.

GENEVA BIBLE: By the words "if anyone cleanses himself" is meant the execution of the matter, and not the cause. For in that we purge ourselves it is not to be attributed to any free will that is in us, but to God, who freely and wholly works in us a good and effectual will. GENEVA BIBLE.[16]

THE HOUSE IS THE WORLD. PAUL GLOCK: The large house is and signifies the whole world, as though Paul said, in this house, there will not only be pious children of God, but also many godless who constantly oppose God and his word and will, as well as the pious who fear God from the heart. That is what you godless magistrates do together with your people, for no righteousness, truth, or faith are to be found among you anymore, but only those works that the prophet points out, and which have often been indicated. Therefore Paul warns us clearly and says that whoever purifies himself from such people will be a vessel sanctified to holiness, useful to the master of the house and prepared for all good works. And so we also say with Paul: whosoever wants to be saved and come to God must leave the whole world (together with the government) and must turn to God and to his house, yes to his church and to the vessels of honor. Thus they will be saved. FIRST DEFENSE.[17]

2:22-26 The Lord's Servant Correcting Opponents

FLEE YOUTHFUL PASSIONS. DAVID DICKSON: Paul admonishes Timothy to moderation of mind and to avoid all youthful affections, and whatsoever may stir up contentions or provoke the minds of others. There are three branches of the admonition.

---

[16]Geneva Bible 1599, NT 95. An alternative Roman Catholic gloss on this text can be seen in Martin, *New Testament*, 590, who comments, "Man then hath free will to make himself a vessel of salvation or damnation: though salvation be attributed to God's mercy principally, the other to his just judgment: neither of both being repugnant to our free will, but working with and by the same, all such effects in us as to his providence and our deserts be agreeable."

[17]CRR 10:322-323*; citing Hos 4:1-2.

---

[15]Vermigli, *Commonplaces*, 3:13-14*; citing Is 42:16.

1. That he avoid all youthful lusts or affections, not only pleasures but also headiness, contention, pride, desire of vainglory, and the like evil affections which young men are usually infected with, who have taken upon them the office of teaching or disputing.

2. That on the other side he follow: "righteousness," which offends none; "faith," which without disputation receives cheerfully the mysteries revealed from God; "charity," which is not envious nor puffed up, is not ambitious, seeks not her own but even those things which conduce to the good of others; "peace" with those who call on the Lord out of a pure heart, that is, with the true worshipers of God.

3. That he shun questions by which no one comes to true wisdom and Christian edification. EXPOSITION OF ALL PAUL'S EPISTLES.[18]

THE LUSTS OF YOUTH. DUTCH ANNOTATIONS: Flee the lusts of youth, that is, which young persons are most subject to, such as are ambition, animosity, unsteadfastness, vainglory, voluptuousness, and the like. DUTCH ANNOTATIONS.[19]

HOW TO BEHAVE TOWARD ADVERSARIES. HEINRICH BULLINGER: With these words he instructs the bishop, prescribing how he should conduct himself toward his adversaries, lest perchance someone infer that these people should be driven away with sharp reproofs. He took up the opportunity from the precept that he already gave, "Reject stupid and ignorant questions, since you know that they produce disputes." Therefore

now he adds, "Rather, it is not fitting that the servant of the Lord should be quarrelsome, but rather should be peaceful and quiet toward friends as well as enemies." For there are some who are readier for reproof and attack than to teach. . . . But the bishop must be *didaktikos* who is able to teach and impel his adversary on by the matter itself and the light of truth rather than to hurt and injure him with insults and witty sayings. He should also be *anexikakon*, that is, tolerant of bad people and things. For in respect of both he refers as much to people as to things. This is to say that the bishop should be such as not to be easily irritated, but one who with gentleness scatters both the insolence of his adversaries, and the adversaries themselves, who does not drive away directly, but educates—with such faith and gentleness that these adversaries understand that it is a question of their own salvation and not of victory and personal advantage.

Finally, Christian love itself prevents us from rashly losing hope in someone. For it can be that those who had been driven away with a sharp rebuke had given themselves entirely in service of the devil to the extent that they had obeyed his authority and desire in everything, now through calm and friendly teaching, having come to themselves, begin to recover and to extricate themselves from the devil's snare, namely, a heresy or any other heinous sin. From these words it is clear how much sin is committed in these days in the excessive ferocity of certain bishops who are quicker to condemn than to teach, to reprove and bite than to take hold and restore to health. It is clear then how vain they are who shout with prayers and contemptible sacred speeches, running as they do to God's decree of providence, "If I am preordained to life, no one can seize it from me." If truly I have been predestined to death, no sacred speech will convert me, and thus there is no need of any sacred speech. The apostle is very far from making such a decree here. COMMENTARY ON ALL THE APOSTOLIC EPISTLES.[20]

---

[18]Dickson, *Exposition*, 174*.

[19]Haak, *Annotations*, s.v.* Jerome D. Quinn and William C. Wacker, *The First and Second Letters to Timothy: A New Translation with Notes and Commentary*, Eerdmans Critical Commentary (Grand Rapids: Eerdmans, 2000), 696-97, comment that "the lusts are not just the sexual excesses to which youths may be particularly inclined but also to that impatience, self-assertion, and self-indulgence (Lock) not to mention the hunger for novelty; the contempt for routine; the obdurate, implacable intransigence; the agitation verging on violence; the lack of prudent measure (Spicq, Boudou, Barclay, Gealy), which mark the immature (of any chronological age). . . . The vices just noted are no monopoly of the young."

[20]Bullinger, *Apostolicas Epistolas*, 611-12.

CORRECTING OPPONENTS WITH GENTLENESS.
DAVID DICKSON: Paul admonishes Timothy to employ meekness in reproving those that are otherwise minded, that he do not presently use sharpness but propound doctrine to them with gentleness and so rebuke them, that they may understand that their salvation and amendment is earnestly sought. The reasons why he should endeavor after this last virtue and use meekness toward those who were otherwise minded are three: (1) Because the conversion of obstinate persons is possible, nor must we hastily despair of it. (2) Because repentance and the acknowledgment of the truth, and every act of faith, is the gift of God. (3) Because their condition is to be pitied, for they abide in the snares of the devil, acting according to his will, so long as it shall seem good to God to suffer it. EXPOSITION OF ALL PAUL'S EPISTLES.[21]

READ SCRIPTURE TO LIVE BETTER NOT FIGHT MORE. THOMAS CRANMER: Among all kinds of contention, none is more hurtful than is contention in matters of religion. "Eschew," says St. Paul, "foolish and unlearned questions, knowing that they breed strife. It becomes not the servant of God to fight or strive, but to be meek toward all." This contention and strife was in St. Paul's time among the Corinthians and is at this time among us English. For there are too many who, upon the ale benches or other places, delight to propound certain questions, not so much pertaining to edification as to vainglory and ostentation, and so unsoberly to reason and dispute that when neither party will give place to the other, they fall to chiding and contention, and sometimes from hot words to further inconvenience. . . .

Let us so read the Scripture that by reading thereof we may be made the better livers, rather than the more contentious disputers. If anything is necessary to be taught, reasoned, or disputed, let us do it with all meekness, softness, and lenity. If anything shall chance to be spoken uncomely, let one bear another's frailty. Those who are faulty, let them rather amend than defend that which they have spoken amiss, lest they fall by contention from a foolish error into an obstinate heresy. For it is better to give place meekly than to win the victory with the breach of charity, which is what happens where everyone will defend their opinion obstinately. FIRST BOOK OF HOMILIES.[22]

MINISTER WITH PATIENCE. PILGRAM MARPECK: No one buries someone who is still alive, nor do they expel from the house someone in the last stage of illness. Rather, one waits with patience and endurance for them to get better. Nor does one give them strong food that would only make them become weaker. For this reason, Paul commands that overseers and bishops be chosen who will uphold the weak and bear with the wicked. Therefore, I desire to be patient with all who are bought with the costly pearl, the death and shed blood of the Lord Jesus Christ, since God requires patience and long-suffering from us through Christ. JUDGMENT AND DECISION.[23]

REPENTANCE IS GOD'S GIFT. PETER MARTYR VERMIGLI: As the apostle teaches us here, even repentance also is the gift of God. For he admonishes a bishop to hold fast sound doctrine and to reprove those who resist, if that is, God might grant it to them to repent. From this it is concluded that it does not lie the hands of all to return into the way, unless it be given them by God. COMMONPLACES.[24]

REPENTANCE IS NOT AS EASY AS MANY PEOPLE THINK. JOHN TRAPP: Repentance is God's gift. Neither is it in the power of any to repent at pleasure. Some vainly conceit that these five words, "Lord have mercy upon me" are as efficacious to send them to heaven, as the papists that their five words of consecration are to transubstantiate the bread . But as many are undone (says one divine) by buying a counterfeit jewel, so many are in hell by mistake of their repentance. A COMMENTARY.[25]

---

[21]Dickson, *Exposition*, 174-75*.

[22]Cranmer, *Certain Sermons or Homelies*, homily 12*.
[23]CRR 2:354.
[24]Vermigli, *Commonplaces*, 3:13*.
[25]Trapp, *Commentary*, 330.

3:1-9 GODLESSNESS IN THE LAST DAYS

But understand this, that in the last days there will come times of difficulty. ²For people will be lovers of self, lovers of money, proud, arrogant, abusive, disobedient to their parents, ungrateful, unholy, ³heartless, unappeasable, slanderous, without self-control, brutal, not loving good, ⁴treacherous, reckless, swollen with conceit, lovers of pleasure rather than lovers of God, ⁵having the appearance of godliness, but denying its power. Avoid such people.

⁶For among them are those who creep into households and capture weak women, burdened with sins and led astray by various passions, ⁷always learning and never able to arrive at a knowledge of the truth. ⁸Just as Jannes and Jambres opposed Moses, so these men also oppose the truth, men corrupted in mind and disqualified regarding the faith. ⁹But they will not get very far, for their folly will be plain to all, as was that of those two men.

Overview: The majority of these early modern exegetes understand the "last days" Paul refers to as the period of time between the first coming of Christ and his second. Some dissent, however, arguing that Paul is referring to the imminent end of the Jewish state in AD 70. All agree, however, that Paul's description of the terrible times aligns with the present experience of the church, as corruption continues to abound and there is no hope of attaining perfection before Christ's eschatological return. The need for Christians to set themselves apart is highlighted in the commentary, as is the need for watchfulness and perseverance in hope. The ungodly, it is argued, are distant from the truth and attack Christ's flock, and so ministers should be on watch and the people of God should seek protection and safety in the Lord.

3:1-5 Avoid Such People

The Last Days of the Jewish Church-State. John Owen: Most expositors suppose that this expression, "the last days," is a periphrasis for the times of the gospel. But it does not appear that they are anywhere so called; nor were they ever known by that name among the Jews, upon whose principles the apostle proceeds. Some seasons, indeed, under the gospel, in reference to some churches, are called "the last days"; but the whole time of the gospel absolutely is nowhere so termed. It is the last days of the Judaical church and state, which were then drawing to their period and abolition, that are here and elsewhere called "the last days," or "the latter days," or "the last hour." Commentary on Hebrews.[1]

There Will Be No State of Perfection Before Christ's Return. John Calvin: By this prediction he intended still more to sharpen his diligence; for, when matters go on to our wish, we become more careless; but necessity urges us keenly. Paul therefore informs him that the church will be subject to terrible diseases, which will require in the pastors uncommon fidelity, diligence, watchfulness, prudence, and unwearied constancy; as if he enjoined Timothy to prepare for arduous and deeply anxious contests that awaited him. And hence we learn that, so far from giving way, or being terrified, on account of any difficulties whatsoever, we ought, on the contrary, to arouse our hearts for resistance.

Under "the last days" he includes the universal condition of the Christian church. Nor does he compare his own age with ours but, on the contrary, informs Timothy what will be the future condition of the kingdom of Christ;† for many imagined

---

[1]Owen, *Works*, 20:11* (commenting on Heb 1:2); citing 1 Tim 4:1; 2 Pet 3:3; 1 Jn 2:18; Jude 18. Cf. *Works* 9:322; 17:542-43.

some sort of condition that would be absolutely peaceful, and free from any annoyance. In short, he means that there will not be, even under the gospel, such a state of perfection, that all vices shall be banished, and virtues of every kind shall flourish; and that therefore the pastors of the Christian church will have quite as much to do with wicked and ungodly people as the prophets and godly priests had in ancient times. Hence it follows, that there is no time for idleness or for repose. COMMENTARY ON 2 TIMOTHY.[2]

GODLESS RULERS SHOULD BE KILLED. THOMAS MÜNTZER: Nebuchadnezzar perceived the divine wisdom in Daniel. He fell down before him after the mighty truth had overcome him. But he was moved like a reed before the wind, as chapter 3 proves. Of the same character are many people now, by far the greatest number, who accept the gospel with great joy as long as everything is going fine and friendly. But when God wishes to put such people to the test or to the trial by fire, oh how they take offense at the smallest weed, as Christ in Mark prophesied. Without doubt inexperienced people will to such an extent anger themselves over this little book for the reason that I say with Christ and with Paul and with the instruction of the whole divine law that the godless rulers should be killed, especially the priests and monks who revile the gospel as heresy for us and wish to be considered at the same time the best Christians. When hypocritical, spurious goodness becomes engaged and embittered beyond the average, it then wishes to defend the godless and says Christ killed no one. . . . And since the friends of God thus quite ineffectually command the wind, then the prophecy of Paul is fulfilled. In the last days the lovers of pleasure will indeed have the form of godliness, but they will denounce its power.

Nothing on earth has a better form and mask that spurious goodness. For this reason all corners are full of nothing but hypocrites, among whom not a one is so bold as to be able to say the real truth. SERMON BEFORE THE PRINCES.[3]

MARKS OF A TIME OF DIFFICULTY. JOHN OWEN: The first thing that makes a season perilous is when the profession of true religion is outwardly maintained under a visible predominance of horrible lusts and wickedness. And the reason why I name it in the first place, is, because it is what the apostle gives his instance in, in this place, "Perilous times shall come." Why? "For many shall be lovers of themselves, covetous, boasters, proud, blasphemers . . ."—maintaining their profession of the truth of religion under a predominance, a visible, open predominance, of vile lusts, and the practice of horrible sins. This rendered the season perilous. Whether this be such a season or not, you judge. And I must say, by the way, we may and ought to witness against it, and mourn for the public sins of the days wherein we live. It is as glorious a thing to be a martyr for bearing testimony against the public sins of an age, as in bearing testimony unto any truth of the gospel whatsoever. SERMON ON 2 TIMOTHY 3:1.[4]

THERE WILL ALWAYS BE WICKED CORRUPTION IN THE CHURCH. GENEVA BIBLE: We may not hope for any church in this world without corruption; but there shall be, rather, great abundance of most wicked people, even in the very bosom of the church, which notwithstanding shall make a show and countenance of great holiness and charity. GENEVA BIBLE.[5]

---

[2]CTS 43:236-37 (CO 52:375-76). †Calvin does not mean that the description here is entirely of a future state to come, since the present-tense verbs in the rest of the chapter show that Paul considered the last days to have already in some sense begun. Cf. William D. Mounce, *The Pastoral Epistles*, Word Biblical Commentary (Nashville: Thomas Nelson, 2000), 543-44.

[3]LCC 25:69*; citing Dan 2:46; 3:5; Lk 8:13; 1 Pet 1:7; Mk 4:17; Lk 19:27; Mt 18:6; 1 Cor 5:7, 13.

[4]Owen, *Works*, 9:323. Despite thinking "the last days" had a particular primary meaning focused on the end of the Jewish church-state, it appears that Owen still considers the warnings in this chapter to be relevant beyond AD 70. See the way he handles 2 Tim 3:12, in *Works*, 9:230; 21:383, 529, which does not imply he considered it to be irrelevant once the destruction of Jerusalem had taken place.

[5]Geneva Bible 1599, NT 95*.

Avoid Those with Only the Form of Godliness. David Dickson: These people have a form of godliness that they make show of in words and profession, the power whereof in their works they so little regard that they seem to abjure and deny it. He commands Timothy to shun these, that is, after admonitions and reproofs by the gentler censures of the church, at length being excluded from the church by excommunication, to beware of them, and restrain them, and by any other prudent course repress them, that the church may not receive any detriment by them. Exposition of All Paul's Epistles.[6]

Self-Love Is the Root of Last Days' Wickedness. Edward Leigh: Self-love is the root of these nineteen vices here mentioned. The apostle begins with self-love, and concludes with love of pleasures. People always abound with self-love, but it shall then prevail more than in times past. Annotations.[7]

Signs of the Antichrist. Matthias Flacius: Indeed such who are enemies of the truth, and are contaminated by the most wretched disease meanwhile rage most violently in the church as holy bishops and monks with their prelates. For they were expelled from the church as heretics. There is thus no doubt that this is a prophecy which shows their true colors. First, their most longstanding corrupt morals are described. Next, their hypocrisies. Thirdly, the injuries, which in truth, they will also inflict upon the Church. The Holy Spirit of the Lord therefore indeed preached this just as he did in chapter 4 in the previous epistle not to be a stumbling block to the godly, but to quicken them against such greater trials, and to teach them to understand, know, and depart from them as well as be able to bear persistent difficulties. Finally, Paul offers comfort against these tribulations. Gloss on 2 Timothy.[8]

3:6-9 Opposing the Truth

Pastors Must Point the Finger at Thieves and Wolves. John Calvin: Let us note well that St. Paul only marks out these wicked people which he speaks of here because he saw that they might do a great deal of damage unless they were impeded and bridled. As he says in another place, such fellows which pervert the grace of God must have the finger pointed at them and not be spared. Ministers especially must cry out with a loud voice when they see their flock set upon. If shepherds suffer their flocks to feed when they see the wolf or the thieves, and hold their peace, and go and hide themselves—if they pretend they saw nothing and turn their backs—what would this be? So then, if we wish to do our duty faithfully we must, when we see corruptions in the church of God, cry out ardently to remedy them and to repel them. Sermons on 2 Timothy.[9]

Always Hearing but Never Really Learning. John Owen: To hear and to learn are good, but not for themselves, for their own sake, but only for the practice of what we hear and learn. The apostle tells us of some who are "always learning, but are never able to come to a knowledge of the truth"; that is, to a practical acknowledgment of it, so as to have an impression of its power and efficacy upon their souls. And such are some who are always learning—such as make it their business to hear and to learn, so that they scarcely do anything else. Gospel truths are *medicina animae*— physic for a sin-sick soul. Now, of what use is it to get a store of medicines and cordials, and never to take them? No more is it to collect, at any price or rate, sermons, doctrines, instructions, if we do not apply them, that they may have their efficacy in us and proper work toward us. There is in some a dropsy of hearing†—the more they hear, the more they desire. But they are only pleased with it at present, and swelled for the future—are neither really refreshed nor strengthened. . . .

---

[6]Dickson, *Exposition*, 175*.
[7]Leigh, *Annotations*, 334.
[8]Flacius, *Glossa Compendaria*, 1080.

[9]CO 54:232.

We should look to sermons as Elijah did to the ravens, that "brought him bread and flesh in the morning, and bread and flesh in the evening." They bring food with them for our souls, if we feed on it; if not, they are lost. When the Israelites gathered manna to eat, it was a precious food, "bread from heaven, angels' meat," food heavenly and angelical— that is, excellent and precious; but when they laid it up by them, "it bred worms and stank." When God scatters truths among people, if they gather them to eat, they are the bread of heaven, angels' food; but if they do it only to lay them by them, in their books, or in the notions of their mind, they will breed the worms of pride and hypocrisy, and make them an offensive savor to God. When, therefore, any truth is proposed to you, learn what is your concernment in it, and let it have its proper and perfect work upon your souls. COMMENTARY ON HEBREWS.[10]

WE MUST DESIRE FREEDOM FROM SINS NOT FLATTERY IN THEM. JOHN CALVIN: Let us note that St. Paul speaks here of women who are burdened with sins. It is true that both men and women are sinners, and the right way to come to God (this is where we need to start) is to feel our sins and our poverty that we may be displeased with ourselves for them. We shall never profit in the gospel unless we have a correct sense of our sins and are ashamed with ourselves. It is for this reason that our Lord Jesus Christ said, "Come to me all who labor and are burdened, and I will relieve you, and you will find rest for your souls." Therefore, if we want to come to the Son of God and find rest in him and in his grace, we must be burdened with sins. It is true. But there are some who are burdened and nevertheless desire allevia- tion while others lie wallowing in their filth. St. Paul speaks here of those women who wish to maintain themselves in their vices and in their sins, and are very happy to be flattered in them and to

have the evil within them covered up. It is neces- sary that God should send these women deceivers, as they deserve, because they do not ask Jesus Christ to take their burden upon him and set them free from the bonds of Satan. They must be held captive because they do not want to come to him who gives us liberty. When the devil has had his foot set on our throats and we have been in this miserable slavery of sin, if we do not ask our Lord Jesus Christ to draw us out of it, shall not that captivity be doubled? SERMONS ON 2 TIMOTHY.[11]

THE UNSETTLED ARE ALWAYS LEARNING. DUTCH ANNOTATIONS: Those who, out of curiosity and unsettledness of mind would always learn something that is new, for this end seek teachers who may satisfy their curiosity. But they are never able to come to a knowledge of the truth, forasmuch as such teachers neither know the foundation themselves nor teach it unto others. They do not know the true and right foundation of Christian religion, in which the right knowledge of sin, and the comfort of consciences against sin, must be sought. DUTCH ANNOTATIONS.[12]

JANNES AND JAMBRES OPPOSED MOSES. JOHN OWEN: It is plain and evident that they were the sort of persons who pretended to a power of miraculous operation, and made use of their skill and reputation in opposition unto Moses. Their chiefs at that time were Jannes and Jambres, mentioned by our apostle, as they are likewise spoken of in the Talmud, and are joined with Moses by Pliny, as persons famous in arts magical.[†] It is not unlikely but that this sort of person might have been cast under some disgrace by failing in the interpretation of the dreams of Pharaoh, the knowledge whereof was of so great importance unto the whole nation. This being done by Joseph, whose eminent exaltation ensued thereon, it is not improbable but that they bore a peculiar malice toward all the Israelites, being,

---

[10]Owen, *Works*, 20:491* (commenting on Heb 3:1-2); citing 1 Kings 17:6; Ex 16:20. [†]Dropsy, or oedema, is a condition characterized by an excess of fluid causing swelling in parts of the body.

[11]CO 54:235; citing Mt 11:28.
[12]Haak, *Annotations, s.v.*

moreover, instigated and provoked by the knowledge and worship of the true God that was among them. This made them vigorously engage in an opposition to Moses, not only in compliance with the king, but, as our apostle speaks, *antestesan*—"they set themselves against him"—which includes more than a mere production of *magical effects* upon the command of Pharaoh, whereby they attempted to obscure the luster of his miracles—even a sedulous, active, industrious opposition to his whole design. And besides, whereas they knew that Moses was skilled in all the learning of the Egyptians, and not perceiving at first any peculiar presence of divine power with him, they thought themselves sufficient for the contest, until they were forced, by the evidence of his miraculous operations, to acknowledge the energy of a divine power above what they could imitate or counterfeit. COMMENTARY ON HEBREWS.[13]

THE MAGICIANS OF EGYPT WERE COMMONLY CALLED JANNES AND JAMBRES. JOHN LIGHTFOOT: When the apostle names the magicians of Egypt, Jannes and Jambres, he does not deliver it for a certain thing, or upon his credit assure them that these were their very names, but alleges only what had been delivered by others, what had been the common tradition among them, well enough known to Timothy, a thing about which neither he nor any other would start any controversy. HEBREW AND TALMUDICAL EXERCITATIONS.[14]

---

[13]Owen, *Works*, 19:256-257. †See Talmud b. Menahot 85a, which

mentions Johana and Mamre; and Pliny, *Natural History* 30.2. Other commentators mention Eusebius, *Praeparatio evangelica* 9.8, who mentions Jannes and Jambres, or Mambres. See Hammond, *A Paraphrase and Annotations*, 711, for a variety of other ancient sources for these names, including Targum Jonathan on Ex 7:11.
[14]Lightfoot, *Horae Hebraicæ et Talmudicæ*, 3:63–64, in comments on Luke 3:36.

3:10-17 ALL SCRIPTURE IS BREATHED BY GOD

[10]*You, however, have followed my teaching, my conduct, my aim in life, my faith, my patience, my love, my steadfastness,* [11]*my persecutions and sufferings that happened to me at Antioch, at Iconium, and at Lystra—which persecutions I endured; yet from them all the Lord rescued me.* [12]*Indeed, all who desire to live a godly life in Christ Jesus will be persecuted,* [13]*while evil people and impostors will go on from bad to worse, deceiving and being deceived.* [14]*But as for you, continue in what you have learned and have firmly believed, knowing from whom*[a] *you learned it* [15]*and how from childhood you have been acquainted with the sacred writings, which are able to make you wise for salvation through faith in Christ Jesus.* [16]*All Scripture is breathed out by God and profitable for teaching, for reproof, for correction, and for training in righteousness,* [17]*that the man of God*[b] *may be complete, equipped for every good work.*

a The Greek for *whom* is plural   b That is, a messenger of God (the phrase echoes a common Old Testament expression)

OVERVIEW: In this passage, Paul contrasts Timothy to those whose lives characterize the difficulties of the times. In this charge, our commentators find much to consider. As Paul reflects on Timothy's imitation of him, our sixteenth-century exegetes note the importance of modeling faithful ministry in order to raise up the next generations of leaders, and Paul's comments on persecution and suffering are directly applied to the church. Considering the centrality of the canonical Scriptures to the Reformation, however, it is unsurprising that Paul's affirmations on its nature and role are the subject of extended reflection. While not articulated as a distinct locus, the doctrine of *sola Scriptura* is clearly operative among these Protestant exegetes, as they argue for the centrality and primacy of Scripture and its authority over the lives of people and the teachings derived from them. The perfection of Scripture and the role of the Holy Spirit in its production and interpretation are emphasized, as is the necessity and sufficiency of Scripture for salvation (against a Roman position that elevated the church, its oral traditions and councils). Through the Scriptures, under the illumination and power of the Holy Spirit, our commentators argue, the people of God are reconciled to the Lord and equipped to serve him with good works.

3:10-13 The Godly Will Be Persecuted

TRAINING IS NOT JUST BY WORDS. JOHN CALVIN: In order to urge Timothy, he employs this argument also, that he is not an ignorant and untaught soldier, because Paul carried him through a long course of training. Nor does he speak of doctrine only; for those things which he likewise enumerates add much weight, and he gives to us, in this sentence, a very lively picture of a good teacher, as one who does not, by words only, train and instruct his disciples, but, so to speak, opens his very breast to them, that they may know that whatever he teaches, he teaches sincerely. This is what is implied in the words "my aim in life." He likewise adds other proofs of sincere and unfeigned affection, such as faith, mildness, love, patience. Such were the early instructions that had been imparted to Timothy in the school of Paul. COMMENTARY ON 2 TIMOTHY.[1]

YOU KNOW HOW TO HANDLE DIFFICULTIES BECAUSE YOU HAVE SEEN ME DO IT. DESIDERIUS ERASMUS: But you (says Paul) who are most unlike those counterfeit fools, see that you purely and constantly spread to others the doctrine of the gospel which I handed down purely to you. Such

[1]CTS 43:243* (CO 52:379).

as my doctrine was, so also was my life. You are the best person to bear witness to this yourself (Timothy) since you have been with me a long time and have by experience seen in me sincerity of doctrine and a demeanor of life agreeable to the same, eagerness of mind that drew back from nothing, strength of faith that could not be moved by any sorrows, gentleness toward heretics, charity that desired to do good even for my enemies, and patience in persecutions and afflictions that, you can testify, happened to me at Antioch, Iconium, and Lystra. You know what grievous storms of persecution I have endured beyond human strength. And yet I have been delivered from them all by the Lord, with whose protection I continued unbroken. PARAPHRASES.[2]

PERSECUTION IS INEVITABLE FOR THE GODLY.
JOHN CALVIN: Having mentioned his own persecutions, he likewise adds now that nothing has happened to him that does not await all the godly. And he says this partly so that believers may prepare themselves for submitting to this condition, and partly so that good people may not view him with suspicion on account of the persecutions that he endures from wicked persons; as it frequently happens that the distresses to which people are subjected lead to unfavorable opinions concerning them; for he whom others regard with aversion is immediately declared by the common people to be hated by God.

By this general statement, therefore, Paul classes himself with the children of God, and, at the same time, exhorts all the children of God to prepare for enduring persecutions; for, if this condition is laid down for "all who wish to live a godly life in Christ," they who wish to be exempt from persecutions must necessarily renounce Christ. In vain shall we endeavor to detach Christ from his cross; for it may be said to be natural that the world should hate Christ even in his members. Now hatred is attended by cruelty, and hence arise persecutions. In short, let us know that we are Christians on this condition, that we shall be liable to many tribulations and various contests.

But it is asked, "Must all be martyrs?" For it is evident that there have been many godly persons who have never suffered banishment, or imprisonment, or flight, or any kind of persecution. I reply, it is not always in one way that Satan persecutes the servants of Christ. But yet it is absolutely unavoidable that all of them shall have the world for their enemy in some form or other, that their faith may be tried and their steadfastness proved; for Satan, who is the continual enemy of Christ, will never suffer any one to be at peace during his whole life; and there will always be wicked people who are thorns in our sides. Moreover, as soon as zeal for God is manifested by a believer, it kindles the rage of all the ungodly; and, although they have not a drawn sword, yet they vomit out their venom, either by murmuring, or by slander, or by raising a disturbance, or by other methods. Accordingly, although they are not exposed to the same assaults, and do not engage in the same battles, yet they have a warfare in common, and shall never be wholly at peace and exempt from persecutions. COMMENTARY ON 2 TIMOTHY.[3]

SUFFERING IS THE THIRD BAPTISM.
BALTHASAR HUBMAIER: For whoever wants to cry with Christ to God: "Abba, pater, dear Father" must do so in faith, and must also be cobaptized in water with Christ and suffer jointly with him in blood. Then they will be a son and heir of God, fellow heir with Christ, and will be jointly glorified with Christ. Therefore no one should be terrified of persecution or suffering, for Christ had to suffer and thus enter into his glory. And also Paul writes: "All who desire to live so devoutly in Christ will be persecuted." This is indeed precisely the third baptism or last baptism in which people should indeed be anointed with the oil of the holy and comforting gospel (in order that we may be meek and ready to suffer). Thus the illness is lightened for us, and we receive forgiveness of sins. A BRIEF APOLOGIA.[4]

---

[2]Erasmus, *Paraphrases*, 98-99.

[3]CTS 43:244* (CO 52:380).
[4]CRR 5:301*; citing Rom 8:17; Lk 24:26; Jas 5:14.

3:14-17 *Sacred Scripture*

ONLY THE SCRIPTURES HAVE GOD'S AUTHORITY. PHILIPP MELANCHTHON: Paul testifies to Timothy that whatever men—whether the church or a priest—legislate outside of Scripture should not be considered an article of faith: "As for you, remain steadfast in what you have learned, knowing from whom you have learned it." He thinks it is important that we know the source of what we have learned. Now how will we know the origin of human opinions unless we can test them against Scripture? For it is quite obvious that whatever the Scriptures confirm has its origin in the Holy Spirit. But whatever is promoted outside of the Scriptures, it is uncertain whether it has its origin in the Spirit of God or from a lying spirit. . . . Scripture alone has the certainty of having been established by the Spirit of God. It is irresponsible to give councils the authority to establish articles of faith, since—to name just one reason—it is possible that there is nobody in the entire council who has the Spirit of God. COMMONPLACES.[5]

IT IS VERY USEFUL TO MEMORIZE SCRIPTURES FROM INFANCY. ENGLISH ANNOTATIONS: There is nothing more profitable than to be exercised in the Scriptures from our infancy; for the vessels that are at the first seasoned with the savor of life, seldom or never lose it. And though while they are very young they cannot come to much understanding, yet the having of Scripture phrases and texts by heart is very useful, and will stand them in good stead after they come to riper years and are able to dive deeper into the meaning of those things they retain perfect in their memories from childhood.

Although the Scripture sufficiently instructs us to salvation, yet we cannot be saved without a lively faith working through love; therefore Paul adds "through faith." Or, by Scriptures he means the Scriptures of the Old Testament, which is all that was extant when Timothy was a child, the knowledge whereof could not save Timothy without faith in Christ, whereby he believed the accomplishment of all those things which were foreshadowed in the Old Testament both by predictions and types. ENGLISH ANNOTATIONS.[6]

THE MEANS OF OUR SALVATION. THE ORDINAL: Most merciful Father, we beseech you, so to send upon these your servants your heavenly blessing, that they may be clad about with all justice,[†] and that your word spoken by their mouths may have such success, that it may never be spoken in vain. Grant also that we may have grace to hear and receive the same as your most holy Word and the means of our salvation, that in all our words and deeds we may seek your glory and increase of your kingdom, through Jesus Christ our Lord. Amen. THE ORDINAL (1549).[7]

SCRIPTURE MOST NECESSARY FOR SALVATION. WESTMINSTER CONFESSION: Although the light of nature, and the works of creation, and providence do so far manifest the goodness, wisdom, and power of God, as to leave men inexcusable; yet are they not sufficient to give that knowledge of God, and of his will, which is necessary unto salvation. Therefore it pleased the Lord, at sundry times, and in divers manners, to reveal himself, and to declare that his will to his church; and afterward for the better preserving and propagating of the truth, and for the more sure establishment and comfort of the church against the corruption of the flesh, and the malice of Satan and of the world, to commit the same wholly unto writing; which makes the holy Scripture to be most necessary; those former ways of God's revealing his will unto his people being now ceased. WESTMINSTER CONFESSION.[8]

DISAGREEMENTS DO NOT MEAN SCRIPTURE IS AMBIGUOUS. PETER MARTYR VERMIGLI:

---

[5]Melanchthon, *Commonplaces*, 78-79.

[6]Downame, ed., *Annotations*, s.v.*; citing Prov 22:6.
[7]*Forme and Maner*, Ordering of Priests*. [†]1549: "clad about with all justice." 1662: "clothed with righteousness."
[8]*Humble Advice of the Assembly of Divines*, 1-2. One of the prooftexts given for this section is 2 Tim 3:15.

When you claim that the Scriptures are twisted in various directions according to how different people are affected, I answer that this is done by the fault of evil or ignorant people, yet they [the Scriptures] must not be blamed as if they are obscure in those things necessary to salvation. When they are brought forth and read simply they fulfil their office well. And the Holy Spirit witnesses that they are profitable to teach, to reprove, and to instruct us, that we may be perfect and equipped for every good work. But if any have doubted, it was their own fault, not Scripture's; and Scripture must not be accused on account of their objections, as though it cannot teach us.... So there is no reason for you to oppose me with men either still living or recently deceased, who disagreed with each other yet shared the Scriptures. Other causes may be found for their disagreement besides the ambiguity of the Scriptures. This is not the place to say how I should judge them; it is enough for me to have defended the function of Scripture. DISPUTATION ON THE EUCHARIST.[9]

THE SUFFICIENCY OF SCRIPTURE. THOMAS CARTWRIGHT: Out of this place we teach the sufficiency of Scripture, without any element of old tradition or new decree.... Our doctrine is that the Scripture is a perfect rule to teach us the way to everlasting life.... But Scripture cannot save or justify us without the grace of God, the righteousness of Christ, and faith to lay hold of them—which are all taught in Scripture. Indeed the knowledge of the Scripture without them shall serve to further condemnation.... The apostle teaches that the Scriptures are able to make us wise for salvation: therefore we need no further counsel or direction thereunto, but out of the Scriptures....

The Scriptures are able to make the man of God, that is, the minister of the Word, perfect and complete for every work of ministry, whether it is by teaching true doctrine, or confuting false doctrine, by exhorting and setting forward that which is good, or dehorting and beating back from that which is

evil. All additions to this bring disgrace and discredit to the holy Scripture, as if it were defective and needy when it actually has such a full and plentiful provision.... The whole Scripture jointly taken is able to make wise every one of the flock, and to furnish the shepherd for all pastoral duties....

If the people of God under the law were through faith in Christ made wise to salvation by the writings of the Old Testament alone, how much more are the Scriptures both of the Old and New together able to make us wise through faith unto salvation, without any other doctrine whatsoever. And if the people under the first times of preaching the gospel had plentiful direction to life when the gospel then preached was not written, how much more have we sufficient address unto it when the same that was then only preached is now both preached and written also? CONFUTATION OF THE RHEMISTS.[10]

SCRIPTURE AND PATRISTIC TRADITION. PETER MARTYR VERMIGLI: There are four things necessary in ecclesiastical doctrine: that is, that we should teach true things; that we should confute false things; that we should instruct people in virtues; and that we should reprove vices. And all these things are to be sought out of the holy Scriptures.... So shall the person of God be perfect, and have all he needs as touching either doctrine or manners. There is also another place in the same chapter: "You have learned the holy Scriptures, out of which you may have salvation." These things manifestly teach that we must not appeal from the Scriptures to the Fathers: for that would be to appeal from certainties to uncertainties, from clear things to obscure, from strong to weak. For although the Fathers saw much, being wise and learned, yet they were but human, and might err. And that which I have said is most of all to be considered, namely, that the Fathers do not always agree among themselves: and indeed, not one of them always agrees with himself.

---

[9]PML 7:211-12.

[10]Cartwright, *Confutation*, 585-86*. Cf. Fulke, *Text of the New Testament*, 389.

But here the adversaries answer: But they must be heard, when they all agree among themselves. But we say, that they must not therefore be heard because they agree among themselves, unless they consent with the word of God.... For even if all the Fathers shall consent among themselves, yet we will not do this injury to the Holy Spirit, that we should rather give credit to them than to the word of God. Indeed, the Fathers themselves would never want themselves to be so believed, as they have sufficiently testified in their writings that they will not have that honor to be given to them, but to the holy Scriptures alone. So those who appeal from the Scriptures to the Fathers, appeal to the Fathers against the Fathers. COMMONPLACES.[11]

THE UNERRING INSPIRED SCRIPTURE. DUTCH ANNOTATIONS: "All Scripture," that is, the whole Scripture, as this word "all" is taken whereby are principally understood the writings of the Old Testament, of which the writings of the New Testament are a further explication and which therefore are also comprehended under it, as may of them as were then written; as Paul wrote this epistle a little before his death, which must also in like manner be understood of the rest which then were not yet written. Scripture is of divine inspiration, that is, by inspiration of the Holy Spirit, who is a Spirit of truth, and led the writers of these writings into all truth, that they could not err. DUTCH ANNOTATIONS.[12]

SCRIPTURE DICTATED BY THE HOLY SPIRIT. JOHN CALVIN: First, he commends the Scripture on account of its authority; and second, on account of the utility that springs from it. In order to uphold the authority of the Scripture, he declares that it is divinely inspired; for, if it be so, it is beyond all controversy that people ought to receive it with reverence. This is a principle that distinguishes our religion from all others, that we know

that God hath spoken to us, and are fully convinced that the prophets did not speak at their own suggestion, but that, being organs of the Holy Spirit, they only uttered what they had been commissioned from heaven to declare. Whoever then wishes to profit in the Scriptures, let them first of all lay down this as a settled point, that the Law and the Prophets are not a doctrine delivered according to the will and pleasure of men, but dictated by the Holy Spirit. COMMENTARY ON 2 TIMOTHY.[13]

THE PERFECTION OF SCRIPTURE WITHOUT UNWRITTEN TRADITION. CHRISTIAN CHEMNITZ: This is a well-known passage, from which we prove the perfection of holy Scripture against the papists. Wherefore also Bellarmine in book four of his *On the Word of God*, chapter ten, calls this saying the Achilles' heel of Brentius and Chemnitius;[†] and in turn in book four of *On the Unwritten Word of God*, he attempts to defend the statement that the Scriptures without traditions are not sufficient, that is, not all things to be believed and done are contained in the Scriptures. But this saying is so very important, that Paul, at the end of his life, wrote it to Timothy, and so testified as to where those things which are necessary for our salvation are to be sought, to wit, from Scripture alone as divinely inspired. And indeed Balduin makes two arguments on this basis: (1) Whatever provides all things that are necessary both in regard to teaching and to practice, that is sufficient and perfect for the instruction of the Christian. But Scripture is divinely inspired. (2) A perfect effect presupposes a perfect cause. The effect of Scripture is perfect. Therefore Scripture that is divinely inspired is perfect.

This can also be formulated as follows: Whatever produces a perfect effect, that too is perfect. Sacred Scripture produces a perfect effect. Therefore, it is perfect. The minor premise is

---

[11]Vermigli, *Commonplaces*, 4:48-49*.
[12]Haak, *Annotations*, s.v.*; citing 1 Cor 13:2; 2 Tim 4:6; 2 Pet 3:16; Rev 1:1; 22:16.

[13]CTS 43:248-49 (CO 52:383); citing 2 Pet 1:20-21. See Calvin, *Institutes*, 4.8.1-9, on "dictation" and the apostles as "sure and genuine scribes of the Holy Spirit."

proved in two ways: (1) From an enumeration of the effects which it produces, with the exception of those in which there is nothing of relevance to Christianity. (2) From clear words: so that the person of God would be made perfect. Therefore, whatever the minister of the church should do, and propose to his hearers, that is contained in the sacred Scripture. A LITTLE COMMENTARY ON ALL PAUL'S EPISTLES.[14]

THE TRUE ESSENCE OF SCRIPTURE. MARTIN LUTHER: We know that the purpose of the whole Scripture is this: to teach, reprove, correct, and train in righteousness, so that the person of God may be perfect for every good work.... Those who fail to observe this purpose, even if they create the impression of erudition among the unlettered by their divinations, nevertheless are ignorant of the true essence of Scripture. Their learning is not unlike bodies infected with dropsy†—inflated by inordinate swelling, they give an appearance of vigor, but the swelling is all corrupt and noxious. EXPOSITION OF SONG OF SONGS.[15]

EQUIPPING THE PASTOR FOR EVERY GOOD WORK. DAVID DICKSON: The Scripture can make the "man of God," or the pastor of the church, perfectly conformed to all the parts of his office, and to every good work, which God requires from him, whether to the saving of himself or others, and the glory of God. Therefore, continue in those things that you have learned from me according to the Scripture, seeing you have the Scripture near you as a treasury, from which you may fetch whatever may make you perfect, and fully render you complete to every good work. EXPOSITION OF ALL PAUL'S EPISTLES.[16]

STUDY THE UNBLEMISHED SCRIPTURES TO FIGHT TEMPTATION AND ADVERSITY. DESIDERIUS ERASMUS: Believe me, dearest beloved brother, there is no attack of the enemy so violent, that is, no temptation so formidable, that an eager study of the Scriptures will not easily beat it off; there is no adversity so sad that it does not render it bearable.... For all holy Scripture was divinely inspired and perfected by God its Author. What is small is the lowliness of the Word, hiding under almost sordid words the greatest mysteries. What is dazzling is no doctrine of mortals, for it is not blemished by any spot of error; the doctrine of Christ alone is wholly snow white, wholly dazzling, wholly pure.... Therefore if you will dedicate yourself wholly to the study of the Scriptures ... you will be fortified and trained against every onslaught of enemies. ENCHIRIDION.[17]

SCRIPTURE IS PROFITABLE FOR SALVATION AND A HOLY LIFE. JOHN CALVIN: Now follows the second part of the commendation, that the Scripture contains a perfect rule of a good and happy life. When he says this, he means that it is corrupted by sinful abuse, when this usefulness is not sought. And thus he indirectly censures the unprincipled who fed the people with vain speculations, as with wind. For this reason we may in the present day, condemn all who, disregarding edification, agitate questions which, though they are ingenious, are also useless. Whenever ingenious trifles of that kind are brought forward, they must be warded off by this shield, that "Scripture is profitable." Hence it follows that it is unlawful to treat it in an unprofitable manner; for the Lord, when he gave us the Scriptures, did not intend either to gratify our curiosity, or to encourage ostentation, or to give occasion for chatting and talking, but to do us good; and, therefore, the right use of Scripture must always tend to what is profitable....

It would be too long to explain what we are to learn from the Scriptures; and, in the preceding

[14]Chemnitz, *Commentariolus*, 62-63. †Robert Bellarmine, *Disputations* 1.4.10. Brentius refers to Johannes Brenz,* and Chemnitius to Christian Chemnitz's great uncle Martin Chemnitz.
[15]LW 15:194 (WA 31/2:589). †Dropsy, or oedema, is a condition characterized by an excess of fluid causing swelling in parts of the body.
[16]Dickson, *Exposition*, 176*; citing Mt 13:52.
[17]Spinka, ed., *Advocates of Reform*, LCC 14:303-4.

verse, he has given a brief summary of them under the word faith. The most valuable knowledge, therefore, is "faith in Christ." Next follows instruction for regulating the life, to which are added the excitements of exhortations and reproofs. Thus the one who knows how to use the Scriptures properly is in want of nothing for salvation, or for a holy life. Reproof and correction differ little from each other, except that the latter proceeds from the former; for the beginning of repentance is the knowledge of our sinfulness, and a conviction of the judgment of God. Instruction in righteousness means the rule of a good and holy life. COMMENTARY ON 2 TIMOTHY.[18]

CHRIST DRIVES AWAY DARKNESS BUT HERETICS MISUNDERSTAND SCRIPTURE.

ALFONSO SALMERÓN: This is "by the faith which is in Christ Jesus." For the Scriptures lead us to eternal salvation. There was a good reason for adding this, because many Jews and heretics without faith in Christ pay attention to the Scriptures, yet they do not accomplish anything. Therefore the very learned Philo—without this faith in Christ—fooled around with the allegories of the Old Testament. He did not enter in by their door, that is, Christ, as Augustine points out in book twelve of *Against Faustus the Manichee*. For really anybody, whether they be Jews, heretics, or Catholics, nevertheless when they are encumbered by the sins of the flesh or the smoke of arrogance, they derive from the Scriptures with which they busy themselves, and which are difficult and obscure, no usefulness or advantage. For no other writing supplies readers who lack the sense of faith so many snares and stumbling blocks, even though it is itself divine. This is because it does not seem to contain anything except what each person presupposes or feels. And obviously without the Spirit giving life the letter kills. Therefore the Lord says to his apostles, "You have been granted to know the mystery of the kingdom of heaven, but to those outside it is in parables." This is also the

source of that growing supply of heretics in Germany and France, where each person resorts to the sacred Scriptures and comments on them according to their own judgment.

Now faith means here whatever we must believe, whether the substance or the end to which faith looks. This is just like how faith is placed on that in which one hopes. Moreover Christ is the light and the sort of sun of all the Scriptures, driving away all darkness and shadows, bringing upon all people light and life, illuminating, justifying, and saving them. DISPUTATION ON PAUL'S EPISTLES.[19]

THE HOLY SPIRIT SPEAKS WITHOUT ERROR IN SCRIPTURE.

LIBERT FROIDMONT: "All Scripture"—this means sacred Scripture, for this without addition and by its own excellence is typically called Scripture—"is divinely inspired." It is inspired by the Spirit of God, inspiring and speaking it to the minds of the prophets and holy authors. The Spirit not only guided them through a bare assistance so that they did not err. He also guides the fathers in a general council. For just as God works in two ways, one immediately as though his particular work (for example when he works miracles), and at the same time through mediating secondary causes, so he endowed their understanding either immediately through the sacred writings, or immediately through other writings, so says St. Thomas. Therefore the apostle shows that the sacred Scripture is the word of God in such a way that all the sentences, words, and syntax are from the Holy Spirit speaking or writing, but that the tongue of the man who spoke, or the pen of the one who wrote were only his instruments.

But then how do we establish that this Scripture is the Word of God rather than certain other writings of pious men? Here Calvin answers that it is from the secret revelation of the Holy Spirit. "For the same Spirit," he says, "who once inspired the prophets now also inspires the minds of the elect so that they recognize the Scripture as the Word of God." But this is a futile argument. For all

---

[18]CTS 43:249-50* (CO 52:383-84).

[19]Salmerón, *Disputationum*, 264-65; citing 2 Cor 3:6; Mk 4:11.

Calvinists believe that they have been elected, and yet they do not all agree as to the number of the books of sacred Scripture. Next, they often disagree in their interpretation of the Scriptures, and one acknowledges one meaning of the Holy Spirit and another a different one. Consequently, because the meaning is like the soul of Scripture, they fashion for themselves discrepant kinds of Scripture, and then the Holy Spirit must contradict himself, if he reveals to each of them their own meaning for sacred Scripture. Therefore, we do not establish that this book is the sacred Scripture rather than that one, based on a private and deceiving spirit but from the declaration of the church—the pillar and foundation of the truth. COMMENTARIES ON THE EPISTLES.[20]

INSPIRATION BEHIND THE LETTER. DAVID JORIS: The Scriptures were breathed into the authors through the Spirit and were given for service, to bring the needy to trust. This does not refer to teaching the letter or exterior of God's word. No. For the mind of God or Christ is not in them. Therefore, I do not know them any longer in this manner. For it is not the letter, but the spirit. He wills that we should fulfill, yes, fulfill what he has called us to do and not merely remember the external words or leave them empty. Instead we are to gladly and willingly fulfill them, having received them with power. For all those who receive the Word of God in this fashion are protected, but not the others who reject it. For it is not taken by the hands or mouth. No. But it is received into a believing, willing, humble heart. Only then will it rise up, working in a mighty and living fashion. A BLESSED INSTRUCTION FOR HUNGERING, BURDENED SOULS.[21]

BISHOPS ARE EQUIPPED BY SCRIPTURE FOR GOOD WORKS. ALFONSO SALMERÓN: This then is the goal of Scripture: "That the man of God may be perfect in righteousness." This means that he might be fully accomplished and endowed with all things required for the perfecting of the man of God. That is, so that the bishop or Christian doctor—for he is the man of God as we mentioned above—might be equipped for every good work. For the goal of the sacred Scriptures is faith, but good works are next to faith and by them he attains eternal life. Not only must he be prepared to understand but also to work, because faith without works is dead. This is something that heretics will not be glad to hear, especially since they rely upon an empty "faith alone." DISPUTATION ON PAUL'S EPISTLES.[22]

---

[20]Froidmont, *Commentaria*, 399.

[21]CRR 7:260*.
[22]Salmerón, *Disputationum*, 266.

4:1-8 PREACH THE WORD

I charge you in the presence of God and of Christ Jesus, who is to judge the living and the dead, and by his appearing and his kingdom: ²preach the word; be ready in season and out of season; reprove, rebuke, and exhort, with complete patience and teaching. ³For the time is coming when people will not endure sound[a] teaching, but having itching ears they will accumulate for themselves teachers to suit their own passions, ⁴and will turn away from listening to the truth and wander off into myths. ⁵As for you, always be sober-minded, endure suffering, do the work of an evangelist, fulfill your ministry.

⁶For I am already being poured out as a drink offering, and the time of my departure has come. ⁷ I have fought the good fight, I have finished the race, I have kept the faith. ⁸Henceforth there is laid up for me the crown of righteousness, which the Lord, the righteous judge, will award to me on that day, and not only to me but also to all who have loved his appearing.

a Or *healthy*

OVERVIEW: For the reformers, the regular, faithful preaching of the Word of God was seen as central to ministry. Alongside the right administration of the sacraments, it was listed by many as one of the two marks of the true church. The significance granted to preaching in the sixteenth century is clear in the way our interpreters read Paul's exhortation to Timothy to preach the Word with patient perseverance. As Paul tells Timothy that his ministry will face opposition, so too do our exegetes recognize that some will dislike and resist true preaching, and they warn that sin will provide a constant challenge to their ministry. Perseverance in ministry will be rewarded, however, and in Paul's reflection on his own work, the reformers find reason for hope and confidence for those who faithfully preach the Word.

4:1-2 Preach the Word in Season and Out

A SERIOUS EXHORTATION TO DILIGENT MINISTRY. DAVID DICKSON: Paul premises to his exhortation (about the discharge of his office) a grave entreaty, wherein he sets before the eyes of Timothy: (1) The majesty of God. (2) The Lord Jesus Christ. (3) The judgment seat of Christ, before whom he was to give an account of his ministry, with others to be judged at the last day. (4) That glory of Christ, which shall show forth itself at his illustrious appearance, and the full manifestation of his kingdom.

In the exhortation itself he requires five duties: (1) Diligence in preaching. (2) Striving against all impediments. (3) That he do not only take all occasions to preach, which may consist not only with his own convenience and the leisure of the slothful people, but that he stir up himself, sparing no pains, and as it were with his hand, restrain the people busied about the vain employments of the world, earnestly exhorting all to seek after that which is mainly necessary. (4) That he leave no means unattempted in exhorting the people that they make progress in the faith and obedience of Christ, not only preaching true doctrine and reproving that which is false, but also reproving and correcting their evil lives, and exhorting them to live in a holy way, justly and soberly. (5) That he mix his reproofs with zeal and fervency, and season them with gentleness, and that he back his confutations of errors with sound doctrine, that his labor may not be in vain. EXPOSITION OF ALL PAUL'S EPISTLES.[1]

---

[1]Dickson, *Exposition*, 176*.

PREACHING IS NEEDED AND NOT JUST READING SCRIPTURE. JOHN CALVIN: It is proper to observe carefully the word "therefore," by means of which he appropriately connects Scripture with preaching. This also refutes certain fanatics, who haughtily boast that they no longer need the aid of teachers, because the reading of scripture is abundantly sufficient. But Paul, after having spoken of the usefulness of Scripture, infers not only that all ought to read it, but that teachers ought to administer it, which is the duty enjoined on them. . . . Let us remember, I say, that the reading of Scripture is recommended to us in Such a manner as not to hinder, in the smallest degree, the ministry of pastors; and, therefore, let believers endeavor to profit both in reading and in hearing; for not in vain hath God ordained both of them. COMMENTARY ON 2 TIMOTHY.[2]

PRAYER FOR MINISTERS. THE ORDINAL: Most merciful Father, we beseech you to send down upon this your servant your heavenly blessing, and so endue him with your Holy Spirit that he, preaching your Word, may not only be earnest to reprove, beseech, and rebuke with all patience and doctrine but also may be to such as believe a wholesome example, in word, in conversation, in love, in faith, in chastity, and purity, that faithfully fulfilling his course at the latter day, he may receive the crown of righteousness laid up by the Lord, the righteous judge, who lives and reigns, one God with the Father and Holy Ghost, world without end. Amen. THE ORDINAL (1549).[3]

A METHOD FOR PREACHING. WESTMINSTER DIRECTORY: Preaching of the word, being the power of God for salvation, and one of the greatest and most excellent works belonging to the ministry of the gospel, should be performed, that the workman need not be ashamed but may save himself and those that hear him.

It is presupposed (according to the rules for ordination) that the minister of Christ is in some

good measure gifted for so weighty a service, by his skill in the original languages, and in such arts and sciences as are handmaids unto divinity; by his knowledge in all the holy Scriptures, having the senses and heart exercised in them above the common sort of believers; and by the illumination of God's Spirit, and other gifts of edification, which (together with reading and studying of the Word) he ought still to seek by prayer and a humble heart, resolving to admit and receive any truth not yet attained, whenever God shall make it known unto him. All which he is to make use of, and improve in his private preparations, before he deliver in public what he has provided.

Ordinarily, the subject of his sermon is to be some text of Scripture, holding forth some principle or head of religion; or suitable to some special occasion emergent; or he may go on in some chapter, psalm, or book of the holy Scripture as he shall see fit.

Let the introduction to his text be brief and perspicuous, drawn from the text itself, or context, or some parallel place, or general sentence of Scripture. If the text be long (as in histories and parables it sometimes must be) let him give a brief sum of it; if short, a paraphrase thereof, if need be. In both, looking diligently to the scope of the text, and pointing at the chief heads and grounds of doctrine which he is to raise from it.

In analyzing and dividing his text, he is to regard more the order of matter than of words, and neither to burden the memory of the hearers in the beginning with too many members of division, nor to trouble their minds with obscure terms of art. In raising doctrines from the text, his care ought to be: first, that the matter be the truth of God; second, that it be a truth contained in, or grounded on that text, that the hearers may discern how God teaches it from thence; third, that he chiefly insist upon those doctrines which are principally intended, and make most for the edification of the hearers. The doctrine is to be expressed in plain terms . . . and the parallel places of Scriptures confirming the doctrine are rather to be plain and pertinent than many. . . .

---

[2]CTS 43:251-52 (CO 52:384-85).
[3]*Forme and Maner*, Consecrating of a Bishop*.

The illustrations of what kind soever ought to be full of light, and such as may convey the truth into the hearers heart with spiritual delight. If any doubt, obvious from Scripture, reason, or prejudice of the hearers seems to arise, it is very requisite to remove it, by reconciling the seeming differences, answering the reasons, and discovering and taking away the causes of prejudice and mistake. Otherwise, it is not fit to detain the hearers with propounding or answering vain or wicked cavils which, as they are endless, so the propounding and answering of them does more hinder than promote edification.

He is not to rest in general doctrine, although never so much cleared and confirmed, but to bring it home to special use, by application to his hearers. Which albeit proves a work of great difficulty to himself, requiring much prudence, zeal, and meditation, and to the natural and corrupt man will be very unpleasant. Yet he is to endeavor to perform it in such a manner that his auditors may feel the word of God to be quick and powerful and a discerner of the thoughts and intentions of the heart. And if any unbeliever or ignorant person be present, he may have the secrets of his heart made manifest, and give glory to God. WESTMINSTER DIRECTORY. OF THE PREACHING OF THE WORD.[4]

THE SERIOUSNESS OF PREACHING. JOHN CALVIN: Here, as in a very weighty matter, Paul adds a solemn charge, exhibiting to Timothy God as the avenger, and Christ as the Judge, if he shall cease to discharge his office of teaching. And, indeed, in like manner as God showed by an inestimable pledge, when he spared not his only begotten Son, how great is the care he has for the church, so he will not suffer to remain unpunished the negligence of pastors, through whom souls, which he has redeemed at so costly a price, perish or are exposed as a prey.

More especially the apostle fixes attention on the judgment of Christ; because, as we are his representatives, so he will demand a more strict account of evil administration. By "the living and the dead" are meant those whom he shall find still alive at his coming, and likewise those who shall have died. There will therefore be none that escape his judgment.

The appearance of Christ and his kingdom mean the same thing; for although he now reigns in heaven and earth, yet hitherto his reign is not clearly manifested, but, on the contrary, is obscurely hidden under the cross, and is violently assailed by enemies. His kingdom will therefore be established at that time when, having vanquished his enemies, and either removed or reduced to nothing every opposing power, he shall display his majesty. COMMENTARY ON 2 TIMOTHY.[5]

PREACHING IN AND OUT OF SEASON. JOHN TRAPP: On the Lord's day, on the weekday. Let people know whether they will or no, that for lack of preaching they shall not perish. The showbread stood all the week before the Lord, to show that preaching is not out of season on any day. A COMMENTARY.[6]

4:3-5 Ministry Among Itching Ears

PEOPLE WHO DISLIKE THE PREACHING. MARTIN BUCER: Obedience to the holy gospel is to be maintained with great earnestness, because there is nothing that the devil and proud flesh oppose so vehemently. And people always want to have teachers and prophets who will not chide them, but tell them what they like to hear. . . .

This is why Christians are first of all to ask the Lord with great earnestness to grant them faithful ministers, and to watch diligently in choosing them to see that they walk in accordance with their calling and serve faithfully; and when these ministers come to warn, punish, teach or exhort in the Lord's name, not to dismiss it thoughtlessly and despise this ministry, as sadly many are wont to do today. Such people are so kind as to object to

---

[4]*Directory*, 13-15*; citing 2 Tim 2:15; 1 Tim 4:16; Heb 4:11; 1 Cor 14:24-25.

[5]CTS 43:252-53* (CO 52:385).
[6]Trapp, *Commentary*, 335; citing Ex 25:30.

and judge the sermons and all the church activities of their ministers, just as if they had been appointed to do so and the reason for hearing sermons was so that they might in the most unfriendly way discuss, distort and run down what had been said in them, or anything else which had been done in the church. In such people you do not observe any thought of approaching sermons in such a way that they might in some way be moved by what they have heard in them to acknowledge their sins more fully, or to commit themselves more wholeheartedly to Christ and seek more earnestly to improve their ways; all they do is to judge and criticize anything which they consider not to fit in with their carnal impudence (and not Christian freedom). And when they praise something in a sermon, it is generally because it applies to other people, whom they like to hear criticized; and they take from such sermons nothing beyond an excuse to run down those they do not like, and not so that they might be warned or built up. CONCERNING THE TRUE CARE OF SOULS.[7]

SIGNS THAT PEOPLE MAY FORSAKE SOUND DOCTRINE. JOHN OWEN: When people grow weary of sound doctrine—when it is too plain, too heavy, too dull, too common, too high, too mysterious, one thing or other that displeases them, and they would hear something new, something that may please—it is a sign that there are in such an age many who are prone to forsake sound doctrine: and many such we know. . . . This proneness to depart from the truth is a perilous season, because it is the greatest evidence of the withdrawing of the Spirit of God from his church: for the Spirit of God is promised to this end, "to lead us into all truth"; and when the efficacy of truth begins to decay, it is the greatest evidence of the departing and withdrawing of the Spirit of God. And I think that this is a dangerous thing; for if the Spirit of God departs, then our glory and our life depart. SERMON ON 2 TIMOTHY 3:1.[8]

PEOPLE WILL NOT LISTEN TO TALK AGAINST SIN. JOHN MAYER: People shall put wholesome doctrine that tends to reformation of life as a grievous burden from off their shoulders, and even as they that have a tickling in the flesh, whereby they are stirred to fornication, so people's minds shall be lasciviously disposed not to hear anything against sin, for that were rough and harsh, but tales and idle illusions whereby their itching ears may be tickled and their minds corrupted from the sincerity of the truth. And these tales shall not be such as stage-players and vain persons tell, but such as Arch-heretics can invent against the Lord, and thus they shall do that shall follow antichrist. These things have almost all been done by heretics in times past, and now there are many who will not endure the sound morality, but do gladly open their ears to stage-player-like fables. COMMENTARY.[9]

ITCHING EARS LEAD TO IMPRUDENT CHOICES. DIRK PHILIPS: Sometimes the sins of the people deserve that God allows a hypocrite and idolater to rule in the place of a shepherd. For since the people are so minded that they hold good teaching in contempt, as Paul says, and have such weak ears that they desire more to hear what is pleasing than fruitful teaching, therefore they chose such teachers for themselves, after whom their ears itch. And then it happens just as the Lord said through the prophet, "It is horrible and dangerous in the land: the prophets teach lies and the priests rule in their office, and my people like to have it that way, but what will you do when the end comes?" THE SENDING OF PREACHERS.[10]

FULFIL YOUR WHOLE MINISTRY. WESTMINSTER DIRECTORY: The servant of Christ, whatever his method be, is to perform his whole ministry:

1. *Painfully*, not doing the work of the Lord negligently.[†]

2. *Plainly*, that the meanest may understand, delivering the truth not in the enticing words of human wisdom, but in demonstration of the Spirit

---

[7]Bucer, *Concerning the True Care of Souls*, 201, 196.
[8]Owen, *Works*, 9:326-27*; citing Jn 16:13.

[9]Mayer, *Commentarie*, 555-56*.
[10]CRR 6:213*; citing Jer 5:30-31.

and of power, lest the cross of Christ should be made of no effect. Abstaining also from an unprofitable use of unknown tongues, strange phrases, and cadences of sounds and words, sparingly citing sentences of ecclesiastical or other human writers ancient or modern, be they never so elegant.

3. *Faithfully*, looking at the honor of Christ, the conversion, edification, and salvation of the people, not at his own gain or glory. Keeping nothing back which may promote those holy ends, giving to everyone his own portion, and bearing impartial respect to all, without neglecting the meanest, or sparing the greatest in their sins.

4. *Wisely*, framing all his doctrines, exhortations, and especially his reproofs, in such a manner as may be most likely to prevail, showing all due respect to each person and place, and not mixing his own passion or bitterness.

5. *Gravely*, as becomes the word of God, shunning all such gesture, voice, and expressions as may occasion the corruptions of humankind to despise him and his ministry.

6. *With loving affection*, that the people may see all coming from his godly zeal, and hearty desire to do them good.

7. *As taught by God*, and persuaded in his own heart that all that he teaches is the truth of Christ; and walking before his flock as an example to them in it, earnestly both in private and public commending his labors to the blessing of God, and watchfully looking to himself and the flock of which the Lord has made him overseer.

So shall the doctrine of truth be preserved uncorrupt, many souls converted and built up, and himself receive manifold comforts of his labors, even in this life, and afterward the crown of glory laid up for him in the world to come.

Where there are more ministers in a congregation than one, and they of different gifts, each may more especially apply himself to doctrine or exhortation, according to the gift wherein he most excels, and as they shall agree between themselves. WESTMINSTER DIRECTORY. OF THE PREACHING OF THE WORD.[11]

4:6-8 I Have Finished the Race

PAUL IS READY TO BE POURED OUT FOR GOD. JOHN TRAPP: He is ready to be poured out as a drink offering upon God's altar. Thus the apostle expresses himself emphatically, pathetically [i.e., with pathos], elegantly, setting forth by what death he should glorify God, namely, by being beheaded.[†] Whether my death be a burnt offering, a drink offering (by fire or sword) or a peace offering (that I die in my bed), I desire it may be a free will offering, a sweet sacrifice to the Lord. A COMMENTARY.[12]

PAUL HAS FOUGHT SUCCESSFULLY, DESPITE APPEARANCES. JOHN CALVIN: Because it is customary to form a judgment from the event, Paul's fight might have been condemned on the ground that it did not end happily. He therefore boasts that it is excellent, whatever may be the light in which it is regarded by the world. This declaration is a testimony of eminent faith; for not only was Paul accounted wretched in the opinion of all, but his death also was to be ignominious. Who then would not have said that he fought without success? But he does not rely on the corrupt judgments of others. On the contrary, by magnanimous courage he rises above every calamity, so that nothing opposes his happiness and glory; and therefore he declares "the fight which he fought" to be good and honorable.

He even congratulates himself on his death, because it may be regarded as the goal or termination of his course. We know that they who run a race have gained their wish when they have reached the goal. In this manner also he affirms that to Christ's combatants death is desirable, because it puts an end to their labors; and, on the other hand, he likewise declares that we ought never to rest in this life, because it is of no advantage to have run well and constantly from the beginning to the middle of the course, if we do not reach the goal.

---

[11] *Directory*, 17-18*. [†]"Painfully" meaning "taking great pains, or care," rather than being an allusion to, e.g., 1 Cor 9:27.

[12] Trapp, *Commentary*, 336*. [†]The early tradition about Paul being beheaded is mentioned in Eusebius, *Church History* 2.25.5 (see NPNF[2] 1:129-30 and the sources listed in n. 6 there).

"I have kept the faith." This may have a twofold meaning, either that to the last he was a faithful soldier to his captain, or that he continued in the right doctrine. Both meanings will be highly appropriate; and indeed he could not make his fidelity acceptable to the Lord in any other way than by constantly professing, the pure doctrine of the gospel. Yet I have no doubt that he alludes to the solemn oath taken by soldiers;† as if he had said that he was a good and faithful soldier to his captain. COMMENTARY ON 2 TIMOTHY.[13]

CONFIDENCE IN A GRACIOUS REWARD. DAVID DICKSON: As for the future, Paul professes his confidence of a free reward, which God has graciously promised to all the faithful; and as a just judge justly and also of grace will reward, not out of any merit of ours but by accumulating his former gracious gifts freely up on the latter. Wherein the apostle presents his example for Timothy's use, and all the faithful, that the crown of righteousness was not to be set upon his head alone, but upon the heads of all, who endeavoring to do those things which are pleasing to the Lord, declare that they expect and love his appearance. EXPOSITION OF ALL PAUL'S EPISTLES.[14]

FAITHFULNESS UNDER AFFLICTION CON-FIRMS JUSTIFICATION. MATTHIAS FLACIUS: Having described his own happy fight, [Paul] now also adds the award, or crown of glory about to be given to him shortly. By this he shows that he does not sweat to such a degree with no effect, nor is he perplexed by perpetual miseries and calamities. What is not discussed here, however, are the causes of justification, as the deceivers plainly with malice

teach who draw away against justifying grace. For it is indeed with the highest diligence that among the sayings of Scripture actions related to the causes of justification and the kinds of actions of the justified, or those done by the godly by obedience under affliction for the heavenly award by the Father must be distinguished. GLOSS ON 2 TIMOTHY.[15]

THE CROWN OF RIGHTEOUSNESS. GIOVANNI DIODATI: The Lord will award a crown, namely, everlasting glory and happiness, which God of his grace has promised, and gives to his servants for a just reward of their righteous and holy works. It is a term taken from games wherein they strive in several exercises. The Lord will award it; that is, not by my own merits, but by the grace which it has pleased and does please him to bestow upon those who are his, whose imperfect and unworthy works he crowns, as if they were perfect and worthy of reward. There were at those games certain judges appointed to take notice of every one of their actions and carriages, and to distribute the rewards. "At that day" means here some certain day, namely, either the day of his death or the day of the last judgment, when believers shall be glorified both in soul and body. "All who have loved his appearing" means those who have fixed all their hopes and intentions upon those eternal rewards, and for them have carried themselves with all loyalty and constancy. Or, who trusting in a good and upright conscience have desired the Lord's day and have not been afraid of it as the wicked are. PIOUS ANNOTATIONS.[16]

PURCHASED BY THE RIGHTEOUSNESS OF CHRIST. JOHN TRAPP: Salvation is called a crown of righteousness, not because it is of right due to us, but because it is purchased for us by the righteousness of Christ, and shall be freely given to those that are justified by faith. A COMMENTARY.[17]

---

[13]CTS 43:260-61* (CO 52:389-390); citing 2 Tim 2:4. †A *sacramentum* was a military oath sworn by soldiers, seen, e.g., in Livy, *Ab urbe condita* 2.32.1, 10.38.2, and 22.38.1-5 (LCL 114:320-21, 191:504-5, and 233:326). This background was also important to another Swiss reformer, Huldrych Zwingli, who in his *De vera et falsa religione* (Zurich, 1529), 197b, mentions the historical background of a Roman soldier leaving a token/*sacramentum* on the altar before battle and reclaiming his reward afterward, in his discussion of the sacrament of baptism. [14]Dickson, *Exposition*, 177.

[15]Flacius, *Glossa Compendaria*, 1085.
[16]Diodati, *Pious Annotations*, 340-41*.
[17]Trapp, *Commentary*, 337*.

4:9-22 PERSONAL INSTRUCTIONS AND FINAL GREETINGS

⁹*Do your best to come to me soon.* ¹⁰*For Demas, in love with this present world, has deserted me and gone to Thessalonica. Crescens has gone to Galatia,ᵃ Titus to Dalmatia.* ¹¹*Luke alone is with me. Get Mark and bring him with you, for he is very useful to me for ministry.* ¹²*Tychicus I have sent to Ephesus.* ¹³*When you come, bring the cloak that I left with Carpus at Troas, also the books, and above all the parchments.* ¹⁴*Alexander the coppersmith did me great harm; the Lord will repay him according to his deeds.* ¹⁵*Beware of him yourself, for he strongly opposed our message.* ¹⁶*At my first defense no one came to stand by me, but all deserted me. May it not*
be charged against them! ¹⁷*But the Lord stood by me and strengthened me, so that through me the message might be fully proclaimed and all the Gentiles might hear it. So I was rescued from the lion's mouth.* ¹⁸*The Lord will rescue me from every evil deed and bring me safely into his heavenly kingdom. To him be the glory forever and ever. Amen.*

¹⁹*Greet Prisca and Aquila, and the household of Onesiphorus.* ²⁰*Erastus remained at Corinth, and I left Trophimus, who was ill, at Miletus.* ²¹*Do your best to come before winter. Eubulus sends greetings to you, as do Pudens and Linus and Claudia and all the brothers.ᵇ*

²²*The Lord be with your spirit. Grace be with you.ᶜ*

a Some manuscripts *Gaul*   b Or *brothers and sisters*. In New Testament usage, depending on the context, the plural Greek word *adelphoi* (translated "brothers") may refer either to *brothers* or to *brothers and sisters*   c The Greek for *you* is plural

OVERVIEW: Paul draws his second letter to Timothy to a close with a series of personal instructions and greetings, and this diverse set of requests, warnings, and messages does not go without comment from our Reformation interpreters. Those who are identified as being in conflict with Paul, Demas and Alexander, are of particular interest, and our exegetes unpack their motivations and the significance of their actions. Paul's request for his books and cloak also draw comment. In the apostle's final affirmations, they meditate on Paul's confidence and focus on the heavenly kingdom as his death draws near.

4:9-12 Demas Loved This Present World

PAUL'S APPROACH TOWARD DEMAS, ALEXANDER, AND OTHERS. RICHARD SIBBES: Blessed St. Paul, being now an old man, and ready to sacrifice his dearest blood for the sealing of that truth which he had carefully taught, sets down in this chapter what diverse reception he found, both
from God and people, in the preaching of it. As for people, he found they dealt most unfaithfully with him when he stood most in need of comfort from them. Demas, a man of great note, in the end forsook him; Alexander the coppersmith did him most mischief—thus it pleases God to try his dearest ones with base oppositions of worthless persons; weaker Christians forsook him.

But mark the wisdom of God's Spirit in the blessed apostle, with regard to his different responses toward these persons. Demas, because his fault was greater, by reason of the eminency of his profession, him he brands to all posterity, for looking back to Sodom and to the world, after he had put his hand to the plow. Alexander's opposing, because it sprung from extremity of malice toward the profession of godliness, him he curses: "The Lord will repay him according to his deeds." Weaker Christians, who failed him from want of some measure of spirit and courage, retaining still a hidden love to the cause of Christ, their names he conceals, with prayer that God would not lay their sin to their charge. The Danger of Backsliding.[1]

Demas Undervalues Paul Compared to His Own Private Advantages. David

Dickson: Timothy should hasten his coming because of the fewness of Paul's companions and helpers, whereof he was now destitute. For Demas, not liking the dangers and afflictions that were incident to Paul's companions, and wherewith they were often exercised (being led by the love of ease, security, and the commodities of this life) undervalues the care of Paul, and the gospel now openly defended by him, in comparison with his own private advantages, he went to Thessalonica, where he might live more securely. Crescens was sent into Galatia, and Titus was gone to Dalmatia, to propagate the gospel. So that he only had Luke the Physician to accompany him. Exposition of All Paul's Epistles.[2]

Demas Cared More for Himself Than for Paul or Christ. John Calvin: It was truly base in such a man to prefer the love of this world to Christ. And yet we must not suppose that he altogether denied Christ or gave himself up either to ungodliness or to the allurements of the world; but he merely preferred his private convenience, or his safety, to the life of Paul. He could not have assisted Paul without many troubles and vexations, attended by imminent risk of his life; he was exposed to many reproaches, and must have submitted to many insults, and been constrained to leave off the care of his own affairs; and, therefore being overcome by his dislike of the cross, he resolved to consult his own interests. Nor can it be doubted, that he enjoyed a propitious gale from the world. That he was one of the leading men may be conjectured on this ground, that Paul mentions him amidst a very few at and likewise in the epistle to Philemon where also he is ranked among Paul's assistants; and, therefore, we need not wonder if he

censures him so sharply on this occasion, for having cared more about himself than about Christ.

Others, whom he afterward mentions, had not gone away from him but for good reasons, and with his own consent.[†] Hence it is evident that he did not study his own advantage, so as to deprive churches of their pastors, but only to obtain from them some relief. Undoubtedly he was always careful to invite to come to him, or to keep along with him, those whose absence would not be injurious to other churches. For this reason he had sent Titus to Dalmatia, and some to one place and some to another, when he invited Timothy to come to him. Not only so, but in order that the church at Ephesus may not be left destitute or forlorn during Timothy's absence, he sends Tychicus thither, and mentions this circumstance to Timothy, that he may know that that church will not be in want of one to fill his place during his absence. Commentary on 2 Timothy.[3]

Labor to Understand the World, That You May Detest It. Richard Sibbes: Those who love the world bring it into the church with them. It is chief in their thoughts, and therefore they carry it about with them in their hearts wherever they go. As it is said of Israel, they carried Egypt into the wilderness, so these bring the world to the ordinances of God, they come to the hearing of the word like drone bees, leaving their stings behind them.

---

[1]Sibbes, *Works*, 7:408-9*.
[2]Dickson, *Exposition*, 177*.

[3]CTS 43:264-65 (CO 52:391-92); citing Col 4:14; Philem 24. [†]This is a conjecture, but one shared by almost all modern commentators. See, e.g., Jerome D. Quinn and William C. Wacker, *The First and Second Letters to Timothy: A New Translation with Notes and Commentary*, Eerdmans Critical Commentary (Grand Rapids: Eerdmans, 2000), 800; I. Howard Marshall, *The Pastoral Epistles*, International Critical Commentary (London: T&T Clark, 2004), 816; George W. Knight III, *The Pastoral Epistles: A Commentary on the Greek Text*, New International Greek Testament Commentary (Carlisle, UK: Paternoster, 1992), 465; William D. Mounce, *The Pastoral Epistles*, Word Biblical Commentary (Nashville: Thomas Nelson, 2000), 590. However, Christopher Green, *Finishing the Race: Reading 2 Timothy Today* (Sydney: Aquila, 2000), 149, notes the absence of a different verb to describe Crescens and Titus, and the fact that they are not mentioned alongside Tychicus, who was "sent" in 2 Tim 4:12, to conclude that it is uncomfortably and "frighteningly plausible" that they may also have in some way deserted Paul.

Paul does not say here "Demas did forsake me" for fear of persecution, but "for love of the world." Faults are in their aggravation as they are in deliberation. Peter denied his Master, but it was not with deliberation, whereas Demas did it in his cold blood. He loved the world; he set up the creature in his heart higher than the Creator.

Labor therefore to know the world, that you may detest it. In religion, the more we know the more we will love; but all the worldly things, the more we know the less we will desire them; as a picture afar off, it will show well, but come near it and it is not so. Let us see, then, what the world is. Alas! It is but the "present world" that will vanish away suddenly. Poor Demas thought a bird in the hand was worth two in the bush, and therefore he would brave it out awhile; but alas, what is become of him now? The worldly often, in seeking these things, lose them-selves and the world too; but a Christian never loses that which they seek after—God and Christ, and the things of a better life. The more we know the vanities of the world and the excellencies of grace, the more we will love the one and hate the other. THE DANGER OF BACKSLIDING.[4]

4:13 Paul's Needs

THE FRUGALITY, HUMILITY, AND DILIGENCE OF PAUL. JOHN MAYER: Note how provident and frugal Paul was. Although a great part of the world was his diocese, yet he studied so not to charge those to whom he preached that he provided him not many coats or cloaks, but if any time he had left his cloak in one place, the weather being warm, he had not another for his necessity against the cold coming on without sending for it. And in that Timothy is appointed to bring it, note the great humility even of bishops then, that none of us now, although we have more outward dignity, may express pride in any thing, and that we may be content with a competency, not expressing so great a desire of base lucre by adding living to living without measure.[†] And let us all learn of him to

study and converse among books, even when we are old, and the time of our departure hence hastens on. COMMENTARY.[5]

PAUL RECOMMENDS CONSTANT READING FOR ALL CHRISTIANS. JOHN CALVIN: It is evident from this that the apostle had not given over reading, though he was already preparing for death. Where are those who think that they have made so great progress that they do not need any more exercise? Which of them will dare to compare himself with Paul? Still more does this expression refute the madness of those men who—despising books, and condemning all reading—boast of nothing but their own divine inspirations. But let us know that this passage gives to all believers a recommendation of constant reading, that they may profit by it. COMMENTARY ON 2 TIMOTHY.[6]

4:14-16 Alexander's Strong Opposition to Paul

COVETOUS BUSINESSMEN OPPOSE THE GOSPEL. ENGLISH ANNOTATIONS: Covetousness is the bane of religion. Two of the greatest enemies St. Paul had were two smiths: the one a silversmith and this coppersmith here. And both of them, as it is conceived, maligned and opposed him and his preaching for the same reason: because the apostle taught they were no gods that were made with hands, and thereby he hindered their gain and marred their handicraft, which was to make silver or copper shrines or images to the heathen gods and goddesses. ENGLISH ANNOTATIONS.[7]

THE LORD WILL REPAY ALEXANDER FOR HIS OPPOSITION. DUTCH ANNOTATIONS: This is no cursing proceeding from a revengeful heart, contrary to the doctrine of Christ and also of

---

[4]Sibbes, *Works*, 7:413*; citing Rom 1:25.

[5]Mayer, *Commentarie*, 559*. [†]Mayer refers to the frowned-on practice of clergy holding more than one "living" or benefice at the same time (in *plurality*), so as to accumulate a larger stipend from the tithes of each parish.
[6]CTS 43:266 (CO 52:392-93).
[7]Downame, ed., *Annotations*, s.v.*; citing Acts 19:24.

Paul himself, but a prophetical threatening out of a godly zeal to God's glory, and inspiration of the Holy Spirit, of the punishment which was approaching Alexander, seeing he showed himself to be altogether impenitent and hardened. DUTCH ANNOTATIONS.[8]

THE RIGHT WAY TO PRONOUNCE SENTENCE ON OTHERS. JOHN CALVIN: So mild and so merciful to all others, how comes it that he shows himself so harsh and inexorable toward Alexander? The reason is this. Because some had fallen through fear and weakness, he desires that the Lord would forgive them; for in this manner we ought to have compassion on the weakness of brethren. But because this man rose against God with malice and sacrilegious hardihood, and openly attacked known truth, such impiety had no claim to compassion.

We must not imagine, therefore, that Paul was moved by excessive warmth of temper, when he broke out into this imprecation; for it was from the Spirit of God, and through a well-regulated zeal that he wished eternal perdition to Alexander and mercy to the others. Seeing that it is by the guidance of the Spirit that Paul pronounces a heavenly judgment from on high, we may infer from this passage how dear to God is his truth, for attacking which he punishes so severely. Especially it ought to be observed how detestable a crime it is to fight with deliberate malice against the true religion.

But lest any person, by falsely imitating the apostle, should rashly utter similar imprecations, there are three things here that deserve notice. First, let us not avenge the injuries done to ourselves, lest self-love and a regard to our private advantage should move us violently, as frequently happens. Second, while we maintain the glory of God, let us not mingle with it our own passions, which always disturb good order. Third, let us not pronounce sentence against every person without discrimination, but only against reprobates, who, by their impiety, give evidence that such is their true character. COMMENTARY ON 2 TIMOTHY.[9]

FEAR OF NERO KEPT CHRISTIANS FROM HELPING PAUL. CARDINAL CAJETAN: "No one stood with me, but all have abandoned me." Note that this is said about those who could have helped him. For he had already said that Luke was with him, and Peter at the time was in Rome. But such men were not among those who would have been able to help them. Yet although there was a great multitude of Christians in Rome then, and some of them could have stood with and helped him, not one of them suffered with Paul—for fear of Nero, most likely. And so he adds "may this not be charged against them." Because Paul suffers with human weakness he wants God not to charge them with this failure. "Yet God stood by me," that is, in place of human beings. "And he strengthened me." THE EPISTLES OF PAUL AND THE OTHER APOSTLES.[10]

4:17-22 Focus on the Heavenly Kingdom

THE LORD RESCUES US FROM THE MOUTHS OF LIONS. RICHARD SIBBES: Blessed St. Paul, being now an old man, and ready to sacrifice his dearest blood for the sealing of that truth that he had carefully taught, sets down in this chapter what diverse reception he found, both from God and people, in the preaching of it. As for people, he found they dealt most unfaithfully with him when he stood most in need of comfort from them.... But while Paul lived in this cold comfort, see what large encouragement he had from heaven! "Though all forsook me, yet," says he, "God did not forsake me, but stood by me, and I was delivered out of the mouth of the lion. And the Lord will deliver me."...

I find that most, both ancient and modern writers, by "lion" understand Nero, that cruel tyrant, thirsty of blood, especially of Christians. Some also understand it to be a proverbial speech, to express extremity of danger, both which are true. But if we take the words in the just breadth of the apostle's intent, we may by lion understand "the whole united company of his cruel enemies," as David in many places has the like; and by the

[8]Haak, *Annotations*, s.v.*; Mt 5:44; Rom 12:14; Neh 4:4; Ps 5:10. [9]CTS 43:268-69* (CO 52:393-94).

[10]Cajetan, *Epistolae Pauli*, 152.

mouth of the lion, the greatest danger he was in by reason of their cruel malice. Whence observe:

1. That enemies of the truth are often for power, always for malice, lions.

2. That God suffers his dearest children to fall into the mouths of these lions.

3. That in this extremity of danger, God delivers them.

The Saint's Safety in Evil Times.[11]

We Should Desire Victory, Not Comfort.
John Calvin: He declares that he hopes the same for the future; not that he will escape death, but that he will not be vanquished by Satan, or turn aside from the right course. This is what we ought chiefly to desire, not that the interests of the body may be promoted, but that we may rise superior to every temptation, and may be ready to suffer a hundred deaths rather than that it should come into our mind to pollute ourselves by any "evil work." Yet I am well aware that there are some who take the expression evil work in a passive sense, as denoting the violence of the wicked, as if Paul had said, "The Lord will not suffer the wicked to do me any injury." But the other meaning is far more appropriate, that he will preserve him pure and unblemished from every wicked action; for he immediately adds, to his heavenly kingdom, by which he means that that alone is true salvation, when the Lord—either by life or by death—conducts us into his kingdom.

This is a remarkable passage for maintaining the uninterrupted communication of the grace of God, in opposition to the papists. After having confessed that the beginning of salvation is from God, they ascribe the continuation of it to free will; so that in this way perseverance is not a heavenly gift, but a human virtue. And Paul, by ascribing to God this work of "preserving us to his kingdom," openly affirms that we are guided by his hand during the whole course of our life, till, having discharged the whole of our warfare, we obtain the victory. And we have a memorable instance of this in Demas, whom he mentioned a little before, because, from

being a noble champion of Christ, he had become a base deserter. All that follows has been seen by us formerly, and therefore does not need additional exposition. Commentary on 2 Timothy 4:18.[12]

Be Much in Heaven in Your Thoughts.
Richard Sibbes: And see here a point of heavenly wisdom: to look, when we are in any danger, with the apostle, to the heavenly kingdom. When we are sick, look not at death. Paul cared not for that, but he says, "The Lord will preserve me to his kingdom." He looked to the bank of the shore. As a person who goes through a river has their eye still on the shore, so the apostle had his eye fixed upon heaven still. I beseech you therefore, in all dangers and distresses whatsoever, if you would keep your souls without discouragement, as you should, be much in heaven in your thoughts, minding the things above, and conversing with God in your spirits. Look to the crown that is held out to us. Let our minds be in heaven before our souls. It is a wondrous help to our weakness in the time of trouble, not to think "I am full of pain. I must be turned into the grave, and rot, and what shall become of me then?" Away with this carnal reasoning. It much weakens faith and damps the hearts of Christians. . . .

"To whom be glory forever and ever." When he had mentioned the heavenly kingdom, and set himself by faith, as it were, in possession of it, he presently begins the employment of heaven, "to praise and glorify God," even while he was on earth. For faith stirs us up to do that which we shall do, when we obtain the things believed. It is called "the evidence of things not seen" and makes them, as it were, present to the soul. Because when we are in heaven indeed, we shall do nothing else but praise God. Faith apprehends it, as if we were now there, for all is sure to faith, God having said it, who will do it. And it sets the soul upon that employment here, which it shall have eternally with God hereafter. The Saint's Safety in Evil Times.[13]

[11]Sibbes, *Works*, 1:314-15*.

[12]CTS 43:271-72* (CO 52:395-96).
[13]Sibbes, *Works*, 1:327, 329*; citing Heb 11:1.

COMMENTARY ON TITUS

1:1-4 INTRODUCTION TO TITUS AND PAUL'S GREETING

Paul, a servant[a] *of God and an apostle of Jesus Christ, for the sake of the faith of God's elect and their knowledge of the truth, which accords with godliness,* [2]*in hope of eternal life, which God, who never lies, promised before the ages began*[b] [3]*and at the proper time manifested in his word*[c] *through the preaching* *with which I have been entrusted by the command of God our Savior;*

[4]*To Titus, my true child in a common faith:*

Grace and peace from God the Father and Christ Jesus our Savior.

a For the contextual rendering of the Greek word *doulos*, see Preface b Greek before *times eternal* c Or *manifested his word*

OVERVIEW: With the third of the so-called Pastoral Epistles being addressed to Titus, our exegetes first attempt to understand who Titus is and why Paul has written to him. The reformers gather together the other texts where Titus is mentioned in the New Testament, and while they agree that he was a Gentile church leader and companion of Paul, there are divergent opinions on his role in the church, leading to suggestions that he might be a bishop, an evangelist, or even an arch-bishop. Despite these differences, there is broad consensus on the purpose of the letter; they argue that Paul was writing to describe the characteristics that should be sought in Christian leaders and his expectations concerning how sound doctrine should be passed down so that Christians can live godly lives as they await the return of Christ. Paul's salutation to Titus is unusually long, and as our commentators note, it is also doctrinally rich. Election and the faithfulness of God are emphasized, as is the need for adherence to divine teaching and practical obedience throughout the Christian life.

Introductory Comments

THE GENERAL INSTRUCTS THE GOVERNOR. MATTHEW POOLE: As a general of an army, who has a large country to conquer, cannot himself stay long in a conquered city, but leaving it with a garrison, under commanders, himself still goes forward in his conquests, and by his letters directs those whom he has left governors in his conquered places how to behave themselves; so the apostle of the Gentiles, having a large field to run over before he could finish his course, could not himself stay long in places where he had brought people into a subjection to the gospel, but after a time, leaving them as a garrison to keep Christ's possession in the place, left them under the conduct of some eminent disciple and minister, to whom he afterward wrote letters directive of such minister, to settle the church in such a place, what and how to preach, and behave himself; thus he left Timothy at Ephesus,

Titus at Crete. ANNOTATIONS UPON THE
Holy Bible.[1]

THE PROVENANCE AND TIMING OF THE
LETTER. JOHN MAYER: Titus was a Greek by
birth, and from Corinth, according to Chrysostom.[†] He, being a man of an excellent life and a
sound teacher, after his conversion by Paul, was by
him made bishop of Crete, according to Theodoret.[‡] St. Paul speaks of him as dear to him, and as
one who labored in other parts also for he says
that Titus had gone to Dalmatia. But he returned
and governed the church in Crete until his death,
he being then aged ninety-four years old, as
Baronius has it.[‡]

To this Titus, St. Paul wrote this epistle when
he was in or near to Nicopolis, as the postscript
shows, and as all generally consent;[§] which place
is also here mentioned, as the place where Paul
purposed to spend the winter. Yet Beza denies him
to have been there then, because speaking of his
intent to winter in Nicopolis, Paul says, "I *purpose*
to winter there." But this is too weak an exception,
because if he were but a mile or two from that city,
to which he was still coming and going, he might
well say this; and therefore we say that this letter
was sent from about Nicopolis in Macedonia.

For the time, it is said by Theodoret to have
been written before the first epistle to Timothy;
and this indeed appears to be so, because at the
time of his wintering in Nicopolis, he had not yet
been prisoner in Rome, as he was when he wrote
first to Timothy. Baronius calculates the time to be
AD 58. The argument of the letter is the same as
that in the epistles to Timothy, of which it is a kind
of epitome. COMMENTARY ON PAUL'S EPISTLES.[2]

TITUS, A GENTILE COMPANION OF PAUL.
GREGORY MARTIN: Titus was a Gentile and not a
Jew. He was part of Paul's retinue by at least the
fourth year after [the apostle's] conversion if not
before from what we understand in Galatians 2.
[Titus] continued with [Paul] until the very end
according to 2 Timothy 4, where [the apostle]
mentions that he sent him from Rome to Dalmatia
when he himself was shortly afterward put to death.

And therefore although St. Luke never names
Titus or himself in Acts, yet he undoubtedly
meant to include him when he spoke in the first
person plural saying, "Immediately we sought to
go into Macedonia." For St. Paul also sent him to
Corinth, between the writing of his first and
second letters to the Corinthians (which time
coincides with Acts 19), by occasion whereof he
makes frequent and honorable mention of him in
2 Corinthians chapters 2 and 7. And again, he sent
him with that epistle, both times about great
matters, so that no doubt he was even then also a
bishop, and received accordingly by the Corinthians, with fear and trembling. But this is plainer in
the epistle to Titus himself where the apostle says,
"For this reason I left you in Crete." By these words
it is also clear that this epistle was not written
during the story of Acts (since no mention is
made there of St. Paul being on the island of
Crete), but after Paul's removal to Rome, out of
his first trouble, and before his second or last
trouble there, as is evident by these words: "When
I shall send to you Artemis or Tychicus, make
haste to come to me at Nicopolis, for there I have
determined to winter."

---

[1]Poole, *Annotations*, s.v.*; citing Acts 26:17-18. This section of
Poole's commentary was completed by "Dr. Collins"—probably
John Collings or Collinges, according to S. A. Alliborne, *A
Critical Dictionary of English Literature and British and American
Authors* (Philadelphia: J. B. Lippincott, 1872), 411, and Samuel
Palmer, *The Nonconformist's Memorial* (London: Button & Son,
1802), 1:170. Cf. A. G. Matthews, *Calamy Revised: Being a Revision
of Edmund Calamy's Account of the Ministers and Others Ejected
and Silenced, 1660–2* (Oxford: Clarendon, 1934), 128.
[2]Mayer, *Commentarie*, 560*; citing 2 Cor 2:13; 2 Tim 4:10; Titus

3:12. [†]See NPNF 13:519. [‡]See his commentary on 1 Tim 3:1 in
Theodoret of Cyrus: Commentary on the Letters of St. Paul, trans.
Robert C. Hill (Brookline, MA: Holy Cross Orthodox Press,
2001), 2:217. See also Eusebius, *Church History* 3.4.6 (NPNF[2]
1:136). [‡]The earliest extant reference to Titus's death aged
ninety-four is in the apocryphal Acts of Titus 12. See Richard I.
Pervo, "'The Acts of Titus': A Preliminary Translation; With an
Introduction, Notes, and Appendices," *Society of Biblical Literature
Seminar Papers* 35 (1996): 455-82. [§]The traditional postscript, or
subscription, to the letter (in Codex Alexandrinus and the Textus
Receptus, for example) says it was written to Titus from
Nicopolis (with some manuscripts adding "of Macedonia").

Therefore he instructs Titus (and in him all bishops) like he does Timothy regarding the qualities that he should require in those whom he would make priest and bishops; the manner in which he was to preach and teach all sorts of people; to encourage them to do good works; and finally, how he himself was to be their example of in all goodness. DOUAY-RHEIMS NEW TESTAMENT. ARGUMENT OF TITUS.[3]

PAUL MIXES TEACHING AND EXHORTATION. MARTIN LUTHER: The epistle to Titus is short, but it is a kind of epitome and summary of other, wordier epistles. We should be imbued with the attitudes that are taught in it. Paul is the sort of teacher who is engaged most of all in these two topics, either teaching or exhorting. Moreover, he never exhorts in such a way that he fails to mingle didactic, that is, doctrinal, instruction with it. And so while this epistle is obviously a hortatory one, yet he writes in such a way that he superbly mingles doctrine with exhortation, and in double measure. He is a true teacher, one who both teaches and exhorts. By his teaching he sets down what is to be believed by faith, and by his exhortation he sets down what is to be done. Thus by doctrine he builds up faith, by exhortation he builds up life. He begins with exhortation, yet he mingles instruction with it. Therefore this is a hortatory epistle, yet not exclusively so. LECTURES ON TITUS.[4]

A SUMMARY OF ALL PAUL'S EPISTLES. EDWARD LEIGH: This epistle is by the learned called *Epitome Paulinarum Epistolarum*, an abridgement of all Paul's epistles. It is filled with such a variety of precepts fitted to all sorts, sexes, ages, and conditions of people, so that whatever he has more largely handled in all his epistles, he seems summarily to have reduced them into this one. This epistle contains three parts. First, the saluta-

tion in the first four verses. Second, the narration or proposition of the matter of it, from the fifth verse of the first chapter to the end of the eleventh verse of the third chapter. Third, the conclusion, containing some private business enjoined on Titus, and then the ordinary salutation of the apostle. ANNOTATIONS.[5]

HOW TO LIVE AS CHRIST'S PEOPLE. WILLIAM TYNDALE: This is a short epistle: yet in it is contained all that is needful for a Christian to know. In the first chapter he shows what kind of man a bishop or curate ought to be: that is, virtuous and learned to preach and defend the gospel, and to confound the doctrine of trusting in works and human traditions which ever fights against the faith and carries away the conscience captive from the freedom that is in Christ into the bondage of their own imaginations and inventions, as though those things (which are to no profit at all) could make a person good in the sight of God.

In the second chapter he teaches all degrees—old, young, men, women, masters, and servants—how to behave as those whom Christ has bought with his blood to be his proper or peculiar people, to glorify God with good works.

In the third chapter he teaches us to honor temporal rulers and to obey them, and yet brings us to Christ again and to the grace that he has purchased for us, that no-one should think that obeying a prince's laws or any other work can justify us before God. And last of all he charges us to avoid the company of the stubborn and of the heretics. NEW TESTAMENT. PREFACE TO TITUS.[6]

ARCHBISHOP TITUS APPOINTED OVER CRETE. DESIDERIUS ERASMUS: The apostle Paul had made his disciple Titus overseer of the Christian congregation on the noble island of Crete, now called Candia. For the excellent gifts that were in him, Paul loved Titus as tenderly as if he had been his own natural son. When Paul left that country,

---

[3]Martin, *New Testament*, 594*; citing Acts 16:10; 2 Cor 7:15; Titus 3:12.
[4]LW 29:3 (WA 25:6).

[5]Leigh, *Annotations*, 338*.
[6]Tyndale, *The Newe Testament*, cccx-cccxi*.

he made him the head overseer of the faithful that were there. Afterward he wrote this epistle or letter to him from a city of Epirus called Nicopolis, lying on the sea coast in a cliff named by the old cosmographers Leucate or the cliff of Actium, at which time all things as it seems were quiet with the Christians, for here is no mention made of any persecution. In this epistle he reminds Titus to finish and perfect those things which he himself had begun among the same people of Crete, and that in every city of the island (of which writers testify there were a hundred) he should ordain overseers, which we now call bishops and here they are by the apostle named elders. And for this reason Paul prescribes to him the true form of a bishop or shepherd of Christ's flock. Furthermore because false apostles had also come into those parts, and were going around putting their Jewish ceremonies into people's heads, Paul here gives him encouragement strongly to confute and reject them.

After these things he shows what the duty of every person and age is, as he did to Timothy: adding this, that no one ought to resist princes and magistrates executing their office and power, even though they were infidels, but rather to tolerate them patiently, that they may the sooner by such modesty be called to the following of the gospel. Last of all he wills Titus to come to him at Nicopolis but not before he had sent Artemas or Tychicus, who were his disciples, into Crete to him. Otherwise, the Cretans would think themselves destitute of the comfort of a head or chief overseer, whom we call an archbishop. PARAPHRASES.[7]

TITUS NO ORDINARY PASTOR. DAVID DICKSON: When Paul had only laid the foundation of a church in the island of Crete, which is also called Candia, making haste to some other place (as was proper for the apostle to the Gentiles), he leaves Titus and enjoins him as an evangelist to prosecute the work. But when Paul understood that he was contemned by some, and that he might be brought into further contempt by those who were obstinate,

as if he had been a common pastor, Paul invests him with authority and puts upon him, as it were, his own person—not only in making ministers but also in the whole administration of the church—and encourages him to go forward in the work of the Lord. EXPOSITION OF ALL PAUL'S EPISTLES.[8]

AUTHORIZING TITUS AMONG THE CRETANS. GIOVANNI DIODATI: Titus, as it appears from Galatians 2:3, having been converted from paganism to the Christian faith, was appointed by St. Paul to be an evangelist, and a companion with him in Crete, to perfect the establishing of the state and government of the churches that St. Paul had founded there. And while he was there, the apostle wrote this epistle to him, to admonish, incite, and strengthen him in the exercise of his charge; and also to authorize him among the Cretans. So then at the very beginning he declares what qualities are required in those persons whom he is to choose for pastors and conductors of the churches in their life, behavior, and domestic government, and especially in their doctrine—it being a most necessary aspect of the work to oppose Jewish false errors and doctrines, the seeds of which were already scattered among those churches. Afterward he appoints him, instead of the vain observations in which false teachers reposed great holiness, to teach and commend the true spiritual sanctification in everyone's vocation. He especially commends obedience to princes and magistrates, according to God's graces presented in the gospel and to the regeneration of the Spirit, which he for that purpose exceedingly extols and lays open. And, on the other hand, he advises him to forbid and suppress all vain disputations, and to shun all obstinate heretics. PIOUS ANNOTATIONS.[9]

ARMING TITUS AGAINST COMPLAINTS. JOHN CALVIN: Paul, having only laid the foundations of the church in Crete, and hastening to go to another place (for he was not the pastor of a single island

---

[7]Erasmus, *Paraphrases*, cccc.ii* (EOO 6:964).

[8]Dickson, *Exposition*, 178* (*Expositio*, 567).
[9]Diodati, *Pious Annotations*, 48*.

only, but the apostle of the Gentiles) had given charge to Titus to prosecute this work as an evangelist. It is evident from this epistle that, immediately after Paul's departure, Satan labored not only to overthrow the government of the church, but likewise to corrupt its doctrine.

There were some who, through ambitious motives, wished to be elevated to the rank of pastors, and who, because Titus did not comply with their wicked desires, spoke unfavorably of him to many persons. On the other hand, there were Jews who, under the presence of supporting the Mosaic law, introduced a great number of trifles; and such persons were listened to with eagerness and with much acceptance. Paul therefore writes with this design, to arm Titus with his authority, that he may be able to bear so great a burden; for undoubtedly there were some who fearlessly despised him as being but one of the ordinary rank of pastors. It is also possible that complaints about him were in circulation, to the effect that he assumed more authority than belonged to him when he did not admit pastors till he had made trial and ascertained their fitness.

Hence we may infer that this was not so much a private epistle of Paul to Titus, as it was a public epistle to the Cretans. It is not probable that Titus is blamed for having with too great indulgence raised unworthy persons to the office of bishop, or that, as an ignorant man and a novice, he is told what is that kind of doctrine in which he ought to instruct the people; but because due honor was not rendered to him, Paul clothes him with his own authority, both in ordaining ministers and in the whole government of the Church. Because there were many who foolishly desired to have another form of doctrine than that which he delivered, Paul approves of this alone—rejecting all others—and exhorts him to proceed as he had begun.

First, then, he shows what sort of persons ought to be chosen for being ministers. Among other qualifications, he requires that a minister shall be well instructed in sound doctrine, that by means of it he may resist adversaries. Here he takes occasion to censure some vices of the Cretans, but especially

rebukes the Jews, who made some kind of holiness to consist in a distinction of food, and in other outward ceremonies. In order to refute their fooleries, he contrasts with them the true exercises of piety and Christian life; and, with the view of pressing them more closely, he describes what are the duties which belong to every one in his calling. These duties he enjoins Titus diligently and constantly to inculcate. On the other hand, he admonishes others not to be weary of hearing them, and shows that this is the design of the redemption and salvation obtained through Christ. If any obstinate person oppose, or refuse to obey, he bids him set that person aside. We now see that Paul has no other object in view than to support the cause of Titus, and to stretch out the hand to assist him in performing the work of the Lord. Commentary on Titus.[10]

1:1-4 Greeting

Paul's Gospel in a Nutshell. David Dickson: The preface contains three things: (1) A description of the penman (vv. 1-3); (2) a description of him to whom he writes; (3) a salutation with an apostolical benediction (vv. 3-4).

In the description of the penman Paul, his authority is asserted from these eight heads. (1) That he is a servant of God, and that is maintained against the Jews, who reproached him as a deserter of the religion of his country. (2) That he is an apostle of Jesus Christ, who by an immediate commission to all nations held the supreme degree of ministry in the church. (3) That his doctrine agrees with the faith of Abraham, and the fathers, and all the elect, which every age of those who are elected would receive, none but reprobates would reject, because it contains nothing but the known and acknowledged truth, instructing people to godliness and the pure worship of God.

In verse 2, he adjoins the remaining commendations of his doctrine and the arguments of his authority. (4) That it brings a lively hope of eternal

[10]CTS 43:277-78 (CO 52:401-2).

life to believers. (5) That it is upheld by the testimony of God who cannot lie, or it is impossible for him to lie, or to speak what is not, or not to be able to effect what he says. (6) That the original of this truth is most ancient, inasmuch as God has promised eternal life, not only in the beginning of the world, preaching it to our first parents in paradise, but also covenanting with his Son (designed to be our mediator) about it before the world was made, in the covenant of redemption. (7) That this truth was most wisely revealed, that is, by degrees, and in convenient seasons, as it seemed good to God, it was made known and now is openly manifested by the preaching of this gospel. Exposition of All Paul's Epistles.[11]

Teaching the Elect in the Face of Tragic Rejection. Martin Luther: It seems that this epistle was written near the end of the apostle's life and that he was sorely troubled. His word was being despised just as that of Jeremiah the prophet had been. He was called a seducer and a heretic; he was accused of destroying Moses and the temple. They stirred up hatred against him among the Gentiles so that people were disgusted at the apostle, as 1 Corinthians 4:13 says, and the false apostles were undermining whole churches. What was one to do? "I preach and pray amid great danger. I give them the greatest of blessings, and this is how they requite me. So the gospel suffers slander, and from our school there arise heretics. Nevertheless, I do not for the sake of all this stop preaching the gospel, even though Jews blaspheme, heathen persecute, and heretics arise. Nevertheless, I shall go on teaching because I know that the elect will accept it." With this word he looks into the tragedy which the Word of God suffers. They will fall by the wayside. "I am doing everything for the sake of the elect." We ought to be acting the same way. Lectures on Titus.[12]

Chosen to Be Given Faith. Moïse Amyraut: Faith does not come from us but is a gift of God. Before foreseeing any faith in us it would be necessary that God had ordained to put it there. And we seek the reason why he has ordained it so. It appears to be enough that God has not ordained to give it to all the world, as the apostle St. Paul says, "Faith does not belong to all." Otherwise, all the world would believe, which is more than refuted by experience. For this reason he calls faith "the faith of God's elect" to show that God has chosen some in particular to give them this grace to believe. But this cannot be the same faith, as a preceding and antecedent thing, which has moved him to elect them to believe rather than any others. Could it therefore ultimately be because he has foreseen that they would use the saving grace which is offered to them in a better way than the others? Not at all. For the good use of saving grace consists either in it being embraced through faith, or that after having been embraced, it is made to bear fruit in good works. Since, therefore, we have shown that this eternal decree to give faith cannot be based on the foreseeing of faith or on good works, it necessarily follows that it certainly cannot be founded either on God having foreseen the good use of grace. Brief Treatise on Predestination.[13]

Many Lose Understanding of the Truth. John Owen: Practical obedience in the course of our walking before God is another means unto the same end [understanding the mind of God]. The gospel is the "truth which is according unto godliness"; and it will not long abide with any who follow not after godliness according unto its guidance and direction. Hence we see so many lose that very understanding which they had of the doctrines of it, when once they begin to give up themselves to ungodly lives. The true notion of holy, evangelical truths will not live, at least not flourish, where they are divided from a holy conversation. Causes, Ways, and Means of Understanding the Mind of God.[14]

---

[11]Dickson, *Exposition*, 178*.
[12]LW 29:8 (WA 25:10); citing 2 Tim 2:10.
[13]Amyraut, *Brief Traitté de la Prédestination*, 113-15; citing 2 Thess 3:2.
[14]Owen, *Works*, 4:206.

JUDGES MUST EXPERIENCE DIRECT DIVINE TEACHING. BALTHASAR HUBMAIER: The judges should be theologians, sound in doctrine, not hooded or capped, but instructed in divine teaching by God himself, carrying the breastplate of Aaron on their breast. The learned ones are still to be listened to, but they are learned who like Josiah daily read the book of the law, who also have Moses and the prophets. They who do not read the book of the law and the prophets, in which the promise to us was long ago given by God the Father, should not hear the process of faith nor can they be judges. THESES AGAINST ECK.[15]

HEAVENLY MINDEDNESS AND THE HOPE OF ETERNAL LIFE. THOMAS TAYLOR: In these words the apostle commends his ministry, partly from the *end* of it, in that it leads the believers of it (by the truth preached) to the hope of eternal life; as also partly from the *effect* of it in them, which is the full furnishing of them with such graces as lead them comfortably to their happiness, adding to the faith of the elect such a hope as makes them not ashamed. And they afford two instructions: (1) That the end of the ministry is to draw people's minds upward, from earth toward heaven. (2) That true faith never goes alone, but is attended with other excellent virtues....

Every faithful teacher must conceive it to be their duty to draw people's hearts from things below, to the contemplation of things of a higher strain.... This was the aim not only of our apostle here but of all the men of God whose faithfulness the Scriptures have recommended unto our imitation.... All other professions further people in their earthly estates: some employed about the health of the body, some about the maintaining of people's outward rights, some about the framing of tender minds in humane disciplines and sciences—all of which further our fellowship and society among people.

Only this of all other professions furthers people in their heavenly estate and fits them ... for their fellowship with God. COMMENTARY ON TITUS.[16]

WHAT COMES FROM THE MOUTH OF GOD IS CERTAIN AND INFALLIBLE TRUTH. JOHN CALVIN: The title that is given to the Word of God brings us a singular consolation. For we are delivered from doubt and wavering when we now know that it is God who speaks to us: for there is nothing in him but certain and infallible truth.... What comes from the mouth of God is certain and entirely trustworthy. It is often declared that the word of God is pure, that there is no dross or impurity mixed in with it. This is why it is compared to gold and silver that has passed through the fire and has been refined. This reassures us so much that we can say people are not responsible for our faith, but that God is the author of it. So we are armed for all the battles that Satan may start against us. SERMONS ON TITUS.[17]

A LIE IS CONTRARY TO GOD'S NATURE. THOMAS TAYLOR: Now to ascribe a lie to God would not only be to impute change to him, but would be contrary to that most simple nature of his. For what is a lie, but to utter something contrary to known truth and that with an evil intention; which wickedness, seeing it implies a contrariety between his will and his word.... How can it be ascribed unto the high majesty of God? COMMENTARY ON TITUS.[18]

TRUST IN GOD WHO DOES NOT LIE. OLYMPIA MORATA: Your health is a great concern to me, and I'm afraid you're worrying night and day as you usually do, and making yourself ill with care.... I suspect, with the war in France, that your husband has left you and you are in pain (that's the way you are). So I've scattered some things, if not all, that relate to your circumstances in the dialogue, as you'll see. I'm also sending you some writings by

---

[15]CRR 5:56-57*; citing Jn 6:1-71; 2 Pet 1:1-21; Ex 28:15; 2 Kings 22:1-20; 2 Chron 34:1-33; Lk 16:29; Deut 18:15; Lk 9:35; Mt 3:1-17; Mk 1:1-45; 1 Cor 1:1-31. In this context, judges refers to those elected within the church to serve as arbiters of doctrinal truth. See CRR 5:52.

[16]Taylor, *A Commentarie*, 23-24*.
[17]CO 54:391; citing Ps 12:6.
[18]Taylor, *A Commentarie*, 33*.

Dr. Martin Luther, which I enjoyed reading. They may be able to move and restore you too. Work hard at these studies, for God's sake; ask that he enlighten you with true religion. You will not lose. You don't think that God lies to you, do you? Why would he have made so many promises, unless he wished to keep them? He invites and summons all the wretched to him. He turns away no one. LETTER 28 TO LAVINIA DELLA ROVERE ORSINI.[19]

THE PROPHETS' OBSCURE PREDICTIONS ARE MADE CLEAR BY CHRIST. JOHN CALVIN: There was indeed some manifestation of this kind, when God in ancient times spoke by his prophets; but because Christ publicly displayed by his coming those things which they had obscurely predicted, and the Gentiles were afterward admitted into the fellowship of the covenant, in this sense Paul says that what had formerly been exhibited in part "has now been manifested." COMMENTARY ON TITUS.[20]

THE ETERNITY AND CERTAINTY OF THE GOSPEL. JOHN MAYER: Note that the gospel does not set forth any new doctrine, but the eternal decree of God touching the saving of sinful humankind by Jesus Christ, which came not so to light as of late years, because the time prefixed by God for the revealing of it was not come. And this is here and in other places inferred, that we might take notice of it, and so be firm in our faith, because as that which is new is deceitful so that which has ever been is more certain and firm. COMMENTARY ON PAUL'S EPISTLES.[21]

BY GRACE, GOD IS NO LONGER OUR ENEMY. JOHN CALVIN: When St. Paul greets the brethren he usually contents himself with these two words, "grace and peace." This signifies (as we have declared on other passages) that all our good and all our happiness consists in this—that we are reconciled to God who holds us in his favor and in his love. Here therefore is the source of all that we should desire—that God loves us and is propitious toward us. For if he is our enemy, woe to us—even if the whole world should conspire to help us! But if God accepts us to himself, even if we are pitiable to human eyes yet all shall be turned to our good and to our salvation.

So it is no small matter, this "grace" of which St. Paul speaks. But note in particular that he calls it "grace" rather than favor or love, because it is a free love; that is to say, that God cannot receive us into his favor unless he has pity upon us. For are we worthy? There is nothing in us but sin! Therefore, if God dealt with us strictly, by rights he would hate us, he would detest us, and he would not recognize us as his creatures. But when it pleases him to have compassion upon our misery, then he begins to love us and that of his free goodness. SERMONS ON TITUS.[22]

---

[19]Morata, *Complete Writings*, 117; citing Heb 6:18; Mt 11:28.
[20]CTS 43:285* (CO 52:406).
[21]Mayer, *Commentarie*, 564-65*.

[22]CO 54:407-8. Calvin continues by speaking about how Paul also adds here the word "mercy," as indeed the Textus Receptus does; yet the word seems to be a scribal emendation to bring Titus into line with the greetings in the other Pastoral Epistles, and so is absent from NA[28] as well as the ESV, NIV, and other modern translations. See Bruce M. Metzger, *A Textual Commentary on the Greek New Testament*, 2nd ed. (Stuttgart: Deutsche Bibelgesellschaft, 1994), 584.

1:5-16 QUALIFICATIONS FOR ELDERS

⁵This is why I left you in Crete, so that you might put what remained into order, and appoint elders in every town as I directed you— ⁶if anyone is above reproach, the husband of one wife,ᵃ and his children are believersᵇ and not open to the charge of debauchery or insubordination. ⁷For an overseer,ᶜ as God's steward, must be above reproach. He must not be arrogant or quick-tempered or a drunkard or violent or greedy for gain, ⁸but hospitable, a lover of good, self-controlled, upright, holy, and disciplined. ⁹He must hold firm to the trustworthy word as taught, so that he may be able to give instruction in soundᵈ doctrine and also to rebuke those who contradict it.

¹⁰For there are many who are insubordinate, empty talkers and deceivers, especially those of the circumcision party.ᵉ ¹¹They must be silenced, since they are upsetting whole families by teaching for shameful gain what they ought not to teach. ¹²One of the Cretans,ᶠ a prophet of their own, said, "Cretans are always liars, evil beasts, lazy gluttons."ᵍ ¹³This testimony is true. Therefore rebuke them sharply, that they may be sound in the faith, ¹⁴not devoting themselves to Jewish myths and the commands of people who turn away from the truth. ¹⁵To the pure, all things are pure, but to the defiled and unbelieving, nothing is pure; but both their minds and their consciences are defiled. ¹⁶They profess to know God, but they deny him by their works. They are detestable, disobedient, unfit for any good work.

a Or *a man of one woman* b Or *are faithful* c Or *bishop*; Greek *episkopos* d Or *healthy*; also verse 13 e Or *especially those of the circumcision* f Greek *One of them* g Probably from Epimenides of Crete

OVERVIEW: Given the ecclesiological divisions of the time, it is unsurprising that our sixteenth- and seventeeth-century commentators begin their exegesis concerning the qualifications of elders with a consideration of what an elder, or *presbyteros*, actually is and how this role relates to others in the church, particularly that of *episkopos*, or overseer. Regardless of whether our interpreters argue for an equal or a hierarchical relationship between the offices in the church, there is little dispute over the type of person expected to hold a position of ecclesial leadership, and Paul's list of qualifications is unpacked with rigor and pastoral sensitivity and applied to contemporary realities. The ability to preach the Word and adhere to sound doctrine is emphasized, particularly as the text turns to Paul's criticism of those in the Cretan church who have fallen away to teach a false message and practice a hypocritical faith. This leads our commentators to an extensive reflection on the need for ministers to preserve the integrity of the message they have received, to oppose and rebuke those who deviate from the truth, and to preach the truth with perseverance in all circumstances.

1:5 The Unfinished Business in Crete

BUILDING A CHURCH IS NEITHER QUICK NOR EASY. JOHN CALVIN: This is what he calls correcting those things that are still wanting. The building of the church is not a work so easy that it can be brought all at once to perfection. How long Paul was in Crete is uncertain; but he had spent some time there, and had faithfully devoted his labors to erect the kingdom of Christ. He did not lack the most consummate skill that can be found in human beings; he was unwearied in toil; and yet he acknowledged that he left the work rough and incomplete. Hence we see the difficulty; and, indeed, we find, by experience, in the present day, that it is not the labor of one or two years to restore fallen churches to a tolerable condition.

Accordingly, those who have made diligent progress for many years must still be attentive to correct many things. Commentary on Titus.[1]

Bishops and Presbyters Are the Same Thing.

Edward Leigh: Since the apostle prosecuting the same argument uses the name of bishop and presbyter indifferently in the same sense (as Jerome and Calvin observe on this place),† thence some infer that there is no difference between them. By the name bishop he means those whom before he called elders; and throughout the New Testament it is indifferently given to all teaching elders, that is pastors and ministers; and so is it here to be taken. It is a title well known in the apostle's days in the tongue then commonly used, to betoken a painful office and a diligent labor; borrowed from such as are set in the watchtower of cities or camps to spy and by a loud voice or sound of a trumpet or otherwise by a bell or warning piece to discover and signify the approaching of the enemy. For such were properly called *episkopoi*, bishops or watchmen. It is attributed to the pastors and teachers of the church; not only the great pastor and archbishop of our souls and the apostles,‡ but the other pastors and teachers. And the word must be generally taken thus in the New Testament, as appears from Philippians 1:1, where the apostle writes to many bishops in one city, Philippi; and Acts 20:28 speaks to many bishops in one city, Ephesus. Annotations.[2]

Godly Consensus in the Election of Ministers.

Martin Bucer: It is necessary to have the consensus of the whole church, because ministers are not only to be blameless in the eyes of the Lord's people, but also well trusted and loved by them. In the second place, however, because it is only possible to receive the necessary testimony as to the suitability of ministers from the whole church, particularly if it is a large one, by the agency of a few who are particularly knowledgeable, the other elders and leaders are to conduct and direct the election and carry out the installation. This comes from the fact that Paul commanded Timothy that he was not to be hasty in laying hands on anyone; and Titus, that he was to appoint elders for the towns, moreover appointing those who were blameless and adorned with such virtues that there was no doubt that the whole congregation would be glad to accept them wholeheartedly as bishops. But this does not mean, as many maintain, that St. Paul commanded Timothy and Titus as the leaders to appoint bishops on the basis of their own authority and will those whom they wanted, irrespective of the will and consensus of the congregation. Because in all the ecclesiastical statutes it is especially laid down that no one should be given to be bishop of any church against its will. Concerning the True Care of Souls.[3]

Bishops as Chief Ministers or Superintendents.

William Fulke: Mere popular elections were never allowable in the church of God, and therefore forbidden by the Council of Laodicea.† Yet long after that council, the people had their elections, moderated by the wisdom and gravity of the clergy, among whom, for order and seemly government, there was always one principal to whom by long use of the church, the name bishop or superintendent has been applied,‡ which office Titus exercised in Crete, Timothy in Ephesus, and others in other places. Therefore, although in the Scripture a bishop and an elder is of one order and authority in preaching the word and administration of the sacraments (as Jerome does often confess) yet in government, by ancient use of speech he is only called a bishop which is in the Scripture called *proistamenos* or *hegoumenois*, that is, chief in government, to whom the ordination or consecration by imposition of hands was always principally committed. Not that imposition of

---

[1] CTS 43:288 (CO 52:408).
[2] Leigh, *Annotations*, 339*; citing 1 Pet 2:25; 5:4; Acts 1:20. †For Jerome's comment, see his *Letter* 146 in NPNF² 6:288. For Calvin, see CTS 43:290 (CO 52:409). ‡The Greek word *episkopēn* in Acts 1:20 is translated "office" in the ESV.

[3] Bucer, *Concerning the True Care of Souls*, 63-64; citing 1 Tim 5:22.

hands belongs only to him, for the rest of the elders that were present at ordination did lay on their hands, or else the bishop did lay on his hands in the name of the rest. Which most ancient form of government, when Aërius would take it away, it was noted among his other errors.†† TEXT OF THE NEW TESTAMENT.[4]

1:6-9 The Qualities Required of Elders

APPOINT BLAMELESS ELDERS. MARTIN BUCER: It is as if he wanted to say: The reason I require elders who are blameless is because these elders are to be bishops, that is, general overseers, and shepherds of the Christians. The episcopal office requires that they should be blameless; because those who are to minister to all the others in order that they should live blameless and holy lives must of necessity themselves be more holy, blameless and free of all reproach than any others.

---

[4]Fulke, *Text of the New Testament*, 392*; citing Rom 12:8; 1 Tim 5:17; Heb 13:17. †Canon 12 of the Council of Laodicea (c. 365) states that "bishops are to be appointed to the ecclesiastical government by the judgment of the metropolitans and neighboring bishops, after having been long proved both in the foundation of their faith and in the conversation of an honest life." Canon 13 adds that "the election of those who are to be appointed to the priesthood is not to be committed to the multitude." See NPNF² 14:131, where the comment of van Espen is also noted: "What the fathers intend to forbid are tumultuous elections, that is, that no attention is paid to riotous demonstrations on the part of the people, when with acclamations they are demanding the ordination of anyone, with an appearance of sedition." ‡Calvin (CTS 43:291; CO 52:409) also notes that "from this passage we do indeed learn that there was not at that time such equality among the ministers of Christ but that some one had authority and deliberative voice above others; but this has nothing to do with the tyrannical and profane custom which prevails in popery." ††Aërius was a fourth-century presbyter in Pontus mentioned by Augustine in *On Heresies to Quodvultdeus* 53 (CCSL 46:323-24 [WSA 1/18:47]). His teaching against the superiority of bishops is addressed by Richard Hooker (1554–1600) in *Of the Laws of Ecclesiastical Polity*, 3:109-11 (bk. 7, chap. 9), where he says Aërius "saw himself unable to rise to that greatness which his ambitious pride did affect" and so "his way of revenge was to try what wit being sharpened with envy and malice could do, in raising a new seditious opinion that the superiority that bishops had was a thing they should not have, that a bishop might not ordain, and that a bishop ought not any way to be distinguished from a presbyter."

From this it can be clearly seen that the apostle here means elders who will be bishops, that is, the proper overseers, carers of souls, and shepherds of the flock of Christ. That is why it is the Holy Spirit's rule that each church should have several elders, who are all shepherds and bishops, that is, overseers to carry out the care of souls and the pastoral office. CONCERNING THE TRUE CARE OF SOULS.[5]

STEWARDS OF THE LORD. THE ORDINAL: You have heard, brethren, in your private examination as well as in the exhortation and the holy lessons taken out of the Gospel and of the writings of the apostles,† of what dignity and of how great importance this office is (to which you have been called). And now we exhort you, in the name of our Lord Jesus Christ, to remember into how high a dignity, and how weighty‡ an office you be called. That is to say, to be the messengers, the watchmen, the pastors, and stewards of the Lord, to teach, to forewarn, to feed and provide for the Lord's family, to seek for Christ's sheep that be dispersed abroad, and for his children, who are in the midst of this naughty world, to be saved through Christ forever.

Have always, therefore, printed in your remembrance, how great a treasure is committed to your charge. They are the sheep of Christ, whom he bought with his death, and for whom he shed his blood. The church and congregation, whom you must serve, is his spouse and his body. And if there is a chance the same church, or any member thereof, will be hurt or hindered by reason of your negligence, you know the greatness of the fault, and also of the horrible punishment that will ensue. Wherefore, consider with yourselves the goal of your ministry toward the children of God, toward the spouse and body of Christ, and see that you never cease your labor, your care and diligence, until you have done all that lies in you, according to your bound duty, to bring all such as are or shall be committed to your charge unto agreement in faith and knowledge of God, and to ripeness and

---

[5]Bucer, *Concerning the True Care of Souls*, 36.

perfectness of age in Christ, that there is no place left among them either for error in religion or for viciousness in life.

Then forasmuch as your office is both of so great excellency and of so great difficulty, you see how great care and study you ought to apply yourselves, and that you may show yourselves dutiful and thankful to that Lord who has placed you in so high a dignity,[††] and also to beware, that neither you yourselves offend nor cause the occasion that others offend. Howbeit, you cannot have a mind and a will thereto of yourselves, for that power and ability is given of God alone. Therefore you ought and have need earnestly to pray for his Holy Spirit. And seeing that you cannot by any other means compass the doing of so weighty a work pertaining to the salvation of humankind, but with doctrine and exhortation taken out of holy Scripture, and with a life agreeable to the same, you perceive how studious you ought to be in reading and learning the holy Scriptures, and in framing the manners both of yourselves and of those who specially pertain unto you, according to the rule of the same Scriptures. And for this self same cause, you see how you ought to forsake and set aside (as much as you may) all worldly cares and studies.

We have a good hope that you have well weighed and pondered these things with yourselves long before this time, and that you have clearly determined, by God's grace, to give yourselves wholly to this vocation, whereunto it has pleased God to call you, so that (as much as lies in you) you apply yourselves wholly to this one thing and draw all your cares and studies this way, and to this end. And that you will continually pray for the heavenly assistance of the Holy Spirit, from God the Father, by the mediation of our only mediator and Savior Jesus Christ, that by daily reading and weighing of the Scriptures you may wax riper and stronger in your ministry. And that you may so endeavor yourselves, from time to time, to sanctify the lives of you and yours, and to fashion them after the rule and doctrine of Christ, and that you may be wholesome and godly examples and

patterns for the rest of the congregation to follow. THE ORDINAL (1549).[6]

TWELVE DESCRIPTIONS OF AN ELDER. DAVID DICKSON: Among the elders, they that labor in the word and doctrine are the chief. The properties of this elder, whom he calls a bishop, are twelve, whereof he spoke in the former epistle to Timothy. (1) They ought to be free from any just blame, lest their authority be diminished, yea so far from blame that nothing is found in them unworthy the steward of God, who ought to be so much the more blameless by how much their office is more holy. (2) They ought not to be self-willed, or such a one who obstinately pleases himself, for he that is too self-willed is ready to displease all others. (3) Not soon angry, for those that are so cannot bear with the infirmities of the people of God or regard them. (4) Not given to wine and drunkenness. (5) Not contentious. No striker. (6) Not given to filthy lucre, free from covetousness. He confirms this in verse 8, because it is requisite that according to their abilities, they are ready to receive strangers, or the banished servants of God. (7) That they esteem and love good people, such as excel others. For it is the sign of a person of little honesty to hate those that are good, upon any pretense. (8) That in all things they are modest, sober, of a sound mind or prudent. (9) That they are just, desirous to restore everyone their own. (10) That they are pious and holy, who by their life and conversation may teach others. (11) That they are continent and temperate, having dominion over their affections and desires. (12) And in verse 9, that they are not a divine only, but that by faith they cleave to the truth, not only able to feed the flock, but to stop the mouths of barking wolves. EXPOSITION OF ALL PAUL'S EPISTLES.[7]

---

[6]*Forme and Maner*, Ordering of Priests*. [†]The readings set for the service of ordination were Acts 20:17-35; 1 Tim 3:1-16; and either Mt 28:18-20 or Jn 10:1-16. In 1662 this was changed to Eph 4:7-13 and either Mt 9:36-38 or Jn 10:1-16. [†]1549: "chargeable." 1662: "weighty an office and charge." [††]1662: "dutiful and thankful unto that Lord." 1549: "kind to that Lord."
[7]Dickson, *Exposition*, 179*; citing 1 Tim 3:1-7.

MARRIAGE RIGHT FOR ALL, INCLUDING PRIESTS.

KATHARINA SCHÜTZ ZELL: God implanted marriage in all people in the first creation, and no one is to be excused from it except the three kinds of people named in Matthew 19. And marriage also is plainly suitable for priests, as Paul says to Timothy and Titus in his epistles to them. But that which God wants to have, the Roman clergy want to condemn and, when they can bring priests who marry into their power, they make them suffer and be martyrs. APOLOGY FOR MATTHEW ZELL.[8]

AN ELDER MUST NOT HAVE INSUBORDINATE CHILDREN.

MATTHEW POOLE: Sons of Belial, ungoverned, disorderly persons, like soldiers that will not keep their ranks, or rather, like cattle untamed, that will not endure any yoke. *Objection:* But why must none be put into the ministry that have such children? The fathers may be good men, though the children be bad. *Solution:* (1) Because the honor and repute of the church is more to be regarded than the interest of any private person. (2) Because it is an ill sign that the parents of such children have not ruled their own houses well, keeping their children in all subjection and gravity under authority, and are therefore very unfit to rule the greater society of a church. ANNOTATIONS UPON THE HOLY BIBLE.[9]

REFUTATION OF ERRORS IN PREACHING.

WESTMINSTER DIRECTORY: In the use of instruction or information in the knowledge of some truth, which is a consequence from his doctrine, he may (when convenient) confirm it by a few firm arguments from the text in hand, and other places of Scripture, or from the nature of that commonplace in divinity, whereof that truth is a branch.

In confutation of false doctrines, he is neither to raise an old heresy from the grave, nor to mention a blasphemous opinion unnecessarily. But if the people be in danger of an error, he is to confute it

soundly, and endeavor to satisfy their judgments and consciences against all objections. . . .

In dissuading, reprimanding, and publicly warning people (which requires special wisdom),[†] let him, as there shall be cause, not only discover the nature and greatness of the sin, with the misery attending it, but also show the danger his hearers are in to be overtaken and surprised by it, together with the remedies and best way to avoid it.

In applying comfort, whether general against all temptation, or particular against some special troubles or terrors, he is carefully to answer such objections, as a troubled heart and afflicted spirit may suggest to the contrary. . . . And, as he needs not always to prosecute every doctrine which lies in his text, so he is wisely to make choice of such uses as, by his residence and conversing with his flock, he finds most needful and seasonable; and, among these, such as may most draw their souls to Christ, the fountain of light, holiness, and comfort. WESTMINSTER DIRECTORY. OF THE PREACHING OF THE WORD.[10]

BISHOPS MUST FEED THE SHEEP AND DEFEND THEM FROM WOLVES.

NIELS HEMMINGSEN: When these words are considered in greater depth, they contain many things. He wants the bishop to hold fast to faithful speech, that is, the word brought forth from the mouth of God, which he calls the faithful word, on account of its truth and certainty. Wherefore it is first to be noted, that although divine scripture has unexhausted depths, nevertheless it is right that the presbyter should be as a shepherd learned in sacred Scripture and in doctrine, so that it sticks so firmly to him that in no way should he allow himself to be torn away from it.

Second, an earnest confession of doctrine is required, so that he should not be frightened by anything, but in the presence of all openly to confess with life and voice that which he holds in his heart.

---

[8]Zell, *Church Mother*, 74; citing Mt 19:12; 1 Tim 3:2.
[9]Poole, *Annotations*, s.v.*

[10]*Directory*, 15-16*. [†]Originally: "In dehortation, reprehension, and public admonition."

When he adds, "according to doctrine," he wants him to teach his hearers, and that he should be eager to be of benefit to them. For it is to this that the office of the bishop pertains, that he teach healthy doctrine, which is of benefit for building up, not that by weighing them down with empty speculations he might at last produce certain abstruse fruit, which has no use in the practice of holiness. From this ministers of the word learn to seek the advancement of the church which has been entrusted to them, and not to seek after their own pleasure and desires. . . .

After the bishop has taught correctly, he needs two things: without doubt, exhortation, so that what the hearers have learned, they might express with their lives, lest he appear to have taught in vain; and refutation, so that he might refute the insolent, that is, those who are enemies of doctrine, lest of course these enemies either deprive the hearers of what he has rightly taught, or by sophistry outright destroy it. For it is the job of the good shepherd not only to feed the sheep, but also to defend from wolves. In this way the bishop feeds the sheep with healthy doctrine, and refutes the heretics with the same. But he calls it "healthy doctrine," either by metonymy, because it frees the mind from errors and sicknesses, namely, those bringing eternal death; or by metalepsis he calls "pure," "healthy," that is, not defiled or corrupted by any human doctrines or by Jewish traditions. COMMENTARY ON THE EPISTLES.[11]

ON THE MEANS OF REFUTING HERESIES.
FRIEDRICH BALDUIN: It is also necessary to give refutation for the benefit of the congregation, that is to say that false teaching should be refuted. This is elsewhere called the office of refutation of the minister, which Paul expressly requires of Timothy. . . . He calls this a Scripture that is useful for *elenchos* [reproof]. This is displeasing to not a few political men, who cannot bear refutation for the benefit of the congregation. By this name they equip the magistrate with edicts against ministers

of the Word, as being quarrelsome and disturbers of the public peace, when they censure false teaching, or when false teachers for that which is brought forth in the assembly, and when they urge their hearers to flee false teachers. But the man of sense will at that time keep his peace, says Amos 5:13. Nor is there great need of much discussion with those smatterers; both a minister's office and his conscience are able to teach any minister of the Word what needs to be done in this generation. To be certain, he who wishes to perform the office of teaching correctly in the church cannot afford to care for thunderbolts of this kind from political men; for that reason he maturely prepares himself for these stripes and whips of the tongue. For this is a good element of ministry, namely, to *elenchein*, "refute" heretics, an element that Paul impresses upon his readers so many times. For this reason ministers are shepherds, who should not only feed the sheep, but also fend off the wolves, which if they did not do, they would be (mere) hired hands, who on the arrival of the wolf flee. . . .

It is permissible to direct refutation not only against doctrine but also against teachers who are particularly obstinate. For thus our Paul in his first letter to Timothy . . . says not only in general, that certain individuals have made a shipwreck of their faith, but also specifies by name that Hymenaeus and Alexander are among their number. Furthermore, in Titus 1:10-11 he writes that those who are boastful and misleading should be contradicted. BRIEF FOUNDATIONS FOR MINISTERS OF THE WORD.[12]

1:10-11 *Silence Empty Talkers*

SILENCING THOSE WHO TEACH FOR SHAME-FUL GAIN. MARTIN LUTHER: Here he gives the reason why he said that it was impossible for a bishop to avoid opposition and enemies. For he will have a domestic Satan who suggests many false thoughts and speculations to him, as well as external enemies, through whom he stirs up sects. . . .

---

[11]Hemmingsen, *Commentaria*, 648-49.

[12]Balduin, *Brevis Institutio Ministrorum Verbi*, 156-57, 161; citing 1 Tim 4:1; 6:3; 2 Tim 3:16; 1 Tim 1:20.

They must be silenced. How can this happen when it is impossible to stop their mouths? For if even the council of the apostles was unable to stop their mouths, much less [can we]. That is, they are not [arising] among our adversaries, but among our own people, so that it is clear that within the church their arguments are undermining the authorities. We cannot make them shut up, but we can persuade our people not to listen to them. And this happens, as was said earlier, when one does not pay attention to their person or their kind. . . .

Any teacher in whom the Holy Spirit dwells seeks the things that are of the Spirit, the glory of God and the salvation of humankind, even at the cost of danger to his own stomach. Therefore the converse also follows: Where the Holy Spirit does not dwell is where the flesh dwells. And where there is the flesh, there is the zeal for one's own glory; they understand the things of earth, and they seek for the earth. Therefore Paul is not a slanderer; he is a completely sure judge. Every wicked teacher seeks his own glory, satisfaction of his own appetite, and base gain. LECTURES ON TITUS.[13]

WE MUST DRAW ATTENTION TO FALSE TEACHERS. JOHN CALVIN: Let us note, therefore, when we see the church of God so troubled by the wicked, that the ministers must strive so much more to keep things in good order, and must be armed not with a physical sword, but with the Word of God, with wisdom and virtue to resist such people. And when we see there are some who conspire to introduce novelties, let us ensure, as far as we can, that the church of God is provided with good governors and those who have it in them to prevent Satan from raising up stumbling blocks. . . .

If there are wicked people who sow any discords, whether false doctrines or wicked talk, to divert the faithful from the right path—if we ignore it or pretend that we saw nothing, the poor people shall be infected, they will not be on their guard, and many simple souls shall be seduced. And there will be a plague which ruins everything.

But if we mark such people, and point the finger at them, everyone will flee them. And so they will be hindered from doing evil. And this is what St. Paul had in mind here. SERMONS ON TITUS.[14]

1:12-14 *The National Sins of Crete*

ALL TRUTH IS GOD'S TRUTH, EVEN IN PROFANE AUTHORS. JOHN CALVIN: I have no doubt that he who is here spoken of is Epimenides, who was a native of Crete; for, when the apostle says that this author was "one of themselves," and was "a prophet of their own," he undoubtedly means that he belonged to the nation of the Cretans. Why he calls him a prophet is doubtful. . . . I think that Paul accommodates his style to the ordinary practice. Nor is it of any importance to inquire on what occasion Epimenides calls his fellow Cretans liars, namely, because they boast of having the sepulcher of Jupiter; but seeing that the poet takes it from an ancient and well-known report, the apostle quotes it as a proverbial saying.[†]

From this passage we may infer that those persons are superstitious, who do not venture to borrow anything from heathen authors. All truth is from God; and consequently, if wicked people have said anything that is true and just, we ought not to reject it; for it has come from God. Besides, all things are of God; and, therefore, why should it not be lawful to dedicate to his glory everything that can properly be employed for such a purpose? COMMENTARY ON TITUS.[15]

OSTENTATIOUS USE OF PROFANE AUTHORS CONDEMNED. JOHN MAYER: Seeing all things are God's, why should it not be lawful to apply for his glory whatsoever may be aptly brought forth for

---

[13]LW 29:34, 37-38 (WA 25:29, 31-32).

[14]CO 54:457-58.
[15]CTS 43:300-301 (CO 52:414-415). [†]Jerome D. Quinn, *The Letter to Titus*, Anchor Bible 35 (New York: Doubleday, 1990), 107, nicely translates the verbless proverb from Epimenides as "Liars always, men of Crete, Nasty brutes that live to eat." The works of Epimenides of Cnossos from the sixth or seventh century BC are not extant, though a fragment of this saying is found in the third-century-BC Greek poet Callimachus of Cyrene (*Hymn to Zeus*, line 8).

that purpose? . . . Yet there is a fault among preachers nowadays in using other authors besides the holy Scriptures, in that many do so for ostentation, and are over frequent herein, as if they propounded to themselves to preach their sayings as well as the dictates of holy Scripture, and so set up an estimation of their great learning and reading in the hearts of their hearers, as well to set forth Christ and his truth. There is no warrant here for such teaching, for the apostle wrote much and taught much, yet he uses such testimonies but once or twice only. . . .

See here the wonderful grace of God in Jesus Christ, in that he set up a church among a people so infamous for vice, that we who are his ministers may take courage to teach and preach the truth even among the vilest, expecting success in so doing. COMMENTARY ON PAUL'S EPISTLES.[16]

BEWARE OF TRADITIONS THAT OVERTURN THE GOSPEL. MATTHIAS FLACIUS: [Paul] expounds on the kind of sound doctrine that he requires from elders as if by describing, through antithesis, contrary diseases raging there at that time, and so similarly sets forth a seventh rule. He therefore names two kinds: Jewish fables and human traditions. They seemed to have been precepts concerning Jewish rituals, some laws, some also chosen from the traditions of the fathers, and all the doctrine of the Nazarenes concerning the necessity of works for salvation. He speaks about these issues in Galatians. He therefore says that they are teachers of trifles and adversaries of truth. Watch out for human traditions that overturn the purity of the gospel. He calls false doctrines fables. GLOSS ON TITUS[17]

NATIONAL SINS AND THE PROGRESS OF THE GOSPEL. JOHN OWEN: The prevalence of the gospel in any nation may be measured by the success it has against known national sins. If these are not in some good measure subdued by it, if the

minds of people are not alienated from them and made watchful against them, if their guilt appear not naked, without the varnish or veil put upon it by commonness or custom, whatever profession is made of the gospel, it is vain and useless. Thus the apostle allows that there were national sins prevalent among the Cretans: "One of the Cretans, a prophet of their own, said, 'Cretans are always liars, evil beasts, lazy gluttons.' This testimony is true. Therefore rebuke them sharply, that they may be sound in the faith." Whatever their profession was, if they were not delivered by the gospel from the power and practice of these national sins they were so prone to, they would not long be sound in the faith nor fruitful in obedience. THE NATURE AND CAUSES OF APOSTASY FROM THE GOSPEL.[18]

BE CAREFUL WITH SHARP REBUKES. PETER MARTYR VERMIGLI: Paul seems to inveigh sharply against the Cretans, when he brings a verse of Epimenides, "Cretans are always liars, evil beasts, lazy gluttons." It might seem to be harshly said, to label the whole nation of the Cretans with so great an infamy. However, the apostle's speech was not intended to this end, but he gave admonition to Titus so that he might understand how earnestly he ought to urge that people. Nevertheless, pastors and schoolmasters must take heed that they do not use such invectives without judgment: for if they often use sharper words, those who are rebuked begin to hate them, whom they ought to love; and by this means admonitions do prevail but a little. Or else another thing follows: that they are not moved by such things, but are in fact hardened, if they often hear bitter words. . . . There must be heed taken, that people are not hurt rashly. COMMONPLACES.[19]

1:15-16 Purity and False Profession

TO THE PURE ALL THINGS ARE PURE. GIOVANNI DIODATI: To the pure all things are

---

[16]Mayer, *Commentarie*, 566*.
[17]Flacius, *Glossa Compendaria*, 1091.

[18]Owen, *Works*, 7:206.
[19]Vermigli, *Commonplaces*, 2:529*.

pure, namely, meats and other of God's creatures in which these false teachers retained the distinction of clean and unclean established by Moses' ceremonial law; which being disannulled by the gospel, the use of them is pure and holy to believers, who are purified by Christ's blood and sanctified by his Spirit. As contrariwise, the spiritual uncleanness of unbelievers makes even those things that were allowed by Moses to be unclean unto them.

"Their minds and their consciences . . ." Namely, those two parts of a person that seem to be most pure after sin, namely, the mind which preserves some light of knowledge, and the conscience which applies that light to testify and judge of a person's actions. Now, by that inward corruption of ignorance and perverseness, everything is made impure to people, because the first hinders them from knowing how they should conform themselves to God's will in what they do and undertake; and the second takes away their will from doing it. By the first they tempt, by the second they offend God. PIOUS ANNOTATIONS.[20]

THOSE WHO TRUST ONLY IN EXTERNAL THINGS CANNOT KNOW GOD. JOHN CALVIN: We see here that people may greatly torment themselves with ceremonies and external things, but until they have integrity of heart they labor in vain; they will only beat the water, as we say. And why? Because the true service of God begins with such sincerity and integrity. So long, then, as we are faithless, we are filthy and stinking before God. All that ever comes from us is no better than filth and dung. . . . When people seek to justify themselves by external things, it is as if they tried to cover up filthy dung with a linen cloth or a sheet. But the dung, nevertheless, remains.

So let us put away the filthiness that is hidden in our hearts, that the evil (I say) be chased from us. And then will our Lord will approve of our life. And here we see what the true knowledge of God is: it is not that we speculate in the air, but that we are truly reformed in obedience to him. For it is

impossible to know God unless we are transformed into his image. SERMONS ON TITUS.[21]

HYPOCRITICAL FEIGNED FAITH. PHILIPP MELANCHTHON: Paul calls an affected faith hypocrisy in 1 Timothy 1: "The end of the commandment is love from a pure heart and a pure conscience and unaffected faith." He is saying, then, that faith is sometimes faked. And he talks about hypocrites in Titus 1:15-16. . . . But if the faith of the godless people spoken of in this passage were truly faith—for Paul is certainly speaking about people who are godly in outward appearance—he should not call them unbelievers, but should say that they lack love, as the Parisians speak. When writing to Timothy, Paul attributes feigned faith to hypocrites, and he calls them unbelievers when writing to Titus. There is, then, no reason to distinguish between formed and unformed faith.[†] For this hypocritical opinion about Christian teachings or divine history, conceived without the Holy Spirit, is clearly not faith. Human nature does not assent to the Word of God, much less is it moved by it. For the sake of teaching I used to call this acquired, unformed faith "historical faith," but now I do not call it faith at all. It is an opinion. COMMONPLACES.[22]

NO FOOD IS UNCLEAN IN ITSELF FOR CHRISTIANS. FRANÇOIS CARRIÈRE: "To the pure all things are pure. But to the defiled and to unbelievers nothing is pure." Verse 16: "Unfit for every good work." But 1 John 1:8: "If we say that we have no sin the truth is not in us." And Acts 28.2: "The pagans showed us a good deal of kindness." I respond that Paul is talking about that selecting that the Judaizers were introducing between foods. For it is obvious from verses 10 and 11 that this passage is dealing with them and their myths. Certain of

---

[20]Diodati, *Pious Annotations*, 347-48*.

[21]CO 54:486, 493.
[22]Melanchthon, *Commonplaces*, 118; citing 1 Tim 1:5. †This is an allusion to the scholastic theologians at the University of Paris, most of whom distinguished between an "unformed faith" received at baptism, and a "formed faith" that yields love, which in turn is the source of other good works.

them were saying that some foods were unclean by the very nature. Later, the Manichees and Marcionites taught the same thing.[†] But others held that some foods were unclean, not in and of themselves but because the law of Moses in Leviticus 11 forbade them, and that Christians should avoid them. Paul here refutes the Judaizers, saying, "Christians must not reject any class of foods or abstain from them because neither in and of themselves nor according to the law of Christ is any food unclean." It is obvious that this is the meaning. First, because he is arguing against Judaizers. Second, because Paul explains himself like this in 1 Timothy 4:3. This letter to Titus is a sort of summary of Timothy. Third, because this is how Chrysostom, Jerome, Theodoret, and Ambrose interpret it. COMMENTARY ON THE WHOLE OF SCRIPTURE.[23]

---

[23]Carrière, *Commentarius in Universam Scripturam*, 778. [†]The Manichees, or Manichaeans, with their leader Mani (c. 216–276), posited a dualistic cosmology in which the spiritual world of light battled against the evil material world of darkness. In their view, Christ was but one among a group of prophets who provided spiritual enlightenment; the Marcionites were followers of Marcion (c. 85–c. 165), who denied the canonicity of the Old Testament as well as much of the New.

2:1-15 TEACH SOUND DOCTRINE

But as for you, teach what accords with sound[a]
doctrine. ²Older men are to be sober-minded,
dignified, self-controlled, sound in faith, in love, and
in steadfastness. ³Older women likewise are to be
reverent in behavior, not slanderers or slaves to much
wine. They are to teach what is good, ⁴and so train
the young women to love their husbands and children,
⁵to be self-controlled, pure, working at home, kind,
and submissive to their own husbands, that the word
of God may not be reviled. ⁶Likewise, urge the
younger men to be self-controlled. ⁷Show yourself in
all respects to be a model of good works, and in your
teaching show integrity, dignity, ⁸and sound speech
that cannot be condemned, so that an opponent may
be put to shame, having nothing evil to say about us.
⁹Bondservants[b] *are to be submissive to their own*

masters in everything; they are to be well-pleasing,
not argumentative, ¹⁰not pilfering, but showing all
good faith, so that in everything they may adorn the
doctrine of God our Savior.

¹¹For the grace of God has appeared, bringing
salvation for all people, ¹²training us to renounce
ungodliness and worldly passions, and to live
self-controlled, upright, and godly lives in the present
age, ¹³waiting for our blessed hope, the appearing of
the glory of our great God and Savior Jesus Christ,
¹⁴who gave himself for us to redeem us from all
lawlessness and to purify for himself a people for his
own possession who are zealous for good works.

¹⁵Declare these things; exhort and rebuke with all
authority. Let no one disregard you.

a Or *healthy*; also verses 2, 8 b For the contextual rendering of the Greek word *doulos*, see Preface

OVERVIEW: As Paul lays out his expectations of various groups in the church to Timothy, our commentators find much of it immediately relevant to the church of the sixteenth and seventeenth centuries. Attention is drawn to the fact that teaching doctrine is not only an abstract, intellectual task, but also involves careful application and modeling, with the life of the teacher needing to exemplify the lessons being taught. Methodologically, Anna Maria van Schurman provides an example of scholastic argumentation in proving the need for women to be educated, while an interesting discussion emerges over the proper interpretation of "all" in verse 11 and whether it asserts that God's grace brings salvation to all people or to all kinds of people. The affirmation of Christ's divinity in verse 13 also does not go unnoticed, and it provides ample evidence for those battling against contemporary anti-trinitarian heresies.

2:1 Teach What Accords with Healthy Doctrine

BE A PEARL IN THE PUDDLE OF THIS WORLD. JOHN TRAPP: The worse others are, the better you must be, keeping a constant countermotion to the corrupt courses that are in the world through lust. A pearl in a puddle retains its preciousness, and fish in the salt waters retain their freshness. A COMMENTARY.[1]

DO NOT PREACH MERE GENERALITIES, BUT CAREFULLY APPLY THE TRUTH. JOHN CALVIN: We have seen previously how St. Paul condemned those who through ambition corrupted God's Word, and did not apply it to the right use, that the people might have been edified by it. For God has not given us his word simply that it might beat against our ears, and for us to let whatever we hear slip away into the air. But he wants us to find

[1]Trapp, *A Commentary*, 342.

pasture there and that our lives might be regulated by it and, to sum it up, that we should show by our deeds that we have not wasted our time being taught in his school. . . .

St. Paul could well have spoken of the law and have told Titus to teach the people to behave themselves as God would have them. But he treats of each person's duty particularly, which is well worth noting. For it may well happen that if people only preach in the abstract, their teaching will be very cold, so that the listeners will not be touched by it. And why? Because we shrink back as much as we possibly can, when God calls us to himself. Therefore he needs to speak to each one, that we may be more deeply touched.

So God approaches this by showing every estate the standard to which they are held, so that he speaks particularly to the old and then to the young; and then he speaks to those who are married, men as well as women; and he speaks to servants and to masters, to rich and to poor. He speaks to those who are in authority, those who sit as judges; and he speaks to those who are charged with preaching his Word. He speaks to those who have households to govern and to those who do not. Now then, when each is spoken to in turn in their own situations then the Word of God stirs us up more, so that we are constrained to think about ourselves more carefully, whereas otherwise it would all slip away from us and vanish into the air, as we see from experience. . . .

So this is why it is useful for us to look carefully when we read holy Scripture, when we come to a sermon—that we think carefully how to apply it to ourselves. SERMONS ON TITUS.[2]

2:2 The Healthy Life for Older Men

BRIEF INSTRUCTIONS. JOHN CALVIN: He begins with particular duties, that the discourse may be better adapted to the instruction of the people. And he does so, not only that he may accommodate himself to their capacity, but that he may press everyone more closely. A general doctrine produces a less powerful impression, but when by holding out a few cases, he has instructed every person about his duty, there is no one who may not easily conclude that the Lord has sufficiently instructed him as to the work in which he ought to be employed. We must not therefore, look for a regular method here; for Paul's design was only to state briefly what were the subjects concerning which godly teachers ought to speak, and not to undertake to treat largely of those subjects.

"Aged men" are mentioned by him in the first place. He wishes them to be "sober," because excessive drinking is a vice too common among the old. "Gravity," which he next mentions, is procured by well-regulated morals. Nothing is more shameful than for an old man to indulge in youthful wantonness, and, by his countenance, to strengthen the impudence of the young. In the life of old men, therefore, let there be displayed *semnotēs*, "a becoming gravity," which shall constrain the young to modesty. This will be followed chiefly by "temperance," which he immediately adds.

I do not know whether the word "sound" or "healthy" contains an indirect allusion to the various diseases of old men, with which he contrasts this health of the soul. I think so, though I do not affirm it. With good reason does he include in these three parts—faith, love, patience—the sum of Christian perfection. By faith we worship God; for neither calling upon him, nor any exercises of godliness, can be separated from it. Love extends to all the commandments of the second table. Next follows patience as the seasoning of "faith" and "love"; for without "patience" faith would not long endure, and many occurrences are taking place every day—instances of unhandsome conduct or evil temper, which irritate us so much that we should not only be languid, but almost dead, to the duties of love toward our neighbor, if the same "patience" did not support us. COMMENTARY ON TITUS 2:2.[3]

[2]CO 54:495, 497, 499-500.

[3]CTS 43:310-11* (CO 53:419).

OLDER MEN MUST CONTINUE TO LEARN IN GOD'S SCHOOL. THOMAS TAYLOR: Our apostle exempts not older men from being subject to the doctrine of God, because of their age; but rather sends them first to school, notwithstanding all that knowledge and experience which they might pretend. For God's school is as well for old as for young, in which men are not only to be initiated in the principles of religion, but also to be led forward unto perfection of wisdom. And seeing no man can attain in this life unto perfection, therefore every man is still to press forward, and to wax old daily learning something. . . .

This condemns the disobedience of many of the elder sort who, although they never learned to know Christ and the way of life when they were young, yet are neither afraid nor ashamed to say that they are now "too old to learn" him. This sort of speech betrays that as yet they never learned him aright, as also that they are very far from salvation. For whosoever is too old to learn the means, is too old also to attain the end. Besides, there is the extreme folly of such an ungodly profession; for would the oldest man that can be, sent on a journey in a way both unknown to him and not easy to be found or held, reason with himself in such a silly way—"I will go forward. I never came this way before, neither do I know it. But I will never ask of it, for I am too old now to learn it"? And yet thus mad are old men in the matters of God and his kingdom. COMMENTARY ON TITUS.[4]

BREAKING DOWN THE COMMAND. MARTIN LUTHER: Temperate means wakeful, not lazy or snoring. They should bestir themselves and not be overly devoted to sleep. Those who are drunk sleep a great deal, but those who are wakeful are able to arise in the morning and are sober.

"Serious" means dignified and honorable, as distinguished from those who are frivolous. It means conducting oneself respectably and earnestly, not making light of things after the manner of those who, when they are presenting a case,

provoke laughter and tickle the carnal senses. It means that one should be serious-minded in word and behavior.

Semnotēs, dignity. This means that an old man should have such manners, actions, and dress that seriousness, not frivolity, is evident. He should not behave as though he wanted to be an adolescent, to dance, and to conduct himself in a way not appropriate to his age. This same thing applies to food.

Sōfrōn: modest, reasonable, a fine, upright man, one who is not intoxicated with is own passions and opinions. . . .

"In love," that is, they ought to have a love without pretense—sincere, honest, and authentic, so that they love friends and enemies equally. A love which discriminates between persons is an inactive love not an active one, an inauthentic love not an inauthentic one. . . . Nevertheless there is nothing which is simulated to a greater extent in the world, because no one would be deceived unless pretense were added.

"In patience." There are three parts of a Christian life. The first is to be temperate and serious. This is still a heathen property, because it really pertains to the outward person and depends on one's behavior. The heart is not involved. But the one who believes has righteousness. A justified person loves their neighbor and does the works of love. There follow the cross, imprisonment, and reproach. There you can see who are the true Christians, those who truly believe, those who love patiently. People say, "If Judas were to hurt me, I could easily bear it. But this is someone near to me, someone for whom I have done many favors!" This is a love that is not upright and sound, but love ought to be authentic. LECTURE ON TITUS 2:2.[5]

THE BEHAVIOR EXPECTED OF OLDER MEN. THOMAS TAYLOR: In the first precept of sobriety, older persons are enjoined to watch against the immoderate use of meat and drink especially, and the use of these (wine and strong drink especially) to moderate themselves within the confines and

---

[4]Taylor, *A Commentarie*, 341-43*; citing 1 Jn 2:13.

[5]LW 29:52-53* (WA 25:42-43); citing Rom 12:9.

precincts of sobriety. And there is great reason of this precept, for this age being full of infirmity, a cold and dry age, it is more desirous to strengthen, warm, and moisten itself with wine and strong drink, and without great watchfulness, easily overshoots itself. The Word teaches how some of the holiest of their age have been foiled and mocked hereby; the infirmity of that age not only being weak to resist, but prone to betray and deliver them up unto the temptation, as with Lot and Noah. . . .

"Dignified." The word signifies a seemly, modest, and gracious carriage, opposed to all lightness, vanity, or viciousness in gesture, speech, apparel, countenance, deeds, or conversation. It is a general virtue befitting every age and every vocation and condition of life. . . . But yet the older sort in all estates ought above others to carry a constant comeliness and grave authority, yea, a fatherly kind of reverent behavior. . . .

"Self-controlled." The older sort especially should become singular patterns and examples of moderation, both in the subduing and extinguishing of all rebellious motions, affections, pastimes, and perturbations [mental imbalances], as also in preserving in them a wise and vigilant care that their minds may be kept in such temper as becomes sobriety and Christianity. . . . Unchaste desires are foul spots in every age, but in old age most of all. . . .

"Sound in faith." Why is soundness of faith required particularly of old men, being a grace that everyone, young as well as old, must strive for? Because they have had the use of the word longer, and therefore their profit should be answerable to their means. . . . Every man must labor to recompense the decay of nature with increase of grace: the weakness of the body with soundness of mind; the failing of the outward man with the fortifying of the inward. . . .

"Love and steadfastness . . ." This third ornament of Christian old age is fitly by the Spirit of God added to the two former, as the preservative of both and most requisite to all Christians. For seeing the virtue [of steadfastness] is nothing else

but a willing and constant suffering of hard and painful things for Christianity and honesty's sake, and further, that affliction follows the faithful who study to testify their love of God in the love of others, even as the shadow follows the body—necessarily must they that would hold out in Christianity get this grace to bear off such calamities as follow upon the keeping of faith and a good conscience. COMMENTARY ON TITUS.[6]

2:3-5 The Healthy Life for Women

OLDER WOMEN TEACHING YOUNGER WOMEN.
PETER MARTYR VERMIGLI: Where in Titus 2 it is commanded that the elder women should admonish the younger women to be temperate, and that they should love their husbands and children, and should likewise be diligent housewives in their family—this must not be understood as touching public doctrine or ecclesiastical sermons, but of private exhortations, which are appropriate to be used by the elder sort toward the younger. COMMONPLACES.[7]

YOUNGER WOMEN SHOULD LOOK AFTER THEIR HUSBANDS AND CHILDREN. MARTIN LUTHER: They should see to it that they take care of their husbands and children. . . . It is their duty. A woman was created for a man and for bearing children. This text is against all monks and nuns. She will not do this work of loving of her own accord, because Satan is present, and the flesh grows weary in less than one year and looks at another man. Therefore it is the greatest gift of God when she takes pleasure in her own husband and not in another, when she does not pay more attention to another man than to her own. . . . These words mean that they should enjoy their husbands' bodies and provide for them.

Thus he instructs matrons to be good teachers and to train younger women to love their husbands and children. I have said what it means to love one's husband, namely, not merely to cohabit

---

[6]Taylor, *A Commentarie*, 344–57*; citing Gen 19:30-35; 9:20-21.
[7]Vermigli, *Commonplaces*, 4:8*.

with him but to respect one's husband, to regard him as lord, to submit to him in all things, not to be domineering. This is a rare quality in a woman, for the female sex inclines naturally toward what is forbidden to it; it wants to reign, to rule, and to judge. From this there come marital discord, blows, and beatings.[†] To love children means not only to educate them for the world but to see to it that they are provided for in body and in soul. For such love the rod and discipline are required. LECTURES ON TITUS.[8]

WOMEN CAN MAKE PROGRESS IN THE GOSPEL. JOHN CALVIN:

When he says that women should be guardians of their home,[†] surely this is a virtue that is already so important to them that it needs no special exhortation. For nature demonstrates this, and even the pagans have declared this, in a crude sort of way, by comparing a woman to a tortoise who always carries her shell with her.[†] ... Since it is so, then, a woman may believe that she has profited greatly in the gospel when she has been able to occupy herself peaceably in her household and when she has scrupulously maintained her home. ...

Paul spoke of the love that wives have for their husbands. Now he also adds subjection. For although women cannot love their husbands without respecting them, there is more to it than that. Because they must not be so very smart that they want to dominate them, but must be conscious that their husbands have been appointed as their heads, so it is not for them to govern. If the men had pushed themselves forward to usurp such authority, it might be said that they were taking advantage. But since God ordained it, and nature agrees, how can we argue? Yet it is a difficult thing, as we know. ... Women need to learn, therefore, that they cannot please God, and their whole lives

cannot be agreeable to him, unless they are first prepared to submit to their husbands, as St. Paul says here. ... But note that it is not said that a woman is to be a slave; rather, she is the life partner of her husband, which is to say that she is part of his body and his person. SERMONS ON TITUS.[9]

WOMEN SHOULD BE EDUCATED. ANNA MARIA VAN SCHURMAN:

Argument: Whosoever is fit for the study of the principal sciences is also fit for the study of instrumental or auxiliary sciences. But the study of the principal sciences is fitting for a Christian woman. ... Therefore. ...

The consequent of the major is valid, since to whomever the end is fitting, the legitimate means by which one may most easily move toward following that end are also fitting.

But the instrumental or auxiliary sciences are legitimate means. ... Therefore. ...

The minor is proved by the study that is fitting to a Christian woman, namely, diligent and serious meditation on the divine word, the knowledge of God, and the consideration of his most beautiful works, as these things apply equally to all Christians.

The study of letters is appropriate for anyone who needs to follow a pastime at home by oneself rather than outside among others.

But for a woman at home by herself rather than outside among others. ... Therefore. ...

The major is very true since studies possess the advantage of always providing a source of pleasure for a companion, even if no comrades

---

[8] LW 29:54-55 (WA 25:44); citing Prov 3:11; 23:13. [†]Luther considered spousal abuse to be vile and cowardly. "This is surely unbecoming to any human being, much more to a Christian," he said. "Therefore I strongly detest those men who are full of courage toward women and, as the saying goes, are lions at home and rabbits outside the home." LW 5:33.

[9] CO 54:514-16; citing Gen 2; Eph 5. [†]The Textus Receptus has here the Greek word for "staying at home" or "overseeing the home" rather than the preferred reading of NA[28], which is a similar word meaning "busy at home." See Bruce M. Metzger, A Textual Commentary on the Greek New Testament, 2nd ed. (Stuttgart: Deutsche Bibelgesellschaft, 1994), 585, and Philip H. Towner, The Letters to Timothy and Titus, New International Commentary on the New Testament (Grand Rapids: Eerdmans, 2006), 717 n. 8. Our commentators generally interpret the word to mean "busy at home" in any case, though Latin translations vary between curam and custodes. [†]This image is used in, e.g., Plutarch, Moralia, 142D and 381E (LCL 222:323 and 306:177). There is another possible quotation from the "pagan" Plutarch, De capienda ex inimicis utilitate 6, later on in this sermon (CO 54:520), which contains several such allusions.

beyond that are available; whence according to the wise Greek proverb, it is said, "Self-choice is also self-experience."

The reason of the minor is no less obvious, since the apostle wants women to be homemakers. Next, experience itself shows that those women whose tongues, ears, eyes are more accustomed to wander and to watch for outside delights, have their faith, diligence, even their chastity called into question by many. WHETHER THE STUDY OF LETTERS IS FITTING FOR A CHRISTIAN WOMAN.[10]

2:6-8 *The Healthy Life for Young Men and Ministers*

YOUNG MEN MUST BE SELF-CONTROLLED. THOMAS TAYLOR: This doctrine reprehends a common error in the world: for generally people think that religion and attendance to the word is for old age; but as for youth, it must sow the wild oats, it must have his course.... But all this is but the wisdom of the flesh, even sensual and devilish, clean contrary to God's wisdom, which urges the young man if ever he would be settled in a good estate, to found it in the remembrance of God. COMMENTARY ON TITUS.[11]

THE APPROPRIATE GRAVITY OF A MINISTER. DAVID DICKSON: Concerning pastors in the person of Titus, to this end, that their doctrine might the better take root, he commands that Titus show himself an example for others to imitate in every good work, but especially that in doctrine he shows forth incorruptness of the sound truth, gravity of authority, and his manner of speech fitted to the edification of his auditors, that the Adversary may have nothing justly to carp at. EXPOSITION OF ALL PAUL'S EPISTLES.[12]

THE MINISTER AS A GODLY EXAMPLE TO OTHERS. JOHN MAYER: Do not only urge others to do and live well, as has been said, but lead your life so as that you may be an example of godly living to them. In your teaching, that is, in preaching the Word of God, to move people the rather, be uncorrupt—that is, be not moved to teach for favor or hatred, and be grave, moving your auditors thus to reverence your teaching the more. Let the word or doctrine you teach be sound, that none may be able to tax it as heretical or erroneous. For the first words alone are sufficient to set forth of what life he should be; that which is added of doctrine then is certainly to be restrained hereunto....

Note that as a preacher is to teach truly and diligently, so that they may prevail the more with the people, they ought in their example to express what in word they teach. It is a long journey (says Seneca) by precepts, but short and effectual by examples. COMMENTARY ON PAUL'S EPISTLES.[13]

THE SOUND SPEECH OF A MINISTER. MATTHEW POOLE: Paul seems to be directing Titus as a minister, and the rest of the ministers in Crete, on how to behave themselves in the ministry, for the last word being plural "you" signifies either the ministry, or else is put for you. He would have Titus not only preach sound doctrine, uncorrupt, and do it gravely, but also preach profitable doctrine, tending to make the souls of others sound and healthy; unless perhaps by *logon* be here meant his style and phrase, which he would have such as none could justly condemn. What was said of Caesar's wife, that she ought not only to be chaste, but so to behave herself as not to be suspected otherwise† is applicable to ministers; their doctrine and phrase used in their ministry ought not only to be sound and grave, but such as none should judge or censure ... that the adversaries of the truth may be ashamed of their casting aspersions upon them, or upon the truth ... and

---

[10]Schurman, *Whether A Christian Woman Should Be Educated*, 29-30*.

[11]Taylor, *A Commentarie*, 404*.

[12]Dickson, *Exposition*, 180*. The ESV here has "show integrity, dignity." The KJV adds a word and changes the order (with the Textus Receptus): "shewing uncorruptness, gravity, sincerity." See Metzger, *Textual Commentary*, 585.

[13]Mayer, *Commentarie*, 568-69*. The quotation is from Seneca, *Ad Lucilium epistulae morales* 6.5 (LCL 75:26-27), *longum iter est per praecepta, breve et efficax per exempla.*

may have no evil thing to charge them with. ANNOTATIONS UPON THE HOLY BIBLE.[14]

THE PASTOR'S LIFE VERIFIES THE GOSPEL.
MATTHIAS FLACIUS: The seventh rule of this chapter is that it demands sound speech in the pastor that is not scurrilous, lewd, or proud, not absurd, or ignorant, but rather established by wisdom, and edifying. Moreover Paul adds the reason from the end, or from the fruit, why he requires these qualities simultaneously in words and deeds in pastors. He says this so that adversaries will not have reason to dispute true doctrine, but rather to confound such accusations by the evidence of experience. GLOSS ON TITUS[15]

2:9-10 The Healthy Life for Slaves

EVEN THE LIFE OF SLAVES CAN ADORN THE GOSPEL OF GOD. JOHN CALVIN: This ought to be a very sharp spur of exhortation to us, when we learn that our becoming conduct adorns the doctrine of God, which, at the same time, is a mirror of his glory. And, indeed, we see that this usually happens; as, on the other hand, our wicked life brings disgrace upon it; for people commonly judge us by our works. But this circumstance ought also to be observed, that God deigns to receive an "ornament" from slaves, whose condition was so low and mean that they were wont to be scarcely accounted human; for he does not mean "servants," such as we have in the present day, but slaves, who were bought with money, and held as property, like oxen or horses. And if the life of those people is an ornament to the Christian name, much more let those who are in honor take care that they do not stain it by their baseness. COMMENTARY ON TITUS.[16]

SLAVES SHOULD BEAR THEIR SERVITUDE WITH PATIENCE AND OBEDIENCE. MARTIN LUTHER: They should give due satisfaction, have regard for what is good, and bear their servitude patiently, considering that this is the will of God and their servile slavery is pleasing to the divine majesty. It should be pleasing to us also, who are only dregs ourselves; that is, we should be willing to be pleased with it too. The second [instruction] is that they carry out their duty in such a way that they avoid offending their masters and that they do what is pleasing to their masters. They should strive to please and please perfectly, serving in such a way that they do not choose certain works in which they are willing to please and others in which they follow their own ideas. LECTURE ON TITUS 2:9.[17]

2:11 The Grace of God Has Appeared

GOD'S GRACE FOR ALL KINDS. DAVID DICKSON: The second part of the chapter touching the doctrine of faith follows, which he subjoins as the fountain from whence virtue is fetched, for the performance of the aforesaid duties. For they cannot be Christian duties except grace to perform them be derived from Christ by faith. For in this the works of regenerate and unregenerate people materially good, do differ: that the works of these are done by the enemies of God, from the corrupt strength of free will, for carnal ends, without any respect to the glory of God; but the works of regenerate people are done by the servants of God, reconciled by faith, from the fountain of saving grace, which administers knowledge and strength to their performances. And this doctrine of faith is propounded by way of confirmation of the precepts or the doctrine of manners, upon four reasons, all of which prove that the aforesaid virtues are to be endeavored after.

1. Because (v. 11) the gospel of the grace of God bringing salvation of all kinds to people, being published and manifested, has appeared to all sorts

---

[14]Poole, *Annotations*, s.v.* †This is noted in various classical sources including Plutarch, *Caesar* 10.6 (LCL 53:466-67) and Cassius Dio, *Roman History* 37.45 (LCL 99:170-71), who writes that Caesar "divorced his wife, telling her that he did not really believe the story, but that he could no longer live with her inasmuch as she had once been suspected of committing adultery; for a chaste wife not only must not err, but must not even incur any evil suspicion."
[15]Flacius, *Glossa Compendaria*, 1093.
[16]CTS 43:316 (CO 52:422).

[17]LW 29:61 (WA 25:48).

of people. Therefore it is meet that people of all sorts show their thankfulness to God in an holy conversation, prosecuting the aforesaid virtues.

2. Because (v. 12) this gospel of God does not only teach us what duties we are bound to perform but also instructs us how to draw strength from the fountain of the grace of Christ, from his death and resurrection, to deny ungodliness and worldly lusts, and to live soberly as to ourselves, justly as to our neighbors, and holily as to God. Therefore we ought to be ready for the performance of these duties.

3. Because (v. 13) we expect eternal life at the second coming of Christ, who is the great God, one with the Father and the Holy Spirit, and our Savior. Therefore it behooves us to be armed and stirred up to follow after all the aforesaid good works, which God requires of us.

4. Because (v. 14) therefore Christ offered up himself for us, that he might effectually redeem us from the bondage of sin, and purchase us to himself, as a peculiar people, that we might follow after good works. Therefore if we would not have that redemption to be void as to us, we must of necessity forsake our sins, and follow after the aforesaid virtues, and newness of life. EXPOSITION OF ALL PAUL'S EPISTLES.[18]

WITH GOD'S STRENGTH WE TURN SOUND DOCTRINE INTO SOUND LIVES. JOHANNES BUGENHAGEN: "Healthy speech" is pure, as before where he spoke of "healthy doctrine," which is blameless and no one can fault, not even from Scripture. In the same way, he talks of "healthy speech," against which no one can object on the grounds that you do not live in a way consistent with what you teach. In this way here the two final points explain the preceding ones. For because he has said, "purity in doctrine," in turn he says, "healthy speech," and because he has said, "dignity or honor," in turn he says, "blameless speech," lest anyone here infer the hypocritical form of dignity, which only trumpets itself to others.

"To all people." That is, both to the Jews, and the Gentiles, both male and female, young and old, masters and slaves, about which he had spoken. Therefore, it is right that all should be taught, that all should live in a way worthy of God, just as it goes on to say: "So that denying" and so on. That is, with all elements which pertain to Adam put to death, we should live a new and spiritual life according to Christ, and this in the present age, not taking regard for those things which are now perishing for us, and are put to death in this life, but waiting for those things which are not seen, for which we have the hope that will come with the coming of the Lord. But here you will say: "How can I deny myself, so as to live in a way worthy of God, so that I may abound in good works, so that I fulfil all those things, when these are not in the power of humankind?" You are correct. Therefore in Christ you find what you do not have in yourself, provided you have him by faith, which is what Paul here takes up in this way. ANNOTATIONS ON PAUL.[19]

IT IS RIDICULOUS TO USE THIS TEXT TO DENY PREDESTINATION. JOHN CALVIN: St. Paul, having spoken of slaves, says that the grace of God has fully appeared to all people. Which is to say that God is not content to choose the great and the noble, and those who are held in high regard; but he has spread his mercy to the least, to those who are rejected, those who are despised, those who are reproached. God has chosen to honor these, admitting them to the rank and status of his children. And we see now why St. Paul speaks here about "all people." And we can also judge from this what stupidity it is in those quarrelers who presume to expound the holy Scripture and do not understand what they are saying, when they assert that, "God wants the whole world to be saved. The grace of God has appeared for the salvation of all the world. It follows that there is free will, and that there is no election, that no one is predestined to salvation!" SERMONS ON TITUS.[20]

---

[18]Dickson, *Exposition*, 180-81*.

[19]Bugenhagen, *Annotationes*, 132.
[20]CO 54:531-32.

LIGHT HAS COME TO SAVE ALL SORTS OF PEOPLE. DUTCH ANNOTATIONS: Now the apostle gives a reason why Titus must exhort all sorts of people, old and young, and even the slaves or servants also, to carry themselves piously. "The saving grace of God," that is, the doctrine of the grace of God shown us by Christ, and contained in the gospel; "has appeared," namely, as a light in the darkness of the shadows of the Old Testament, and of the ignorance of Gentilism; "to all people," that is, all sorts of people, men and women, old, young, free and bondservants, as appears from what goes before. See the like in 1 Timothy 2:1-4. Some join these words "all people" to the word "saving," in this sense: "The grace of God saving all people has appeared." DUTCH ANNOTATIONS.[21]

UNIVERSAL GRACE TO BE ACCEPTED. MOÏSE AMYRAUT: The misery of humankind is equal and universal, and the desire that God has had of delivering them by such a great Redeemer proceeds from the compassion which he has for them as his creatures who have fallen into such a great ruin. They are equally his creatures, so the grace of redemption which he has procured and offered to them ought also to be equal and universal, provided that they also are found to be equally disposed to receive it. And to this extent there is no difference between them. The Redeemer has been taken from their race and made a participant in the same flesh and the same blood with all of them, which is to say, of one and the same human nature conjoined in him with the divine nature in a unity of person. The sacrifice that he has offered for the propitiation of their offenses has been equally offered for all, and the salvation which he has received from his Father to communicate to people in the sanctification of the Spirit and in the glorification of the body is equally intended for all, provided, I say, that the disposition necessary to receive it is, in the same way, equal. . . .

Yet it is not necessary to think that there is either any people group or even any person excluded by the will of God from the salvation which he has acquired for the human race, provided that they make use of the testimonies of mercy which God has given to them. . . .

Even though someone does not distinctly know the name of Christ, and has learned nothing of the way in which he has obtained redemption for us, nevertheless, they would not be left out from participating in the remission of their sins, in the sanctification of their spirit, and in the glorious immortality. For these words are an eternal and universal truth, that "it is he who is the propitiation for our sins, and not only for ours but also for the sins of the whole world." And this, again, that "God desires that all people might be saved and come to the knowledge of his truth, since there is only one God and only one mediator between God and humankind—namely, the man Jesus Christ, who has given himself as a ransom for all." This is to say that not only does he not exclude any, but that it would be very easy for all the world to approach him, seeing that he here invites the whole world, as to a grace which he has intended for all the human race—if it is not shown to be unworthy. And this is why St. Paul calls it "the grace of salvation to all people." TREATISE ON PREDESTINATION.[22]

GRACE HAS APPEARED TO ALL CLASSES OF PEOPLE. LIBERT FROIDMONT: "For it has appeared" (it has now shown forth through the proclamation of the mystery of the incarnation and of the redemption of the human race) "the grace of God." Love is merciful, which Paul in 3:4 below calls kindness, that is, the uncreated grace of God, and source from which his created grace flows to men. "Of our savior." In Greek the meaning is

---

[21]Haak, *Annotations*, s.v.*; citing Is 42:7, 16; Acts 26:18; Eph 5:8; 1 Pet 2:9; 1 Jn 2:8

[22]Amyraut, *Brief Traitté de la Prédestination*, 77-83; citing 1 Jn 2:2; 1 Tim 2:5-6. In the 1658 reissue of this treatise, Amyraut made some subtle changes in this chapter, removing each occurrence of the word "equal," for example, and changing the word "equally" to "indifferently/impartially" (*egalement, indifferemment*) or skipping it altogether, in response to controversy over his doctrine of hypothetical universalism. See also comments on 1 Tim 2:4, 6.

"bearer of salvation," although St. Jerome in his day read "savior" as we have. This is why Sasbout[†] thinks that the Greek text we have today has been corrupted. "To all people." Not only to one people, as once was the case under the old law, but to all sorts of people, Jews, Gentiles, slaves, free, and so on. Therefore it is not surprising that the apostles and bishops even stooped to instructing slaves in morality. The word "all," therefore, applies to classes of individuals, and not to individuals of each class. So then, this passage does not support those who teach that a grace sufficient for salvation is given to individual men, says van Est.[†] Next, the apostle speaks specifically about the grace of the New Testament. But those authors [i.e., Protestant writers] teach that in the law—both of nature and of Scripture—sufficient grace has appeared and has been given to all and to individuals. COMMENTARIES ON THE EPISTLES.[23]

2:12 The Grace of God Trains Us

RENOUNCING UNGODLINESS AND WORLDLY LUSTS. ENGLISH ANNOTATIONS: "Denying ungodliness," that is, renouncing and forsaking them. Under the name "ungodliness," Paul comprises all breaches of the first table of the law; under "worldly lusts," all inordinate desires against the second table of the law. They are called worldly, both in respect of their object—because they are concerned with such things as belong to the present estate of this life and world—and with respect to their subject, namely, such lusts as are found and reign in worldly and unregenerate people. ENGLISH ANNOTATIONS.[24]

GRACE TEACHES US TO DENY UNGODLINESS AND PURSUE GOOD. THOMAS TAYLOR: Whosoever has truly received the grace of God is taught thereby to deny all ungodliness. And whereas

ungodliness seeks both to fix deep roots in the heart, as also to display the branches abroad in the life, so grace teaches us to strive two ways against it: (1) In purging the heart. (2) In striking off the arms which are (as we say) above ground, so as neither root nor branch is spared. . . .

The doctrine of grace teaches not only to abstain from evil but also to do good; and is the mistress of true sanctification in both parts of it— both the mortification of sins, as also quickening in righteousness.[†] For as it is in the lighting of a dark house first darkness must give place and light must succeed, so it is in the shining of this light of grace: the night must pass, and then the day must come; the old nature must be cast off with its lusts, and then the new nature put on. The gospel is the teacher of both these. COMMENTARY ON TITUS.[25]

2:13 Waiting for Our Great God and Savior

AWAITING HIS RETURN. MARTIN LUTHER: Our life ought to be one of such modesty in relation to ourselves, to our neighbor, and to God that we can confidently expect the appearing of our Lord. Is this not the most ample comfort? If a slave believes in Christ and obeys their master, they can confidently expect the appearing of Christ. If a husband does his duty, if a wife loves her husband and takes care of the house, they can be confident too; for they know that they are most certainly pleasing to God. Thus a preacher who pays attention to his office is confident; for he is completely sure that he serves God and does what God wishes, even though Satan certainly attacks him. . . . A servant girl can say this: "I have washed the pots, lit the fire in the oven, and made the beds." She confidently expects the appearing of Christ because she has done these works in Christ, and they are certainly

---

[23]Froidmont, *Commentaria*, 412-13; citing Titus 3:4. [†]Probably Sasbout Vermeer, second archbishop of Utrecht (1548–1614). [†]Willem Hessels van Est (1542–1613). [24]Downame, ed., *Annotations*, s.v.*; citing Eph 2:2-3; 4:17-19; 1 Pet 4:3; 1 Jn 2:16.

[25]Taylor, *A Commentarie*, 458, 465*. [†]See the two parts of conversion in question 88 of the Heidelberg Catechism, and the two parts of sanctification in question 35 of the Westminster Shorter Catechism, which says that "sanctification is the work of God's free grace, whereby we are renewed in the whole man after the image of God, and are enabled more and more to die unto sin, and live unto righteousness."

[pleasing to him]. So it is with a son who is obedient to his father. If he is sent to do his lessons, he does them and thinks, "This is my father's command, and it is pleasing to God." It is unavoidable that Satan will attack you if you obey your brother or love your husband. But he wants the very opposite. Thus the doctrine of God is adorned by our life, but not in the sense that we are justified by this. It is a great thing that he is willing to grant eternal life for the washing of pots. No, but he does give it to those who have lived in this way. . . . This is how a Christian waits. These are magnificent words, and this is not a temporal hope that crucifies instead of bringing blessing. Then he will be revealed in his glory and greatness and divine majesty. Christ is God; this is the first part. The second is that he has given and administered his gifts. Christ strengthens the conscience, lest it despair of eternal life. LECTURES ON TITUS.[26]

THE INFINITE POWER OF JESUS CHRIST.

ENGLISH ANNOTATIONS: To the confutation and confusion of all that deny the deity of Christ, the apostle here calls him not only God, but the great God—that is, immense and of infinite power. For as life when it is attributed to God signifies immortality, and wealth all sufficiency, and age eternity, and strength omnipotence, so greatness signifies immensity. ENGLISH ANNOTATIONS.[27]

CHRIST IS HERE BOTH GOD AND SAVIOR.

JOHN CALVIN: It is uncertain whether these words should be read together thus, "the glory of our Lord Jesus Christ, the great God and our Savior," or separately, as of the Father and the Son, "the glory of the great God, and of our Savior, the Lord Jesus Christ."[†] The Arians, seizing on this latter sense, have endeavored to prove from it that the Son is less than the Father, because here Paul calls the Father "the great God" by way of distinction from the Son. The orthodox teachers of the church, for the purpose of shutting out this slander, eagerly

contended that both are affirmed of Christ.[†] But the Arians may be refuted in a few words and by solid argument; for Paul, having spoken of the revelation of the glory of "the great God," immediately added "Christ," in order to inform us, that that revelation of glory will be in his person; as if he had said that, when Christ shall appear, the greatness of the divine glory shall then be revealed to us. COMMENTARY ON TITUS.[28]

WE MUST NOT DIVIDE THE FATHER AND THE SON.

JOHN CALVIN: Now when St. Paul speaks of the "great God" and of "our Savior Jesus Christ," we must not divide God the Father from his Son. But St. Paul understands that God will appear in the person of our Lord Jesus Christ, just as he says that then God will be all in all. And this must be noted well against those who wish to deny the divinity of Jesus Christ and who imagine him as a newly made God; of such was the detestable man who was punished in this city,[†] who confessed rightly that Jesus Christ was God but said that he had not always been so, but that he had only begun his divine essence at the creation of the world, and that God the Father made him pass through an alembic (as he called it),[‡] and then he appeared to be God when he was born into the world. Here we have a god forged in haste!

Now those who have had a similar opinion, like the ancient heretics, have armed themselves with this passage. "O!" they say, "St. Paul here names a great God, and *then* Jesus Christ. So it follows then

---

[26]LW 29:65-66 (WA 25:52-53).
[27]Downame, ed., *Annotations*, s.v.*

[28]CTS 43:320-21 (CO 52:423-24). [†]The KJV speaks of "the glorious appearing of the great God and our Savior Jesus Christ." The Geneva Bible renders it the "appearing of that glorie of that mighty God, and of our Savior Jesus Christ" (including a comma after God) but comments in the margin that "Christ is here most plainly called that mighty God." The adjective "mighty" may be suggested by Is 9:6. [‡]E.g., Chrysostom (344/354–407) said, "But can he have said 'appearing' of the Father? Nay, that he may the more convince you, he has added with reference to the appearing 'of the great God.' Is it then not said of the Father? By no means. For the sequel suffers it not which says, 'The appearing of our great God and Savior Jesus Christ.' See, the Son is great also" (NPNF 13:207). Theodoret of Cyrus (c. 393–466) comments of Paul that "here he calls the same one both Savior and great God and Jesus Christ" (NPNF² 3:319).

that Jesus Christ is an inferior and subordinate god." These people, I tell you, are good at mocking the holy Scripture. For St. Paul demonstrates that we must not conceive of any majesty of God apart from Jesus Christ, for there (as he says in other passages) is enclosed all divinity. Sermons on Titus.[29]

2:14 Christ Gave Himself to Redeem His People

The Double Fruit of Christ's Death for Us. Thomas Taylor: In verse 14 our apostle uses another forcible argument to urge the denial of unrighteousness and practice the former virtues of sobriety, justice, and piety. For the gospel not only teaches these things, which while we profess it we must adorn, but also if we look for ay benefit by the death of Christ, we may not, like riven vessels, let this doctrine slip. For to what other end did Christ so willingly give himself to death for believers in his name, but that they should reap the double fruit of it mentioned in this verse? First, redemption from sin; and second, sanctification: the which (1) inwardly purges believers to become the Lord's own peculiar, and (2) causes them outwardly to shine out in the zealous practice of good works. Commentary on Titus.[30]

Christ Died to Save His Special Posses-sion. Matthew Poole: Our great God and Savior Jesus Christ was not only sent and given by the Father but freely gave up himself to be incarnate, and to die for us, *hyper hēmōn*, in our stead to die. "That he might redeem us from all iniquity"; that by that price he might purchase salvation for us, delivering us both from the guilt and power of sin, who were slaves and captives to our lusts. "And purify unto himself a peculiar people . . ." We translate it a peculiar people; some translate it an egregious, famous, principal people;

others say it signifies something got by our own labor and industry, and laid up for our own use. Others say it signifies something we have set our hearts and affections upon, in a special peculiar manner. "Zealous of good works." Studious to do, and warmly pursuing all such works as are acceptable to God, and profitable to ourselves, and others. Annotations upon the Holy Bible.[31]

Christ the Object of God's Wrath for Believers Only. Thomas Taylor: First, the giver is noted in the words immediately going before, to be Jesus Christ our Savior. *Objection:* But God the Father gave Christ for us, and therefore he gave not himself. *Answer:* God the Father gave his Son, and Christ the Son gave himself by one and the selfsame will, and one joint and inseparable operation of them both, together with the Holy Spirit. . . . The Lord of life gave himself to death, not ignominiously only before people, but accursed before God. The Father's delight and darling became the object of such wrath, as would have crushed all creatures in heaven and earth to pieces. . . . Thus did the Son of God make exchange of the greatest glory above all comprehension, with the greatest infamy, and the greatest joys with the greatest sorrows that can be imagined, even the sorrows of hell.

"He gave himself for us." The which words by the latter part of the verse, must be expounded only of believers, of which number the apostle was; and are not to be meant of all humankind, as though Christ gave himself for a universal salvation of every particular person, or intended to save all if they would believe, as they who are termed the Lutheran divines contend.[†] But this place plainly restrains it to his people, his church, such as are redeemed from iniquity, such as are purged, such as are a chosen and peculiar people and such as are zealous for good works. For such Christ gave himself and for no other. Commentary on Titus.[32]

---

[29]CO 54:547; citing 1 Cor 15:28; Col 1:19; 2:9. [†]He is speaking here of Michael Servetus (1509–1553), his most infamous anti-trinitarian opponent. See *Institutes* 2.14.5-8, where he refutes that "deadly monster." [‡]An alembic was a kind of distillation apparatus.
[30]Taylor, *A Commentarie*, 498*.

[31]Poole, *Annotations*, s.v.*; citing Jn 3:16.
[32]Taylor, *A Commentarie*, 499-500, 505*. [†]See D. Scaer, "The Nature and Extent of the Atonement in Lutheran Theology," *Bulletin of the Evangelical Theological Society* 10, no. 4 (1967): 179-87. Writing

2:15 Exhort and Rebuke with All Authority

Let No One Despise You. Edward Leigh:
Titus should not suffer any to condemn him. Paul
does not speak here to Titus as he did to Timothy,
"Let no one despise your youth"; whence it is
collected that Titus was older than Timothy. The
Greek word here rendered "despise" is not the same
as that in Timothy. Annotations.[33]

The Authority of Titus. John Calvin:
Titus should claim authority and respect for
himself in teaching these things. For people given
to curious inquiries, and eager about trifles, dislike
the commandments to lead a pious and holy life as

---

before the Synod of Dort, Taylor identifies this position with
Lutheran theologians, rather than (as later commentators might)
with Arminian or Amyraldian writers within the Reformed
churches themselves. See the comments on 1 Tim 2:4, 6.

[33]Leigh, *Annotations*, 341; citing 1 Tim 4:12. The Greek word in
Titus 2:15 is *periphroneitō*, "let no one *disregard* you," as in, reject
your authority; in 1 Tim 4:12 it is *kataphoneitō*, "let no one *despise*
you," as in, look down on you.

being too common and vulgar. In order that Titus
may meet this disdain, he is enjoined to add the
weight of his authority to his doctrine. It is with
the same view (in my opinion) that he immediately
adds, "Let no one despise you."

Others think that Titus is instructed to gain the
ear of others, and their respect for him, by the
integrity of his life; and it is indeed true that holy
and blameless conduct imparts authority to
instruction. But Paul had another object in view;
for here he addresses the people rather than Titus.
Because many had ears so delicate, that they
despised the simplicity of the gospel; because they
had such an itch for novelty, that hardly any space
was left for edification; he beats down the haughtiness of such people, and strictly charges them to
desist from despising, in any way, sound and useful
doctrine. This confirms the remark which I made
at the outset, that this epistle was written to the
inhabitants of Crete rather than to any single
individual. Commentary on Titus.[34]

---

[34]CTS 43:323* (CO 52:425).

3:1-15 ENCOURAGEMENT TO GOOD WORKS AND FINAL INSTRUCTIONS

Remind them to be submissive to rulers and authorities, to be obedient, to be ready for every good work, ²to speak evil of no one, to avoid quarreling, to be gentle, and to show perfect courtesy toward all people. ³For we ourselves were once foolish, disobedient, led astray, slaves to various passions and pleasures, passing our days in malice and envy, hated by others and hating one another. ⁴But when the goodness and loving kindness of God our Savior appeared, ⁵he saved us, not because of works done by us in righteousness, but according to his own mercy, by the washing of regeneration and renewal of the Holy Spirit, ⁶whom he poured out on us richly through Jesus Christ our Savior, ⁷so that being justified by his grace we might become heirs according to the hope of eternal life. ⁸The saying is trustworthy, and I want you to insist on these things, so that those who have believed in God may be careful to devote themselves to good works. These things are excellent and profitable for people. ⁹But avoid foolish controversies, genealogies, dissensions, and quarrels about the law, for they are unprofitable and worthless. ¹⁰As for a person who stirs up division, after warning him once and then twice, have nothing more to do with him, ¹¹knowing that such a person is warped and sinful; he is self-condemned.

¹²When I send Artemas or Tychicus to you, do your best to come to me at Nicopolis, for I have decided to spend the winter there. ¹³Do your best to speed Zenas the lawyer and Apollos on their way; see that they lack nothing. ¹⁴And let our people learn to devote themselves to good works, so as to help cases of urgent need, and not be unfruitful.

¹⁵All who are with me send greetings to you. Greet those who love us in the faith.

Grace be with you all.

OVERVIEW: In a final series of exhortations, Paul addresses Christian behavior within the wider community. Against certain Anabaptists and "Libertines," who saw the gospel as abolishing the need for civil magistrates and obedience to them, magisterial commentators reaffirmed the place and role of the state, whether ruled by Christians or not. Further, while asserting that good works do not contribute to salvation, the reformers follow Paul's teaching on the necessity of good works, which should be motivated by the loving and merciful example of Christ. The rich theology of Titus 3:4-8 and its relation to baptism draws significant interest, and though there are differences concerning its appropriate timing, the washing and new birth of the sacrament are viewed as foundational to the Christian life. Paul's instructions on avoiding foolish controversies and those who stir them up also draw significant attention, and our exegetes consider the nature of heresy and how it is to be identified and handled within the church. Paul's closing salutations are seen by most of our sixteenth-century interpreters as referring primarily to the Christians of Crete, although one suggests it is addressed to other pastors and Luther finds in it a "gibe" toward the insincere.

3:1 Obey the Authorities

THE GOSPEL DOES NOT OVERTHROW POLITICAL INSTITUTIONS. PETER MARTYR VERMIGLI: This subject is treated frequently and accurately in the New Testament, and mostly for the following reason: the children of God sometimes think that, being governed by the Spirit and Word of God, it is somehow beneath their dignity to be subject to external powers.... Now Christ conducted himself much differently, for he paid the tribute money and taught to "render unto Caesar the things that are Caesar's." . . . Paul wrote the same thing to Titus: "Remind them to be submissive to rulers and authorities, to be obedient to the magistrates." And in the letters to the Ephesians, to Timothy and to Titus, he commends servants to obey their masters diligently. In his letter to Timothy he commands Christians to pray for their magistrates. From all these passages it is readily apparent what we have often said, and which is written by Chrysostom on this topic,[†] namely, that evangelical doctrine was not given to overthrow political constitutions but rather to confirm them and to improve them. COMMENTARY ON ROMANS.[1]

CHRISTIANITY DOES NOT DESTROY CIVIL AUTHORITY. THOMAS TAYLOR: Christianity does not eat up magistracy, nor destroy government and civil authority, but ratifies and confirms it. For Christians are here called to subjection and obedience to civil authority. The reason is: (1) The kingdom of Christ is not of this world, his authority divides not civil inheritances, his crown and scepter detract not from earthly crowns and scepters, his weapons are not carnal, the keys of his kingdom are no temporal jurisdiction, he could not be the true and lawful King of the Jews and yet convey himself away when they would have given him his right. (2) For one ordinance of God to destroy another would argue a lack of wisdom in God the ordainer, the very thought whereof would be blasphemous. . . .

Every Christian is bound to take heed to the mouth of the king in all things and so far as he has power to command. Now because the civil magistrate is always bound to command in the Lord, and is the father of our bodies in a way, and of all our outward person: hence two grounds of great moment are concluded. The former is that everyone must obey all possible commandments

that are not against the law of nature and the law of God. For the magistrate in all his commandments as well as executions must be the minister of God, only using that upon his subjects which God himself, whose place he sustains, would urge. COMMENTARY ON TITUS.[2]

IT IS GOD'S WILL THAT WE SUBMIT, EVEN TO UNWORTHY RULERS. JOHN CALVIN: Now, if Christians were commanded to obey and be subject to the principalities and powers at a time when those who bore the sword of justice were unbelievers and enemies of God . . . if we were under the Turks, under tyrants, or under mortal enemies of the gospel, we would still be commanded to be subject to them. Why? Because it pleases God. SERMONS ON TITUS.[3]

3:2-3 Show Perfect Courtesy Toward All

SHOWING MEEKNESS TO SINNERS. ENGLISH ANNOTATIONS: Though all sinners are not alike to be handled, but on some we are to have compassion, others to save with fear, pulling them out of the fire, yet the ministers of God must do nothing in rage or passion, but with the spirit of meekness, showing all meekness to all people, Gentiles as well as Jews, enemies as well as friends; and that especially out of this consideration, that the best of Christians before their conversion were as bad as the worst of them, whose carriage is most offensive to the church (v. 3). ENGLISH ANNOTATIONS.[4]

REASONS TO BE MILD AND LOVING. GIOVANNI DIODATI: He gives a reason why believers should be mild and loving: namely, because the Lord has showed abundance of mercy toward them, being most corrupt and wretched. Or generally, because they should addict themselves to good works, that being the end of their redemption. PIOUS ANNOTATIONS.[5]

---

[1]Donnelly, James, and McLelland, eds., *Peter Martyr Reader*, 224; citing Mt 17:27; 22:21; Eph 6:5; 1 Tim 6:1; Titus 2:9-10; 1 Tim 2:1-4. [†]Chrysostom, *In Epist. ad Rom.*, homily 23.1 (PG 60:613-14).

[2]Taylor, *A Commentarie*, 544, 549*.
[3]CO 54:557.
[4]Downame, ed., *Annotations*, s.v.*; Jude 23.
[5]Diodati, *Pious Annotations*, 348.

WE WERE ONCE AS OTHERS ARE NOW. DAVID DICKSON: He gives two reasons why gentleness should be showed toward some. 1. Because we, before our conversion, were such as they now are. We are all of us by nature, upon many considerations to be blamed, yet we desired to be treated courteously and mildly by all. Therefore let us deal accordingly with those who are not yet converted.

He sets down five diseases of our natures: (i) We were "foolish," because all the wisdom of humankind is mere vanity, so long as we do not know God, for we are ignorant of the right rule and the true fountain and the due end of our affections. (ii) "Disobedient": because people by nature do none of those things which either God or conscience command, but that which pleases themselves. (iii) "Straying," namely, from the true way, which leads to eternal life and being deceived with errors, they go further off from God daily. (iv) "Serving," with delight, diverse lusts and pleasures, which reign together and, as it were, by turns challenge for dominion over all the unregenerate. (v) We were destitute of the true love of God, living in malice and envy, rejoicing in the hurt, and sorry for the good that befalls our neighbor; hating one another, when all of us were most worthy to be hated of God.

2. Because we, although perverse, yet at length were converted by the grace of God, therefore we ought to use gentleness toward those that are unconverted, and hope well of them who may possibly be converted by the same divine grace. EXPOSITION OF ALL PAUL'S EPISTLES.[6]

3:4-8 The Kindness of God Our Savior

THE GOODNESS AND LOVINGKINDNESS OF CHRIST. MARTIN LUTHER: A man is kind or sweet when he is friendly and well-disposed, easily approachable, not harsh, but pleasant and joyful. He makes an effort to have people enjoy being about him. They are glad to hear him speak. He is companionable, affable, and easy for everyone to get

along with. He is a brother to every man you can think of. This is a sweet manner. This text sets forth Christ as one who had *chrēstotēs*, the sweetness of golden virtue and of deity. God dwelt in Christ, He was in Christ....

Goodness, that most gracious treatment of us and attitude toward us in Christ. Whoever was with him preferred his company to that of the Pharisees. *Philanthropia* ... means lovingkindness toward human beings; that is, he lived among us in the sweetest of ways, offended no one, and tolerated everyone. With this sweetness he did not serve himself but sought to show love and the effects of love toward blind people by giving them sight, as Matthew 11:5 says; for this was the purpose and effect of his *philanthropia*, that he was eager to serve people out of generosity and friendliness. These virtues we see in Christ and in God ... that God is so disposed in Christ, he who treats us sweetly, who does everything to help us, who gives his gifts, who gives teachers to teach the brethren and to help and strengthen us in bearing evils, who is present at death to receive our souls—in short, who wants to love people. LECTURES ON TITUS.[7]

PURE GRACE SHOWN TO THOSE WHO COULD DO NOTHING BUT SIN. JOHN CALVIN: Let us remember that here Paul addresses his discourse to believers, and describes the manner in which they entered into the kingdom of God. He affirms that by their works they did not at all deserve that they should become partakers of salvation, or that they should be reconciled to God through faith; but he says that they obtained this blessing solely through the mercy of God. We therefore conclude from his words that we bring nothing to God, but that he goes before us by his pure grace, without any regard to works. For when he says—"Not by works which we have done," he means that we can do nothing but sin till we have been renewed by God. This negative statement depends on the former affirmation, by which he said that they were foolish

---

[6]Dickson, *Exposition*, 181*.

[7]LW 29:78-79 (WA 25:61-62).

and disobedient, and led away by various desires, till they were created anew in Christ; and indeed, what good work could proceed from so corrupt a Mass? COMMENTARY ON TITUS.[8]

SALVATION IS NOT CAUSED BY WORKS OF ANY KIND. DUTCH ANNOTATIONS: "He saved us, not by works," namely, as causes that should merit or be worthy of salvation. It is not by works of righteousness, that is, works that are done according to the law of God, which is the rule of all righteousness. So that here are clearly excluded all good works done, not only according to the ceremonial law, but also according to the moral law, or the Ten Commandments.[†] These are "works that we had done," namely, not only before our conversion and justification, as if by the same we had prepared ourselves thereunto, but also those which were done after our conversion, seeing to these works are not opposed works after conversion but God's mercy, which excludes all works. We are saved by regeneration and renewing of the Holy Spirit, which is as a bath, whereby the filthiness of our sins are washed and purified whereof the bath of baptism is a sign and seal. See the like phrase in Romans 9:11. DUTCH ANNOTATIONS.[9]

SPIRITUAL REBIRTH IN BAPTISM. PHILIPP MELANCHTHON: Clearly Baptism signifies a transition through death into life, the drowning to death of the old Adam and the raising to life of the new Adam. And its proper function is also understood by this signification. This is why Paul calls it a "washing of regeneration." This definition will be understood most easily in reference to a type. Baptism was foreshadowed by the crossing of the Israelites through the Arabian Sea. They were doing nothing less than walking into death when they entrusted themselves to the waters. By faith

they crossed through the waters, through death, until they escaped to the other side. In this historical account the very thing that baptism signifies happened—the Israelites crossed through death to life. So also the entire Christian life is a putting to death of the flesh and a rebirth of the Spirit. Thus the very thing that Baptism signifies actually happens up to the day when we finally rise from the dead. COMMONPLACES.[10]

WASHING A NEWBORN BABY. EDWARD LEIGH: The Spirit of God alludes to the practice of all civilized people at the birth of a child: they first wash to from its natural uncleanness. So the Spirit of God cleanses us from our spiritual pollution. Baptism is sacramentally the "laver of regeneration,"[†] not by the work wrought, but by the grace of God's Spirit by which we are justified. ANNOTATIONS.[11]

CHILDREN CANNOT EXPERIENCE THE NEW BIRTH OF BAPTISM. DIRK PHILIPS: True believers in Christ, then, are the regenerated children of God. But baptism is a bath of the born again. That is, there the newborn children of God are bathed and washed, not by the power of the elements or natural water, but through the blood and Spirit of Christ Jesus. For this is he, as John says, "who comes with water and blood, not with water only but with water and blood. And the Spirit is witness that the Spirit is truth. For there are three who give testimony here on earth, the Spirit, the water, and the blood; and these three agree," the Spirit through which the person believes, the water with which the believer is baptized, and the blood of Christ Jesus with which the believing and baptized Christians are sprinkled in their souls and consciences, of which sprinkling of the blood of Jesus Christ the apostles clearly testify in their writings. Therefore, on the cross Christ also allowed his side to be pierced through and water and blood to flow from it as a testimony of his true

---

[8]CTS 43:330-31 (CO 52:429-30).
[9]Haak, *Annotations*, s.v.*; Rom 9:16; 11:6; Ezek 36:25-27. †See Lee Gatiss, *Cornerstones of Salvation: Foundations and Debates in the Reformed Tradition* (Welwyn, UK: Evangelical Press, 2017), 88-91, on the Reformation-era use of the distinction between the ceremonial and the moral law with regard to salvation.

[10]Melanchthon, *Commonplaces*, 171-72.
[11]Leigh, *Annotations*, 341*; citing 1 Pet 3:21. †The laver is the basin used by priest to wash when entering the tent of meeting. See Ex 30:18.

humanity and that he has with his blood sprinkled, washed, and cleansed his congregation (which is taken out of his side, flesh of his flesh and bone of his bone) from all her sins, and has poured the water of the Spirit over her, of which baptism is a sacramental sign.

Since then believers are born again of God and baptism is a both of this new birth, and young children have not come to this new birth so long as they still lack understanding and do not believe, baptism does not apply to them. For baptism belongs to no one and may not be given rightly to anyone except the born again children of God, that is, to believers who have been inwardly renewed after the image and likeness of God, to those forsaking the old Adam so that the new person, yes, Christ lives and works in them through faith. To such Christians baptism applies, for there baptism is a bath of regeneration and gives testimony of the new creature in Christ Jesus. THE BAPTISM OF OUR LORD JESUS CHRIST.[12]

BAPTISM AS THE INSTRUMENTAL CAUSE OF SALVATION. THOMAS CARTWRIGHT: By "the laver of regeneration" the apostle understands both the outward element of water and the grace of God signified thereby, which is the whole sacrament of baptism, and therefore he calls it the laver of new birth of the Holy Spirit. In which regard we speak of it as an instrumental cause whereby we are saved,[†] but in regard of the Holy Spirit, the very *formal cause* of our salvation, both in applying unto us the righteousness of Jesus Christ, and in the merit thereof sanctifying us daily more and more until such time as by death first, and after by resurrection from the dead, he shall have abolished sin and made us wholly holy both body and soul. And even the outward element in the sacrament of baptism we confess frankly that it is an instrumental cause of our salvation, of which the apostle might in that sort truly say to the faithful who are already baptized that by it they were saved, because

it was a worthy mean to assure them of the Holy Spirit, the Spirit of adoption; but thereof to conclude that none can be saved that are not baptized when they cannot conveniently come by it, or that every one which is baptized has forgiveness of sins and receives the Spirit of adoption, has no ground to stand upon this place. CONFUTATION OF THE RHEMISTS.[13]

PAUL SENDS US QUICKLY FROM THE SIGN TO THE SPIRIT. JOHN CALVIN: I have no doubt that he alludes, at least, to baptism, and even I will not object to have this passage expounded as relating to baptism; not that salvation is contained in the outward symbol of water, but because baptism seals to us the salvation obtained by Christ. Paul treats of the exhibition of the grace of God, which, we have said, has been made by faith. Since therefore a part of revelation consists in baptism, that is, so far as it is intended to confirm our faith, he properly makes mention of it. Besides, baptism—being the entrance into the church and the symbol of our ingrafting into Christ—is here appropriately introduced by Paul, when he intends to show in what manner the grace of God appeared to us; so that the strain of the passage runs thus: "God has saved us by his mercy, the symbol and pledge of which he gave in baptism, by admitting us into his church, and engrafting us into the body of his Son."

Now the apostles are wont to draw an argument from the sacraments, to prove that which is there exhibited under a figure, because it ought to be held by believers as a settled principle, that God does not sport with us by unmeaning figures, but inwardly accomplishes by his power what he exhibits by the outward sign; and therefore, baptism is fitly and truly said to be "the washing of regeneration." . . .

---

[12]CRR 6:79-80*; citing 1 Pet 3:21; 1 Jn 5:6-8; 1 Pet 1:2; Jn 19:34; Eph 5:29-30; Jn 4:2; 2 Cor 3:18; Col 3:10; Eph 4:24; Mt 16:10; Gal 5:6.

[13]Cartwright, *Confutation*, 592*. [†]Cartwright is here using the common technical terminology of causation, which originated with Aristotle, on which see Richard C. Muller, *Dictionary of Latin and Greek Theological Terms Drawn Principally from Protestant Scholastic Theology*, 2nd ed. (Carlisle, UK: Paternoster, 2000), 61-62. Cf. Aristotle, *Metaphysics* 1.3, 5.2.

Though he mentioned the sign, that he might exhibit to our view the grace of God, yet, that we may not fix our whole attention on the sign, he immediately sends us to the Spirit, that we may know that we are washed by his power, and not by water, agreeably to what is said—"I will sprinkle on you clean waters, even my Spirit."

And indeed, the words of Paul agree so completely with the words of the prophet that it appears clearly that both of them say the same thing. For this reason I said at the commencement that Paul, while he speaks directly about the Holy Spirit, at the same time alludes to baptism. It is therefore the Spirit of God who regenerates us, and makes us new creatures; but because his grace is invisible and hidden, a visible symbol of it is beheld in baptism. COMMENTARY ON TITUS.[14]

IMPUTATION OF RIGHTEOUSNESS BY GOD'S GRACE ALONE. THOMAS TAYLOR: The righteousness of a sinner before God is not any quality in the believer, but that which the Lord imputes and accepts through his Son. For the apostle here speaking of renewing of believers inwardly and in truth, yet ascribes not their righteousness thereto, but attributes it wholly to grace. And if we speak of the righteousness of a sinner before God, regeneration is indeed a companion of it, but no part of it. Besides, he says not we are justified by grace, but by "his grace"; which is even his gracious accepting of us in his Son and not for those graces which he works in us, which are *ours* after he has once given them. COMMENTARY ON TITUS.[15]

GOOD WORKS, MERIT, AND SUPERNATURAL LIFE IN BAPTISM. LIBERT FROIDMONT: "Not from works of righteousness" (i.e., righteous or good works) "that we have done." This means not by our efforts before the first grace was given, that by which we have been called to faith and baptism. Rather, works that precede this first grace are wicked, if not always according to their immediate goal, at least by

the weakness of their connection to the end toward which they should be directed, as Augustine repeatedly insists. Nevertheless, the merits of good works are not for this reason eliminated, as the Calvinists argue. For our good works themselves, those by which we are either inclined to justification or ones that as righteous persons we work are the effects of grace and mercy of God. "But according to his own mercy." This is from his own infinite mercy with which he marvelously has pitied human nature that fell into an undistinguished mass of damnation by the sin of our first parent. "He has saved us," by the salvation of grace on earth which the salvation of eternal glory in the heavens replaces. "Through washing" (baptism) "of regeneration." By this we are again reborn not to that natural life by which we were born from our parents in sin, but to supernatural life, that is, sanctifying grace. By it we are made sharers in the divine nature. COMMENTARIES ON THE EPISTLES.[16]

3:9-11 *Avoid Foolish Controversies and Heretics*

THE DEFINITION OF A HERETIC. THOMAS TAYLOR: A heretic is one who professes Christ yet invents or maintains any errors against the foundation of religion, and that with obstinacy. For the opening of which description three things are to be noted. First, that a heretic must profess Christ. For Jews, Turks, or pagans cannot properly be heretics, although they fight against Christ and all religion in all the foundations of it. These are more properly called heathens, infidels, and atheists without God in the world. But the person whom Titus has here to deal with is one within the church, and cast off from a foundation upon which they seemed to stand.

Second, they must maintain an error in doctrine (for if people err in practice they are rather hypocrites and profane wretched) and this error must be fundamental, that is, overturning some ground or article of our faith. . . .

---

[14]CTS 43:332-34 (CO 52:430-31); citing Ezek 36:25, 27.
[15]Taylor, *A Commentarie*, 669*.

[16]Froidmont, *Commentaria*, 415; citing 2 Pet 1:4.

Third, this error must be willfully and obstinately maintained. For they must reject admonition, and strive after conviction. And this properly makes a heretic. For everyone that holds a heretical opinion is not a heretic. Someone may by simplicity, levity, or rashness or gentleness of nature be drawn into such an opinion; but if admonished of their error they contend not, but are ready to yield up themselves to the persuasion of truth, they are no heretic. For these three things make up a heretic: (1) error, (2) conviction, (3) obstinacy or weddedness to their opinion. Commentary on Titus.[17]

Excommunicate Heretics and Don't Waste Time on Them. David Dickson: In verse 10 the apostle enjoins Titus to reject by excommunication the person who is a heretic, or who holds contrary to sound doctrine, and makes a division or sect in the church, or breaks the unity of the church by any error of theirs (when they are openly convicted before the presbytery, and admonished the first and second time) and neither trouble himself and the church more than necessary with the disputations of such kind of people or spend that time which is appointed for instructing the church, in vain disputations with these perverse people. Exposition of All Paul's Epistles.[18]

Let Heretics Rant to Their Own Destruction. Balthasar Hubmaier: Heretics are those who wantonly resist the holy Scripture. The first of them was the devil, who spoke to Eve: "By no means will you die." Together with his followers. Likewise are those persons heretics who blind the Scripture, and who exposit it otherwise than the Holy Spirit demands, such as [interpreting] "a wife" as a prebend, "pasturing" as ruling, "a stone" as the rock, "church" as Rome, who proclaim this everywhere and force us to believe such nonsense. Those who are such should be overcome with holy instruction, not contentiously but gently, even though the holy Scripture also includes wrath. But the wrath of Scripture is truly a spiritual flame and a loving zeal, which burns only with the Word of God. Should they not yield to words of authority or gospel reasons, then avoid them and let them go on to rant and rage, so that those who are filthy may become yet more filthy. On Heretics and Those Who Burn Them.[19]

Ministers Are Drawn into Battles with Heretics for Various Reasons. John Calvin: Such is the cunning of Satan that, by the impudent talkativeness of heretics, he entangles good and faithful pastors, so as to draw them away from diligence in teaching. We must therefore beware lest we become engaged in quarrelsome disputes; for we shall never have leisure to devote our labors to the Lord's flock, and contentious people will never cease to annoy us.

When Paul commands Titus to avoid such persons, it is as if he said that he must not toil hard to satisfy them. . . . This is a highly necessary admonition; for even they who would willingly take no part in strifes of words are sometimes drawn by shame into controversy, because they think that it would be shameful cowardice to quit the field. Besides, there is no temper, however mild, that is not liable to be provoked by the fierce taunts of enemies, because they look upon it as intolerable that those men should attack the truth (as they are accustomed to do) and that none should reply. Nor are there wanting men who are either of a combative disposition, or excessively hot-tempered, who are eager for battle. On the contrary, Paul does not wish that the servant of Christ should be much and long employed in debating with heretics. Commentary on Titus.[20]

Be Careful Not to Read Later Meanings into the Words Here. Matthew Poole: Two things make up a heretic according to the

[17]Taylor, *A Commentarie*, 701-2*.
[18]Dickson, *Exposition*, 182*.
[19]CRR 5:59-60*; citing Gen 3:4; Rev 22:11.
[20]CTS 43:340-41* (CO 52:434-35).

common acceptation of the term now. (1) An error in some matters of faith; (2) stubbornness and contumacy in the holding and maintaining of it. Whether it so signified so early I cannot tell; it seems to refer to the former verse, supposing some, that notwithstanding all the endeavors of Titus, would be striving and contending for niceties about questions, genealogies, and so on, "After the first and second admonition reject." For such (says the apostle) admonish them once and again; if they will not have done, refuse them, reject them. Whether excommunication can be certainly built upon this text, may be doubted; *paraiteomai* signifies no more than to avoid, reject, or refuse. ANNOTATIONS UPON THE HOLY BIBLE.[21]

A CHURCH COUNCIL IS NOT REQUIRED TO CONDEMN SOMEONE AS A HERETIC. WILLIAM FULKE: A person may be convicted to be a heretic without a general council, if they do obstinately defend any grievous error against the manifest authority of the holy Scriptures. So were many heretics and heresies condemned against which there were no councils gathered. Many godly people and the truth itself by councils have been condemned for heretics and heresies.... [But] no opinion is to be taken for heresy that is agreeable to the holy Scriptures, though it be condemned by all people in the world. TEXT OF THE NEW TESTAMENT.[22]

AVOIDING HERETICS AND SCHISMATICS. JOHN MAYER: A heretic is one who prefers false doctrine, so as they will not be reclaimed, but are addicted to

their own error against the whole church of God. Thus Anselm also describes them, distinguishing between a heretic and a schismatic, in that the latter goes from the church upon some episcopal dissension, yet it is commonly on a difference in opinion also. But by "an error held against the truth" I take it that any error is not to be understood, but any error opposite to the grace of God in Christ, or against the analogy of faith set forth in the Apostles' Creed.... Calvin will not have any distinction here between heretics and schismatics, for schismatics are such, says he, as rest not in the doctrine of the church but trouble the peace thereof with their contrary opinions and disputes. But howsoever the schismatics here specially spoken against were heretics, yet every schismatic is not so, because some make a trouble in the church about circumstances, for which they are not to be avoided, but to be borne withal, till they outgrow this weakness and become stronger. COMMENTARY ON PAUL'S EPISTLES.[23]

WE MUST HATE HERESY BECAUSE IT THREATENS THE UNITY OF THE CHURCH. JOHN CALVIN: We must now see what he means by the word "heretic." There is a common and well-known distinction between a heretic and a schismatic.[†] But here, in my opinion, Paul disregards that distinction: for, by the term "heretic" he describes not only those who cherish and defend an erroneous or perverse doctrine, but in general all who do not yield assent to the sound doctrine that he laid down a little before. Thus under this name he includes all ambitious, unruly, contentious persons, who, led away by sinful passions, disturb the peace of the church, and raise disputings. In short, every person who, by their overweening pride, breaks up the unity of the church is pronounced by Paul to be "heretic."

But we must exercise moderation so as not instantly to declare everyone to be a "heretic" who

---

[21]Poole, *Annotations*, s.v.*
[22]Fulke, *Text of the New Testament*, 393*. Martin, *New Testament*, 599, had affirmed on this text that "not everyone that errs in religion is a heretic, but he only that after the church's determination willfully and stubbornly stands in his false opinion, not yielding to decree of council or the chief pastors of the church therein.... They that in the church of Christ have a crazed or perverse opinion, if being admonished to be of a sound and right opinion, they resist obstinately and will not amend their pestiferous opinions, but persist in defending them, are thereby heretics.... Let our Protestants behold themselves in this glass ... and they shall find all definitions and marks of a heretic to fall upon themselves."

[23]Mayer, *Commentarie*, 570-71*. See Aquinas, *Summa Theologiae* II-II, q. 11, a. 3, which looks at how 2 Tim 2:24-25 relates to Titus 3:10-11 on this question, and refers to heresy as a capital crime, which indeed it was in England from 1401 to 1677.

does not agree with our opinion. There are some matters on which Christians may differ from each other without being divided into sects. . . . But whenever the obstinacy of any person grows to such an extent that, led by selfish motives, they either separate from the body, or draw away some of the flock, or interrupts the course of sound doctrine, in such a case we must boldly resist.

In a word, a heresy or sect and the unity of the church—are things totally opposite to each other. Since the unity of the church is dear to God, and ought to be held by us in the highest estimation, we ought to entertain the strongest abhorrence of heresy. COMMENTARY ON TITUS.[24]

THE CONGREGATION MUST SHUN EVIL PEOPLE. DIRK PHILIPS: The Lord Jesus Christ has given his congregation the power and has established the ordinance that it shall separate, shun, and avoid false brothers, the unlawful and disobedient, the quarrelsome and heretical persons, yes, all who are found to be evil within the congregation, as was said before. What happens beyond this is not Christian, nor evangelical, nor apostolic. THE CONGREGATION OF GOD.[25]

3:12-15 Final Instructions and Greetings

DETAILS IN PAUL'S FINAL INSTRUCTIONS. HUGO GROTIUS: "Zenas the lawyer." This is a contracted form of the name "Zenodorus." *Nomikos* . . . means one skilled in the law. . . . The Stoics defined *nomikos* as an interpreter of the law. Greeks also learned Roman law, such as Tryphoninus, Callistratus, Menander, and Arcadius. Nor do I doubt that many of the priests of the law became priests of Christ, because they saw that all the precepts of the law were contained in that religion. Among them was Tertullian, who was replete with phrases from Roman law. . . .

"And Apollos." I suspect that this man was at Rome with Paul: for the imprisoned man had need of many helpers in such a great city. Speed them. . . . They, if I am not mistaken, traveled from Rome by way of Crete to Judea and Syria, on a mission of Paul's.

The word *propempein* means to care for them [Zenas and Apollos] so as to be able to get on their way, that is, having been supplied, as follows, with the things which are necessary for the journey, such as a ship, travel money, and food. In the same way the word *propempein* is used in Wisdom 19:2, 1 Corinthians 16:11, and elsewhere. ANNOTATIONS.[26]

BELIEVERS IN OUR CHURCHES MUST BE FRUITFUL IN GOOD WORKS. THOMAS TAYLOR: Of whom are good works called for? "Let ours," called in verse 8 "believers in God." "Ours," who are converted and confirmed in the faith by thy labor and mine; of these call for good works. For this is the first condition of any good work, that the worker must be a believer in Christ. For make the tree good and then the fruit will. Be good. They must be people that have learned by the doctrine of the gospel to do a good work, as the words of the verse imply. COMMENTARY ON TITUS.[27]

EDUCATION IS ESSENTIAL TO CHRISTIAN CHARACTER AND SERVICE. MATTHIAS FLACIUS: [Paul] also teaches that Christians are not to be bereft of such virtues and benefits, but also that they be learned in the liberal arts which the common society of humanity has produced so that they would not be ignorant bellies and weighed down by the unprofitable things of the world. And it is in this way that I understand the prescribed works above in verse 8. For there he said that they believed in God. This here he says to us. And also, since in the manner of Zeno's jurisprudence by honestly treating the mention he makes, it can be plainly seen that he enjoins to younger Christians the study of law and other liberal arts with which

[24]CTS 43:341-42* (CO 52:435-436). †Aquinas, *Summa Theologiae* II-II, q. 39, a. 1, makes the distinction between schism and heresy, based on Augustine, *Contra Faustum* 20.3 and *Contra Crescon* 2.4.
[25]CRR 6:374*; citing Rom 16:17; 1 Cor 5:10; 1 Thess 5:14.
[26]Grotius, *Annotationes*, 7:337-38.
[27]Taylor, *A Commentarie*, 734*.

they might be able to become profitable and serve the common life of humanity. GLOSS ON TITUS[28]

LET OUR PASTORS LEARN TO DEVOTE THEM-SELVES TO GOOD WORKS. DAVID DICKSON: Titus is to instruct not only the faithful among the people, but also the preachers of the gospel, or those that are of the pastoral order, that they go before others in the communication of their goods and distributing according to necessity. The reason whereof is given: lest while they exhort others to good works, they themselves should be without fruit. EXPOSITION OF ALL PAUL'S EPISTLES.[29]

SALUTATIONS FROM OTHERS ARE AN EN-COURAGEMENT TO TITUS. THOMAS TAYLOR: "All who are with me send greetings." In these words our apostle would have Titus to know that all the Christians who were with him embraced him with all Christian and loving affection, and would have their mindfulness of him witnessed by a kind and familiar salutations. The use whereof was: (1) To testify their love toward him. (2) To knit the bond of it more firm and closely. (3) To encourage Titus in his godly course, when he should hear from the apostle's mouth that for the same all good people approved him and wished him all good proceedings. And hence we may note what is the use of this most ancient and approved custom of saluting one another by writing; namely, to signify a loving remembrance of the party saluted, with an earnest desire of their good and welfare. For that is a common affection to all salutations to signify such a desire. COMMENTARY ON TITUS.[30]

PAUL GREETS THOSE WHO LOVE HIM AND JESUS SINCERELY. MARTIN LUTHER: This is a gibe. Since the entire epistle was written to preserve godly Christians against ravenous wolves, he at least makes some distinction. Everyone, he says, loves us, but deceitfully and only in words. We do not want to be loved by those who despise Jesus, in whom and for the sake of whom we want to be loved, regardless of how much the heretics may flatter and pretend love, as the fanatics do. I do not want their love. In fact, of course, they do not love, but hate most ardently. Therefore we do not care, because they tread our Lord underfoot; he ought to be loved first of all, then we in Christ and for his sake. We have this epistle, which is brief but is filled with very good instruction and admonitions, so that there is almost nothing in the church that is not treated here. Let everyone see to it that he abides in the Christian message that Christ has been given for us, and in [works of] love that are not vain. LECTURES ON TITUS.[31]

PROVIDE FOR TRAVELERS AND GIVE ALMS. CARDINAL CAJETAN: Paul orders Titus to provide for travelers things that are necessary for the journey. "Moreover, let them learn." Here we read "your people" for "our people." Obviously this means those Christians who have been converted from the Gentiles, instructing them in the imitation of the Jews who cared for the needs of their teachers. "To excel in good works in instances of pressing need." Paul calls the giving of alms "good works," and he wants them to excel in almsgiving not for excess but for the pressing needs of guests and travelers. "That they not be unfruitful." They would be unfruitful if they did not offer as fruit alms for pressing needs. THE EPISTLES OF PAUL AND THE OTHER APOSTLES.[32]

SUBSTITUTE MINISTERS AND SUBSIDIZED TRAVEL. CASPAR CRUCIGER: See here how the apostle feared for himself, that somehow there would be no civility without both a faithful and discrete minister of God. By no means is he willing to invite Titus to himself, unless he replaces him with others who had also been put to the test. This industry is much to be desired today, lest many run off on account of another hope, that is, one of

[28]Flacius, *Glossa Compendaria*, 1097.
[29]Dickson, *Exposition*, 182*.
[30]Taylor, *A Commentarie*, 745-46*.

[31]LW 29:89 (WA 25:69); citing Mt 7:15.
[32]Cajetan, *Epistolae Pauli*, 155.

greater profit, having heedlessly abandoned their own affairs.

Let him assiduously conduct Zenas the lawyer and Apollos, so that they lack nothing. But let our people also learn to be preeminent in good works for doing what is needful, in order that they not be unfruitful. Travel should be subsidized from the church coffers, lest travelling teachers be in want, as far as necessity and not extravagance requires. The *pompē*, "conduct," of their guests was a most noble practice also among the gentiles. Homer's *Odyssey* contains many examples of this. For this reason he encourages the devout to be as generous as possible toward the treasury of the church, to be kept for the sake of its ministers, teachers, and its poor people. COMMENTARY ON 1 TIMOTHY.[33]

---

[33]Cruciger, *Commentarius*, 313-14.

COMMENTARY ON PHILEMON

1-7 INTRODUCTION TO PHILEMON AND PAUL'S GREETING

Paul, a prisoner for Christ Jesus, and Timothy our brother,

To Philemon our beloved fellow worker ²and Apphia our sister and Archippus our fellow soldier, and the church in your house:

³Grace to you and peace from God our Father and the Lord Jesus Christ.

⁴I thank my God always when I remember you in my prayers, ⁵because I hear of your love and of the faith that you have toward the Lord Jesus and for all the saints, ⁶and I pray that the sharing of your faith may become effective for the full knowledge of every good thing that is in us for the sake of Christ.ᵃ ⁷For I have derived much joy and comfort from your love, my brother, because the hearts of the saints have been refreshed through you.

a Or *for Christ's service*

OVERVIEW: In Paul's shortest letter, to Philemon, who was the owner of Onesimus, a runaway slave who had become a Christian, our commentators find much of value for their audiences. While modern exegetes reflect more readily on the institution of slavery, this was not a pressing issue in the sixteenth century. Instead, Paul's concern for a slave, a person of little significance in worldly terms, is emphasized, and this posture of mercy and love is given general application as a model and expectation for all Christians. The interpreters recognize Paul's address to Philemon as a fellow Christian, leading him to omit the references to his authority that commonly appear at the beginning of his letters. Paul's praise for Philemon's virtues is echoed by many of our commentators, although Luther provides a more critical reading, seeing Paul's kind words as preparation for his following request.

Introductory Comments

A GODLY EXAMPLE OF CHRISTIAN LOVE. WILLIAM TYNDALE: In this epistle St. Paul shows a godly example of Christian love. Herein we see how Paul takes poor Onesimus to him and makes intercession for him to his master and helps him with all that he may, and behaves as though he himself were the said Onesimus. Yet he does not do this with power and authority, as he well might have: but he puts off all authority and whatsoever he might by right do, so that Philemon might do likewise toward Onesimus, and with great meekness and wisdom he teaches Philemon to see his duty in Christ Jesus. THE PROLOGUE TO THE EPISTLE OF ST. PAUL UNTO PHILEMON.[1]

THE LOFTINESS OF THE MIND OF PAUL IN A SHORT LETTER. JOHN CALVIN: The singular

---

[1] *Tyndale's New Testament*, 323*.

loftiness of the mind of Paul, though it may be seen to greater advantage in his other writings that treat of weightier matters, is also attested by this epistle, in which, while he handles a subject otherwise low and mean, he rises to God with his wonted elevation. Sending back a runaway slave and thief, he asks pardon for him. But in pleading this cause, he speaks about Christian forbearance with such ability that he appears to speak about the interests of the whole church rather than the private affairs of a single individual. In behalf of a man of the lowest condition, he demeans himself so modestly and humbly that nowhere else is the meekness of his temper painted in a more lively manner. COMMENTARY ON PHILEMON.[2]

PHILEMON IN THE CANON FOR THE GOOD OF THE CHURCH. DAVID DICKSON: Philemon, one of the Colossian pastors, had a servant called Onesimus, who being guilty of theft came to Rome, and by the special providence of God, upon his hearing of Paul (who preached the gospel at Rome in bonds), he is converted to the faith. This Onesimus the apostle sends back to his master Philemon, and earnestly with many arguments pleads his pardon, that he might be received into favor; and because the Holy Ghost, in the business of Onesimus, would set forth an instance both of his divine love and of our duty toward penitent sinners, though of the meanest rank among human beings; therefore for the universal and perpetual edification of the church, God would admit this among other canonical epistles. THE EPISTLE OF PAUL TO PHILEMON.[3]

GOD'S CARE FOR THE CHURCH. VIKTORIN STRIGEL: All households ought to be domestic churches. And then under the care of God the universal church is dispersed over all the earth; thus there is no doubt that individual churches are divinely protected and preserved, just as were the families of Joseph, Mary, Zechariah, Anna, and Simeon, a flock having roamed bitterly to Judea, of which the mark was wantonness. ON THE LETTER TO PHILEMON.[4]

A PRIVATE AND DOMESTIC LETTER. MARTIN LUTHER: Paul cannot refrain from inculcating the general doctrine concerning Christ even here in treating a private matter. "In the faith." This is how he urges and insists in order to preserve this doctrine in the church. He reconciles a slave to his master in such a way that it seems that he will not accomplish anything. But you will see the outstanding doctrines, which Cicero did not see. We will set these forth diligently in order to see that one can say nothing so ordinary that Christ is not present. LECTURES ON PHILEMON.[5]

1-3 Greetings

TIMOTHY A COWORKER IN THE GOSPEL. DAVID DICKSON: Philemon had no doubt of Paul's apostleship. Therefore the apostle makes no mention of it, but of this bond which he accounted honorable for the gospel of Christ, he adjoins his brother Timothy to himself, as a partner in his request. First, he calls Philemon "Beloved," then his "fellow laborer," that is, in the preaching of the gospel, that he might make way for the reconciling of Philemon's mind. THE EPISTLE OF PAUL TO PHILEMON.[6]

TEACHERS ARE SOLDIERS IN AN ACUTE SENSE. JOHN CALVIN: Although the condition of a soldier belongs to all Christians universally, yet because teachers may be regarded as standard-bearers in the warfare, they ought to be ready more than all others to fight, and Satan usually gives them greater annoyance. It is also possible, that Archippus attended and shared in some contests that Paul maintained; and, indeed, this is the very word that Paul makes use of whenever he mentions persecutions. COMMENTARY ON PHILEMON.[7]

---

[2]CTS 43:347-48* (CO 52:441).
[3]Dickson, *Exposition*, 183.

[4]Strigel, *Omnes Libros Novi Testamenti*, 594* (pdf 772).
[5]LW 29:93; citing Titus 3:15.
[6]Dickson, *Exposition*, 183*.
[7]CTS 43:348-49 (CO 52:442).

PHILEMON ADVOCATES FOR ONESIMUS.
CARDINAL CAJETAN: Being about to ask for a
kindness for Onesimus, he begins with a remem-
brance, indeed, with a recognition of the services of
Philemon himself toward the faithfulness of Christ.
And therefore he mentions that he gives thanks to
God, and prays for Philemon. ON THE LETTER OF
PAUL TO PHILEMON.[8]

4-7 *Philemon's Love and Faith*

**PAUL'S FOUR ARGUMENTS IN THE OPENING OF
THE LETTER.** DAVID DICKSON: [First argument:]
He gives thanks for the gifts of the Holy Spirit
bestowed on Philemon, and also praises for the
increase of his gifts. . . . [Second argument:]
Particularly from the commendation of his faith in
Christ, and his love flowing therefrom toward all
people, especially toward the saints, which two
comprehend the whole perfection of a Christian
person, and this is the matter of his thanksgiving
for Philemon. [Third argument:] By way of prayer,
that his faith might show its efficacy in good fruits,
that to the honor of Christ, the sincere grace of
Christ abiding in him and his wife might be
known to all, and this is the matter of his prayer
for Philemon. [Fourth argument:] From the
rejoicing that he had in that Philemon was so
helpful to the necessity of the saints, that they all
acknowledged to be refreshed by him. THE
EPISTLE OF PAUL TO PHILEMON.[9]

ALWAYS GIVING THANKS TO GOD. JOHN
CALVIN: The arrangement of the passage is
somewhat confused; but there is no obscurity in
the meaning, except that it is doubtful whether the
adverb "always" is connected with the first clause, "I
give thanks always to my God," or with the second
clause, "making mention of you always in my
prayers." The meaning may be brought out in this
manner, that whenever the apostle offered prayer
for Philemon, he interwove thanksgiving with it;

that is, because Philemon's piety afforded ground
of rejoicing, for we often pray for those in whom
nothing is to be found but what gives occasion for
grief and tears. Yet the second mode of pointing is
generally preferred, that Paul "gives thanks for
Philemon, and always makes mention of him in his
prayers." Let my readers be at full liberty to judge
for themselves; but, for my own part, I think that
the former meaning is more appropriate. COM-
MENTARY ON PHILEMON.[10]

**WE SHOULD BE THANKFUL WHEN WE HEAR
THE WORD TRULY PREACHED.** MARTIN
LUTHER: "Because I hear [of your love and of the
faith that you have toward the Lord Jesus Christ
and all the saints]." This is Paul's general method of
arranging his epistles, to begin with thanksgiving.
But he adapts this rule to his purpose here, since
he wants to motivate Philemon to a good work.
Look at the individual words. "I thank my [God]
always." You know that these things are taught by
the felling that comes from the Holy Spirit himself.
For Paul had suffered from false prophets and had
heard that many were forsaking the faith and were
stirring up heresies and sects, just as is happening
to us. It is a rare thing to hear a preacher who is
constant in the Word. But if we hear one, this is a
cause for prayer and thanksgiving. The very nature
of the gospel or the Spirit produces this in us. So
we are trained by hearing evil everywhere to give
thanks when we hear something good. LECTURES
ON PHILEMON.[11]

FAITH AND LOVE ARE THE HIGHEST VIRTUES.
JOHANNES BRENZ: This is the praise from which
Paul seeks the benevolence of Philemon in order to
prepare the way for pleading with him on behalf of
his runaway slave. For Paul commends Philemon's
faith and love, saying, "I give thanks to my God
when I hear about your faith, which you have from
the Lord Jesus, and for your love which you have
for all the saints." However, Paul cannot commend

---

[8]Cajetan, *In Omnes*, 326 (pdf 333).
[9]Dickson, *Exposition*, 183.

[10]CTS 43:349-50 (CO 52:442).
[11]LW 29:95-96.

Philemon for greater and more excellent virtues. Neither could Philemon at any time do anything better, useful, or more greatly necessary than to believe or love. Some are wont to be commended for prudence, others for power, some for physical beauty, and others for good fortune. Heroes are commended for conspicuous deeds in war. Those who are commended for miracles which are produced. Others have a prophetic spirit for which they are commended. These, having such great praise and fame in the presence of people, have their own certain use in the church, but they are not those by which one stands in blessedness. Faith in Christ alone and love for neighbor are necessary for salvation. Whoever has these virtues can have all. Whoever lacks these virtues has none even though that person can have all other things. For first faith in Christ is the organ with which Christ is received and placed. Moreover, where Christ is, there is all righteousness, holiness, and salvation. For to whom Christ is given, how can it be that all good things do not come with it? Wherefore it is through faith that we are regarded as righteous before God and preserved. Furthermore it is by love for our neighbor that we serve our neighbor and conserve human society. It is therefore through love that we are regarded righteous before humanity. EXPLICATION ON PHILEMON.[12]

EFFECTIVE EVANGELISM. JOHN CALVIN: "That the communication of your faith may be effectual." This clause is somewhat obscure; but I shall endeavor to elucidate it in such a manner that my readers may somewhat understand Paul's meaning. First, it ought to be known that the apostle is not continuing to give the praise of Philemon, but that, on the contrary, he expresses those blessings for which he prays to God. These words are connected with what he had formerly said, that he "makes mention of him in his prayers." What blessing then did he ask for Philemon? That his faith, exercising itself by good works, might be proved to be true, and not unprofitable. He calls it "the communica-

tion of faith" because it does not remain inactive and concealed within, but is manifested to men by actual effects. Although faith has a hidden residence in the heart, yet it communicates itself to people by good works. It is, therefore, as if he had said, "That your faith, by communicating itself, may demonstrate its efficacy in every good thing." COMMENTARY ON PHILEMON.[13]

PAUL'S HEART IS FILLED, THUS HE SPEAKS ABOUT CHRIST. MARTIN LUTHER: Yesterday we dealt with the topic that Paul is fond of setting forth everywhere, so that he is not able to keep silence about it even in an epistle written about private matters. "Out of the abundance of the heart [the mouth speaks]." His heart is filled, and therefore he always speaks and writes about Christ. We do not find such things in the theologians after the apostles; nor do we find them among the other apostles. Our concern and entire light ought to be concentrated on this, that this knowledge may become firm. For this we need the Holy Spirit, to know what has been given to us, namely, salvation, righteousness, redemption from every evil, life eternal, a status as a brother of Christ, as a fellow heir of Christ, an heir of God. These things are expressed in short words; therefore the Holy Spirit is needed to make the knowledge grow. He always instructs about faith and redemption. LECTURES ON PHILEMON.[14]

PRAYER FOR SPIRITUAL GROWTH. MATTHIAS FLACIUS: Following this latter point: For this is the reason why he later prays so much for members: that his faith should be built up by the sharing of good works, so that he may bring other brothers and sisters to himself, and share his fruit. He also adds the final reason as to why he seeks it, to which he says that he makes known the gifts and operations of Jesus for his glory. Observe that the good works of the godly glorify Christ, and are to be brought about through him also as though he were

---

[12]Brenz, *Explicatio epistolarum*, 220.

[13]CTS 43:350-51 (CO 52:443).
[14]LW 29:97-98; citing Mt 12:34; Rom 8:17.

the fountain of all good things, who is the source of life, or the head, sprinkling all his own branches and members everywhere as depicted by the Holy Spirit in Scripture. GLOSS ON PHILEMON.[15]

PHILEMON PROVIDED RELIEF FOR THE GODLY.
JOHN CALVIN: "For your love." It is plain enough what he means: that he has great joy and consolation, because Philemon administered relief to the necessities of the godly. This was singular love, to feel so much joy on account of the benefit received by others. Besides, the apostle does not only speak of his personal joy, but says that many rejoiced on account of the kindness and benevolence with which Philemon had aided religious people. COMMENTARY ON PHILEMON.[16]

THE REFRESHING VIRTUES OF PHILEMON.
JOHANNES PISCATOR: An appropriate introduc-

tion to the benevolence to be acquired and to be maintained. For he testifies concerning Philemon's own benevolent works, and he praises his virtues. And he gives testimony to certain testimony by speaking of his deeds, which he might do for the sake of Philemon. Truly that he might do good things for with God for him, and he implores the same for himself, and continually. He expounds that matter of good deeds in verse 5 and thus also the works and strengths of Philemon he praises. For example, his faith in Christ, and his charity on account of the saints, truly the destitute and afflicted Christians. He expounds the matter of prayer in verse 6. For example, the faith of Philemon and the love through the sharing of duties, and so that his kindness might increase and be made known to all. In verse 7, he praises the charity and kindness of Philemon which has been demonstrated. COMMENTARY ON PHILEMON.[17]

---

[15]Flacius, *Glossa Compendaria*, 1099.
[16]CTS 43:351-52 (CO 52:443-44).

[17]Piscator, *Commentarii in Omnes Libros Novi Testamenti*, 672.

8-25 PAUL'S PLEA
ON BEHALF OF ONESIMUS

⁸Accordingly, though I am bold enough in Christ to command you to do what is required, ⁹yet for love's sake I prefer to appeal to you—I, Paul, an old man and now a prisoner also for Christ Jesus— ¹⁰I appeal to you for my child, Onesimus,ᵃ whose father I became in my imprisonment. ¹¹(Formerly he was useless to you, but now he is indeed useful to you and to me.) ¹²I am sending him back to you, sending my very heart. ¹³I would have been glad to keep him with me, in order that he might serve me on your behalf during my imprisonment for the gospel, ¹⁴but I preferred to do nothing without your consent in order that your goodness might not be by compulsion but of your own accord. ¹⁵For this perhaps is why he was parted from you for a while, that you might have him back forever, ¹⁶no longer as a bondservantᵇ but more than a bondservant, as a beloved brother—especially to me, but how much more to you, both in the flesh and in the Lord.

¹⁷So if you consider me your partner, receive him as you would receive me. ¹⁸If he has wronged you at all, or owes you anything, charge that to my account. ¹⁹I, Paul, write this with my own hand: I will repay it—to say nothing of your owing me even your own self. ²⁰Yes, brother, I want some benefit from you in the Lord. Refresh my heart in Christ.

²¹Confident of your obedience, I write to you, knowing that you will do even more than I say. ²²At the same time, prepare a guest room for me, for I am hoping that through your prayers I will be graciously given to you.

²³Epaphras, my fellow prisoner in Christ Jesus, sends greetings to you, ²⁴and so do Mark, Aristarchus, Demas, and Luke, my fellow workers.

²⁵The grace of the Lord Jesus Christ be with your spirit.

a *Onesimus* means *useful* (see verse 11) or *beneficial* (see verse 20)   b For the contextual rendering of the Greek word *doulos*, see Preface; twice in this verse

---

OVERVIEW: Paul's plea to Philemon on behalf of Onesimus makes up the heart of this brief epistle, and as the apostle lays out his reasoning, our commentators find much to discuss. Luther continues in his belief that Paul is flattering Philemon with the hope of ensuring a positive outcome, while others find Paul's appeals to be more genuine, based on his identification with Onesimus, the latter's newfound faith, and Paul's trust in Philemon to act mercifully as a fellow believer. Paul's personal assurances and the obligation he holds Philemon under as a Christian also draw significant comment, and they are generally seen by our interpreters as an opportunity to recognize the significance of fellowship and the importance of acting in consonance with our professed beliefs.

8-12 Paul's Appeal Based on Love

PAUL COMPARED TO THE POPE. MARTIN LUTHER: I do not want this to be a matter of obligation, but of entreaty. But I have also experienced how laws usually take away desires. A man is more easily drawn than pushed, and compulsion brings with it a rebellious will. A Christian, however, does not act that way. Nevertheless, Paul flatters him in such a sweet manner that even in addressing a Christian he avoids a domineering tone. To be sure, there is not this danger among Christians, for the matter proceeds in love and there is pure love in you, not compulsion. Therefore it is my wish that you do this out of love, not out of compulsion. . . . When did the pope and the other officials act this way, when do they humble themselves this way, as Paul becomes a young man with the young, an equal with equals? LECTURES ON PHILEMON.[1]

THE RIGHT OF APOSTLESHIP. DAVID DICKSON: [First argument:] By the right of an apostle I can command that which is thy duty. Therefore Onesimus is to be received into favor, when I shall have showed you your duty in this matter.

[Second argument:] Though I could command you I this matter, I would rather out of love to you lay aside commands and humbly request you. Therefore you ought to grant what I request touching Onesimus. [Third argument:] Though I ought to do that for Paul, now aged, and in bonds for Christ, which is acceptable to him, seeing he humbly requests of you that which is honest and may easily by done. Therefore you ought to grant what I require concerning Onesimus.

[Fourth argument:] My request is for Onesimus your servant, whom, while I lay in bonds, I have set at liberty from the bonds of Satan, by the gospel, to the faith of Christ, and whom I esteem no less than my own son. Therefore receive him.

[Fifth argument:] Although formerly before his conversation, Onesimus was unprofitable to you, hereafter he will prove a faithful and diligent servant in performing the duties of his condition.

[Sixth argument:] You shall refresh my heart if you courteously receive Onesimus, but if you do otherwise, you are discourteous toward me. THE FIRST EPISTLE OF PAUL TO THE THESSALONIANS.[2]

ONESEMUS LIVES UP TO HIS NAME. THE ENGLISH ANNOTATIONS: He evidently alludes to the name *honēsimus*, Onesimus, which in the Greek means "profitable." Wile he was a servant before and an unbeliever, he was contrary to his name; utterly unprofitable. But now, upon his conversion, he will make good and prove himself truly Onesimus, that is, profitable to you and to me. ANNOTATIONS ON PHILEMON 1:11.[3]

WHAT DOES IT MEAN TO BE BEGOTTEN BY ANOTHER PERSON? JOHN CALVIN: When he says that Onesimus has been "begotten" by him, this must be understood to mean that it was done by his ministry, and not by his power. To renew the soul of a man and form it anew to the image of God is not a human work, and it is of this spiritual regeneration that he now speaks. Yet because the soul is regenerated by faith, and "faith is by hearing," on that account he who administers the doctrine holds the place of a parent. Moreover, because the Word of God preached by human beings is the seed of eternal life, we need not wonder that he from whose mouth we receive that seed is called a father. Yet, at the same time, we must believe that while the ministry of a person is efficacious in regenerating the soul, yet, strictly speaking, God himself regenerates by the power of his Spirit. These modes of expression, therefore, do not imply any opposition between God and humankind, but only show what God does by means of human beings. When he says that he had "begotten him in his bonds," this circumstance adds weight to the commendation. COMMENTARY ON PHILEMON.[4]

TO RECEIVE ONESIMUS IS TO RECEIVE PAUL'S VERY HEART. JOHN CALVIN: "Receive him, that is, my heart." Nothing could have been more powerful for assuaging the wrath of Philemon; for if he had refused to forgive his slave, he would thus have used cruelty against "the heart" of Paul. This is remarkable kindness displayed by Paul, that he did not hesitate to receive, as it were into his heart, a contemptible slave, and thief, and runaway, so as to defend him from the indignation of his master. And, indeed, if the conversion of a person to God were estimated by us, at its proper value, we too would embrace in the same manner those who should give evidence that they had truly and sincerely repented. COMMENTARY ON PHILEMON.[5]

[1]LW 29:99.
[2]Dickson, *Exposition*, 183-84.
[3]Downame, ed., *Annotations*, 3M1r*.

[4]CTS 43:353-54* (CO 52:445); citing Rom 10:17.
[5]CTS 43:354 (CO 52:445).

THE POINT OF THE EPISTLE. MARTIN LUTHER: "I am sending him back." This is the [point] of the epistle. He is doing this to reconcile the slave to his master. He says, "I am simply sending him back. I do not ask that you grant him his freedom, but that he might return to the original servitude, so that he might serve you twice as well as he did before." You see that slavery is not being abrogated here. LECTURES ON PHILEMON.[6]

13-16 *Now, a Beloved Brother*

PAUL COMMENDS ONESIMUS. DAVID DICKSON: [Argument seven:] I have so great an opinion of Onesimus's faithfulness in his service that I should commit myself and affairs to his fidelity, and should make use of him, had I not rather obtain that courtesy upon your offer, than extort it upon any necessity.... [Argument eight:] You yourself, Philemon, are bound to minister to me in my bonds, in no way to refuse your servant again at my request, for your own proper benefit....

[Argument nine:] By the providence of God, Onesimus's running away for a time will turn to your advantage, by his constant abiding with you for the future.

[Tenth argument:] Onesimus will not return to you a servant only, but also a faithful brother in Christ, and therefore to be loved of you, as well according to the flesh, because your household servant, as in the Lord, because a Christian. For seeing I love him, though I make no use of him, how much more ought he to be loved by you, who are to receive the benefit of his fidelity. THE EPISTLE OF PAUL TO PHILEMON.[7]

THE DEFENSE OF THE GOSPEL BELONGS TO ALL. JOHN CALVIN: "That he might minister to me instead of you in the bonds of the gospel." He now mentions other circumstances: First, Onesimus will supply the place of his master, by performing this service; second, Paul himself, through modesty, was unwilling to deprive Philemon of his right; and third, Philemon will receive more applause if, after having had his slave restored to him, he shall willingly and generously send him back. From this last consideration we infer that we ought to aid the martyrs of Christ by every kind office in our power, while they are laboring for the testimony of the gospel; for if exile, imprisonment, stripes, blows, and violent seizing of our property are believed by us to belong to the gospel, as Paul here calls them, whoever refuses to share and partake of them separates himself even from Christ. Undoubtedly the defense of the gospel belongs alike to all. Accordingly, he who endures persecution for the sake of the gospel ought not to be regarded as a private individual, but as one who publicly represents the whole church. Hence it follows that all believers ought to be united in taking care of it, so that they may not, as is frequently done, leave the gospel to be defended by one person. COMMENTARY ON PHILEMON.[8]

A MINISTRY IN THE BONDS OF THE GOSPEL. MARTIN LUTHER: In addition "[in order that he might serve me on your behalf] during my imprisonment of the gospel." Such fine words! Is the gospel imprisoned? As though Christ and the gospel were imprisoned for my own sake; for it will redound to the glory of the gospel, for this expansion and dissemination. These are pure Hebraisms. Rejoice when Christ binds or has commanded to be bound. I am referring to imprisonment "for" or to the praise of the gospel. I need a ministry in the bonds of the gospel, through which you have been saved; therefore those bonds are precious in the sight of the Lord. I have a twofold obligation, you see. So do you, who are likewise in a most precious ministry, namely, in the cause of the gospel. Christ would have been satisfied with this. Therefore you should be also. Nevertheless I yield to you. LECTURES ON PHILEMON.[9]

---

[6]LW 29:101.
[7]Dickson, *Exposition*, 184.

[8]CTS 43:354-55 (CO 52:445-46).
[9]LW 29:101.

FREE WILL OF THE HUMAN BEING. BALTHASAR
HUBMAIER: "I wanted to keep Onesimus with me
so that he might serve me in your place in the
bonds of the gospel. However, without your will I
did not want to do anything so that your goodness
might be forced but voluntary." Whoever wants
should look at Jerome concerning these words,
though in themselves they testify more than clearly
about the free will of the human being. FREEDOM
OF THE WILL.[10]

THINGS DONE THROUGH MALICE HAVE BEEN
TURNED TO A DIFFERENT PURPOSE. JOHN
CALVIN: "For perhaps he was separated." If we are
angry on account of offenses committed by
human beings, our minds ought to be soothed,
when we perceive that those things which were
done through malice have been turned to a
different end by the purpose of God. A joyful
result may be regarded as a remedy for evils,
which is held out to us by the hand of God for
blotting out offenses. Thus Joseph—when he
takes into consideration that the wonderful
providence of God brought it about that though
he was sold as a slave, yet he was elevated to that
high rank, from which he could provide food for
his brethren and his father—forgets the treachery
and cruelty of his brothers, and says that he was
sent before on their account.

Paul therefore reminds Philemon that he ought
not to be so greatly offended at the flight of his
slave, for it was the cause of a benefit not to be
regretted. So long as Onesimus was at heart a
runaway, Philemon, though he had him in his
house, did not actually enjoy him as his property;
for he was wicked and unfaithful, and could not be
of real advantage. He says, therefore, that he was a
wanderer for a little time, that by changing his
place he might be converted and become a new
man. And he prudently softens everything by
calling the flight a departure, and adding that it was
only "for a time." COMMENTARY ON PHILEMON.[11]

ELECT OFTEN BROUGHT TO FAITH VIA
CIRCUITOUS ROUTES. JOHN CALVIN: "Especially
to me." Lest the heart of Onesimus, wounded by
the offense that was still fresh, should be reluctant
to admit the brotherly appellation, Paul claims
Onesimus first of all as his own "brother." Hence he
infers that Philemon is much more closely related
to him, because both of them had the same
relationship in the Lord according to the Spirit, but,
according to the flesh, Onesimus is a member of
his family. Here we behold the uncommon
modesty of Paul, who bestows on a worthless slave
the title of a brother, and even calls him a dearly
beloved brother to himself. And indeed, it would
be excessive pride if we should be ashamed of
acknowledging as our brother those whom God
accounts to be his sons.

"How much more to you." By these words he
does not mean that Philemon is higher in rank
according to the Spirit; but the meaning is, "Seeing
that he is especially a brother to me, he must be
much more so to you; for there is a twofold
relationship between you."

We must hold it to be an undoubted truth that
Paul does not rashly or lightly (as many people do)
answer for a man of whom he knows little, or extol
his faith before he has ascertained it by strong
proofs, and therefore in the person of Onesimus
there is exhibited a memorable example of repentance. We know how wicked the dispositions of
slaves were, so that scarcely one in a hundred ever
came to be of real use. As to Onesimus, we may
conjecture from his flight that he had been
hardened in depravity by long habit and practice. It
is therefore uncommon and wonderful virtue to lay
aside the vices by which his nature was polluted, so
that the apostle can truly declare that he has now
become another man.

From the same source proceeds a profitable
doctrine, that the elect of God are sometimes
brought to salvation by a method that could not
have been believed, contrary to general expectation,
by circuitous windings, and even by labyrinths.
Onesimus lived in a religious and holy family, and
being banished from it by his own evil actions, he

---

[10]CRR 5:463.
[11]CTS 43:356 (CO 52:446); citing Gen 45:5.

deliberately, as it were, withdraws far from God and from eternal life. Yet God, by hidden providence, wonderfully directs his pernicious flight, so that he meets with Paul. COMMENTARY ON PHILEMON[12]

17-22 Paul as a Partner in the Gospel

PAUL APPEALS TO PHILEMON. DAVID DICKSON: [Twelfth argument:] By way of an answer to an objection, the damage that you have sustained by his theft, whereby Onesimus has become a debtor, I Paul am ready to answer. In testimony of which, I will that you set to my account what Onesimus might have cost you; to that end, keep this epistle written with my own hand as an obligation. Therefore he is to be received again.

[Thirteenth argument:] You owe yourself to me, because converted by my ministry, and are bound to lay out yourself, and all you have, in my service, much more to receive a fugitive servant upon such equal terms. THE EPISTLE OF PAUL TO PHILEMON.[13]

PHILEMON ASKED TO NOT REQUIRE ANYTHING FROM ONESIMUS. JOHN CALVIN: There remains one question. How does Paul—who, if he had not been aided by the churches, did not have the means of living sparingly and frugally—promise to pay money? Amid such poverty and want this does certainly appear to be a ridiculous promise; but it is easy to see that, by this form of expression, Paul beseeches Philemon not to ask anything back from his slave. Though he does not speak ironically, yet, by an indirect figure, he requests him to blot out and cancel this account. The meaning, therefore, is—"I wish that you should not contend with your slave, unless you choose to have me for your debtor in his stead." For he immediately adds that Philemon is altogether his own; and he who claims the whole man as his property need not be uneasy about paying money. COMMENTARY ON PHILEMON.[14]

PHILEMON OWES PAUL HIS VERY LIFE. MARTIN LUTHER: What an exaggeration! This is how intensely Christian hearts feel. This is to be a special memorandum, and I want to put my seal upon it, so that you may have a testimony. Because we want to proceed in a completely legal manner, you ought to give me a free Onesimus to pay your debt. Nevertheless, you owe me your own self. If you demand your rights, I will do the same. You do not owe me your house, but yourself. My brother, let me enjoy you. Augustine says that a creature is not meant to be enjoyed but to be used.[†] This is the supreme argument. I want to find my consolation in you, that is, in you as a Christian, not in you as Philemon. LECTURES ON PHILEMON.[15]

PAUL EXPECTS THE FRUIT OF PHILEMON'S FAITH. DAVID DICKSON: I shall receive fruit of your faith in the Lord if you grant this to me: you shall refresh his heart and mine for Christ's sake. Therefore Onesimus ought to be received into favor. THE EPISTLE OF PAUL TO PHILEMON.[16]

THE QUESTION OF CIVIL GOVERNMENT AND PAUL'S PERSUASION. JOHN CALVIN: "Refresh my heart in the Lord." He again repeats the same form of expressions that he had previously employed. Hence we infer that the faith of the gospel does not overturn civil government, or set aside the power and authority that masters have over slaves. For Philemon was not a man of the ordinary rank, but a fellow laborer of Paul in cultivating Christ's vineyard; and yet that power over a slave which was permitted by the law is not taken away, but he is only commanded to receive him kindly by granting forgiveness, and is even humbly besought by Paul to restore him to his former condition.

When Paul pleads so humbly in behalf of another, we are reminded how far distant they are from true repentance who obstinately excuse their vices, or who without shame and without tokens of humility acknowledge indeed that they have sinned,

[12]CTS 43:357-58 (CO 52:446-47).
[13]Dickson, *Exposition*, 184*.
[14]CTS 43:358-59* (CO 52:446-47).

[15]LW 29:104. [†]Augustine, *Teaching Christianity* 1.22-23.
[16]Dickson, *Exposition*, 184*.

but in such a manner as if they had never sinned. When Onesimus saw so distinguished an apostle of Christ plead so eagerly in his behalf, he, must undoubtedly have been much more humbled, that he might bend the heart of his master to be merciful to him. To the same purpose is the excuse he offers for writing so boldly, because he knew that Philemon would do more than he had been requested. COMMENTARY ON PHILEMON.[17]

ALL CHRISTIANS NEED THE PRAYERS OF OTHERS. MARTIN LUTHER: Here again you see that although Paul is a saint and a "chosen instrument," nevertheless he everywhere requests prayers and support for himself and asks that others stand by him in battle. Thus every one of us needs the prayer of others even more, we who are conscious of being in the same Christ, but are far inferior to him. "Not only am I sending Onesimus, but you will have me as well." LECTURES ON PHILEMON.[18]

23-25 Final Greetings

DEMAS FORSAKES PAUL. JOHN CALVIN: This [i.e., Demas] is the same person who afterward forsook him, as he complains in the second epistle to Timothy. And if one of Paul's assistants, having become weary and discouraged, was afterward drawn aside by the vanity of the world, let no one reckon too confidently on the zeal of a single year; but considering how large a portion of the journey still remains to be accomplished, let him pray to God for steadfastness. COMMENTARY ON PHILEMON.[19]

PAUL'S COWORKERS SAFEGUARD THE GOSPEL AND CARE FOR THE CHURCHES. MARTIN LUTHER: Epaphras is the one who has established and given birth to the Colossians. . . . He was certainly a pious person and one who receives great praise from Paul. Mark, whom he once wanted to take along as a companion on his journey. Demas is still a man of sincere faith because he mentions Luke after him. This must have been shortly before [the apostasy of Demas], because Paul is already in prison. He was a great man, since he is mentioned before Luke, who is a great man in preaching, expounding, and writing the Gospel. As long as the Roman Empire stood, there was completely free passage throughout the world. Therefore he had many such with him, to see to it that nothing evil [befell the gospel]. They were his messengers and visitors. Timothy, Titus, Crescens, and Luke had to run in order to resist the false prophets and to see Philemon and Archippus. Thus we have a private epistle from which much should be learned about how the brethren are to be commended, that is, that an example might be provided to the church how we ought to take care of those who fall and restore those who err, for the kingdom of Christ is a kingdom of mercy and grace, while the kingdom of Satan is a kingdom of murder, error, darkness, and lies. LECTURE ON PHILEMON 23-25.[20]

PERSEVERING GRACE GIVEN BY GOD. HEINRICH BULLINGER: Rightly Jerome believed therefore that the apostle mentioned hospitality since he expected that what he had asked might soon take place. But in fact he needed faithfully to trust in his prayers, which certainly in the presence of the Lord were efficacious. Elsewhere mention was made of those of which here he remembered—of these illustrious men. Demas had not yet defected [from the faith]. The Lord granted to all faithful men a strong spirit, and thus therefore revived, they might persevere in gospel profession all the way to the end. Amen. COMMENTARY ON PHILEMON.[21]

---

[17]CTS 43:359-60 (CO 52:448).
[18]LW 19:104-5; citing Acts 9:15.
[19]CTS 43:360-61 (CO 52:450); citing 2 Tim 4:10.

[20]LW 29:105* (WA 25:78); citing Col 1:7; 4:12; 4:10; 2 Tim 4:10.
[21]Bullinger, *Ad Philemenon*, 236.

Map of Europe at the Time of the Reformation

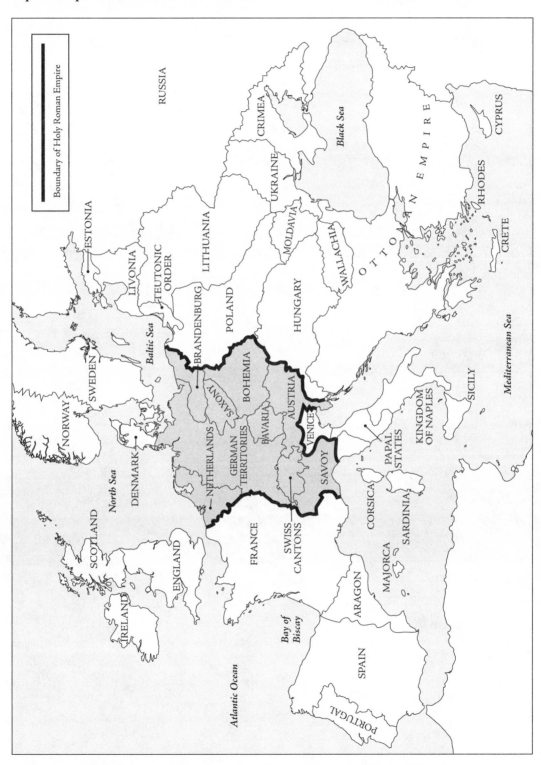

Timeline of the Reformation

	German Territories	France	Spain	Italy	Switzerland	Netherlands	British Isles
1309–1377		Babylonian Captivity of the Papacy					
1337–1453		d. Nicholas of Lyra Hundred Years' War	b. Paul of Burgos (Solomon ha-Levi)(d. 1435) Alonso Tostado (1400–1455)				Hundred Years' War
1378–1415		Western Schism (Avignon Papacy)		Western Schism			
1384							d. John Wycliffe
1414–1418					Council of Basel (1431–1437)		
1415				Council of Constance; d. Jan Hus; Martin V (r. 1417–1431); Council of Florence (1438–1445)			
1450	Invention of printing press						
1452				b. Leonardo da Vinci (d. 1519)			
1453				Fall of Constantinople			
1455–1485	b. Johannes Reuchlin (d. 1522)						War of Roses; rise of House of Tudor
1456	Gutenberg Bible						
1460				Pope Pius II issued *Execrabilis*			
1466		b. Jacques Lefèvre d'Étaples (d. 1536)					
1467						b. Desiderius Erasmus (d. 1536)	b. John Colet (d. 1519)
1469	b. Antoius Broickwy von Königstein (d. 541)						
1470				b. Santes Pagninus (d. 1541)			b. John (Mair) Major (d. 1550)
1475				b. Michelangelo (d. 1564)			
1478	b. Wolfgang Capito (d. 1541)		Ferdinand and Isabella	b. Jacopo Sadoleto (d. 1547)			b. Thomas More (d. 1535)

	German Territories	France	Spain	Italy	Switzerland	Netherlands	British Isles
1480	b. Balthasar Hubmaier (d. 1528); b. Andreas Bodenstein von Karlstadt (d. 1541)						
1481–1530			Spanish Inquisition				
1482					b. Johannes Oecolampadius (d. 1531)		
1483	b. Martin Luther (d. 1546)						
1484	b. Johann Spangenberg (d. 1550)				b. Huldrych Zwingli (d. 1531)		
1485	b. Johannes Bugenhagen (d. 1554)						b. Hugh Latimer (d. 1555)
1486	r. Frederick the Wise, Elector (d. 1525); b. Johann Eck (d. 1543)						
1488	b. Otto Brunfels (d. 1534)						b. Miles Coverdale (d. 1568)
1489	b. Thomas Müntzer (d. 1525); b. Kaspar von Schwenckfeld (d. 1561)						b. Thomas Cranmer (d. 1556)
1491	b. Martin Bucer (d. 1551)		b. Ignatius Loyola (d. 1556)				
1492			Defeat of Moors in Grenada; Columbus discovers America; expulsion of Jews from Spain	Alexander VI (r. 1492–1503)			
1493	b. Justus Jonas (d. 1555)						
1494							b. William Tyndale (d. 1536)
1496	b. Andreas Osiander (d. 1552)					b. Menno Simons (d. 1561)	
1497	b. Philipp Melanchthon (d. 1560); b. Wolfgang Musculus (d. 1563) b. Johannes (Ferus) Wild (d. 1554)						

	German Territories	France	Spain	Italy	Switzerland	Netherlands	British Isles
1498				d. Girolamo Savonarola	b. Conrad Grebel (d. 1526)		
1499	b. Johannes Brenz (d. 1570) b. Justus Menius (d. 1558)			b. Peter Martyr Vermigli (d. 1562)			
1500			b. Charles V (–1558)				
1501	b. Erasmus Sarcerius (d. 1559)						
1502	Founding of University of Wittenberg			Julius II (r. 1503–1513)		b. Frans Titelmans (d. 1537)	
1504					b. Heinrich Bullinger (d. 1575)		
1505	Luther joins Augustinian Order			b. Benedict Aretius (d. 1574)			
1506		b. Augustin Marlorat (d. 1562)		Restoration of St. Peter's begins			
1507				Sale of indulgences approved to fund building			
1508	b. Lucas Lossius (d. 1582)						
1509		b. John Calvin (d. 1564)					r. Henry VIII (–1547)
1510	Luther moves to Rome			b. Immanuel Tremellius (d. 1580)			b. Nicholas Ridley (d. 1555)
1511	Luther moves to Wittenberg						
1512				Sistine Chapel completed			
1512–1517				Fifth Lateran Council; rejection of conciliarism			
1513	Luther lectures on Psalms			r. Pope Leo X (–1521)			b. John Knox (d. 1572)
1515	Luther lectures on Romans	r. Francis I (–1547); b. Peter Ramus (d. 1572)					
1516		Est. French National Church (via Concordat of Bologna)		Concordat of Bologna		Publication of Erasmus's Greek New Testament	
1517	Tetzel sells indulgences in Saxony; Luther's Ninety-five Theses						

	German Territories	France	Spain	Italy	Switzerland	Netherlands	British Isles
1518	Heidelberg Disputation; Luther examined by Cajetan at Diet of Augsburg			Diet of Augsburg			
1519	Leipzig Disputation	b. Theodore Beza (d. 1605)	Cortés conquers Aztecs; Portuguese sailor Magellan circumnavigates the globe		Zwingli appointed pastor of Grossmünster in Zurich; b. Rudolf Gwalther (d. 1586)		
1520	Publication of Luther's "Three Treatises"; burning of papal bull in Wittenberg		Coronation of Charles V	Papal Bull v. Luther: *Exsurge Domine*			
1521	Luther excommunicated; Diet/Edict of Worms—Luther condemned; Luther in hiding; Melanchthon's *Loci communes*	French-Spanish War (–1526)	French-Spanish War; Loyola converts	Papal excommunication of Luther			Henry VIII publishes *Affirmation of the Seven Sacraments* against Luther; awarded title "Defender of the Faith" by Pope
1521–1522	Disorder in Wittenberg; Luther translates New Testament						
1521–1525		First and Second Habsburg–Valois War					
1522	Luther returns to Wittenberg; Luther's NT published; criticizes Zwickau prophets; b. Martin Chemnitz (d. 1586)		Publication of Complutensian Polyglot Bible under Cisneros		Sausage Affair and reform begins in Zurich under Zwingli		b. John Jewel (d. 1571)
1523	Knight's Revolt	Bucer begins ministry in Strasbourg	Loyola writes Spiritual Exercises	r. Pope Clement VII (–1534)	Iconoclasm in Zurich		
1524	Luther criticizes peasants; d. Johann von Staupitz					Erasmus's disputation on free will	
1524–1526	Peasants' War						
1525	Luther marries; execution of Thomas Müntzer; publication of Luther's *Bondage of the Will*				Abolition of mass in Zurich; disputation on baptism; first believers' baptism performed in Zurich		

	German Territories	France	Spain	Italy	Switzerland	Netherlands	British Isles
1526					Zurich council mandates capital punishment of Anabaptists	Publication of Tyndale's English translation of NT	
1527	d. Hans Denck (b. c. 1500) d. Hans Hut (b. 1490) b. Tilemann Hesshus (d. 1588)			Sack of Rome by mutinous troops of Charles V	First Anabaptist executed in Zurich; drafting of Schleitheim Confession		
1528	Execution of Hubmaier						
1529	Second Diet of Speyer; evangelical "protest"; publication of Luther's catechisms; Marburg Colloquy; siege of Vienna by Turkish forces	Abolition of mass in Strasbourg			d. Georg Blaurock (b. 1492)		Thomas More appointed chancellor to Henry VIII
1530	Diet of Augsburg; Confession of Augsburg	d. Francois Lambert (Lambert of Avignon) (b. 1487)	Charles V crowned Holy Roman Emperor				
1531	Formation of Schmalkaldic League				d. H. Zwingli; succeeded by H. Bullinger		
1532		Publication of Calvin's commentary on Seneca; conversion of Calvin	b. Francisco de Toledo (d. 1596)				
1533	b. Valentein Weigel (d. 1588)	Nicholas Cop addresses University of Paris; Cop and Calvin implicated as "Lutheran" sympathizers	b. Juan de Maldonado (d. 1583)				Thomas Cranmer appointed as Archbishop of Canterbury; Henry VIII divorces
1534	First edition of Luther's Bible published	Affair of the Placards; Calvin flees d. Guillame Briçonnet (b. 1470)		Jesuits founded; d. Cardinal Cajetan (Thomas de Vio) (b. 1469)			Act of Supremacy; English church breaks with Rome
1535	Bohemian Confession of 1535; Anabaptist theocracy at Münster collapses after eighteen months				b. Lambert Daneau (d. 1595)		d. Thomas More; d. John Fisher

	German Territories	France	Spain	Italy	Switzerland	Netherlands	British Isles
1536	Wittenberg Concord; b. Kaspar Olevianus (d. 1587)				First edition of Calvin's *Institutes* published; Calvin arrives in Geneva (–1538); First Helvetic Confession	Publication of Tyndale's translation of NT; d. W. Tyndale	d. A. Boleyn; Henry VIII dissolves monasteries (–1541)
1537					Calvin presents ecclesiastical ordinances to Genevan Council		
1538					Calvin exiled from Geneva; arrives in Strasbourg (–1541)		
1539		Calvin publishes second edition of *Institutes* in Strasbourg		d. Felix Pratensis			Statute of Six Articles; publication of Coverdale's Great Bible
1540				Papal approval of Jesuit order			d. Thomas Cromwell
1541	Colloquy of Regensburg	French translation of Calvin's *Institutes* published	d. Juan de Valdés (b. 1500/1510)		d. A. Karlstadt; Calvin returns to Geneva (–1564)		
1542	d. Sebastian Franck (b. 1499)			Institution of Roman Inquisition			War between England and Scotland; James V of Scotland defeated; Ireland declared sovereign kingdom
1543	Copernicus publishes *On the Revolutions of the Heavenly Spheres*; d. Johann Eck (Johann Maier of Eck) (b. 1486)						
1545–1547	Schmalkaldic Wars; d. Martin Luther			First session of Council of Trent			b. Richard Bancroft (d. 1610)
1546	b. Johannes Piscator (d. 1625)						
1547	Defeat of Protestants at Mühlberg	d. Francis I; r. Henri II (–1559)					d. Henry VIII; r. Edward VI (–1553)
1548	Augsburg Interim (–1552) d. Caspar Cruciger (b. 1504) b. David Pareus (d. 1622)						

	German Territories	France	Spain	Italy	Switzerland	Netherlands	British Isles
1549	d. Paul Fagius (b. 1504)	d. Marguerite d'Angoulême (b. 1492)			Consensus Tigurinus between Calvin and Bullinger		First Book of Common Prayer published
1550	b. Aegidius Hunnius (d. 1603)						
1551–1552				Second session of Council of Trent			
1552	d. Sebastian Münster (b. 1488) d. Friedrich Nausea (b. c. 1496)						Book of Common Prayer revised
1553	d. Johannes Aepinus (b. 1449)				Michael Servetus executed in Geneva		Cranmer's Forty-Two Articles; d. Edward VI; r. Mary I (d. 1558)
1554							Richard Hooker (d. 1600)
1555	Diet of Augsburg; Peace of Augsburg establishes legal territorial existence of Lutheranism and Catholicism b. Johann Arndt (d. 1621)	First mission of French pastors trained in Geneva				b. Sibbrandus Lubbertus (d. 1625)	b. Lancelot Andrewes (d. 1626) b. Robert Rollock (d. 1599); d. Hugh Latimer; d. Nicholas Ridley d. John Hooper
1556	d. Pilgram Marpeck (b. 1495) d. Konrad Pellikan (b. 1478) d. Peter Riedemann (b. 1506)		Charles V resigns			d. David Joris (b. c. 1501)	d. Thomas Cranmer
1557							Alliance with Spain in war against France
1558			d. Charles V				b. William Perkins (d. 1602); d. Mary I; r. Elizabeth I (–1603)
1559		d. Henry II; r. Francis II (–1560); first national synod of French reformed churches (1559) in Paris; Gallic Confession		First index of prohibited books issued	Final edition of Calvin's *Institutes*; founding of Genevan Academy	b. Jacobus Arminius (d. 1609)	Elizabethan Settlement

	German Territories	France	Spain	Italy	Switzerland	Netherlands	British Isles
1560	d. P. Melanchthon	d. Francis II; r. Charles IX (1574); Edict of Toleration created peace with Huguenots	d. Domingo de Soto (b. 1494)		Geneva Bible		Kirk of Scotland established; Scottish Confession
1561-1563				Third session of Council of Trent			
1561						Belgic Confession	
1562	d. Katharina Schütz Zell (b. 1497/98)	Massacre of Huguenots begins French Wars of Religion (–1598)					The Articles of Religion—in Elizabethan "final" form (1562/71); publication of Latin edition of Jewel's *Apology*
1563	Heidelberg Catechism						
1564				b. Galileo (d. 1642)	d. J. Calvin		b. William Shakespeare (d. 1616); publication of Lady Ann Bacon's English translation of Jewel's *Apology*
1566	d. Johann Agricola (b. 1494)			Roman Catechism	Second Helvetic Confession		
1567						Spanish occupation	Abdication of Scottish throne by Mary Stuart; r. James VI (1603–1625)
1568						d. Dirk Phillips (b. 1504) Dutch movement for liberation (–1645)	*Bishops' Bible*
1570		d. Johannes Mercerus (Jean Mercier)		Papal Bull *Regnans in Excelsis* excommunicates Elizabeth I			Elizabeth I excommunicated
1571	b. Johannes Kepler (d. 1630)		Spain defeats Ottoman navy at Battle of Lepanto				b. John Downame (d. 1652)
1572		Massacre of Huguenots on St. Bartholomew's Day		r. Pope Gregory XIII (1583–1585)		William of Orange invades	b. John Donne (d. 1631)
1574		d. Charles IX; r. Henri III (d. 1589)					

	German Territories	France	Spain	Italy	Switzerland	Netherlands	British Isles
1575	d. Georg Major (b. 1502); Bohemian Confession of 1575						
1576		Declaration of Toleration; formation of Catholic League		b. Giovanni Diodati (d. 1649)		Sack of Antwerp; Pacification of Ghent	
1577	Lutheran Formula of Concord						England allies with Netherlands against Spain
1578	Swiss Brethren Confession of Hesse d. Peter Walpot	Truce with Ottomans					Sir Francis Drake circumnavigates the globe
1579			Expeditions to Ireland			Division of Dutch provinces	
1580	Lutheran Book of Concord						
1581			d. Teresa of Avila				Anti-Catholic statutes passed
1582				Gregorian Reform of calendar			
1583							b. David Dickson (d. 1663)
1584		Treaty of Joinville with Spain	Treaty of Joinville; Spain inducted into Catholic League; defeats Dutch at Antwerp			Fall of Antwerp; d. William of Orange	
1585	d. Josua Opitz (b. c. 1542)	Henri of Navarre excommunicated		r. Pope Sixtus V (–1590)			
1586							Sir Francis Drake's expedition to West Indies; Sir Walter Raleigh in Roanoke
1587	d. Johann Wigand (b. 1523)	Henri of Navarre defeats royal army					d. Mary Stuart of Scotland
1588		Henri of Navarre drives Henri III from Paris; assassination of Catholic League Leaders	Armada destroyed				English Navy defeats Spanish Armada
1589		d. Henri III; r. Henri (of Navarre) IV (–1610)	Victory over England at Lisbon				Defeated by Spain in Lisbon
1590		Henri IV's siege of Paris		d. Girolamo Zanchi (b. 1516)			Alliance with Henri IV

	German Territories	France	Spain	Italy	Switzerland	Netherlands	British Isles
1592	d. Nikolaus Selnecker (b. 1530)						
1593		Henri IV converts to Catholicism					Books I-IV of Hooker's *Laws of Ecclesiastical Polity* published
1594		Henri grants toleration to Huguenots					
1595		Henri IV declares war on Spain; received into Catholic Church		Pope Sixtus accepts Henri IV into Church			Alliance with France
1596		b. René Descartes (d. 1650) b. Moïse Amyraut (d. 1664)					
1597							Book V of Hooker's *Laws of Ecclesiastical Polity* published
1598		Edict of Nantes; toleration of Huguenots; peace with Spain	Treaty of Vervins; peace with France				
1600	d. David Chytraeus (b. 1531)						
1601							b. John Trapp (d. 1669)
1602					d. Daniel Toussain (b. 1541)		
1603							d. Elizabeth I; r. James I (James VI of Scotland) (–1625)
1604	d. Cyriacus Spangenberg (b. 1528)						d. John Whitgift (b. 1530)
1605						b. Rembrandt (d. 1669)	Guy Fawkes and gunpowder plot
1606							Jamestown Settlement
1607							b. John Milton (d. 1674)
1608							
1610		d. Henri IV; r. Louis XIII (–1643)	d. Benedict Pererius (b. 1535)			The Remonstrance; Short Confession	

	German Territories	France	Spain	Italy	Switzerland	Netherlands	British Isles
1611							Publication of Authorized English Translation of Bible (AV/KJV); George Abbot becomes Archbishop of Canterbury (–1633)
1612							b. Richard Crashaw (d. 1649)
1616							b. John Owen (d. 1683)
1617							b. Ralph Cudworth (d. 1689)
1618–1619						Synod of Dordrecht	
1618–1648	Thirty Years' War						
1620							English Sepratists land in Plymouth, Massachusetts
1621							d. Andrew Willet (b. 1562)
1628							Puritans establish Massachusetts Bay colony
1633	d. Christoph Pelargus (b. 1565)						Laud becomes Archbishop of Canterbury
1637	d. Johann Gerhard (b. 1582)					*Statenvertaling*	
1638							d. Joseph Mede (b. 1638)
1640				Diodati's Italian translation of Bible published			
1642–1649							English civil wars; d. Charles I; r. Oliver Cromwell (1660)
1643		d. Louis XIII; r. Louis XIV (–1715)					
1643–1649							Westminster Assembly
1645							d. William Laud (b. 1573)

	German Territories	France	Spain	Italy	Switzerland	Netherlands	British Isles
1648		Treaty of Westphalia ends Thirty Years' War					Books VI and VIII of Hooker's *Laws of Ecclesiastical Polity* posthumously published
1656	d. Georg Calixtus (b. 1586)						
1658							d. Oliver Cromwell
1659							Richard Cromwell resigns
1660							English Restoration; r. Charles II (–1685)
1662							Act of Uniformity; Book VII of Hooker's *Laws of Ecclesiastical Polity* posthumously published
1664						d. Thieleman Jans van Braght (b. 1625)	d. John Mayer (b. 1583)
1671							d. William Greenhill (b. 1591)
1677							d. Thomas Manton (b. 1620)
1678						d. Anna Maria von Schurman (b. 1607)	
1688							Glorious Revolution; r. William and Mary (-1702); d. John Bunyan (b. 1628)
1691							d. Richard Baxter (b. 1615)

BIOGRAPHICAL SKETCHES OF

REFORMATION-ERA FIGURES AND WORKS

This list is cumulative, including all the authors cited in the Reformation Commentary on Scripture
to date as well as other people relevant to the Reformation and Reformation-era exegesis.
For works consulted, see "Sources for Biographical Sketches," p. 403.

Cornelius À Lapide (1567–1637). Flemish biblical exegete. A Jesuit, Lapide served as professor of Holy Scripture and Hebrew at Louvain for twenty years before taking a similar role in Rome, where he taught until his death. He is best known for his extensive commentaries on the Scriptures. Encompassing all books of the Bible except Job and the Psalms, his work employs a fourfold hermeneutic and draws heavily on the work of patristic and medieval exegetes.

Thomas Adams (1583–1653). Anglican minister and author. He attended the University of Cambridge where he received his BA in 1601 and his MA in 1606. Following his ordination in 1604, Adams served as curate at Northill in Bedfordshire. In 1611, he became vicar of Willmington. Three years later he served the parish of Wingrave, Buckinghamshire, where he remained until 1618. From 1618 to 1623 Adams was preacher at St. Gregory by St. Paul's. He also served as chaplain to Henry Montague, First Earl of Manchester, and Lord Chief Justice of England. Among his most important works are the *Happiness of the Church* (1618) and an extensive commentary on 2 Peter (1638).

Johannes Aepinus (1499–1553). German Lutheran preacher and theologian. Aepinus studied under Martin Luther,* Philipp Melanchthon* and Johannes Bugenhagen* in Wittenberg. Because of

his Lutheran beliefs, Aepinus lost his first teaching position in Brandenburg. He fled north to Stralsund and became a preacher and superintendent at Saint Peter's Church in Hamburg. In 1534, he made a diplomatic visit to England but could not convince Henry VIII* to embrace the Augsburg Confession.* His works include sermons and theological writings. Aepinus became best known as leader of the Infernalists, who believed that Christ underwent torment in hell after his crucifixion.

Johann Agricola (c. 1494–1566). German Lutheran pastor and theologian. An early student of Martin Luther,* Agricola eventually began a controversy over the role of the law, first with Melanchthon* and then with Luther himself. Agricola claimed to defend Luther's true position, asserting that only the gospel of the crucified Christ calls Christians to truly good works, not the fear of the law. After this first controversy, Agricola seems to have radicalized his views to the point that he eliminated Luther's *simul iustus et peccator* ("at the same time righteous and sinful") paradox of the Christian life, emphasizing instead that believers have no need for the law once they are united with Christ through faith. Luther responded by writing anonymous pamphlets against antinomianism. Agricola later published a recantation of his views, hoping to assuage relations with Luther, although they were never personally reconciled. He published a commentary on Luke, a series of sermons on Colossians, and a massive collection of German proverbs.

Henry Ainsworth (1571–1622/1623). English Puritan Hebraist. In 1593, under threat of persecution, Ainsworth relocated to Amsterdam, where he served as a teacher in an English congregation. He composed a confession of faith for the community and a number of polemical and exegetical works, including annotations on the Pentateuch, the Psalms and Song of Songs.

Henry Airay (c. 1560–1616). English Puritan professor and pastor. He was especially noted for his preaching, a blend of hostility toward Catholicism and articulate exposition of English Calvinism. He was promoted to provost of Queen's College Oxford (1598) and then to vice chancellor of the university in 1606. He disputed with William Laud* concerning Laud's putative Catholicization of the Church of England, particularly over the practice of genuflection, which Airay vehemently opposed. He also opposed fellow Puritans who wished to separate from the Church of England. His lectures on Philippians were his only work published during his lifetime.

Albert the Great (1201–1280). German theologian, philosopher, scientist, and ecclesiastic. Albert was born in Lauingen, located in the Bavarian-Swabian region. After completing his studies at Padua, Albert joined the Dominicans in 1220s. Upon finishing further theological studies at Cologne, Albert became a conventual lecturer during the 1230s at Hildesheim, Freiberg (Saxony), Regensburg, and Strasbourg. In the early 1240s, Albert was sent to Paris where he became a master of theology, and regent of the university in 1245. He served as regent until 1248. While at Paris, Albert commenced his paraphrases of Aristotle's works. Furthermore, Albert authored a systematic theology, and lectured on the four Gospels and nine books of the Old Testament. Albert is best known for having taught Thomas Aquinas,* who, as his assistant, transcribed his course on the works of Dionysius and Aristotle's *Nicomachean Ethics*.

Alexander (Ales) Alesius (1500–1565). Scottish Lutheran theologian. Following the martyrdom of his theological adversary Patrick Hamilton (c. 1504–1528), Alesius converted to the Reformation and fled to Germany. In 1535 Martin Luther* and Philipp Melanchthon* sent him as an emissary to Henry VIII* and Thomas Cranmer.* He taught briefly at Cambridge, but after the Act of Six Articles reasserted Catholic sacramental theology he returned to Germany, where he lectured at Frankfurt an der Oder and Leipzig. Alesius composed many exegetical, theological and polemical works, including commentaries on John, Romans, 1–2 Timothy, Titus and the Psalms.

Andreas Althamer (c. 1500–1539). German Lutheran humanist and pastor. Forced from the chaplaincy at Schwäbisch-Gmünd for teaching evangelical ideas, Althamer studied theology at Wittenberg before serving as a pastor in Eltersdorf, Nuremberg, and Ansbach. A staunch Lutheran, he contended against Reformed theologians at the 1528 disputation at Bern and delivered numerous polemics against Anabaptism. He also composed an early Lutheran catechism, published at Nuremberg in 1528.

William Ames (1576–1633). English Puritan theologian. Heavily influenced by William Perkins* while at Cambridge, Ames was unable to find employment in the English church due to his Puritan commitments. Most of his life was spent in exile in the Netherlands, where he served as chaplain to English forces at The Hague and was the pastor of a small congregation. Best known as a controversialist during his early career, Ames was the theological advisor to the president of the Synod of Dort (1618–1619) and was later installed as chair of theology at the University of Franeker in Friesland. *The Marrow of Theology* (1627) is viewed as a model of seventeenth-century Puritan theology.

Moïse Amyraut (1596–1664). French Reformed pastor and professor. Originally intending to be a lawyer, Amyraut turned to theology after an encounter with several Huguenot pastors and having read Calvin's* *Institutes*. After a brief stint as a parish pastor, Amyraut spent the majority of his career at the Saumur Academy. He was well known for his irenicism and ecumenicism (for example, in advocating intercommunion with Lutherans). Certain aspects of his writings on justification, faith, the covenants and especially predestination proved controversial among the Reformed. His doctrine of election is often called hypothetical universalism or Amyraldianism, stating that Christ's atoning work was intended by God for all human beings indiscriminately, although its effectiveness for salvation depends on faith, which is a free gift of God given only to those whom God has chosen from eternity. Amyraut was charged with grave doctrinal error three times before the National Synod but was acquitted each time. Aside from his theological treatises, Amyraut published paraphrases of almost the entire New Testament and the Psalms, as well as many sermons.

Anabaptists of Trieste (1539). Following a meeting between Swiss Brethren and the Hutterites at Steinabrunn on December 6, 1536, around 140 radicals were arrested and imprisoned in Falkenstein Castle. After six weeks in captivity, the ninety men of the group were forced to march to Trieste to be sold as galley slaves. Twelve days after arrival, all but twelve prisoners managed to escape and return to Moravia, where they published a confession of their beliefs.

Jakob Andreae (1528–1590). German Lutheran theologian. Andreae studied at the University of Tübingen before being called to the diaconate in Stuttgart in 1546. He was appointed ecclesiastical superintendent of Göppingen in 1553 and supported Johannes Brenz's* proposal to place the church under civil administrative control. An ecclesial diplomat for the duke of Württemberg, Andreae debated eucharistic theology, the use of images, and predestination with Theodore Beza* at the Colloquy of Montbéliard (1586) to determine whether French Reformed exiles would be required to submit to the Formula of Concord.* Andreae coauthored the Formula of Concord. He and his wife had eighteen children.

Lancelot Andrewes (1555–1626). Anglican bishop. A scholar, pastor and preacher, Andrews

prominently shaped a distinctly Anglican identity between the poles of Puritanism and Catholicism. He oversaw the translation of Genesis to 2 Kings for the Authorized Version.* His eight-volume collected works—primarily devotional tracts and sermons—are marked by his fluency in Scripture, the Christian tradition and classical literature.

Thomas Aquinas (1225–1274). Dominican medieval theologian. Thomas Aquinas was born into a noble family in Rocasecca, Italy. In 1230 Thomas's father sent him to the abbey at Monte Casino as a child oblate. When, at age fourteen, Thomas was given the choice between taking his final vows and leaving, he chose to go to Naples to study at the school recently founded by the Holy Roman Emperor. While studying at Naples, Thomas came into contact with the Dominicans, and joined this order in 1244. Although his family objected to his decision at first, to the point of actually imprisoning Thomas, they came to accept his decision the following year. Afterwards, Aquinas traveled to Paris where he began his formal studies under Albert the Great (1200–1280). Aquinas followed his teacher to Cologne in 1248 where he was ordained a priest, and completed his course in theology. Four years later, he was appointed a bachelor in the Dominican convent in Paris where he lectured on Peter Lombard's (1096–1160)* Sentences. In 1256, Thomas was incepted as a master of the sacred page, and he taught in Paris until 1259. In 1261, he was appointed lecturer at a school in Orvieto. Four years later, Aquinas was transferred to Rome, and in 1268 returned to Paris. In 1272, the Dominican order appointed Aquinas to start a new school in Naples. A mystical experience reportedly caused Aquinas to abruptly cease his writing. Aquinas died at a monastery in Fossanova. In addition to his major works, *Summa Theologia* and *Summa Contra Gentiles*, Aquinas's voluminous corpus includes extensive commentaries on Jeremiah, Lamentations, Isaiah, Job, and an incomplete one on the Psalms. Aquinas also wrote commentaries on the Gospels of Matthew and John as well as the Pauline Epistles. Furthermore, at the request of the pope, Aquinas produced the *Catena Aurea*, a commentary on the four Gospels consisting of exegetical statements by the Latin and Greek fathers. One of the most significant features of Aquinas's biblical commentaries is his emphasis on the literal meaning of a Scriptural text. As a representation of medieval Catholic theology, Aquinas's theology was regularly challenged by the Protestant reformers.

Benedict Aretius (d. 1574). Swiss Reformed professor. Trained at the universities of Bern, Strasbourg and Marburg, Aretius taught logic and philosophy as well as the biblical languages and theology. He advocated for stronger unity and peace between the Lutheran and Reformed churches. Aretius joined others in denouncing the antitrinitarian Giovanni Valentino Gentile (d. 1566). He published commentaries on the New Testament, as well as various works on astronomy, botany and medicine.

Aristotle (388–322 BC). Ancient Greek philosopher and scientist. Aristotle was born in Stagira, Chalkdice, northern Greece. He is considered the "Father of Western Philosophy" along with his teacher, Plato, because his teaching produced the bases for almost every discipline studied in the Western world. After his father's death while he was still a child, Aristotle was raised by his guardian, Proxenus of Atarneus. At the age of about eighteen, Aristotle joined Plato's Academy in Athens, where he remained until his was thirty-seven. Aristotle's writings cover a wide range of subjects: physics, biology, zoology, metaphysics, logic, ethics, aesthetics, poetry, theater, music, rhetoric, psychology, linguistics, and politics. Shortly after Plato's death, King Philip II of Macedonia requested his services as a tutor to his son, Alexander the Great. Aristotle began tutoring the young prince in 343 BC. While teaching Alexander, Aristotle was able to acquire hundreds of books for the library of what would become his Lyceum. Aristotle's work profoundly shaped scholarship during the Middle Ages and early modern period as his logic was employed in the exegesis of Scripture and forma-

tion of theology. Among the major theologians who incorporated Aristotle's methods into their theological systems was Thomas Aquinas.* Aristotle's methods and categories would also be utilized by many Protestant theologians throughout the sixteenth and seventeenth centuries.

Jacobus Arminius (1559–1609). Dutch Remonstrant pastor and theologian. Arminius was a vocal critic of high Calvinist scholasticism, whose views were repudiated by the Synod of Dordrecht. Arminius was a student of Theodore Beza* at the academy of Geneva. He served as a pastor in Amsterdam and later joined the faculty of theology at the university in Leiden, where his lectures on predestination were popular and controversial. Predestination, as Arminius understood it, was the decree of God determined on the basis of divine foreknowledge of faith or rejection by humans who are the recipients of prevenient, but resistible, grace.

Johann Arndt (1555–1621). German Lutheran pastor and theologian. After a brief time teaching, Arndt pastored in Badeborn (Anhalt) until 1590, when Prince Johann Georg von Anhalt (1567–1618) began introducing Reformed ecclesial policies. Arndt ministered in Quedlinberg, Brunswick, Eisleben and Celle. Heavily influenced by medieval mysticism, Arndt centered his theology on Christ's mystical union with the believer, out of which flows love of God and neighbor. He is best known for his *True Christianity* (1605–1609), which greatly influenced Philipp Jakob Spener (1635–1705) and later Pietists.

John Arrowsmith (1602–1659). English Puritan theologian. Arrowsmith participated in the Westminster Assembly, and later taught at Cambridge. His works, all published posthumously, include three sermons preached to Parliament and an unfinished catechism.

Articles of Religion (1562; revised 1571). The Articles underwent a long editorial process that drew from the influence of Continental confessions in England, resulting in a uniquely Anglican blend of Protestantism and Catholicism. In their final form, they were reduced from Thomas Cranmer's*

Forty-two Articles (1539) to the Elizabethan Thirty-Nine Articles (1571), excising polemical articles against the Anabaptists and Millenarians as well as adding articles on the Holy Spirit, good works and Communion. Originating in a 1535 meeting with Lutherans, the Articles retained a minor influence from the Augsburg Confession* and Württemberg Confession (1552), but showed significant revision in accordance with Genevan theology, as well as the Second Helvetic Confession.*

Anne Askew (1521–1546). English Protestant martyr. Askew was forced to marry her deceased sister's intended husband, who later expelled Askew from his house—after the birth of two children—on account of her religious views. After unsuccessfully seeking a divorce in Lincoln, Askew moved to London, where she met other Protestants and began to preach. In 1546, she was arrested, imprisoned and convicted of heresy for denying the doctrine of transubstantiation. Under torture in the Tower of London she refused to name any other Protestants. On July 16, 1546, she was burned at the stake. Askew is best known through her accounts of her arrests and examinations. John Bale (1495–1563), a bishop, historian and playwright, published these manuscripts. Later John Foxe (1516–1587) included them in his *Acts and Monuments*, presenting her as a role model for other pious Protestant women.

Augsburg Confession (1530). In the wake of Luther's* stand against ecclesial authorities at the Diet of Worms (1521), the Holy Roman Empire splintered along theological lines. Emperor Charles V sought to ameliorate this—while also hoping to secure a united European front against Turkish invasion—by calling together another imperial diet in Augsburg in 1530. The Evangelical party was cast in a strongly heretical light at the diet by Johann Eck.* For this reason, Philipp Melanchthon* and Justus Jonas* thought it best to strike a conciliatory tone (Luther, as an official outlaw, did not attend), submitting a confession rather than a defense. The resulting Augsburg Confession was approved by many of the rulers of the northeastern Empire; however, due to differences in eucharistic

theology, Martin Bucer* and the representatives of Strasbourg, Constance, Lindau and Memmingen drafted a separate confession (the Tetrapolitan Confession). Charles V accepted neither confession, demanding that the Evangelicals accept the Catholic rebuttal instead. In 1531, along with the publication of the Augsburg Confession itself, Melanchthon released a defense of the confession that responded to the Catholic confutation and expanded on the original articles. Most subsequent Protestant confessions followed the general structure of the Augsburg Confession.

Augustine of Hippo (354–430 AD). North African bishop and theologian. Augustine was born in Thagaste (Ahras, Algeria), a small town in the Roman province to Numidia, the son of a Christian mother, Monica, and a non-Christian father, Patricius, a local official of modest means. Enabled by local patronage, Augustine received a classical education, which afforded him the opportunity to pursue advanced training in rhetoric at Carthage. Upon completing his education at Carthage, Augustine taught rhetoric there as well as in Rome and Milan, where he was appointed official rhetorician of that city. Inspired by his reading of Cicero's *Hortensius*, Augustine embarked upon a quest for wisdom. While in Carthage, Augustine was repulsed by the seemingly simplistic Christianity he encountered, and therefore joined the Manicheans. Having become disillusioned by the Manichaeans' failure to lead him to the wisdom they promised, Augustine was eventually drawn to orthodox Christianity by the preaching of Ambrose (340–397) and his reading of the Neo-Platonist philosopher Plotinus (204–270). As a result of his conversion in 386, Augustine abandoned his secular ambitions in favor of a celibate life fully committed to intellectual and spiritual devotion to God. Towards this end, Augustine returned to north Africa to establish a semi–monastic community. However, in 391, while visiting Hippo Regius, he was forcibly ordained into the priesthood, and made bishop of that church in 396. In addition to his many duties as a bishop, Augustine engaged in controversies against the Manicheans, Donatists, and Pelagians, which took up the remainder of his life and career. He died in 430 while the Vandals besieged Hippo. Among his many works, Augustine devoted several to exegesis. He outlines exegetical principles in his *De Doctrina Christiana* ("On Christian Doctrine"), and he authored extensive series of homilies on most of the books of the New Testament as well as the Old Testament books of Psalms and Genesis (incomplete). During the Reformation era, both Catholic and Protestant theologians appealed to and engaged with Augustine's theology, especially his emphases upon original sin and humanity's need for God's grace.

Authorized Version (1611). In 1604 King James I* commissioned this new translation—popularly remembered as the King James Version—for uniform use in the public worship of the Church of England. The Bible and the Apocrypha was divided into six portions and assigned to six companies of nine scholars—both Anglicans and Puritans—centered at Cambridge, Oxford and Westminster. Richard Bancroft, the general editor of the Authorized Version, composed fifteen rules to guide the translators and to guard against overly partisan decisions. Rather than offer an entirely fresh English translation, the companies were to follow the Bishops' Bible* as closely as possible. "Truly (good Christian Reader)," the preface states, "we neuer thought from the beginning that we should need to make a new Translation, nor yet to make of a bad one a good one . . . but make a good one better, or out of many good ones, one principall good one, not iustly to be excepted against: that hath bene our endeauour, that our mark." Other rules standardized spelling, dictated traditional ecclesial terms (e.g., *church*, *baptize* and *bishop*), and allowed only for linguistic marginal notes and cross-references. Each book of the Bible went through a rigorous revision process: first, each person in a company made an initial draft, then the company put together a composite draft, then a supercommittee composed of representatives from each company reviewed these drafts, and finally two bishops and Bancroft scrutinized the final edits. The text and

translation process of the Authorized Version have widely influenced biblical translations ever since.

Robert Bagnall (b. 1559 or 1560). English Protestant minister. Bagnall authored *The Steward's Last Account* (1622), a collection of five sermons on Luke 16.

Friedrich Balduin (1575–1627). German Lutheran theologian. After spending time in the pastorate at Freiberg and Oelsnitz, Balduin was appointed professor of theology at Wittenberg in 1604, where he remained until the end of his life. He also served as head of the theology faculty, superintendent of churches, and assessor of the consistory. Known for his commitment to Lutheran orthodoxy, Balduin's major works include a commentary on the Pauline letters and writings on exegesis, homiletics, and casuistry.

John Ball (1585–1640). English Puritan theologian. Ball was a respected educator. He briefly held a church office until he was removed on account of his Puritanism. He composed popular catechisms and tracts on faith, the church and the covenant of grace.

John Barlow (1580/1581?–1629/1630). English Protestant minister. Educated at Oxford, Barlow ministered in Plymouth, Halifax, and Chester. A number of his sermons have been preserved, including his teachings on 2 Timothy 1 and 1 Thessalonians 4:18.

Thomas Bastard (c. 1565–1618). English Protestant minister and poet. Educated at Winchester and New College, Oxford, Bastard published numerous works, including collections of poems and sermons; his most famous title is *Chrestoleros* (1598), a collection of epigrams. Bastard was alleged to be the author of an anonymous work, *An Admonition to the City of Oxford*, which revealed the carnal vices of many clergy and scholars in Oxford; despite denying authorship, he was dismissed from Oxford in 1591. Bastard was recognized as a skilled classical scholar and preacher. He died impoverished in a debtor's prison in Dorchester.

Jeremias Bastingius (1551–1595). Dutch Reformed theologian. Educated in Heidelberg and Geneva, Bastingius pastored the Reformed church in Antwerp for nearly a decade until the

Spanish overran the city in 1585; he later settled in Dordrecht. He spent the last few years of his life in Leiden on the university's board of regents. He wrote an influential commentary on the Heidelberg Catechism that was translated into English, Dutch, German and Flemish.

Johann (Pomarius) Baumgart (1514–1578). Lutheran pastor and amateur playwright. Baumgart studied under Georg Major,* Martin Luther* and Philipp Melanchthon* at the University of Wittenberg. Before becoming pastor of the Church of the Holy Spirit in 1540, Baumgart taught secondary school. He authored catechetical and polemical works, a postil for the Gospel readings throughout the church year, numerous hymns and a didactic play (*Juditium Salomonis*).

Richard Baxter (1615–1691). English Puritan minister. Baxter was a leading Puritan pastor, evangelist and theologian, known throughout England for his landmark ministry in Kidderminster and a prodigious literary output, producing 135 books in just over forty years. Baxter came to faith through reading William Perkins,* Richard Sibbes* and other early Puritan writers and was the first cleric to decline the terms of ministry in the national English church imposed by the 1662 Act of Uniformity; Baxter wrote on behalf of the more than 1700 who shared ejection from the national church. He hoped for restoration to national church ministry, or toleration, that would allow lawful preaching and pastoring. Baxter sought unity in theological, ecclesiastical, sociopolitical and personal terms and is regarded as a forerunner of Noncomformist ecumenicity, though he was defeated in his efforts at the 1661 Savoy Conference to take seriously Puritan objections to the revision of the 1604 Prayer Book. Baxter's views on church ministry were considerably hybrid: he was a paedo-baptist, Nonconformist minister who approved of synodical Episcopal government and fixed liturgy. He is most known for his classic writings on the Christian life, such as *The Saints' Everlasting Rest* and *A Christian Directory*, and pastoral ministry, such as *The Reformed Pastor*. He also produced *Catholick Theology*, a large volume squaring current Reformed, Lutheran, Arminian and Roman Catholic systems with each other.

Thomas Becon (1511/1512–1567). English Puritan preacher. Becon was a friend of Hugh Latimer,* and for several years chaplain to Archbishop Thomas Cranmer.* Becon was sent to the Tower of London by Mary I and then exiled for his controversial preaching at the English royal court. He returned to England upon Elizabeth I's* accession. Becon was one of the most widely read popular preachers in England during the Reformation. He published many of his sermons, including a postil, or collection of sermon helps for undertrained or inexperienced preachers.

Belgic Confession (1561). Written by Guy de Brès (1523–1567), this statement of Dutch Reformed faith was heavily reliant on the Gallic Confession,* although more detailed, especially in how strongly it distances the Reformed from Roman Catholics and Anabaptists. The Confession first appeared in French in 1561 and was translated to Dutch in 1562. It was presented to Philip II (1527–1598) in the hope that he would grant toleration to the Reformed, to no avail. At the Synod of Dordrecht* the Confession was revised, clarifying and strengthening the article on election as well as sharpening the distinctives of Reformed theology against the Anabaptists, thus situating the Dutch Reformed more closely to the international Calvinist movement. The Belgic Confession in conjunction with the Heidelberg Catechism* and the Canons of Dordrecht were granted official status as the confessional standards (the Three Forms of Unity) of the Dutch Reformed Church.

Robert Bellarmine (1542–1621). Italian Catholic cardinal. A Jesuit, Bellarmine first taught at Louvain before being appointed chair of polemical theology at the Roman College. Much of Bellarmine's career was devoted to the refutation of Protestant teachings, and his three volume work, the *Controversies* (1586–93), was widely disseminated in the post-Tridentine era as the foremost refutation of the evangelical message. He was influential in the official revision of the Vulgate* text during the reign of Pope Clement VIII

(1536–1605), with the resulting version, the Sixto-Clementine Vulgate, providing the basic biblical text for Catholics until Vatican II. Bellarmine is also a controversial figure in the history of science. Appointed to the Holy Office, also known as the Inquisition, by Pope Paul V (1550–1621), it was he who examined Galileo Galilei (1564–1642) and ordered him to treat heliocentrism as a hypothesis rather than a reality, believing the evidentiary threshold had not yet been met. Later in his career, Bellarmine's attention turned to works on devotion and piety, and include his extensive commentary on the Psalms (1611).

Bernard of Clairvaux (1090–1153). French abbot and theologian. Born the son of a Bugundian knight, Bernard became interested in the new reforming movement at Citeaux, and thus abandoned his preparation for a secular career in favor of monastic life there. Towards this end, Bernard persuaded thirty-one of his friends and relatives to follow him to Citeaux, and join the Cistercian order. Among this group were four of Bernard's brothers. In 1115, Bernard went with others of his order to found a Cistercian monastery at Claivaux. Bernard's austere approach to the monastic life attracted many followers to the point that by the time of his death there were sixty-eight Cistercian houses. Throughout his career, Bernard preached, mediated theological disputes, and advised. Bernard is best known for having preached the Second Crusade (1147–1150) as well as advising his former student, Pope Eugenius III (r. 1145–1153), and engaging in theological controversies with Peter Abelard (1079–1142) and Gilbert of Poitiers (1085–1154). One of the distinguishing characteristics of Bernard's theology is his Christocentric mysticism. Among Bernard's most important works are his treatises *On Consideration* and *On Loving God* along with his *Sermons on the Song of Songs* as well as many other sermons on the liturgical year and other subject. Many of the reformers in the sixteenth century cited Bernard extensively, especially Martin Luther* and John Calvin*.

Theodore Beza (1519–1605). French pastor and professor. Beza was compatriot and successor to John Calvin* as moderator of the Company of Pastors in Geneva during the second half of the sixteenth century. He was a noteworthy New Testament scholar whose *Codex Bezae* formed the basis of the New Testament section of later English translations. A leader in the academy and the church, Beza served as professor of Greek at the Lausanne Academy until 1558, at which time he moved to Geneva to become the rector of the newly founded Genevan Academy. He enjoyed an international reputation through his correspondence with key European leaders. Beza developed and extended Calvin's doctrinal thought on several important themes such as the nature of predestination and the real spiritual presence of Christ in the Eucharist.

Theodor Bibliander (1504?–1564). Swiss Reformed Hebraist and theologian. Professor of Old Testament at the Zurich Academy from 1531, Bibliander published two Hebrew grammars, a collection of letters by Zwingli* and Oecolampadius*, commentaries on Isaiah, Ezekiel, and Nahum, a Latin translation of the Qur'an, and a tract warning Christians against the threat of Islam. He taught a universalist view of predestination, arguing that God saved all people unless they rejected divine grace. Following a dispute with double-predestinarian Peter Martyr Vermigli*, he was forced into retirement in 1560.

Thomas Bilson (1546/1547?–1616). English Anglican Bishop and theologian. A celebrated preacher and theologian, Bilson served as canon of Winchester Cathedral and warden of Winchester College before becoming bishop of Worcester. He held this position for only one year, however, before his appointment to the wealthier see of Winchester. As an advisor to King James I,* he preached at his coronation, and he was involved with the publication of the 1611 Authorized Version,* being part of the Cambridge company responsible for translating the Apocrypha, the author of part of the front matter, and one of the text's final editors. His extant writings defend the episcopacy against Erastianism, condemn rebellion, and argue for a literal understanding of Christ's descent into hell.

Hugh Binning (1627–1653). Scottish Presbyterian theologian. At the age of eighteen, Binning became a professor of philosophy at the University of Glasgow. In his early twenties he left this post for parish ministry, and died of consumption a few years later. His commentary on the Westminster Confession and a selection of his sermons were published after his death.

Samuel Bird (d. 1604). Anglican minister and author. A native of Essex, Bird matriculated at Queen's College, Cambridge, where he received his BA in 1570 and his MA in 1573, at which time he was also elected a fellow of Corpus Christi College, Cambridge. For reasons unknown, Bird resigned his fellowship sometime in 1576. He spent nearly the entirety of his post-university career as rector of St. Peter's in Ipswich until his death in 1604. Among Bird's major works are *A Friendlie Communication or Dialogue Betweene Paule and Demas, wherein is Disputed How We are to Use the Pleasures of This Life* (1580), *Lectures upon the 11. Chapter of Hebrews and upon the 38. Psalme* (1598), and *Lectures upon the 8 and 9 Chapters of the Second Epistle to the Corinthians* (1598).

Bishops' Bible (1568). Anglicans were polarized by the two most recent English translations of the Bible: the Great Bible (1539) relied too heavily on the Vulgate* and was thus perceived as too Catholic, while the Geneva Bible's* marginal notes were too Calvinist for many Anglicans. So Archbishop Matthew Parker (1504–1575) commissioned a new translation of Scripture from the original languages with marginal annotations (many of which, ironically, were from the Geneva Bible). Published under royal warrant, the Bishops' Bible became the official translation for the Church of England. The 1602 edition provided the basis for the King James Bible (1611).

Georg Blaurock (1492–1529). Swiss Anabaptist. Blaurock (a nickname meaning "blue coat," because of his preference for this garment) was one of the first leaders of Switzerland's radical reform movement. In the first public disputations on baptism in Zurich, he argued for believer's baptism and was the first person to receive adult believers' baptism there, having been baptized by Conrad Grebel* in 1525. Blaurock was arrested several times for performing mass adult baptisms and engaging in social disobedience by disrupting worship services. He was eventually expelled from Zurich but continued preaching and baptizing in various Swiss cantons until his execution.

Bohemian Confession (1535). Bohemian Christianity was subdivided between traditional Catholics, Utraquists (who demanded Communion in both kinds) and the *Unitas Fratrum*, who were not Protestants but whose theology bore strong affinities to the Waldensians and the Reformed. The 1535 Latin edition of this confession—an earlier Czech edition had already been drafted—was an attempt to clarify and redefine the beliefs of the *Unitas Fratrum*. This confession purged all earlier openness to rebaptism and inched toward Luther's* eucharistic theology. Jan Augusta (c. 1500–1572) and Jan Roh (also Johannes Horn; c. 1490–1547) presented the confession to King Ferdinand I (1503–1564) in Vienna, but the king would not print it. The *Unitas Fratrum* sought, and with slight amendments eventually obtained, Luther's advocacy of the confession. It generally follows the structure of the Augsburg Confession.*

Bohemian Confession (1575). This confession was an attempt to shield Bohemian Christian minorities—the Utraquists and the *Unitas Fratrum*—from the Counter-Reformation and Habsburg insistence on uniformity. The hope was that this umbrella consensus would ensure peace in the midst of Christian diversity; anyone who affirmed the 1575 Confession, passed by the Bohemian legislature, would be tolerated. This confession was, like the Bohemian Confession of 1535, patterned after the Augsburg Confession.* It emphasizes both justification by faith alone and good works as the fruit of salvation. Baptism and the Eucharist are the focus of the sacramental section, although the five traditional Catholic sacraments are also listed for the Utraquists.

Though it was eventually accepted in 1609 by Rudolf II (1552–1612), the Thirty Years' War (1618–1648) rendered the confession moot.

Book of Common Prayer (1549; 1552). After the Church of England's break with Rome, it needed a liturgical manual to distinguish its theology and practice from that of Catholicism. Thomas Cranmer* drafted the Book of Common Prayer based on the medieval Roman Missal, under the dual influence of the revised Lutheran Mass and the reforms of the Spanish Cardinal Quiñones. This manual details the eucharistic service, as well as services for rites such as baptism, confirmation, marriage and funerals. It includes a matrix of the epistle and Gospel readings and the appropriate collect for each Sunday and feast day of the church year. The 1548 Act of Uniformity established the Book of Common Prayer as *the* authoritative liturgical manual for the Church of England, to be implemented everywhere by Pentecost 1549. After its 1552 revision, Queen Mary I banned it; Elizabeth I* reestablished it in 1559, although it was rejected by Puritans and Catholics alike.

The Book of Homilies (1547; 1563; 1570). This collection of approved sermons, published in three parts during the reigns of Edward VI and Elizabeth I,* was intended to inculcate Anglican theological distinctives and mitigate the problems raised by the lack of educated preachers. Addressing doctrinal and practical topics, Thomas Cranmer* likely wrote the majority of the first twelve sermons, published in 1547; John Jewel* added another twenty sermons in 1563. A final sermon, *A Homily Against Disobedience*, was appended to the canon in 1570. Reprinted regularly, the *Book of Homilies* was an important resource in Anglican preaching until at least the end of the seventeenth century.

Martin (Cellarius) Borrhaus (1499–1564). German Reformed theologian. After a dispute with his mentor Johann Eck,* Borrhaus settled in Wittenberg, where he was influenced by the radical Zwickau Prophets. He travelled extensively, and finally settled in Basel to teach philosophy and Old Testament. Despite his objections, many accused Borrhaus of Anabaptism; he argued that baptism was a matter of conscience. On account of his association with Sebastian Castellio (1515–1563) and Michael Servetus (1511–1553), some scholars posit that Borrhaus was an antitrinitarian. His writings include a treatise on the Trinity and commentaries on the Torah, historical books, Ecclesiastes and Isaiah.

John Bowle (d. 1637). Anglican pastor. After matriculating from Cambridge, Bowle was household pastor to Sir Robert Cecil (1563–1612) and held a pastorate at Tilehurst in Berkshire. He was appointed dean of Salisbury in 1620 and bishop of Rochester in 1629.

John Boys (1571–1625). Anglican priest and theologian. Before doctoral work at Cambridge, Boys pastored several parishes in Kent; after completing his studies he was appointed to more prominent positions, culminating in his 1619 appointment as the Dean of Canterbury by James I.* Boys published a popular four-volume postil of the Gospel and epistle readings for the church year, as well as a companion volume for the Psalms.

John Bradford (1510-1555). English Reformer, prebendary of St. Paul's, and martyr. Bradford was born in Blackley, Manchester, to an affluent family. After grammar school, Bradford at first began legal studies at the Inner Temple in London. However, while there, he heard the preaching of a fellow student, and thus converted to an evangelical faith. This conversion caused Bradford to abandon his study of law and enroll at St. Catherine's Hall, Cambridge, to study theology. He completed his MA in 1549, and in the same year, received an appointment of fellow at Pembroke Hall, Cambridge. In August, 1550, Bishop Nicholas Ridley ordained Bradford a deacon, and appointed him his personal chaplain. Bradford's exceptional preaching moved King Edward VI to select him as his chaplain and prebendary at St. Paul's Cathedral. After Mary Tudor succeeded her half-brother to throne, Bradford was tried and convicted of heresy on January 31, 1555. He was executed at the stake on July 1 of the same year.

Anne Bradstreet (1612–1672). English-American Puritan poet. Born in Northampton, Bradstreet married at sixteen and emigrated to the Massachusetts Bay Colony, of which both her father and husband would serve as governors. Mother to eight children, Bradstreet also wrote poetry. Much of her verse reflects on marriage, children, and her Puritan faith. While her writing received a mixed reception from contemporaries, many of whom viewed poetry as outside a woman's purview, she is today celebrated as the most significant early English poet in North America.

Thieleman Jans van Braght (1625–1664). Dutch Radical preacher. After demonstrating great ability with languages, this cloth merchant was made preacher in his hometown of Dordrecht in 1648. He served in this office for the next sixteen years, until his death. This celebrated preacher had a reputation for engaging in debate wherever an opportunity presented itself, particularly concerning infant baptism. The publication of his book of martyrs, *Het Bloedigh Tooneel of Martelaersspiegel* (1660; *Martyrs' Mirror*), proved to be his lasting contribution to the Mennonite tradition. *Martyrs' Mirror* is heavily indebted to the earlier martyr book *Offer des Heeren* (1562), to which Braght added many early church martyrs who rejected infant baptism, as well as over 800 contemporary martyrs.

Johannes Brenz (1499–1570). German Lutheran theologian and pastor. Brenz was converted to the reformation cause after hearing Martin Luther* speak; later, Brenz became a student of Johannes Oecolampadius.* His central achievement lay in his talent for organization. As city preacher in Schwäbisch-Hall and afterward in Württemberg and Tübingen, he oversaw the introduction of reform measures and doctrines and new governing structures for ecclesial and educational communities. Brenz also helped establish Lutheran orthodoxy through treatises, commentaries and catechisms. He defended Luther's position on eucharistic presence against Huldrych Zwingli* and opposed the death penalty for religious dissenters.

Guillaume Briçonnet (1470–1534). French Catholic abbot and bishop. Briçonnet created a short-lived circle of reformist-minded humanists in his diocese under the sponsorship of Marguerite d'Angoulême. His desire for ecclesial reform developed throughout his prestigious career (including positions as royal chaplain to the queen, abbot at Saint-Germain-des-Prés and bishop of Meaux), influenced by Jacques Lefèvre d'Étaples.* Briçonnet encouraged reform through ministerial visitation, Scripture and preaching in the vernacular and active study of the Bible. When this triggered the ire of the theology faculty at the Sorbonne in Paris, Briçonnet quelled the activity and departed, envisioning an ecclesial reform that proceeded hierarchically.

Thomas Brightman (1562–1607). English Puritan pastor and exegete. Under alleged divine inspiration, Brightman wrote a well known commentary on Revelation, influenced by Joachim of Fiore (d. 1202). In contrast to the putatively true churches of Geneva and Scotland, he depicted the Church of England as a type of the lukewarm Laodicean church. He believed that the Reformation would result in the defeat of the Vatican and the Ottoman Empire and that all humanity would be regenerated through the spread of the gospel before Christ's final return and judgment.

Otto Brunfels (c. 1488–1534). German Lutheran botanist, teacher and physician. Brunfels joined the Carthusian order, where he developed interests in the natural sciences and became involved with a humanist circle associated with Ulrich von Hutten and Wolfgang Capito.* In 1521, after coming into contact with Luther's* teaching, Brunfels abandoned the monastic life, traveling and spending time in botanical research and pastoral care. He received a medical degree in Basel and was appointed city physician of Bern in 1534. Brunfels penned defenses of Luther and Hutten, devotional biographies of biblical figures, a prayer book, and annotations on the Gospels and the Acts of the Apostles. His most influential contribution, however, is as a Renaissance botanist.

Martin Bucer (1491–1551). German Reformed theologian and pastor. A Dominican friar, Bucer was influenced by Desiderius Erasmus* during his doctoral studies at the University of Heidelberg, where he began corresponding with Martin Luther.* After advocating reform in Alsace, Bucer was excommunicated and fled to Strasbourg, where he became a leader in the city's Reformed ecclesial and educational communities. Bucer sought concord between Lutherans and Zwinglians and Protestants and Catholics. He emigrated to England, becoming a professor at Cambridge. Bucer's greatest theological concern was the centrality of Christ's sacrificial death, which achieved justification and sanctification and orients Christian community.

Johannes Bugenhagen (1485–1558). German Lutheran pastor and professor. Bugenhagen, a priest and lecturer at a Premonstratensian monastery, became a city preacher in Wittenberg during the reform efforts of Martin Luther* and Philipp Melanchthon.* Initially influenced by his reading of Desiderius Erasmus,* Bugenhagen grew in evangelical orientation through Luther's works; later, he studied under Melanchthon at the University of Wittenberg, eventually serving as rector and faculty member there. Bugenhagen was a versatile commentator, exegete and lecturer on Scripture. Through these roles and his development of lectionary and devotional material, Bugenhagen facilitated rapid establishment of church order throughout many German provinces.

Heinrich Bullinger (1504–1575). Swiss Reformed pastor and theologian. Bullinger succeeded Huldrych Zwingli* as minister and leader in Zurich. The primary author of the First and Second Helvetic Confessions,* Bullinger was drawn toward reform through the works of Martin Luther* and Philipp Melanchthon.* After Zwingli died, Bullinger was vital in maintaining adherence to the cause of reform; he oversaw the expansion of the Zurich synodal system while preaching, teaching and writing extensively. One of Bullinger's lasting legacies was the development of a federal view of the divine covenant with humanity, making baptism and the Eucharist covenantal signs.

John Bunyan (1628–1688). English Puritan preacher and writer. His *Pilgrim's Progress* is one of the best-selling English-language titles in history. Born to a working-class family, Bunyan was largely unschooled, gaining literacy (and entering the faith) through reading the Bible and such early Puritan

devotional works as *The Plain Man's Pathway to Heaven* and *The Practice of Piety*. Following a short stint in Oliver Cromwell's parliamentary army, in which Bunyan narrowly escaped death in combat, he turned to a preaching ministry, succeeding John Gifford as pastor at the Congregational church in Bedford. A noted preacher, Bunyan drew large crowds in itinerant appearances and it was in the sermonic form that Bunyan developed his theological outlook, which was an Augustinian-inflected Calvinism. Bunyan's opposition to the Book of Common Prayer and refusal of official ecclesiastical licensure led to multiple imprisonments, where he wrote many of his famous allegorical works, including *Pilgrim's Progress*, *The Holy City*, *Prison Meditations* and *Holy War*.

Michelangelo Buonarroti (1475–1564). Italian Catholic artist and poet. Michelangelo was born in Florence but spent the majority of his career in Rome, completing artworks commissioned by the popes of the early sixteenth century. One of the most recognized artists of all time, his artworks include the *Pietà* (1499), *David* (1501–1504), the ceiling of the Sistine Chapel (1508–1512), *Moses* (1515), and the *Last Judgment* (1536–1541), which remain famous and have done much to shape Western aesthetics. Toward the end of his life, his interests shifted toward architecture, culminating with his contributions to the designs of St. Peter's Basilica in Rome. Michelangelo is thought to have been devoutly Catholic throughout his life, but recent scholarship has considered the complexity of his relationship with the Catholic Reformation and the Protestant movement.

Jeremiah Burroughs (c. 1600–1646). English Puritan pastor and delegate to the Westminster Assembly. Burroughs left Cambridge, as well as a rectorate in Norfolk, because of his nonconformity. After returning to England from pastoring an English congregation in Rotterdam for several years (1637–1641), he became one of only a few dissenters from the official presbyterianism of the Assembly in favor of a congregationalist polity. Nevertheless, he was well known and respected by presbyterian colleagues such as Richard Baxter* for his irenic tone and conciliatory manner. The vast majority of Burroughs's corpus was published posthumously, although during his lifetime he published annotations on Hosea and several polemical works.

Anthony Cade (d. 1641). Anglican pastor. Cade served as tutor and chaplain to George Villiers, First Duke of Buckingham (1592–1628), a close confidante of King James I* before holding a number of pastoral positions in Leicestershire and Northamptonshire.

Cardinal Cajetan (Thomas de Vio) (1469–1534). Italian Catholic cardinal, professor, theologian and biblical exegete. This Dominican monk was the leading Thomist theologian and one of the most important Catholic exegetes of the sixteenth century. Cajetan is best-known for his interview with Martin Luther* at the Diet of Augsburg (1518). Among his many works are polemical treatises, extensive biblical commentaries and most importantly a four-volume commentary (1508–1523) on the *Summa Theologiae* of Thomas Aquinas.*

Georg Calixtus (1586–1656). German Lutheran theologian. Calixtus studied at the University of Helmstedt where he developed regard for Philipp Melanchthon.* Between his time as a student and later as a professor at Helmstedt, Calixtus traveled through Europe seeking a way to unite and reconcile Lutherans, Calvinists and Catholics. He attempted to fuse these denominations through use of the Scriptures, the Apostles' Creed, and the first five centuries, interpreted by the Vincentian canon. Calixtus's position was stamped as syncretist and yielded further debate even after his death.

John Calvin (1509–1564). French Reformed pastor and theologian. John Calvin was born in Noyon, France. After receiving his primary education in the aristocratic family of Charles de Hangest, he attended the University of Paris to prepare for further study of theology. However, after completing his BA degree, as per his father's instructions, Calvin proceeded to the study of the law at Orleans of Bourges. While at Orleans, Calvin's interests in Greek and Latin literature were reawakened. Upon his father's death, Calvin resumed his study of classical literature at the newly founded College of Royal Readers in Paris under the direction of Guillaume Bude. The product of these studies was his commentary on Seneca's *De Clementia* (1532). Sometime between 1533 and 1534 Calvin experienced a "sudden conversion" due largely to the influence to Martin Luther's 1520 treatises. Calvin's embracing of an evangelical faith forced him to flee France. From there he went to Basel, where he wrote the first edition of his *Institutes of the Christian Religion* in 1536. The *Institutes* became a theological dogmatics for the Reformed churches. Calvin spent most of his career in Geneva (excepting a three-year ministry in Strasbourg with Martin Bucer*). In Geneva, Calvin reorganized the structure and governance of the church and established an academy that became an international center for theological education. He was a tireless writer, revising his *Institutes* several times, and authoring theological treatises as well as biblical commentaries. Calvin is also known for his debates with his contemporaries, including Michael Servetus, whose anti-Trinitarian views led to his execution in Geneva in 1553. Calvin also maintained friendly correspondence with many reformers, including Melanchthon* and Bullinger*, the latter of whom he was able to come to an agreement with regarding the presence of Christ in the Lord's Supper with the signing of the *Consensus Tigurinus* in 1551, which brought a degree of unity between Geneva and Zurich and to the Reformed tradition. One of the foremost figures during the Reformation period, Calvin has an extensive exegetical and theological legacy.

Wolfgang Capito (1478?–1541). German Reformed humanist and theologian. Capito, a Hebrew scholar, produced a Hebrew grammar and published several Latin commentaries on books of the Hebrew Scriptures. He corresponded with Desiderius Erasmus* and fellow humanists. Capito translated Martin Luther's* early works into Latin for the printer Johann Froben. On meeting Luther, Capito was converted to Luther's vision, left Mainz and settled in Strasbourg, where he lectured on Luther's theology to the city clergy. With Martin Bucer,* Capito reformed liturgy, ecclesial life and teachings, education, welfare, and government.

Capito worked for the theological unification of the Swiss cantons with Strasbourg.

Pietro Carnesecchi (1508–1567). Italian humanist. Carnesecchi rose in the papal bureaucracy under Medici patronage, but after the death of Clement VII* he began to deviate from Catholic orthodoxy, aligning himself with Juan de Valdés.* While he retained relations with the established church, he also read Protestant works by theologians such as Luther,* Calvin,* and Bucer,* and his only extant doctrinal writing defends Bucer's view of the Eucharist over that of Zwingli.* Carnesecchi was able to avoid arrest by the Inquisition for a time, and his condemnation to death in absentia was pardoned under Pope Pius IV (1499–1565). However, Pius V (1504–1572) was a longtime opponent of Carnesecchi, and upon his election to the papal office, reopened the case and those of a number of others suspected of Protestant leanings. While seeking refuge in Florence, Carnesecchi was betrayed to the Inquisition by Cosimo I de' Medici, and following trial he was beheaded.

François Carrière (d. 1665). French Catholic theologian. A Franciscan doctor of theology, Carrière composed a commentary on the whole Bible, a summary of Catholic doctrine, and a history of the papacy.

Thomas Cartwright (1535–1606). English Puritan preacher and professor. Cartwright was educated at St. John's College, Cambridge, although as an influential leader of the Presbyterian party in the Church of England he was continually at odds with the Anglican party, especially John Whitgift.* Cartwright spent some time as an exile in Geneva and Heidelberg as well as in Antwerp, where he pastored an English church. In 1585, Cartwright was arrested and eventually jailed for trying to return to England despite Elizabeth I's* refusal of his request. Many acknowledged him to be learned but also quite cantankerous. His publications include commentaries on Colossians, Ecclesiastes, Proverbs and the Gospels, as well as a dispute against Whitgift on church discipline.

Mathew Caylie (unknown). English Protestant minister. Caylie authored *The Cleansing of the Ten Lepers* (1623), an exposition of Luke 17:14-18.

John Chardon (d. 1601). Irish Anglican bishop. Chardon was educated at Oxford. He advocated Reformed doctrine in his preaching, yet opposed those Puritans who rejected Anglican church order. He published several sermons.

Christian Chemnitz (1615–1666). German Lutheran theologian. Grandnephew of Martin Chemnitz,* Christian Chemnitz was principal at the high school in Jena before serving the church as a deacon and archdeacon in Weimer and Braunschweig then as superintendent in Eisenach. Returning to Jena, he received his doctorate and replaced John Major as professor of theology, also serving as dean of the theology faculty and rector of the university. He wrote on numerous biblical, pastoral, and controversial topics, with his works including a defense of Lutheranism, instructions for young ministers, and a series of sermons on judgement.

Martin Chemnitz (1522–1586). German Lutheran theologian. A leading figure in establishing Lutheran orthodoxy, Chemnitz studied theology and patristics at the University of Wittenburg, later becoming a defender of Philipp Melanchthon's* interpretation of the doctrine of justification. Chemnitz drafted a compendium of doctrine and reorganized the structure of the church in Wolfenbüttel; later, he led efforts to reconcile divisions within Lutheranism, culminating in the Formula of Concord*. One of his chief theological accomplishments was a modification of the christological doctrine of the *communicatio idiomatium*, which provided a Lutheran platform for understanding the sacramental presence of Christ's humanity in the Eucharist.

David Chytraeus (1531–1600). German Lutheran professor, theologian and biblical exegete. At the age of eight Chytraeus was admitted to the University of Tübingen. There he studied law, philology, philosophy, and theology, finally receiving his master's degree in 1546. Chytraeus befriended Philipp Melanchthon* while sojourning in Wittenberg, where he taught the *Loci communes*. While teaching exegesis at the University of Rostock Chytraeus became acquainted with Tilemann Heshusius,* who strongly influenced Chytraeus away from Philippist theology. As a defender of Gnesio-Lutheran theology Chytraeus helped organize churches throughout Austria in accordance with the Augsburg Confession.* Chytraeus coauthored the Formula of Concord* with Martin Chemnitz,* Andreas Musculus (1514–1581), Nikolaus Selnecker* and Jakob Andreae.* He wrote commentaries on most of the Bible, as well as a devotional work titled *Regula vitae* (1555) that described the Christian virtues.

David Clarkson (1622–1686). English Puritan theologian. After his dismissal from the pastorate on account of the Act of Uniformity (1662), little is known about Clarkson. At the end of his life he ministered with John Owen* in London.

Robert Cleaver (1571–1613). English Puritan pastor. Cleaver served as rector at Drayton in Oxfordshire until silenced by Archbishop Richard Bancroft for advocating Nonconformity. Despite opposition from ecclesiastical authorities, Cleaver enjoyed a reputation as an excellent preacher. His published works include sermons on Hebrews 4 and Song of Songs 2 as well as one on the last chapter of Proverbs. Cleaver also authored *The Parsimony of Christian Children*, which contained a defense of infant baptism against Baptist criticisms.

Michael Cobabus (d. 1686). German Lutheran theologian and mathematician. Trained in philosophy, mathematics, and theology at the University of Rostock, Cobabus remained in the city, serving as rector of the city school until appointed professor of mathematics at the university. He later received a doctorate in theology from the University of Griefswald and exchanged his position in the Rostock mathematics faculty for a professorship in theology.

Johannes Cocceius (1603–1669). German Reformed theologian. Cocceius first served as professor of biblical philology in his hometown of Bremen before moving to Franeker, where he taught Hebrew and theology, and finally to Leiden, where he spent the majority of his career as professor of theology. Cocceius is perhaps best remembered for his exposition of Reformed

federal theology, defining the relationship between humanity and God in terms of progressive covenants. His critics, chief among them Gisbertus Voetius (1589–1676), argued that Cocceius's view of salvation history ignored the unity of the Scriptures and spiritualized the Old Testament. His other writings are extensive, including commentaries on all the books of the Bible, an influential Hebrew and Aramaic lexicon, and numerous works on theology, ethics, and philology.

John Colet (1467–1519). English Catholic priest, preacher and educator. Colet, appointed dean of Saint Paul's Cathedral by Henry VII, was a friend of Desiderius Erasmus,* on whose classical ideals Colet reconstructed the curriculum of Saint Paul's school. Colet was convinced that the foundation of moral reform lay in the education of children. Though an ardent advocate of reform, Colet, like Erasmus, remained loyal to the Catholic Church throughout his life. Colet's agenda of reform was oriented around spiritual and ethical themes, demonstrated in his commentaries on select books of the New Testament and the writings of Pseudo-Dionysius the Areopagite.

Vittoria Colonna (1490–1547). Italian Renaissance poet. Born into a noble family, Colonna was betrothed at three years of age to Fernando d'Ávalos (1489–1525), and they married in 1509. D'Ávalos was largely absent on military campaigns during their marriage, while she exercised his governorship of Benvenuto and became involved in the literary circles of Rome and Naples. One of the most important writers of her age, her friends included Pietro Bembo (1470–1547), Marguerite de Navarre,* and Michelangelo Buonarroti.* Writing primarily in the Petrarchan style, Colonna's reputation as a poet grew after the death of her husband, and much of her poetry was dedicated to his memory. Spiritual concerns form a major element of Colonna's writings, promoting contemplation and the ascetic life. While denied her desire to take holy orders in widowhood, Colonna spent much of her life residing in religious communities, and she was actively involved in movements seeking their improvement, collaborating with reformers such as Reginald Pole,* Juan de Valdés,* and Bernardo Ochino.*

Gasparo Contarini (1483–1542). Italian statesman, theologian and reform-minded cardinal. Contarini was an able negotiator and graceful compromiser. Charles V requested Contarini as the papal legate for the Colloquy of Regensburg (1541), where Contarini reached agreement with Melanchthon* on the doctrine of justification (although neither the pope nor Luther* ratified the agreement). He had come to a similar belief in the priority of faith in the work of Christ rather than works as the basis for Christian life in 1511, though unlike Luther, he never left the papal church over the issue; instead he remained within it to try to seek gentle reform, and he adhered to papal sacramental teaching. Contarini was an important voice for reform within the Catholic Church, always seeking reconciliation rather than confrontation with Protestant reformers. He wrote many works, including a treatise detailing the ideal bishop, a manual for lay church leaders, a political text on right governance and brief commentaries on the Pauline letters.

Christoph Corner (1518–1594). German Lutheran theologian. Professor of philosophy, rhetoric, and theology at the University of Frankfurt, Corner participated in the drafting of the Formula of Concord.* He also served as superintendent of churches in Mark Brandenberg.

Antonio del Corro (1527–1591). Spanish Reformed pastor and theologian. After encountering the ideas of Martin Luther* and other reformers, Corro abandoned the Hieronymite order. Leaving Spain to avoid charges of heresy, he traveled through Europe, spending time in Geneva and Lausanne before pastoring churches in France and the Low Countries. The arrival of Spanish armies in the Netherlands saw Corro and his family relocate to England, where he pastored a church of Spanish exiles in London and taught at Temple Church and Oxford. Corro courted controversy throughout his career, entering into debates with a wide array of Protestant theologians. In England, he was suspended from his pastorate for slander

and examined a number of times for heresy, with some finding suggestions of Arianism in his Christology. Although these charges were never upheld, they clouded his later career and legacy.

Antonius Corvinus (1501–1553). German Lutheran theologian, pastor, and church administrator. Influenced by evangelical ideas, Corvinus left the Cistercian order to study at Wittenberg. He held a number of pastoral and administrative positions and published numerous works, including exegetical postils on Genesis, the Psalms, the Gospels, and Letters. Perhaps his greatest influence was his role in the composition of numerous church orders, including Northeim, Calenberg, Wolfenbüttel, and Hildesheim, giving the organizational foundation for the Lutheran church in Northern Germany and establishing its autonomy from regional rulers.

John Cosin (1594–1672). Anglican preacher and bishop. Early in his career Cosin was the vice chancellor of Cambridge and canon at the Durham cathedral. But as a friend of William Laud* and an advocate for "Laudian" changes, he was suspected of being a crypto-Catholic. In 1640 during the Long Parliament a Puritan lodged a complaint with the House of Commons concerning Cosin's "popish innovations." Cosin was promptly removed from office. During the turmoil of the English Civil Wars, Cosin sojourned in Paris among English nobility but struggled financially. Cosin returned to England after the Restoration in 1660 to be consecrated as the bishop of Durham. He published annotations on the Book of Common Prayer* and a history of the canon.

John Cotton (1584–1652). New England Puritan minister. Cotton was born to Puritan parents in Derby, England. He entered Trinity College, Cambridge, graduating with his bachelor's degree in 1603. Afterward, Cotton became a fellow at Emmanuel College, Cambridge, which at the time was heavily influenced by Puritanism. There, Cotton finished his master's degree in 1606. Cotton then served as head lecturer, dean, and catechist for the college. It was in this period that he heard the preaching of Richard Sibbes,* which proved instrumental in Cotton's personal conversion. Cotton received a bachelor of divinity in 1610 from Cambridge and was shortly thereafter ordained into the priesthood of the Church of England. However, Cotton's increasing nonconformity brought him into conflict with episcopal authorities, which prompted him to move to the colony of Massachusetts in July 1633. Upon his arrival, he immediately assumed a position of leadership as the teacher of the First Church of Boston. Throughout his tenure, Cotton exerted significant influence in the civic and ecclesiastical affairs of the colony. He continued in his ministry at First Church until his death on December 23, 1652. Over the course of his ministry, Cotton wrote nearly forty works. Among these were the *Keys of the Kingdom of Heaven, and the Power Thereof* (1644) and *Exposition upon the Thirteenth Chapter of Revelation* (1655).

Council of Constance (1414–1418). Convened to resolve the Western Schism, root out heresy and reform the church in head and members, the council asserted in *Sacrosancta* (1415) the immediate authority of ecumenical councils assembled in the Holy Spirit under Christ—even over the pope. Martin V was elected pope in 1417 after the three papal claimants were deposed; thus, the council ended the schism. The council condemned Jan Hus,* Jerome of Prague (c. 1365–1416) and, posthumously, John Wycliffe. Hus and Jerome, despite letters of safe conduct, were burned at the stake. Their deaths ignited the Hussite Wars, which ended as a result of the Council of Basel's concessions to the Bohemian church. The council fathers sought to reform the church through the regular convocation of councils (*Frequens*; 1417). Martin V begrudgingly complied by calling the required councils, then immediately disbanding them. Pius II (r. 1458–1464) reasserted papal dominance through *Execrabilis* (1460), which condemned any appeal to a future council apart from the pope's authority.

Council of Trent (1545–1563) Convoked by Pope Paul III (r. 1534–1549) with the support of Charles V*, the nineteenth ecumenical council was convened in the northern Italian city of Trent.

Attended primarily by Italian clerics, it met in three distinct phases. Beginning in December 1545, during its first eight sessions, the council issued doctrinal decrees, asserting the authority of tradition alongside Scripture, the authenticity of the Vulgate, the prerogative of the church in interpretation, and the necessity of human cooperation in the work of salvation. Ecclesial abuses were also addressed, as attempts were made to eliminate absenteeism and pluralism and devolve power from Rome to bishoprics and parishes. The council was suspended following the outbreak of the plague in Trent in March 1547. A number of Protestant delegates were present during the second phase of the council, which met between May 1551 and April 1552 under the supervision of Pope Julius III (r. 1550–1555). The primary achievement of this period of the council was the clarification of teachings on the seven sacraments, with transubstantiation, the objective efficacy of the Eucharist, and the necessity of auricular confession confirmed as dogma. Reconvened by Pope Pius IV (r. 1559–1565) in 1561, the third phase of the council addressed the relationship between bishops and Rome, resulting in affirmations of the divine appointment of the church hierarchy and the obligation of bishops to reside in their dioceses. Clerical education, the regulation of marriage, and teachings on purgatory, indulgences, the use of images, and the saints were also addressed.

Miles Coverdale (1488–1568). Anglican bishop. Coverdale is known for his translations of the Bible into English, completing William Tyndale's* efforts and later producing the Great Bible commissioned by Henry VIII* (1539). A former friar, Coverdale was among the Cambridge scholars who met at the White Horse Tavern to discuss Martin Luther's* ideas. During Coverdale's three terms of exile in Europe, he undertook various translations, including the Geneva Bible*. He was appointed bishop of Exeter by Thomas Cranmer* and served as chaplain to Edward VI. Coverdale contributed to Cranmer's first edition of the Book of Common Prayer.*

William Cowper (Couper) (1568–1619). Scottish Puritan bishop. After graduating from the University of St. Andrews, Cowper worked in parish ministry for twenty-five years before becoming bishop. As a zealous Puritan and advocate of regular preaching and rigorous discipline, Cowper championed Presbyterian polity and lay participation in church government. Cowper published devotional works, sermon collections and a commentary on Revelation.

Walter Cradock (1606–1659). Welsh Anglican minister. Cradock was born in Llangwm, Monmouthshire, Wales. After completing his education at the University of Oxford, Cradock assumed his first position as curate at Peterson-super-Ely, Glamorgan. In 1633, Cradock, along with some other Welsh ministers, was reported to Archbishop William Laud* and the Court of High Commission for preaching nonconformity and for refusing the *Book of Sports*. In 1634 Cradock traveled throughout Wexham and Herefordshire encouraging the establishment of Welsh Nonconformist congregations. Cradock later became pastor of an Independent congregation at Llanfair Waterdine in 1639. When the English Civil War began, Cradock and his conventicle moved to Bristol, but when Royalist forces came to occupy the city, he and some of his group departed for All-Hallows-the-Great, where he preached regularly with Henry Jessey (1603–1663). In 1641, Cradock was among the group of preachers for Wales commissioned by the Long Parliament. Later, he served as regular preacher for the Barebones Parliament. Throughout this period, Cradock was an ardent supporter of Oliver Cromwell. Cradock lived the remainder of his life quietly while ministering to a congregation at Llangwm. Throughout his career, Cradock authored a number of devotional works, among which were *Gospel Liberty* (1648) and *Gospel Holiness* (1655).

Thomas Cranmer (1489–1556). Anglican archbishop and theologian. Cranmer supervised church reform and produced the first two editions of the Book of Common Prayer.* As a doctoral student at Cambridge, he was involved in the discussions at the White Horse Tavern. Cranmer contributed to a religious defense of Henry VIII's* divorce; Henry then appointed him Archbishop of Canterbury. Cranmer cautiously steered the course of reform, accelerating under Edward VI. After supporting the attempted coup to prevent Mary's assuming the throne, Cranmer was convicted of treason and burned at the stake. Cranmer's legacy is the splendid English of his liturgy and prayer books.

Richard Crashaw (1612–1649). English Catholic poet. Educated at Cambridge, Crashaw was fluent in Hebrew, Greek and Latin. His first volume of poetry was *Epigrammatum sacrorum liber* (1634). Despite being born into a Puritan family, Crashaw was attracted to Catholicism, finally converting in 1644 after he was forced to resign his fellowship for not signing the Solemn League and Covenant (1643). In 1649, he was made a subcanon of Our Lady of Loretto by Cardinal Palotta.

Herbert Croft (1603–1691). Anglican bishop. As a boy Croft converted to Catholicism; he returned to the Church of England during his studies at Oxford. Before the English Civil Wars, he served as chaplain to Charles I. After the Restoration, Charles II appointed him as bishop. Croft ardently opposed Catholicism in his later years.

John Crompe (d. 1661). Anglican priest. Educated at Cambridge, Crompe published a commentary on the Apostles' Creed, a sermon on Psalm 21:3 and an exposition of Christ's passion.

Oliver Cromwell (1599–1658). Commander of the Parliamentary forces during the English Civil War. Lord Protector of the Commonwealth of England, Scotland, and Ireland. Cromwell was born in Huntingdon, East Anglia, the only surviving son of Robert Cromwell. In 1616, he enrolled at the University of Cambridge as a fellow commoner. However, he withdrew from the university the following year due to his father's death. He represented Huntingdon in Parliament in 1628, and later Cambridge in the Short and Long Parliaments. During the Civil War, he commanded the Parliamentary forces, which he led to victory at the Battles of Marston Moor

(1644) and Naseby (1645). After the execution of King Charles I in 1649, he became a member of the Council of State. It was at this time that the monarchy was abolished. In 1653, he was elevated to the position of Lord Protector of the Commonwealth. He declined the crown, though it was offered him in 1657. As Lord Protector, he endeavored to lead the postwar recovery, suppress military resistance, and advance British influence throughout Europe and the world. Moreover, he promoted a limited religious toleration in the kingdoms of England, Scotland, and Ireland. After his death in 1658, his son Richard (1626–1712) succeeded him as Lord Protector. However, due to incompetence, Richard was forced to resign, which paved the way for the Restoration of the monarchy in 1660 with the ascension of Charles II (1630–1685) to the throne. One year after the Restoration, Oliver Cromwell's body was disinterred from Westminster Abbey, hung on the gallows at Tyburn, and cast into an unmarked grave.

Caspar Cruciger (1504–1548). German Lutheran theologian. Recognized for his alignment with the theological views of Philipp Melanchthon,* Cruciger was a scholar respected among both Protestants and Catholics. In 1521, Cruciger came Wittenberg to study Hebrew and remained there most of his life. He became a valuable partner for Martin Luther* in translating the Old Testament and served as teacher, delegate to major theological colloquies and rector. Cruciger was an agent of reform in his birthplace of Leipzig, where at the age of fifteen he had observed the disputation between Luther and Johann Eck.*

Elisabeth Cruciger (c. 1500–1535). German Lutheran hymnist. Following her conversion to Lutheranism, Cruciger left the Praemonstratensian order and relocated to Wittenberg, where she married Caspar Cruciger.* While her authorship has been contested, recent scholarship has assigned Cruciger the place of the first female Lutheran hymnist for her composition of "Lord Christ is the Only Son of God" (Herr Christ der einig Gotts Sohn) (1524).

Ralph Cudworth (d. 1624) English Protestant minister. Father of noted Cambridge Platonist Ralph Cudworth (1617–1688), the elder Cudworth was a fellow of Emanuel College, Cambridge and rector of Aller in Somersetshire.

Marguerite d'Angoulême (1492–1549). French Catholic noblewoman. The elder sister of King Francis I of France, Marguerite was the Queen of Navarre and Duchess of Alençon and Berry. She was a poet and author of the French Renaissance. She composed *The Mirror of a Sinful Soul* (1531)—condemned by the theologians of the Sorbonne for containing Lutheran ideas—and an unfinished collection of short stories, the *Heptaméron* (1558). A leading figure in the French Reformation, Marguerite was at the center of a network of reform-minded individuals that included Guillame Briçonnet,* Jacques Lefèvre d'Etaples,* Gérard Roussel (1500–1550) and Guillaume Farel (1489–1565).

Jakob Dachser (1486–1567). German Anabaptist theologian and hymnist. Dachser served as a Catholic priest in Vienna until he was imprisoned and then exiled for defending the Lutheran understanding of the Mass and fasting. Hans Hut* rebaptized him in Augsburg, where Dachser was appointed as a leader of the Anabaptist congregation. Lutheran authorities imprisoned him for nearly four years. In 1531 he recanted his Radical beliefs and began to catechize children with the permission of the city council. Dachser was expelled from Augsburg as a possible insurrectionist in 1552 and relocated to Pfalz-Neuberg. He published a number of poems, hymns and mystical works, and he versified several psalms.

Jean Daillé (1594–1670). French Reformed pastor. Born into a devout Reformed family, Daillé studied theology and philosophy at Saumur under the most influential contemporary lay leader in French Protestantism, Philippe Duplessis-Mornay (1549–1623). Daillé held to Amyraldianism—the belief that Christ died for all humanity inclusively, not particularly for the elect who would inherit salvation (though only the elect are in fact saved). He wrote a controversial treatise on the church fathers that aggravated many Catholic and

Anglican scholars because of Daillé's apparent demotion of patristic authority in matters of faith.

Lambert Daneau (1535–1595). French Reformed pastor and theologian. After a decade of pastoring in France, following the St. Bartholomew's Day Massacre, Daneau fled to Geneva to teach theology at the Academy. He later taught in the Low Countries, finishing his career in southern France. Daneau's diverse works include tracts on science, ethics and morality as well as numerous theological and exegetical works.

John Davenant (1576–1641). Anglican bishop and professor. Davenant attended Queen's College, Cambridge, where he received his doctorate and was appointed professor of divinity. During the Remonstrant controversy, James I* sent Davenant as one of the four representatives for the Church of England to the Synod of Dordrecht.* Following James's instructions, Davenant advocated a *via media* between the Calvinists and the Remonstrants, although in later years he defended against the rise of Arminianism in England. In 1621, Davenant was promoted to the bishopric of Salisbury, where he was generally receptive to Laudian reforms. Davenant's lectures on Colossians are his best-known work.

William Day (1605–1684). Anglican theologian. Born and raised in Windsor, Berkshire, Day received his early education from Eton College. Afterward, he matriculated at King's College, Cambridge, where he was elected a fellow in 1624. Day received his BA in 1629, and MA in 1632. In 1635, Day was incorporated MA at Oxford and in 1637 became vicar of Mapledurham, Oxfordshire. Throughout his long career, Day conformed to all the ecclesiastical changes dictated by the government through the Restoration, during which he retained his vicarage. Finally, Day was made divinity reader at the King's Chapel, Windsor Chapel. He published two commentaries, *An Exposition of the Book of the Prophet Isaiah* (1654) and *A Paraphrase and Commentary upon the Epistle of St. Paul to the Romans* (1666).

Defense of the Augsburg Confession (1531). See *Augsburg Confession.*

Hans Denck (c. 1500–1527). German Radical theologian. Denck, a crucial early figure of the German Anabaptist movement, combined medieval German mysticism with the radical sacramental theology of Andreas Bodenstein von Karlstadt* and Thomas Müntzer.* Denck argued that the exterior forms of Scripture and sacrament are symbolic witnesses secondary to the internally revealed truth of the Sprit in the human soul. This view led to his expulsion from Nuremberg in 1525; he spent the next two years in various centers of reform in the German territories. At the time of his death, violent persecution against Anabaptists was on the rise throughout northern Europe.

Stephen Denison (unknown). English Puritan pastor. Denison received the post of curate at St. Katherine Cree in London sometime in the 1610s, where he ministered until his ejection from office in 1635. During his career at St. Katherine Cree, Denison waded into controversy with both Puritans (over the doctrine of predestination) and Anglicans (over concerns about liturgical ceremonies). He approached both altercations with rancor and rigidity, although he seems to have been quite popular and beloved by most of his congregation. In 1631, William Laud* consecrated the newly renovated St. Katherine Cree, and as part of the festivities Denison offered a sermon on Luke 19:27 in which he publicly rebuked Laud for fashioning the Lord's house into a "den of robbers." Aside from the record of his quarrels, very little is known about Denison. In addition to *The White Wolf* (a 1627 sermon against another opponent), he published a catechism for children (1621), a treatise on the sacraments (1621) and a commentary on 2 Peter 1 (1622).

Marie Dentière (1495–1561). Belgian Reformed theologian. Dentière relinquished her monastic vows and married Simon Robert (d.1533), a former priest, in Strasbourg. After Robert died, she married Antoine Froment (1508–1581), a reformer in Geneva, and became involved in the reform of that city. Her best-known writings are a tract addressed to Marguerite d'Angoulême,* the *Very Useful Epistle* (1539), in which she espoused the evangelical faith and the right of women to interpret and teach scripture, and a preface to Calvin's sermon on 1 Timothy 2:8-12. Dentière is the only woman to have her name inscribed on the International Monument to the Reformation in Geneva.

Edward Dering (c.1540–1576). English Puritan preacher. An early Puritan, Dering's prospects of advancement in the Elizabethan church were effectively ended after a sermon in front of the Queen in which he described her as an "untamed and unruly heifer" while criticizing the state of the church and clergy. While continuing with intemperate and critical attacks throughout his career, Dering established himself as a preacher at St. Paul's Cathedral in London, where he became known for his pastoral concern and desire to teach the assurance of salvation.

David Dickson (1583?–1663). Scottish Reformed pastor, preacher, professor and theologian. Dickson defended the Presbyterian form of ecclesial reformation in Scotland and was recognized for his iteration of Calvinist federal theology and expository biblical commentaries. Dickson served for over twenty years as professor of philosophy at the University of Glasgow before being appointed professor of divinity. He opposed the imposition of Episcopalian measures on the church in Scotland and was active in political and ecclesial venues to protest and prohibit such influences. Dickson was removed from his academic post following his refusal of the oath of supremacy during the Restoration era.

Veit Dietrich (1506–1549). German Lutheran preacher and theologian. Dietrich intended to study medicine at the University of Wittenberg, but Martin Luther* and Philipp Melanchthon* convinced him to study theology instead. Dietrich developed a strong relationship with Luther, accompanying him to the Marburg Colloquy (1529) and to Coburg Castle during the Diet of Augsburg (1530). After graduating, Dietrich taught on the arts faculty, eventually becoming dean. In 1535 he returned to his hometown, Nuremberg, to pastor. Later in life, Dietrich worked with Melanchthon to reform the church in Regensburg. In 1547, when Charles V arrived in Nuremberg, Dietrich was suspended from the pastorate; he resisted the imposition of the Augsburg Interim to no avail. In addition to transcribing some of Luther's lectures, portions of the Table Talk and the very popular *Hauspostille* (1544), Dietrich published his own sermons for children, a manual for pastors and a summary of the Bible.

Louis de Dieu (1590–1642). Dutch Reformed pastor and linguist. Committed to his pastoral and teaching ministry in Leiden, Dieu turned down the opportunity to teach theology and Old Testament at the University of Utrecht. He published grammars of Hebrew (1626) and Persian (1639); a comparative grammar of Hebrew, Aramaic, and Syriac (1628); and a collection of writings on the New Testament text.

Giovanni Diodati (1576–1649). Italian Reformed theologian. Diodati was from an Italian banking family who fled for religious reasons to Geneva. There he trained under Theodore Beza;* on completion of his doctoral degree, Diodati became professor of Hebrew at the academy. He was an ecclesiastical representative of the church in Geneva (for whom he was a delegate at the Synod of Dordrecht*) and an advocate for reform in Venice. Diodati's chief contribution to the Italian reform movement was a translation of the Bible into Italian (1640–1641), which remains the standard translation in Italian Protestantism.

John Dod (c. 1549–1645). English Puritan pastor. Over the course of his lengthy pastoral career (spanning roughly sixty years), Dod was twice suspended for nonconformity and twice reinstated. A popular preacher, he published many sermons as well as commentaries on the Ten Commandments and the Lord's Prayer; collections of his sayings and anecdotes were compiled after his death.

John Donne (1572–1631). Anglican poet and preacher. Donne was born into a strong Catholic family. However, sometime between his brother's death from the plague while in prison in 1593 and the publication of his *Pseudo-Martyr* in 1610, Donne joined the Church of England. Ordained to the Anglican priesthood in 1615 and already widely recognized for his verse, Donne quickly rose to prominence as a preacher—some have deemed him the best of his era. His textual corpus is an amalgam of erotic *and* divine poetry (e.g., "Batter My Heart"), as well as a great number of sermons.

Dordrecht Confession (1632). Dutch Mennonite confession. Adriaan Cornelisz (1581–1632) wrote the Dordrecht Confession to unify Dutch Mennonites. This basic statement of Mennonite belief and practice affirms distinctive doctrines such as nonresistance, shunning, footwashing and the refusal to swear oaths. Most continental Mennonites subscribed to this confession during the second half of the seventeenth century.

John Downame (c. 1571–1652). English Puritan pastor and theologian. See *English Annotations.*

Charles Drelincourt (1595–1669). French Reformed pastor, theologian and controversialist. After studying at Saumur Academy, Drelincourt pastored the Reformed Church in Paris for nearly fifty years. He was well known for his ministry to the sick. In addition to polemical works against Catholicism, he published numerous pastoral resources: catechisms, three volumes of sermons and a five-volume series on consolation for the suffering.

The Dutch Annotations (1657). See *Statenvertaling.*

Daniel Dyke (d. 1614). English Puritan preacher. Born of nonconformist stock, Dyke championed a more thorough reformation of church practice in England. After the promulgation of John Whitgift's* articles in 1583, Dyke refused to accept what he saw as remnants of Catholicism, bringing him into conflict with the bishop of London. Despite the petitions of his congregation and some politicians, the bishop of London suspended Dyke from his ministry for refusing priestly ordination and conformity to the Book of Common Prayer.* All of his work was published posthumously; it is mostly focused on biblical interpretation.

Johann Eck (Johann Maier of Eck) (1486–1543). German Catholic theologian. Though Eck was not an antagonist of Martin Luther* until the dispute over indulgences, Luther's Ninety-five Theses (1517) sealed the two as adversaries. After their debate at the Leipzig Disputation (1519),

Eck participated in the writing of the papal bull that led to Luther's excommunication. Much of Eck's work was written to oppose Protestantism or to defend Catholic doctrine and the papacy; his *Enchiridion* was a manual written to counter Protestant doctrine. However, Eck was also deeply invested in the status of parish preaching, publishing a five-volume set of postils. He participated in the assemblies at Regensburg and Augsburg and led the Catholics in their rejection of the Augsburg Confession.

Edward VI of England (1537–1553). English monarch. Son of Henry VIII* and Jane Seymour (1508–1537), Edward ascended to the throne as a minor, leaving the practical power of the monarchy in the hands of those appointed by the Regency council as Lord Protector of the Realm, first, his uncle, Edward Seymour, duke of Somerset (1500–1552), and afterwards, John Dudley, duke of Northumberland (1504–1553). Under Somerset and Northumberland, and with Thomas Cranmer* installed as Archbishop of Canterbury, the eclectic reforms made during the reign of Henry VIII were drawn into the service of a thoroughly Protestant transformation. During the reign of Edward, communion in two kinds was instituted, all services were held in the vernacular, and a series of ecclesiastical visitations oversaw the suppression of Catholic religion. Alongside the flood of Protestant refugees from the continent that sheltered in the kingdom, the publication of the revised Book of Common Prayer*, the Book of Homilies* and the Forty–Two Articles (1553) helped establish the future direction of Anglicanism.

Elizabeth I of England (1533–1603) English monarch. The daughter of Henry VIII* (r. 1509–1547) and Anne Boleyn (c. 1501–1536), Elizabeth outwardly conformed to Catholicism during the reign of her sister Mary I (r. 1553–1558), but her Protestant upbringing encouraged the hopes of many reformers upon her accession in 1558. With the 1559 Elizabethan Settlement, Elizabeth redefined England as a Protestant country, with the Act of Supremacy asserting the monarch as the head of the English church, and the Act of

Uniformity establishing the 1559 *Book of Common Prayer** as the valid order of service within the realm. However, Elizabeth resisted the aggressive persecution of Catholics for political reasons, while also allowing some traditional vestments, furniture and ceremonies to be retained. Her moderate and pragmatic reforms frustrated many who wished for more thorough change and led to the emergence of the Puritan movement. Elizabeth faced numerous threats during her reign, including the machinations of Scottish Catholics and claims to the throne of Mary Stuart (1542–1547), leading to her rival's imprisonment and execution in 1587; the attempted invasion of England by Spain, which culminated in the celebrated defeat of the Spanish Armada in 1588; and a Catholic rebellion in Ireland that was suppressed during the Nine Years War (1594–1603). Elizabeth never married, and was succeeded on the throne by James I* following her death in 1603.

Edward Elton (1569–1624). Puritan minister. Elton served as pastor of St. Mary Magdalen's Church in Bermondsey, Surrey. Richard Baxter* praised him for his exegetical works, among which were *Three Excellent Pious Treatises in Sundry Sermons upon the Whole Seventh, Eighth, and Ninth Chapters of the Epistle to the Romans* and *An Exposition of the Epistle of St. Paul to the Colossians*.

English Annotations (1645; 1651; 1657). Under a commission from the Westminster Assembly, the editors of the English Annotations—John Downame* along with unnamed colleagues—translated, collated and digested in a compact and accessible format several significant Continental biblical resources, including Calvin's* commentaries, Beza's* *Annotationes majores* and Diodati's* *Annotations*.

Desiderius Erasmus (1466–1536). Dutch Catholic humanist and pedagogue. Erasmus, a celebrated humanist scholar, was recognized for translations of ancient texts, reform of education according to classical studies, moral and spiritual writings and the first printed edition of the Greek New Testament. A former Augustinian who never left the Catholic Church, Erasmus addressed deficiencies he saw in the church and society, challenging numerous prevailing doctrines but advocating reform. He envisioned a simple, spiritual Christian life shaped by the teachings of Jesus and ancient wisdom. He was often accused of collusion with Martin Luther* on account of some resonance of their ideas but hotly debated Luther on human will.

Paul Fagius (1504–1549). German Reformed Hebraist and pastor. After studying at the University of Heidelberg, Fagius went to Strasbourg where he perfected his Hebrew under Wolfgang Capito.* In Isny im Allgäu (Baden-Württemberg) he met the great Jewish grammarian Elias Levita (1469–1549), with whom he established a Hebrew printing press. In 1544 Fagius returned to Strasbourg, succeeding Capito as preacher and Old Testament lecturer. During the Augsburg Interim, Fagius (with Martin Bucer*) accepted Thomas Cranmer's* invitation to translate and interpret the Bible at Cambridge. However, Fagius died before he could begin any of the work. Fagius wrote commentaries on the first four chapters of Genesis and the deuterocanonical books of Sirach and Tobit.

Guillaume Farel (1489–1565) French Reformed preacher and theologian. At the vanguard of the French Reformation, Farel was a student of Jacques Lefèvre d'Étaples* and member of Archbishop Briçonnet's* circle in Meaux until his desire for more rapid change saw him depart in 1523 to preach the Protestant message in Basel, Montbéliard, Strasbourg, Bern, and Aigle. During this period of his ministry, he composed the first French Protestant book, an evangelical commentary on the Lord's Prayer and the Apostle's Creed, as well as the first French Confession of Faith. A catalyst in Geneva's acceptance of the Reformation in 1536, it was Farel who persuaded Calvin* to settle in the city. After he and Calvin were banished from Geneva in 1538, Farel accepted the pastorate in Neuchâtel, a position he held until his death while continuing to travel and support the Reformation in the French-speaking lands.

John Fary (unknown). English Puritan pastor. Fary authored *God's Severity on Man's Sterility* (1645), a sermon on the fruitless fig tree in Luke 13:6-9.

Margaret Fell (1614–1702). English Quaker. Known as the "Mother of Quakerism," Fell was born at Dalton-in-Furness in northern England. The daughter of a local judge, she married Thomas Fell, who was a judge as well as a member of Parliament, representing Lancashire. In 1652, under the preaching of George Fox (1624–1691), Fell and her daughters became members of the Society of Friends (the Quakers). From that time onward, she became a pivotal figure in the subsequent development of the Quaker movement. Throughout her extensive correspondence to powerful members of the nobility, including King Charles II (r. 1660–1685), she pleaded for the release of imprisoned Quakers. Fell was arrested in 1664 for leading Quaker meetings and for her refusal to swear the Oath of Obedience, and she was sentenced to four and a half years imprisonment. After her release, she married George Fox in 1669, her first husband having died eleven years earlier. In addition to her advocacy for incarcerated Quakers, Fell enhanced the work of the Quaker Women's Meeting, which consisted of caring for the sick and elderly as well as orphans and prisoners. Her exegetical works include *For Mannaseth Ben Israel* and *A Loving Salutation to the Seed of Abraham*, both published in 1656, and translated into Hebrew (the latter believed to have been translated by the Jewish philosopher Benedict Spinoza). Moreover during her imprisonment, she authored her most famous treatise, *Women's Speaking Justified, Proved and Allowed of by the Scriptures.*

William Fenner (1600–1640). English Puritan pastor. After studying at Cambridge and Oxford, Fenner ministered at Sedgley and Rochford. Fenner's extant writings, which primarily deal with practical and devotional topics, demonstrate a zealous Puritan piety and a keen interest in Scripture and theology.

Charles Ferme (1566–1617). Scottish Reformed pastor and educator. After studying and teaching at the University of Edinburgh, Ferme pastored in Philorth, where he later served as the principal of a newly chartered university. The reconstitution of the episcopacy brought challenges for Ferme, and his resistance saw him imprisoned a number of times, including a three-year incarceration on the Isle of Bute. His only extant writing is a logical analysis of Romans.

First Helvetic Confession (1536). Anticipating the planned church council at Mantua (1537, but delayed until 1545 at Trent), Reformed theologians of the Swiss cantons drafted a confession to distinguish themselves from both Catholics and the churches of the Augsburg Confession.* Heinrich Bullinger* led the discussion and wrote the confession itself; Leo Jud, Oswald Myconius, Simon Grynaeus and others were part of the assembly. Martin Bucer* and Wolfgang Capito* had desired to draw the Lutheran and Reformed communions closer together through this document, but Luther* proved unwilling after Bullinger refused to accept the Wittenberg Concord (1536). This confession was largely eclipsed by Bullinger's Second Helvetic Confession.*

John Fisher (1469–1535). English Catholic bishop and theologian. This reputed preacher defended Catholic orthodoxy and strove to reform abuses in the church. In 1521 Henry VIII* honored Fisher with the title *Fidei Defensor* ("defender of the faith"). Nevertheless, Fisher opposed the king's divorce of Catherine of Aragon (1485–1536) and the independent establishment of the Church of England; he was convicted for treason and executed. Most of Fisher's works are polemical and occasional (e.g., on transubstantiation, against Martin Luther*); however, he also published a series of sermons on the seven penitential psalms. In addition to his episcopal duties, Fisher was the chancellor of Cambridge from 1504 until his death.

Matthias Flacius (1520–1575). Lutheran theologian. A native of Croatia, Matthias Flacius commenced his studies at the University of Tubingen, and completed them at Wittenberg, where through Luther's influence, he embraced the university's evangelical theology. Flacius began his career as instructor of Hebrew at the University of Wittenberg in 1544, and remained in this post until 1549. As a devoted follower of Luther's teachings, Flacius sought to defend them in their purity which drove him and Nikolaus von Amsdorf as leaders of the Gnesio-Lutherans to oppose the more moderate positions of Philipp Melanchthon and his sympathizers, the Philippists, in several controversies concerning the role of free will and good works in justification as well as relations with Calvinism. After serving as a professor at the University of Jena (1557–1561), Flacius spent the remainder of his life as an independent scholar, frequently moving from one city to another to escape persecution. Flacius died in Frankfurt am Main in 1575. His important exegetical works are *De vocabula Dei* (1549), *Clavis Scripturae Sacrae* (1567), and *Glossa Novi Testamenti* (1570). Flacius also published two historical works, *Catalogus Testium Veritatis* (1556) and the *Magdeburg Centuries*.

Marcantonio Flaminio (1498–1550). Italian humanist and poet. Flaminio was dependent on patronage, and he spent much of his life in the houses of noble benefactors in Bologna, Genoa, and Verona. While he never left the Roman church, he was drawn to intellectual currents that sought reform. In Naples, he participated in an intellectual circle that included Juan de Valdés* and Pietro Carnesecchi* before joining the house of Cardinal Pole* in Viterbo. Alongside his poetry and humanistic writings, Flaminio also edited one of the most significant Italian texts of the Reformation, Benedetto de Mantova's* *The Benefit of Christ* (1543).

John Flavel (c. 1630–1691). English Puritan pastor. Trained at Oxford, Flavel ministered in southwest England from 1650 until the Act of Uniformity in 1662, which reaffirmed the compulsory use of the Book of Common Prayer. Flavel preached unofficially for many years, until his congregation was eventually allowed to build a meeting place in 1687. His works were numerous, varied and popular.

Giovanni Battista Folengo (1490–1559). Italian Catholic exegete. In 1528 Folengo left the Benedictine order, questioning the validity of monastic vows; he returned to the monastic life in 1534. During this hiatus Folengo came into contact with the Neapolitan reform-minded circle founded by Juan de Valdés.* Folengo published commentaries on the Psalms, John, 1–2 Peter and James. Augustin Marlorat* included Folengo's comment in his anthology of exegesis on the Psalms. In 1580 Folengo's Psalms commentary was added to the Index of Prohibited Books.

John Forbes (1568?–1634). Scottish Reformed pastor. While minister at Alford in Aberdeenshire, Forbes was appointed moderator of the Presbyterian Aberdeen Assembly, which met against the orders of King James I.* Refusing to accept the monarch's jurisdiction, he was exiled to the Continent and settled in the Netherlands, where he pastored English congregations at Middleburg and Delft until forced out under the reforms of Archbishop Laud.*

Formula of Concord (1577). After Luther's* death, intra-Lutheran controversies between the Gnesio-Lutherans (partisans of Luther) and the Philippists (partisans of Melanchthon*) threatened to cause a split among those who had subscribed to the Augsburg Confession.* In 1576, Jakob Andreae,* Martin Chemnitz,* Nikolaus Selnecker,* David Chytraeus* and Andreas Musculus (1514–1581) met with the intent of resolving the controversies, which mainly regarded the relationship between good works and salvation, the third use of the law, and the role of the human will in accepting God's grace. In 1580, celebrating the fiftieth anniversary of the presentation of the Augsburg Confession to Charles V (1500–1558), the *Book of Concord* was printed as the authoritative interpretation of the Augsburg Confession; it included the three ancient creeds, the Augsburg Confession, its Apology (1531), the Schmalkald Articles,* Luther's *Treatise on the Power and Primacy of the Pope* (1537) and both his Small and Large Catechisms (1529).

John Foxe (1516–1587). English Protestant martryrologist, historian. John Foxe was born in Boston, Lincolnshire. After completing his early education, Foxe became a fellow at Magdalen College, Oxford, where he completed his BA degree in 1537, and MA in 1543. Also he was lecturer in logic from 1539 to 1540. However, in 1545, Foxe was forced to resign from Magdalen because he had adopted Protestant beliefs. After leaving Oxford, Foxe became tutor to the children of the Earl of Surrey. During this time Foxe made the acquaintance of John Bale (1495–1562) who fostered his interest in history. When Mary Tudor ascended the throne of England in 1553, Foxe fled to the continent. While there, Foxe traveled to Frankfurt, where in 1555 he met Edmund Grindal (1519–1583), who had been composing accounts of Protestant martyrs. Foxe later joined Grindal in Basel, where he translated his narratives into Latin. Foxe published the book resulting from his labors in Basel in 1559. After Elizabeth I* succeeded to the throne in the same year, Foxe returned to England. Upon his return he began working with the printer, John Day, who published the first English edition of Foxe's work. This voluminous work, *The Acts and Monuments*, underwent four editions during the remainder of the author's lifetime. *The Acts and Monuments* contributed significantly to the development of the national identity and piety of Elizabethan England. Shorter versions of this work are known simply as *Foxe's Book of Martyrs*.

Francis I of France (1494–1547). French monarch. Francis ascended to the French throne following the death of Louis XII (1462–1515), who was both his cousin and father-in-law. Much of Francis's reign was dominated by warfare. In Italy, victory over the Swiss allowed him to assert his dynastic claim to the Duchy of Milan, and extract liberties for the French church from Pope Leo X* through the Concordat of Bologna. His campaign against Charles V* was less successful, however, as Milan was lost and following defeat at the Battle of Pavia, Francis was taken prisoner. His release was negotiated by his sister, Marguerite d'Angouleme*, though he reneged in its terms once reaching safety, ensuring continued conflict with the Holy Roman Emperor throughout his reign. Francis fostered humanistic learning within his kingdom, and while he resisted Lutheran and other evangelical thought, he gave some space for its expression, giving protection to scholars such as those gathered around his sister and Bishop Guillaume Briçonnet* at Meaux. His desire for social order saw him take increasingly strident steps against the Reformation, however, particularly after his bedchamber was pamphleted during the Affair of the Placards, and the final years of his reign saw a significant increase in attempts to reassert Catholic doctrine and stamp out Protestantism with persecution.

Sebastian Franck (1499–1542). German Radical theologian. Franck became a Lutheran in 1525, but by 1529 he began to develop ideas that distanced him from Protestants and Catholics. Expelled from Strasbourg and later Ulm due to his controversial writings, Franck spent the end of his life in Basel. Franck emphasized God's word as a divine internal spark that cannot be adequately expressed in outward forms. Thus he criticized religious institutions and dogmas. His work consists mostly of commentaries, compilations and translations. In his sweeping historical *Chronica* (1531), Franck supported numerous heretics condemned by the Catholic Church and criticized political and church authorities.

Leonhard Frick (d. 1528). Austrian Radical martyr. See *Kunstbuch*.

John Frith (1503–1533). English reformer, author, and martyr. Frith was born in Westerham, Kent. He was the son of Richard Frith, the innkeeper of the White Horse Inn. After receiving his earlier education at Sevenoaks Grammar School and Eton College, Frith matriculated at Queen's College, Cambridge, where Stephen Gardiner (1497–1555), future bishop of Winchester, and opponent of the English Reformation, was his tutor. Frith graduated with his BA degree in 1525, having obtained proficiency in Latin and mathematics. While still a student, Frith met Thomas Bilney (1495–1531), who most likely introduced him to evangelical faith. After graduating, Frith became a junior canon at Christ Church, Oxford. However, while at Oxford, Frith along with nine others was imprisoned in a fish cellar for possessing what ecclesiastical authorities considered "heretical books." Upon his release, Frith traveled to the Continent, where he assisted William Tyndale* with his translation work. Also while on the Continent, Frith translated some antipapal polemical works, and authored *A Disputation of Purgatory*. Upon Frith's return to England in 1532, he was arrested and imprisoned several times for publicly preaching against transubstantiation and purgatory. Eventually, Frith was imprisoned in the Tower of London, and later transferred to Newgate Prison. He was burned at the stake on July 4, 1533.

Libert Froidmont (1587–1653). Belgian philosopher, scientist, and theologian. A childhood friend of Cornelius Jansen (1585–1638), Froidmont entered the Society of Jesus and his early career was focused on philosophy and the sciences, teaching at Antwerp, Saint-Michel, and Louvain. Drawn to the rigorous but controversial Augustinianism of Jansen, Froidmont earned his doctorate in theology in 1628 and succeeded Jansen as chair of theology at Louvain. While publishing a number of theological and exegetical works, including a commentary on Paul's letters, Froidmont was also active in the scientific and philosophical debates of his era. He published against Nicolas Copernicus (1473–1543) and Galileo Galilei (1564–1642), whom he argued were wrong but not heretical, and was one of the first to engage with the thought of René Descartes (1596–1650).

William Fulke (1538–1589). English Protestant theologian. Responsible for preaching and lecturing on Old Testament and other subjects, William Fulke courted controversy during his tenure as fellow at Cambridge. He was briefly expelled for his advocacy of Vestarians and later resigned until acquitted of being in an incestuous marriage. He left Cambridge to serve as chaplain to Robert Dudley, Earl of Leicester (1532–1588), returning almost a decade later as master of Pembroke College. He is best remembered as a controversialist and was the author of numerous anti-Catholic tracts.

Gallic Confession (1559). This confession was accepted at the first National Synod of the Reformed Churches of France (1559). It was intended to be a touchstone of Reformed faith but also to show to the people of France that the Huguenots—who faced persecution—were not seditious. The French Reformed Church presented this confession to Francis II (1544–1560) in 1560, and to his successor, Charles IX (1550–1574), in 1561. The later Genevan draft, likely written by Calvin,* Beza* and Pierre Viret (1511–1571), was received as the true Reformed confession at the seventh National Synod in La Rochelle (1571).

Geneva Bible (originally printed 1560). During Mary I's reign many English Protestants sought safety abroad in Reformed territories of the Empire and the Swiss Cantons, especially in Calvin's* Geneva. A team of English exiles in Geneva led by William Whittingham (c. 1524–1579) brought this complete translation to press in the course of two years. Notable for several innovations—Roman type, verse numbers, italics indicating English idiom and not literal phrasing of the original languages, even variant readings in the Gospels and Acts—this translation is most well known for its marginal notes, which reflect a strongly Calvinist theology. The notes explained Scripture in an accessible way for the laity, also giving unlearned clergy a new sermon resource. Although controversial because of its implicit critique of royal power, this translation was wildly popular; even after the publication of the Authorized Version (1611) and James I's* 1616 ban on its printing, the Geneva Bible continued to be the most popular English translation until after the English Civil Wars.

Johann Gerhard (1582–1637). German Lutheran theologian, professor and superintendent. Gerhard is considered one of the most eminent Lutheran theologians, after Martin Luther* and Martin Chemnitz.* After studying patristics and Hebrew at Wittenberg, Jena and Marburg, Gerhard was appointed superintendent at the age of twenty-four. In 1616 he was appointed to a post at the University of Jena, where he reintroduced Aristotelian metaphysics to theology and gained widespread fame. His most important work was the nine-volume *Loci Theologici* (1610–1625). He also expanded Chemnitz's harmony of the Gospels (*Harmonia Evangelicae*), which was finally published by Polykarp Leyser (1552–1610) in 1593. Gerhard was well-known for an irenic spirit and an ability to communicate clearly.

George Gifford (c. 1548–1600). English Puritan pastor. Gifford was suspended for nonconformity in 1584. With private support, however, he was able to continue his ministry. Through his published works he wanted to help develop lay piety and biblical literacy.

George Gifford (d. 1620). English Puritan minister. A celebrated preacher in Maldon, Essex, Gifford was removed from the pulpit when he refused to subscribe to Articles of Conformity drawn up by Archbishop John Whitgift.* Allowed to continue ministry in the office of lecturer, he also served as a representative for Essex at Puritan synods. He published numerous works, including a primer for common Christians, a dialogue between a Catholic and a Protestant, and two works on witchcraft.

Anthony Gilby (c. 1510–1585). English Puritan translator. During Mary I's reign, Gilby fled to Geneva, where he assisted William Whittingham (c. 1524–1579) with the Geneva Bible.* He returned to England to pastor after Elizabeth I's* accession. In addition to translating numerous continental Reformed works into English—especially those of John Calvin* and Theodore Beza*—Gilby also wrote commentaries on Micah and Malachi.

Bernard Gilpin (1517–1583). Anglican theologian and priest. In public disputations, Gilpin defended Roman Catholic theology against John Hooper (c. 1495-1555) and Peter Martyr Vermigli.* These debates caused Gilpin to reexamine his faith. Upon Mary I's accession, Gilpin resigned his benefice. He sojourned in Belgium and France, returning to pastoral ministry in England in 1556. Gilpin dedicated himself to a preaching circuit in northern England, thus earning the moniker "the Apostle to the North." His zealous preaching and almsgiving roused royal opposition and a warrant for his arrest. On his way to the queen's commission, Gilpin fractured his leg, delaying his arrival

in London until after Mary's death and thus likely saving his life. His only extant writing is a sermon on Luke 2 confronting clerical abuses.

Paul Glock (c. 1530–1585). German Radical preacher. A teenage convert to Hutterite Anabaptism, Glock spent nineteen years imprisoned at Hohenwittlingen, unwilling to recant. While incarcerated, he wrote hymns, a confession and defense of his beliefs, and numerous letters that proved influential in the development of Anabaptist thought. After helping extinguish a fire at the prison in 1576, Glock was freed and settled with the Brethren in Moravia.

Glossa ordinaria. This standard collection of biblical commentaries consists of interlinear and marginal notes drawn from patristic and Carolingian exegesis appended to the Vulgate*; later editions also include Nicholas of Lyra's* *Postilla*. The *Glossa ordinaria* and the *Sentences* of Peter Lombard (c. 1100–1160) were essential resources for all late medieval and early modern commentators.

Thomas Goodwin (1600–1679). Puritan minister. Goodwin was born October 5, 1600, in Norfolk. After receiving his early education from local schools, Goodwin matriculated at Christ College, Cambridge, which was a prime center of Puritan influence. He graduated with the BA degree in 1616 and MA in 1620. Upon receiving his MA, Goodwin became a fellow and lecturer at the university. In October 1620, Goodwin experienced a profound conversion on his twentieth birthday. After his conversion, Goodwin joined the Puritan party at Cambridge. He was licensed to preach in the Church of England in 1625. Three years later, Goodwin became lecturer at Trinity Church. He served as vicar of this church from 1632 to 1634. Unwilling to comply with Archbishop William Laud's* directives for conformity, Goodwin was forced to resign all of his ecclesiastical and academic positions, and leave Cambridge. During the remainder of the 1630s, due to John Cotton's* influence, Goodwin came to adopt the principles of Independency. In 1639, in order to escape the increasing restrictions of unauthorized preachers, Goodwin fled to the

Netherlands, where he worked with other English Independent exiles. In 1641, Goodwin returned to England per Parliament's request, and preached before it on April 27, 1642. Goodwin was later appointed a delegate to the Westminster Assembly. In the Assembly, Goodwin proved himself to be one of the foremost advocates of Independency. After the Westminster Assembly adjourned, Goodwin was appointed a lecturer at Oxford, and a year later became president of Magdalen College. Furthermore, Goodwin served as an advisor to Oliver Cromwell (1599–1658) and as the Lord Protector's Oxford commissioner. Goodwin also tended to Cromwell on his deathbed. In addition to his university and advisory duties, Goodwin pastored an Independent church at Oxford. Notably, Goodwin was one of the primary authors of the Savoy Declaration of Faith (1658), which served as the confession of faith for the Independent/Congregational churches. When Charles II ascended to the throne of England in 1660, Goodwin withdrew from Oxford to London, where he pastored an Independent congregation until his death at the age of eighty. Throughout his career, Goodwin produced an enormous literary corpus, which includes many exegetical works. Best known among these are his expositions of Ephesians and Revelation.

Marie le Jars de Gournay (1565–1645). French Catholic writer and editor. Born into the minor nobility, the early death of Gournay's father led her family to relocate to their estate in Picardy, where she taught herself Latin and Greek. After reading the *Essais* (1580) of Michel de Montaigne (1533–1592), she committed herself to a life of literature and became active in the intellectual circles of Paris. While she translated many classical writings, she is best known for her editorial work on Montaigne's essays and her advocacy for the rights of women, laid out in a number of writings including *The Equality of Men and Women* (1622) and *The Ladies' Grievance* (1626).

Simon Goulart (1543–1628) French Reformed pastor, translator, and theologian. Goulart spent most of his career as a pastor in Geneva and its surrounds, particularly at the city parish of St. Gervais, and was the leader of the Company of Pastors during the last decades of his life. A prolific translator, he published numerous French editions of classical, patristic, and contemporary works from diverse authors including Plutarch, Seneca, Chrysostom, Cyprian, Tertullian, Beza*, Perkins* and Vermigli*. He also composed numerous devotional writings, important histories of early French Protestantism, and polemical treatises supporting the Huguenot cause.

Conrad Grebel (c. 1498–1526). Swiss Radical theologian. Grebel, considered the father of the Anabaptist movement, was one of the first defenders and performers of believers' baptism, for which he was eventually imprisoned in Zurich. One of Huldrych Zwingli's* early compatriots, Grebel advocated rapid, radical reform, clashing publicly with the civil authorities and Zwingli. Grebel's views, particularly on baptism, were influenced by Andreas Bodenstein von Karlstadt* and Thomas Müntzer.* Grebel advocated elimination of magisterial involvement in governing the church; instead, he envisioned the church as lay Christians determining their own affairs with strict adherence to the biblical text, and unified in volitional baptism.

William Greenhill (1591–1671). English Puritan pastor. Greenhill attended and worked at Magdalen College. He ministered in the diocese of Norwich but soon left for London, where he preached at Stepney. Greenhill was a member of the Westminster Assembly of Divines and was appointed the parliament chaplain by the children of Charles I. Oliver Cromwell included him among the preachers who helped draw up the Savoy Declaration. Greenhill was evicted from his post following the Restoration, after which he pastored independently. Among Greenhill's most significant contributions to church history was his *Exposition of the Prophet of Ezekiel*.

Catharina Regina von Greiffenberg (1633–1694). Austrian Lutheran poet. Upon her adulthood her guardian (and half uncle) sought to marry her; despite her protests of their consanguinity and her desire to remain celibate, she relented in 1664. After the deaths of her mother and husband, Greiffenberg abandoned her home to debtors and joined her friends Susanne Popp (d. 1683) and Sigmund von Birken (1626–1681) in Nuremberg. During her final years she dedicated herself to studying the biblical languages and to writing meditations on Jesus' death and resurrection, which she never completed. One of the most important and learned Austrian poets of the Baroque period, Greiffenberg published a collection of sonnets, songs and poems (1662) as well as three sets of mystical meditations on Jesus' life, suffering and death (1672; 1683; 1693). She participated in a society of poets called the Ister Gesellschaft.

Lady Jane Grey (1537–1554). English Protestant monarch, sometimes known as "the Nine Days Queen." The eldest daughter of Henry Grey and Frances Brandon, the daughter of Henry VIII's* younger sister Mary, Jane received an extensive Protestant and humanist education. She married Lord Guildford Dudley (c. 1535–1554), son of Edward VI's* chief minister John Dudley, Duke of Northumberland (1504–1553). Seeking to avoid succession by Edward's Catholic half-sister Mary I, Edward and Northumberland conspired to alter the order of succession, naming Jane as heir in the king's will. Following Edward's death, Jane reluctantly took the crown on July 9, 1553, but Northumberland and other Protestants were unable to raise adequate support for her claim and the Privy Council proclaimed Mary queen on July 19. Upon Mary's accession, Jane was imprisoned in the Tower of London and after trial was executed alongside her husband for treason. A handful of her writings exist demonstrating her religious affections, while the story of her martyrdom is prominent in John Foxe's Acts and Monuments.

Hugo Grotius (1583–1645). Dutch lawyer, statesman, and humanist. Grotius began practicing law at The Hague in 1599, was appointed Advocate-General of the Fisc for the provinces of Holland, Zeeland, and West Friesland in 1607 and in 1613 became pensionary of Rotterdam. As debates between Calvinists and Arminians came to national significance, Grotius sided with the Remonstrants, especially in his rejection of Reformed arguments for the independence of the church, defending the right of the state to appoint ministers and adjudicate over matters of doctrine. Following the victory of Maurice of Orange (1567–1635) over Grotius's patron Johan van Oldenbarnevelt (1547–1619) and the condemnation of Arminianism at the Synod of Dordrecht* (1618–1619), Grotius was imprisoned, though only briefly, as he escaped in a book chest and fled to Paris. Unable to secure return from exile, Grotius became a Swedish ambassador to France while seeking religious toleration and the establishment of a Christian republic. A number of his works from this period, in particular De Jure Belli ac Pacis (On the law of war and peace, 1625) made a significant contribution to the establishment of international law.

Argula von Grumbach (c. 1490–c. 1564) German Lutheran noblewoman. Grumbach, an attendant of Queen Kunigunde of Austria (1465–1520), was one of the first women to publish in support of the Reformation. She is best known for letters from 1523 and 1524 written in defense of Arsacius Seehofer (1503–1545), a lecturer at the university of Ingolstadt accused of Lutheranism. For unknown reasons, Grumberg ceased to publish after 1524, although her private correspondence after this time demonstrates a continued effort to support evangelical reform.

Johann Jacob Grynaeus (1540–1617). Swiss Reformed theologian. Raised Lutheran, Grynaeus replaced his father as pastor at Rotelen. After becoming professor of Old Testament at Basel, however, Grynaeus caused conflict by embracing Reformed theology. He avoided controversy by spending two years at the University of Heidelberg. Upon his return to Basel, his opponents had largely died, and he was made superintendent of the church in the city and professor of New Testament. Grynaeus aligned the Basel church with his Reformed convictions and reorganized the city's educational system while preaching regularly and composing numerous theological, exegetical, and practical works.

William Guild (1586–1657). Scottish Reformed minister and theologian. Guild was born in Aberdeen and educated at Marischal College. He was licensed to preach in 1605 and ordained to serve as minister of the parish of King Edward in 1608. In 1617, Guild joined the protest for the liberties of the Scottish national church. While in Edinburgh, Guild met the acquaintance of Bishop Lancelot Andrewes,* who was accompanying King James VI/I* on his royal visit to the city. Moreover, Guild dedicated his best-known work, *Moses Unveiled* (1620), to both Andrewes and the king. He was later appointed chaplain to Charles I, and shortly thereafter received the degree of doctor of divinity. In 1631, Guild was given his second charge in Aberdeen. When he assumed this charge, Guild expressed his support for episcopacy. He signed the National Covenant in 1638 with some conditions. However, when in 1640 an army came to Aberdeen to enforce full subscription to the Covenant, Guild fled to the Netherlands. After returning to Scotland later that year, he was appointed Guild Principal for King's College Aberdeen, but was deprived of this post by Oliver Cromwell's (1599–1658) military commissioners in 1651. Following his deprivation, Guild lived in retirement until his death in Aberdeen.

Rudolf Gwalther (1519–1586). Swiss Reformed preacher. Gwalther was a consummate servant of the Reformed church in Zurich, its chief religious officer and preacher, a responsibility fulfilled previously by Huldrych Zwingli* and Heinrich Bullinger.* Gwalther provided sermons and commentaries and translated the works of Zwingli into Latin. He worked for many years alongside Bullinger in structuring and governing the church in Zurich. Gwalther also strove to strengthen the connections to the Reformed churches on the Continent and England: he was a participant in the Colloquy of Regensburg (1541) and an opponent of the Formula of Concord.*

Matthias Hafenreffer (1561–1619). German Lutheran theologian. After holding pastoral positions in Herenberg, Ehingen, and Stuttgart, Hafenreffer was appointed professor of theology at Tübingen, a position he held for more than twenty-five years. He composed exegetical works on Nahum, Habakkuk, and Ezekiel, a number of polemical works, and a theological *loci communes* that served as a common textbook within the Lutheran churches for much of the seventeenth century.

Hans Has von Hallstatt (d. 1527). Austrian Reformed pastor. See *Kunstbuch.*

Henry Hammond (1605–1660). Anglican priest. After completing his studies at Oxford, Hammond was ordained in 1629. A Royalist, Hammond helped recruit soldiers for the king; he was chaplain to Charles I. During the king's captivity, Hammond was imprisoned for not submitting to Parliament. Later he was allowed to pastor again, until his death. Hammond published a catechism, numerous polemical sermons and treatises as well as his *Paraphrase and Annotations on the New Testament* (1653).

Jörg Haug (Unknown) German Anabaptist leader. Haug was a radical preacher during the 1525 Peasant's Revolt and composed a tract entitled *A Christian Order of a True Christian* (1524) enumerating seven degrees of faith reached by Christians.

Peter Hausted (d. 1645). Anglican priest and playwright. Educated at Cambridge and Oxford, Hausted ministered in a number of parishes and preached adamantly and vehemently against Puritanism. He is best known for his play *The Rival Friends*, which is filled with invective against the Puritans; during a performance before the king and queen, a riot nearly broke out. Haustead died during the siege of Banbury Castle.

Erhart Hegenwald (Unknown). Swiss Protestant teacher and doctor. A teacher at the Pfäffen Monastery in St. Gallen and at the Schola Carolina in Zurich, Hegenwald recorded the minutes of Zwingli's* First Zurich Disputation in 1523. Correspondence demonstrates he remained in contact with the Zurich reformers while he studied medicine at Wittenberg, and after graduating in 1526, he may have practiced as a physician in Frankfurt.

Heidelberg Catechism (1563). This German Reformed catechism was commissioned by the elector of the Palatinate, Frederick III (1515–1576) for pastors and teachers in his territories to use in instructing children and new believers in the faith. It was written by theologian Zacharias Ursinus (1534–1583) in consultation with Frederick's court preacher Kaspar Olevianus* and the entire theology faculty at the University of Heidelberg. The Heidelberg Catechism was accepted as one of the Dutch Reformed Church's Three Forms of Unity—along with the Belgic Confession* and the Canons of Dordrecht—at the Synod of Dordrecht,* and became widely popular among other Reformed confessional traditions throughout Europe.

Ursula Hellrigel (b. c. 1521). Austrian Anabaptist. Imprisoned for her heterodox beliefs at 17, authorities sought Hellrigel's recantation, but she refused to acquiesce. After five years she was released from prison and exiled from the Tyrol. The thirty-sixth hymn in the first known Anabaptist hymnal, the *Ausbund* (1654), is commonly attributed to her.

Niels Hemmingsen (1513–1600). Danish Lutheran theologian. Hemmingsen studied at the University of Wittenberg, where he befriended Philipp Melanchthon.* In 1542, Hemmingsen returned to Denmark to pastor and to teach Greek, dialectics and theology at the University of Copenhagen. Foremost of the Danish theologians, Hemmingsen oversaw the preparation and publication of the first Danish Bible (1550). Later in his career he became embroiled in controversies because of his Philippist theology, especially regarding the Eucharist. Due to rising tensions with Lutheran nobles outside of Denmark, King Frederick II (1534–1588) dismissed Hemmingsen from his university post in 1579, transferring him to a prominent but less internationally visible Cathedral outside of Copenhagen. Hemmingsen was a prolific author, writing commentaries on the New Testament and Psalms, sermon collections and several methodological, theological and pastoral handbooks.

Henry IV of France (1553–1610). French monarch. Son of Jeanne of Navarre* and Antoine de Bourbon (1518–1562), Henry's religious loyalties wavered throughout his life. Raised Protestant at the behest of his mother, he practiced Catholicism while attending the Valois court. After his mother's death in 1572, Henry succeeded her as King of Navarre and soon afterwards married Margaret of Valois (1553–1615), the daughter of Henry II of France (1519–1559) and Catherine de' Medici (1519–1589). Their wedding provided the occasion for the St. Bartholomew's Day Massacre, when Catholic forces seized the opportunity to decimate the Huguenot leadership gathered to celebrate the nuptials in Paris, leading to an outbreak of mob violence that devastated the Huguenot movement. A great proportion of the Protestants in France were killed in the weeks that followed the wedding, while many others, including Henry, reconverted to Catholicism. In 1576, Henry escaped the influence of the Valois court, returned his allegiance to Protestantism and took a leadership role amongst the Huguenots. Following the assassination of Henry III of France (1551–1589), Henry was the presumptive heir, but French Catholics were unwilling to accept his rule and Henry was unable to assert his prerogative outside Huguenot strongholds. In 1593, therefore, Henry converted again to Catholicism, with legend claiming he justified his decision with the phrase "Paris is worth a mass." Over the following years, Henry established his authority throughout his kingdom, and while remaining Catholic, provided some relief to Protestants, particularly through the Edict of Nantes (1598), essentially ending the Religious Wars. Henry's pragmatic reign ended with his assassination by a Radical Catholic in 1610.

King Henry VIII of England (1491–1547). English monarch. The second son of Henry VII (r. 1485–1509) and Elizabeth of York (1466–1503), Henry VIII succeeded his father to the English throne, his elder brother Edward having died in 1502. Soon after accession, he married his brother's widow, Catherine of Aragon (1485–1536). Following several stillbirths and the birth of a daughter, Mary, Henry, who was desperate for a male heir to head off dynastic challenges, wished separation from Catherine in order to marry Anne

Boleyn (c. 1501–1536). Believing his marriage cursed as it transgressed the commands in Leviticus against marrying a brother's widow, Henry sought dispensation from the church for his annulment and remarriage. While the case was first heard by a papal legate in England, it was transferred to Rome upon the order of Pope Clement VII*, who wished to placate Charles V, Catherine's nephew, whose troops had recently sacked Rome and held the pope under house arrest. Henry asserted praemunire, arguing that as king, he was supreme in his own kingdom. With the formation of the Reformation Parliament in 1529, the legislative process to disentangle the English Church from the Roman was begun. The issue of Henry's divorce was finalized in 1533, after Thomas Cranmer* became Archbishop of Canterbury and declared his marriage to Catherine invalid. While Henry's divorce, assertion of royal supremacy, and subversion of Catholic institutions gave impetus to English Protestantism, Henry's beliefs remained essentially Catholic, and these continued to be enforced by law. He ultimately married six times, and was succeeded by Edward VI*, his son by his third wife, Jane Seymour (1508–1537). Elizabeth I*, Henry's daughter by Anne Boleyn, later became Queen and with the Elizabethan Settlement in 1559, redefined England as a Protestant country.

George Herbert (1593–1633). Anglican minister, theologian, and poet. Herbert was born in Montgomery Powys, Wales, on April 3, 1593, to a noble family. After completing his early education at Westminster School, Herbert matriculated at Trinity College, Cambridge, in 1609. He graduated with both his bachelor's and master's degrees. Shortly thereafter Herbert was elected a fellow of the college, and then became Reader of Rhetoric. From 1620 to 1627, Herbert was Public Orator for the University of Cambridge. In 1624, Herbert was elected to Parliament. However, after the death of King James I,* and of his other major patrons, Herbert withdrew from politics to pursue a career in the church. Toward this end, Herbert was ordained to the priesthood of the

Church of England in 1630, and appointed rector of Fugglestone St. Peter and later Bemerton St. Andrews in Wiltshire near Salisbury. While at St. Andrews, Herbert composed his collection of poems titled *The Temple* and his guide for rural ministers, *A Priest to the Temple, or The Country Parson: His Character and Rule of Holy Life*. Twice a week Herbert traveled to Salisbury, where he attended services at Salisbury Cathedral. Following the services, Herbert would compose music with the cathedral musicians. Herbert died of consumption in 1633.

Tilemann Hesshus (1527–1588). German Lutheran theologian and pastor. Hesshus studied under Philipp Melanchthon* but was a staunch Gnesio-Lutheran. With great hesitation—and later regret—he affirmed the Formula of Concord.* Heshuss ardently advocated for church discipline, considering obedience a mark of the church. Unwilling to compromise his strong convictions, especially regarding matters of discipline, Hesshus was regularly embroiled in controversy. He was expelled or pressed to leave Goslar, Rostock, Heidelberg, Bremen, Magdeburg, Wesel, Königsberg and Samland before settling in Helmstedt, where he remained until his death. He wrote numerous polemical tracts concerning ecclesiology, justification, the sacraments and original sin, as well as commentaries on Psalms, Romans, 1–2 Corinthians, Galatians, Colossians and 1–2 Timothy, and a postil collection.

Cornelis Hoen (c. 1460–1524). Dutch humanist, jurist, and theologian. A lawyer at the Court of Holland at the Hague, Hoen was prosecuted in 1523 over his sympathy for the evangelical message. He proposed a symbolic interpretation of Christ's presence in the Eucharist justified with reference to Matthew 24:23 in an influential, posthumously-published treatise.

Melchior Hoffman (1495?–1543). German Anabaptist preacher. First appearing as a Lutheran lay preacher in Livonia in 1523, Hoffman's claim to direct revelation, his perfectionist teachings and his announcements that the end of the world would occur in 1533 saw him alienated from both

Lutheran and Reformed circles. After converting to Anabaptism in Strasbourg in 1530, a city he claimed would rise as the spiritual Jerusalem, Hoffman escaped brief arrest and fled to the Netherlands, where his preaching made him the first to bring the radical faith to the Low Countries. Believing himself to be Elijah, Hoffman gathered numerous followers, including future Anabaptist leaders Obbe Philips* and Jan Mathijs (d. 1534), until his arrest in Strasbourg in 1533, whereupon he was imprisoned for the final decade of his life. A tendency toward mystical allegory and apocalyptic exegesis supported by direct revelation is found in his writings, which include commentaries on Romans, Revelation, and Daniel 12 alongside numerous tracts, pamphlets, and letters.

Nathaniel Holmes (1599–1678). English Puritan theologian. Educated at Oxford, Holmes was a preacher in the Anglican Church until his millenarian views led him to establish an independent congregation. His publications include defenses of infant baptism and exclusive psalmody; treatises against witchcraft, usury, and astrology; and a commentary on the Song of Solomon.

Christopher Hooke (unknown). English Puritan physician and pastor. Hooke published a treatise promoting the joys and blessings of childbirth (1590) and a sermon on Hebrews 12:11-12. To support the poor, Hooke proposed a bank funded by voluntary investment of wealthy households.

Richard Hooker (c. 1553–1600). Anglican priest. Shortly after graduating from Corpus Christi College Oxford, Hooker took holy orders as a priest in 1581. After his marriage, he struggled to find work and temporarily tended sheep until Archbishop John Whitgift* appointed him to the Temple Church in London. Hooker's primary work is *The Laws of Ecclesiastical Polity* (1593), in which he sought to establish a philosophical and logical foundation for the highly controversial Elizabethan Religious Settlement (1559). The Elizabethan Settlement, through the Act of Supremacy, reasserted the Church of England's independence from the Church of Rome, and,

through the Act of Uniformity, constructed a common church structure based on the reinstitution of the Book of Common Prayer.* Hooker's argumentation strongly emphasizes natural law and anticipates the social contract theory of John Locke (1632–1704).

Thomas Hooker (1586–1647) English-American Puritan Preacher. Hooker ministered at churches in Surrey and Essex and established a school to teach pastors until threatened with arrest as Archbishop Laud* worked to suppress Puritanism. Fleeing to Holland and then New England, he pastored a church in New Town (later Cambridge), Massachusetts before playing an important role in the foundation of Hartford, Connecticut and assisting with the composition of the state constitution.

John Hooper (d. 1555). English Protestant bishop and martyr. Impressed by the works of Huldrych Zwingli* and Heinrich Bullinger,* Hooper joined the Protestant movement in England. However, after the Act of Six Articles was passed, he fled to Zurich, where he spent ten years. He returned to England in 1549 and was appointed as a bishop. He stoutly advocated a Zwinglian reform agenda, arguing against the use of vestments and for a less "popish" Book of Common Prayer.* Condemned as a heretic for denying transubstantiation, Hooper was burned at the stake during Mary I's reign.

Rudolf Hospinian (Wirth) (1547–1626). Swiss Reformed theologian and minister. After studying theology at Marburg and Heidelberg, Hospinian pastored in rural parishes around Zurich and taught secondary school. In 1588, he transferred to Zurich, ministering at Grossmünster and Fraumünster. A keen student of church history, Hospinian wanted to show the differences between early church doctrine and contemporary Catholic teaching, particularly with regard to sacramental theology. He also criticized Lutheran dogma and the Formula of Concord*. Most of Hospinian's corpus consists of polemical treatises; he also published a series of sermons on the Magnificat.

Hans Hotz (dates unknown). Swiss Anabaptist leader. Born in Grüningen, near Zurich, Hotz was an associate of Georg Blaurock.* He defended Anabaptism as spokesman for the Swiss Brethren at disputations in Zofingen (1532) and Bern (1538).

Caspar Huberinus (1500–1553). German Lutheran theologian and pastor. After studying theology at Wittenberg, Huberinus moved to Augsburg to serve as Urbanus Rhegius's* assistant. Huberinus represented Augsburg at the Bern Disputation (1528) on the Eucharist and images. In 1551, along with the nobility, Huberinus supported the Augsburg Interim, so long as communion of both kinds and regular preaching were allowed. Nevertheless the people viewed him as a traitor because of his official participation in the Interim, nicknaming him "Buberinus" (i.e., scoundrel). He wrote a number of popular devotional works as well as tracts defending Lutheran eucharistic theology against Zwinglian and Anabaptist detractions.

Balthasar Hubmaier (1480/5–1528). German Radical theologian. Hubmaier, a former priest who studied under Johann Eck,* is identified with his leadership in the peasants' uprising at Waldshut. Hubmaier served as the cathedral preacher in Regensberg, where he became involved in a series of anti-Semitic attacks. He was drawn to reform through the early works of Martin Luther*; his contact with Huldrych Zwingli* made Hubmaier a defender of more radical reform, including believers' baptism and a memorialist account of the Eucharist. His involvement in the Peasants' War led to his extradition and execution by the Austrians.

Aegidius Hunnius (1550–1603). German Lutheran theologian and preacher. Educated at Tübingen by Jakob Andreae (1528–1590) and Johannes Brenz,* Hunnius bolstered and advanced early Lutheran orthodoxy. After his crusade to root out all "crypto-Calvinism" divided Hesse into Lutheran and Reformed regions, Hunnius joined the Wittenberg theological faculty, where with Polykarp Leyser (1552–1610) he helped shape the university into an orthodox stronghold. Passionately confessional, Hunnius developed and nuanced the orthodox

doctrines of predestination, Scripture, the church and Christology (more explicitly Chalcedonian), reflecting their codification in the Formula of Concord.* He was unafraid to engage in confessional polemics from the pulpit. In addition to his many treatises (most notably *De persona Christi*, in which he defended Christ's ubiquity), Hunnius published commentaries on Matthew, John, Ephesians and Colossians; his notes on Galatians, Philemon and 1 Corinthians were published posthumously.

Jan Hus (d. 1415). Bohemian reformer and martyr. This popular preacher strove for reform in the church, moral improvement in society, and an end to clerical abuses and popular religious superstition. He was branded a heretic for his alleged affinity for John Wycliffe's writings; however, while he agreed that a priest in mortal sin rendered the sacraments inefficacious, he affirmed the doctrine of transubstantiation. The Council of Constance* convicted Hus of heresy, banned his books and teaching, and, despite a letter of safe conduct, burned him at the stake.

Hans Hut (1490–1527). German Radical leader. Hut was an early leader of a mystical, apocalyptic strand of Anabaptist radical reform. His theological views were shaped by Andreas Bodenstein von Karlstadt,* Thomas Müntzer* and Hans Denck,* by whom Hut had been baptized. Hut rejected society and the established church and heralded the imminent end of days, which he perceived in the Peasants' War. Eventually arrested for practicing believers' baptism and participating in the Peasants' War, Hut was tortured and died accidentally in a fire in the Augsburg prison. The next day, the authorities sentenced his corpse to death and burned him.

George Hutcheson (1615–1674). Scottish Puritan pastor. Hutcheson, a pastor in Edinburgh, published commentaries on Job, John and the Minor Prophets, as well as sermons on Psalm 130.

Roger Hutchinson (d. 1555). English reformer. Little is known about Hutchinson except for his controversies. He disputed against the Mass while at Cambridge and debated with Joan Bocher (d. 1550), who affirmed the doctrine of the celestial flesh. During the Marian Restoration he was deprived of his fellowship at Eton because he was married.

Andreas Hyperius (1511–1564). Dutch Protestant theologian. After a peripatetic humanist education that encompassed studies in theology, canon law, and medicine, Hyperius became professor of theology at Marburg in 1541 and held this position until his death. Often viewed as mediating between Lutheran and Reformed thought, Hyperius was particularly concerned with the practical application of theology, demonstrated in his composition of the first Protestant text on homiletic method.

Abraham Ibn Ezra (1089–c. 1167). Spanish Jewish rabbi, exegete and poet. In 1140 Ibn Ezra fled his native Spain to escape persecution by the Almohad Caliphate. He spent the rest of his life as an exile, traveling through Europe, North Africa and the Middle East. His corpus consists of works on poetry, exegesis, grammar, philosophy, mathematics and astrology. In his commentaries on the Old Testament, Ibn Ezra restricts himself to *peshat* (see *quadriga*).

Valentin Ickelshamer (c. 1500–1547). German Radical teacher. After time at Erfurt, he studied under Luther,* Melanchthon,* Bugenhagen* and Karlstadt* in Wittenberg. He sided with Karlstadt against Luther, writing a treatise in Karlstadt's defense. Ickelshamer also represented the Wittenberg guilds in opposition to the city council. This guild committee allied with the peasants in 1525, leading to Ickelshamer's eventual exile. His poem in the Marpeck Circle's *Kunstbuch*terixsd is an expansion of a similar poem by Sebastian Franck.*

Thomas Jackson (1579–1640). Anglican theologian and priest. Before serving as the president of Corpus Christi College at Oxford for the final decade of his life, Jackson was a parish priest and chaplain to the king. His best known work is a twelve-volume commentary on the Apostles' Creed.

King James I of England (VI of Scotland) (1566–1625). English monarch. The son of Mary, Queen of Scots, James ascended to the Scottish throne in 1567 following his mother's abdication.

In the Union of the Crowns (1603), he took the English and Irish thrones after the death of his cousin, Elizabeth I.* James's reign was tumultuous and tense: Parliament and the nobility often opposed him, church factions squabbled over worship forms and ecclesiology, climaxing in the Gunpowder Plot. James wrote treatises on the divine right of kings, law, the evils of smoking tobacco and demonology. His religious writings include a versification of the Psalms, a paraphrase of Revelation and meditations on the Lord's Prayer and passages from Chronicles, Matthew and Revelation. He also sponsored the translation of the Authorized Version*—popularly remembered as the King James Version.

Jeanne of Navarre (1528–1572) French Reformed noblewoman. Daughter of Henry II, King of Navarre (1503–1555) and Marguerite d'Angoulême*, Jeanne was forced into a strategic marriage at age 12 by her uncle, Francis I* to William, Duke of Cleves (1516–1592). Shifting political alignments allowed her an annulment after four years and in 1548 she wed the first Prince of the Blood, Antoine de Bourbon (1518–1562). Jeanne took the throne of her father, and after making a public announcement of her conversion to the evangelical faith, established a Reformed community at Béarn. A regular correspondent of reformers such as Calvin* and Beza* and an advocate for the reformation of her lands, Jeanne nevertheless remained largely neutral and advocated tolerance during the first years of religious war. At the outbreak of the Third War of Religion (1569–1570), however, she recognized her moderate position was untenable, and from the Protestant stronghold of La Rochelle served as political head for the Huguenot cause alongside Gaspard de Coligny (1519–1572), commander of the Huguenot armed forces.

John Jewel (1522–1571). Anglican theologian and bishop. Jewel studied at Oxford where he met Peter Martyr Vermigli.* After graduating in 1552, Jewel was appointed to his first vicarage and became the orator for the university. Upon Mary I's accession, Jewel lost his post as orator because of his Protestant views. After the trials of Thomas Cranmer* and Nicholas Ridley,* Jewel affirmed Catholic teaching to avoid their fate. Still he had to flee to the continent. Confronted by John Knox,* Jewel publicly repented of his cowardice before the English congregation in Frankfurt, then reunited with Vermigli in Strasbourg. After Mary I's death, Jewel returned to England and was consecrated bishop in 1560. He advocated low-church ecclesiology, but supported the Elizabethan Settlement against Catholics and Puritans. In response to the Council of Trent, he published the *Apoligia ecclesiae Anglicanae* (1562), which established him as the apostle for Anglicanism and incited numerous controversies.

St. John of the Cross (Juan de Yepes y Álvarez) (1542–1591). Spanish Catholic mystic. Born into poverty, Álvarez entered the Carmelite order in Medina del Campo, where, after studying theology at Salamanca, he met the famed mystic Teresa of Ávila (1515–1582). Drawn to her vision of the contemplative life, with two others, he established the first house of Discalced (barefoot) Carmelite Friars and became a leader in the Catholic reform movement. An exceptional administrator and spiritual leader, for more than twenty years, John of the Cross sought to return his order to its original vision of asceticism and prayer while establishing many new reformed Carmelite houses. He encountered significant resistance in his work for renewal, however, and spent nine months imprisoned and tortured by his Carmelite superiors. Considered among the foremost poets in Spanish literary history, his poems, including *The Spiritual Canticle, Ascent of Mount Carmel*, and *The Dark Night of the Soul* demonstrate his overriding desire for spiritual growth and closeness to God.

Justus Jonas (1493–1555). German Lutheran theologian, pastor and administrator. Jonas studied law at Erfurt, where he befriended the poet Eobanus Hessus (1488–1540), whom Luther* dubbed "king of the poets"; later, under the influence of the humanist Konrad Muth, Jonas focused on theology. In 1516 he was ordained as a priest, and in 1518 he became a

doctor of theology and law. After witnessing the Leipzig Disputation, Jonas was converted to Luther's* cause. While traveling with Luther to the Diet of Worms, Jonas was appointed professor of canon law at Wittenberg. Later he became its dean of theology, lecturing on Romans, Acts and the Psalms. Jonas was also instrumental for reform in Halle. He preached Luther's funeral sermon but had a falling-out with Melanchthon* over the Leipzig Interim. Jonas's most influential contribution was translating Luther's *The Bondage of the Will* and Melanchthon's *Loci communes* into German.

William Jones (1561–1636). Anglican minister and theologian. After teaching at Cambridge, Jones ministered at East Bergholt in Suffolk for forty-four years, publishing a commentary on Philemon and Hebrews and tracts on suffering, the nativity, and arrangements to be made before one's death.

David Joris (c. 1501–1556). Dutch Radical pastor and hymnist. This former glass painter was one of the leading Dutch Anabaptist leaders after the fall of Münster (1535), although due to his increasingly radical ideas his influence waned in the early 1540s. Joris came to see himself as a "third David," a Spirit-anointed prophet ordained to proclaim the coming third kingdom of God, which would be established in the Netherlands with Dutch as its *lingua franca*. Joris's interpretation of Scripture, with his heavy emphasis on personal mystical experience, led to a very public dispute with Menno Simons* whom Joris considered a teacher of the "dead letter." In 1544 Joris and about one hundred followers moved to Basel, conforming outwardly to the teaching of the Reformed church there. Today 240 of Joris's books are extant, the most important of which is his *Twonder Boek* (1542/43).

Jörg Haugk von Jüchsen (unknown). German Radical preacher. Nothing is known of Haugk's life except that during the 1524–1525 Peasants' War in Thuringia, he was elected as a preacher by the insurrectionists in his district. He composed one extant tract, titled *A Christian Order of a True Christian: Giving an Account of the Origin of His*

Faith, published in 1526 but likely written before the Peasants' War. While lacking reference to most distinctive Anabaptist doctrines, this pamphlet became popular among radicals as it set out the stages of Christian growth toward perfection.

Andreas Bodenstein von Karlstadt (Carlstadt) (1486–1541). German Radical theologian. Karlstadt, an early associate of Martin Luther* and Philipp Melanchthon* at the University of Wittenberg, participated alongside Luther in the dispute at Leipzig with Johann Eck.* He also influenced the configuration of the Old Testament canon in Protestantism. During Luther's captivity in Wartburg Castle in Eisenach, Karlstadt oversaw reform in Wittenberg. His acceleration of the pace of reform brought conflict with Luther, so Karlstadt left Wittenberg, eventually settling at the University of Basel as professor of Old Testament (after a sojourn in Zurich with Huldrych Zwingli*). During his time in Switzerland, Karlstadt opposed infant baptism and repudiated Luther's doctrine of Christ's real presence in the Eucharist.

Edward Kellett (d. 1641). Anglican theologian and priest. Kellett published a sermon concerning the reconversion of an Englishman from Islam, a tract on the soul and a discourse on the Lord's Supper in connection with Passover.

David Kimchi (Radak) (1160–1235). French Jewish rabbi, exegete and philosopher. Kimchi wrote an important Hebrew grammar and dictionary, as well as commentaries on Genesis, 1–2 Chronicles, the Psalms and the Prophets. He focused on *peshat* (see *quadriga*). In his Psalms commentary he attacks Christian interpretation as forced, irrational and inadmissible. While Sebastian Münster* censors and condemns these arguments in his *Miqdaš YHWH* (1534–1535), he and many other Christian commentators valued Kimchi's work as a grammatical resource.

Moses Kimchi (Remak) (1127–1190). French Jewish rabbi and exegete. He was David Kimchi's* brother. He wrote commentaries on Proverbs and Ezra-Nehemiah. Sebastian Münster* translated Kimchi's concise Hebrew grammar into Latin; many sixteenth-century Christian exegetes used this resource.

Andreas Knöpken (c. 1468–1539). German Lutheran pastor. Knöpken worked in Pomerania as assistant to Johannes Bugenhagen* before relocating to Riga. Here he served as pastor of St. Peter's, and after a brief setback that saw him return to his previous position, he returned and won a disputation before the authorities, which allowed him to undertake the evangelical reform of the city. Knöpken oversaw the reorganization of the churches and schools, composed the church order, wrote a commentary on Romans, and arranged a number of hymns based on the Psalms.

John Knox (1513–1572). Scottish Reformed preacher. Knox, a fiery preacher to monarchs and zealous defender of high Calvinism, was a leading figure of reform in Scotland. Following imprisonment in the French galleys, Knox went to England, where he became a royal chaplain to Edward VI. At the accession of Mary, Knox fled to Geneva, studying under John Calvin* and serving as a pastor. Knox returned to Scotland after Mary's death and became a chief architect of the reform of the Scottish church (Presbyterian), serving as one of the authors of the Book of Discipline and writing many pamphlets and sermons.

Antonius Broickwy von Königstein (1470–1541). German Catholic preacher. Very little is known about this important cathedral preacher in Cologne. Strongly opposed to evangelicals, he sought to develop robust resources for Catholic homilies. His postils were bestsellers, and his biblical concordance helped Catholic preachers to construct doctrinal loci from Scripture itself.

Kunstbuch. In 1956, two German students rediscovered this unique collection of Anabaptist works. Four hundred years earlier, a friend of the recently deceased Pilgram Marpeck*—the painter Jörg Probst—had entrusted this collection of letters, tracts and poetry to a Zurich bindery; today only half of it remains. Probst's redaction arranges various compositions from the Marpeck Circle into a devotional anthology focused on the theme of the church as Christ incarnate (cf. Gal 2:20).

Osmund Lake (c. 1543–1621). English Pastor

who ministered at Ringwood in Hampshire.

François Lambert (Lambert of Avignon) (1487–1530). French Reformed theologian. In 1522, after becoming drawn to the writings of Martin Luther* and meeting Huldrych Zwingli,* Lambert left the Franciscan order. He spent time in Wittenberg, Strasbourg, and Hesse, where Lambert took a leading role at the Homberg Synod (1526) and in creating a biblically based plan for church reform. He served as professor of theology at Marburg University from 1527 to his death. After the Marburg Colloquy (1529), Lambert accepted Zwingli's symbolic view of the Eucharist. Lambert produced nineteen books, mostly biblical commentaries that favored spiritual interpretations; his unfinished work of comprehensive theology was published posthumously.

Eitelhans Langenmantel (d. 1528). German Radical writer. The son of the mayor of Augsburg, Langenmantel was converted to Anabaptism and was rebaptized by Hans Hut* in 1527. Arrested for his heterodox views later that year, he was freed after accepting the validity of infant baptism during a debate, but after renouncing his recantation in 1528, he was rearrested and beheaded. Seven tracts he composed during 1526 and 1527 survive, focusing on the Lord's Supper and the moral life.

Hugh Latimer (c. 1485–1555). Anglican bishop and preacher. Latimer was celebrated for his sermons critiquing the idolatrous nature of Catholic practices and the social injustices visited on the underclass by the aristocracy and the individualism of Protestant government. After his support for Henry's petition of divorce he served as a court preacher under Henry VIII* and Edward VI. Latimer became a proponent of reform following his education at Cambridge University and received license as a preacher. Following Edward's death, Latimer was tried for heresy, perishing at the stake with Nicholas Ridley* and Thomas Cranmer.*

William Laud (1573–1645). Anglican archbishop, one of the most pivotal and controversial figures in Anglican church history. Early in his career, Laud

offended many with his highly traditional, anti-Puritan approach to ecclesial policies. After his election as Archbishop of Canterbury in 1633, Laud continued to strive against the Puritans, demanding the eastward placement of the Communion altar (affirming the religious centrality of the Eucharist), the use of clerical garments, the reintroduction of stained-glass windows, and the uniform use of the Book of Common Prayer.* Laud was accused of being a crypto-Catholic—an ominous accusation during the protracted threat of invasion by the Spanish Armada. In 1640 the Long Parliament met, quickly impeached Laud on charges of treason, and placed him in jail for several years before his execution.

Ludwig Lavater (1527–1586). Swiss Reformed pastor and theologian. Under his father-in-law Heinrich Bullinger,* Lavater became an archdeacon in Zurich. In 1585 he succeeded Rudolf Gwalther* as the city's Antistes. He authored a widely disseminated book on demonology, commentaries on Chronicles, Proverbs, Ecclesiastes, Nehemiah and Ezekiel, theological works, and biographies of Bullinger and Konrad Pellikan.*

Laws and Liberties of the Inhabitants of Massachusetts (1647). North American colonial constitution. The first printed set of laws in the American colonies, the 1647 *Laws and Liberties of the Inhabitants of Massachusetts* was a revision of the *Massachusetts Body of Liberties* (1641), a legal code collected by Puritan minister Nathaniel Ward (1578–1652). The *Laws and Liberties* codified Puritan expectations of doctrine and morality, and included provision for the punishment for heresy, stipulating banishment for Anabaptism. The majority of the document consists of practical clauses addressing general and specific aspects of communal and commercial life.

John Lawson (unknown). Seventeenth-century English Puritan. Lawson wrote *Gleanings and Expositions of Some of Scripture* (1646) and a treatise on the sabbath in the New Testament.

Jacques Lefèvre d'Étaples (Faber Stapulensis) (1460?–1536). French Catholic humanist, publisher and translator. Lefèvre d'Étaples studied classical literature and philosophy, as well as patristic and medieval mysticism. He advocated the principle of *ad fontes*, issuing a full-scale annotation on the corpus of Aristotle, publishing the writings of key Christian mystics, and contributing to efforts at biblical translation and commentary. Although he never broke with the Catholic Church, his views prefigured those of Martin Luther,* for which he was condemned by the University of Sorbonne in Paris. He then found refuge in the court of Marguerite d'Angoulême, where he met John Calvin* and Martin Bucer.*

Edward Leigh (1602–1671). English Puritan biblical critic, historian and politician. Educated at Oxford, Leigh's public career included appointments as a Justice of the Peace, an officer in the parliamentary army during the English Civil Wars and a member of Parliament. Although never ordained, Leigh devoted himself to the study of theology and Scripture; he participated in the Westminster Assembly. Leigh published a diverse corpus, including lexicons of Greek, Hebrew and juristic terms, and histories of Roman, Greek and English rulers. His most important theological work is *A Systeme or Body of Divinity* (1662).

John Lightfoot (1602–1675). Anglican priest and biblical scholar. After graduating from Cambridge, Lightfoot was ordained and pastored at several small parishes. He continued to study classics under the support of the politician Rowland Cotton (1581–1634). Siding with the Parliamentarians during the English Civil Wars, Lightfoot relocated to London in 1643. He was one of the original members of the Westminster Assembly, where he defended a moderate Presbyterianism. His best-known work is the six-volume *Horae Hebraicae et Talmudicae* (1658–1677), a verse-by-verse commentary illumined by Hebrew customs, language and the Jewish interpretive tradition.

Wenceslaus Linck (1482–1547). German Lutheran theologian and preacher. As dean of the theology faculty at the University of Wittenberg and successor to Johannes von Staupitz* as the prior of the Augustinian Monastery, Linck

worked closely with Martin Luther* and attended the Heidelberg Disputation with him. He replaced Staupitz as vicar-general of the Augustinian order in 1520 in Germany, a capacity in which he pronounced all members free from their vows before renouncing the order himself. After periods of ministry in Munich and Altenburg, Linck settled in Nuremberg, where he became known as an exemplary preacher and an advisor to cities undertaking Protestant reform. He published a significant number of sermons and practical tracts as well as a paraphrase and annotations on the Old Testament.

Peter Lombard (1095–1160). Scholastic theologian, bishop of Paris. Though little is known about his life, some records indicate that Lombard came from the region of Novara in Lombardy. Bernard of Clairvaux* patronized his studies at Reims, and later recommended him for further study at St. Victor in Paris. In 1144, Lombard participated in an examination of the writings of Gilbert of Poitiers for heresy. Lombard became a canon at Notre Dame in 1145, and an archdeacon there in 1156. Meanwhile he spent a year and a half in Rome as an assistant to Theobald, bishop of Paris. Lombard was elected bishop of Paris in 1159. He died less than a year later. Lombard's most important work was the *Four Books of the Sentences*, which served as the standard textbook for theology throughout the remainder of the Middle Ages, and at the beginning of the early modern period. Additionally, Lombard produced commentaries on the Psalms and Pauline epistles.

Johannes Lonicer (1499–1569). German Lutheran theologian and linguist. After studying in Erfurt and Wittenberg, Lonicer renounced his Augustinian vows. He briefly taught Hebrew at the University of Freiburg, but controversy saw him flee to Strasburg, where he worked with a printer, translating some early Lutheran vernacular works into Latin. At the opening of the University of Marburg, Lonicer was appointed to teach Greek and Hebrew, and he later also served as professor of theology.

Lucas Lossius (1508–1582). German Lutheran teacher and musician. While a student at Leipzig and Wittenberg, Lossius was deeply influenced by Melanchthon* and Luther,* who found work for him as Urbanus Rhegius's* secretary. Soon after going to work for Rhegius, Lossius began teaching at a local gymnasium (or secondary school), *Das Johanneum*, eventually becoming its headmaster. Lossius remained at *Das Johanneum* until his death, even turning down appointments to university professorships. A man of varied interests, he wrote on dialectics, music and church history, as well as publishing a postil and a five-volume set of annotations on the New Testament.

Sibrandus Lubbertus (c. 1555–1625). Dutch Reformed theologian. Lubbertis, a key figure in the establishment of orthodox Calvinism in Frisia, studied theology at Wittenburg and Geneva (under Theodore Beza*) before his appointment as professor of theology at the University of Franeker. Throughout his career, Lubbertis advocated for high Calvinist theology, defending it in disputes with representatives of Socinianism, Arminianism and Roman Catholicism. Lubbertis criticized the Catholic theologian Robert Bellarmine and fellow Dutch reformer Jacobus Arminius*; the views of the latter he opposed as a prominent participant in the Synod of Dordrecht.*

Martin Luther (1483–1546). German Lutheran priest, professor, and theologian. Martin Luther was born in Eisleben, Saxony, to an entrepreneurial minor. Upon completing his earlier education at Eisenach, Luther matriculated at the University of Erfurt where he completed his BA in 1502, and MA in 1505. While at Erfurt, Luther studied the philosophy of William of Ockham (1285–1347), and his disciple, Gabriel Biel (1420–1495). After receiving his MA, Luther proceeded to the study of law. However, a number of events culminating in his promise to St. Anne (the patron saint of minors) to become a monk compelled Luther to withdraw from law school and join the Augustinian monastery at Erfurt in 1505. At this monastery, Luther was ordained a priest. Later, the Augustinians sent Luther to the University of Wittenberg to study theology. In 1512, Luther received his doctorate, and took up the post of lecturer in Bible at Wittenberg, a position he would hold the rest of his life. While a professor at this university, Luther reinterpreted the doctrine of justification. Convinced that righteousness comes only from God's grace, he disputed the sale of indulgences with his *Ninety–Five Theses*, which he reportedly posted to the door of All Saints' Church in Wittenberg on October 31, 1517. Luther's positions brought conflict with Rome. He challenged the Mass, transubstantiation, and communion in one kind, and his denial of papal authority led to excommunication. Though Luther was condemned by the Diet of Worms, Frederick III, the Elector of Saxony, provided him safe haven. Luther later returned to Wittenberg with public order collapsing under Andreas Bodenstein von Karlstadt* and steered a more cautious path of reform. Among his most influential works are three treatises published in 1520: *To the Christian Nobility of the German Nation, On the Babylonian Captivity of the Church*, and *On the Freedom of a Christian*. His rendering of the Bible and liturgy in the vernacular, as well as his hymns and sermons, proved extensively influential.

Georg Major (1502–1574). German Lutheran theologian. Major was on the theological faculty of the University of Wittenberg, succeeding as dean Johannes Bugenhagen* and Philipp Melanchthon.* One of the chief editors on the Wittenberg edition of Luther's works, Major is most identified with the controversy bearing his name, in which he stated that good works are necessary to salvation. Major qualified his statement, which was in reference to the totality of the Christian life. The Formula of Concord* rejected the statement, ending the controversy. As a theologian, Major further refined Lutheran views of the inspiration of Scripture and the doctrine of the Trinity.

John (Mair) Major (1467–1550). Scottish Catholic philosopher. Major taught logic and theology at the universities of Paris (his alma mater), Glasgow and St Andrews. His broad interests and impressive work drew students from all over Europe. While disapproving of evangelicals (though he did teach John Knox*), Major advocated reform programs for Rome. He supported collegial episcopacy and even challenged the curia's teaching on sexuality. Still he was a nominalist who was critical of humanist approaches to biblical exegesis. His best-known publication is *A History of Greater Britain, Both England and Scotland* (1521), which promoted the union of the kingdoms. He also published a commentary on Peter Lombard's *Sentences* and the Gospel of John.

Juan de Maldonado (1533–1583). Spanish Catholic biblical scholar. A student of Francisco de Toledo,* Maldonado taught philosophy and theology at the universities of Paris and Salamanca. Ordained to the priesthood in Rome, he revised the Septuagint under papal appointment. While Maldonado vehemently criticized Protestants, he asserted that Reformed baptism was valid and that mixed confessional marriages were acceptable. His views on Mary's immaculate conception proved controversial among many Catholics who conflated his statement that it was not an article of faith with its denial. He was intrigued by demonology (blaming demonic influence for the Reformation). All his work was published posthumously; his Gospel commentaries were highly valued and important.

Thomas Manton (1620–1677). English Puritan minister. Manton, educated at Oxford, served for a time as lecturer at Westminster Abbey and rector of St. Paul's, Covent Garden, and was a strong advocate of Presbyterianism. He was known as a rigorous evangelical Calvinist who preached long expository sermons. At different times in his ecclesial career he worked side-by-side with Richard Baxter* and John Owen.* In his later life, Manton's Nonconformist position led to his ejection as a clergyman from the Church of England (1662) and eventual imprisonment (1670). Although a voluminous writer, Manton was best known for his preaching. At his funeral in 1677, he was dubbed "the king of preachers."

Benedetto da Mantova (c. 1495–c. 1556). Italian Catholic monk. Benedetto entered the Benedictine order in Mantua and served as dean at San Giorgio Maggiore in Venice. At San Nicolò l'Arena on Mt. Etna, he became acquainted with Waldensian and Protestant thought, which influenced his composition of *The Benefit of Christ*, one of the most significant Italian writings of the Reformation. Marcantonio Flaminio* was asked to rewrite the text in more elegant prose before its anonymous publication in 1543, and although the work drew the ire of the Inquisition, Benedetto's authorship was not uncovered during his lifetime. His increasingly radical spiritualism saw him arrested in Padua, though nothing of his later life is known.

Felix Mantz (d. 1527). Swiss Anabaptist Leader. An early supporter of Zwingli* in Zurich, Mantz's frustration with the pace of the magisterial Reformation led him to found an independent congregation, the Swiss Brethren, with Conrad Grebel,* Georg Blaurock,* and others. Mantz and Grebel represented the Brethren in two disputations with Zwingli over infant baptism in 1525. Defeated, the Brethren refused to cease meeting and rebaptizing adults, which they considered a first baptism, leading to suppression by the Zurich authorities. Mantz was able to spread his message for a time, traveling through a number of Swiss regions despite several arrests. Imprisoned by the Zurich authorities in March 1526 with Grebel and Blaurock, he briefly escaped, but having broken his commitment not to rebaptize adults, he was executed by drowning, the stipulated punishment for Anabaptism, in January 1527.

Augustin Marlorat (c. 1506–1562). French Reformed pastor. Committed by his family to a monastery at the age of eight, Marlorat was also ordained into the priesthood at an early age in 1524. He fled to Geneva in 1535, where he pastored until the Genevan Company of Pastors sent him to France to shepherd the nascent evangelical congregations. His petition to the young Charles IX (1550–1574) for the right to public evangelical worship was denied. In response to a massacre of evangelicals in Vassy (over sixty dead, many more wounded), Marlorat's congregation planned to overtake Rouen. After the crown captured Rouen,

Marlorat was arrested and executed three days later for treason. His principle published work was an anthology of New Testament comment modeled after Thomas Aquinas's* *Catena aurea in quatuor Evangelia.* Marlorat harmonized Reformed and Lutheran comment with the church fathers, interspersed with his own brief comments. He also wrote such anthologies for Genesis, Job, the Psalms, Song of Songs and Isaiah.

Pilgram Marpeck (c. 1495–1556). Austrian Radical elder and theologian. During a brief sojourn in Strasbourg, Marpeck debated with Martin Bucer* before the city council; Bucer was declared the winner, and Marpeck was asked to leave Strasbourg for his views concerning paedobaptism (which he compared to a sacrifice to Moloch). After his time in Strasbourg, Marpeck traveled throughout southern Germany and western Austria, planting Anabaptist congregations. Marpeck criticized the strict use of the ban, however, particularly among the Swiss brethren. He also engaged in a christological controversy with Kaspar von Schwenckfeld.*

Gregory Martin (1542?–1582). English Catholic priest and translator. After studying at Oxford, Martin tutored the sons of the Duke of Norfolk until leaving for the college of Douai, where he received his doctorate. He taught for two years at the English college in Rome before returning to the college of Douai, which was temporarily based at Rheims. While he composed a number of polemical writings, he is best known as the primary translator of the Douai-Rheims Bible, an English translation of the Vulgate with commentary and notes intended to provide a Catholic alternative to the influx of Protestant annotated English Bibles. The New Testament was published at Douai in 1582 and the Old Testament at Rheims in 1609–1610.

Mary I of England (1516–1558). English monarch. Daughter of Henry VIII* and his first wife Catherine of Aragon (1509–1553), Mary was raised in the strict Catholicism of her mother. Her succession of Edward VI, her half-brother, was briefly contested by Lady Jane Grey*, daughter of Henry VIII's younger sister, in whom Protestants placed their hopes, but unable to raise adequate support, this challenge was quickly dismissed. Upon her ascent, Mary set about the task of restoring the Catholic religion, a reversal of royal policy that was positively received by much of the populace. While able to reestablish relations with the Pope and reassert the mass and other aspects of Catholicism, the impoverishment of the church following the dissolution of the monasteries and the closure of the chantries was difficult to overcome. Other aspects of popular piety, including the cult of the saints, pilgrimages, and the doctrine of purgatory, were not restored during her reign. Mary looms large in the Protestant imagination, and her persecution of evangelicals led to the moniker "Bloody Mary." The accounts of martyrs such as Thomas Cranmer*, Hugh Latimer*, and Nicholas Ridley* were immortalized in John Foxe's (1516–1587) *Acts and Monuments** and became a mainstay of Protestant propaganda.

Johannes Mathesius (1504–1565). German Lutheran theologian and pastor. After reading Martin Luther's* *On Good Works*, Mathesius left his teaching post in Ingolstadt and traveled to Wittenberg to study theology. Mathesius was an important agent of reform in the Bohemian town of Jáchymov, where he pastored, preached and taught. Over one thousand of Mathesius's sermons are extant, including numerous wedding and funeral sermons as well as a series on Luther's life. Mathesius also transcribed portions of Luther's Table Talk.

Anthony Maxey (d. 1618). Anglican minister. Maxey was born in Essex and educated at Westminster School. After completing his early education at Westminster, Maxey matriculated at Trinity College, Cambridge, in 1578. Maxey graduated Cambridge with the BA (1581), MA (1585), BD (1594), and DD (1608) degrees. However, he was unable to obtain a fellowship at Trinity. King James I* appointed Maxey as his chaplain and dean of Windsor on June 21, 1612. Maxey was also inducted into the Order of the Garter. He died on May 3, 1618. Maxey's published works consist of three sermons: *The Churches Sleep*; *The Golden Chain of Man's Salvation*; and *The Fearful Point of Hardening*.

John Mayer (1583–1664). Anglican priest and biblical exegete. Mayer dedicated much of his life to biblical exegesis, writing a seven-volume commentary on the entire Bible (1627–1653). Styled after Philipp Melanchthon's* *locus* method, Mayer's work avoided running commentary, focusing instead on textual and theological problems. He was a parish priest for fifty-five years. In the office of priest Mayer also wrote a popular catechism, *The English Catechisme, or a Commentarie on the Short Catechisme* (1621), which went through twelve editions in his lifetime.

Joseph Mede (1586–1638). Anglican biblical scholar, Hebraist and Greek lecturer. A man of encyclopedic knowledge, Mede was interested in numerous fields, varying from philology and history to mathematics and physics, although millennial thought and apocalyptic prophesy were clearly his chief interests. Mede's most important work was his *Clavis Apocalyptica* (1627, later translated into English as *The Key of the Revelation*). This work examined the structure of Revelation as the key to its interpretation. Mede saw the visions as a connected and chronological sequence hinging around Revelation 17:18. He is remembered as an important figure in the history of millenarian theology. He was respected as a mild-mannered and generous scholar who avoided controversy and debate, but who had many original thoughts.

Philipp Melanchthon (1497–1560). German Lutheran educator, reformer, and theologian. Philipp Melanchthon was born in the Palatinate, the son of an armorer. He attended the Latin school in Pforzheim, where he lived with the sister of Johannes Reuchlin* to whom he was related by marriage. Having completed his early education, Melanchthon went on to attend the University of Heidelberg, where he received his BA in 1511. Afterwards, he earned his MA from the University of Tubingen in 1514. In 1518, Reuchlin recommended Melanchthon for the new professorship of Greek at the University of Wittenberg, where he

remained for the rest of his life. There, Melanchthon taught Greek, rhetoric, and logic. Melanchthon is known as the partner and successor to Martin Luther* in reform in Germany and for his pioneering *Loci Communes*, which served as a theological textbook. Melanchthon participated with Luther in the Leipzig disputation, helped implement reform in Wittenberg, and was a chief architect of the Augsburg Confession.* Later, Melanchthon and Martin Bucer* worked for union between reformed and Catholic churches. On account of Melanchthon's ecumenical disposition and his modification of several of Luther's doctrines, he was held in suspicion by some.

Andrew Melville (1545–1622). Scottish Reformed theologian. Melville was born at Baldovie on August 1, 1545, to an evangelical family. After finishing his early education at Montrose Grammar School, he matriculated at St. Mary's College, St. Andrews, in 1559. Melville graduated St. Andrews in 1564, after which he traveled to Paris, where he studied Greek, Hebrew, mathematics, and other languages. While in Paris, Melville came under the influence of Petrus Ramus,* whose pedagogical methods he would later utilize in Scotland. From there, he proceeded to Poitiers to study law. There, he became regent of the College of St. Marceon. However, when Poitiers came under siege, Melville departed the city for Geneva, where Theodore Beza* warmly received him. Shortly after Melville's arrival in Geneva, he assumed the chair of humanities at the academy. Melville remained in this position at the academy until 1573, when he returned to Scotland. In 1574, Melville was appointed principal of the College of Glasgow. While in this post, Melville led in the reform of the college's curriculum, and engaged in ecclesiastical controversy. He served on the committee that drafted the Second Book of Discipline, and was elected moderator of the General Assembly in 1578. In 1580, Melville became principal of St. Mary's College, St. Andrews, where he initiated the same types of reform as he did at Glasgow. Throughout his career, Melville denounced royal ecclesiastical supremacy, arguing strongly for the autonomy of the national church. For this he was summoned to the Privy Council in Edinburgh in 1584 on the possible charge of treason for his resistance to royal ecclesiastical authority. Though they could not charge Melville with sedition, the Privy Council still determined to consign him to trial, but Melville managed to escape to England. While in England, he visited Puritan leaders at Oxford and Cambridge. He also lectured on Genesis in London. Melville returned to Scotland in 1585, and became rector of the University of St. Andrews in 1590. He was eventually deprived of this rectorship in 1587 for his opposition to episcopacy. In 1606, along with several ministers, he was summoned to appear before Hampton Court, where he gave some uncompromising speeches. These speeches resulted in Melville's imprisonment in several places, including the Tower of London. Melville was released from the Tower on April 19, 1611, and from there traveled to France. Having arrived in France, Melville proceeded through Paris and Rouen to Sedan, where he assumed the chair of theology. He remained in Sedan until his death in 1622. Melville authored an extensive literary corpus, which includes a commentary on Romans.

Justus Menius (1499–1558). German Lutheran pastor and theologian. Menius was a prominent reformer in Thuringia. He participated in the Marburg Colloquy and, with others, helped Martin Luther* compose the Schmalkald Articles.* Throughout his career Menius entered into numerous controversies with Anabaptists and even fellow Lutherans. He rejected Andreas Osiander's (d. 1552) doctrine of justification—that the indwelling of Christ's divine nature justifies, rather than the imputed alien righteousness of Christ's person, declared through God's mercy. Against Nikolaus von Amsdorf (1483–1565) and Matthias Flacius (1520–1575), Menius agreed with Georg Major* that good works are necessary to salvation. Osiander's view of justification was censored in Article 3 of the Formula of Concord*; Menius's understanding of the relationship

between good works and salvation was rejected in Article 4. Menius translated many of Luther's Latin works into German. He also composed a handbook for Christian households and an influential commentary on 1 Samuel.

Johannes Mercerus (Jean Mercier) (d. 1570). French Hebraist. Mercerus studied under the first Hebrew chair at the Collège Royal de Paris, François Vatable (d. 1547), whom he succeeded in 1546. John Calvin* tried to recruit Mercerus to the Genevan Academy as professor of Hebrew, once in 1558 and again in 1563; he refused both times. During his lifetime Mercerus published grammatical helps for Hebrew and Chaldean, an aid to the Masoretic symbols in the Hebrew text, and translated the commentaries and grammars of several medieval rabbis. He himself wrote commentaries on Genesis, the wisdom books, and most of the Minor Prophets. These commentaries—most of them only published after his death—were philologically focused and interacted with the work of Jerome, Nicholas of Lyra,* notable rabbis and Johannes Oecolampadius.*

Peter Moffett (d. 1617). English Protestant clergyman. Rector at Fobbing, Essex, Moffett published a commentary on the Song of Solomon and a sermon on 1 Timothy 1:16.

Ambrose Moibanus (1494–1554). German Lutheran bishop and theologian. Moibanus helped reform the church of Breslau (modern Wroclaw, Poland). He revised the Mass, bolstered pastoral care and welfare for the poor, and wrote a new evangelical catechism.

Olympia Morata (1526/27–1555). Italian Protestant humanist and theologian. Daughter of a humanist scholar, her father taught in the court of Ferrara, and she was raised alongside Anna d'Este (1531–1607), daughter of Protestant Renée of France (1510–1574) and later wife of Francis, Duke of Guise (1519–1563), a central antagonist in the St. Bartholomew's Day Massacre. A precocious scholar, Morata's classical, humanist, and biblical studies drew her toward the evangelical currents of the court, but these Protestant leanings also raised the constant suspicion of the Inquisition. In 1550, Morata married Andreas

Grundler (unknown), a German Protestant doctor, and moved to his native Schweinfurt, where, facing limited opportunities due to her gender, she continued her studies and privately tutored in Greek and the classics. She developed an extensive correspondence with friends, especially noblewomen she had met at court, and Protestant leaders including Luther*, Melanchthon* and Matthias Flacius (1520–1575), whom she asked to translate some of Luther's work into Italian. Most of Morata's writings were destroyed during the siege of Schweinfurt in 1553–1554, and while she was able to resettle in Frankfurt, she died of tuberculosis soon afterwards. In her writings that survived the siege, her scholarly erudition is clear, and her letters demonstrate a ministerial care for her correspondents and desire for the spread of the Reformation message.

Thomas More (1478–1535). English Catholic lawyer, politician, humanist and martyr. More briefly studied at Oxford, but completed his legal studies in London. After contemplating the priesthood for four years, he opted for politics and was elected a member of Parliament in 1504. A devout Catholic, More worked with church leaders in England to root out heresy while he also confronted Lutheran teachings in writing. After four years as Lord Chancellor, More resigned due to heightened tensions with Henry VIII* over papal supremacy (which More supported and Henry did not). Tensions did not abate. More's steadfast refusal to accept the Act of Supremacy (1534)—which declared the King of England to be the supreme ecclesial primate not the pope—resulted in his arrest and trial for high treason. He was found guilty and beheaded with John Fisher (1469–1535). Friends with John Colet* and Desiderius Erasmus,* More was a widely respected humanist in England as well as on the continent. Well-known for his novel *Utopia* (1516), More also penned several religious treatises on Christ's passion and suffering during his imprisonment in the Tower of London, which were published posthumously.

Sebastian Münster (1488–1552). German Reformed Hebraist, exegete, printer, and geographer. After converting to the Reformation in 1524, Münster taught Hebrew at the universities of Heidelberg and Basel. During his lengthy tenure in Basel he published more than seventy books, including Hebrew dictionaries and rabbinic commentaries. He also produced an evangelistic work for Jews titled *Vikuach* (1539). Münster's *Torat ha-Maschiach* (1537), the Gospel of Matthew, was the first published Hebrew translation of any portion of the New Testament. Despite his massive contribution to contemporary understanding of the Hebrew language, Münster was criticized by many of the reformers as a Judaizer.

Thomas Müntzer (c. 1489–1525). German Radical preacher. As a preacher in the town of Zwickau, Müntzer was influenced by German mysticism and, growing convinced that Martin Luther* had not carried through reform properly, sought to restore the pure apostolic church of the New Testament. Müntzer's radical ideas led to expulsions from various cities; he developed a highly apocalyptic theology, in which he heralded the last days that would establish the pure community out of suffering, prompting Müntzer's proactive role in the Peasants' War, which he perceived as a crucial apocalyptic event. Six thousand of Müntzer's followers were annihilated by magisterial troops; Müntzer was executed.

John Murcot (1625–1654). English Puritan pastor. After completing his bachelor's at Oxford in 1647, Murcot was ordained as a pastor, transferring to several parishes until in 1651 he moved to Dublin. All his works were published posthumously.

Simon Musaeus (1521–1582). German Lutheran theologian. After studying at the universities of Frankfurt an der Oder and Wittenberg, Musaeus began teaching Greek at the Cathedral school in Nuremberg and was ordained. Having returned to Wittenberg to complete a doctoral degree, Musaeus spent the rest of his career in numerous ecclesial and academic administrative posts. He opposed Matthias Flacius's (1505–1575) view of original sin—that the formal essence of human beings is marred by original sin—even calling the pro-Flacian faculty at Wittenberg "the devil's latrine." Musaeus published a disputation on original sin and a postil.

Wolfgang Musculus (1497–1563). German Reformed pastor and theologian. Musculus produced translations, biblical commentaries and an influential theological text, *Loci communes Sacrae Theologiae* (*Commonplaces of Sacred Theology*), outlining a Zwinglian theology. Musculus began to study theology while at a Benedictine monastery; he departed in 1527 and became secretary to Martin Bucer* in Strasbourg. He was later installed as a pastor in Augsburg, eventually performing the first evangelical liturgy in the city's cathedral. Displaced by the Augsburg Interim, Musculus ended his career as professor of theology at Bern. Though Musculus was active in the pursuit of the reform agenda, he was also concerned for ecumenism, participating in the Wittenberg Concord (1536) and discussions between Lutherans and Catholics.

Georg Mylius (1548–1607). German Lutheran pastor and theologian. Mylius began his career as a preacher in Augsburg, rising to superintendent of the churches in the city after receiving his doctorate in theology. He was arrested and ejected from the city by the Catholic-dominated council for his opposition to the Gregorian calendar, returning briefly to learn of the death of his pregnant wife and child. After grieving in Ulm, Mylius spend the remainder of his career as a preacher and professor of theology at Wittenberg, with a brief hiatus teaching at Jena.

Hans Nadler (unknown). German Radical layperson. An uneducated and illiterate needle salesman, after receiving baptism from Hans Hut* in 1527, Nadler sought to share the faith with those he met during his extensive travels. He is remembered through the records of his arrest and examination, recorded by a court reporter, which give insight into his beliefs and activities as a committed Anabaptist layperson, whereby he affirmed believer's baptism, the spiritual reception of the Eucharist, and nonresistance.

Friedrich Nausea (c. 1496–1552). German Catholic bishop and preacher. After completing his studies at Leipzig, this famed preacher was appointed priest in Frankfurt but was run out of town by his congregants during his first sermon. He transferred to Mainz as cathedral preacher. Nausea was well connected through the German papal hierarchy and traveled widely to preach to influential ecclesial and secular courts. Court preacher for Ferdinand I (1503–1564), his reform tendencies fit well with royal Austrian theological leanings, and he was enthroned as the bishop of Vienna. Nausea thought that rather than endless colloquies only a council could settle reform. Unfortunately he could not participate in the first session of Trent due to insufficient funding, but he arrived for the second session. Nausea defended the laity's reception of the cup and stressed the importance of promulgating official Catholic teaching in the vernacular.

Melchior Neukirch (1540–1597). German Lutheran pastor and playwright. Neukirch's pastoral career spanned more than thirty years in several northern German parishes. Neukirch published a history of the Braunschweig church since the Reformation and a dramatization of Acts 4–7. He died of the plague.

Nicholas of Lyra (1270–1349). French Catholic biblical exegete. Very little is known about this influential medieval theologian of the Sorbonne aside from the works he published, particularly the *Postilla litteralis super totam Bibliam* (1322–1333). With the advent of the printing press this work was regularly published alongside the Latin Vulgate and the *Glossa ordinaria*. In this running commentary on the Bible Nicholas promoted literal interpretation as the basis for theology. Despite his preference for literal interpretation, Nicholas also published a companion volume, the *Postilla moralis super totam Bibliam* (1339), a commentary on the spiritual meaning of the biblical text. Nicholas was a major conversation partner for many reformers though many of them rejected his exegesis as too literal and too "Jewish" (not concerned enough with the Bible's fulfillment in Jesus Christ).

John Norden (1547–1625). English devotional writer. Norden was born at Somerset, and in 1564 entered Hart Hall, Oxford where he graduated with his BA in 1568, and MA in 1573. Norden spent most of his life Middlesex, moving later to St. Giles in the Fields in 1619, where he remained until his death in 1625. Throughout his life, Norden distinguished himself also as a cartographer, chorographer, and antiquarian. His best known devotional work was his Progress of Piety (1596).

Alexander Nowell (1517–1602). Anglican theologian. Born in Lancashire, Nowell was educated at Brasenose College, Oxford where he shared a room with the future martyrologist John Foxe. Nowell was elected a fellow at the same college, where he spent thirteen years. In 1543, he was appointed master of Westminster School, and in December, 1551, a prebendary of Westminster Abbey. Though elected to the House of Commons in 1553, Nowell was permitted to assume his seat because as a prebendary, he had a seat in Convocation. Because of his evangelical convictions, Nowell lost prebendary in 1554, after which he fled to the Continent, traveling first to Strasbourg, and then to Frankfurt. When Elizabeth I ascended the throne, Nowell returned to England where he afterwards served as chaplain to Edmund Grindal. In 1561 Nowell became Dean of St. Paul's Cathedral, a post which he held until his death. Nowell's best known work was his Catechism originally written in Latin (1563), and translated into English by Thomas Norton in 1570.

Bernardino Ochino (1487–1564). Italian Reformed theologian. After serving as vicar general of the Franciscan order, Ochino left the foundation of the Capuchins, where he assisted in the composition of their constitution and served as vicar general. A famed preacher, his teaching came to the attention of the Inquisition as it began to reflect the thought of Juan de Valdés. Summoned to Rome in 1542, he fled to Geneva with Peter Martyr Vermigli* where his Reformed orthodoxy, tinged with Franciscan mysticism, was brought into the open. Following his flight, Ochino led an unstable life, with brief stays in Basel, Strasbourg, and Augsburg before moving to England with Vermigli in 1548 where he was able to compose a significant treatise against the Roman church. His doctrinal orthodoxy was questioned by the pastor of the Italian congregation in London, but his case left unresolved when he departed for Geneva, then Basel and Zurich, at the accession of Mary*. As pastor of a congregation of Italian refugees in Zurich, Ochino courted considerable controversy. He refused to have his works approved by the city magistrates before publication, and his opponents alleged that his *Dialogi XXX* (1563) included questionable teachings on the Trinity and divorce while seeming to advocate polygamy. Expelled from Zurich in 1563, he died in Moravia the following year.

Johannes Oecolampadius (Johannes Huszgen) (1482–1531). Swiss-German Reformed humanist, reformer and theologian. Oecolampadius (an assumed name meaning "house light") assisted with Desiderius Erasmus's* Greek New Testament, lectured on biblical languages and exegesis and completed an influential Greek grammar. After joining the evangelical cause through studying patristics and the work of Martin Luther,* Oecolampadius went to Basel, where he lectured on biblical exegesis and participated in ecclesial reform. On account of Oecolampadius's effort, the city council passed legislation restricting preaching to the gospel and releasing the city from compulsory Mass. Oecolampadius was a chief ally of Huldrych Zwingli,* whom he supported at the Marburg Colloquy (1529).

Kaspar Olevianus (1536–1587). German Reformed theologian. Olevianus is celebrated for composing the Heidelberg Catechism and producing a critical edition of Calvin's *Institutes* in German. Olevianus studied theology with many, including John Calvin,* Theodore Beza,* Heinrich Bullinger* and Peter Martyr Vermigli.* As an advocate of Reformed doctrine, Olevianus oversaw the shift from Lutheranism to Calvinism throughout Heidelberg, organizing the city's churches after Calvin's Geneva. The Calvinist ecclesial vision of Olevianus entangled him in a dispute with another Heidelberg reformer over the rights of ecclesiastical discipline, which Olevianus felt belonged to the council of clergy and elders rather than civil magistrates.

Josua Opitz (c. 1542–1585). German Lutheran pastor. After a brief stint as superintendent in Regensburg, Opitz, a longtime preacher, was dismissed for his support of Matthias Flacius's (1520–1575) view of original sin. (Using Aristotelian categories, Flacius argued that the formal essence of human beings is marred by original sin, forming sinners into the image of Satan; his views were officially rejected in Article 1 of the Formula of Concord.*) Hans Wilhelm Roggendorf (1533–1591) invited Opitz to lower Austria as part of his Lutheranizing program. Unfortunately Roggendorf and Opitz never succeed in getting Lutheranism legal recognition, perhaps in large part due to Opitz's staunch criticism of Catholics, which resulted in his exile. He died of plague.

Lucas Osiander (1534–1604). German Lutheran pastor. For three decades, Osiander— son of the controversial Nuremberg reformer Andreas Osiander (d. 1552)—served as pastor and court preacher in Stuttgart, until he fell out of favor with the duke in 1598. Osiander produced numerous theological and exegetical works, as well as an influential hymnal.

John Owen (1616–1683). English Puritan theologian. Owen trained at Oxford University, where he was later appointed dean of Christ Church and vice chancellor of the university, following his service as chaplain to Oliver Cromwell. Although Owen began his career as a Presbyterian minister, he eventually departed to the party of Independents. Owen composed many sermons, biblical commentaries (including seven volumes on the book of Hebrews), theological treatises and controversial monographs (including disputations with Arminians, Anglicans, Catholics and Socinians).

Santes Pagninus (c. 1470–1541). Italian Catholic biblical scholar. Pagninus studied under Girolamo Savonarola* and later taught in Rome, Avignon and Lyons. He translated the Old Testament into Latin according to a tight, almost wooden, adherence to the Hebrew. This translation and his Hebrew lexicon *Thesaurus linguae sanctae* (1529) were important resources for translators and commentators.

Johann Pappus (1549–1610). German Lutheran theologian. After a decade as a teacher of Hebrew and professor of theology at the Strasbourg academy, Pappus was appointed president of the city's company of pastors. Despite resistance from the Reformed theologian Johann Sturm (1507–1589), he led the city away from its Swiss Reformed alliances and toward subscription to the Lutheran Formula of Concord. A talented humanist, Pappus published more than thirty works on controversial, theological, historical, and exegetical subjects.

David (Wängler) Pareus (1548–1622). German Reformed pastor and theologian. Born at Frankenstein in Lower Silesia, Pareus studied theology at Heidelberg under Zacharias Ursinus (1534–1583), the principal author of the Heidelberg Catechism.* After reforming several churches, Pareus returned to Heidelberg to teach at the Reformed seminary. He then joined the theological faculty at the University of Heidelberg, first as a professor of Old Testament and later as a professor of New Testament. Pareus edited the *Neustadter Bibel* (1587), a publication of Martin Luther's* German translation with Reformed annotations—which was strongly denounced by Lutherans, especially Jakob Andreae* and Johann Georg Sigwart (1554–1618). In an extended debate, Pareus defended the orthodoxy of Calvin's exegesis against Aegidius Hunnius,* who accused Calvin of "judaizing" by rejecting many traditional Christological interpretations of Old Testament passages. Towards the end of his career, Pareus wrote commentaries on Genesis, Hosea, Matthew, Romans, 1 Corinthians, Galatians, Hebrews and Revelation.

Catherine Parr (1512–1548). The last of King Henry VIII's* six wives, Catherine Parr was Queen Consort to Henry from 1543 until his death in 1547. She enjoyed a close relationship with two of her step children, Elizabeth and Edward (the future Queen Elizabeth I* and King

Edward VI), involving herself extensively in their education. Having married three more times after the death of Henry VIII, Catherine died in 1548. Her published works are *Psalms or Prayers* (1543) and a *Lamentation of a Sinner* (1548).

Paul of Burgos (Solomon ha-Levi) (c. 1351–1435). Spanish Catholic archbishop. In 1391 Solomon ha-Levi, a rabbi and Talmudic scholar, converted to Christianity, receiving baptism with his entire family (except for his wife). He changed his name to Paul de Santa Maria. Some have suggested that he converted to avoid persecution; he himself stated that Thomas Aquinas's* work persuaded him of the truth of Christian faith. After studying theology in Paris, he was ordained bishop in 1403. He actively and ardently persecuted Jews, trying to compel them to convert. In order to convince Jews that Christians correctly interpret the Hebrew Scriptures, Paul wrote *Dialogus Pauli et Sauli contra Judaeos, sive Scrutinium Scripturarum* (1434), a book filled with vile language toward the Jews. He also wrote a series of controversial marginal notes and comments on Nicholas of Lyra's* *Postilla*, many of which criticized Nicholas's use of Jewish scholarship.

Christoph Pelargus (1565–1633). German Lutheran pastor, theologian, professor and superintendent. Pelargus studied philosophy and theology at the University of Frankfurt an der Oder, in Brandenburg. This irenic Philippist was appointed as the superintendent of Brandenburg and later became a pastor in Frankfurt, although the local authorities first required him to condemn Calvinist theology, because several years earlier he had been called before the consistory in Berlin under suspicion of being a crypto-Calvinist. Among his most important works were a four-volume commentary on *De orthodoxa fide* by John of Damascus (d. 749), a treatise defending the breaking of the bread during communion, and a volume of funeral sermons. He also published commentaries on the Pentateuch, the Psalms, Matthew, John and Acts.

Konrad Pellikan (1478–1556). German Reformed Hebraist and theologian. Pellikan attended the University of Heidelberg, where he mastered Hebrew under Johannes Reuchlin. In 1504

Pellikan published one of the first Hebrew grammars that was not merely a translation of the work of medieval rabbis. While living in Basel, Pellikan assisted the printer Johannes Amerbach, with whom he published some of Luther's* early writings. He also worked with Sebastian Münster* and Wolfgang Capito* on a Hebrew Psalter (1516). In 1526, after teaching theology for three years at the University of Basel, Huldrych Zwingli* brought Pellikan to Zurich to chair the faculty of Old Testament. Pellikan's magnum opus is a seven-volume commentary on the entire Bible (except Revelation) and the Apocrypha; it is often heavily dependent upon the work of others (esp. Desiderius Erasmus* and Johannes Oecolampadius*).

William Pemble (1591–1623). Puritan theologian and author. Pemble was born in Egerton, Kent. He was educated at Magdalen College, Oxford, where he graduated with his BA degree in 1614. Afterward he moved to Magdalen Hall, where he became a reader and tutor in divinity. He received his MA in 1618. Primarily a Hebrew scholar, Pemble authored commentaries on Ecclesiastes (1629), the first nine chapters of Zechariah (1629), and portions of Ezra, Nehemiah, and Daniel. Pemble also wrote *An Introduction to the Worthy Receiving the Sacrament* (1628), as well as treatises on predestination and justification. He died of a fever on April 14, 1623.

Benedict Pererius (1535–1610). Spanish Catholic theologian, philosopher and exegete. Pererius entered the Society of Jesus in 1552. He taught philosophy, theology, and exegesis at the Roman College of the Jesuits. Early in his career he warned against neo-Platonism and astrology in his *De principiis* (1576). Pererius wrote a lengthy commentary on Daniel, and five volumes of exegetical theses on Exodus, Romans, Revelation and part of the Gospel of John (chs. 1–14). His four-volume commentary on Genesis (1591–1599) was lauded by Protestants and Catholics alike.

William Perkins (1558–1602). English Puritan preacher and theologian. Perkins was a highly regarded Puritan Presbyterian preacher and biblical commentator in the Elizabethan era. He studied at Cambridge University and later became a fellow of Christ's Church college as a preacher and professor, receiving acclaim for his sermons and lectures. Even more, Perkins gained an esteemed reputation for his ardent exposition of Calvinist reformed doctrine in the style of Petrus Ramus,* becoming one of the first English reformed theologians to achieve international recognition. Perkins influenced the federal Calvinist shape of Puritan theology and the vision of logical, practical expository preaching.

François Perrault (1577–1657). French Reformed pastor for over fifty years. His book on demonology was prominent, perhaps because of the intrigue at his home in 1612. According to his account, a poltergeist made a commotion and argued points of theology; a few months later Perrault's parishioners slew a large snake slithering out of his house.

Dirk Philips (1504–1568). Dutch Radical elder and theologian. This former Franciscan monk, known for being severe and obstinate, was a leading theologian of the sixteenth-century Anabaptist movement. Despite the fame of Menno Simons* and his own older brother Obbe, Philips wielded great influence over Anabaptists in the Netherlands and northern Germany where he ministered. As a result of Philips's understanding of the apostolic church as radically separated from the children of the world, he advocated a very strict interpretation of the ban, including formal shunning. His writings were collected and published near the end of his life as *Enchiridion oft Hantboecxken van de Christelijcke Leere* (1564).

Obbe Philips (1500–1568) Dutch radical leader. Trained as a physician, Philips was drawn to mystical Anabaptism, as taught by Melchior Hoffman (1495–1543) in his hometown of Leewarden. After adult rebaptism and ordination, he preached in Amsterdam, Delft, Appingedam, and Grongen, and he ordained other leaders including his brother Dirk Philips*, David Joris*, and Menno Simmons*. Disillusioned with the growth of revolutionary, enthusiastic, and apocalyptic elements within Anabaptism and unable to reconcile any visible church with the church of God, Philips withdrew from the radical movement in 1540, after which nothing is known of his life. His only extant writing, entitled *The Confession of Obbe Philips*, was published after his death and recounts elements of the history of the Anabaptist movement and defends his departure from the movement.

James Pilkington (1520-1576). Protestant bishop of Durham and Elizabethan author. Born in Lancashire, Pilkington received his early education at Manchester Grammar School. Afterwards, he entered Pembroke College, Cambridge, and later transferred to St. John's College, Cambridge, from where he graduated with his BA degree in 1539, and MA in 1542. Pilkington was appointed vicar of Kendal in 1545, but resigned this position shortly thereafter in order to return to Cambridge. While there, Pilkington was granted a license to preach, and was awarded the degree of Bachelor of Theology in 1551. In this same year, Pilkington became president of the college. When Mary Tudor succeeded her half-brother, Edward VI, in 1553, Pilkington fled to the Continent where he traveled to Zurich, Geneva, Frankfurt, and Strasbourg. He returned to England in 1559 when Elizabeth I ascended the throne of England. After returning to England, Pilkington became Regius Professor of Divinity at Cambridge and after, bishop of Durham in 1560. Pilkington's major work was his voluminous commentary on the Prophet Haggai.

Charles Pinner (Unknown). English Protestant pastor. Pinner studied at New College, Oxford, and served as rector at Wootton Bassett in Wiltshire. His extant writings include two sermons on 1 Timothy and two on 1 Peter.

Hector Pinto (c. 1528–1584). Portuguese Catholic theologian and exegete. A member of the order of Saint Jerome, Pinto taught theology and Scripture at the Universities of Sigüenza and Coimbra. A respected theologian and exegete, he published commentaries on Daniel, Nahum, Jeremiah, and Isaiah and an influential devotional work, *The Image of the Christian Life*.

Caritas Pirckheimer (1466–1532). German Catholic nun. Sister of famed humanist Wilibald

Pirckheimer (1470–1530), Caritas received a humanistic education before entering the Franciscan convent at Nuremberg. Extolled by Erasmus* as one of the most learned women in Europe, Pirckheimer served as abbess at the advent of the Reformation, and her experiences are recorded in a journal covering the pivotal years of 1524–1528. While Nuremberg accepted Lutheran theology under the leadership of the city council and preachers such as Andreas Osiander (1498–1552), Pirckheimer defended the right of her order to continue in their vocation. She ultimately won a concession after a visit from Philip Melanchthon* in 1525, who recommended that the council allow those who wished to remain in the cloister to live out their vows in peace.

Johannes Piscator (1546–1625). German Reformed theologian. Educated at Tübingen (though he wanted to study at Wittenberg), Piscator taught at the universities of Strasbourg and Heidelberg, as well as academies in Neustadt and Herborn. His commentaries on both the Old and New Testaments involve a tripartite analysis of a given passage's argument, of scholia on the text and of doctrinal loci. Some consider Piscator's method to be a full flowering of Beza's* "logical" scriptural analysis, focused on the text's meaning and its relationship to the pericopes around it.

Constantino Ponce de la Fuente (1502–1559). Spanish Protestant theologian and preacher. A priest in Seville, Ponce de la Fuente was a critic of the established church and associated with the evangelical circle in the city. A popular preacher, he authored a catechism and a number of books on doctrine and the Christian life that focused on the work of Christ. Charged with heresy by the Inquisition, he admitted to the authorship of a number of heretical writings and died in prison awaiting trial while his works were added to the Index of Prohibited Books.

Matthew Poole (1624–1679). English Nonconformist minister. Having made known his preference for simplicity in worship, Matthew Poole was rector of St Michael-le-Querne until the passing of the 1662 Act of Uniformity led him to resign.

Living off his inheritance, he preached occasionally and composed some brief tracts but devoted much of his effort to the compilation of Latin biblical commentary in the *Synopsis criticorum* (1669) and the composition of his own annotations on Scripture. He died in Amsterdam, having fled London during the Popish Plot (1678–1681). He believed his life was in danger for his anti-Catholic writings as part of a Catholic conspiracy to kill Charles II, which was ultimately revealed as a fiction concocted by Titus Oates (1649–1705).

Gabriel Powell (1575–1611). Puritan minister. Powell was born at Ruabon in Denbigshire in 1575. Having completed his studies at Jesus College, Oxford, Powell became master of the free-school in Ruthen. During his tenure at Ruthen, Powell closely studied the writings of the church fathers as well as philosophy, and afterward endeavored to publish several works based on this research. Finding his present location to be a hinderance to his literary objectives, Powell relocated to Oxford, entering St. Mary's Hall, where he finished his anticipated projects. Powell is chiefly known for his literary debate with Thomas Bilson (1547–1619) concerning Christ's descent into hell. Later, Richard Vaughan (1550–1607), bishop of London, appointed Powell his domestic chaplain. Powell died on December 31, 1611. In addition to many controversial and polemical works, Powell wrote a commentary on Romans 1.

Vavasor Powell (1617–1670). Welsh Puritan minister and author. Powell was born at Knucklas, Radnorshire, Wales. After completing his education at Jesus College, Oxford, Powell returned to Wales to assume the position of a local schoolmaster. During this time, Powell came under the influence of Walter Cradock's* preaching as well as the writings of Richard Sibbes* and William Perkins,* resulting in his conversion to Puritanism. Soon thereafter he became an itinerant preacher, traveling throughout Wales. He was arrested twice for nonconformity. During the Civil War, Powell first preached in London, and shortly thereafter pastored an Independent congregation in Wales. On December 26, 1641,

Royalist forces arrested and imprisoned Powell. In 1646, as victory for the Puritans appeared inevitable, Powell was released, and allowed to return to Wales, having received a letter of endorsement from the Westminster Assembly. Back in Wales, Powell played a prominent role in the Westminster Assembly's 1650 commission for the better propagation of the gospel throughout Wales. In 1653, Powell returned to London, where he preached at St. Ann Blackfriars. It was at this time that Powell denounced Oliver Cromwell (1599–1658) for assuming the position of Lord Protector. For this reason, he was arrested and imprisoned. At the Restoration in 1660, Powell was again arrested and imprisoned for unauthorized preaching for seven years. Though released in 1667, Powell was once more arrested and incarcerated. He remained in custody until his death on October 27, 1660. Powell authored many poems and a concordance to the Bible.

Felix Pratensis (d. 1539). Italian Catholic Hebraist. Pratensis, the son of a rabbi, converted to Christianity and entered the Augustinian Hermits around the turn of the sixteenth century. In 1515, with papal permission, Pratensis published a new translation of the Psalms based on the Hebrew text. His *Biblia Rabbinica* (1517–1518), printed in Jewish and Christian editions, included text-critical notes in the margins as well as the Targum and rabbinic commentaries on each book (e.g., Rashi* on the Pentateuch and David Kimchi* on the Prophets). Many of the reformers consulted this valuable resource as they labored on their own translations and expositions of the Old Testament.

John Preston (1587–1628). Puritan minister and author. Preston was born at Upper Heyford, Northamptonshire, on October 27, 1587. He studied philosophy at King's College and Queen's College, Cambridge, earning his bachelor's degree in 1607. He became a fellow at Queen's in 1609, and a prebendary at Lincoln Cathedral a year later. During this period, Preston studied medicine and astronomy. In 1611, he received the MA degree. Sometime afterward, he experienced a conversion

under the preaching of John Cotton.* After his conversion, Preston went on to study theology, concentrating mainly on Thomas Aquinas,* Duns Scotus, and William of Ockham. From there, he proceeded to the reformers, especially John Calvin.* Preston was appointed court chaplain in 1615. In this position he was influential in the promotion of Puritans to high civil office. Preston later assumed the positions of dean and catechist at Queen's College, Cambridge, where he distinguished himself by preaching a series of sermons that formed the basis of his body of divinity. In 1622, he received the degree of bachelor of divinity, becoming thereafter master of Emmanuel College, Cambridge. While at Emmanuel, Preston participated in the conflict between Calvinism and Arminianism. Moreover, in the same year, Preston succeeded John Donne* as preacher at Lincoln's Inn. Two years later, Preston accepted the lectureship at Trinity Church. He died at the age of forty in 1628. Throughout his prodigious career, Preston authored a sizable corpus, which includes published sermons on Romans.

Quadriga. The *quadriga*, or four senses of Scripture, grew out of the exegetical legacy of Paul's dichotomy of letter and spirit (2 Cor 3:6), as well as church fathers like Origen (c. 185–254), Jerome (c. 347–420) and Augustine* (354–430). Advocates for this method—the primary framework for biblical exegesis during the medieval era—assumed the necessity of the gift of faith under the guidance of the Holy Spirit. The literal-historical meaning of the text served as the foundation for the fuller perception of Scripture's meaning in the three spiritual senses, accessible only through faith: the allegorical sense taught what should be believed, the tropological or moral sense taught what should be done, and the anagogical or eschatological sense taught what should be hoped for. Medieval Jewish exegesis also had a fourfold interpretive method—not necessarily related to the *quadriga*—called *pardes* ("grove"): *peshat*, the simple, literal sense of the text according to grammar; *remez*, the allegorical sense; *derash*, the moral sense; and *sod*, the mystic sense related to

Kabbalah. Scholars hotly dispute the precise use and meaning of these terms.

Edward Rainbow[e] (1608–1684). Anglican minister, scholar, and bishop. Rainbow was born at Lincolnshire on April 20, 1608. After completing his education, Rainbow matriculated at Corpus Christi College, and later transferred to Magdalene College, Cambridge, where he graduated with the BA (1627), MA (1630), BD (1637), and DD (1643). He was elected a fellow at Magdalene in 1633 and a master there in 1642. In 1630, Rainbow accepted the mastership of the Kirton-in-Lindsey but shortly afterward moved to London. In 1632, Rainbow took holy orders and preached his first sermon in April of that year. His first appointment was that of curate of Savoy Hospital. Rainbow was recalled to Cambridge in 1633 and elected a fellow. Four years later he became dean of Magdalene and master of the same college in 1642. Though dismissed from his mastership by Parliament in 1650, Rainbow was restored to it in the year of the Restoration (1660). At the same time, he was appointed chaplain to the king. In 1661, Rainbow became dean of Peterborough, and appointed vice chancellor of Cambridge a year later. Rainbow was elected bishop of Carlisle in 1664. As bishop, Rainbow led in the systemic reform of his diocese. Rainbow died March 26, 1684. His published works consist of three published sermons and an incomplete treatise, *Verba Christi*.

Petrus Ramus (1515–1572). French Reformed humanist philosopher. Ramus was an influential professor of philosophy and logic at the French royal college in Paris; he converted to Protestantism and left France for Germany, where he came under the influence of Calvinist thought. Ramus was a trenchant critic of Aristotle and noted for his method of classification based on a deductive movement from universals to particulars, the latter becoming branching divisions that provided a visual chart of the parts to the whole. His system profoundly influenced Puritan theology and preaching. After returning to Paris, Ramus died in the Saint Bartholomew's Day Massacre.

Rashi (Shlomo Yitzchaki) (1040–1105). French Jewish rabbi and exegete. After completing his studies, Rashi founded a yeshiva in Troyes. He composed the first comprehensive commentary on the Talmud, as well as commentaries on the entire Old Testament except for 1–2 Chronicles. These works remain influential within orthodox Judaism. Late medieval and early modern Christian scholars valued his exegesis, characterized by his preference for peshat (see quadriga).

Reformatio Legum Ecclesiasticarum (1552). Under the leadership of Archbishop of Canterbury Thomas Cranmer,* Edward VI* established a committee of thirty-two bishops, theologians, and lawyers including Nicholas Ridley,* John Hooper,* Peter Martyr Vermigli,* Matthew Parker (1504–1575), and William Cecil (1520–1598) to align the laws of the English church with Reformed theology and English civil law. Completed in 1552, it touched on diverse topics, including church organization, doctrine and heresy, qualifications for ministry, and marriage and divorce. It was brought before Parliament in 1553, where it was blocked by John Dudley, Duke of Northumberland (1504–1553), who wished to decrease church powers, and then dropped upon the accession of Mary I. A manuscript of the proposal revised by John Foxe (1516/1517–1587) was published in 1671, and while some elements of the Reformatio Legum Ecclesiasticarum were adopted under Elizabeth I, thoroughgoing reform of ecclesiastical law was not brought about until the *Book of Canons* (1604).

Remonstrance (1610). See *Synod of Dordrecht*.

Johannes Reuchlin (1455–1522). German Catholic lawyer, humanist and Hebraist. Reuchlin held judicial appointments for the dukes of Württemberg, the Supreme Court in Speyer and the imperial court of the Swabian League. He pioneered the study of Hebrew among Christians in Germany, standing against those who, like Johannes Pfefferkorn (1469–1523), wanted to destroy Jewish literature. Among his many works he published a Latin dictionary, an introductory Greek grammar, the most important early modern

Hebrew grammar and dictionary (*De rudimentis hebraicis*; 1506), and a commentary on the penitential psalms.

Edward Reynolds (1599–1676). Anglican bishop. Reynolds succeeded John Donne* as the preacher at Lincoln's Inn before entering parish ministry in Northamptonshire. During the English Civil Wars, he supported the Puritans because of his sympathy toward their simplicity and piety—despite believing that Scripture demanded no particular form of government; later he refused to support the abolition of the monarchy. Until the Restoration he ministered in London; afterward he became the bishop of Norwich. He wrote the general thanksgiving prayer which is part of the morning office in the *Book of Common Prayer.**

Urbanus Rhegius (1489–1541). German Lutheran pastor. Rhegius, who was likely the son of a priest, studied under the humanists at Freiburg and Ingolstadt. After a brief stint as a foot soldier, he received ordination in 1519 and was made cathedral preacher in Augsburg. During his time in Augsburg he closely read Luther's* works, becoming an enthusiastic follower. Despite his close friendship with Zwingli* and Oecolampadius,* Rhegius supported Luther in the eucharistic debates, later playing a major role in the Wittenberg Concord (1536). He advocated for peace during the Peasants' War and had extended interactions with the Anabaptists in Augsburg. Later in his career he concerned himself with the training of pastors, writing a pastoral guide and two catechisms. About one hundred of his writings were published posthumously.

Lancelot Ridley (d. 1576). Anglican preacher. Ridley was the first cousin of Nicholas Ridley,* the bishop of London who was martyred during the Marian persecutions. By Cranmer's* recommendation, Ridley became one of the six Canterbury Cathedral preachers. Upon Mary I's accession in 1553, Ridley was defrocked (as a married priest). Ridley returned to Canterbury Cathedral after Mary's death. He wrote commentaries on Jude, Ephesians, Philippians and Colossians.

Nicholas Ridley (c. 1502–1555). Anglican bishop. Ridley was a student and fellow at Cambridge University who was appointed chaplain to Archbishop Thomas Cranmer* and is thought to be partially responsible for Cranmer's shift to a symbolic view of the Eucharist. Cranmer promoted Ridley twice: as bishop of Rochester, where he openly advocated Reformed theological views, and, later, as bishop of London. Ridley assisted Cranmer in the revisions of the Book of Common Prayer.* Ridley's support of Lady Jane Grey against the claims of Mary to the throne led to his arrest; he was tried for heresy and burned at the stake with Hugh Latimer.*

Peter Riedemann (1506–1556). German Radical elder, theologian and hymnist. While traveling as a Silesian cobbler, Riedemann came into contact with Anabaptist teachings and joined a congregation in Linz. In 1529 he was called to be a minister, only to be imprisoned soon after as part of Archduke Ferdinand's efforts to suppress heterodoxy in his realm. Once he was released, he moved to Moravia in 1532 where he was elected as a minister and missionary of the Hutterite community there. His *Account of Our Religion, Doctrine and Faith* (1542), with its more than two thousand biblical references, is Riedemann's most important work and is still used by Hutterites today.

John Robinson (1576–1625). English Puritan pastor. After his suspension for nonconformity, Robinson fled to the Netherlands with his congregation, eventually settling in Leiden in 1609. Robinson entered into controversies over Arminianism, separation and congregationalism. Most of his healthy congregants immigrated to Plymouth in 1620; Robinson remained in Leiden with those unable to travel.

John Rogers (1505–1555). English Protestant Bible translator. Rogers was born in Deritend, Birmingham. After receiving his early education at the Guild School of St. John the Baptist, Rogers matriculated at Pembroke Hall, Cambridge, where he graduated with the BA degree in 1526. He served as rector of Holy Trinity the Less in London from 1532 to 1534, when he left for the

Continent to serve as chaplain to the English merchants of the Company of the Merchant Adventurers. It was at this time that he met William Tyndale,* under whose influence he came to embrace an evangelical faith. After Tyndale's death, Rogers completed his late colleague's translation of the Old Testament, which had ended with 2 Chronicles, by adding Miles Coverdale's translation of the remainder, including the Apocrypha. The resulting work, known as the "Matthew Bible" (Rogers published it under the pseudonym "Thomas Matthew") was published in 1537. It has the distinction of being the first complete English Bible translated essentially from the original languages to be printed. "Matthew's Bible" served as the basis for the Great Bible (1540), which in turn was used by those who prepared the Bishops' Bible (1568), on which later the King James Version (1611) was produced. In 1540, Rogers enrolled at the University of Wittenberg, where he became close friends with Philipp Melanchthon.* During his three years at Wittenberg, Rogers was a superintendent of the Lutheran Church in northern Germany. When Rogers returned to England in 1548, he published a translation of Melanchthon's *Considerations of the Augsburg Interim*, and later served in a variety of ecclesiastical roles. Rogers was burned at the stake for heresy during the reign of Mary Tudor on February 4, 1555.

Nehemiah Rogers (1593–1660). Anglican priest. After studying at Cambridge, Rogers ministered at numerous parishes during his more than forty-year career. In 1643, he seems to have been forced out of a parish on account of being a Royalist and friend of William Laud.* Rogers published a number of sermons and tracts, including a series of expositions on Jesus' parables in the Gospels.

Thomas Rogers (d. 1616). Anglican theologian and translator. Rogers attended Christ Church, Oxford, where he completed his BA degree in 1573 and MA in 1576. Later he served as rector of Horrigner in Suffolk, and chaplain to Archbishop of Canterbury, Richard Bancroft. He died at Horringer and was buried in his church. Among his many works were an exposition of the Thirty-Nine Articles as well as a paraphrase of the Psalms and a translation of Niels Hemmingsen's commentary on Psalm 84.

Robert Rollock (c. 1555–1599). Scottish Reformed pastor, educator and theologian. Rollock was deeply influenced by Petrus Ramus's* system of logic, which he implemented as a tutor and (later) principal of Edinburgh University and in his expositions of the Bible. Rollock, as a divinity professor and theologian, was instrumental in diffusing a federalist Calvinism in the Scottish church; he lectured on theology using the texts of Theodore Beza* and articulated a highly covenantal interpretation of the biblical narratives. He was a prolific writer of sermons, expositions, commentaries, lectures and occasional treatises.

David Runge (1564–1604). German Lutheran theologian. First appointed professor of Hebrew at the University of Greifswald, Runge supported and later replaced his father in teaching philosophy and theology. After receiving his doctorate, he was named to the theological faculty at Wittenberg, where he also served as dean and rector of the university.

Johann Rurer (1480–1542) German Lutheran pastor. Rurer was court chaplain to Margrave Casimir of Brandenberg–Kulmbach (1481–1527), and the first Protestant pastor in Ansbach. Conflict over church order and his desire for reform led to his expulsion, but he was recalled after Casimir's death by his successor, George (1484–1543), who sought a throughgoing Lutheran reformation of the town and appointed Rurer preacher at the collegiate church.

Samuel Rutherford (1600–1661). Scottish Reformed theologian. Rutherford was born in Nisbet, Roxburghshire. After completing his early education at Jedborough, Rutherford enrolled at the University of Edinburgh, where he received his MA degree in 1621. In 1623, Rutherford was appointed professor of humanities at Edinburgh. Two years later, he was dismissed from his position on account of misbehavior with the woman who would later be his wife. Sometime after this incident, he underwent a spiritual conversion. In 1625, Rutherford commenced the study of theology at Edinburgh. Upon finishing his studies, Rutherford was called to pastor a church in Antwoth by Solway in Kirkcudbrightshire. Throughout his ministry, Rutherford proved to be an ardent opponent to episcopacy. For this, he was summoned to appear before the Court of High Commission in 1630. Despite the court's warnings to cease and desist, Rutherford continued his nonconformity. Rutherford also participated extensively in the Arminian controversy, writing treatises against Arminius as well as the Jesuits. Since Rutherford's virulent opposition to Arminianism placed him in direct opposition with the English episcopacy, he was once again summoned by the Court of High Commission in 1636. After a three-day trial, Rutherford was deprived of his ministerial office and ordered not to preach anywhere in Scotland. Meanwhile he was confined to Aberdeen. In 1638, when the National Covenant was signed and Presbyterianism restored in Scotland, Rutherford left Aberdeen and assumed the post of professor of theology at St. Mary's College, St. Andrews. Later, Rutherford served as a commissioner to the Westminster Assembly, where he contributed to the discussions related to the Shorter Catechism. In 1647, Rutherford returned to Scotland, where he was appointed principal of St. Mary's College, and rector of the university in 1651. After the monarchy was restored, Rutherford was charged with treason, and deprived of all his ecclesiastical and university positions. He died on March 30, 1661. Throughout his career, Rutherford published many sermons and theological works, most famous of which is *Lex Rex* (The law is king), a treatise arguing against the divine right of kings.

Jacopo Sadoleto (1477–1547). Italian Catholic Cardinal. Sadoleto, attaché to Leo X's court, was appointed bishop in 1517, cardinal in 1536. He participated in the reform commission led by Gasparo Contarini.* However, he tried to reconcile with Protestants apart from the commission, sending several letters to Protestant leaders in addition to his famous letter to the city of Geneva, which John Calvin* pointedly answered. Sadoleto published a commentary on Romans that was censored as semi-Pelagian. His insufficient treatment of prevenient grace left him vulnerable to this charge. Sadoleto emphasized grammar as the rule and norm of exegesis.

Alfonso Salmerón (1515–1585). Spanish Catholic exegete and theologian. While studying at the Sorbonne, Salmerón met Ignatius Loyola (1491–1556) and, with five others, took a vow of poverty and service to church and pope. After ministering in France, the group traveled to Rome, where they were given papal approval to form the Society of Jesus. Salmerón helped write the constitutions of the order, and following the priorities of the Jesuits, spent much of his career focused on education. He lectured throughout Italy, served briefly on the faculty of the University of Ingolstadt, and, in Naples, founded one of the first Jesuit colleges. He also undertook a number of missions as a papal emissary and served as a papal theologian at all three meetings of the Council of Trent. His primary works are his commentaries on the New Testament, which cover the Gospels, Acts, and Paul's letters.

Heinrich Salmuth (1522–1576). German Lutheran theologian. After earning his doctorate from the University of Leipzig, Salmuth served in several coterminous pastoral and academic positions. He was integral to the reorganization of the University of Jena. Except for a few disputations, all of Salmuth's works—mostly sermons— were published posthumously by his son.

Robert Sanderson (1587–1663). Anglican bishop and philosopher. Before his appointment as professor of divinity at Oxford in 1642, Sanderson pastored in several parishes. Because of his loyalty to the Crown during the English Civil Wars, the Parliamentarians stripped Sanderson of his post at Oxford. After the Restoration he was reinstated at Oxford and consecrated bishop. He wrote an influential textbook on logic.

Edwin Sandys (1519–1588). Anglican bishop. During his doctoral studies at Cambridge, Sandys befriended Martin Bucer.* Having supported the Protestant Lady Jane Grey's claim to the throne, Sandys resigned his post at Cambridge upon Mary I's accession. He was then arrested and imprisoned in the Tower of London. Released in 1554, he sojourned on the continent until Mary's death. On his return to England he was appointed to revise the liturgy and was consecrated bishop. Many of his sermons were published, but his most significant literary legacy is his work as a translator of the Bishop's Bible (1568), which served as the foundational English text for the translators of the King James Bible (1611).

Erasmus Sarcerius (1501–1559). German Lutheran superintendent, educator and pastor. Sarcerius served as educational superintendent, court preacher and pastor in Nassau and, later, in Leipzig. The hallmark of Sarcerius's reputation was his ethical emphasis as exercised through ecclesial oversight and family structure; he also drafted disciplinary codes for regional churches in Germany. Sarcerius served with Philipp Melanchthon* as Protestant delegates at the Council of Trent, though both withdrew prior to the dismissal of the session; he eventually became an opponent of Melanchthon, contesting the latter's understanding of the Eucharist at a colloquy in Worms in 1557.

Michael Sattler (c. 1490–1527). Swiss Radical leader. Sattler was a Benedictine monk who abandoned the monastic life during the upheavals of the Peasants' War. He took up the trade of weaving under the guidance of an outspoken Anabaptist. It seems that Sattler did not openly join the Anabaptist movement until after the suppression of the Peasants' War in 1526. Sattler interceded with Martin Bucer* and Wolfgang Capito* for imprisoned Anabaptists in Strasbourg. Shortly before he was convicted of heresy and executed, he wrote the definitive expression of Anabaptist theology, the Schleitheim Articles.*

Girolamo Savonarola (1452–1498). Italian Catholic preacher and martyr. Outraged by clerical corruption and the neglect of the poor, Savonarola traveled to preach against these abuses and to prophesy impending judgment—a mighty king would scourge and reform the church. Savonarola thought that the French invasion of Italy in 1494 confirmed his apocalyptic visions. Thus he pressed to purge Florence of vice and institute public welfare, in order to usher in a new age of Christianity. Florence's refusal to join papal resistance against the French enraged Alexander VI (r. 1492–1503). He blamed Savonarola, promptly excommunicating him and threatening Florence with an interdict. After an ordeal by fire turned into a riot, Savonarola was arrested. Under torture he admitted to charges of conspiracy and false prophecy; he was hanged and burned. In addition to numerous sermons and letters, he wrote meditations on Psalms 31 and 51 as well as *The Triumph of the Cross* (1497).

Leupold Scharnschlager (d. 1563). Austrian Radical elder. See *Kunstbuch.*

Leonhard Schiemer (d. 1528) Austrian radical martyr. Troubled by the hypocrisies he experienced, Scheimer left the Franciscan order and spent a period of time wandering. Attracted to the teachings of Hans Hut* after hearing him debate Balthasar Hubmaier* in Moravia, he was rebaptized and traveled widely throughout Austria and Southern Germany, spreading the Anabaptist message until he was arrested in Rattenberg, where he was condemned to death and beheaded. A number of his essays and hymns survive, dispersed among the *Kunstbuch** and other collections of radical writings.

Hans Schlaffer (c. 1490–1528). Austrian Radical martyr. Drawn by Luther's theology, Schlaffer resigned his priesthood in 1526 only to turn to Anabaptism soon afterward. While contemporaries recognized his ability as a preacher, he never settled in a ministry position. He spent time among Radical congregations in Freistadt, Nicholsburg, Augsburg, Nuremberg, and Regensburg before his arrest in Schatz, where he was executed. Nine writings by Schlaffer remain, most of which were composed during his imprisonment. They include confessions of his beliefs and devotional works, which have been preserved among Hutterite churches.

Schleitheim Articles (1527). After the death of Conrad Grebel* in 1526 and the execution of Felix Manz (born c. 1498) in early 1527, the young Swiss Anabaptist movement was in need of unity and direction. A synod convened at Schleitheim under the chairmanship of Michael Sattler,* which passed seven articles of Anabaptist distinctives—likely defined against both magisterial reformers and other Anabaptists with less orthodox and more militant views (e.g., Balthasar Hubmaier*). Unlike most confessions, these articles do not explicitly address traditional creedal interests; they explicate instead the Anabaptist view of the sacraments, church discipline, separatism, the role of ministers, pacifism and oaths. Throughout the document there is a resolute focus on Christ's example. Also referred to as the Schleitheim Confession and the Schleitheim Brotherly Union, the Schleitheim Articles are considered the definitive statement of Anabaptist theology, particularly regarding separatism.

Schmalkald Articles (1537). In response to Pope Paul III's (1468–1549) 1536 decree ordering a general church council to solve the Protestant crisis, Elector John Frederick (1503–1554) commissioned Martin Luther* to draft the sum of his teaching. Intended by Luther as a last will and testament—and composed with advice from well-known colleagues Justus Jonas,* Johann Bugenhagen,* Caspar Cruciger,* Nikolaus von Amsdorf (1483–1565), Georg Spalatin (1484–1545), Philipp Melanchthon* and Johann Agricola*—these articles provide perhaps the briefest and most systematic summary of Luther's teaching. The document was not adopted formally by the Lutheran Schmalkald League, as was hoped, and the general church council was postponed for several years (until convening at Trent in 1545). Only in 1580 were the articles officially received, by being incorporated into the *Book of Concord* defining orthodox Lutheranism.

Sebastian Schmidt (1617–1696). German Lutheran theologian. After serving as pastor in Entzheim and rector of the high school in Lindau, Schmidt became professor of theology at Strasbourg. His body of writings is extensive and includes commentaries on many of the Pauline letters, Hebrews, John, and Jeremiah.

Dietrich Schnepff (1525–1586). German Lutheran pastor and theologian. Schnepff taught briefly at the city school in Tübingen while working toward his theological doctorate before taking pastorates in Derendingen and Nürtingen. Returning to Tübingen as professor of theology, Schnepff also took on additional roles as rector of the university and pastor of the Collegiate Church.

Anna Maria van Schurman (1607–1678). Dutch Reformed polymath. Van Schurman cultivated talents in art, poetry, botany, linguistics and theology. She mastered most contemporary European languages, in addition to Latin, Greek, Hebrew, Arabic, Farsi and Ethiopian. With the encouragement of leading Reformed theologian Gisbertus Voetius (1589–1676), van Schurman attended lectures at the University of Utrecht—although she was required to sit behind a wooden screen so that the male students could not see her. In 1638 van Schurman published her famous treatise advocating female scholarship, *Amica dissertatio . . . de capacitate ingenii muliebris ad scientias*. In addition to these more polemical works, van Schurman also wrote hymns and poems, including a paraphrase of Genesis 1–3. Later in life she became a devotee of Jean de Labadie (1610–1674), a former Jesuit who was also expelled from the Reformed church for his separatist leanings. Her *Eucleria* (1673) is the most well known defense of Labadie's theology.

Kaspar von Schwenckfeld (1489–1561). German Radical reformer. Schwenckfeld was a Silesian nobleman who encountered Luther's* works in 1521. He traveled to Wittenberg twice: first to meet Luther and Karlstadt,* and a second time to convince Luther of his doctrine of the "internal word"—emphasizing inner revelation so strongly that he did not see church meetings or the sacraments as necessary—after which Luther considered him heterodox. Schwenckfeld won his native territory to the Reformation in 1524 and later lived in Strasbourg for five years until Bucer* sought to purify the city of less traditional theologies. Schwenckfeld wrote numerous polemical and exegetical tracts.

Scots Confession (1560). In 1560, the Scottish Parliament undertook to reform the Church of Scotland and to commission a Reformed confession of faith. In the course of four days, a committee—which included John Knox*—wrote this confession, largely based on Calvin's* work, the Confession of the English Congregation in Geneva (1556) and the Gallic Confession.* The articles were not ratified until 1567 and were displaced by the Westminster Confession (1646), adopted by the Scottish in 1647.

Abraham Scultetus (1566–1625). Silesian Reformed theologian. Scultetus spent the majority of his career in service of the Palatinate, holding a number of pastoral roles before becoming court preacher to Elector Frederic V (1596–1632). Appointed professor of theology at Heidelberg in 1618, he represented the Palatinate at the Synod of Dordrecht* (1618–1619), where he opposed the theology of the Remonstrants. Scultetus is often vilified for encouraging Reformed Frederic V to take the crown of Lutheran Bohemia, an act that led to war and the defeat of Frederic V, but his exegetical, historical, and pastoral teachings nevertheless garnered significant respect from his contemporaries.

Second Helvetic Confession (1566). Believing he would soon die, Heinrich Bullinger* penned a personal statement of his Reformed faith in 1561 as a theological will. In 1563, Bullinger sent a copy of this confession, which blended Zwingli's and Calvin's theology, to the elector of the Palatinate, Frederick III (1515–1576), who had asked for a complete explication of the Reformed faith in order to defend himself against aggressive Lutheran attacks after printing the Heidelberg Confession.* Although not published until 1566, the Second Helvetic Confession became the definitive sixteenth-century Reformed statement of faith. Theodore Beza* used it as the organizing confession for his *Harmonia Confessionum* (1581), which sought to

emphasize the unity of the Reformed churches. Bullinger's personal confession was adopted by the Reformed churches of Scotland (1566), Hungary (1567), France (1571) and Poland (1571).

Obadiah Sedgwick (c. 1600–1658). English Puritan minister. Educated at Oxford, Sedgwick pastored in London and participated in the Westminster Assembly. An ardent Puritan, Sedgwick was appointed by Oliver Cromwell (1599–1658) to examine clerical candidates. Sedgwick published a catechism, several sermons and a treatise on how to deal with doubt.

Nikolaus Selnecker (1530–1592). German Lutheran theologian, preacher, pastor and hymnist. Selnecker taught in Wittenberg, Jena and Leipzig, preached in Dresden and Wolfenbüttel, and pastored in Leipzig. He was forced out of his post at Jena because of suspicions that he was a crypto-Calvinist. He sought refuge in Wolfenbüttel, where he met Martin Chemnitz* and Jakob Andreae.* Under their influence Selnecker was drawn away from Philippist theology. Selnecker's shift in theology can be seen in his *Institutio religionis christianae* (1573). Selnecker coauthored the Formula of Concord* with Chemnitz, Andreae, Andreas Musculus (1514–1581), and David Chytraeus.* Selnecker also published lectures on Genesis, the Psalms, and the New Testament epistles, as well as composing over a hundred hymn tunes and texts.

Short Confession (1610). In response to some of William Laud's* reforms in the Church of England—particularly a law stating that ministers who refused to comply with the Book of Common Prayer* would lose their ordination—a group of English Puritans immigrated to the Netherlands in protest, where they eventually embraced the practice of believer's baptism. The resulting Short Confession was an attempt at union between these Puritans and local Dutch Anabaptists ("Waterlanders"). The document highlights the importance of love in the church and reflects optimism regarding the freedom of the will while explicitly rejecting double predestination.

Richard Sibbes (1577–1635). English Puritan

preacher. Sibbes was educated at St. John's College, Cambridge, where he was converted to reforming views and became a popular preacher. As a moderate Puritan emphasizing interior piety and brotherly love, Sibbes always remained within the established Church of England, though opposed to some of its liturgical ceremonies. His collected sermons constitute his main literary legacy.

Menno Simons (c. 1496–1561). Dutch Radical leader. Simons led a separatist Anabaptist group in the Netherlands that would later be called Mennonites, known for nonviolence and renunciation of the world. A former priest, Simons rejected Catholicism through the influence of Anabaptist disciples of Melchior Hoffmann and based on his study of Scripture, in which he found no support for transubstantiation or infant baptism. Following the sack of Anabaptists at Münster, Simons committed to a nonviolent way of life. Simons proclaimed a message of radical discipleship of obedience and inner purity, marked by voluntary adult baptism and communal discipline.

Henry Smith (c. 1550–1591). English Puritan minister. Smith stridently opposed the Book of Common Prayer* and refused to subscribe to the Articles of Religion,* thus limiting his pastoral opportunities. Nevertheless he gained a reputation as an eloquent preacher in London. He published sermon collections as well as several treatises.

Domingo de Soto (1494–1560). Spanish Catholic theologian. Soto taught philosophy for four years at the University in Alcalá before entering the Dominican order. In 1532 he became chair of theology at the University of Salamanca; Soto sought to reintroduce Aristotle in the curriculum. He served as confessor and spiritual advisor to Charles V, who enlisted Soto as imperial theologian for the Council of Trent. Alongside commentaries on the works of Aristotle and Peter Lombard (c. 1100–1160), Soto commented on Romans and wrote an influential treatise on nature and grace.

Fausto Sozzini (1539–1604). Italian theologian. Without a formal education, Sozzini used his inherited wealth to travel widely throughout Europe after his family came under the suspicion of the Inquisition for Lutheranism. Spending time in Lyons, Zurich, and Geneva, he published his first work, an explanation of the prologue to John's Gospel, claiming Christ was not divine, but a human worthy of respect due his divinely appointed office. Returning to Italy, Sozzini served at the Florentine court of Isabella de Medici (1542–1576) for more than a decade, departing for Basel, then Transylvania and Poland after her death. His thoroughgoing rationalism saw him elevate human reason over divine revelation and traditional doctrine. He rejected the doctrine of the Trinity and Nicene orthodoxy, instead arguing that Christ was not divine and did not make atonement for humanity, but rather served as a model of victory over death for all people.

Cyriacus Spangenberg (1528–1604). German Lutheran pastor, preacher and theologian. Spangenberg was a staunch, often acerbic, Gnesio-Lutheran. He rejected the Formula of Concord* because of concerns about the princely control of the church, as well as its rejection of Flacian language of original sin (as constituting the "substance" of human nature after the fall). He published many commentaries and sermons, most famously seventy wedding sermons (*Ehespiegel* [1561]), his sermons on Luther* (*Theander Luther* [1562–1571]) and Luther's hymns (*Cithara Lutheri* [1569–1570]). He also published an analysis of the Old Testament (though he only got as far as Job), based on a methodology that anticipated the logical bifurcations of Peter Ramus.*

Johann Spangenberg (1484–1550). German Lutheran pastor and catechist. Spangenberg studied at the University of Erfurt, where he was welcomed into a group of humanists associated with Konrad Muth (1470–1526). There he met the reformer Justus Jonas,* and Eobanus Hessius (1488–1540), whom Luther* dubbed "king of the poets." Spangenberg served at parishes in Stolberg (1520–1524), Nordhausen (1524–1546) and, by Luther's recommendation, Eisleben (1546–1550). Spangenberg published one of the best-selling postils of the sixteenth century, the *Postilla Teütsch*, a six-volume work meant to prepare children to understand the lectionary readings. It borrowed the question-answer form of Luther's *Small Catechism* and was so popular that a monk, Johannes Craendonch, purged overt anti-Catholic statements from it and republished it under his own name. Among Spangenberg's other pastoral works are *ars moriendi* ("the art of dying") booklets, a postil for the Acts of the Apostles and a question-answer version of Luther's *Large Catechism*. In addition to preaching and pastoring, Spangenberg wrote pamphlets on controversial topics such as purgatory, as well as textbooks on music, mathematics and grammar.

Georg Spindler (1525–1605). German Reformed theologian and pastor. After studying theology under Caspar Cruciger* and Philipp Melanchthon,* Spindler accepted a pastorate in Bohemia. A well-respected preacher, Spindler published postils in 1576 which some of his peers viewed as crypto-Calvinist. To investigate this allegation Spindler read John Calvin's* *Institutes*, and subsequently converted to the Reformed faith. After years of travel, he settled in the Palatinate and pastored there until his death. In addition to his Lutheran postils, Spindler also published Reformed postils in 1594 as well as several treatises on the Lord's Supper and predestination.

Statenvertaling (1637). The Synod of Dordrecht* commissioned this new Dutch translation of the Bible ("State's Translation"). The six theologians who undertook this translation also wrote prefaces for each biblical book, annotated obscure words and difficult passages, and provided cross-references; they even explained certain significant translation decisions. At the request of the Westminster Assembly, Theodore Haak (1605–1690) translated the *Statenvertaling* into English as *The Dutch Annotations Upon the Whole Bible* (1657).

Johann von Staupitz (d. 1524). German Catholic theologian, professor and preacher. Frederick the Wise summoned this Augustinian monk to serve as professor of Bible and first dean of the theology faculty at the University of Wittenberg. As Vicar-General of the Reformed Augustinian

Hermits in Germany, Staupitz sought to reform the order and attempted unsuccessfully to reunite with the conventional Augustinians. While in Wittenberg, Staupitz was Martin Luther's* teacher, confessor and spiritual father. He supported Luther in the early controversies over indulgences, but after releasing Luther from his monastic vows (to protect him), he distanced himself from the conflict. He relocated to Salzburg, where he was court preacher to Cardinal Matthäus Lang von Wellenburg (d. 1540) and abbot of the Benedictine monastery. Staupitz wrote treatises on predestination, faith and the love of God. Many of his sermons were collected and published during his lifetime.

Petrus Stevartius (1549–1624). German Catholic theologian. A Jesuit, Stevartius spent most of his career as professor of exegesis at the University of Ingolstadt, also serving as rector and procurator. He also established a library for the school and an orphanage in the city. His writings include commentaries on most Pauline letters and James and a defense of the Jesuits.

Michael Stifel (1486–1567). German Lutheran mathematician, theologian and pastor. An Augustinian monk, Stifel's interest in mysticism, apocalypticism and numerology led him to identify Pope Leo X as the antichrist. Stifel soon joined the reform movement, writing a 1522 pamphlet in support of Martin Luther's* theology. After Luther quelled the fallout of Stifel's failed prediction of the Apocalypse—October 19, 1533 at 8 a.m.—Stifel focused more on mathematics and his pastoral duties. He was the first professor of mathematics at the University of Jena. He published several numerological interpretations of texts from the Gospels, Daniel and Revelation. However, Stifel's most important work is his *Arithmetica Integra* (1544), in which he standardized the approach to quadratic equations. He also developed notations for exponents and radicals.

John Stoughton (1593?–1639). English Puritan minister. Stoughton pastored at Aller in Somerset and St. Mary Aldermanbury in the city of London. A Puritan, he was briefly arrested by Archbishop Laud, accused of financially supporting the Puritan cause. A collection of his sermons and other writings was published after his death.

Viktorin Strigel (1524–1569). German Lutheran theologian. Strigel taught at Wittenberg, Erfurt, Jena, Leipzig and Heidelberg. During his time in Jena he disputed with Matthias Flacius (1520–1575) over the human will's autonomy. Following Philipp Melanchthon,* Strigel asserted that in conversion the human will obediently cooperates with the divine will through the Holy Spirit and the Word of God. In the Weimar Disputation (1560), Strigel elicited Flacius's opinion that sin is a substance that mars the formal essence of human beings. Flacius's views were officially rejected in Article 1 of the Formula of Concord*; Strigel's, in Article 2. In 1567 the University of Leipzig suspended Strigel from teaching on account of suspicions that he affirmed Reformed Eucharistic theology; he acknowledged that he did and joined the Reformed confession on the faculty of the University of Heidelberg. In addition to controversial tracts, Strigel published commentaries on the entire Bible (except Lamentations) and the Apocrypha.

Johann Sutell (1504–1575). German Lutheran pastor. After studying at the University of Wittenberg, Sutell received a call to a pastorate in Göttingen, where he eventually became superintendent. He wrote new church orders for Göttingen (1531) and Schweinfurt (1543), and expanded two sermons for publication, *The Dreadful Destruction of Jerusalem* (1539) and *History of Lazarus* (1543).

Swiss Brethren Confession of Hesse (1578). Anabaptist leader Hans Pauly Kuchenbecker penned this confession after a 1577 interrogation by Lutheran authorities. This confession was unusually amenable to Lutheran views—there is no mention of pacifism or rejection of oath taking.

Synod of Dordrecht (1618–1619). This large Dutch Reformed Church council—also attended by English, German and Swiss delegates—met to settle the theological issues raised by the followers of Jacobus Arminius.* Arminius's theological disagreements with mainstream Reformed

teaching erupted into open conflict with the publication of the *Remonstrance* (1610). This "protest" was based on five points: that election is based on foreseen faith or unbelief; that Christ died indiscriminately for all people (although only believers receive salvation); that people are thoroughly sinful by nature apart from the prevenient grace of God that enables their free will to embrace or reject the gospel; that humans are able to resist the working of God's grace; and that it is possible for true believers to fall away from faith completely. The Synod ruled in favor of the Contra-Remonstrants, its Canons often remembered with a TULIP acrostic—total depravity, unconditional election, limited atonement, irresistible grace, perseverance of the saints—each letter countering one of the five Remonstrant articles. The Synod also officially accepted the Belgic Confession,* Heidelberg Catechism* and the Canons of Dordrecht as standards of the Dutch Reformed Church.

Arcangela Tarabotti (1604–1652). Italian Catholic nun. At the age of eleven, Tarabotti entered a Benedictine convent as a student-boarder; three years later her father forced her to take monastic vows. The dignity of women and their treatment in the male-controlled institutions of early modern Venice concerned Tarabotti deeply. She protested forced cloistering, the denial of education to women, the exclusion of women from public life and the double standards by which men and women were judged. Tarbotti authored numerous polemical works and an extensive correspondence.

Johannes Tauler (c. 1300–1361) German mystical theologian. A Dominican friar and disciple of Meister Eckhart (c. 1260–c. 1328), Tauler spent most of his career as a mendicant preacher in Strasburg and Basel. Known through a collection of about eighty German sermons, Tauler taught a practical spirituality, accessible to those outside the cloister and intended to draw his audience to deeper contemplation of the divine nature.

Richard Taverner (1505–1575). English Puritan humanist and translator. After graduating from

Oxford, Taverner briefly studied abroad. When he returned to England, he joined Thomas Cromwell's (1485–1540) circle. After Cromwell's beheading, Taverner escaped severe punishment and retired from public life during Mary I's reign. Under Elizabeth I,* Taverner served as justice of the peace, sheriff and a licensed lay preacher. Taverner translated many important continental Reformation works into English, most notably the Augsburg Confession* and several of Desiderius Erasmus's* works. Some of these translations—John Calvin's* 1536 catechism, Wolfgang Capito's* work on the Psalms and probably Erasmus Sarcerius's* postils— he presented as his own work. Underwritten by Cromwell, Taverner also published an edited version of the Matthew Bible (1537).

Jeremy Taylor (1613–1667) Anglican theologian, preacher, and author. Son of a barber, Taylor studied at Cambridge before the patronage of Archbishop Laud* drew him into the work of the English church. After serving as chaplain to Laud and King Charles I (1600–1649), he entered parish ministry. Following the outbreak of the Civil War (1642–51), his commitment to the Royalist cause saw him imprisoned at least three times. Withdrawing to Wales, he ran a school preparing students for university while serving as chaplain to the earl of Carbery. Known for his skill as a writer, it was here that Taylor composed many of his best known works, including his popular devotional manuals, *The Rules and Exercises of Holy Living* (1650), and *The Rules and Exercises of Holy Dying* (1651). After the Restoration, Taylor was made Bishop of Down and Connor in Ireland and served as vice-chancellor of the University of Dublin.

Thomas Taylor (1576–1633). English Puritan pastor. Taylor ministered in Watford and Reading before becoming minister at St. Mary Aldermanbury in the city of London. He wrote more than fifty works on diverse topics, including a commentary on Titus, a response to the Gunpowder Plot, and an explanation of the role of the law under the gospel.

Thomas Taylor (1576–1632). Puritan minister and commentator. Taylor was born in Richmond, Yorkshire. He was educated at Christ's College, Cambridge, where he earned the degrees of Bachelor of Arts (1595) and Master of Arts (1598). Prior to entering pastoral ministry, Taylor served as a fellow and lecturer in Hebrew at the university. Throughout his academic career, Taylor was significantly influenced by the writings of William Perkins.* At the age of twenty-five, Taylor preached a virulent sermon against the papacy before Queen Elizabeth I.* As a Puritan, Taylor denounced the ecclesiastical policies of Archbishop Richard Bancroft.* In 1612, Taylor became minister of a church in Watford, Hertfordshire. While serving this charge, Taylor preached regularly in Berkshire and Reading. Moreover, Taylor formed and led a Puritan seminary, where he personally trained Nonconformist preachers. In the early 1620s, Taylor served as a chaplain to Edward Conway (1564–1631), secretary of state under James VI/I* (1566–1625). In 1625, Taylor was called to be curate and lecturer at St. Aldermanbury, London. While there, he organized and ran another Puritan seminary. Two years later, Taylor joined several other Puritans' efforts to send relief to oppressed Reformed ministers on the Continent. Taylor retired from his labors in 1630 due to ill health. He died of pleurisy in 1632. His main works include *Christ Revealed; or The Old Testament Explained* and *An Exposition of Titus*.

Thirty-Nine Articles. See *Articles of Religion*.

Thomas Thorowgood (1595–1669). English Puritan pastor. Thorowgood was a Puritan minister in Norfolk and the chief financier of John Eliot (1604–1690), a Puritan missionary among the Native American tribes in Massachusetts. In 1650, under the title *Jews in America, or, Probabilities that Americans be of that Race*, Thorowgood became one of the first to put forward the thesis that Native Americans were actually the ten lost tribes of Israel.

Frans Titelmans (1502–1537). Belgian Catholic philosopher. Titelmans studied at the University of Leuven, where he was influenced by Petrus Ramus.* After first joining a Franciscan monastery, Titelmans realigned with the stricter Capuchins and moved to Italy. He is best known for his advocacy for the Vulgate and his debates with Desiderius Erasmus* over Pauline theology (1527–1530)—he was deeply suspicious of the fruits of humanism, especially regarding biblical studies. His work was published posthumously by his brother, Pieter Titelmans (1501–1572).

Francisco de Toledo (1532–1596). Spanish Catholic theologian. This important Jesuit taught philosophy at the universities of Salamanca and Rome. He published works on Aristotelian philosophy and a commentary on Thomas Aquinas's* work, as well as biblical commentaries on John, Romans and the first half of Luke. He was also the general editor for the Clementine Vulgate (1598).

Laurence Tomson (1539–1608). English Reformed politician and translator. Tomson was born in Northhamptonshire and educated at Magdalen College, Oxford. He graduated with his BA degree (1559) and MA degree (1564). Tomson was a fellow at Magdalen until he resigned in 1569. Prior to this resignation, Tomson was part of a diplomatic delegation to France. From 1575 to 1587, Tomson served in the House of Commons and attended the royal court at Windsor in 1582. He went on further embassies throughout Europe, where he occasionally lectured on Hebrew. Tomson died on March 29, 1608. Tomson's chief exegetical contribution was his revised text and annotations of the New Testament of the Geneva Bible.

Alonso Tostado (1400–1455). Spanish Catholic bishop and exegete. Tostado lectured on theology, law and philosophy at the University of Salamanca, in addition to ministering in a local parish. Tostado entered into disputes over papal supremacy and the date of Christ's birth. Tostado's thirteen-volume collected works include commentaries on the historical books of the Old Testament and the Gospel of Matthew.

Daniel Toussain (1541–1602). Swiss Reformed pastor and professor. Toussain became pastor at Orléans after attending college in Basel. After the third War of Religion, Toussain was exiled, eventually returning to Montbéliard, his birthplace. In 1571, he faced opposition there from the strict Lutheran rulers and was eventually exiled due to his influence over the clergy. He returned

to Orléans but fled following the Saint Bartholomew's Day Massacre (1572), eventually becoming pastor in Basel. He relocated to Heidelberg in 1583 as pastor to the new regent, becoming professor of theology at the university, and he remained there until his death.

John Trapp (1601–1669). Anglican biblical exegete. After studying at Oxford, Trapp entered the pastorate in 1636. During the English Civil Wars he sided with Parliament, which later made it difficult for him to collect tithes from a congregation whose royalist pastor had been evicted. Trapp published commentaries on all the books of the Bible from 1646 to 1656.

Immanuel Tremellius (1510–1580). Italian Reformed Hebraist. Around 1540, Tremellius received baptism by Cardinal Reginald Pole (1500–1558) and converted from Judaism to Christianity; he affiliated with evangelicals the next year. On account of the political and religious upheaval, Tremellius relocated often, teaching Hebrew in Lucca; Strasbourg, fleeing the Inquisition; Cambridge, displaced by the Schmalkaldic War; Heidelberg, escaping Mary I's persecutions; and Sedan, expelled by the new Lutheran Elector of the Palatine. Many considered Tremellius's translation of the Old Testament as the most accurate available. He also published a Hebrew grammar and translated John Calvin's* catechism into Hebrew.

Richard Turnbull (d. 1593). English minister. A preacher in London, Richard Turnbull published sermons on James, Jude, and Psalm 15.

William Tyndale (Hychyns) (1494–1536). English reformer, theologian and translator. Tyndale was educated at Oxford University, where he was influenced by the writings of humanist thinkers. Believing that piety is fostered through personal encounter with the Bible, he asked to translate the Bible into English; denied permission, Tyndale left for the Continent to complete the task. His New Testament was the equivalent of a modern-day bestseller in England but was banned and ordered burned. Tyndale's theology was oriented around justification, the authority of

Scripture and Christian obedience; Tyndale emphasized the ethical as a concomitant reality of justification. He was martyred in Brussels before completing his English translation of the Old Testament, which Miles Coverdale* finished.

Guillaume du Vair (1556–1621). French Catholic priest, lawyer, and writer. While du Vair took holy orders in his youth, much of his life was spent serving the state as a counselor of the parliament of Paris, a representative of King Henry IV both in France and abroad, and as Keeper of the Seals, the highest legal office in the country. The last four years of his life were spent as the bishop of Lisieux. His studies on Epictetus and the Stoics, and attempts to relate Stoicism to the Christian faith, were influential in the dissemination of this philosophy during the seventeenth and eighteenth centuries. He also wrote significant works on politics, the moral life, prayer, and the use and abuse of the French language.

Juan de Valdés (1500/10–1541). Spanish Catholic theologian and writer. Although Valdés adopted an evangelical doctrine, had Erasmian affiliations and published works that were listed on the Index of Prohibited Books, Valdés rebuked the reformers for creating disunity and never left the Catholic Church. His writings included translations of the Hebrew Psalter and various biblical books, a work on the Spanish language and several commentaries. Valdés fled to Rome in 1531 to escape the Spanish Inquisition and worked in the court of Clement VII in Bologna until the pope's death in 1534. Valdés subsequently returned to Naples, where he led the reform- and revival-minded Valdesian circle.

Thomas Venatorius (c. 1490–1551). German Lutheran theologian, mathematician, and humanist. Following a humanistic education, Venatorius spent the majority of his career in Nuremberg, where he advocated for reform as the head of the city's school system and as a preacher and pastor in the city's churches. His theological and pastoral works include one of the first Protestant works on ethics, a short catechism, and a commentary on 1 Timothy. He also edited the

first Greek edition of Archimedes's writings and translated Aristophanes's *Plutus*.

Peter Martyr Vermigli (1499–1562). Italian Reformed humanist and theologian. Vermigli was one of the most influential theologians of the era, held in common regard with such figures as Martin Luther* and John Calvin.* In Italy, Vermigli was a distinguished theologian, preacher and advocate for moral reform; however, during the reinstitution of the Roman Inquisition Vermigli fled to Protestant regions in northern Europe. He was eventually appointed professor of divinity at Oxford University, where Vermigli delivered acclaimed disputations on the Eucharist. Vermigli was widely noted for his deeply integrated biblical commentaries and theological treatises.

Juan Luis Vives (1492?–1540). Spanish Catholic humanist. Born into a Jewish family but baptized Catholic, Vives spent most of his life outside Spain following the persecution of his family by the Inquisition. After studying in Paris, he lived in Bruges, where he became part of the intellectual circle around Erasmus,* and taught at Oxford toward the end of his life. Vives largely avoided entering into religious controversies, and his works received a mixed reception from both Catholics and Protestants. He is best known for his educational and social writings, including an influential Latin primer, works on pedagogy and women's education, and arguments for pacifism and poor relief.

Gisbertus Voetius (1589–1676). Dutch Reformed theologian. Voetius pastored at Vlijmen and Heusden and served as the youngest delegate at the Synod of Dordrecht* before becoming professor of theology and Oriental languages at the University of Utrecht. While Voetius's writings demonstrate concern for missions, practical piety, and personal purity, he also entered into numerous theological controversies during his career. His Reformed commitments led to ongoing conflicts with Arminians and Catholics, and he sought to uphold the importance of the Old Testament against Johannes Cocceius's (1603–1669) formulation of the covenants. He also entered into debate with René Descartes (1596–1650) and his followers, arguing from an Aristotelian perspective that to accept Cartesian skepticism was to reject biblical truth and the Christian tradition.

Conradus Vorstius (1569–1622). Dutch Arminian-Socinian theologian. A student of David Paraeus* and Johannes Piscator,* Vorstius's Socinian tendencies emerged during his tenure as professor of theology at Steinfurt. After an apology and examination, he was allowed to replace Arminius* as professor of theology at Leiden though never permitted to teach, as his questioning of the doctrine of atonement and the eternity, fore-knowledge, and omnipresence of God drew wide censure, ultimately from King James I of England.* Exiled to Gouda and deposed at the Synod of Dordrecht,* Vorstius published numerous theological works and a commentary on the Pauline letters.

Vulgate. In 382 Pope Damasus I (c. 300–384) commissioned Jerome (c. 347–420) to translate the four Gospels into Latin based on Old Latin and Greek manuscripts. Jerome completed the translation of the Gospels and the Old Testament around 405. It is widely debated how much of the rest of the New Testament was translated by Jerome. During the Middle Ages, the Vulgate became the Catholic Church's standard Latin translation. The Council of Trent recognized it as the official text of Scripture.

George Walker (1581–1651). Puritan minister. Walker was born at Hawkshead, Lancashire, and educated at St. John's College, Cambridge. After graduating Cambridge, Walker moved to London, where he became rector of St. John the Evangelist on Watling Street in 1614. He served this parish for nearly forty years. Throughout his ministry, Walker showed himself to be an ardent opponent of the papacy and practices within the Church of England that he deemed not sufficiently reformed. Toward this end, Walker engaged numerous disputations and literary debates with both conformists and Catholics. For his sermons that were critical of the Church of England, he was

summoned to appear before Archbishop Laud in 1635 and the Star Chamber in 1638, which fined and imprisoned him for twelve weeks. On another occasion, Walker was incarcerated for as long as two years for his nonconformity until released by the Long Parliament. In 1643, Walker was selected to serve in the Westminster Assembly and to participate in the trial of Laud. Walker died in London. Among his many published sermons and polemical works is a treatise on justification.

Thomas Walkington (d. 1621). Anglican minister and author. Born in Lincoln, he was educated at Cambridge, graduating with his BA in 1597 and his MA in 1600. Walkington was elected a fellow at St. John's College, Cambridge, in 1602. Later, he received a BD from Oxford and a DD from Cambridge. He served as rector of parishes in Northamptonshire, Lincolnshire, and Middlesex. A prolific author, Walkington published works on diverse subjects. Among his biblical works are *An Exposition of the First Two Verses of the Sixth Chapter to the Hebrews in form of a Dialogue* (1609) and *Theologicall Rules to Guide Us in the Understanding and Practice of Holy Scripture* (1615).

Peter Walpot (d. 1578). Moravian Radical pastor and bishop. Walpot was a bishop of the Hutterite community after Jakob Hutter, Peter Riedemann* and Leonhard Lanzenstiel. Riedemann's *Confession of Faith* (1545; 1565) became a vital authority for Hutterite exegesis, theology and morals. Walpot added his own *Great Article Book* (1577), which collates primary biblical passages on baptism, communion, the community of goods, the sword and divorce. In keeping with Hutterite theology, Walpot defended the community of goods as a mark of the true church.

Valentin Weigel (1533–1588). German Lutheran pastor. Weigel studied at Leipzig and Wittenberg, entering the pastorate in 1567. Despite a strong anti-institutional bias, he was recognized by the church hierarchy as a talented preacher and compassionate minister of mercy to the poor. Although he signed the Formula of Concord,* Weigel's orthodoxy was questioned so openly that he had to publish a defense. He appears to have tried to synthesize several medieval mystics with the ideas of Sebastian Franck,* Thomas Müntzer* and others. His posthumously published works have led some recent scholars to suggest that Weigel's works may have deeply influenced later Pietism.

Hieronymus Weller von Molsdorf (1499–1572). German Lutheran theologian. Originally intending to study law, Weller devoted himself to theology after hearing one of Martin Luther's* sermons on the catechism. He boarded with Luther and tutored Luther's son. In 1539 he moved to Freiburg, where he lectured on the Bible and held theological disputations at the Latin school. In addition to hymns, works of practical theology and a postil set, Weller published commentaries on Genesis, 1–2 Samuel, 1–2 Kings, Job, the Psalms, Christ's passion, Ephesians, Philippians, 1–2 Thessalonians and 1–2 Peter.

Westminster Assembly (1643–1652). English church council. Called by English Parliament to advise on church reform, the Westminster Assembly was made up of more than 120 clergymen, thirty parliamentary observers, and a delegation from the Church of Scotland. Beginning with a review of the Articles of Religion,* the most heated debates were undertaken over ecclesiology, as factions argued for presbyterianism, congregationalism, Erastianism, and episcopalianism, with the council ultimately recommending presbyterianism to the parliament. Much of the legacy of the assembly is held in the major documents it produced, the *Directory for Public Worship* (1644), *The Form of Presbyterial Church Government* (1645), the *Westminster Confession of Faith* (1646), the *Shorter Catechism* (1647), and the *Larger Catechism* (1648), which became foundational for the English and Scottish churches and many of the Reformed denominations.

John Whitgift (1530–1604). Anglican archbishop. Though Whitgift shared much theological common ground with Puritans, after his election as Archbishop of Canterbury (1583) he moved decisively to squelch the political and ecclesiastical threat they posed during Elizabeth

I's* reign. Whitgift enforced strict compliance to the Book of Common Prayer,* the Act of Uniformity (1559) and the Articles of Religion.* Whitgift's policies led to a large migration of Puritans to Holland. The bulk of Whitgift's published corpus is the fruit of a lengthy public disputation with Thomas Cartwright,* in which Whitgift defines Anglican doctrine against Cartwright's staunch Puritanism.

Johann Wigand (1523–1587). German Lutheran theologian. Wigand is most noted as one of the compilers of the *Magdeburg Centuries*, a German ecclesiastical history of the first thirteen centuries of the church. He was a student of Philipp Melanchthon* at the University of Wittenburg and became a significant figure in the controversies dividing Lutheranism. Strongly opposed to Roman Catholicism, Wigand lobbied against innovations in Lutheran theology that appeared sympathetic to Catholic thought. In the later debates, Wigand's support for Gnesio-Lutheranism established his role in the development of confessional Lutheranism. Wigand was appointed bishop of Pomerania after serving academic posts at the universities in Jena and Königsburg.

Thomas Wilcox (c. 1549–1608). English Puritan theologian. In 1572, Wilcox objected to Parliament against the episcopacy and the Book of Common Prayer,* advocating for presbyterian church governance. He was imprisoned for sedition. After his release, he preached itinerantly. He was brought before the courts twice more for his continued protest against the Church of England's episcopal structure. He translated some of Theodore Beza* and John Calvin's* sermons into English, and he wrote polemical and occasional works as well as commentaries on the Psalms and Song of Songs.

Johann (Ferus) Wild (1495–1554). German Catholic pastor. After studying at Heidelberg and teaching at Tübingen, this Franciscan was appointed as lector in the Mainz cathedral, eventually being promoted to cathedral preacher— a post for which he became widely popular but also controversial. Wild strongly identified as Catholic but was not unwilling to criticize the curia. Known for an irenic spirit—criticized in fact as *too kind*—he was troubled by the polemics between all parties of the Reformation. He preached with great lucidity, integrating the liturgy, Scripture and doctrine to exposit Catholic worship and teaching for common people. His sermons on John were pirated for publication without his knowledge; the Sorbonne banned them as heretical. Despite his popularity among clergy, the majority of his works were on the Roman Index until 1900.

Andrew Willet (1562–1621). Anglican priest, professor, and biblical expositor. Willet was a gifted biblical expositor and powerful preacher. He walked away from a promising university career in 1588 when he was ordained a priest in the Church of England. For the next thirty-three years he served as a parish priest. Willet's commentaries summarized the present state of discussion while also offering practical applications for preachers. They have been cited as some of the most technical commentaries of the early seventeenth century. His most important publication was *Synopsis Papismi, or a General View of Papistrie* (1594), in which he responded to many of Robert Bellarmine's critiques. After years of royal favor, Willet was imprisoned in 1618 for a month after presenting to King James I* his opposition to the "Spanish Match" of Prince Charles to the Infanta Maria. While serving as a parish priest, he wrote forty-two works, most of which were either commentaries on books of the Bible or controversial works against Catholics.

Thomas Wilson (d. 1586). English Anglican priest. A fellow of St John's, Cambridge, Wilson fled to Frankfurt to escape the Marian Persecution. After his return to England, he served as a canon and Dean of Worcester.

George Wither (1588–1667). English poet, satirist, and hymn writer. Wither was born in Bentworth, Hampshire. After finishing his early education under the tutelage of a local minister, Wither continued his studies at Magdalen College, Oxford. Afterward, he studied law at the Inns of Chancery. Wither commenced his literary career with the publication of an elegy on the occasion of the death of Henry Frederick, Prince of Wales (1594–1612). Most of Wither's literary works consist of satirical pamphlets for which he was regularly arrested, imprisoned, and released. He fought in the Parliamentary Army during the Civil War. A conforming Anglican, Wither composed numerous hymns as well as translations of the Psalms. Two of Wither's major works are *Preparation to the Psalter* (1619), in which he explores various literary aspects of the Bible, and *Hymns and Songs of the Church* (1622/1623). He died in London.

John Woolton (c. 1535–1594). Anglican bishop. After graduating from Oxford, Woolton lived in Germany until the accession of Elizabeth I.* He was ordained as a priest in 1560 and as a bishop in 1578. Woolton published many theological, devotional and practical works, including a treatise on the immortality of the soul, a discourse on conscience and a manual for Christian living.

John Wycliffe (c. 1330–1384). English theologian, philosopher, and reformer known as "the Morning Star of the Reformation." While holding benefices from a number of parishes, Wycliffe spent the majority of his career at Oxford, where he studied, taught, and served as head of Balliol College. His early work focused on logic and metaphysics, but after entering into the service of John of Gaunt, Duke of Lancaster (1340–1399) and serving as a royal envoy to discuss taxes with papal representatives, Wycliffe turned his attention to more practical concerns. His criticism of papal power and wealth drew initially civil and ecclesiastical approval, but application of his principle that any headship profiting the governor rather than the governed is illegitimate to the English church brought controversy and censure. This criticism increased as he rejected transubstantiation, criticized monasticism, argued along Augustinian lines that only the invisible body of the elect constituted the true church, that Scripture belongs to the body of the elect rather than the institutional church, and that as many leaders of the visible church were likely reprobate, their offices and sacraments were invalid. While dismissed from Oxford in 1381, powerful defenders protected Wycliffe from further consequences during his lifetime, but he was condemned as a heretic at the Council of Constance (1515), whence he was exhumed and his remains burned. While largely condemned by contemporaries, Wycliffe, and his followers, the Lollards, are often viewed as forerunners of the Reformation who prepared the way for the tumult of the sixteenth century.

Girolamo Zanchi (1516–1590). Italian Reformed theologian and pastor. Zanchi joined an Augustinian monastery at the age of fifteen, where he studied Greek and Latin, the church fathers and the works of Aristotle and Thomas Aquinas.* Under the influence of his prior, Peter Martyr Vermigli,* Zanchi also imbibed the writings of the Swiss and German reformers. To avoid the Inquisition, Zanchi fled to Geneva where he was strongly attracted to the preaching and teaching of John Calvin.* Zanchi taught biblical theology and the *locus* method at academies in Strasbourg, Heidelberg, and Neustadt. He also served as pastor of an Italian refugee congregation. Zanchi's theological works, *De tribus Elohim* (1572) and *De natura Dei* (1577), have received more attention than his commentaries. His commentaries comprise about a quarter of his literary output, however, and display a strong typological and christological interpretation in conversation with the church fathers, medieval exegetes, and other reformers.

Katharina Schütz Zell (1497/98–1562). German Reformed writer. Zell became infamous in Strasbourg and the Empire when in 1523 she married the priest Matthias Zell, and then published an apology defending her husband against charges of impiety and libertinism. Longing for a united church, she called for toleration of Catholics and Anabaptists, famously writing to Martin Luther* after the failed Marburg Colloquy

of 1529 to exhort him to check his hostility and to be ruled instead by Christian charity. Much to the chagrin of her contemporaries, Zell published diverse works, ranging from polemical treatises on marriage to letters of consolation, as well as editing a hymnal and penning an exposition of Psalm 51.

Martha Elizabeth Zitter (Unknown). German Catholic nun. Zitter entered the Ursuline convent in Erfurt during her teenage years. Most of what is known about her is drawn from a letter she composed to her mother, explaining her decision to leave the order and become Lutheran, which focuses on aspects of her vows and Roman Catholic piety she believes to be unbiblical. Despite this public departure from the Roman church, however, Zitter returned toward the end of her life.

Ulrich Zwingli (1484–1531). Swiss Reformed humanist, preacher and theologian. Zwingli studied at the University of Vienna, and afterwards the University of Basel, where he received his BA and MA in 1504 and 1506. Ordained in September 1506, Zwingli became priest of the church in Glarus where he taught himself Greek, and read deeply in the church fathers. During this period, Zwingli was also greatly impacted by the writings of Desiderius Erasmus*. In 1516, Zwingli accepted the position of priest at the Benedictine Abbey at Einsiedeln in Schwyz, where he intently studied the Greek New Testament, and learned Hebrew. When he became a preacher in the city cathedral at Zurich, Zwingli enacted reform through sermons, public disputations, and conciliation with the town council, abolishing the Mass and images in the church. Zwingli broke with the lectionary preaching tradition, instead preaching serial expository biblical sermons. He later was embroiled in controversy with Anabaptists over infant baptism and with Martin Luther* at the Marburg Colloquy (1529) over their differing views of the Eucharist. Zwingli, serving as chaplain to Zurich's military, was killed in the Second Battle of Kappel.

SOURCES FOR
BIOGRAPHICAL SKETCHES

General Reference Works

Allgemeine Deutsche Biographie. 56 vols. Leipzig: Duncker & Humblot, 1875–1912; reprint, 1967–1971. Accessible online via deutsche -biographie.de/index.html.

Baskin, Judith R., ed. *The Cambridge Dictionary of Judaism and Jewish Culture.* New York: Cambridge University Press, 2011.

Benedetto, Robert, ed. *The New Westminster Dictionary of Church History.* Vol. 1. Louisville: Westminster John Knox Press, 2008.

Bettenson, Henry and Chris Maunder, eds. *Documents of the Christian Church.* 3rd ed. Oxford: Oxford University Press, 1999.

Betz, Hans Dieter, Don Browning, Bernd Janowski and Eberhard Jüngel, eds. *Religion Past & Present: Encyclopedia of Theology and Relgion.* 13 vols. Leiden: Brill, 2007–2013.

Bremer, Francis J. and Tom Webster, eds. *Puritans and Puritanism in Europe and America: A Comprehensive Encyclopedia.* 2 vols. Santa Barbara, CA: ABC-CLIO, 2006.

Gritsch, Eric W. *A History of Lutheranism.* Minneapolis: Fortress Press, 2002.

Haag, Eugene and Émile Haag. *La France protestante ou vies des protestants français.* 2nd ed. 6 vols. Paris: Sandoz & Fischbacher, 1877–1888.

Hillerbrand, Hans J., ed. *Oxford Encyclopedia of the Reformation.* 4 vols. New York: Oxford University Press, 1996.

Kolb, Robert, and Timothy J. Wengert, eds. *The Book of Concord: The Confessions of the Evangelical Lutheran Church.* Translated by Charles Arand et al. Minneapolis: Fortress, 2000.

McKim, Donald K., ed. *Dictionary of Major Biblical Interpreters.* Downers Grove, IL: InterVarsity Press, 2007.

Müller, Gerhard, et al., ed. *Theologische Realenzyklopädie.* Berlin: Walter de Gruyter, 1994.

Neue Deutsche Biographie. 28 vols. projected. Berlin: Duncker & Humblot, 1953–. Accessible online via deutsche-biographie.de/index.html.

New Catholic Encyclopedia. 15 vols. New York: McGraw-Hill, 1967; 2nd ed., Detroit: Thomson-Gale, 2002.

Oxford Dictionary of National Biography. 60 vols. Oxford: Oxford University Press, 2004.

Pelikan, Jaroslav. *The Christian Tradition.* 5 vols. Chicago: University of Chicago Press, 1971–1989.

Stephen, Leslie, and Sidney Lee, eds. *Dictionary of National Biography.* 63 vols. London: Smith, Elder and Co., 1885–1900.

Terry, Michael, ed. *Reader's Guide to Judaism.* New York: Routledge, 2000.

Wordsworth, Christopher, ed. *Lives of Eminent Men connected with the History of Religion in England.* 4 vols. London: J. G. & F. Rivington, 1839.

Additional Works for Individual Sketches

Akin, Daniel L. "An Expositional Analysis of the Schleitheim Confession." *Criswell Theological Review* 2 (1988): 345-70.

Bald, R. C. *John Donne: A Life.* Oxford: Oxford University Press, 1970.

Beeke, Joel, and Randall J. Pederson. *Meet the Puritans.* Grand Rapids: Reformation Heritage Books, 2006.

Bireley, Robert, *The Refashioning of Catholicism, 1450–1700,* Washington, DC: Catholic University of America Press, 1999.

Blok, P. J., and P. C. Molhuysen, eds. *Nieuw Nederlandsch Biografisch Woordenboek.* 10 vols.

Brackney, William H. *A Genetic History of Baptist Thought: With Special Reference to Baptists in Britain and North America.* Atlanta: Mercer University Press, 2004.

Brook, Benjamin. *The Lives of the Puritans.* 3 vols. London: James Black, 1813. Reprint, Pittsburgh, PA: Soli Deo Gloria, 1994.

Brown, Peter. *Augustine of Hippo: A Biography.* Berkeley & Los Angeles, CA: University of California Press, 1967.

Burke, David G. "The Enduring Significance of the KJV." *Word and World* 31, no. 3 (2011): 229-44.

Campbell, Gordon. *Bible: The Story of the King James Version, 1611–2011*. Oxford: Oxford University Press, 2010.

Charles, Amy. *A Life of George Herbert*. Ithaca, NY: Cornell University Press, 1977.

Coffey, John. *Politics, Religion, and the British Revolutions: The Thought of Samuel Rutherford*. Cambridge: Cambridge University Press, 1997.

Colish, Marcia. *Peter Lombard*, 2 vols. Leiden, Netherlands: Brill, 1993.

Doornkaat Koolman, J ten. "The First Edition of Peter Riedemann's 'Rechenschaft.'" *Mennonite Quarterly Review* 36, no. 2 (1962): 169-70.

Emerson, Everett H. *John Cotton*. New York: Twayne, 1990.

Fischlin, Daniel and Mark Fortier, eds. *Royal Subjects: Essays on the Writings of James VI and I*. Detroit: Wayne State University Press, 2002.

Fishbane, Michael A. "Teacher and the Hermeneutical Task: A Reinterpretation of Medieval Exegesis." *Journal of the American Academy of Religion* 43, no. 4 (1975): 709-21.

Friedmann, Robert. "Second Generation Anabaptism as Illustrated by the Walpot Era of the Hutterites." *Mennonite Quarterly* 44, no. 4 (1970): 390-93.

Frymire, John M. *The Primacy of the Postils: Catholics, Protestants, and the Dissemination of Ideas in Early Modern Germany*. Leiden: Brill, 2010.

Furcha, Edward J. "Key Concepts in Caspar von Schwenckfeld's Thought, Regeneration and the New Life." *Church History* 37, no. 2 (1968): 160-73.

Gordon, Bruce, *The Swiss Reformation*. Manchester: Manchester University Press, 2002.

Greaves, Richard L. *Society and Religion in Elizabethan England*. Minneapolis: University of Minnesota, 1981.

Greiffenberg, Catharina Regina von. *Meditations on the Incarnation, Passion and Death of Jesus Christ*. Edited and translated by Lynne Tatlock. The Other Voice in Early Modern Europe. Chicago: University of Chicago Press, 2009.

Grendler, Paul. "Italian biblical humanism and the papacy, 1515-1535." In *Biblical Humanism and Scholasticism in the Age of Erasmus*. Edited by Erika Rummel, 225-76. Leiden: Brill, 2008.

Haemig, Mary Jane. "Elisabeth Cruciger (1500?–1535): The Case of the Disappearing Hymn Writer." *Sixteenth Century Journal* 32, no. 1 (2001): 21-44.

Harpley, W., ed. *Report and Transactions of the Devonshire Association for the Advancement of Science, Literature and Art* 24 (July 1882). Plymouth: William Brendon and Son, 1892.

Heiden, Albert van der. "Pardes: Methodological Reflections on the Theory of the Four Senses." *Journal of Jewish Studies* 34, no. 2 (1983): 147-59.

Hendrix, Scott H., ed. and trans. *Early Protestant Spirituality*. New York: Paulist Press, 2009.

Hvolbek, Russell H. "Being and Knowing: Spiritualist Epistelmology and Anthropology from Schwenckfeld to Böhme." *Sixteenth Century Journal* 22, no. 1 (1991): 97-110.

Kahle, Paul. "Felix Pratensis—a Prato, Felix. Der Herausgeber der Ersten Rabbinerbibel, Venedig 1516/7." *Die Welt des Orients* 1, no. 1 (1947): 32-36.

Kelly, Joseph Francis. *The Ecumenical Councils of the Catholic Church: A History*. Collegeville, MN: Liturgical Press, 2009.

Lake, Peter. *The Boxmaker's Revenge: "Orthodoxy", "Heterodox" and the Politics of the Parish in Early Stuart London*. Stanford, CA: Stanford University Press, 2001.

Lane, Anthony N. S. *Calvin and Bernard of Clairvaux*. Princeton, NJ: Princeton Theological Seminary, 1996.

Lane, Belden C. *Ravished by Beauty: The Surprising Legacy of Reformed Spirituality*. Oxford: Oxford University Press, 2011.

Lockhart, Paul Douglas. *Frederick II and the Protestant Cause: Denmark's Role in the Wars of Religion, 1559–1596*. Leiden: Brill, 2004.

Lubac, Henri de. *Medieval Exegesis: The Four Senses of Scripture*. 3 vols. Translated by Mark Sebanc and E. M. Macierowski. Grand Rapids: Eerdmans, 1998–2009.

Manetsch, Scott, *Calvin's Company of Pastors: Pastoral Care and the Emerging Reformed Church, 1536–1609*. Oxford: Oxford University Press, 2013.

Manschereck, Clyde Leonard. *Melanchthon, the Quiet Reformer*. New York: Abingdon, 1958.

Matheson, Peter, *Argula von Grumbach: A Woman's Voice in the Reformation*. Edinburgh: T&T Clark, 1995.

McGuire, Daniel Patrick. *The Difficult Saint: Bernard of Clairvaux and his Tradition*. Collegeville, MN: Cistercian Publication, 1991.

McKinley, Mary B. "Volume Editor's Introduction." In *Epistle to Marguerite of Navarre and Preface to a Sermon by John Calvin*, edited and translated by Mary B. McKiney. Chicago: University of Chicago Press, 2004.

M'Crie, Thomas. *The Life of Andrew Melville.* 2 vols. Edinburgh: William Blackwood, 1819.

Norton, David. *A Textual History of the King James Bible.* New York: Cambridge University Press, 2005

Nuttall, Geoffrey. *The Welsh Saints, 1640–1660: Walter Cradock, Vavasor Powell, Morgan Llwyd.* Cardiff: University of Wales Press, 1957.

Oberman, Heiko A. *Luther: Man Between God and the Devil.* New York, NY: Doubleday, 1989.

O'Meara, Thomas F. *Albert the Great: Theologian and Scientist.* Chicago: New Priory Press, 2013.

Packull, Werner O. "The Origins of Peter Riedemann's Account of Our Faith." *Sixteenth Century Journal* 30, no. 1 (1999): 61-69.

Papazian, Mary Arshagouni, ed. *John Donne and the Protestant Reformation: New Perspectives.* Detroit: Wayne State University Press, 2003.

Paulicelli, Eugenia. "Sister Arcangela Tarabotti: Hair, Wigs and Other Vices." In *Writing Fashion in Early Modern Italy: From Sprezzatura to Satire,* by idem, 177-204. Farnham, Surrey, UK: Ashgate, 2014.

Pragman, James H. "The Augsburg Confession in the English Reformation: Richard Taverner's Contribution." *Sixteenth Century Journal* 11, no. 3 (1980): 75-85.

Rashi. *Rashi's Commentary on Psalms.* Translated by Mayer I. Gruber. Atlanta: Scholars Press, 1998.

Raynor, Brian. *John Frith: Scholar and Martyr.* Kent, UK: Pond View Books, 2000.

Reid, Jonathan A. *King's Sister—Queen of Dissent: Marguerite of Navarre (1492–1549) and her Evangelical Network.* Leiden: Brill, 2009.

Schmidt, Josef, "Introduction" in Johannes Tauler, *Sermons.* New York: Paulist Press, 1985, 1-34.

Spinka, Matthew. *John Hus: A Biography.* Princeton, NJ: Princeton University Press, 1968.

———. *John Hus at the Council of Constance.* New York: Columbia University Press, 1968.

———. *John Hus and the Czech Reform.* Hamden, CT: Archon Books, 1966.

Steinmetz, David C. *Reformers in the Wings: From Geiler von Kayserberg to Theodore Beza.* Oxford: Oxford University Press, 2000.

———. "The Superiority of Pre-Critical Exegesis." *Theology Today* 37, no. 1 (1980): 27-38.

Stjerna, Kirsi. *Women of the Reformation.* Malden, MA: Blackwell Publishing, 2009.

Synder, C. Arnold. "The Confession of the Swiss Brethren in Hesse, 1578." In *Anabaptism Revisited: Essays on Anabaptist/Mennonite Studies in Honor of C. J. Dyck.* Edited by Walter Klaassen, 29-49. Waterloo, ON; Scottdale, PA: Herald Press, 1992.

———. "The Schleitheim Articles in Light of the Revolution of the Common Man: Continuation or Departure?" *Sixteenth Century Journal* 16, no. 4 (1985): 419-30.

Todd, Margo. "Bishops in the Kirk: William Cowper of Galloway and the Puritan Episcopacy of Scotland." *Scottish Journal of Theology,* 57 (2004): 300-312.

Thornton, Wallace. *John Foxe and His Monument: A Theological-Historical Perspective.* Birmingham, AL: Aldersgate Heritage Press, 2013.

Van Liere, Frans. *An Introduction to the Medieval Bible.* New York: Cambridge University Press, 2014.

Voogt, Gerrit. "Remonstrant-Counter-Remonstrant Debates: Crafting a Principled Defense of Toleration after the Synod of Dordrecht (1619–1650)." *Church History and Religious Culture* 89, no. 4 (2009): 489-524.

Wallace, Dewey D. Jr. "George Gifford, Puritan Propaganda and Popular Religion in Elizabethan England." *Sixteenth Century Journal* 9, no. 1 (1978): 27-49.

Wawrykow, Joseph P. *The Westminster Handbook to Thomas Aquinas.* Louisville, KY: Westminster John Knox, 2005.

Wendel, Francois. *Calvin: The Origins and Development of His Religious Thought.* New York: Harper & Row, 1963.

Wengert, Timothy J. "'Fear and Love' in the Ten Commandments." *Concordia Journal* 21, no. 1 (1995): 14-27.

Wiesner-Hanks, Merry, ed. *Convents Confront the Reformation: Catholic and Protestant Nuns in Germany.* Translated by Joan Skocir and Merry Wiesner-Hanks. Milwaukee: Marquette University Press, 1996.

———. "Philip Melanchthon and John Calvin against Andreas Osiander: Coming to Terms with Forensic Justification." In *Calvin and Luther: The Continuing Relationship,* edited by R. Ward Holder, 63-87. Göttingen: Vandenhoeck & Ruprecht, 2013.

Wilkinson, Robert J. *Tetragrammaton: Western Christians and the Hebrew Name of God.* Leiden: Brill, 2015.

BIBLIOGRAPHY

Primary Sources and Translations Used in This Volume

Acta Synodi Nationalis . . . Dordrechti habitae Anno MDCXVIII et MDCXIX. Leiden: Isaac Elzevir, 1620.

Amyraut, Moïse. *Brief Traitté de la Prédestination*. Saumur: Jean Lesnier and Isaac Desbordes, 1634. Digital copy online at books.google.com.

———. *Paraphrase sur Les Epistres de L'Apostre S. Paul a Timothee*. Saumur: Jean Lesnier, 1646. Digital copy online at books.google.com.

Aretius, Benedict. *Commentarii in Epistolas D. Pauli Ad Philippenses, Colossenses, and in utramque, ad Thessalonicenses*. Bern, 1580.

Arminius, Jacobus. *The Works of James Arminius*. The London Edition. Translated by James Nichols and William Nichols. 3 vols. Kansas City, MO: Beacon Hill Press, 1986.

———. *The Writings of James Arminius: Translated from the Latin in Three Volumes*. Edited by James Nicholls and W. R. Bagnall. Grand Rapids: Baker, 1956. Digital copy online at www.ccel.org.

Balduin, Friedrich. *Brevis Institutio Ministrorum Verbi, potissimum ex Priore Epistola D. Pauli ad Timotheum Conscripta*. Wittenberg, 1622.

Barlow, John. *An Exposition of the First and Second Chapters of the Latter Episte Of the Apostle Paul to Timothy*. London, 1632. Digital copy online at EEBO.

Baxter, Richard. *The Reformed Pastor*. Edinburgh: Banner of Truth, 1974.

Beza, Theodore. *The New Testament of Our Lord Jesus Christ, Translated out of Greeke by Theodore Beza: With Brief Summaries and Expositions upon the Hard Places by the Said Author*. Translated by L. Tomson. London, 1599.

———. *Novum Domini Nostri Iesu Christi Testamentum*. Basel, 1559. Digital copy online at EEBO.

Bilson, Thomas. *The Perpetual Government of Christ's Church* (1593). Edited by Robert Eden. Oxford: Oxford University Press, 1842. Digital copy online at archive.org.

Bray, Gerald, ed. *Tudor Church Reform: The Henrician Canons of 1535 and the Reformatio Legum Ecclesiasticarum*. Church of England Record Society 8. Woodbridge, UK: Boydell Press, 2000.

Brenz, Johannes. *Explicatio Epistolarum Saint Pauli Apostoli*. Frankfurt, 1570.

Bromiley, Geoffrey W., ed. and trans. *Zwingli and Bullinger*. LCC 24. London: SCM Press, 1953.

Bucer, Martin. *Common Places of Martin Bucer*. The Courtenay Library of Reformation Classics 4. Translated and edited by David F. Wright. Appleford, UK: Sutton Courtenay Press, 1972.

———. *Concerning the True Care of Souls*. Translated by Peter Beale. Edinburgh: Banner of Truth, 2009.

Bugenhagen. Johannes. *Annotationes Io. Bugenhagii Pomerani in Epistolas Pauli*. Strassburg: Knobloch, 1525. Digital copy online at digitale.bibliothek.uni-halle.de.

Bullinger, Heinrich. *Apostoli Pauli Ad Thessalonicences, Timotheum, Titum and Philemon epistolas*. Froschouerum, 1536. Digital copy at www.prdl.org.

———. *A Commentary upon the Second Epistle of St. Paul to the Thessalonians*. Translated by R. H. Printed in Soutwarke, England. 1538.

———. *Fifty Godly and Learned Sermons*. Translated by H. I., "student in Divinitie." London: Ralph Newberie, 1584. Digital copy online at EEBO.

———. *Fiftie Godlie and Learned Sermons Divided into Five Decades*. London: Ralph Newberrie, 1577. Digital copy online at EEBO.

———. *In Omnes Apostolicas Epistolas*. Zurich: Christophorum Froschoverum, 1537. Digital copy available from www.e-rara.ch.

———. *Sermonum Decas Quinta . . . Tomus Tertius*. Zurich: Christophorum Froschoverum, 1551. Digital copy online at books.google.com.

Cajetan, Cardinal (Thomas de Vio). *Epistolae Pauli et Aliorum Apostolorum ad Graecam Veritatem Castigatae*. Venice, 1531.

———. *Epistolae Pauli et Aliorum Apostolarum. Ad graecam veritatem castigate, & per reverendissimum dominum Thomas de vio, Caitanum, Cardinalem sancti Xisti, iuxta sensum literalem enarratae. Recens in lucem editae*. Paris: Jehan Petit, 1540.

Calvin, John. *Commentaries on the Epistles to Timothy, Titus, and Philemon*. Translated by William Pringle. CTS 21. Grand Rapids: Baker, 1993.

———. *Commentarius in Epistolam Pauli ad Thessalonioenses I et ad Thessalonioenses II*. CO 52. Edited by G. Baum, E. Cunitz, and E. Reuss. Brunswick: C. A. Schwetschke, 1863. Digital copy online at archive-ouverte.unige.ch/unige:650.

———. *Commentary on the Second Epistle to the Thessalonians*. Translated by William Pringle. CTS 21. Edinburgh: Calvin Translation Society, 1848–1948. Reprinted Grand Rapids: Baker, 2003. Digital copy online at www.ccel.org.

———. *Institutes of the Christian Religion* (1559). Edited by John T. McNeill. Translated by Ford Lewis Battles. LCC 20–21. Philadelphia: Westminster, 1960. Latin text available in CO 2 (1864). Digital copy online at archive-ourverte.unige.ch/unige:650.

———. *Sermons sur La Premiere Epitre à Timothée*. Edited by G. Baum, E. Cunitz, and E. Reuss. CO 53. Brunswick: C. A. Schwetschke, 1895. Digital copy online at archive-ouverte.unige.ch/unige:650.

———. *Sermons sur La Seconde Epitre à Timothée et Sermons sur L'Epitre à Tite*. Edited by G. Baum, E. Cunitz, and E. Reuss. CO 54. Brunswick: C. A. Schwetschke, 1895. Digital copy online at archive-ouverte.unige.ch/unige:650.

Cartwright, Thomas. *A Confutation of the Rhemists Translation, Glosses and Annotations on the New Testament*. Leiden: W. Brewster, 1618. Digital copy online at EEBO.

Chemnitz, Christian. *Commentariolus in Omnes Epistolas D. Pauli*. Jena, 1667.

Cranmer, Thomas, ed. *Certain Sermons or Homilies [The First Book of Homilies]*. London, 1547. Digital copy online at EEBO.

Cruciger, Caspar. *In Epistolam Pauli ad Timotheum priorem Commentarius*. Mylius, 1542. Digital copy online at PRDL.

Daneau, Lambert. *The Judgement of that Reverend and Godly Learned Man . . . contained in his preface before his commentary upon the first Epistle to Timothie*. Edinburgh: R. Waldegrave, 1590. Digital copy online at EEBO.

Davenant, John. *Expositio Epistolae D. Pauli ad Colossenses*. Cambridge: Thomas and John Bucke, 1627. Digital copy online at EEBO.

Dentière, Marie. *Epistle to Marguerite de Navarre and Preface to a Sermon by John Calvin*. Edited and translated by Mary B. McKinley. The Other Voice in Early Modern Europe. Chicago: University of Chicago Press, 2004.

Dickson, David. *An exposition of all St. Paul's epistles together with an explanation of those other epistles . . . wherein the sense of every chapter and verse is analytically unfolded and the text enlightened.* London: Eglesfield,1659.

———. *Expositio analytica omnium apostolicarum epistolarum.* Glasgow: George Anderson, 1645.

Diodati, Giovanni. *Pious Annotations upon the Holy Bible.* London: Nicholas Fussell, 1643.

A Directory for the Publique Worship of God. London: Printed by G. M. and I. F. for the Company of Stationers, 1645. Digital copy online at EEBO.

Donnelly, John P., Frank A. James, and Joseph C. McLelland, eds. *The Peter Martyr Reader.* Kirksville, MO: Truman State University Press, 1999.

Downame, John, ed. *Annotations upon All the Books of the Old and New Testament.* London: John Legatt and John Raworth, 1645. Digital copy online at EEBO.

Erasmus, Desiderius. *Desiderii Erasmi Roterodami Opera Omnia.* 10 vols. Edited by Jean LeClerc. Leiden: Van der Aa, 1706. Reprint, Hildersheim: Georg Olms, 1961–1962. Digital copy online at babel.hathitrust.org.

———. *Paraphrases in Epistolas Pauli, ad Timotheum duas, ad Titum unam, et ad Philemonem unam.* Basel, 1520. Digital copy online at daten.digitale-sammlungen.de.

Fell, Margaret. *Women's Speaking Justified, Proved and Allowed of by the Scriptures.* London, 1666.

Forbes, John. *Four Sermons Which doe manifest the true sense of the 1. Epistle to Timothie 6. Chapter 13. 14. 15. & 16. verses of that Chapter.* Delph, 1635. Digital copy online at EEBO.

———. *A Sermon Discursing the true meaning of these words: The 1. Epistle of Timothy, the 2. chapt. vers. The 4.* Delph, 1632. Digital copy online at EEBO.

The Forme and Maner of Makyng and Consecratying of Archebishoppes, Bishoppes, Priests, and Deacons. London: Richard Grafton, 1549. Digital copy online at EEBO.

Froidmont, Libert. *Commentaria in Omnes B. Pauli Apostoli et Septem Canonicas Aliorum Apostolorum Epistolas.* Louvain, 1663.

Fulke, William. *The text of the New Testament . . . with a confutation of all such arguments, glosses, and annotations as contain manifest impiety, treason, and slander.* London: Christopher Barker, 1589. Digital copy online at EEBO.

Gifford, George. *Foure Sermons Upon Severall partes of Scripture.* London, 1598. Digital copy online at EEBO.

Gournay, Marie le Jars de. *Apology for the Woman Writing and Other Works.* Edited and translated by Richard Hillman and Colette Quesnell. The Other Voice in Early Modern Europe. Chicago: University of Chicago Press, 2002.

Grotius, Hugo. *Annotationes in Novem Testamentum: Denuo Emendatius Editae.* 8 vols. Groningen: W. Zuidema, 1826–1830. Digital copy online at books.google.com.

Grumbach, Argula von. *A Woman's Voice in the Reformation.* Edited by Peter Matheson. Edinburgh: T&T Clark, 1995.

Haak, Theodore. *The Dutch Annotations upon the Whole Bible.* London: Henry Hills for John Rothwell, Joshua Kirton, and Richard Tomlins, 1657. Digital copy available from EEBO.

Hammond, Henry. *A Paraphrase and Annotations Upon all the Books of the New Testament.* London, 1659. Digital copy online at EEBO.

Hemmingsen, Niels. *Commentaria in omnes Epistolas Apostolorum.* Frankfurt, 1579. Digital copy online at books.google.com.

Hesshus, Tilemann. *Commentarius in Priorem Epistolam Apostoli Pauli ad Timotheum.* Helmstedt: Iacobus Lucius, 1586. Digital copy online at books.google.com.

Hooker, Richard. *Of the Laws of Ecclesiastical Polity: A Critical Edition with Modern Spelling*. Edited by Arthur Stephen McGrade. 3 vols. Oxford: Oxford University Press, 2013.

Hubmaier, Balthasar. *Balthasar Hubmaier: Theologian of Anabaptism*. Translated and edited by H. Wayne Pipkin and John H. Yoder. CRR 5. Scottdale, PA: Herald Press, 1989.

The Humble Advice of the Assembly of Divines Now by Authority of Parliament Sitting at Westminster, Concerning a Confession of Faith. London: Printed for the Company of Stationers, 1647. Digital copy online at EEBO.

Hunnius, Aegidius. *Thesaurus Apostolicus complectens Commentarios in Omnes Novi Testamenti Epistolas et Apocalypsin Iohannis*. Edited by Jo. Henrico Feustkingio. Wittenberg: Mayer, 1705. Digital copy online at diglib.hab.de/.

Jackson, Samuel M., ed. *Selected Works of Huldreich Zwingli*. Philadelphia: Longmans, Green, 1901.

Jewel, John, ed. *The Second Tome of Homilees*. London: Richard Jugge and John Cawood, 1571. Digital copy online at EEBO.

Joris, David. *The Anabaptist Writings of David Joris*. Translated and edited by Gary K. Waite. CRR 7. Waterloo, ON: Herald Press, 1994.

Karlstadt, Andreas Bodenstein von. *The Essential Carlstadt*. Translated and edited by E. J. Furcha. CRR 8. Waterloo, ON: Herald Press, 1995.

Ketley, Joseph, ed. *The Two Liturgies with other Documents Set Forth by Authority in the Reign of Edward the Sixth*. Cambridge: Cambridge University Press, 1844.

Klaassen, Walter, Werner O. Packull, C. Arnold Snyder, and F. Friesen, eds. *Sources of South German/ Austrian Anabaptism*. CRR 10. Kitchener, ON: Pandora Press, 2001.

Leigh, Edward. *Annotations upon All the New Testament Philologicall and Theologicall*. London: W. W. and E. G. for William Lee, 1650. Digital copy online at EEBO.

Lefèvre d'Étaples, Jacques. *In Omneis D. Pauli Epistolas Commentarioris libri XIII*. Cologne: Eucharius Cervicornus, 1531.

Lightfoot, John. *Horae Hebraicæ et Talmudicæ: Hebrew and Talmudical Exercitations . . . in Four Volumes. First published between 1658–1674*. Oxford: Oxford University Press, 1859. Digital copy online at books.google.com.

Luther, Martin. *Complete Sermons of Martin Luther*. Edited by John Nicholas Lenker. 7 vols. Grand Rapids: Baker, 2000.

———. *D. Martin Luthers Werke, Kritische Gesamtausgabe*. 73 vols. Weimar: Hermann Böhlaus Nachfolger, 1883–2009. Digital copy online at archive.org.

———. *Luther's Works [American edition]*. 82 volumes planned. St. Louis: Concordia; Philadelphia: Fortress, 1955–1986, 2009–.

Maler, Jörg. *Jörg Maler's Kunstbuch: Writings of the Pilgram Marpeck Circle*. Translated and edited by John D. Rempel. CRR 12. Kitchener, ON: Pandora, 2010.

Marpeck, Pilgram. *The Writings of Pilgram Marpeck*. Edited and Translated by William Klassen and Walter Klassen. CRR 2. Scottdale, PA: Herald Press, 1978.

Martin, Gregory. *The New Testament of Jesus Christ, Translated Faithfully into English . . . with Arguments of books and chapters, Annotations, and other necessary helps*. Rhemes, 1582. Digital copy online at EEBO.

Mayer, John. *A Commentarie upon All the Epistles of the Apostle Saint Paul*. London: John Haviland for John Grismond, 1631. Digitally copy online at EEBO.

Melanchthon, Philip. *Commonplaces: Loci Communes 1521*. Translated by Christian Preus. St. Louis: Concordia, 2014.

Moffett, Peter. *The Excellencie of the Mysterie of Christ Jesus. Declared in an exposition or meditation upon the 16th verse of the first epistle of Saint Paul unto Timothie.* London, 1590. Digital copy online at EEBO.

Morata, Olympia. *The Complete Writings of an Italian Heretic.* Edited and translated by Holt N. Parker. The Other Voice in Early Modern Europe. Chicago: University of Chicago Press, 2003.

Müntzer, Thomas. *The Collected Works of Thomas Müntzer.* Translated and edited by Peter Matheson. Edinburgh: T&T Clark, 1994.

Musculus, Wolfgang. *In Divi Pauli Epistolas ad Philippenses, Colossenses, Thessalonicenses ambas, et primum ad Timotheum.* Basel: Hervagius, 1578. Digital copy online at books.google.com.

Owen, John. *The Works of John Owen.* Edited by W. H. Goold. 24 volumes. London: Johnstone and Hunter, 1850–1855. Digital copy online at www.prdl.org.

Philips, Dirk. *The Writings of Dirk Philips, 1504–1568.* Translated and edited by Cornelius J. Dyck, William E. Keeney, and Alvin J. Beachy. CRR 6. Scottdale, PA: Herald Press, 1992.

Pinner, Charles. *A Sermon preached at Marlborow, 6 October 1596, to the public assembly of ministers at the visitation, on 1 Tim. 4:16.* Oxford, 1597.

———. *Sermon upon the Wordes of Paul the Apostle unto Timothie, Epist. 1. Chap. 4. vers. 8.* Oxford, 1597.

Piscator, Johann. *Commentarii in Omnes Libros Novi Testamenti.* Herborn: Nassouiorum, 1613. Digital copy available from digital.slub-dresden.de.

Poole, Matthew. *Annotations upon the Holy Bible. Vol. II . . . being a continuation of Mr. Pool's work by certain judicious and learned divines.* London: Printed for Thomas Parkhurst, 1685. Digital copy online at EEBO.

———. *Annotations upon the Holy Bible, Wherein the Sacred Text is Inserted, and Various Readings Annexed, Together with the Parallel Scriptures.* Vol. 3. Robert Carter and Brothers: New York, 1852.

Preston, John. *Sermons Preached Before His Majesty.* London, 1631. Digital copy online at EEBO.

Riedemann, Peter. *Peter Riedemann's Hutterite Confession of Faith.* Translated and edited by John J. Friesen. CRR 9. Waterloo, ON: Herald Press, 1999.

Rollock, Robert. *In Utramque Epistolam Pauli Ad Thessalonicenses Commentarius.* Herborn: Christopher Corvinus, 1601.

Salmerón, Alfonso. *Disputationum in Epistolas Divi Pauli: Tomus Tertius.* Madrid, 1602.

Sarcerius, Erasmus. *In Epistolas D. Pauli ad Philippenses, Colossenses, and Thessalonicenses, pia and erudite Scholia.* Frankfort: Christianus Egenolphus, 1542.

Sattler, Michael. *The Legacy of Michael Sattler.* Translated and edited by John H. Yoder. CRR 1. Scottdale, PA: Herald Press, 1973.

Schaff, Philip, ed. *Bibliotheca Symbolica Ecclesiae Universalis: The Creeds of Christendom.* 3 vols. New York: Harper and Brothers, 1877. 6th ed., by David S. Schaff. Reprint ed. Grand Rapids: Baker, 1990. Available online at www.ccel.org.

Schurman, Anna Maria van. *Whether a Christian Woman Should Be Educated and Other Writings from Her Intellectual Circle.* Edited and translated by Joyce L. Irwin. The Other Voice in Early Modern Europe. Chicago: University of Chicago Press, 1998.

Scultetus, Abraham. *The Determination of the Question concerning the Divine Right of Episcopacie . . . Faithfully translated out of his Observations upon the Epistles to Timothy and Titus.* London: Nathaniel Butter, 1641. Digital copy online at EEBO.

Sibbes, Richard. *The Complete Works of Richard Sibbes.* Edited by Alexander B. Grosart. 7 vols. Edinburgh: James Nichol, 1862. Digital copy online at archive.org.

Spinka, Matthew, ed. *Advocates of Reform: From Wyclif to Erasmus.* London: SCM Press, 1953.

Stevartius, Petrus. *Commentarius in Priorem D. Pauli Apostoli Ad Timeotheum Epistolam.* Ingolstadt, 1611.

Stoughton, John. *A Forme of Wholsome Words; or, An Introduction to the Body of Divinity: In three Sermons on 2 Timothy 1.13.* London, 1640. Digital copy online at EEBO.

Strigel, Viktorin. *Omnes Libros Novi Testamenti.* Leipzig, 1566.

Tappert, Theodore G., ed. *The Book of Concord: The Confessions of the Evangelical Lutheran Church.* Philadelphia: Mühlenberg, 1959.

Taylor, Thomas. *A Commentarie Upon the Epistle of S. Paul written to Titus.* Cambridge, 1612. Digital copy online at EEBO.

Trapp, John. *A Commentary or Exposition upon All the Epistles and the Revelation of John the Divine.* London: A. M. for John Bellamy, 1647. Digital copy online at EEBO.

Tyndale, William. *The Newe Testament Diligently Corrected and Compared with the Greek.* Antwerp: Marten Emperowr, 1534. Digital copy online at EEBO.

———. *The Obedience of a Christian Man.* Edited by David Daniell. Harmondsworth, UK: Penguin, 2000.

———. *Tyndale's New Testament.* Edited by by David Daniell. New Haven, CT: Yale University Press, 1989.

Venatorius, Thomas. *In Divi Pauli Apostoli Priorem ad Timotheum Epistolam Distributiones XX.* Basel, 1533.

Vermigli, Peter Martyr. *The Common Places of the Most Famous and Renowned Divine Doctor Peter Martyr.* London: Henry Denham and Henry Middleton, 1583. Digital copy online at EEBO.

———. *The Oxford Treatise and Disputation on the Eucharist, 1549.* PML 7. Translated by Joseph C. McLelland. Kirksville, MO: Truman State University Press, 2000.

Vorstius, Conradus. *Commentarius in Omnes Epistolas Apostolicas.* Amsterdam: Guilielmum Blaev, 1631. Digital copy online at books.google.com.

Whittingham, William. *The Bible and Holy Scriptures conteined in the Olde and Newe Testament.* London: Christopher Barkar, 1576. Digital copy online at EEBO.

———. *The Bible and Holy Scriptures conteyned in the Olde and Newe Testament.* Geneva: Rouland Hall, 1560. Digital copy online at EEBO.

Wiesner-Hanks, Merry, ed. *Convents Confront the Reformation: Catholic and Protestant Nuns in Germany.* Translated by Merry Wiesner-Hanks and Joan Skocir. Milwaukee: Marquette University Press, 1996.

Williams, George H., and Angel M. Mergal, eds. *Spiritual and Anabaptist Writers.* LCC 25. Philadelphia: Westminster, 1957.

Wycliffe, John. *Trialogus.* Translated by Stephen E. Lahey. Cambridge: Cambridge University Press, 2013.

Zanchi, Jerome. *In D. Pauli Apostoli Epistolas Ad Phillipenses, Colossenses, Thessalonicenses, Et Duo priora capita primae Epistolae D. Ioahannis.* Neustadt, 1601.

Zell, Katharina Schütz. *Church Mother: The Writings of a Protestant Reformer in Sixteenth-Century Germany.* Translated by Elsie McKee. The Other Voice in Early Modern Europe. Chicago: University of Chicago Press, 2006.

Zwingli, Ulrich. *De Vera et Falsa Religione.* Zurich, 1529.

Other Works Consulted

Acton, Lord. *Lectures on Modern History.* London: Macmillan, 1930.

Allen, Michael, and Jonathan A. Linebaugh, eds. *Reformation Readings of Paul: Explorations in History and Exegesis.* Downers Grove, IL: IVP Academic, 2015.

Alliborne, S. A. *A Critical Dictionary of English Literature and British and American Authors.* Philadelphia: J. B. Lippincott, 1872.

Ambrosiaster. *Commentaries on Galatians–Philemon.* Edited and translated by Gerald L. Bray. Ancient Christian Texts. Downers Grove, IL: IVP Academic, 2009.

Arnold, Thomas, ed. *Select English Works of John Wyclif*. Vol. 3, *Miscellaneous Works*. Oxford: Clarendon, 1871.

Arrizabalaga, Jon, John Henderson, and Roger French. *The Great Pox: The French Disease in Renaissance Europe*. New Haven, CT: Yale University Press, 1997.

Augustine. *Arianism and Other Heresies*. Translated by Roland J. Teske. Works of Saint Augustine: A Translation for the 21st Century 1/18. Hyde Park, NY: New City Press, 1995.

———. *Teaching Christianity*. Translated by Edmund Hill. The Works of Saint Augustine: A New Translation for the 21st Century 1/11. Hyde Park, NY: New City Press, 1997.

Ayres, Lewis. *Nicaea and Its Legacy: An Approach to Fourth-Century Trinitarian Theology*. Oxford: Oxford University Press, 2006.

Babbitt, F. C., ed. *Plutarch: Moralia II*. LCL 222. Cambridge, MA: Harvard University Press, 1928.

———. *Plutarch: Moralia V*. LCL 306. Cambridge, MA: Harvard University Press, 1936.

Barnes, Jonathan, ed. *The Complete Works of Aristotle: The Revised Oxford Translation*. 2 vols. Princeton, NJ: Princeton University Press, 1984.

Baronio, Cesare. *Annales Ecclesiastici*. 12 vols. Antwerp: John Moritz, 1588–1607.

———. *Epitome Annalium Ecclesiasticorum Cæsaris Baronii*. 12 vols. Venice, 1588–1607.

Beale, Gregory K. "The Eschatological Conception of New Testament Theology." In *"The Reader Must Understand": Eschatology in Bible and Theology*, edited by Kent E. Brower and Mark W. Elliott, 11-52. Leicester, UK: Apollos, 1997.

———. *1–2 Thessalonians*. IVP New Testament Commentary. Downers Grove, IL: InterVarsity Press, 2003.

———. *A New Testament Biblical Theology: The Unfolding of the Old Testament in the New*. Grand Rapids: Baker Academic, 2011.

Bedouelle, Guy. "Lefèvre d'Étaples, Jacques." In *The Oxford Encyclopedia of the Reformation*, edited by Hans J. Hillerbrand, 2:415-16. New York: The Oxford University Press, 1996.

Bellarmine, Robert. *De Controversiis Fidei Christiani contra Haereticos Nostri Tempori: Tomus Primus, De Ecclesia*. Ingolstadt, 1588.

———. *De Controversiis Fidei Christiani: De Ecclesia Militante*. Ingolstadt: David Satori, 1588

Belloc, Hilaire. *The Great Heresies*. London: Sheed and Ward, 1938. Reprint, Milwaukee, WI: Cavalier, 2015.

Bouyer, Louis. *The Spirit and Forms and Protestantism*. Translated by A. V. Littledale. San Francisco: Ignatius, 2017.

Bray, Gerald. "In Conclusion: The Story of Reformation Readings." In *Reformation Readings of Paul: Explorations in History and Exegesis*, edited by Michael Allen and Jonathan A. Linebaugh, 255-74. Downers Grove, IL: IVP Academic, 2015.

Bruce, F. F. *The Canon of Scripture*. Downers Grove, IL: InterVarsity Press, 1988.

———. *Paul: Apostle of the Heart Set Free*. Grand Rapids: Eerdmans, 1977.

Calvin, John, and Jacopo Sadoleto. *A Reformation Debate*. Edited by John C. Olin. Grand Rapids: Baker, 1976.

Cary, E., ed. *Dio's Roman History III*. LCL 99. New York: Macmillan, 1914.

Chester, Stephen J. *Reading Paul with the Reformers: Reconciling Old and New Perspectives*. Grand Rapids: Eerdmans, 2017.

Chong-Gossard, J. H. Kim On. *Gender and Communication in Euripides' Plays: Between Song and Silence*. Leiden: Brill, 2008.

Corley, Bruce. "Interpreting Paul's Conversion—Then and Now." In *The Road from Damascus: The Impact of Paul's Conversion on His Life, Thought, and Ministry*, edited by Richard N. Longenecker, 1-17. Grand Rapids: Eerdmans, 1997.

Eck, Johannes. *Enchiridion Locorum Communium adversus Lutherum et alios Hostes Ecclesiae*. Ingolstadt, 1536.

———. *Enchiridion of Commonplaces Against Luther and Other Enemies of the Church*. Translated by Ford Lewis Battles. Grand Rapids: Baker, 1979.

Ehrman, Bart G. *Forgery and Counterforgery: The Use of Literary Deceit in Early Christian Polemics*. Oxford: Oxford University Press, 2013.

Ellis, E. Earle. *Christ and the Future in New Testament History*. Leiden: Brill, 2001.

———. *The Making of the New Testament Documents*. Leiden: Brill, 2002.

———. *The Old Testament in Early Christianity: Canon and Interpretation in the Light of Modern Research*. Tübingen: Mohr Siebeck, 1991. Reprint, Grand Rapids: Baker, 1992.

Engelbrecht, Edward A. *Friends of the Law: Luther's Use of the Law for the Christian Life*. St. Louis: Concordia, 2011.

Fee, Gordon D. *1 and 2 Timothy, Titus*. New International Biblical Commentary. Carlisle, UK: Paternoster, 1995.

Foord, Martin. "God Wills All People to Be Saved—Or Does He? Calvin's Reading of 1 Timothy 2:4." In *Engaging with Calvin: Aspects of the Reformer's Legacy for Today*, edited by Mark D. Thompson, 179-203. Nottingham, UK: Apollos, 2009.

Foster, B. O., ed. *Livy: Books I and II*. LCL 114. London: Heinemann, 1967.

———. *Livy: Books VIII-X*. LCL 191. London: Heinemann, 1926.

———. *Livy: Books XXI-XXII*. LCL 233. London: Heinemann, 1929.

Gaffin, Richard. "The New Testament as Canon." In *Inerrancy and Hermeneutic: A Tradition, a Challenge, a Debate*, edited by Harvie Conn, 165-83. Grand Rapids: Baker, 1988.

Gatiss, Lee. *Cornerstones of Salvation: Foundations and Debates in the Reformed Tradition*. Welwyn, UK: Evangelical Press, 2017.

———. *For Us and For Our Salvation: "Limited Atonement" in the Bible, Doctrine, History, and Ministry*. London: Latimer Trust, 2012.

———. "Grace Tasted Death for All: Thomas Aquinas on Hebrews 2:9." *Tyndale Bulletin* 63, no. 2 (2012): 228-231.

Gazal, Andre A. "'Profit That Is Condemned by the Word of God': John Jewel's Theological Method in His Opposition to Usury." *Perichoresis* 13, no. 1 (2015): 37-54.

Geist, Charles R. *Beggar Thy Neighbor: A History of Usury and Debt*. Philadelphia: University of Pennsylvania Press, 2013.

George, Timothy. *Reading Scripture with the Reformers*. Downers Grove, IL: IVP Academic, 2011.

Green, Christopher. *Finishing the Race: Reading 2 Timothy Today*. Sydney: Aquila Press, 2000.

Gregory, Brad S. *The Unintended Reformation: How a Religious Revolution Secularized Society*. Cambridge, MA: Belknap Press of Harvard University Press, 2012.

Gumerlock, Francis. *Fulgentius of Ruspe: On the Saving Will of God; The Development of a Sixth-Century African Bishop's Interpretation of 1 Timothy 2:4 During the Semi-Pelagian Controversy*. Lewiston, NY: Mellen, 2009.

Gummere, Richard M., ed. *Seneca: Ad Lucilium Epistulae Morales I*. LCL 75. London: Heinemann, 1925.

Guthrie, Donald. *The Pastoral Epistles*. Tyndale New Testament Commentaries. Downers Grove, IL: InterVarsity Press, 1990.

Harley, Thomas. *Matthew Poole: His Life, His Times, His Contributions*. New York: iUniverse, 2009.

Hart, D. G. "Hyper About Pluralism: A Review Essay." *Humanitas* 27, nos. 1 and 2 (2014): 153-61.

Hillerbrand, Hans J. *The Oxford Encyclopedia of the Reformation*. 4 vols. New York: Oxford University Press, 1996.

Holder, R. *A Companion to Paul in the Reformation*. Brill's Companions to the Christian Tradition. Leiden: Brill, 2009.

Jansen, Katherine Ludwig. *The Making of Mary Magdalene: Preaching and Popular Devotion in the Later Middle Ages*. Princeton, NJ: Princeton University Press, 2000.

Jewel, John. "Commentary on 1 Thessalonians 4:4" and "A Paper on Usury," translated and edited by Andre A. Gazal, *Journal of Markets and Morality* 15, no. 1 (2012): 273-313.

Johnson, Luke Timothy. *The First and Second Letters to Timothy: A New Translation with Introduction and Commentary*. Anchor Yale Bible 35A. New Haven, CT: Yale University Press, 2008.

Jones, David W. *Reforming the Morality of Usury: A Study of the Differences That Separated the Protestant Reformers*. Lanham, MD: University Press of America, 2004.

Jones, Norman. *God and the Moneylenders: Usury and Law in Early Modern England*. Oxford: Blackwell, 1989.

Kerridge, Eric. *Usury, Interest, and the Reformation*. Aldershot: Ashgate, 2002.

Knight, George W., III. *The Pastoral Epistles: A Commentary on the Greek Text*. New International Greek Testament Commentary. Carlisle, UK: Paternoster, 1992.

Köstenberger, Andreas J., and Thomas R. Schreiner, eds. *Women in the Church: An Analysis and Application of 1 Timothy 2:9-15*. 3rd ed. Wheaton, IL: Crossway, 2016.

Kruger, Michael J. *Canon Revisited: Establishing the Origins and Authority of the New Testament Books*. Wheaton, IL: Crossway, 2012.

————. *The Question of Canon: Challenging the Status Quo in The New Testament Debate*. Downers Grove, IL: IVP Academic, 2013.

Ladd, George Eldon. *Gospel of the Kingdom: Scriptural Studies in the Kingdom of God*. Grand Rapids: Eerdmans, 1990.

————. *A Theology of the New Testament*. Edited by Donald A. Hagner. 2nd ed. Cambridge: Lutterworth, 2001.

Lewis, Charlton T. *A Latin Dictionary*. Oxford: Clarendon, 1984.

Liddel, H. G., and R. Scott. *A Lexicon, Abridged from Liddell and Scott's Greek-English Lexicon*. Oxford: Clarendon, 1976.

Linebaugh, Jonathan. "The Texts of Paul and the Theology of Cranmer." In *Reformation Readings of Paul: Explorations in History and Exegesis*, edited by Michael Allen and Jonathan A. Linebaugh, 235-54. Downers Grove, IL: IVP Academic, 2015.

Longenecker, Richard N., ed. *The Road from Damascus: The Impact of Paul's Conversion on His Life, Thought, and Ministry*. Grand Rapids: Eerdmans, 1997.

Luther, Martin. "Preface to the Epistle of St. Paul to the Romans." In *Martin Luther: Selections from His Writings*, edited by John Dillenberger, 19-34. New York: Doubleday, 1962.

Macdonald, C., ed. *Cicero: Orations. In Catilinam 1-4. Pro Murena. Pro Sulla. Pro Flacco*. LCL 324. Cambridge, MA: Harvard University Press, 1976.

Manetsch, Scott M., ed. *1 Corinthians*. Reformation Commentary on Scripture, NT IXa. Downers Grove, IL: IVP Academic, 2017.

Marshall, I. Howard. *The Pastoral Epistles*. International Critical Commentary. London: T&T Clark, 2004.

Matthews, A. G. *Calamy Revised: Being a Revision of Edmund Calamy's Account of the Ministers and Others Ejected and Silenced, 1660–2*. Oxford: Clarendon, 1934.

Metzger, Bruce M. *The Canon of the New Testament: Its Origin, Development, and Significance*. Oxford: Clarendon, 1992.

———. *A Textual Commentary on the Greek New Testament.* 2nd ed. Stuttgart: Deutsche Bibelgesell-schaft, 1994.

Migne, J. P., ed. *Sancti Ambrosii Mediolanensis Episcopi Opera Omnia. Tomus Secundi et Ultimi Pars Posterior.* PL 17. Paris: Migne, 1845.

———. *Sancti Aurelii Augustini, Hipponensis Episcopi, Opera Omnia. Tomus Tertius. Pars Prior.* PL 34. Paris: Migne, 1865.

———. *Sancti Prosperi Aquitani . . . Opera Omnia. Tomus Unicus.* PL 51. Paris: Migne, 1846.

———. *SS. Gelasii I Papæ, Aviti, Faustini, necnon Joannis Diaconi, Juliani Pomerii et Duorum Anony-morum Opera Omnia.* PL 59. Paris: Migne, 1862.

Mounce, William D. *Pastoral Epistles.* Word Biblical Commentary 46. Nashville: Thomas Nelson, 2000.

Muller, Richard A. *Dictionary of Latin and Greek Theological Terms Drawn Principally from Protestant Scholastic Theology.* 2nd ed. Carlisle, UK: Paternoster, 2000.

Norlin, George, ed. *Isocrates: With an English Translation.* Vol. 2. LCL 229. London: Heinemann, 1929.

Null, Ashley. "Thomas Cranmer's Reading of Paul's Letters." In *Reformation Readings of Paul: Explora-tions in History and Exegesis,* edited by Michael Allen and Jonathan A. Linebaugh, 211-33. Downers Grove, IL: IVP Academic, 2015.

O'Brien, Peter T. *Colossians, Philemon.* Word Biblical Commentary 44. Waco, TX: Word, 1982.

Palmer, Samuel. *The Nonconformist's Memorial.* London: Button & Son, 1802.

Payne, Philip B. *Man and Woman, One in Christ: An Exegetical and Theological Study of Paul's Letters.* Grand Rapids: Zondervan, 2009.

Perrin, B., ed. *Plutarch's Lives. Volume 7: Demosthenes and Cicero. Alexander and Caesar.* LCL 53. Cam-bridge, MA: Harvard University Press, 1967.

Pervo, Richard I. "'The Acts of Titus': A Preliminary Translation; With an Introduction, Notes, and Appendices." *Society of Biblical Literature Seminar Papers* 35 (1996): 455-82.

Peter Lombard. *The Sentences.* Vol. 1, *The Mystery of the Trinity.* Translated by Giulio Silano. Toronto: Pontifical Institute of Mediaeval Studies, 2007.

———. *The Sentences.* Vol. 3, *On the Incarnation of the Word.* Translated by Giulio Silano. Toronto: Pontifical Institute of Mediaeval Studies, 2008.

Quinn, Jerome D. *The Letter to Titus: A New Translation with Notes and Commentary and an Intro-duction.* Anchor Bible 35. New York: Doubleday, 1990.

Quinn, Jerome D., and Wacker, William C. *The First and Second Letters to Timothy: A New Transla-tion with Notes and Commentary.* Eerdmans Critical Commentary. Grand Rapids: Eerdmans, 2000.

Rackham, H., ed. *Pliny: Natural History. Volume 2: Libri III–VII.* LCL 352. London: Heinemann, 1961.

Ridderbos, Herman. *Paul: An Outline of His Theology.* Translated by John Richard De Witt. Grand Rapids: Eerdmans, 1997.

Rittgers, Ronald K., ed. *Hebrews, James.* Reformation Commentary on Scripture, NT XIII. Downers Grove, IL: IVP Academic, 2017.

Sanders, E. P. *Paul: A Very Short Introduction.* Oxford: Oxford University Press, 1991.

Scaer, D. "The Nature and Extent of the Atonement in Lutheran Theology." *Bulletin of the Evangelical Theological Society* 10, no. 4 (1967): 179-87.

Schroeder, H. J. *The Canons and Decrees of the Council of Trent.* Rockford, IL: Tan, 1978.

Schweitzer, Albert. *Paul and His Interpreters: A Critical History.* Translated by W. Montgomery. New York: Schocken, 1964.

Skeat, T. C. "'Especially the Parchments': A Note on 2 Timothy IV.13." *Journal of Theological Studies* 30 (1979): 173-77.

Sloan, Robert B. "Unity in Diversity: A Clue to the Emergence of the New Testament as Sacred Literature." In *New Testament Criticism and Interpretation*, edited by David Alan Black and David S. Dockery, 437-68. Grand Rapids: Zondervan, 1991.

Stark, Rodney. *The Rise of Christianity: How the Obscure, Marginal Jesus Movement Became the Dominant Religious Force in the Western World in a Few Centuries*. San Francisco: HarperSanFrancisco, 1997.

Stelten, Leo F. *Dictionary of Ecclesiastical Latin*. Peabody, MA: Hendrickson, 1995.

Stendahl, Krister. "The Apostle Paul and the Introspective Conscience of the West." *Harvard Theological Review* 56 (1963): 199-215.

Suelzer, Josephine. *Julianus Pomerius: The Contemplative Life*. Westminster, MA: Newman, 1947.

Teske, Roland. "1 Timothy 2:4 and the Beginnings of the Massalian Controversy." In *Grace for Grace: The Debates After Augustine and Pelagius*, edited by Alexander Y. Hwang, Brian J. Matz, and Augustine Casiday, 14-34. Washington, DC: Catholic University of America Press, 2014.

Thackeray, H., St. J. *Josephus with an English Translation. II—The Jewish War, Books I–III*. LCL 203. London: Heinemann, 1956.

Thiselton, Anthony. *1 and 2 Thessalonians Through the Centuries*. Chichester, UK: Wiley-Blackwell, 2010.

Thomas Aquinas. *Commentaries on St. Paul's Epistles to Timothy, Titus, and Philemon*. Translated by Chrysostom Baer. South Bend, IN: St. Augustine's Press, 2007.

———. *Commentary on the Letters of Saint Paul to the Philippians, Colossians, Thessalonians, Timothy, Titus, and Philemon*. Translated by Fabian R. Larcher. Edited by John Mortensen and Enrique Alarcón. Latin-English Edition of the Works of St. Thomas Aquinas 40. Lander, WY: Aquinas Institute, 2012.

———. *Summa theologiae*. Translated by Laurence Shapcote. Edited by John Mortensen and Enrique Alarcón. 18 vols. Latin-English Edition of the Works of St. Thomas Aquinas 13–20. Lander, WY: Aquinas Institute, 2012.

Thornton, Dillon. *Hostility in the House of God: An Investigation of the Opponents in 1 and 2 Timothy*. Bulletin for Biblical Research, Supplements 15. Winona Lake, IN: Eisenbrauns, 2016.

Towner, Philip H. *1–2 Timothy and Titus*. IVP New Testament Commentary. Leicester, UK: InterVarsity Press, 1994.

———. *The Letters to Timothy and Titus*. New International Commentary on the New Testament. Grand Rapids: Eerdmans, 2006.

Trueman, Carl. "Pay No Attention to That Man Behind the Curtain! Roman Catholic History and the Emerald City Protocol." Reformation 21. April 2012. www.reformation21.org/articles/pay-no-attention-to-that-man-behind-the-curtain-roman-catholic-history-and-the-e.php.

Twomey, Jay. *The Pastoral Epistles Through the Centuries*. Oxford: Wiley-Blackwell, 2009.

Vos, Geerhardus. *The Pauline Eschatology*. Phillipsburg, NJ: P&R, 1979.

Warfield, B. B. *Calvin and Augustine*. Edited by Samuel G. Craig. Philadelphia: P&R, 1956.

Wengert, Timothy J. *Reading the Bible with Martin Luther*. Grand Rapids: Baker Academic, 2013.

Williams, Rowan. *Arius: Heresy and Tradition*. 2nd ed. Grand Rapids: Eerdmans, 2002.

Wright, N. T. *Paul and the Faithfulness of God*. 2 vols. Christian Origins and the Question of God 4. Minneapolis: Fortress, 2013.

Zwingli, Huldrych. *De vera et falsa religione*. Zurich, 1529.

Author and Writings Index

Subject Index

abomination of desolation,
70, 86
See also antichrist
Adam and Eve, 148-50, 153-
54, 156
agency, human, 10, 315
Alexander, 260, 262-63
See also Hymenaeus and
Alexander
ambition, foolish vs. right, 29
angels, 63-65, 172-73, 196-97
antichrist
bondage to, 97
coming of precedes
Christ's coming, 72-73
compared to Christ, 83,
86, 92-93
and deception, 80, 95-96,
98
destruction of, 13, 86,
92-94
as head of universal
apostasy, 75, 77
ministers of, 162
miracles, signs, and
wonders of, 96
Nero as, 74
other names of, 75
recognition of, 76-77, 80,
85, 89
restraint of by Roman
Empire, 80-82, 91, 94
revealing of, 75, 77, 86
signs of, 86, 243
worship of as God, 76, 87,
89-90
See also Muhammad:
identified with
antichrist; pope:
identified with
antichrist
apostasy, 72-74, 77, 225, 236-
37, 264
causes of, 175
and covetousness, 204
See also doctrine, false
apostles
as ambassadors, 18-19
authority of, 113
persecution of, 18
archangels, 41-43
armor, in spiritual battle, 47
baptism, 107, 230, 299-301
suffering as a, 247
body, soul, and spirit, 57
calling, of Christians by God,
18, 58, 66, 99, 221

Christ, return of, 10, 60, 64, 256
with authority, 41
church will be drawn up
into the clouds at, 41-42
destruction of wicked at,
45, 65
doctrine of, 68-69
as encouragement, 65, 292
method and order of,
40-41
preparation for, 44-46, 293
signs preceding, 70
timing of, 10, 40, 44-46,
72-73, 75
church
appropriate secession of,
87-88
authority of to judge of, 55
corruption within in the
last days, 242
fellowship of with Father
and Son, 2
founded on God, 3
God's care for, 308
head of is Christ, 85
as household of God,
169-70
as pillar of truth, 18, 169-
71, 211
unity of, 3, 304
Communion. *See* Lord's Supper
conscience
binding of by bishops,
174, 177
good, 131, 281
seared, 174-75
creation, wise use of, 177-78
Cretans, 279-80
Day of the Lord. *See* Christ:
return of
deacons
prayer for, 167
qualifications for, 165-67
role of, 166-68
worthy of honor, 168
dead, state of the
knowledge of assuages
grief, 35-39
as not separated from
Christ, 38
as not suffering, 38
compared to sleeping,
36-37, 39
death
believers pass from into
life, 49
of Christ for believers, 49,
142, 294

grief over, 35-36, 40, 52
as leading to almsgiving, 10
as reminder of God's
coming, 10
and resurrection, 36-38
deceit
arguments for avoidance
of, 31-32
by spirits, 175
fruits of, 33
in measures and weights, 32
as opposed to true
doctrine, 71, 177, 203
as a result of persecution,
229
and usury, 32-33
See also antichrist: and
deception; women:
deception of
Demas, 260-62, 264, 317
devil. *See* Satan
divinity, of Christ, 293
doctrine
false, 68, 71, 280-81
true, 71, 222-24, 243-44,
257-58, 278, 286, 288-
90, 308
education, necessity of for
Christians, 304
election
of believers by God, 47, 97,
142, 236-37, 270
as manifest in fruit, 7
simplicity of, 221
various views of, 7
See also predestination;
salvation: pertains to
the elect only
eternal life, 43
Eve. *See* Adam and Eve
excommunication. *See* wicked,
separation from
exhortation, 15
faith
as active, 6
alone, 253
apprehends Christ, 120
benefits of limited to
those in fellowship with
Christ, 3, 11, 142
certainty of, 222
in Christ as Son of God, 10
Christ's death and
resurrection an axiom
of, 38
and conscience, 131
curiosity as adversary
of, 121

definition of, 252
fight of, 207
general vs. particular, 26
God as source of, 27, 101,
270
hypocritical, 281
justification by, 64, 127
lively, 223
and love, as highest virtues,
310
patience as fruit of, 62
perfection of, 27, 66
profession of, 208
relationship of to
preaching, 8
sincere, 7
as work of God, 66
faith, hope, and love, 8
as definition of true
Christianity, 6
fluctuation of, 26
resting on God alone, 9
as spiritual armor, 47
fall, of humanity, 58, 153-56
family, care for, 190
First Thessalonians
multiple authors of, 2
Paul's purpose in writing, 2
topics of, 1-2
First Timothy
audience of, 110-15
contents of, 110, 114
provenance of, 112
purpose of, 110-11, 114
foreknowledge, of God, 52
fruit(s)
forbidden, eating of, 58,
153-56
of the gospel, 228-29, 270,
304, 309
judgment of people by in
time, 51, 56-57, 119
results from growth in
faith, 62, 316
gentleness, toward all people,
297-98
glory
of Christ, 173, 293
of God, 129, 293
godliness
and contentment, 203
definition of, 180
training in, 179-80, 182
and ungodliness, 292
See also sanctification
good works
abounding in, 29, 290,
304-5

Scripture Index